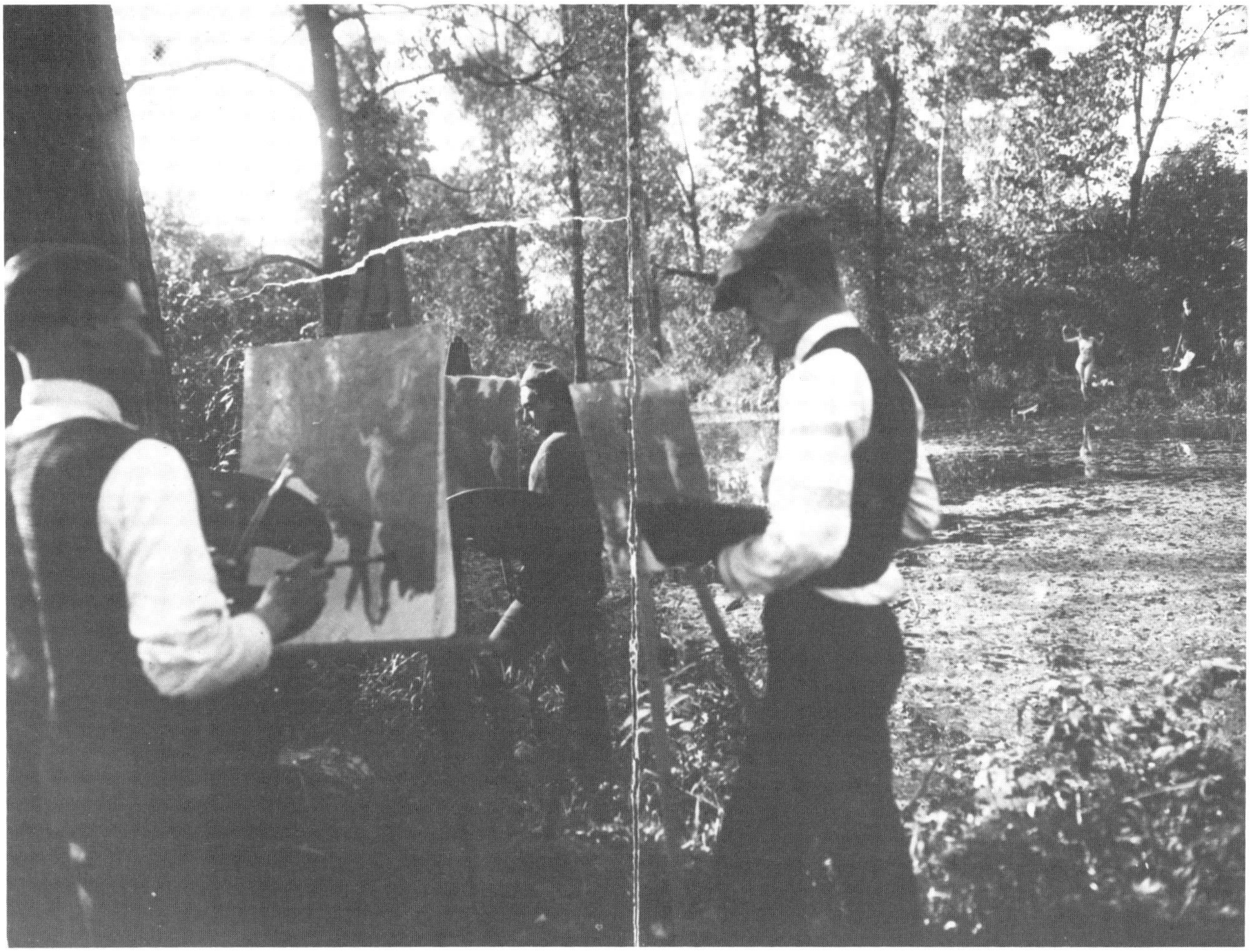

Artists working in the vicinity of Rochester, ca. 1910. The Archives of American Art, Giacomo Spicuzza Papers.

ARTISTS IN MICHIGAN, 1900–1976

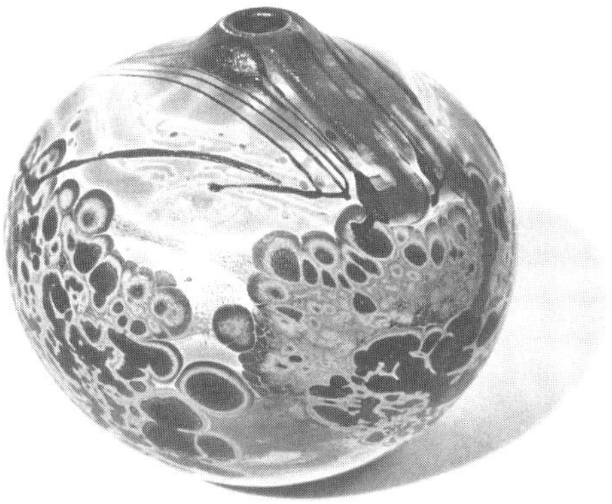

A Biographical Dictionary

*Introduction by **D**ennis **B**arrie*

Biographies Compiled by
Jeanie Huntley Bentley,
Cynthia Newman Helms,
and Mary Chris Rospond

Wayne State University Press, Detroit,
in association with the Archives of American Art,
Smithsonian Institution, and
the Founders Society Detroit Institute of Arts
1989

93 92 91 90 89 5 4 3 2 1

Library of Congress Cataloging-in-Publication Data

Artists in Michigan, 1900–1976 : a biographical dictionary / introduction by Dennis Barrie : biographies compiled by Jeanie Huntley Bentley, Cynthia Newman Helms, and Mary Chris Rospond. — Great Lakes Books ed.

p. cm.

"In association with the Archives of American Art, Smithsonian Institution and the Founders Society, Detroit Institute of Arts."

Bibliography: p.

ISBN 0-8143-1907-6

1. Artists—Michigan—Biography—Dictionaries. 2. Art—Michigan—Societies, etc. 3. Art patronage—Michigan. I. Barrie, Dennis. II. Bentley, Jeanie Huntley. III. Helms, Cynthia Newman. IV. Rospond, Mary Chris.

N6530.M5A78 1989

709'.2'2—dc19

[B] 88-14832

CIP

Sponsors

The financial assistance of the following institutions in the compilation and publication of this volume is gratefully acknowledged:

The Founders Society Detroit Institute of Arts
The Michigan Council for the Arts
The McGregor Fund
The National Endowment for the Arts, a Federal Agency
The Stroh Foundation

CONTENTS

ILLUSTRATIONS

FOREWORD

It is a special pleasure to participate with the Founders Society of the Detroit Institute of Arts and Wayne State University Press in the publication of this important reference work on artists in Michigan. Although the Archives of American Art has grown into a national institution with regional offices in major cities, our original home is Detroit, where Edgar P. Richardson, Lawrence A. Fleischman, and others founded the Archives in 1954 as a much needed instrument for research. From the first, we have concentrated on collecting and preserving original records as the base for research, and our publications tend to be guides to help researchers use our vast collections. But our mission of promoting research is also well served by publications that provide biographical and historical information that is not otherwise readily available.

There is another, perhaps more basic, reason for this publication. The Archives of American Art is a national resource, collecting and preserving documentation from many places. We encourage the recognition that art develops not from one geographic center toward the "regions," but that artists become artists because they must, no matter where they live. In fact, if the extraordinary compilation of information in this book is surveyed, it is understood that Michigan produced, and is still producing art and artists who feel no special compulsion to find a "center" of art other than their own. They work where they feel the most productive, at home. This essential fact must be recognized: To construct a clear and accurate picture of art in America, the art and artists of many different places, not just the supposed center of art, must be known. Otherwise, the historian falls into the solipsistic rut of thinking that one place represents all others.

Michigan is where the Archives of American Art began its work. This publication, then, is our contribution to making better known the art and artists of our original home. Researchers will find the entries of great value and usefulness, and the Archives staff invites perusal of the many documents in our collections that throw yet more light on the artists of Michigan. But surely as important as the individual biographical entries is the introduction by Dennis Barrie. It is, in fact, the most up-to-date history of the visual arts in Michigan and records an extraordinary amount of information hitherto unknown. Taken together, the introduction and the individual biographical entries form an indispensable resource for study of the visual arts in the state.

More than the usual note of appreciation is due Dennis Barrie, who for ten years was the Archives Midwest Regional Director in Detroit and who worked with our dedicated staff to assemble and write the biographical entries. It was a work of the most enjoyable kind. I also thank the many staff members and volunteers who worked on this publication for their tireless efforts in assembling the many details into a coherent whole.

RICHARD N. MURRAY
Director, 1983–1987,
Archives of American Art

PREFACE

Wayne State University Press in 1975 published *Artists of Early Michigan: A Biographical Dictionary of Artists Native to or Active in Michigan, 1701–1900* by Arthur Hopkin Gibson. This volume, a checklist of some 1,800 artists who were born or who worked in Michigan in the years between the founding of Detroit and the beginning of the twentieth century, was the first substantial effort to gather together and make accessible information on Michigan's artists. It also provided the inspiration for the present volume.

The Michigan Council for the Arts underwrote the publication of Gibson's book, and it was a member of the Council's staff, James Crawford, who first suggested to me that the Archives of American Art oversee the compilation of a second volume covering artists active in the state in the twentieth century. Also involved from the very early stages of the project was the Detroit Institute of Arts, which not only made available its considerable resources in terms of research material but also, through the agency of the Founders Society, provided financial assistance for both the research phase and the publication of the book. Furthermore, Susan F. Rossen, formerly Senior Editor and Coordinator of Publications at the Institute, was of great assistance in the development of the concept of the book as well as its format.

Also crucial to the implementation of the project was the establishment of an advisory board consisting of individuals from various areas of the state, all of whom have been actively involved in the Michigan art scene for periods ranging from ten to twenty years. The members of this advisory board were Joy Hakanson Colby, art critic for the *Detroit News*; Frederick J. Cummings, former director of the Detroit Institute of Arts; Charles Meyer, chairman of the art department at Western Michigan University; Sadayoshi Omoto, professor of art at Michigan State University; Charles H. Sawyer, former director of the University of Michigan Museum of Art; and William E. Woolfenden, former national director of the Archives of American Art and staff member at the Detroit Institute of Arts (1947–56). The guidance of these six individuals was invaluable. They suggested possible avenues for research, assisted in formulating the criteria by which artists were chosen for inclusion in the book (see Compilers' Note), and generously shared their knowledge of the history and development of Michigan's art community.

Research for the book began in the fall of 1976, when Cynthia Newman Helms was hired as research coordinator. She was soon joined by Jeanie Huntley Bentley and later by Mary Chris Rospond. Over the next four years an exhaustive research effort was conducted in which this basic three-member team was assisted primarily by student interns from Wayne State University and Henry Ford Community College. Included in this group of interns were: Danuta Boczar, Renate Dix, Judy Dyki, Jeannine M. Head, Kay Kazora, Anne Fisher Kidder, Steven Kowalik, Beryl Krasner, Jean O'Korn, Nancy Rade, Cathy Robinson, Melissa Speck, and Victoria Van Leigh. In addition, Judith Schulman, former assistant librarian at the Detroit Institute of Arts, investigated the archives of the Cranbrook Academy of Art, and Allison Day, a summer intern at the Detroit Institute of Arts, assisted in the final confirmation of all bibliographic citations.

It soon became clear that despite numerous trips around the state by myself, Ms. Helms, and Ms. Bentley, the resources of the various areas could only be sufficiently investigated by on-site researchers. We were ably assisted in this regard by Gail Beke (Lansing), Olive Craig and Anita Meyland (the Upper Peninsula), Kathy Estep (Flint, Saginaw), June Gorman and Nellie A. Curry (Grand Rapids), Loretta Grellner (Saugatuck), Kathryn Keillor (Muskegon), Helen Sheridan and Mildred Pritchard (Kalamazoo), and Ellen Shaller (Ann Arbor).

A particular difficulty in compiling this volume was the lack of traditional published sources. Although a few book-length treatments of specific institutions or individuals and vast numbers of news clippngs existed, much of the state's artistic history had never been written down. To capture this unwritten history, the Archives, in line with its established oral history program, instigated a series of taped interviews with artists, museum professionals, educators, art critics, and the representatives of various arts organizations in Michigan. I thank the following individuals for confidmuseum, (b) a juried exhibition at a major museum, (c) an invitational at a Michigan museum, or (d) three or more juried shows at Michigan museums.

4) The artist's work has won (a) a prize in a nationally-oriented juried show or the Founders Society Purchase Prize (FSPP) at the "Exhibition for Michigan Artists" or the "Exhibition for Michigan Artist-Craftsmen" at the Detroit Institute of Arts, or (b) prizes other than the FSPP at the DIA or a prize in a regionally-oriented juried show.
5) The artist has completed a commission for a work of art in a public place.
6) The artist has been an influential teacher or has made significant contributions to the state's artistic life other than the creation of his or her art.

To be included in the final volume, an artist had to show representation in at least two of the six categories as well as achieving a minimum total "score."

The criteria on which the formula is based are admittedly traditional and generally involve in some way the sanction of the state's formal art organizations. But until the early 1970s, such criteria constituted a fairly accurate reflection of the means by which an artist's stature was judged.

A few comments on how to use this book: The appearance of a name in boldface type in the Introduction or within a biographical entry indicates that the individual cited is listed in a separate biographical entry in this volume. Each biographical entry contains four section: (a) a short summary of the artist's education and career; (b) an enumeration of one-person and group exhibitions; (c) a listing of collections in which the artist's work is represented, and/or major commisssions, and (d) a bibliographic citation of the sources used in compiling the information. It is emphasized that the exhibitions and collections/commissions sections of each entry are selective rather than exhaustive and intentionally emphasize the artist's Michigan activities.

In the exhibition portions, an asterisk (*) after a date indicates that the catalogue for a particular exhibition contains biographical information and/or criticism that is of interest to the researcher. In the citation of dates, the solidus (/) between years indicates that the indicated exhibition covered a continuous time period, whereas a dash (–) means that consecutive exhibitions were held in each year during the period cited.

In the exhibitions and collections/commissions portions, the location of institutions such as colleges, universities, museums, and large businesses is cited only if not well known. No cities are cited for colleges or universities within Michigan.

The "Classification of Artists by Medium," which appears at the end of the volume, serves as cross-index to the 258 Michigan artists included.

INTRODUCTION

Artists in Michigan, 1900–1976

DENNIS BARRIE

Historical Perspective

During most of the nineteenth century, Michigan was a cultural backwater. The area was a little too far north of the main patterns of settlement, and as towns in Ohio and Illinois grew rapidly into cities, Michigan's towns languished. Although Detroit is one of the oldest cities in America, in 1860 it had a population of only 45,000, whereas Cincinnati had 150,000 inhabitants and New York 800,000. By 1880, Detroit's population had grown to 200,000, but the city still ranked a mere seventeenth in size nationally.

Throughout history, visual artists have needed cities in order to thrive. Patronage has usually come from the wealthy classes, government, and religious institutions, all of which are most often concentrated in urban areas. Lacking cities of any commanding size, Michigan could not support much cultural activity. The few artists working in the state were generally untrained itinerant portrait painters, although occasionally a professional artist would set up shop in a town and paint everything from street signs and barroom murals to portraits of mayors and governors.

As the state became increasingly industrialized in the last twenty years of the nineteenth century, the cities of Michigan began to grow. Detroit, Flint, Grand Rapids, and other cities of the Lower Peninsula became manufacturing centers, attracting thousands of immigrants from Europe, as well as Canadians and Americans from the surrounding countryside. In just a few years, fields gave way to factories, and the institutions of a more urbanized, sophisticated America began to develop. In this climate of change, the first signs of an emerging art community can be seen.

The Detroit business community, under the leadership of William Brearly, advertising manager of the *Evening News* (later the *Detroit News*), sponsored an exhibition in 1883 that was known as the "Detroit Art Loan." This effort to change the cultural complexion of the city brought together hundreds of privately owned works of art in a specially constructed pavilion. For two and one-half months, nearly 135,000 visitors toured the exhibition, many coming from across Michigan on special trains.

The incredible success of the "Art Loan" exhibition was the impetus for further activity, and many of the organizers of the "Art Loan" joined together in 1885 to incorporate the state's first art museum, the Detroit Museum of Art. Within three years the museum's trustees had succeeded in building a Gothic-style edifice on fashionable East Jefferson Avenue and had begun to fill it with everything from old master paintings (both authentic and imagined ones) to carved coconuts. The Art School of the Detroit Museum of Art was added to the complex a year later. These were major accomplishments for Michigan in that few places west of the Appalachians could boast of such cultural institutions.

Most of the energy that could be mustered for the arts had been spent in the act of creating the museum, and in the next few years there was no proliferation of galleries, collectors, or patrons of art in Michigan, nor did the number of artists increase significantly. Commissions were still practically nonexistent, except perhaps in the realm of portraiture, and most individuals who considered themselves artists had to resort to commercial art to make a living. Detroit had a few collectors, such as newspaper baron James Edmund Scripps and industrialist Charles Lang Freer, but they had little or no interest in the work of local artists. Scripps, founder and publisher of the *Evening News,* had begun collecting European "old master" paintings in the 1870s and in 1889 gave seventy of these works to the Detroit Museum of Art. Freer, a railroad car manufacturer, collected Oriental art and the works of American artists James McNeill Whistler (1834–1903) and Thomas Dewing (1851–1938). He later donated his collection to the Smithsonian Institution in Washington, D.C.

In the first years of the twentieth century, however, the forces and conditions that would give rise to a thriving artistic climate began to come together. Economically, the state was booming. Michigan's first automobile manufacturer, Oldsmobile, was incorporated in 1899 and by 1905 was turning out more than 5,000 cars a year. The Ford Motor Company was founded in 1903 and was soon outselling every other automobile manufacturer in the country. By 1910 Michigan was well on its way to becoming the heart of one of the nation's largest industries. This economic growth drew people with all kinds of interests and skills to Michi-

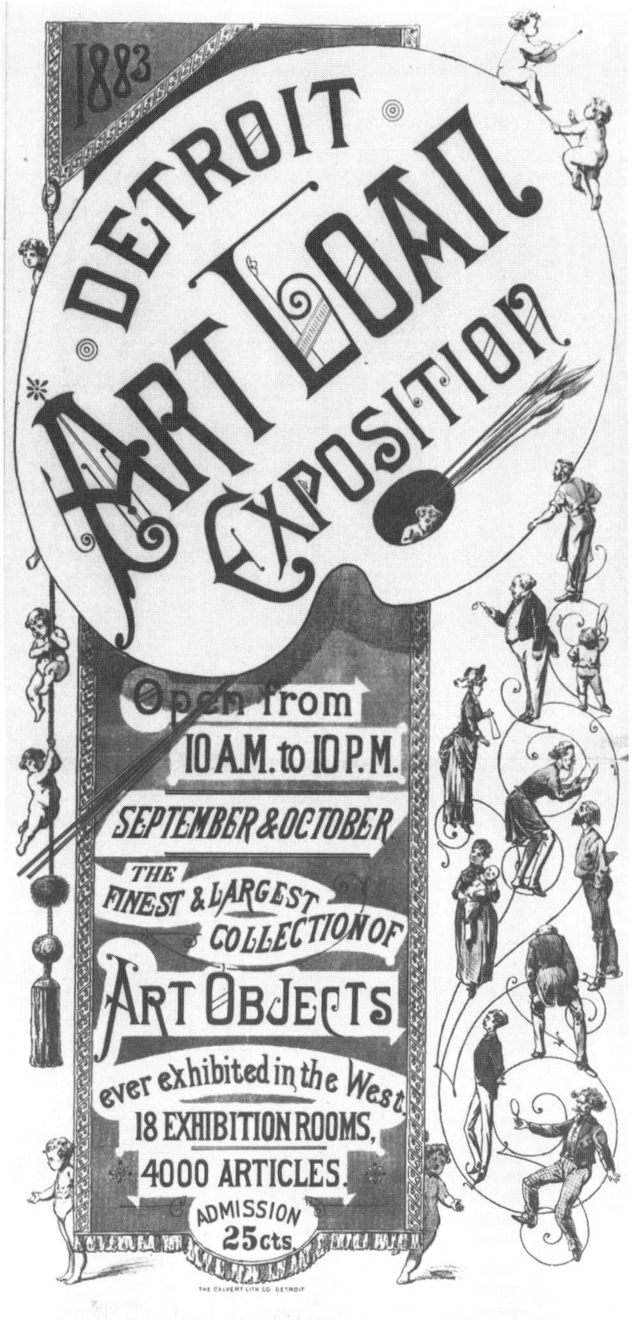

Advertisement for the "Art Loan Exhibition." Calvert Lithography Company, Detroit, 1883. The Detroit Institute of Arts, Museum Archives.

gan, charging the area with the kind of "electricity" that only boom-town conditions provide.

Furthermore, by 1900 there were a sizable number of merchants and industrialists in the state for whom the making of money was no longer an all-consuming concern. Having established their fortunes in the late nineteenth century, these individuals now sought other socially acceptable outlets for their energies and turned their attentions to charitable works, civic improvement, and cultural activities. They were willing to buy art and make it accessible to the public; they were also willing to put money into the building of museums, galleries, and art schools.

Among these patrons were George Gough Booth, a newspaper publisher who sponsored the founding of the Detroit Society of Arts and Crafts and was instrumental in the establishment of the Cranbrook Academy of Art; Horace Caulkins, a manufacturer of kilns who backed the Pewabic Pottery in its early years; and Frederick Stearns, who made a fortune in pharmaceuticals and was one of the chief supporters of the Detroit Museum of Art.

The growth in the arts in Michigan was phenomenal during the first decade of the twentieth century. Several important artist associations were founded, including the Detroit Society of Women Painters (1903), the Scarab Club (1910), the Detroit Society of Arts and Crafts (1906), and the Ann Arbor Art Association (1909). The state's most influential pottery, the Pewabic Pottery, was established in 1903, and in 1910 the Oxbow Summer School of Painting became the first summer art school in the Midwest.

Michigan's art world was dominated in the first years of the new century by painters who had studied in Europe in the 1880s. These artists had been trained in the aesthetics and techniques taught by the European art academies which emphasized naturalistic portraiture and figure painting. The skills and sophistication they had gained abroad dazzled their Michigan audiences, and it was to these artists that most commissions came, and they to whom the public and other artists deferred.

Among the artists who set the pace in Michigan early in the century were **Joseph Gies**, **Percy Ives**, **Gari Melchers**, **Francis Petrus Paulus**, and **Julius Rolshoven**. Gies had studied in Munich and Paris; he co-founded the Detroit Academy of Art in 1895 with Paulus, helped found the Scarab Club, and was renowned for his portraits of women. Ives, a student of the great French painter Léon Gérôme, was a member of the board of trustees of the Detroit Museum of Art and painted the portraits of mayors, governors, and other leading Michigan citizens. Melchers had attended the Royal Academy of Düsseldorf, the École des Beaux-Arts, and the Académie Julian, and was internationally known for his figure painting.

Although Melchers remained in Europe, returning only infrequently to Michigan, his influence in the state was pronounced. Melchers and Ives were looked upon as the state's great "native sons," and they were awarded the most prestigious commissions, exhibitions, and prizes. Paulus had been a student at the École des Beaux-Arts and eventually gained a considerable international reputation for his scenes of the medieval Belgian city of Bruges. Rolshoven, a frequent

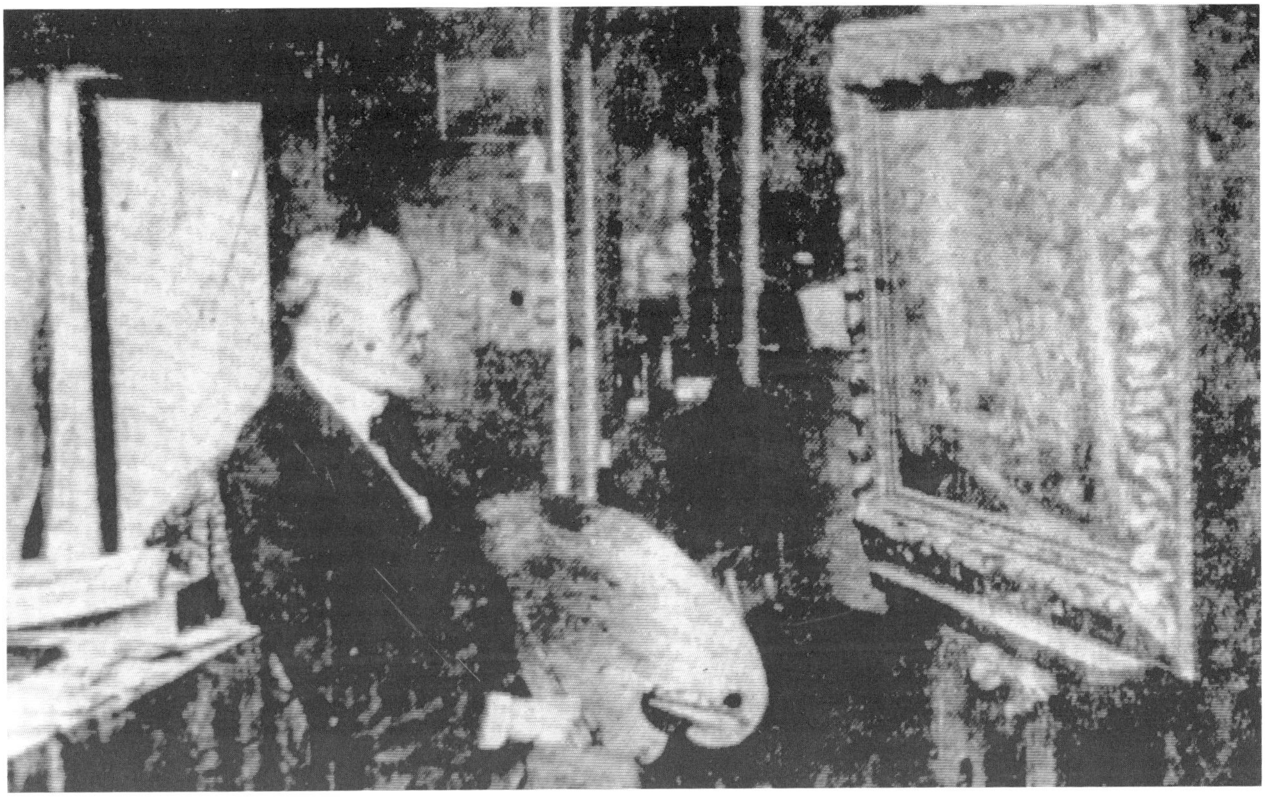

Joseph Gies (1860–1935) in his studio. Detroit Free Press, *Sunday, January 17, 1926. Courtesy the* Detroit Free Press.

and popular exhibitor in Detroit, had been trained in Düsseldorf, Munich, Paris, and Florence. His favorite subjects were romantic figures from myth and legend, as well as sensuous nudes, and picturesque European scenes.

All of these painters worked in a naturalistic style based on an academic aesthetic that was already twenty or thirty years old by the turn of the century, but that was nonetheless acceptable to most of the artists working in the state and very popular with the general public. By the teens, impressionism, the oldest and most accepted challenge to the tenets of academic art, had a few adherents in Michigan, but the other artistic movements associated with the coming of the modern age—post-impressionism, cubism, and expressionism—had no supporters at all.

Painters held sway over the Michigan art world, for few artists in the state could find the training, facilities, or commissions to sustain a career in sculpture, and work in ceramics, metal, fiber, and other traditional craft media was held in relatively low esteem. Even the renewed interest in the crafts that had been inspired by the English Arts and Crafts Movement had not elevated the status of silversmithing or ceramics to that of painting. Only **Mary Chase Stratton**, the founder of the Pewabic Pottery, received the kind of recognition and had the degree of influence that painters such as Ives and Melchers achieved.

Meanwhile, in New York City and elsewhere in America, artistic styles were changing. By 1908 a group of American artists, led by Robert Henri (1865–1929), had joined together under the banner of "The Eight" to rebel against European aestheticism and had called for an art that spoke more directly to its time and place. The "Armory Show" held in New York City in 1913 put before the American art world the radical work of Europe's new modernist masters and in so doing changed the thinking of scores of artists and patrons about the possibilities and limits of art, while outraging the majority of the public. At around the same time, New York photographer Alfred Stieglitz (1864–1946) founded the Photo-Secession Gallery, also known by its address, "291," to showcase the works of American artists who had taken up the concerns of the cubists and the Fauves and who used color, form, and composition in ways unimaginable to artists of Gies and Rolshoven's generation.

The impact of European modernism was not felt in Michigan until the end of the 1920s, when a number of younger artists, many of them still students, began

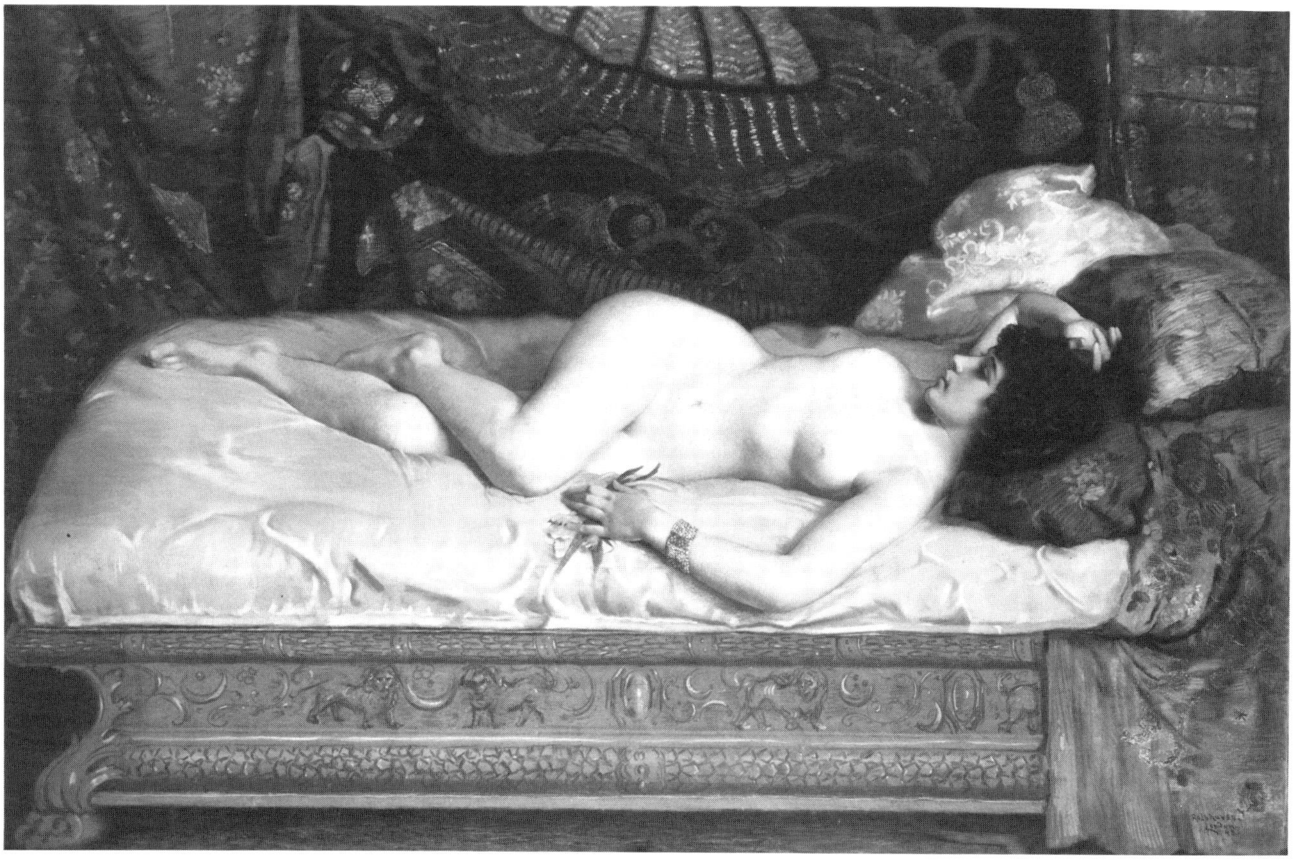

Julius Rolshoven (1854–1930). The Brunette Venus. *1892. Oil on canvas. Private Collection. The Detroit Institute of Arts, Research Library.*

incorporating abstract elements into their work. Some turned to the bright, bold, unnatural colors that characterized the painting of the Fauves; others rejected the use of naturalistic imagery in their painting, utilizing the simplified forms of the cubists, or turned to an almost architectural emphasis on line. Among these early Michigan modernists were **Jay Boorsma**, who painted landscapes that were highly stylized abstractions, and **Edgar Yaeger**, whose still lifes were influenced by Picasso's cubist period works, while other of his paintings were reminiscent of the dream-like quality found in the works of the surrealist Giorgio di Chirico. Perhaps most influential of all was Samuel Halpert, a New York artist of considerable reputation, who was brought to Michigan to head the painting department of the Art School of the Detroit Society of Arts and Crafts. Halpert painted in a modernist vein that was influenced by the French post-impressionist masters, in particular Paul Cézanne. The moment of glory for these painters came in 1928, when out-of-state jurors for the prestigious "Exhibition for Michigan Artists" at the Detroit Institute of Arts chose works by these younger artists, while the work of the "old guard" was excluded. This 1928 exhibition, like the "Armory Show" of 1913, outraged much of the art community and most of the public, although it was an accurate indicator of the changes in taste that were taking place.

By the late 1920s, many young Michigan artists were products of American schools, often those located in Michigan or some other part of the Midwest. Their experience was American, not European, and their art was less dependent on tradition. The more radical of the modernist styles, however, did not prevail. Michigan was not overrun with derivative cubists and pseudo-surrealists. Painting and sculpture remained solidly representational, with work varying only in the way in which color might be used, or in a particular artist's stylized handling of form. At the same time, a unique regional style did not develop in Michigan as it did in other parts of the country, such as the central Midwest, where artists such as Thomas Hart Benton (1889–1975) and Grant Wood (1892–1942) looked to farms, fields, and people connected with the land for their inspiration.

The greatest influence on Michigan art in the 1930s was not to be found in the philosophies of the various art movements, but rather in the economic disaster of the Depression and in the federal government's response to it. The majority of Michigan's artists joined the rolls of such federally sponsored art projects as the Public Works of Art Project, the Federal Art Project of the Works Progress Administration, and a number of others during this time. These projects enabled artists to survive the Depression years, supplying much-needed income. The directors of these programs were in a position to dictate the kind of art they wanted to see produced, and the stress in subject matter was placed on subjects drawn from the American scene. Edward Rowan, director of the Public Works of Art Project, outlined it directly to his regional heads, stating that:

> Any artist who feels that he can only find the picturesque and the paintable and the imaginative in foreign subject matter had better be dropped from the project and an opportunity be given to the man or woman with enough imagination and vision to see the beauty and possibility for aesthetic expression in the subject matter of his own country.[1]

As a result, most of the Michigan painters and sculptors employed by the projects looked to folk tales, scenes of local color and interest, and symbols of American traditions for their subject matter. In the ten years between 1933 and 1943, more "noble Redmen," muscular lumberjacks, and steadfast farmers were depicted in art than at any time before or since.

Stylistically, this work was direct, easily understood, and the subject matter often narrative in nature. It was intended to appeal to the vast public and, for the most part, it did so. Proposals that deviated from this norm were usually rejected by the various panels of artists or clients before getting very far. Along with style and content, the federal arts projects also dictated form and size, and work on a large scale became the rule rather than the exception. Murals and large-scale sculpture seemed to saturate the state. Artists on these projects learned to work in dimensions that would have been unimaginable for most of them a decade earlier.

Younger artists, such as **Gerald Mast**, **David Fredenthal**, and **Frank Cassara** got their first major commissions through the Federal Art Project, painting murals for some of the state's major government buildings. More established artists like **Jean Paul Slusser**, **Zoltan Sepeshy**, and **Charles Pollock** found in the projects the patronage they needed to continue their work.

The crafts did not flourish in Michigan in the 1930s. Although the government sponsored some crafts projects, these were mainly directed at the training and eventual employment of the nonprofessional. The Cranbrook Academy of Art, which had been founded in 1927, the Pewabic Pottery, and the Art School of the Detroit Society of Arts and Crafts were,

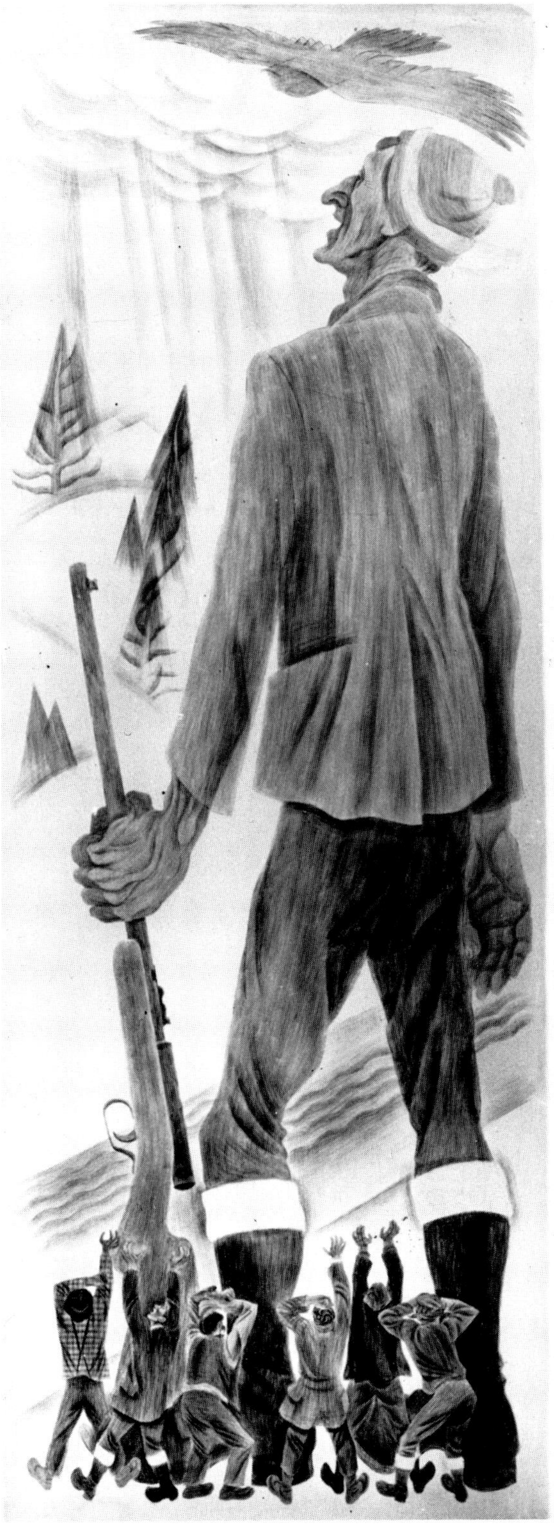

Francis Danovitch (1920–). Paul Bunyan. *Mural, egg tempera. 4 × 7 feet. Collection of the University of Michigan Dental School. The Detroit Institute of Arts, Research Library.*

for all practical purposes, the only places in the state where any significant work was done. Even then, only a handful of individuals were active, and the most important of them worked at Cranbrook. In this time when most artists were working in very American styles, treating "American scene" subject matter, the Cranbrook faculty was producing work based on the European philosophy of good design, which aimed for compatibility between the crafts and architecture. The work they produced was international in design and concept, and touched only slightly by the Michigan environment.

Among the Cranbrook faculty who dominated the crafts scene in Michigan was metalsmith **Arthur Neville Kirk**, an Englishman whose work was finely crafted and highly decorative, with an almost Gothic quality, characteristics especially suitable for the ecclesiastical objects he most often created. **Loja Saarinen** headed the textile department of the Academy; together with her assistants **Lillian Holm** and **Marianne Strengell**, she was responsible for some of the finest textile design in Michigan for the next two decades, bringing a strong use of color and geometric imagery to the medium and working with combinations of natural and synthetic fibers. Internationally recognized ceramicist **Maija Grotell** came to Cranbrook in 1938 and had perhaps the greatest impact of all. Grotell emphasized the principle that ceramics should be viewed as an art form, an attitude that most Americans did not share at this time. Her own simply shaped, beautifully glazed works dramatically illustrate her concepts and made her one of the most sought-after potters in Michigan for the next thirty years.

Another influential potter whose work matured in the mid-1930s was **John Foster**, who had studied with **Mary Chase Stratton**. His clay pieces are both beautiful and functional, often displaying a simplicity evocative of Oriental ceramics. Foster's concern for the aesthetics of functional objects would be later transmitted to several generations of students at Wayne State University and at the Art School of the Detroit Society of Arts and Crafts.

Artistic activity was greatly reduced everywhere in America during the years of World War II, as artists were drafted or became involved in defense work. Art schools and museums in Michigan operated at a minimal level. Michigan did not experience the influx of European artists fleeing Nazi domination that so en-

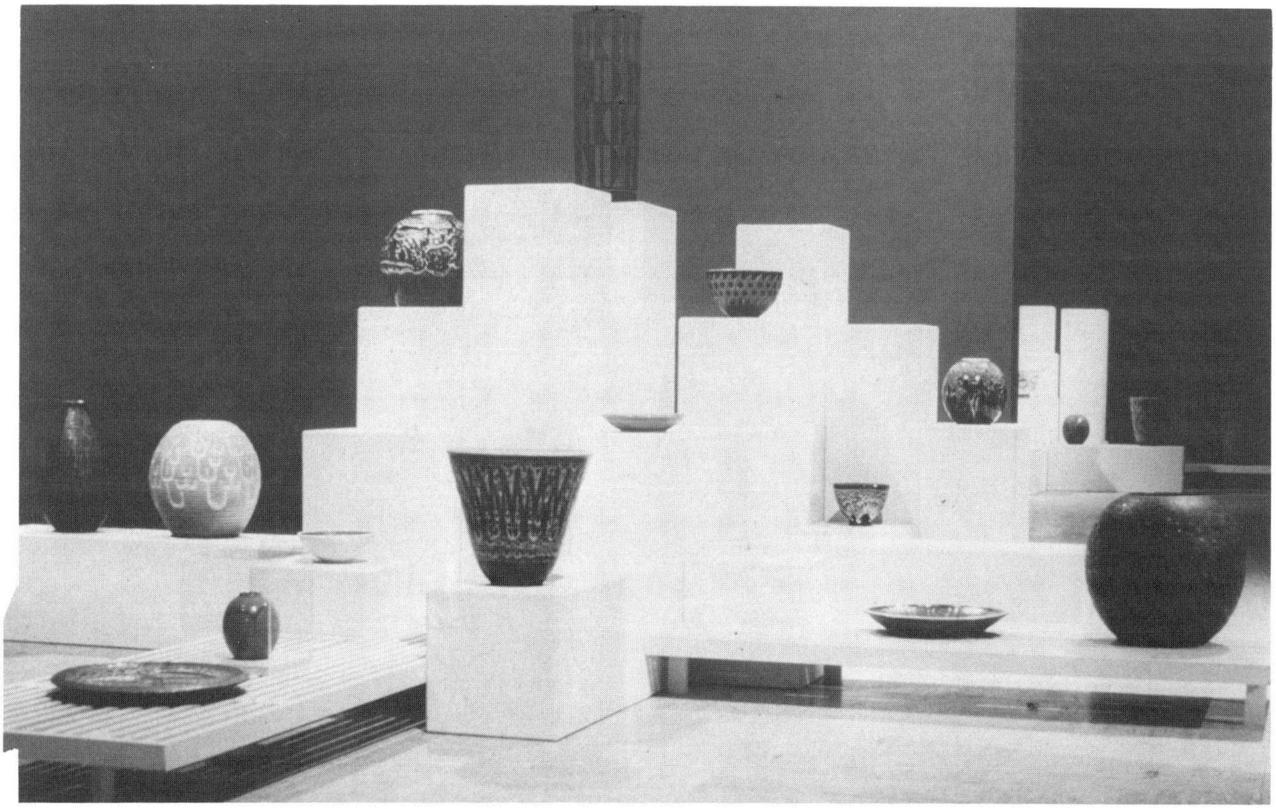

Maija Grotell (1899–1973). Installation at the Cranbrook Academy of Art Museum. Courtesy the Cranbrook Academy of Art Museum.

riched the American art scene in New York and Chicago. During the 1940s the artists who were important in Michigan remained isolated and were not, for the most part, involved in avant-garde experiments.

Zoltan Sepeshy was typical of the artists who were celebrated in the 1940s. Head of the painting department at the Cranbrook Academy of art from 1930 until he became director in 1947, Sepeshy won prize after prize for his paintings in tempera. His subject matter focused, for the most part, on Michigan scenes, but his style ranged from straightforwardly representational to more abstract. Another of the premier figures of this time was **Constance Richardson**. She likewise turned to the Midwestern landscape for her subject matter, but employed light and atmosphere in ways that softened and romantically transformed the landscape. **Charles Culver**, a painter who spent much of his time in the northern Lower Peninsula, gained renown throughout the state for his simplified watercolors of animals and insects. **Sarkis Sarkisian**, an artist who emigrated from Turkey in the 1920s, drew upon stylistic references to Byzantine painting, particularly its flatness, geometry, and heavily defined lines, to create strong, direct portraits and figure studies. Sarkisian was director of the Art School of the Detroit Society of Arts and Crafts during the war years. Although sculptural activity almost ceased at this time, **Marshall Fredericks** was one of the most sought-after sculptors in Michigan both before and after the war. Frederick's stylized, heroic bronze figures were the kind of monumental sculpture that came into demand once metals were again available for use in art.

The increasing mobility of the American populace after World War II brought new artists, ideas, and energies to Michigan. The growth in communications and media in the state made the latest developments in art more available than they had ever been before. More Americans in this period were turning to professional careers, which produced an explosion in art activity in the area.

Perhaps the most dramatic change in the art styles of the 1950s was the sudden and very real presence of abstraction as a major force in the work produced. The wave of abstract expressionism that began to build in New York City in the late 1940s hit Michigan in the early 1950s. By the mid-1950s, the impact was far-reaching and pronounced as scores of Michigan artists experimented with elements of abstraction in their work. Progressive painters and sculptors were working in wholly nonrepresentational styles and even the more conservative artists were often willing to include abstract elements in their work.

In 1955 the director of the Detroit Institute of Arts, Edgar P. Richardson, observed: "It is obvious that Abstract Expressionism is now the idiom in which most artists of the state (as well as the world) choose to work. One cannot say that the artists of Michigan lack a varied point of view, heaven knows, but abstraction in its various forms is certainly the most popular and widespread point of view among them."[2] The artists who emerged as major figures in this period were those painters and sculptors most successful in incorporating elements of abstraction into their work. **Guy Palazzola** produced the first semi-abstract painting to win the coveted Founders Society Purchase Prize in the 1950 "Exhibition for Michigan Artists" at the Detroit Institute of Arts. **Stefan Davidek** employed bold color and collage in his abstract paintings and won acclaim in Flint, Detroit, and elsewhere in the state. **Richard Kozlow**, who painted abstract landscapes with rich textural effects, became a favorite of Michigan collectors. **Gerome Kamrowski** was influenced by the surrealists working in New York in the 1940s, and **Wallace Mitchell**, who was later to become the head of the

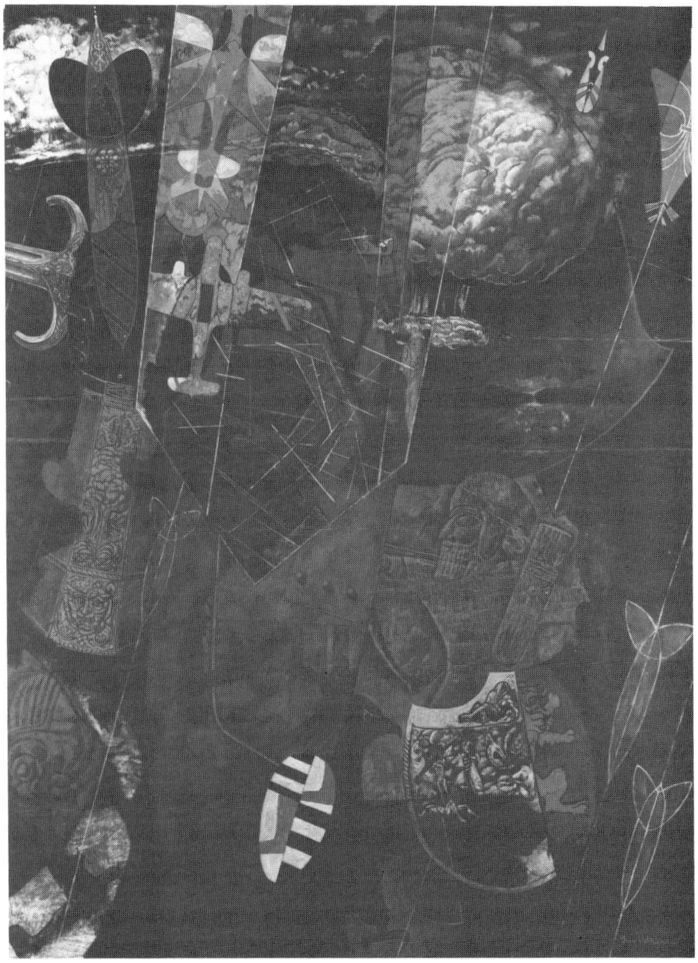

Guy Palazzola (1919–1978). The Black Knight. *1951. Oil on canvas 40 × 31 inches. Collection of the Detroit Institute of Arts, Founders Society Purchase Prize, "Exhibition for Michigan Artists," 1951.*

Cranbrook Academy of Art, experimented with geometrical forms and color relationship. Many sculptural honors and commissions went to artists like **Walter Midener**, whose sculpture reduced the figure to boldly carved planar surfaces; **Thomas McClure**, one of the first artists in Michigan to follow David Smith's lead in constructing sculpture out of welded metal; and **Morris Brose**, whose work in sculpture consisted of simplified forms and planes.

The commanding position of abstraction in painting and sculpture in Michigan lasted well into the 1960s, as museums, galleries, and group shows paid little attention to artists not working in an abstract vein. The 1962 "Exhibition for Michigan Artists" at the Detroit Institute of Arts was almost entirely filled with nonrepresentational work.

The increased level of activity and interest in the traditional craft media in the 1950s was a national phenomenon. In Michigan, the continued presence of a number of the key figures from the 1930s, along with a matured generation of their students and strong craft programs at the Cranbrook Academy of Art, the Art School of the Detroit Society of Arts and Crafts, and several university art departments, combined to produce a particularly energetic scene.

The annual "Exhibition for Michigan Artist-Craftsmen" at the Detroit Institute of Arts was established in 1946 and grew in importance as more artists began to express themselves in the various craft media. Nowhere was the activity greater than in ceramics. In the 1950s both **Maija Grotell** and **John A. Foster** remained strong leaders, producing quality work and influencing scores of students. **Robert Diebboll**, a Foster student, produced classically shaped salt-glazed pieces, often with calligraphically painted surfaces. **J. T. Abernathy**, one of the founders of the Ann Arbor Potters Guild, gained wide recognition for thrown pieces of enormous size with distinctive matte glazes. **Marc Hansen** perfected several crystalline glazes and strongly influenced the work of potters in Ann Arbor and Kalamazoo, while New Yorker **William Pitney** made the Wayne State University ceramics department his own.

Metalsmithing, which languished in the war years because of the scarcity of materials, dramatically blossomed in the postwar period. Among the leaders in the field were **Fred Kenney-Eagen** and **Marion Kenny-Eagen**, a husband and wife team who came from the art program of Cass Technical High School in Detroit. The Kenney-Eagens turned out pieces of jewelry that drew upon classic forms for their beauty. **Richard Thomas** took over the dormant metalsmithing department at Cranbrook in 1947 and organized the first college degree program in metalsmithing there, attracting to Michigan some of the finest students in the field. **Earl Krentzin**, a graduate of Wayne State University, captured the fancies of the public and critics alike with small playful figures of hammered sterling silver. **Robert Engstrom** and **Audrey Engstrom**, working in Kalamazoo, created fine jewelry, often working with the process of copper enameling.

Artists connected with Cranbrook continued to dominate the realm of fiber art in the 1950s. Pipsin Saarinen Swanson designed textiles for industry and architectural use. **Ruth Adler Schnee** opened one of the first Michigan studios devoted to textile design and printing, and **Lillian Holm** continued the tradition of tapestry weaving as well as fabricating unusual linens and other handmade textiles.

In painting and sculpture, the momentum gained by abstraction in the 1950s was carried over into the 1960s. It was during this period that the influence of art being made in New York City had its greatest impact on Michigan's artists. Scores of them were working in ways derivative of styles then current in New York that were so widely promoted by the national media. Art institutions in Michigan reinforced the belief that artists who fit the perception of what was important in New York were better. Out-of-state jurors for the various museums' annual exhibitions between 1962 and 1972 tended to select those artists whose works most closely fit the New York mold, no matter how unoriginal. The more developed and independent artists of the Michigan community were frequently either juried out or were aware of the jurors' biases and chose not to enter.

Nonetheless, Michigan had its share of strong painters and sculptors in the 1960s. Many artists managed to remain aware of national trends and movements while still creating works with personal integrity. **Robert Wilbert** painted in a representational style exploring the figure and still life and was an influential member of the Wayne State University faculty. **Sheldon Iden**'s painted canvases explored the various qualities of black, utilizing some of the concepts of minimalism. **Anthony DeBlasi**, of the Michigan State University faculty, developed large color-field paintings, often applying his paint directly from the tube. **Murray Jones**, also of Michigan State, created large-scale abstract paintings that were highly influenced by oriental formats.

In sculpture, **Julius Schmidt**, head of the department of sculpture at Cranbrook, gained national recognition for cast-iron totem-like columns that reflected the technology and forms of the machine age. **David Barr** took up the cause of structurism, a movement related to constructivism, and made wooden reliefs exploring the underlying order of natural systems. **Carole Harrison**, who established the sculpture department at Western Michigan University in 1960, worked with bronze, brass, concrete, and other materials to create imposing large-scale figurative works.

The growth in the crafts in the 1960s was once again paced by ceramics. Courses were offered everywhere and potters were turned out by the hundreds. Art fairs developed in the 1960s and joined galleries in offering vast arrays of ceramic art, ranging from traditionally functional pieces to Pop Art miniatures and sculptured forms that expanded the traditional boundaries of ceramics. A number of Michigan potters gained national recognition during this decade. **John Glick**, a student of both Foster and Grotell, established a one-man production studio in Farmington and began turning out award-winning functional pieces that were characterized by the rich use of glazes and brushwork. Taking the opposite approach, **Richard DeVore**, a teacher at both Flint Junior College and Cranbrook, stressed aestheticism over functionality and created delicate, asymmetrical ceramic pieces that were sculptural in feeling. In the Ann Arbor and Ypsilanti areas, **John Stephenson** turned to the expressive use of ceramics as three-dimensional sculpture and incorporated metal into his clay pieces, and **Suzanne Stephenson** created highly lustered nonfunctional clay forms partially thrown and partially slab-built.

Fiber art was also a strong field in the 1960s and into the 1970s. **Robert Kidd**, a Cranbrook graduate who returned to head the Academy's fiber department from 1967 to 1970, produced deep-piled, multifibered rugs and hangings characterized by their sculptural surfaces and landscape-like quality. One of Kidd's students, **Urban Jupena**, also used deep piles and sculptural surfaces in both functional and nonfunctional pieces. Between 1961 and 1971 **Eleen Auvil** taught in fiber programs at almost every institution in southeastern Michigan. Her work with organic materials and natural fibers and dyes was highly influential. In 1970 **Gerhardt Knodel** became head of the Cranbrook fiber department. Knodel created large environmental pieces for major structures around the United States, demonstrating some of the ways that fiber can complement architectural features.

Glassmaking gained a new status in the 1960s. Glass had been a solely industrial medium for half a century; the revitalization of glass as a medium for personal expression in art began with a series of workshops held in Ohio at the Toledo Museum of Art in the 1960s. Many Michigan artists found their way to Toledo and were subsequently influential in developing glassmaking as an art in the state. **Sylvia Vigiletti** and Herbert Babcock attended these workshops and were soon established as significant glassmakers associated with the Art School of the Detroit Society of Arts and Crafts.

Although there had been printmakers of note in Michigan throughout the century, most notably **Emil Weddige**, **James Lee**, and **Reynold Weidenaar**, the impact of the medium on the rest of the art world remained negligible until the 1960s. Printmaking then experienced a national resurgence, partly because prints remained affordable at a time when prices for

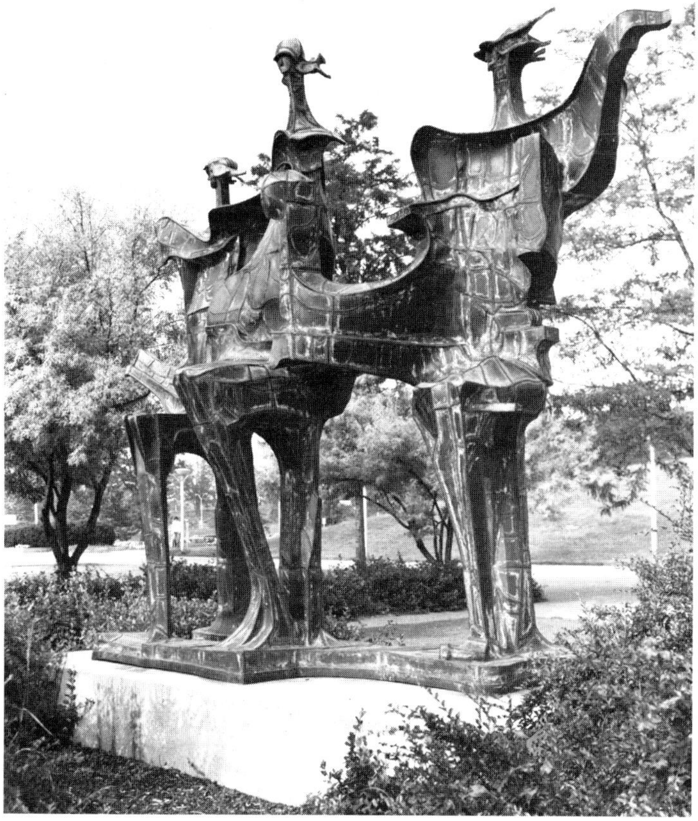

Carole Harrison (1933–). Three Figures. *1972. Welded brass. h. 14 feet. Collection of Western Michigan University. Courtesy the Fay L. Hendry Outdoor Sculpture Collection, MSU Archives and Historical Collection. Balthazar Korab, Photographer.*

paintings and sculpture had risen far beyond what most collectors could afford. Print workshops and printmaking classes began to develop everywhere, as artists who had previously worked mainly as painters took up graphic arts.

Laurence Barker, head of the printmaking department at Cranbrook between 1960 and 1970, set up the first fine-arts papermaking program in the United States and collaborated with many artists on print and papermaking projects. One of Barker's students, **Aris Koutroulis**, was responsible for a number of print projects in the area, among them a workshop at Wayne State University that played an important role in the American revival of cliché-verre, a printmaking method first used in the early nineteenth century. His most ambitious project, the Detroit (later Michigan) Workshop of Fine Prints, provided Michigan artists with facilities for all sorts of printmaking activities, including the production of major suites.

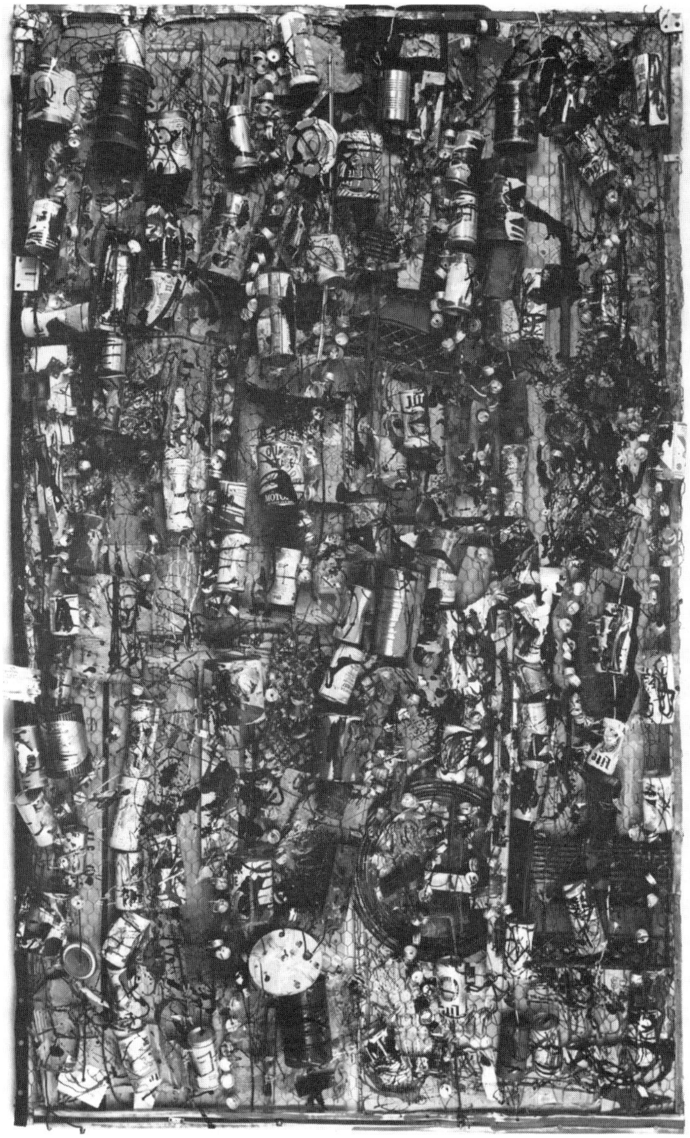

Robert Sestok (1946–). Meogeesic. 1978. Metal, cardboard, paint, wood, plastic. 60 × 96 inches. Collection of James F. Duffy, Jr. Courtesy Feigenson-Rosenstein Gallery, Detroit.

From the time of its founding in 1885 as the Detroit Museum of Art, it has been the state's premier museum. In size, quality of collections, and reputation, the Art Institute has had no close rival in the state. It has been the one Michigan museum of national and international standing.

The Detroit Institute of Arts, in spite of its location in Detroit, has served as a museum for the entire state since its earliest days. Through its sponsorship of exhibitions for Michigan artists, traveling shows, and various service programs, the Detroit Institute of Arts has affected the lives of artists and the public in even the most remote corners of Michigan.

In the 1890s, under the directorship of Armand Griffith, a self-styled promoter of the arts, the museum began to emerge as a place of excitement and interest. The museum, in the first few years of its existence had functioned mainly as a somewhat fusty repository for a small collection of paintings, plaster casts of famous sculptures, and orientalia. Griffith felt strongly that a museum should be an integral part of the community. With that aim in mind, he established a free admission policy, made great efforts to publicize the museum's activities on an almost daily basis by keeping the local newspapers informed, and instituted a series of lectures on popular topics that managed to entice tremendous numbers of Detroiters into the museum. On any given Sunday during his twenty-year tenure, crowds numbering several thousand filled the galleries to hear lectures on such diverse topics as "The Art of the Red Man," "Van Dyke and His Portraits," and "Not Money But Taste." Griffith's understanding of what "sold" art to the public was very important in popularizing the museum and its collections.

In 1901 Griffith appointed Clyde Burroughs, a schoolteacher with an interest in contemporary art, as his assistant. This appointment was a fortuitous choice for the art community, as Burroughs was particularly interested in working with Michigan artists. Over the course of the forty-five years he spent at the museum, during which he served variously as administrator and director of the museum, curator of American art, and secretary of the city's Arts Commission, Burroughs worked to develop the museum's connections with the artists of Detroit and the surrounding communities. He actively sought their work for special exhibitions as well as for inclusion in the permanent collection. His highly visible presence provided evidence of the museum's support as he became involved in the causes, projects, and organizations of the Michigan art community.

Perhaps the most lasting legacy of Burroughs's involvement and the activity that, more than any other, represented the museum's commitment to Michigan artists was the establishment of the "Exhibition for Michigan Artists." This prestigious annual show was held at the museum over a period of nearly sixty years.

The "Exhibition for Michigan Artists." An annual exhibition sponsored by and for the membership of a local artist organization known as the "Hopkin Club" (later renamed the "Scarab Club") evolved into the prestigious "Exhibition for Michigan Artists." First held, at Burroughs's invitation, in the galleries of the Detroit Museum of Art in 1911, the "Scarab Club Annual" began as a simple unjuried event that was designed to showcase the work of the club's membership.

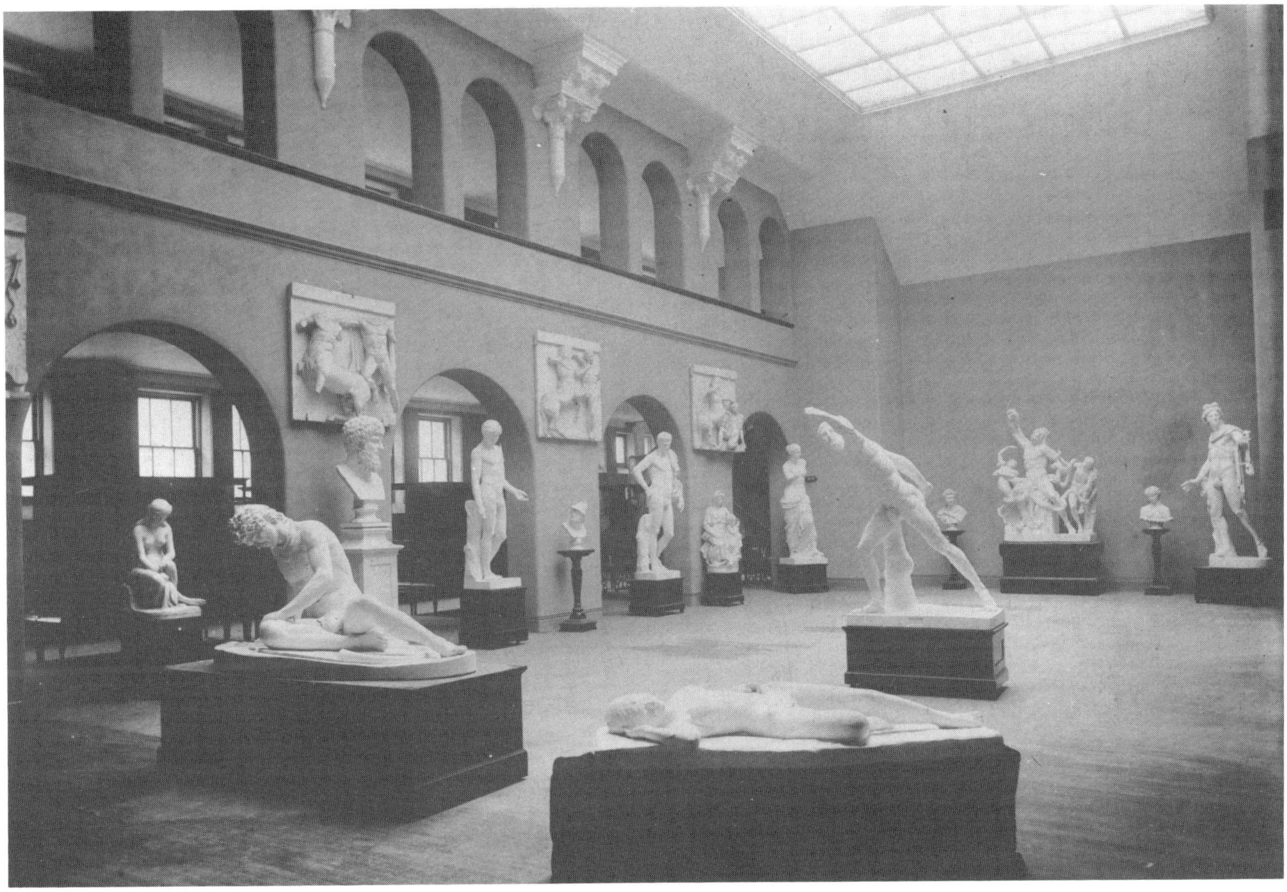

Sculpture Court of the Detroit Museum of Art, ca. 1890. The Detroit Institute of Arts, Museum Archives.

In those days, the membership roster was virtually a "Who's Who" of Detroit and Michigan's professional art community.

The scope of this annual exhibition began to widen in 1915. Entrance eligibility was expanded beyond the membership of the club to include, as the catalogue stated, "the entire coterie of Michigan painters, including those living abroad."[3] In that same year, a dual jury system was added: one jury selecting the works to be exhibited, and another awarding prizes in various categories.

Eventually the jurying process itself was expanded. Originally, both the selection jury and the awards jury had been made up of Scarab Club members, but in the 1920s a decision was made to invite some of the best-known figures in the American art world to serve on the awards jury. Included were Robert Reid (1862–1929), a member of the group of American impressionists known as "The Ten," who painted murals for the Library of Congress; Leon Kroll (1884–1974), a well-known painter of cityscapes who taught at the Art Students League and the School of the Art Institute of Chicago; and Charles Hawthorne (1872–1930), founder of the Cape Cod School of Art in Provincetown, Massachusetts. These painters were typical of the caliber of artist brought to Michigan over a period of several years to choose the award-winners.

The Detroit Institute of Arts also began in the 1920s to take a more active role in the exhibition, and the Scarab Club relinquished some of the responsibilities for what was rapidly becoming an overwhelming undertaking. In 1926 the Detroit Institute of Arts made its increased interest in the exhibition very clear by creating a major prize, the Founders Society Prize, which was to be given each year to the best work in any medium. A substantial cash award (two-hundred dollars) and the prestige of an award from the trustees of the museum soon made the Founders Society Prize, along with the Scarab Club's Gold Medal, an award, established in 1917, which was given to the artist whose work was "the most important contribution to the success of the exhibition," the most coveted of honors.[4]

The Scarab Club's direct involvement with the exhibition ended in 1928. In that year, for the first time, outside jurors were responsible for selection of all the work to be shown, not just for the awards. Nationally known painters Samuel Halpert (1884–1930), Elizabeth McCord Pitts, and Paul Trebilcock (b. 1902) overwhelmingly favored artists who were considered by Michigan's artistic establishment to be "modernists and radicals." Such mainstays of previous exhibitions as **Percy Ives**, **Julius Rolshoven**, and **Joseph Gies**, all very established but conservative artists, were eliminated and these exclusions tore the art community apart. The jurors were attacked from all sides. Critics lashed out at their decisions; for example, one wrote that many of the works were "so obviously worthless from any point of view that their presence is a complete mystery."[5] A group of the rejected artists, many of them Scarab Club members, set up Michigan's first "Salon des Refusés," a rival exhibition held at the Scarab Club. The jurors were every bit as vociferous in defense of their decisions. Halpert stated to the press that "Some of the men whose work we threw out had been dead for twenty years and didn't know it."[6]

Thus the Scarab Club show was confronted with the problem that it and other regional exhibitions would continue to face throughout their histories: finding a selection process responsive to the needs of the community, yet retaining high enough standards to make the exhibition meaningful. In 1929 two changes were made, in the hope of assuring that the exhibition would function without controversy. First, the responsibility for the show was turned over to the Detroit Institute of Arts, a truly regional institution which would be responsible to all factions of the art community. In addition, a committee composed of representatives from art organizations throughout the state was developed to run the exhibition, and jurying was done by individuals selected from these various organizations. That same year the show was retitled the "Exhibition for Michigan Artists."

These changes did not, however, remove controversy and dissension from the "Exhibition for Michigan Artists." Throughout the early 1930s a group of artists, known as the "Society of Independents," continued to run their own rival unjuried exhibition in the same fashion as the 1928 "Salon des Refusés." In 1933, in response to the Society of Independents, the organizers of the "Exhibition for Michigan Artists" experimented by holding an unjuried annual. The exhibition was opened to everyone, and 466 artists entered 816 works. This experiment was a disastrous one; it was attacked by the critics as the worst annual ever. A critic from the *Detroit Times* wrote: "For the most part the show is utterly and completely independent of perspective, anatomy, color laws, or anything. . . . as it appears to the non-alcoholic laity," and summed up by stating that "Art with no standards is no better than an individual without them."[7] Only the ever-buoyant Clyde Burroughs found something nice to say about the exhibition, headlining a review for the *Detroit News*: "Michigan Artist Free-for-all Abounds in Fun."[8] The artists themselves were displeased in general, and the 1933 annual was the first and last unjuried "Exhibition for Michigan Artists."

In the years that followed this debacle, the "Exhibition for Michigan Artists" quickly regained its stature as the important regional competition in Michigan. The month-long show once again became a cornerstone of the state's artistic life. An artist's inclusion in the exhibition gave his or her work the stamp of community approval, which was even further enhanced if the work won a prize, since many such winners were purchased for the museum's collection. Controversy, however, was avoided, and the exhibition became a rather sedate affair. For the rest of the 1930s and the 1940s, the "Exhibition for Michigan Artists" was dominated by artists who worked representationally, though with occasional hints of abstraction. Prizes were awarded consistently to such leading figures as **Zoltan Sepeshy**, **John Carroll**, **Sarkis Sarkisian**, **Emil Weddige**, **Edgar Yaeger**, and **Donald Gooch**. Students were discouraged from entering, and those few artists producing work considered by their contemporaries to be extremely modern or radical had little success.

As the director of the Detroit Institute of Arts, Edgar P. Richardson, noted in his introduction to the catalogue for the 1948 "Exhibition for Michigan Artists":

> There is no dominant fashion or style in the exhibition. Instead, there are a gratifying number of interesting personal talents. Some of these have distinguished reputations, others are yet only locally recognized. But they are going their own road. You cannot judge this exhibit by seeing if it conforms to what is already familiar in some famous European or American artists. You must judge these artists as men and women creating a fresh and lively creative life here among us, for themselves and for this part of America.[9]

In 1946 the Detroit Institute of Arts instituted an annual "Exhibition for Michigan Artist-Craftsmen" in its schedule. Originally organized in cooperation with the Detroit Artists Market (discussed later), this exhibition focused on those artists working in ceramics, metal, fiber, wood, and glass—all media not normally included in the "Exhibition for Michigan Artists." The early exhibitions were small and low-key. The jurors were local, usually well-known patrons and collectors, and most of the artist-craftsmen selected were from Detroit or Cranbrook. The prizes, which included purchase prizes for the Detroit Institute of Arts' collection, were minimal.

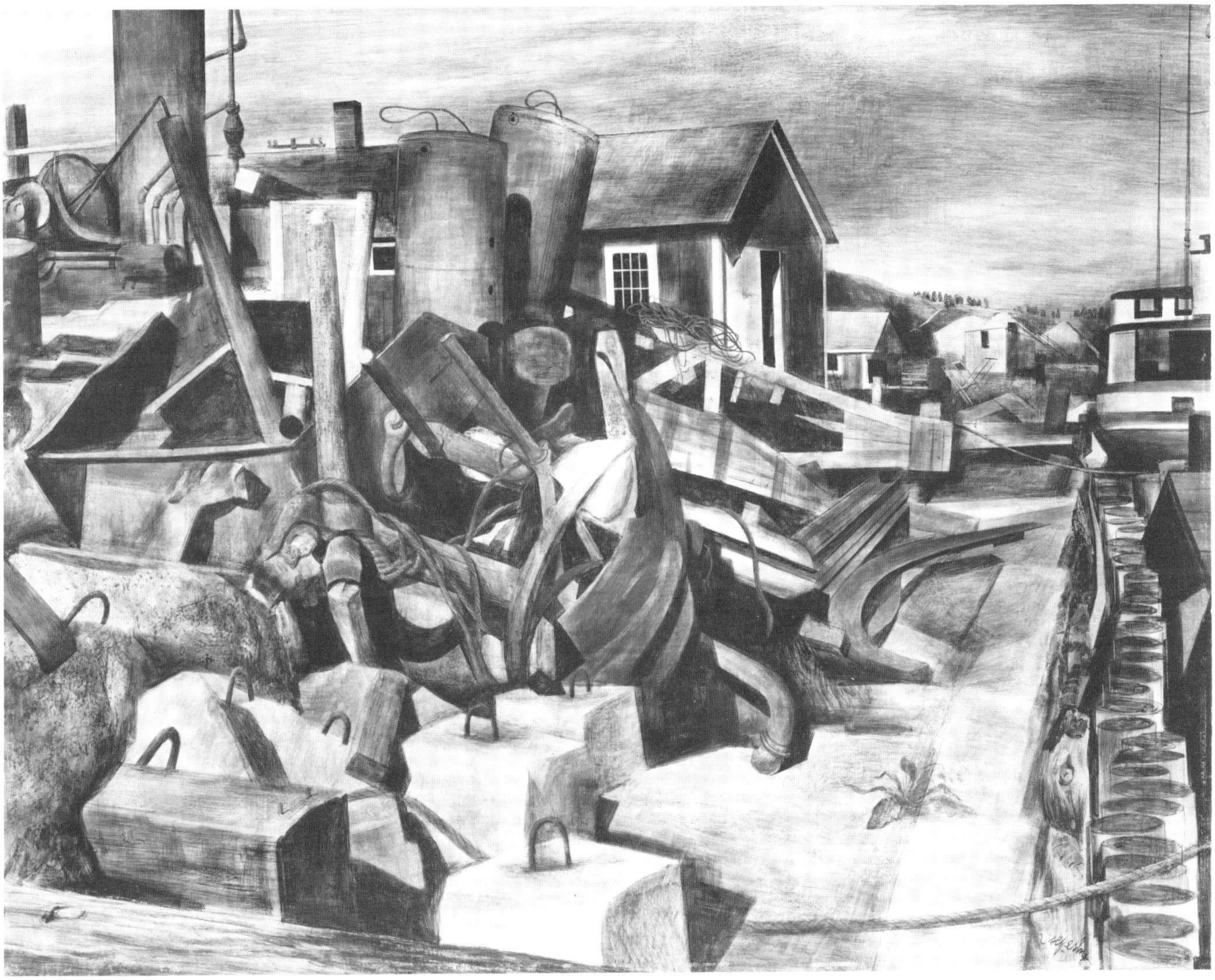

Zoltan Sepeshy (1889–1974). Marine Still Life. *Tempera on masonite. 30 × 38 inches. Collection of the Detroit Institute of Arts, Gift of Dr. and Mrs. George Kamperman. Winner of the Scarab Club Prize, "Exhibition for Michigan Artists," Detroit Institute of Arts, 1946.*

By the early 1950s, however, the "Exhibition for Michigan Artist-Craftsmen" had blossomed into a show of considerable size and prestige, with hundreds of entrants. The exhibition drew participants from practically every active center for crafts in the state. Judging was given over to leading designers, craftsmen, and decorative arts curators from around the country. An increased number of prizes were awarded in a wide range of categories and offered by some of the community's most important patrons. The quality of the work exhibited consistently matched that found in the best national shows.

Chief among the prizes in the 1950s, the Founders Society Purchase Prize became an award of singular distinction. Artists chosen for the prize were more often than not individuals of considerable achievement who were regarded to be among the leaders in their fields. Textile artists **Lillian Holm** and **Liselotte Moser**, ceramicists **Maija Grotell** and **John Foster**, and metalsmiths such as **Earl Krentzin**, **Marion Kenney-Eagen**, and **Fred Kenney-Eagen**—all among the state's most respected names in craft media—were so honored.

The tranquility that had characterized the "Exhibition for Michigan Artists" in the 1940s ended abruptly in 1951, when Michigan was forced to recognize the growing importance of abstract art. The two jurors for that year's show, painter Walter Stuempfig (1914–1970) and Museum of Modern Art curator Dorothy Miller, chose a number of works which utilized abstract elements, and awarded the coveted Founders Society Prize for the first time to a semi-abstract work, *The Black Knight*, by Guy Palazzola. The jurors' selections produced a considerable uproar, with the public and many artists attacking the exhibition as being "too modern," and the critics and museum staff once again defending their choices.

Despite this controversy, it soon became evident that abstraction was to be the mainstream of artistic endeavor and would attract the most critical interest in Michigan. Those established artists whose work did not incorporate the developing forms of abstract art eventually found themselves more often than not excluded by the jurors of the "Exhibition for Michigan Artists" during the last years of the 1950s.

The exhibition reached a critical juncture in 1962, when the jury, nationally recognized artists Gabriel Kohn and Adja Junkers, selected an exhibition that was almost exclusively abstract. Much of the work was done by students or other new artists on the scene. More than any previous "Exhibition for Michigan Artists," the 1962 exhibition placed an emphasis on what was new and what fit into the current mode of experimentation in New York. Although there was much protest once again from the art community, this show set the course for those to follow. Subsequent jurors applied much the same criteria that Kohn and Junkers had applied, weighing the art of Michigan artists against that of artists based in New York. The concept of the exhibition as an annual outing for Michigan's art establishment was abandoned, as the exhibition became a showcase for experimental and provocative work along with works that were imitative of those done by national figures. Many artists who had been yearly participants withdrew from the competition rather than face rejection. Claims were made by the artists, with a considerable amount of justification, that the exhibitions were no longer truly representative of the range of works being done by Michigan artists.

The late 1960s and early 1970s constituted a period of crisis for the "Exhibition for Michigan Artists." No one seemed completely satisfied with the annual, and this dissatisfaction peaked in 1973 when the 59th annual, judged by Dean Swanson, John Varian, and James Monte, three museum professionals from outside the state, produced a greal deal of ire and showed little art. Of the 1,500 works submitted, the jury chose seventy pieces, twenty of which were photographs. The reaction of the art community, particularly the critics, was overwhelmingly negative. Everyone seemed to realize that an exhibition of only seventy works to represent the output of all Michigan artists

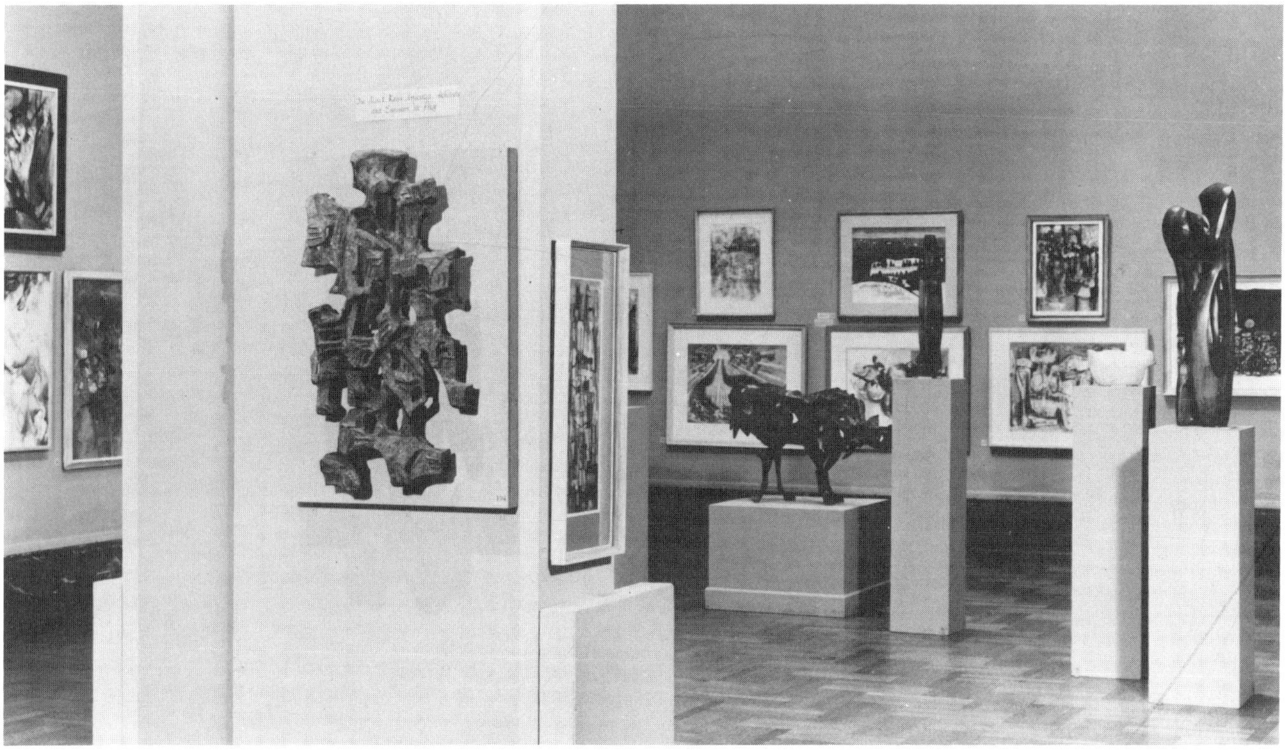

"52nd Annual Exhibition for Michigan Artists," 1962. The Detroit Institute of Arts, Museum Archives.

for a year was ludicrous. *Detroit News* critic Joy Hakanson wrote:

> At issue is the DIA's increasing neglect of the local art community. This neglect shows up in the condescending biennial Michigan exhibitions; in a refusal to search out and encourage really creative artists who work here; in a disregard for informing the public about local art and in a generally negative attitude toward the best galleries which often provide the only consistent platform for contemporary art.[10]

To make matters worse, the 1973 exhibition was also plagued by censorship. Members of the museum's board of trustees objected to the content of two of the photographs in the exhibition, maintaining that they were obscene, and demanded their removal. The museum's administration gave in to these demands and the works were removed. Their removal immediately set off a wave of protest from the two artists involved and their sympathizers, resulting in several other artists removing their works from the exhibition. The exhibition became the focus of media attention and much bad press resulted. Michigan artists in general found the Detroit Institute of Arts' actions inexcusable. Thus, it was finally clear to all concerned that the annual was no longer viable in its traditional form. Over the next few years, as discussed later, various means of presenting the work of Michigan's artists would be explored in an attempt to find a satisfactory formula. But for all practical purposes, the "Exhibition for Michigan Artists" had met its demise.

The period from the late 1960s into the early 1970s also brought trouble for the "Exhibition for Michigan Artist-Craftsmen." In 1966 the exhibition became a biennial and soon after began to show signs of strain. Like the "Exhibition for Michigan Artists," the "Exhibition for Michigan Artist-Craftsmen" became immersed in controversy over the attitudes of its jurors. Many of the state's top artisans refused to participate in the exhibition because they felt the jurors were no longer sensitive to the traditional concerns of craftsmen, relying instead on criteria formerly reserved for the "fine arts."

The final "Exhibition for Michigan Artist-Craftsmen" was held in 1976. By then, the exhibition had little representation from large segments of the craft community. More than twenty-five percent of the thirty-nine artists included in the show were not strongly associated with the traditional craft media. They were, in fact, painters, sculptors, and graphic artists who occasionally tried their hands at ceramics, weaving, or metalwork. At the same time, the exhibition did not include many of Michigan's best-known names in the crafts. These individuals had either been juried out or had not even bothered to enter. The works in the show tended to be nonfunctional and most often sculptural in nature. The exhibition served no special constituency and offered little that could not be seen in a dozen other exhibitions around the state. Like the "Exhibition for Michigan Artists" before it, the crafts show appeared to be moribund.

Other Activities of the Detroit Institute of Arts. Although the two annual exhibitions for Michigan artists and craftsmen were the most visible manifestations of the Detroit Institute of Art's support of the regional art community, other activities have had significant impact as well. Throughout its entire history, beginning with the Art School of the Detroit Museum of Art, the museum has provided educational opportunities for developing young artists. Beginning in the 1930s a whole range of classes was provided by studios and workshops located within the building. Works of art from the collections were used as teaching aids, and members of the education department were made available for lectures and demonstrations. By the 1950s this involvement with art instruction extended to the use of public television. Programs such as "A TV History of Art" and "Inside the DIA" dealt with a wide range of both historical and contemporary topics, utilizing the resources of the art community as a whole as well as those of the museum.

The Detroit Institute of Arts also engaged artists, critics, and scholars to lecture on art. In 1946 the Friends of Modern Art, one of the museum's many support groups, launched a series of lectures on contemporary movements in art which became a continuing and important feature on the community's art calendar. From Yasuo Kuniyoshi to Robert Motherwell to Claes Oldenberg, major figures of the American and international art worlds came to Detroit to exchange their thoughts and ideas about contemporary art with the Michigan art community.

The museum, in the late 1930s, established a separate gallery for exhibiting works by Michigan artists. Located near the museum's modern art galleries, this space featured the works of Michigan artists who were represented in the Detroit Institute of Art's permanent collection. The gallery was small but its pieces were rotated frequently so that, at any given moment, the works shown were fairly representative of what was happening in the art community. For nearly thirty years the museum's administration strongly supported the idea of having a gallery devoted to Michigan artists. Edgar P. Richardson, who served as director from 1943 until 1962, was particularly adamant about maintaining the museum's responsibility to provide the artists of the community with much-needed exposure and prestige. However, in 1963 the Michigan Artists Gallery was dismantled because of a space shortage within the museum.

The nature of the commitment by the Detroit Institute of Arts to Michigan artists changed somewhat in the late 1960s and early 1970s as the museum's focus came to be directed toward exhibitions and programs that would give it recognition in the international art world. At the same time, the growth of other institutions, organizations, and galleries reduced the regional art scene's dependence on the Detroit Institute of Arts. The museum continued to show and purchase the work of the state's artists, and staff members such as Sam Wagstaff, Curator of Modern Art from 1969 to 1972, were particularly helpful in recognizing and encouraging young artists from the region. However, the Detroit Institute of Arts was perceived by the art community, in this period, to be less supportive of regional art than it had once been, and at times even indifferent to the plight of regional artists.

Among the earliest actions taken to combat this perception of the museum was the formation of a Michigan Artists Committee in 1973. In response to the hostile reception granted the "Exhibition for Michigan Artists" of that year, this group, made up of artists and museum staff members, held a public meeting to discuss the museum's problematic relationship with the state's artists. In 1974, the Detroit Institute of Arts, the Flint Institute of Arts, and the Grand Rapids Art Museum joined forces in a project that was intended to address some of the issues raised by this committee. More than 3,400 works by 1,400 artists were assembled in a Detroit warehouse for scrutiny by a panel of four top out-of-state jurors. The actual presentation of the exhibition, entitled "Michigan Focus," was divided into three segments—painting, sculpture, and works on paper—with each segment presented simultaneously in one of the three participating museums. The state's resources were committed to its artists on an unprecedented level for this exhibition in the hope that it would be more representative of the range of art being produced in Michigan.

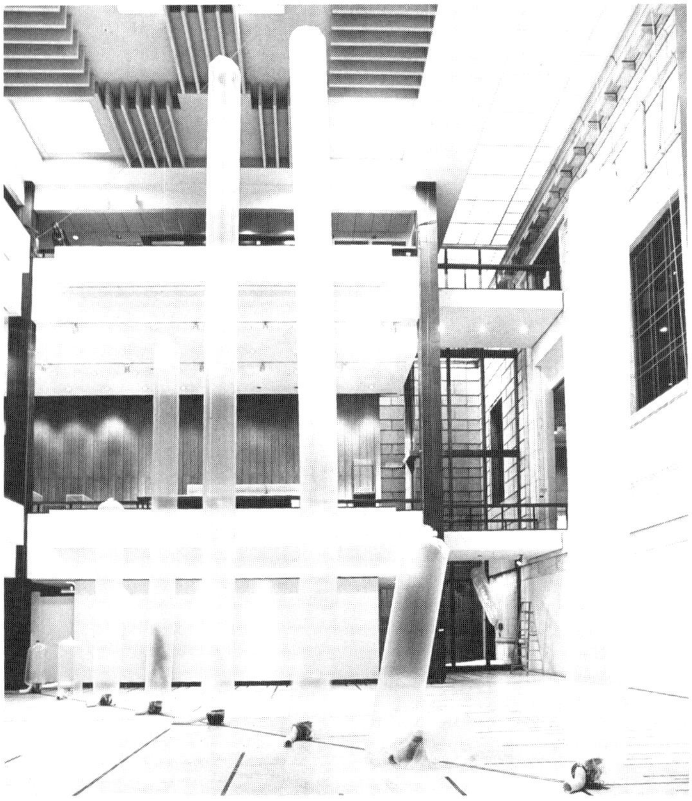

Jim Pallas (1941–). Tube Dance. *Installation from "Works in Progress IV," Detroit Institute of Arts, 1978. The Detroit Institute of Arts, Department of Twentieth-Century Art.*

"Michigan Focus" remained, however, the type of regional competition that in the past had not satisfied the needs of the art community. Despite the scale, the region's artists were still confronted with a one-show survey selected by a jury which, although sympathetic, had little understanding of the local context and its effect on the art produced. "Michigan Focus" complicated matters further by making the exhibition difficult to view; its audience was forced to travel from city to city in order to see it in its entirety. With the show divided in this way, it was virtually impossible for anyone to grasp the range and scope of works by Michigan artists.

The great logistical problems and the less than satisfactory results of "Michigan Focus" prompted the staff of the Detroit Institute of Arts to look for other alternatives. John H. Neff, Curator of Modern Art from 1974 to 1978, instituted a series of programs that helped to reestablish the museum's role in the Michigan art community. He and his staff spent many hours visiting the studios of artists across the state. They also organized exhibitions that focused on historic aspects of the Michigan art community, most notably "Arts and Crafts in Detroit 1906–1976." The museum's rental gallery, which had functioned for many years as a minor outlet for some of Michigan's artists, was upgraded, with Neff curating a number of small exhibitions. He also organized a day-long symposium that explored the problems experienced by Michigan artists and the possibilities of collaboration with the museum in resolving some of them. Neff's most notable contribution, however, was the institution of "Works in Progress," a series of exhibitions intended as an alternative to the annual "Exhibition for Michigan Artists." "Works in Progress" were one-person exhibitions and small invitational shows that were held between 1975 and 1979.

The "Works in Progress" series, in its first year, provided major exhibitions for Michigan painter **Aris Koutroulis** and environmental artist **Germaine Keller**. The following year eleven artists, among them Ivy Sky Rutzky, **David Barr**, and **John Egner**, were part of a group show entitled "Detroit Area Artists." Sculptor **Michael Hall** soon followed with the installation of a series of massive on-site structures which occupied one of the main courts of the museum for nearly five months. Many other one-person shows were presented and catalogues of the "Works in Progress" shows were published, with critical essays, including one written by New York critic Robert Pincus-Witten.

The principal drawback of this series was its inability to give exposure to more than a half-dozen or so artists per year. The great majority of Michigan artists still did not have the opportunity to present their work in the state's largest museum. Nevertheless, the program received a great deal of praise from many significant sections of the art community, and the Detroit Institute of Arts' commitment to the art of its own place and time was well demonstrated. National media coverage was given to some of the shows, and museums in other states, most significantly the Albright-Knox Museum in Buffalo, adopted similar policies for the exhibition of regional art.

Regional Museums

The Detroit Institute of Arts, of course, is not the only Michigan art museum to have affected Michigan artists. Virtually all of the state's art museums have involved themselves in some way in the contemporary art scene. Indicative of the kinds of activities undertaken by these institutions are those of the four oldest municipal museums: the Muskegon Museum of Art (formerly the Hackley Art Gallery), the Grand Rapids Art Museum, the Kalamazoo Institute of Arts, and the Flint Institute of Arts.

The Hackley Art Gallery. The small western Michigan city of Muskegon was the first community to follow Detroit's lead and establish its own art museum. The Hackley Art Gallery, re-named the Muskegon Museum of Art in 1981, was established in 1912 and owes its existence to the philanthropy of the city's wealthiest citizen, Charles M. Hackley. Hackley provided the funds to construct a library, hospital, training school, and parks, and left a small bequest of $150,000 for the purchase of "pictures of the best kind."[11] This bequest allowed Muskegon to be the first city in the United States with a population under 30,000 to create and maintain a public art gallery. The gallery soon developed programs aimed at enhancing the local art scene. Children's classes in art were offered and the work of local artists was displayed.

In 1927 the Hackley Art Gallery established the "Annual West Michigan Juried Competition," more popularly called "The Regional." This competition, along with exhibitions held at the Kalamazoo Institute of Arts and the Grand Rapids Art Museum, developed into one of the most important annual competitions for artists living in the southwest section of the state. "The Regional" has continued to be a mainstay of the Muskegon Museum of Art's program for local artists.

The Grand Rapids Art Museum. As in many American cities, the development of a cultural center in Grand Rapids was related to the activities of various women's organizations. In 1911 the Grand Rapids Art Association was established as an outgrowth of the Federation of Women's Clubs. The association sponsored exhibitions and lectures throughout the teens, and by 1924 was able to open the Grand Rapids Art Gallery. Under the direction of Mary Swarthout, the first exhibitions of work by local artists were held, and by the end of her tenure in 1935, the groundwork also had been laid for an art school under the auspices of the gallery. A little more than a decade later, the gallery enhanced its professional image by affiliating with the University of Michigan extension and by establishing an annual juried exhibition, the "West Michigan Annual."

The "West Michigan Annual" drew hundreds of entries from artists throughout southwestern Michigan each year during its existence from 1946 to 1962. Its impact on the region was so great, in fact, that it was decided that the museum could better serve the artists by dividing the exhibition in half. In 1963 the first "Michigan Painters-Printmakers Exhibition" was held, followed a year later by the "Michigan Artists-Craftsmen Exhibition." These two exhibitions continued to alternate throughout the 1960s and 1970s. The gallery changed its name to the Grand Rapids Art Museum in 1963.

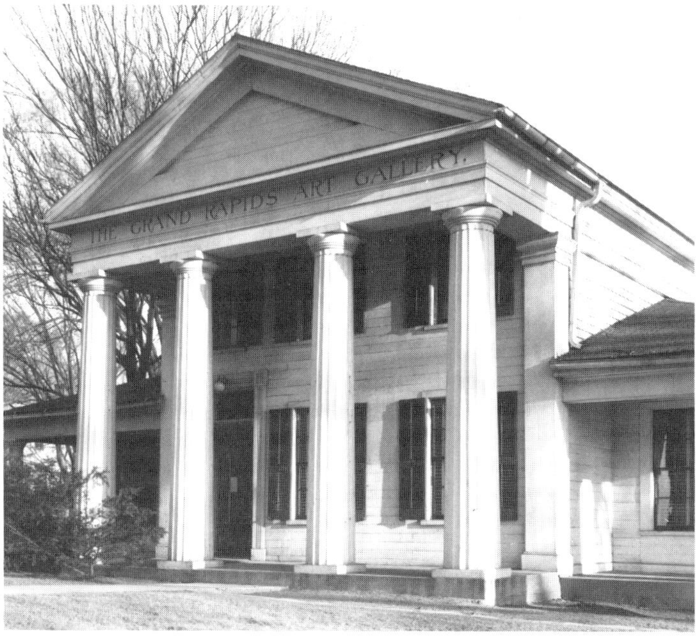

The Grand Rapids Art Gallery, forerunner of the Grand Rapids Art Museum, ca. 1940. Courtesy the Grand Rapids Art Museum.

In the late 1960s and throughout the 1970s the Grand Rapids Art Museum came to be a key force behind a number of events that brought new life to the art scene in the city. A small volunteer group, the museum's Women's Committee, put together a series of exhibitions that intensified the city's contact with twentieth-century art: "Twentieth Century Painting" in 1967, "Sculpture of the '60s" in 1969, and "Spatial Discoveries" in 1971. The climactic event was the staging of a major outdoor sculpture exhibition in 1974, "Sculpture off the Pedestal." This last show involved thirteen nationally known sculptors: Stephen Antanakos, Mark Di Suvero, Dale Eldred, **Michael Hall**, John Henry, William King, Lyman Kipp, Clement Meadmore, Boyd Medford, Robert Morris, Robert Murray, and Steven Urry. All of the artists were invited to come to Grand Rapids to fabricate and construct their pieces, and eight actually did so. The Women's Committee enlisted the aid of all segments of the community to execute the project, so that local millwrights, construction workers, and welders were used. Grand Rapids artists helped in the planning and logistics, and housing for the artists was offered by local residents. Thus the exhibition became a community-wide experience, and its success was a major boost for the artists of Grand Rapids, as it produced a more receptive atmosphere for their work. Grand Rapids gained a wide reputation for its contemporary art enterprises, thanks to the leading role played by its museum.

The Kalamazoo Institute of Arts. The history of the Kalamazoo Institute of Arts reflects its strong involvement with working artists. Its evolution was partly a result of the efforts of the Kalamazoo chapter of the American Federation of the Arts, whose main activities in the 1920s consisted of art classes taught by Nina Ward. The actual formation of the institute came when two organizations joined together: the Art League, a group that staged exhibitions and sponsored lectures, and the Palette and Chisel Club, a group of artists who conducted various art classes under the direction of painter Frank Oliver. These two organizations incorporated in 1924 as the Kalamazoo Institute of Arts. For the next two years, the institute struggled along, seeking financing, a permanent home, and a director. By the 1930s it had emerged as an effective center for the arts, having found a building, some financial support, and an energetic director who was a working artist, Sylvester Jerry. A painter from Wisconsin, Jerry was hired as director in 1931. His responsibilities included teaching art classes, arranging exhibitions, opening and closing the building, and stoking the furnace. Jerry's presence reinforced the emphasis on contemporary art that had marked the institute's activities from its inception. The Kalamazoo Institute of Arts' first exhibition in 1929 had been a show of contemporary American art, and a year later it staged its first presentation of work by area artists.

The Kalamazoo Institute of Arts in the 1930s initiated a lecture series that brought some of the most influential figures in art, including Thomas Hart Benton, Holger Cahill, Le Corbusier, Diego Rivera, and Frank Lloyd Wright, to the city. Jerry left the Kalamazoo Institute of Arts in 1935 to become director of the Works Progress Administration/Federal Arts Project in Michigan, but in the years that followed, the institution continued to have working artists as its directors, such as George Rickey, Ulfert Wilke, and Karl Priebe. Indeed, the Kalamazoo Institute of Arts was one of the few art centers in the state to be headed by artists in the 1930s and 1940s.

An innovative "artist-in-residence" program was sponsored nationally in the late 1930s and early 1940s by the Carnegie Corporation, and both Olivet and Kalamazoo Colleges were involved with this project. Selected artists of promising or proven ability were invited to make their art in educational settings, and talented artists such as Alexander Brooks, George Rickey, and Philip Evergood came to the city. Within a short time, most of these artists found themselves involved in teaching classes at the Kalamazoo Institute of Arts as well, thus becoming available to many of the area's developing artists.

At the end of World War II, the Kalamazoo Institute of Arts continued its practice of hiring studio artists as directors. Painters, printmakers, and sculptors guided the institution through the next three decades. The presence of painter Alfred Maurice, sculptor **Kirk Newman**, and printmaker Harry Greaver assured the continued involvement with contemporary art and with such exhibitions as the Kalamazoo Area Show for the region's artists.

The Flint Institute of Arts. The Flint Institute of Arts grew out of the small Flint School of Art and Design. From the time of the Institute's founding in 1928, its programs stressed art education. **Jaroslav Brozik**, a painter with a strong academic background, was hired as assistant director, with the duties of teaching both adult and childrens' classes, and these became one of the main strengths of the institute.

The Flint Institute's exhibition schedule in its early years was strongly oriented toward contemporary American art, with shows featuring the work of artists such as Alexander Archipenko, Rockwell Kent, and Ivan Olinsky. Michigan artists were also given both one-person and group exhibitions. In 1931 the Flint Institute of Arts staged its first juried regional exhibition, the "Flint Artists Show," which became an important part of the area's cultural life, and remains the principal exhibition for Flint artists.

One of the innovations of the Flint Institute of Arts was the development of the Flint Artists Market in 1946. Designed to showcase and sell the work of the area's artists, this was the first such gallery located within a Michigan museum. In 1956 the Flint Institute of Arts moved into its present building, the DeWaters Art Center, giving it enlarged gallery and exhibition space.

Artist Groups and Associations

Artists form associations for a number of reasons: to foster professionalism, promote the work of members, help with public relations, ease the burden of expenses, and often simply to provide comradeship. Many of the associations formed in Michigan have been short-lived and extremely limited in their effectiveness, but others have survived for scores of years and played important roles in the development of the artistic climate in Michigan.

Artist Groups

The Detroit Society of Women Painters and Sculptors. It is ironic that in a profession so dominated by men, the first organization in the state formed exclusively for painters was organized by women. Lillian Meeser, a painter with considerable training and professional experience, was both the spiritual and organizing force behind the founding of the Detroit Society of Women Painters in 1903. The Society was expanded to include women sculptors in 1930.

During the first years of its existence, the Society included almost every woman artist of note in the city. Although many were amateurs, others were professionals, including Alexandrine McEwen and **Katherine McEwen**, **Letta Crapo Smith**, and ceramicist **Mary Chase Stratton**. At no point during the period from 1903 to 1913 did the Society's membership exceed thirty, yet it had considerable impact upon the community as a whole, offering group discussions, exhibitions, and studio classes.

The Detroit Society of Women Painters was the first art organization in Michigan to hold an annual exhibition of its members' works. In 1904 Meeser put together the first such exhibition, a credible show of landscapes and portraits, held at the Detroit Museum of Art. The *Detroit Free Press* wrote: "Up until a year ago such a thing as a society of women artists was unknown in Detroit. Indeed, it was thought impossible that such a thing could exist, as it was believed that there were too few women painters to keep up an organization. But this exhibition certainly proves otherwise." The highest accolade, perhaps, came from the *News-Tribune:* "Better than some of the men painters have done," which was certainly high praise for the times.

For seven years the annual exhibition of the Detroit Society of Women Painters remained the only annual show of any kind that originated in Michigan. As time passed, however, the location was moved from the Detroit Museum of Art to less prestigious spaces and the quality of the work exhibited fluctuated.

Esther Longyear McGraw and several other members brought a new momentum to the society in 1928 by staging an exhibition of small paintings by the membership at the J. L. Hudson Company department store. This exhibit was instantly successful in sales and critical reception and became an annual affair. That same year, Longyear was also the force behind the organization of a two-week show of the Society's work at the Holt Gallery in New York.

The Detroit Society of Women Painters began what was to become a long association with the Scarab Club in 1932. Using the Scarab Club as a base of operation, the Society thrived. Its membership included art instructors in the public schools, members of college art department faculties, and women who combined their artistic production with running a home. Although the significance of the Society lessened in the 1970s, it retained a membership of over 100 women artists from the Detroit area.

The Pewabic Pottery. Two of the most influential organizations founded in the early years of the twentieth century were centered on the crafts rather than the fine arts. Influenced by the ideas of British designer and social critic William Morris (1834–1896), individuals in Detroit and dozens of other American cities became concerned about the lack of good design and craftsmanship in many American commercial products of the time. To reestablish high-quality production in the crafts, societies were formed to sponsor lectures, exhibitions, and classes. The principal Michigan adherents to the philosophies of the Arts and Crafts Movement were the organizers of the Detroit Society of Arts and Crafts and the Pewabic Pottery.

Not only was the Pewabic Pottery the outstanding commercial success of the Arts and Crafts Movement in Michigan, it also served as a focus for ceramic activity in the state. Opened in 1903 by **Mary Chase** Perry (later **Stratton**) and Horace J. Caulkins, the Pottery's intent was to provide objects for everyday use that would reflect good design and workmanship. The Pottery made vases, lamps, bowls, candlesticks, and other useful objects and developed several unique iridescent glazes. The bulk of the Pottery's business, however, was in the production of ceramic tiles for both interior and exterior use.

For many decades the Pewabic Pottery's facilities on East Jefferson Avenue were without equal in Michigan and attracted ceramicists and ceramic students from all over the southeastern part of the state. Perry taught classes there, and for some time ceramic courses

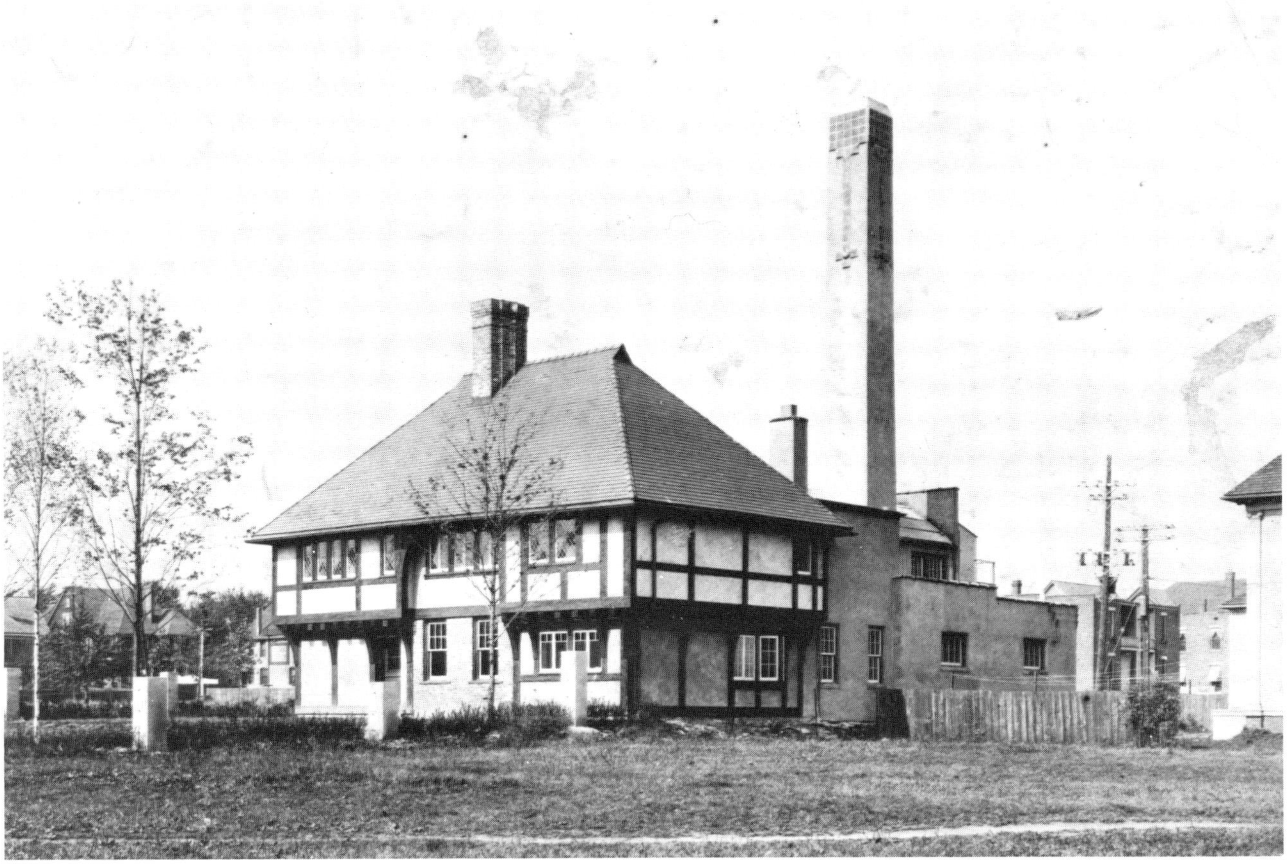

Pewabic Pottery on Jefferson Avenue, Detroit, ca. 1910. Courtesy Thomas Brunk.

offered by both the Art School of the Detroit Society of Arts and Crafts and Wayne State University were taught at Pewabic. Until the rapid growth of ceramic departments in universities and art schools during the post-World War II period, the Pewabic Pottery was the most important ceramic facility in the state.

Key patrons of the Detroit art community, such as Charles Lang Freer, the renowned collector of Asian and American art, were particularly supportive, bringing many architects to review the Pottery's work for possible use in commissions. By the second decade of the century, architects of considerable stature like Ralph Adams Cram (1863–1942) and Cass Gilbert (1854–1934) were using Pewabic tile to decorate important buildings. During the building boom that swept Michigan and the rest of the country in the 1920s, the Pottery's architectural commissions reached an apex. Major structures like the National Shrine of the Immaculate Conception in Washington, D.C., and local buildings like the Detroit Institute of Arts and the Guardian Building, along with scores of the finest private homes being built throughout Michigan, were decorated with Pewabic tile.

The Pewabic Pottery's influence was also felt in the art community. In 1918 Mary Chase Perry married architect William Buck Stratton; by then she had become a sought-after teacher and lecturer and her style was widely copied. She was involved as a faculty member, board member, or was active in other capacities in virtually every art institution in Detroit.

The Pottery's influence began to wane in the 1930s as the demand for the kind of architectural decorative work that had been its financial mainstay lessened, but the Pottery survived as an operating concern until Stratton's death in 1964. In 1966 Michigan State University acquired the Pottery and reopened it as an extension center offering classes in ceramics.

The Detroit Society of Arts and Crafts. Officially founded in 1906, the Detroit Society of Arts and Crafts grew out of a crafts exhibition organized a few years earlier at the Detroit Museum of Art by patrons George Booth, Albert Kahn, and Horace Caulkins, ceramicist Mary Chase Perry and architect William Stratton. The success of this exhibition led to the organization of a permanent society dedicated to advancing the cause of good design. The Detroit Society of Arts and

Crafts initiated an exhibition program that presented the works of European and American craftsmen, a lecture series, and a showroom for the sale of contemporary crafts. Although the Society vigorously promoted all three of these aspects, the exhibition program was to have the greatest impact.

From 1906 to 1931 the Society staged more than 100 exhibitions, offering Michigan residents the opportunity to see major works by many distinguished artisans. Tapestries from the Herter Looms, the jewelry of May Morris, silver by Georg Jensen, pottery by Charles Binns, and textiles by various Swedish artists were all exhibited. In one spectacular year in the 1930s, the Society not only presented an exhibition of the work of world-renowned English potter Bernard Leach, but also held one of the few American showings of objects from the 1925 "International Paris Exposition of Modern Decorative and Industrial Arts," the pivotal exhibition that introduced Art Deco and shaped American design for the next decade.

Backed by funds from Booth and Caulkins, the Society expanded rapidly in the two decades after its founding. An ambitious building was constructed at 47 Watson Street in 1916, incorporating offices, showrooms, a little theater, and a central courtyard surrounded by workshops for the various crafts. The Society hosted the Ninth Annual Conference of the American Federation of Arts in 1918, and more than 4,000 delegates from 229 chapters across the nation found the Arts and Crafts Movement in Detroit as strong as any in the nation.

The Art School of the Detroit Society of Arts and Crafts was opened in the building on Watson Street in 1926, and most of the Society's efforts and resources were diverted to this endeavor. The showrooms closed in 1931, and the exhibition program was handed over to one of its most active supporters, collector Robert Tannahill. Tannahill changed the exhibition policy, eliminating the contemporary crafts shows, and bringing instead what he considered to be the best of twentieth-century painting and sculpture to Detroit. Although working with a small budget, for the next nine years Tannahill exhibited works by such artists as Henri Matisse, George Rouault, Georgia O'Keeffe, John Marin, and Charles Sheeler, thus providing the Michigan art community with the only continuing opportunity to see examples of the major avant-garde works of the time. Although few of these exhibitions ever drew more than several hundred people, they had an important impact on a small number of local collectors such as Edsel and Eleanor Ford, Mr. and Mrs. George Kamperman, and John Newberry. Many works purchased at these exhibitions would later find their way into the Detroit Institute of Arts and form the basis for its modern art collection.

The economic and social strains of World War II forced the closing of the gallery in 1941, although the art school continued in operation. All of the Society's further efforts from this time on would be made in the area of art education.

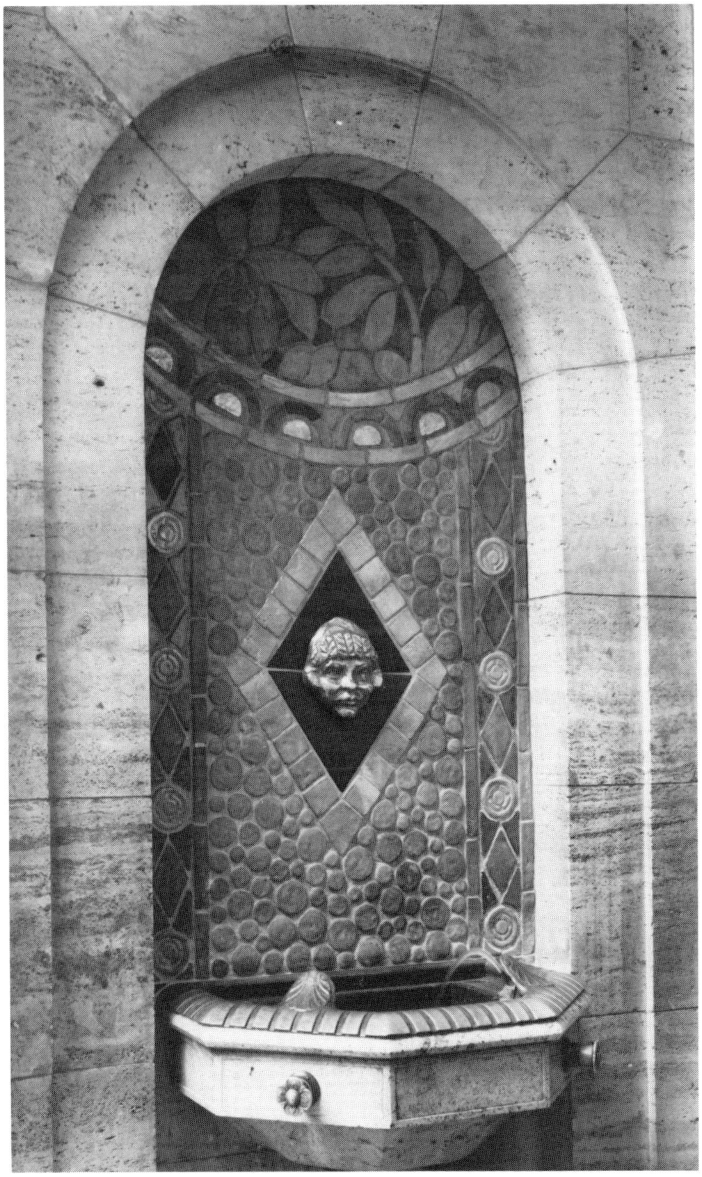

Gwen Lux (1910–). Pewabic Pottery commission for the Detroit Institute of Arts. The Detroit Institute of Arts, Museum Archives.

The Scarab Club (Hopkin Club). The Hopkin Club evolved out of informal gatherings in the Detroit studio of marine painter Robert Hopkin (1832–1909). This grand old man of Michigan painting provided younger artists with a place where they could enjoy good fellowship, discuss art, and eat a meal together. In a city where there were few such sympathetic meeting spots, the Hopkin studio soon became the center of

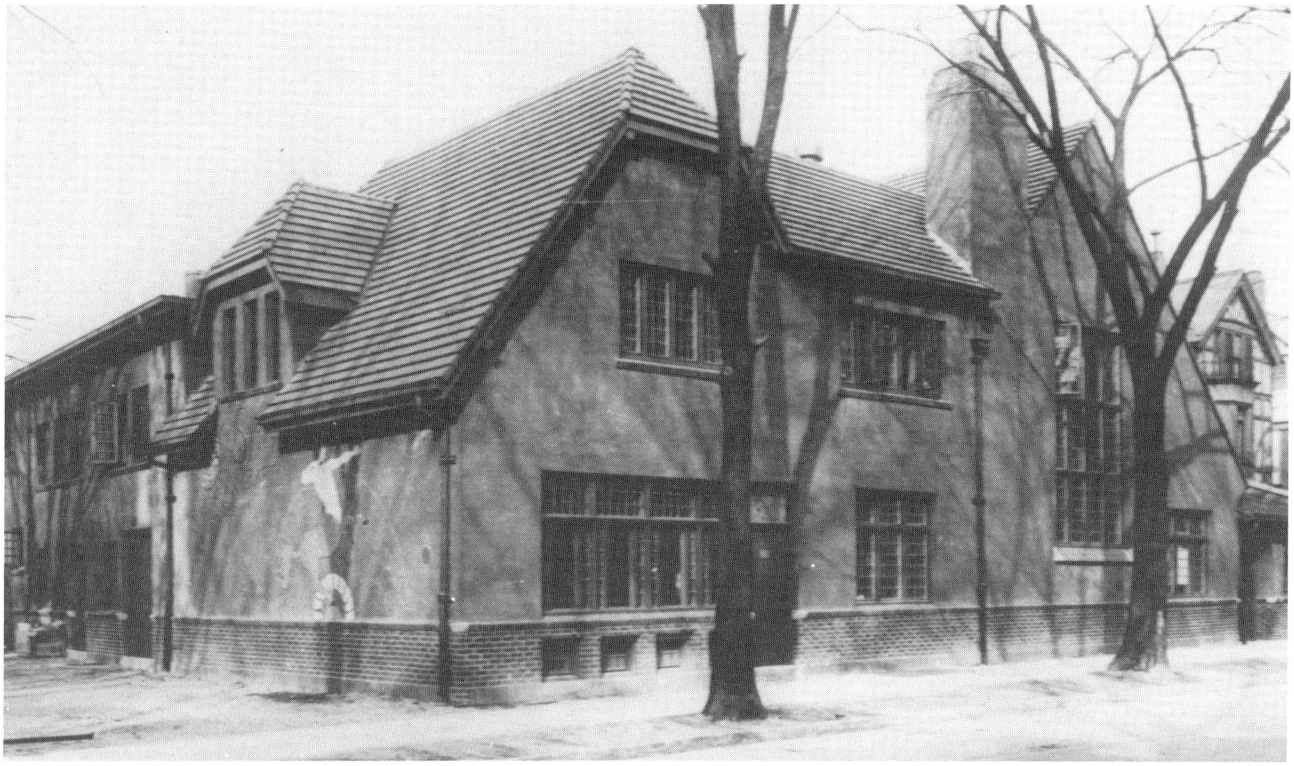

The Detroit Society of Arts and Crafts, 47 Watson Street, 1916. The Archives of American Art, DSAC Scrapbook.

social life for many of the region's best-known artists. In 1907 this group decided to organize, calling themselves the "Hopkin Club," and began to meet in various clubhouses and beer-halls around Detroit. Despite its rather unassuming nature, the Hopkin Club soon became the only artist organization that, in fact, wielded a measure of power. Its membership included artists of considerable reputation, such as **Myron Barlow**, **Joseph Gies**, **Percy Ives**, **Francis Petrus Paulus**, and **Julius Rolshoven**, as well as influential supporters of the city's art scene, like the administrator of the Detroit Museum of Art, Clyde Burroughs.

Within a few years of the Hopkin Club's founding, Burroughs and James Swan succeeded in organizing an exhibition of 155 pieces representing the works of sixteen artists. The "Hopkin Club Exhibition" of 1911, held in the main gallery of the Detroit Museum of Art, was a great success, drawing crowds of viewers, capturing the attention of the media, and selling many works. Perceived as a major cultural achievement for Michigan artists and as a sign that the community had reached a certain level of maturity, it would become an annual event.

A year after the death of Robert Hopkin, the Hopkin Club's members voted to change its name to the "Scarab Club," taking the name from the scarab beetle, which in ancient Egyptian culture symbolized immortality. The Scarab Club remained a powerful force in the Michigan art world throughout the teens and 1920s. Its annual show, which eventually came to be known as the "Scarab Club Exhibition for Michigan Artists," was the most prestigious show in the state.

In 1928, however, a controversy arose which led to the demise of the Club as a major power. As the annual exhibition had grown in importance, it had also burgeoned in size, and the Detroit Institute of Arts had assumed a greater portion of control. Jurying, once the exclusive preserve of Scarab Club members, was opened to nonmembers and eventually became a function that was filled by artists from outside Michigan.

Although the Club's members had chosen the out-of-state jurors for the 1928 show, those jurors were overwhelmingly "modern" in their point of view. The jury selected pieces by younger, more radical artists, eliminating the works of a majority of the Scarab Club members. This placed the Club in the unhappy and untenable position of being the sponsor of a show that was an open affront to most of the Club's members. The only realistic course of action possible was for the club to withdraw from further sponsorship of the annual show. Left without its greatest source of influence and dominated by an aging group of artists

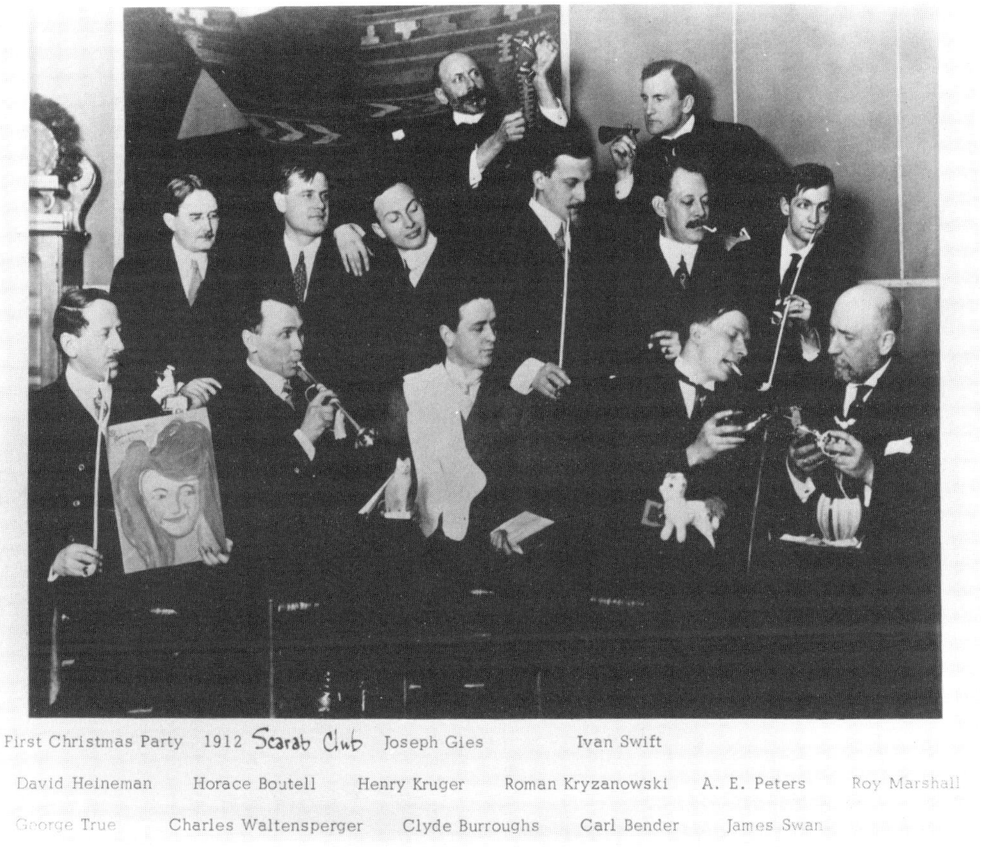

Scarab Club Christmas Party, 1912. The Detroit Institute of Arts, Museum Archives.

who were, for the most part, out of step with the times, the Scarab Club functioned more and more as a social gathering place. It still included major figures of the Michigan art scene among its membership, and still hosted bohemian social events such as masked balls and tradition-filled parties for important visitors, but it no longer functioned as a place where the latest ideas about art were generated and discussed.

The membership of the Scarab Club came to be dominated by men in the commercial arts in the 1940s and 1950s. Some of the top artists in the fields of advertising and design made the Club the center for their professional activities. The "fine" artists who remained among the membership tended toward the conservative end of the spectrum, and most younger artists shied away. In an effort to increase its membership, the Club was opened to women in 1962. Threatened with the demolition of its building in the late 1970s, the members managed to get an historic designation for the clubhouse, an important step toward revitalization of the group.

The Ann Arbor Art Association. The Ann Arbor Art Association was founded in 1909. Among its early organizers were potter H. C. Markham; painter Alice Hunt; director of the Detroit Museum of Art, Armand Griffith; and the head of the University of Michigan College of Architecture, Emil Lorch. The Association sponsored exhibitions and a lecture series; it also served as an auxiliary teaching resource for the University of Michigan, holding classes in university buildings and even receiving a subsidy from the university's Board of Regents. Because the University had no fine arts department until 1920, members of the Association also served as an adjunct faculty for the University, teaching classes in printmaking and drawing.

The Association's inaugural exhibition in 1910 featured an impressive display of oriental and American art, including a section for Michigan artists, with works by **Myron Barlow**, **Della Garretson**, **Gari Melchers**, **Julius Rolshoven**, and **John P. Wicker**. In the 1920s, some of the top names in Michigan art exhibited: **Ernest Harrison Barnes**, **Leon Makielski**, Geza Maroti, Gerrit Benneker, and **David Fredenthal**. By arrangement with New York art dealer Edith Halpert, in 1934 the Association broadened its scope and presented works by John Marin and Georgia O'Keeffe. A year later the Association shook Ann Arbor with an exhibition of the works of Pablo Picasso, Henri Matisse, Fernand Léger, André Masson, and Marie Laurencin. By the 1930s the Association had begun to acquire works for a permanent collection.

The 1946 opening of the University's Museum of Art made the Association's exhibition program, which in many ways was representative of the kind of general exhibition program for which a museum is usually responsible, somewhat of a duplication of effort. It was subsequently decided that a policy committee would be set up to steer a course for the Association which would complement yet not compete with the changing and expanding role of the University in the community's art life. The policy committee, which included a number of individuals who were members of both the Association and the University's art faculty, pushed for a program which heavily emphasized lectures, workshops, tours, and films, and sought to increase the Association's role in adult education. The Association's exhibition policy began to stress regional exhibitions rather than those that were national or international in scope. Annual group exhibitions for members and one- and two-person shows for artists from southeastern Michigan dominated the exhibition schedule.

The activities of the Association in the 1970s centered on the acquisition of a permanent headquarters. In its previous sixty-odd years of existence, the Association had always operated out of makeshift facilities at the university or various leased spaces around the city. The establishment of new, permanent headquarters in downtown Ann Arbor allowed the Association to greatly expand its programs and its visibility.

Other Artist Groups

The Pen and Palette Club. Formed in Detroit in 1926, the Pen and Palette Club was the state's first black artists' organization. It was sponsored by the Detroit Urban League as part of a larger effort to enhance the cultural efforts of Michigan blacks. Programs for writers, musicians, and dramatists were begun by the League at that time also.

The driving forces behind the Pen and Palette Club were painter Henry Stevens; head of the Detroit Urban League, John Dancy; and art dealer and patron, Albert DeSalle. These three, plus the others they gathered about them, sought to provide black artists with access to good artistic training, adequate studio space, and artistic interchange. Most of all, however, they sought to make the Pen and Palette Club a means by which the black artists of the community could achieve some notice and professional respectability in a period when it was extremely difficult to get their art before the public, much less to have it treated seriously.

DeSalle made the Pen and Palette Club a cause among the members of the white art establishment. Through his influence, white artists and patrons lent their support to the activities of the club. Artists such as **Paul Honoré**, **Reginald Bennett**, and **Francis DeErdely**, for example, taught classes at the Club. Others, such as painter **Zoltan Sepeshy**, patron George Kamperman, and Detroit Institute of Arts director William Valentiner, lent their prestige to the Club's annual exhibition by acting as sponsors and jurors.

Central to the Club's efforts on behalf of black artists was an annual exhibition for its members. The exhibition, which was always staged in an important location in the city and always supported by the white art establishment, focused the art community's attention on the works of black artists. For many of the Pen and Palette's members, this was the only real exposure their work received outside the black community during the year, and for many young black artists it was the first exhibition of their works in a professional way. Year after year the "Pen and Palette Annual Exhibition" brought to the public's attention the works of such talented artists as **Hughie Lee-Smith**, **Charles McGee**, **Henri Umbaji King**, and **Leroy Foster**. The Pen and Palette Club remained a strong, vital organization throughout most of the 1930s and 1940s, when it served as a training ground and meeting place for young artists who would figure prominently in the next two decades.

The Arts Extended Groupe. Still, in fact, segregated by the social norms of the 1950s, a group of younger black artists who had been connected with the Pen and Palette Club decided to set up a center in Detroit where they could share studios, equipment, and gallery space, and conduct classes. The Arts Extended Groupe was composed of Charles Finger, Laverne Finger, Alice Lightfoot, Myrtle Hall, Richard Kinney, Mae Morris, Cledie Taylor, Rodney Warren, and James Wilson, among others. In 1956 the Arts Extended Groupe opened the state's first gallery showing the works of black artists. Their operation was an immediate success, and soon classes were offered and black artists from across the state were attracted to the group's activities. The gallery operation was so successful that the space could not accommodate the number of artists who wished to show. Arts Extended maintained a gallery operation exhibiting the works of black artists throughout the 1960s and 1970s.

The Contemporary Studio. The success of Arts Extended led to the establishment of a third black artist association in Detroit known as the Contemporary Studio. In 1958 painters **Henry Umbaji King** and **Harold Neal**, together with such leading black artists as **Leroy Foster**, **Ernest Hardman**, and **Charles McGee**, established headquarters in a second-floor flat near the

YOUNG ARTISTS AT WORK 1942

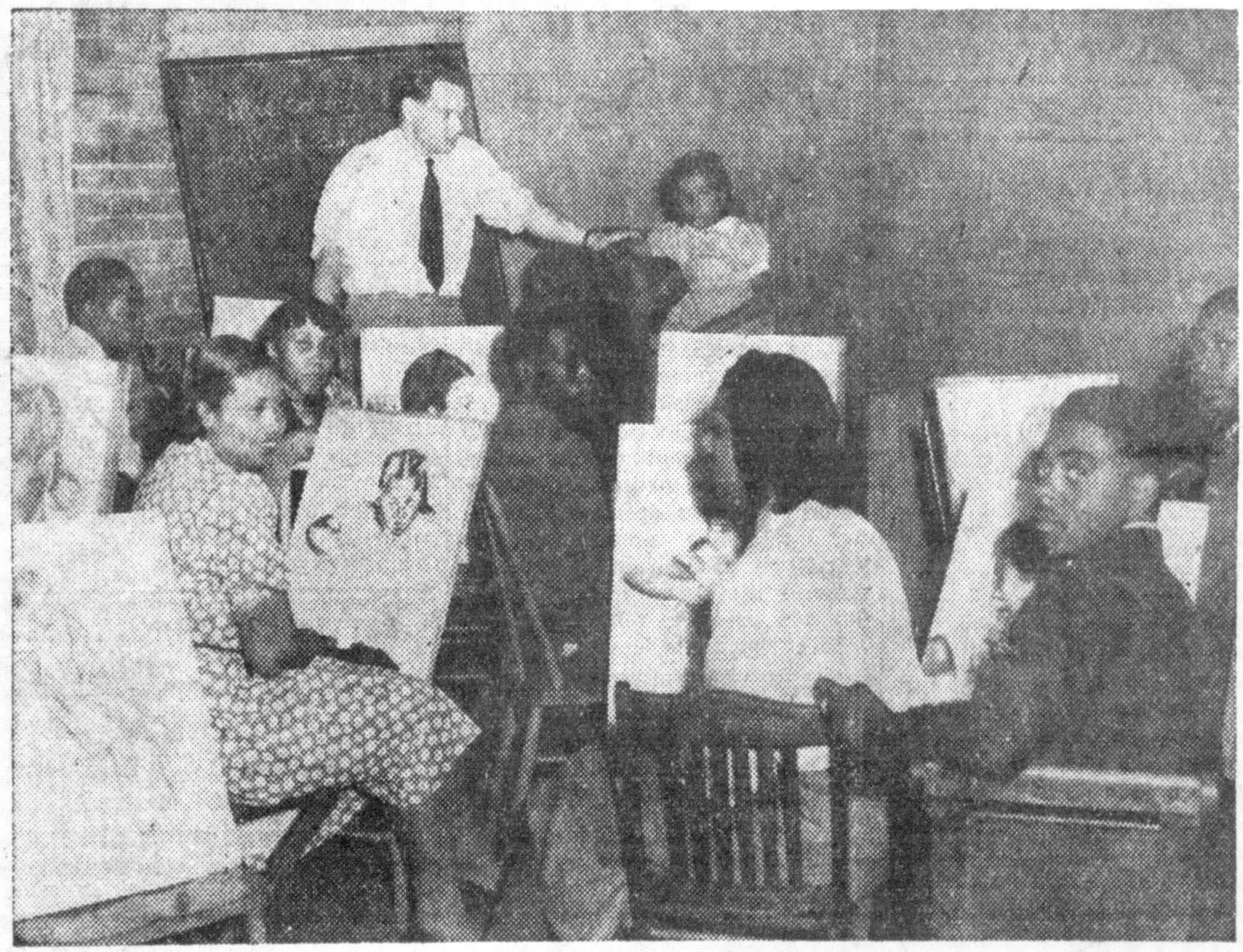

Members of the Pen and Palette Art club which is sponsored by the Detroit Urban league are shown at work while instructor Francis de Erdley is directing the model. Mr. Erdley is a distinguished artist who is volunteering his service for this important work. The Pen and Palette group meets regularly at the Chestnutt Street center of the Urban league which is headed by John Dancy.

Francis DeErdely (1909–1959) teaching a class at the Pen and Palette Club, Detroit, 1942. Courtesy the Detroit Free Press.

John C. Lodge expressway and held exhibitions, auctions, classes, seminars, and discussions. Newspaper critics praised the efforts and exhibitions of the group's members, and they began to plan for the establishment of a major gallery and center of operation for the association. Unfortunately, the momentum of the organization lasted only for a few years, and by the end of the 1960s, the Contemporary Studio had ceased to function.

The Michigan Water Color Society. Seventy artists interested in promoting watercolor as an artistic medium joined together in 1946 to develop a regional organization. The organizers of the Michigan Water Color Society, drawn mostly from the University of Michigan, Wayne State University, and the Scarab Club, included some of the best known watercolorists in the state: Donald Brackett, **Mary Jane Bigler**, **Wayne Claxton**, **Donald Gooch**, **Louise Nobili**, **Jean Paul Slusser**, and **Emil Weddige**. The Society organized a lecture series, established a prize for watercolor to be awarded at the annual "Exhibition for Michigan Artists" at the Detroit Institute of Arts, and sponsored a number of watercolor exhibitions, including a juried annual show held in various locations in Michigan, that was particu-

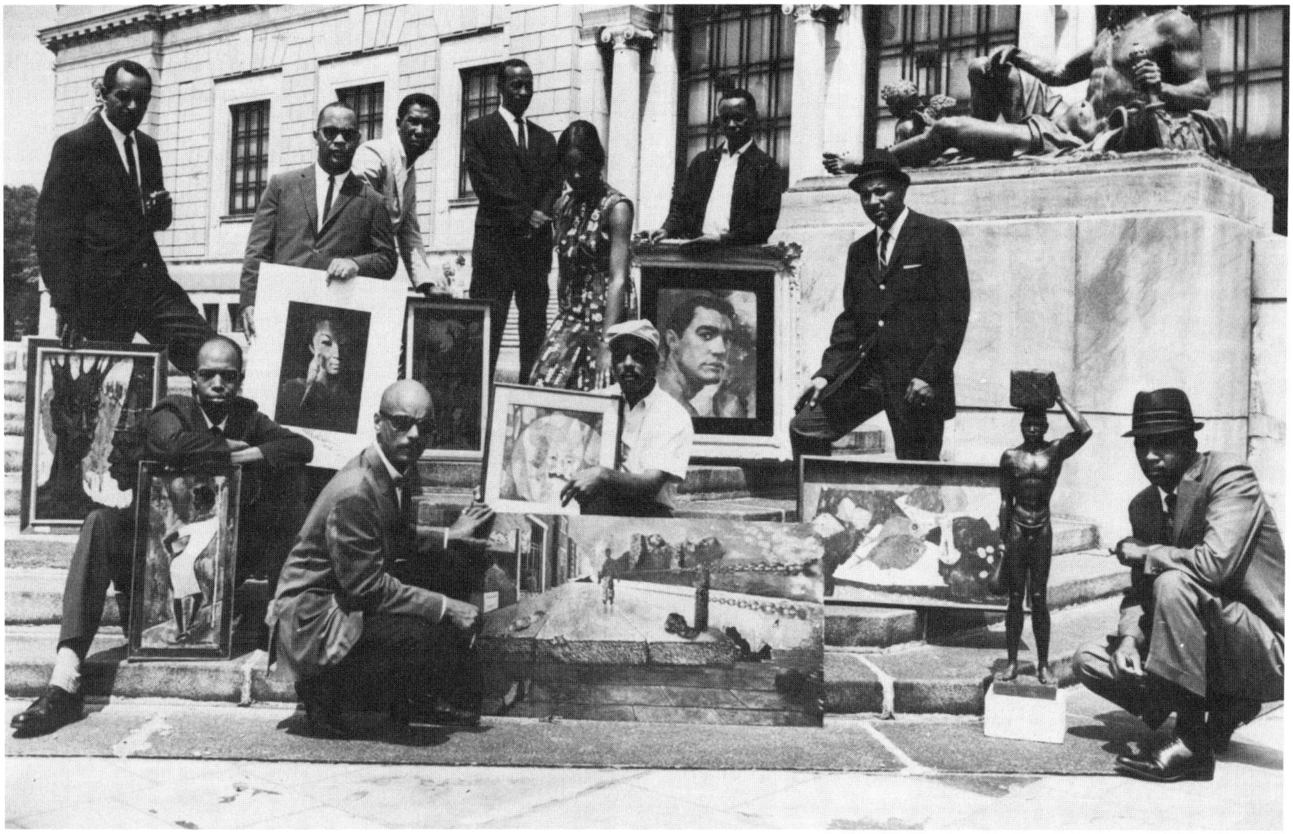

Contemporary Studio artists in front of the Detroit Institute of Arts, 1962. Top row, left to right: *Henry Umbaji King, gallery director; Coleman Hill; Omar Shabazz; Clarence Nelson; Maude Bennet; Leroy Foster; Ernest Alston, president.* Bottom row, left to right: *James Malone, assistant gallery director; Cesant Alrey, board chairman; Harold Neal; Oscar Graves. James D. Wilson, Photographer.*

larly successful. In addition, a traveling exhibition composed of works selected by the jury from the principal show was sent to public and college art galleries throughout the Midwest.

The Society was particularly active in the 1950s and 1960s, even staging a national watercolor exhibition in 1966. Despite some waning of interest in the medium of watercolor during the 1970s, the Society kept a strong membership throughout that decade.

The Michigan Printmakers Society. Michigan printmakers also began to organize in the early 1950s as printmaking began to receive greater recognition. The printmaker was no longer seen as simply a craftsman carrying out someone else's ideas, but rather as an artist who originated and realized ideas.

Aware of the changing status of the graphic media, printmakers around the country sought greater professionalism. In 1953, **Emil Weddige**, one of the state's most respected graphic artists, and Richard David, the director of the Saginaw Museum of Art, organized the Michigan Printmakers Society.

Although its membership never numbered more than twenty-five, the Michigan Printmakers Society included most of the top graphic artists in the state. Among its members were Thomas Woodward of Detroit, **Reynold Weidenaar** of Grand Rapids, and **Frank Cassara** of Ann Arbor. Also included in the membership were younger, less established artists who were admitted to the Society in a sort of apprentice role. It was hoped that these younger members would insure the future of the profession in the state.

The Society's most important yearly program was an exhibition for its membership. The exhibitions usually featured about forty works which, in the Society's first years, were juried by other members. In its last two years outside jurors selected the works. The exhibition was held in one Michigan location for a month and then traveled to other states for the next ten months, providing wide exposure for the participating members. Organizational problems caused the demise of the Society in 1958.

The Michigan Association of Printmakers. Founded and organized in 1959 by **Robert Broner** of Wayne State University and members of the Detroit Institute of Arts staff, the Michigan Association of Printmakers was most active in the 1960s, when the interest in printmaking was at a peak. A series of five open juried biennial exhibitions were held at the Detroit Institute of Arts; these focused attention on the work of some of Michigan's best-known printmakers. Interest in graphics waned throughout the nation in the 1970s. The Association remained inactive until 1977 when the organization revived its exhibition. The 1977 exhibition was well juried and well funded and once again drew considerable attention to the exhibiting artists.

Crafts Organizations

The resurgence of interest in crafts media throughout the United States in the years immediately following World War II resulted in the formation of a number of artists organizations devoted to furthering and supporting the crafts. The first such associations to be founded in Michigan were the Ann Arbor Potters Guild and the Michigan Silversmiths Guild, both established in 1949.

The Ann Arbor Potters Guild was founded by a group of ceramicists who met informally in a workshop known as the "Goat's Nest." It was originally intended as a noncommercial cooperative for serious amateur ceramicists. Members built a studio, potter's wheels, and other equipment and set up classes taught by artists of national reputation. Leading Michigan artists such as **J. T. Abernathy**, Mary Kring, **William Lewis**, Harvey Littleton, and **Marie Woo** were active in the Guild. Although its activity remained primarily local, the Guild had a significant impact on the state as a model for community-oriented, nonprofit craft organizations.

Marion Kenney-Eagen, **Fred Kenney-Eagen**, and Reginald Brewer were the driving personalities behind the formation of the Michigan Silversmiths Guild. Under their guidance and with the support of other artists, including **Michael Vizzini** and Virginia Lowrie, as well as sympathetic members of the art community, such as William Woolfenden, Curator of Education at the Detroit Institute of Arts, the Guild sponsored lectures, workshops, and exhibitions. These activities brought to Michigan such major names in the field as Arthur Pulos of the University of Illinois; Baron Erick Fleming, Court Silversmith to the King of Sweden; and Frederick Miller of the Cleveland Institute of Arts. The Guild has remained active, holding their first group exhibition in 1977.

As the 1950s progressed, associations of artists working in the crafts proliferated. Among the most important of these in Michigan were the Midwest Designer-Craftsmen, founded in 1953; the Michigan Potters' Association, established in 1958; and the Michigan League of Handweavers, organized in 1959.

In the late 1950s the movement to organize the state's craftsmen reached the Upper Peninsula. In 1958 Michael Church, Director of the University of Michigan Adult Extension Service, Charles Sawyer, Regional Director of the University of Michigan Extension Service, and Aare Lahti, who had served as director of a crafts project for the Upper Peninsula in the 1930s, organized a conference designed to encourage the revival of the traditional crafts of the Finns and other Scandinavians living in the region. One aim of the conference was to use such a revival to help combat the economic deprivation brought about by the shrinking of the local mining industry. David Crawford of the Museum of Contemporary Crafts (now the American Craft Museum) in New York was asked to address interested individuals from all over the Upper Peninsula at the conference in Marquette, which was jointly sponsored by the University of Michigan Extension in Escanaba, Michigan State University in Marquette, Northern Michigan University, Michigan Technological University, and Suomi College. Subsequently, between 1960 and 1965, conferences were held annually in an attempt to sustain interest in the crafts.

A permanent Upper Peninsula Crafts Council was created in 1965, involving most of the major figures in the crafts from that part of the state. The Council held meetings, sponsored workshops, and created a directory of Upper Peninsula craftsmen to stimulate sales and contact between artists. The creation of this council brought organization to the artists of the Upper Peninsula for the first time since the federal art projects during the Depression.

Experimental Groups

The ONCE Group. Formed in Ann Arbor in 1960, the ONCE Group was the brainchild of University of Michigan faculty members Mary Ashley, Robert Ashley, Milton Cohen, and George Manupelli, and architects Harold Borkin and Joseph Wehrs. This was Michigan's first experiment with the possibilities of multimedia performances utilizing film, experimental music, light, and live action. One of the most celebrated moments of the ONCE Group occurred when they took over an Ann Arbor parking ramp and rooftop and constructed an elaborate scaffolding, complete with movie screens and trap doors, as the setting for

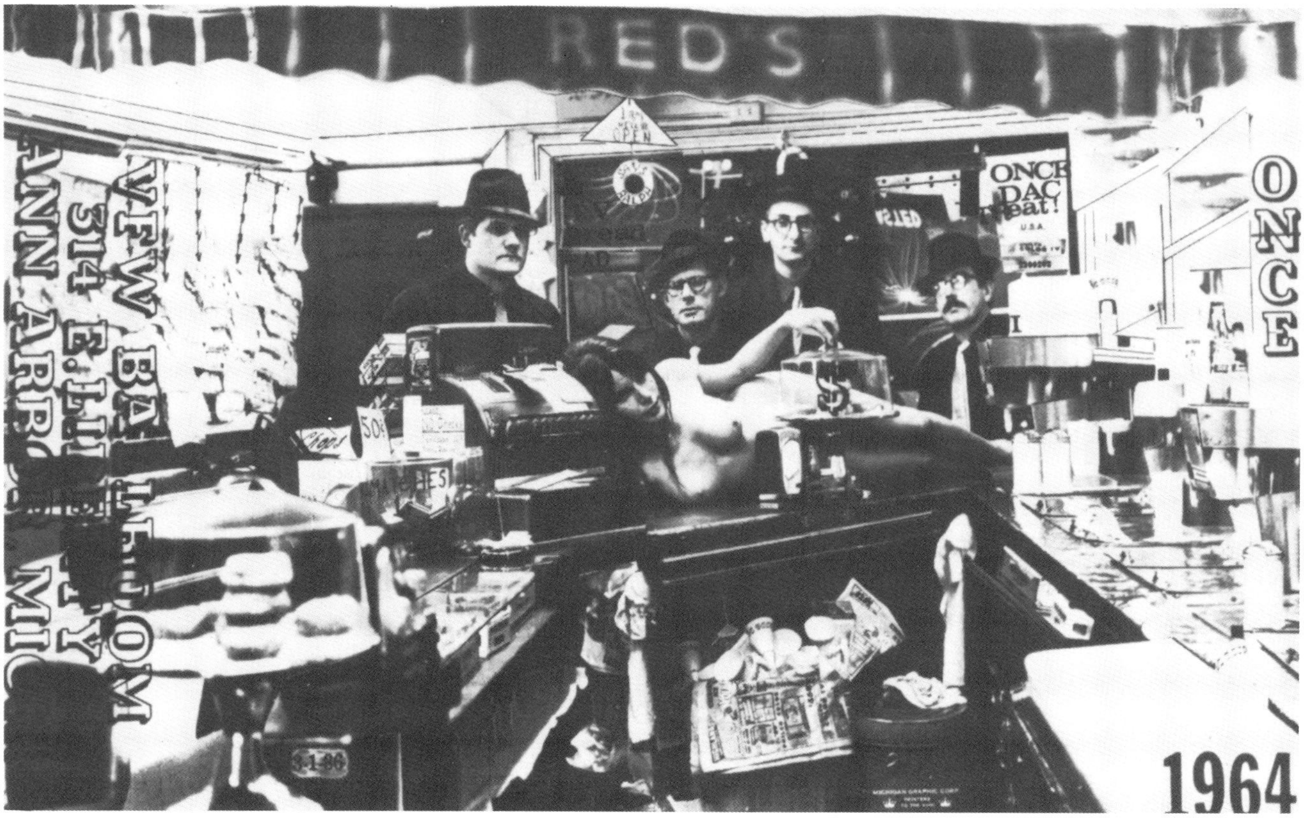

The ONCE Group, Ann Arbor, 1964. The Archives of American Art.

their performance. For three nights the ONCE Group presented Ginger Rogers and Fred Astaire on screen, while dozens of bizarre activities took place off screen. Weather balloons expanded and floated above, a trap door opened to reveal a woman dressed in a black dress changing into a white one, performers emptied and filled garbage cans, and multicolored lights blinked on and off, all to the bewildered eyes of an amazed audience.

The ONCE Group's activities paralleled in their style and atmosphere the "happenings" or spontaneous performances staged in New York by such artists as Jim Dine, Allen Kaprow, Claes Oldenburg, and Robert Whitmore in the same period. The ONCE Group, however, placed as much emphasis on avant-garde music as they did on visual imagery. Unfortunately, the Group's serious efforts to stretch the boundaries of visual and musical expression were later obscured by the merely theatrical antics of the innumerable rock groups that emerged in popular music in the mid-1960s. In its four years of existence, however, the ONCE Group introduced the Michigan art community to new possibilities and methods for visual experiences that would resurface in the performance art of the late 1970s.

The Common Ground for the Arts. The Common Ground for the Arts, an experimental association of artists, was opened in Detroit in 1962. Originally the concept of city planner Charles Blessing, Common Ground was intended to be a planned studio cooperative, a Bauhaus-like complex where artists, craftsmen, architects, and planners would share space and ideas. Eventually, however, the space was wholly occupied by painters, sculptors, printmakers, and craftsmen so that the quality of cooperation between artists and designers never materialized. Nonetheless, over the seventeen years of its existence, Common Ground generated a genuine excitement in the Michigan art community and attracted some of the state's best known artists to its studios. Lynn Bonner, **Robert Broner**, **Stan Dolega**, Bradley Jones, **Aris Koutroulis**, **G. Alden Smith**, and **Michael Vizzini**, among dozens of others, shared space, ideas, and projects at the Common Ground. After two moves from one inner-city building to another, the Common Ground was the first artist-run organization in the nation to receive a National Endowment for the Arts grant and settled in a warehouse on Cass Avenue in 1968.

The Common Ground was an important force in the development of the Cass Corridor neighborhood as

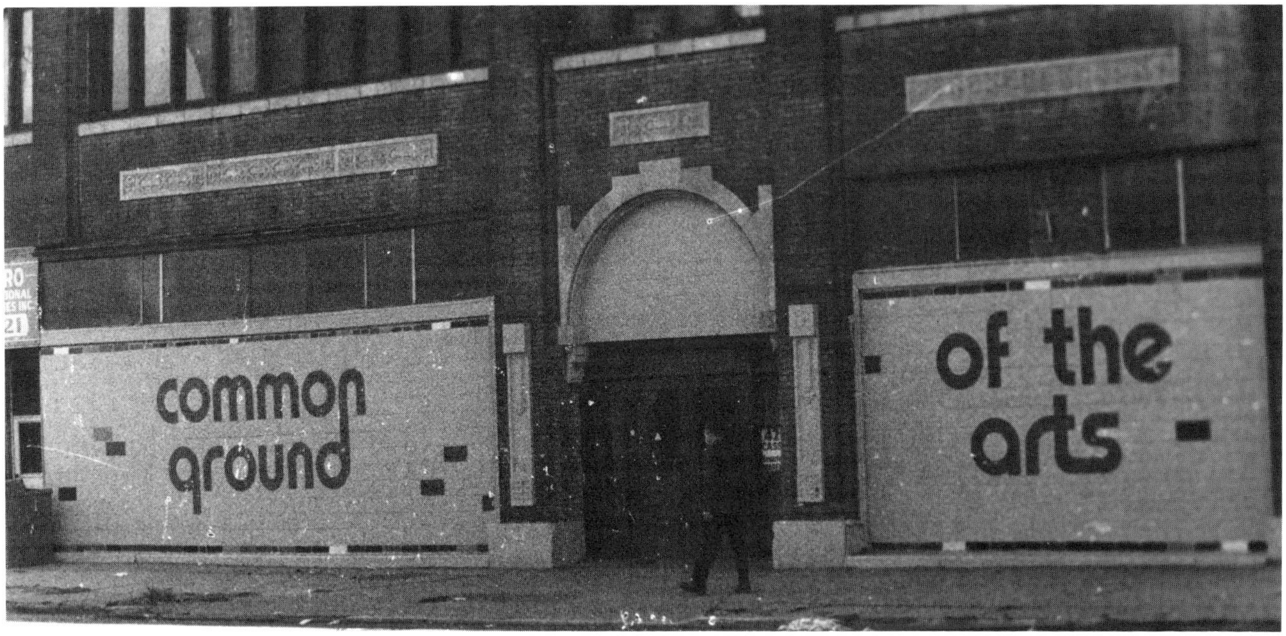

Common Ground for the Arts, Cass Avenue, Detroit, ca. 1965. The Archives of American Art.

a center of art activity in Detroit. Between 1968 and 1977, the Common Ground sponsored exhibitions, workshops, tours, lectures, and other forums, as well as providing studio space in a stimulating communal atmosphere. As the Cass Corridor art community began to disperse in the late 1970s, the Common Ground became less significant as a gathering place, and it too moved from the neighborhood in 1977 to a Second Avenue warehouse. In 1979 the cooperative lost its lease and disbanded. Although the Common Ground never functioned as the ideal center for the arts that the planners had envisioned, it was nonetheless, as one critic put it, "the place where Picasso would be found if he were living in Detroit."[12]

Outstate Organizations

Although most of the organizations discussed so far have been based within the Detroit metropolitan area, there has been, of course, much organizational activity among artists throughout the state. Although not all of the wide variety of artists associations can be reviewed here, a few groups deserve mention as indications of larger trends.

Artists North. Northern lower Michigan experienced an influx of artists from Michigan's urban centers to the south in the 1960s and 1970s. These artists, like many other members of their generation, felt that the north country offered a simple, less harried lifestyle, which was more conducive to their creativity. However, northern Michigan had its drawbacks, including little or no support system for the artists who located there. Confronted with the difficulties of obtaining supplies, disseminating information, and attracting potential customers, in 1979 Sue Bolt and Russell Bolt were instrumental in organizing an association called "Artists North." The many achievements of this confederation included the establishment of a group insurance plan for artists, the cooperative buying of materials to save on costs, and the arranging of workshops and lectures to provide information on everything from framing and matting to income tax preparation. This group also established an annual automobile tour of members' studios and published a map and a guide listing their locations.

Mid-Michigan Association of Working Artists. In the 1960s and 1970s, artists also began to become more politically active than at perhaps any time since the 1930s. One organization that represents this new political involvement is the Mid-Michigan Association of Working Artists. Although this association has worked in diverse ways to create a more favorable climate for the arts in Michigan, its main thrust is legislative. Centered in Lansing, the Association has lobbied for legislative bills that provide support to the state's artists and has sponsored a number of programs to make legislators aware of what Michigan's artists are doing. One of its long-range goals is the creation of a visual and performing arts center in Lansing to provide a focus for the arts in the state's capital.

Urban Institute for Contemporary Art. One of the more influential artist-run organizations to develop in an urban center outside Detroit has been the

Urban Institute for Contemporary Art. Located in Grand Rapids, the Institute was established in the spring of 1977. Initially located on the banks of the Grand River in an old warehouse, the Urban Institute contained exhibition, meeting, and even some studio space. It developed a continuous program of lectures, workshops, exhibitions, and performances, and sought to act as an agent for art-related programs in the community, taking on everything from fundraising to referral services. By the end of the decade, the Urban Institute had become an integral part of the Grand Rapids art community.

Despite the lack of a formal membership and adequate staff, the Urban Institute has managed to reach hundreds of artists working in and around Grand Rapids. Under the direction of **Ronald Watson**, the Institute has presented the new works of artists from both the Grand Rapids area and outside the region. One-person exhibitions, group shows, and joint exhibitions with other organizations and institutions are continuing aspects of the Urban Institute's visual arts programming.

Education of Artists in Michigan

Private Art Schools

In the late nineteenth century professional art education in Michigan was dominated by private art schools. Some schools were the independent creations of one or two dedicated individuals, others were affiliated with various museums or arts organizations. This situation continued well into the twentieth century. Colleges and universities did not offer fine arts programs of significance because training in the arts was regarded as a special field that did not require the intellectual discipline of higher education nor the degree that certified that such discipline had been attained. When college-level institutions began to expand their programs in art in the mid-twentieth century, Michigan's private art schools remained competitive, for they offered a more intimate atmosphere and one more intensely concentrated on art than the larger and more diverse institutions.

The Art School of the Detroit Museum of Art. The first private art school of any significance in Michigan was operated under the auspices of the Detroit Museum of Art. Known as the Detroit Museum of Art School, it was opened in 1889, with John Ward Dunsmore serving as its director as well as a teacher of life drawing. The school had a small faculty, usually numbering no more than five, drawn from well-respected names of the Detroit art community. **Percy Ives**, Emil Lorch, **Alice Guysi**, and **Jeannette Guysi** were among the artists who offered students the basics of a fine arts education.

The Art School of the Detroit Museum of Art, despite a real need for the services it offered, failed to survive to the end of the century. In 1899, combined shortages of space and money, as well as a very nonsupportive attitude on the part of museum director Armand Griffith, ended the school's operation.

The Detroit Academy of Art. A small independent art school, the Detroit Academy of Art was opened in 1895 by painters **Francis Petrus Paulus** and **Joseph Gies**. Offering courses in drawing, painting, and related areas, the school had a small but devoted student body. In 1911 painter **John P. Wicker** took over the Academy and continued its tradition of offering training to competent students, of whom the most well known was **Sarkis Sarkisian**. Wicker ran the school until his death in 1931.

The Detroit School of Design. The most significant of the early private art schools, however, was the Detroit School of Design, founded in 1911 with the backing of some of Detroit's most influential patrons of art and architecture. George Booth, publisher of the *Detroit News*, Gustavus Pope, businessman and civic leader, Horace Caulkins, industrialist and philanthropist, and H. J. Maxwell Grylls, the city's leading architect, all gave time, money, and direction to the school. Their aim was to offer training in skills that could be used in Detroit's many industries, so design, drawing, interior decoration, illustration, and architecture were among the many courses taught.

Seeking a stronger base of support and greater prestige, the trustees of the Detroit School of Design decided to merge the school with the Detroit Museum of Art in 1913, thus re-establishing the museum's involvement with studio art training. The merger enabled the school to receive an operating subsidy from the City of Detroit which at the time was providing subsidies for the museum's operation.

The collections and operation of the Detroit Museum of Art were taken over by the City of Detroit in 1919. The newly created Detroit Institute of Arts became a department of city government. The change of the museum's status also changed the status of the Detroit School of Design, and it was incorporated into the city's public education system. The School of Design then became the Art Department of Cass Technical High School, an experimental school which drew top students from all over the city.

Over the last sixty years, Cass Technical High School has offered training in the fine arts but has emphasized the commercial arts. Its staff has included such well-respected artists as Greta Pach, who was known for her work in metalsmithing, and Irving Berg, who concentrates on constructivist sculpture. Scores of Michigan artists, including sculptor **Harry Bertoia**, printmaker **James Lee**, painter **David Fredenthal**, and metalsmiths **Fred Kenney-Eagen**, **Marion Kenney-**

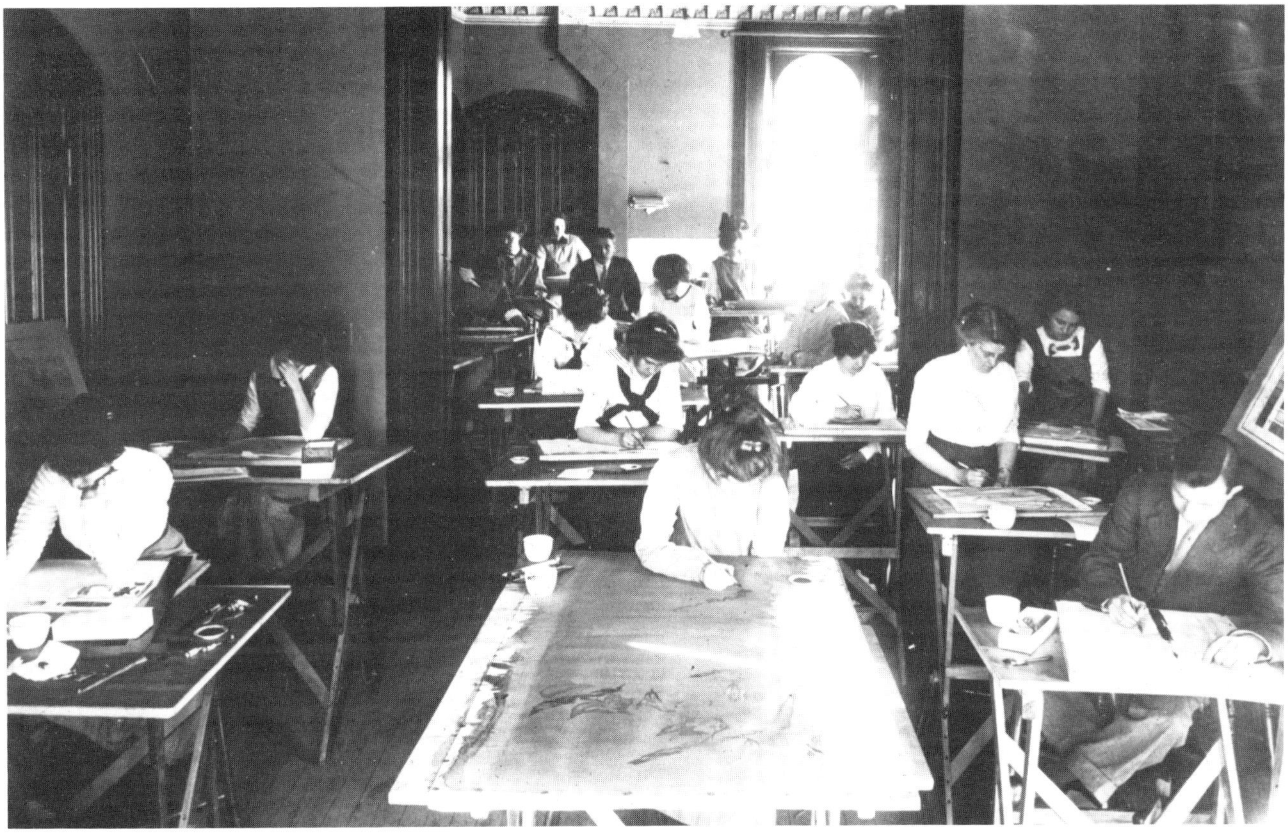

Class at the Detroit School of Design, 1912. The Archives of American Art, DSAC Scrapbook.

Eagen, and **Michael Vizzini**, received their initial training at Cass.

The Oxbow Summer School of Painting. Since the nineteenth century, artists from Chicago, Milwaukee, Detroit, and elsewhere have been drawn to Michigan's extensive lakeshores to work during the summer months. The Lake Michigan shoreline, with its high dunes and relative accessibility to urban centers, has long been the most popular destination for the summer migration of midwestern artists. This summer migration led to the establishment of an art school which, like a number of similar schools of America's Atlantic Coast, capitalized on an environmental setting to bring creative people together.

The Oxbow Summer School of Painting was founded in 1910 on the shore of Lake Michigan at Saugatuck by artists **Frederick Fursman** of Milwaukee and Walter Marshall Clute of Chicago, with the financial backing of architect Thomas Eddy Talmadge. Oxbow quickly became a thriving summer colony for artists who were attracted by its 110 acres of secluded land and the companionship of other artists in a natural setting. However, the economic and artistic forces behind Oxbow were based in Chicago and Milwaukee, and relatively few Michigan artists took advantage of this institution until the 1960s.

Fursman served as academic director for thirty-three years. He was followed in this position by a number of others, most notably Else Ulbricht, also a Milwaukee artist. Throughout the first fifty years of its existence, the colony, which changed its name to the Oxbow Summer School of Art in the 1960s, had a rather dichotomous existence. Serious artists like Claes Oldenberg, Carl Holty, Leon Golub, Joan Mitchell, **Phillip Fike**, and **Zubel Kachadoorian** came to work and exchange ideas in the relaxed communal atmosphere; yet the school's resort-like setting also drew many "Sunday painters," who created an atmosphere of superficiality. In the late 1960s the school's board of directors sought to make Oxbow a more professional institution without losing the informal structure and good comradeship that had always been an important part of Oxbow's appeal. Artists-in-residence from around the country were asked to come, among them Janet Fish, Enrico Natale, and Ed Paschke. The school also opened its grounds to special conferences and veloping artist with the opportunity to experience the creative process. He envisioned bringing to Cranbrook a core group of nationally and internationally known artists who would be given studios and housing as well as salaries and would be asked in return to serve as artists-in-residence, working at their profession and sharing their knowledge and expertise with a select group of students. The students would be chosen from all over the country, given scholarships, and provided with a place to live and work. Their only responsibility would be to avail themselves of all that was offered around them. Booth's plan, in essence, was modeled after the master craftsman-apprentice relationship of the medieval guild system, and it was such an atmosphere that he sought for Cranbrook.

Booth had hired the internationally celebrated architect Eliel Saarinen in 1924 to develop the architectural plans for the Cranbrook complex. Saarinen shared a special enthusiasm with Booth for the academy project. He moved his architectural offices to Cranbrook upon Booth's request and assumed the role of the academy's architect-in-residence. Within a short time, he became Booth's most trusted advisor on the development of the academy. In 1932 Booth formally founded the Cranbrook Academy of Art and made Saarinen its first president.

Saarinen was a highly respected, opinionated, and flamboyant character, with the reputation needed to draw top-rated artists to Cranbrook to head the various departments. Textile artist **Marianne Strengell** joined **Loja Saarinen**, Eliel's wife, in directing the textile department. **Maija Grotell**, whose work had been widely exhibited in both the United States and Europe, came to work in ceramics. Painter **Zoltan Sepeshy** was lured away from the Art School of the Detroit Society of Arts and Crafts. Most importantly, however, Saarinen was able to convince Swedish sculptor **Carl Milles**, one of the period's most celebrated sculptors of public monuments, to move to Cranbrook as sculptor-in-residence.

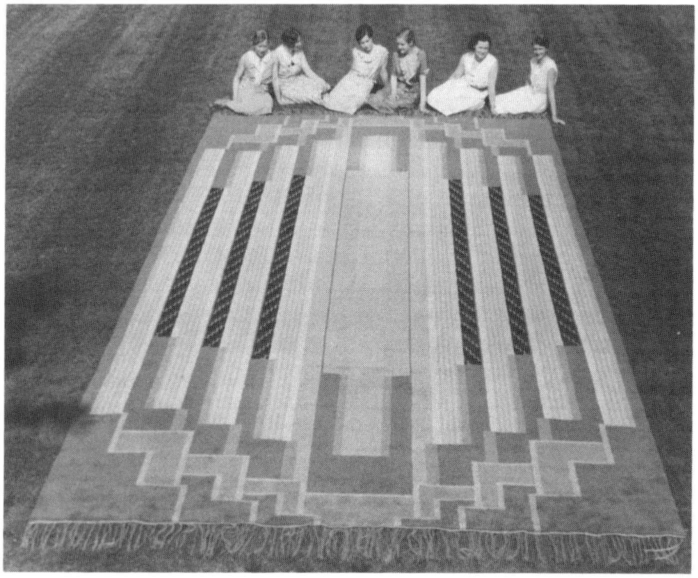

Kingswood students with rug designed by Loja Saarinen (1879–1968). Courtesy the Cranbrook Academy of Art Museum.

Moreover, Saarinen was an articulate spokesman who was able to combine his own architectural and aesthetic philosophy with Booth's educational philosophy to make an even stronger case for the experiment in the arts taking place at Cranbrook. Saarinen was a proponent of "total architecture," in which the architect assumed responsibility for the design of all aspects of a structure, including landscaping, furniture, appointments, and artwork. With this view in mind, Saarinen felt it was essential for the architect and artisan to work closely together to achieve a harmonious creation. The educational approach of the academy, with its close, informal contact between faculty and students in an unstructured learning situation were complementary to Saarinen's vision of artisans and architects working together to achieve a harmonious creation.

Saarinen, however, could not endorse all that Booth envisioned. He saw, for example, that there was no room in the modern world for medieval systems. He emphasized that Cranbrook's purpose should be to foster an understanding of the basic principles of art, so that students could develop a "true and expressive art for their time." He was able to shift the emphasis of the school from good craftsmanship toward good design, modifying Booth's ideas to give them a more practical, up-to-date form with a stress on his own concepts of totally integrated architecture and design.

Saarinen and Booth together set the pace and style of the Academy in the 1930s and 1940s. The two men turned the Cranbrook facility into one of the most exciting centers for art education in the nation. The Academy, its artists, and its programs generated national and international interest. Individuals connected with all facets of the visual arts were drawn to Cranbrook to study, lecture, participate in workshops or panels, or simply to see what was going on there.

The Academy's physical development was certainly one of the key reasons for Cranbrook's renown during the period. From 1927 to 1937 Saarinen worked on the design and oversaw the construction of an art school facility that was unmatched at that time by any in the country, creating an intimate yet functional campus of studios, workshops, faculty residences, student housing, a library, museum, and gardens. By the mid-1930s the Cranbrook complex provided the world with one of the finest examples of modern integrated architectural planning.

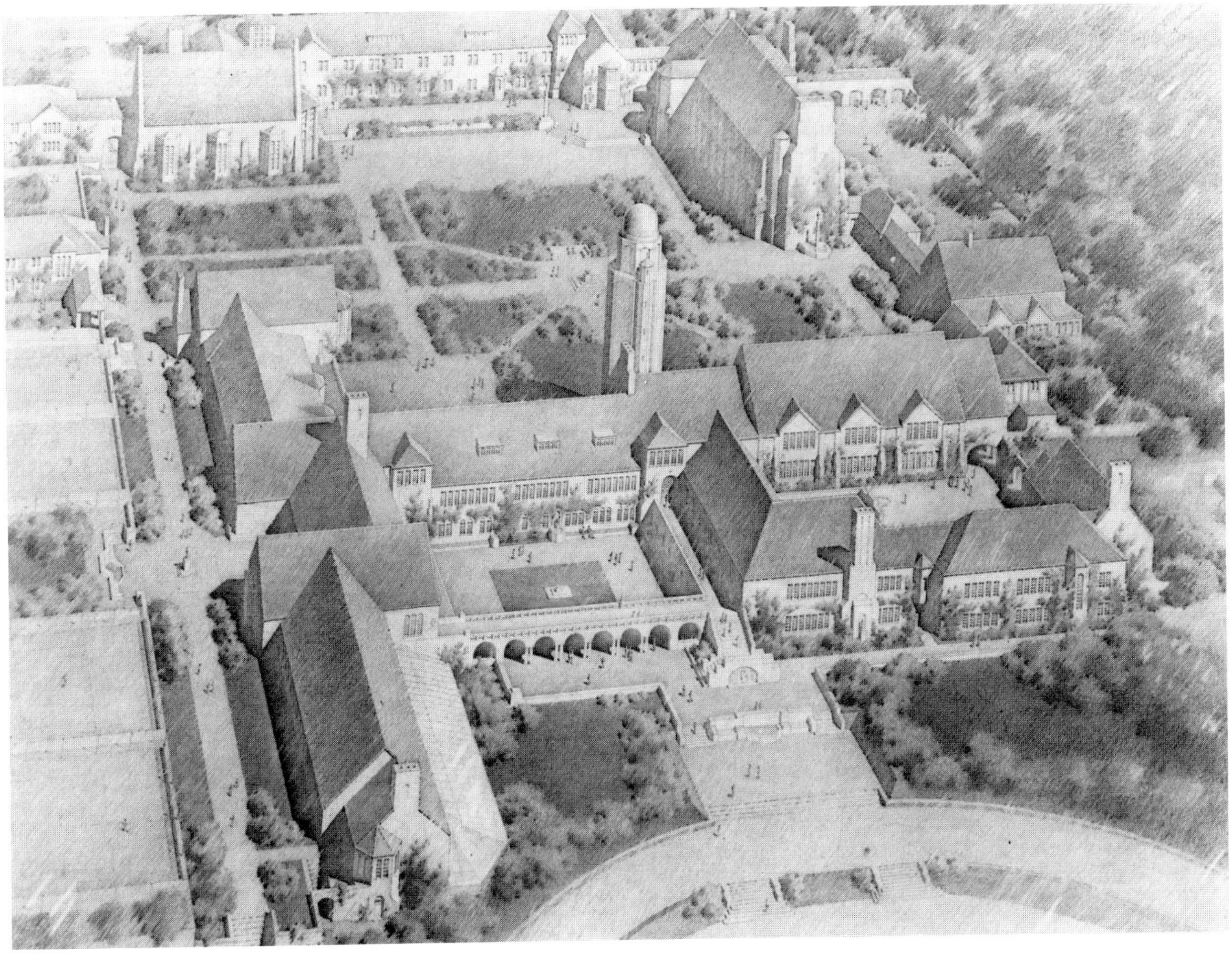

Eliel Saarinen 1873–1950). Design for Cranbrook School. *1925. Aerial perspective (detail). Pencil on paper. 21½ × 25⅜ inches. Collection of the Cranbrook Academy of Art Museum. Courtesy the Cranbrook Academy of Art Museum. Dirk Bakker, Photographer.*

The achievements of faculty and students also brought fame. During the 1930s and 1940s Saarinen received many national awards for his contribution to architecture and his work was featured in exhibitions at the Metropolitan Museum of Art and the Architectural League of New York. Alone, and later in partnership with his son Eero, Saarinen turned out some of the era's most acclaimed buildings. At the same time, Milles won the commissions for several major public sculptures and produced a striking set of bronzes to enhance the grounds at Cranbrook. Strengell's textiles were included in prestigious exhibitions, and Grotell received prizes for her ceramics at international shows.

As these established artists continued to add to their acclaim, a number of younger artists, now well known, got their start at the Academy. **Harry Bertoia,** whose delicate work in metal sculpture received critical attention in the 1950s and 1960s, began seriously to work in metal while a student at the Academy and singlehandedly revived its dormant metalsmithing department. The internationally known designer Charles Eames was given his first major position at Cranbrook in 1939 as head of the experimental design department. Award-winning architect Harry Weese, known for his design of the Arena Stage Theater in Washington, D.C. as well as other buildings, studied under Saarinen, and furniture designer Florence Knoll, founder of Knoll & Associates, was a student in design. Sculptor **Marshall Fredericks**, the creator of *The Spirit of Detroit* and a score of other landmark public monupractically synonymous with the University's art department, joined Kamrowski in teaching. In 1949 sculptor **Thomas McClure** was hired to establish a sculpture program; in 1950 ceramicist **J. T. Abernathy** arrived to do the same for ceramics.

The University established a museum of art in 1948 under the direction of faculty member Jean Paul Slusser. The establishment of the new museum not only offered faculty, students, and the community access to the art of many periods and cultures but provided the department with an important local gallery for viewing works created by its own members.

A new visual arts program was established for the Department of Architecture in the postwar years. For the first time the University offered a degree in fine arts that was independent of any studies in architecture. The new program also opened courses in the fine arts to the general student. The fine arts department's expansion continued throughout the 1950s and 1960s; in fact, the growth in the number of degree students and faculty sorely taxed the overcrowded and aging facilities. Despite these difficulties, the department developed and encouraged all sorts of activities. In 1959 a printmaking seminar was organized with such top graphic artists as Gabor Peterdi, Garo Antreasian, and Rudy Pozzatti participating. The presence of such fine printmakers as **Paul Stewart**, **Frank Cassara**, and **Emil Weddige** on the faculty made this area a strong one.

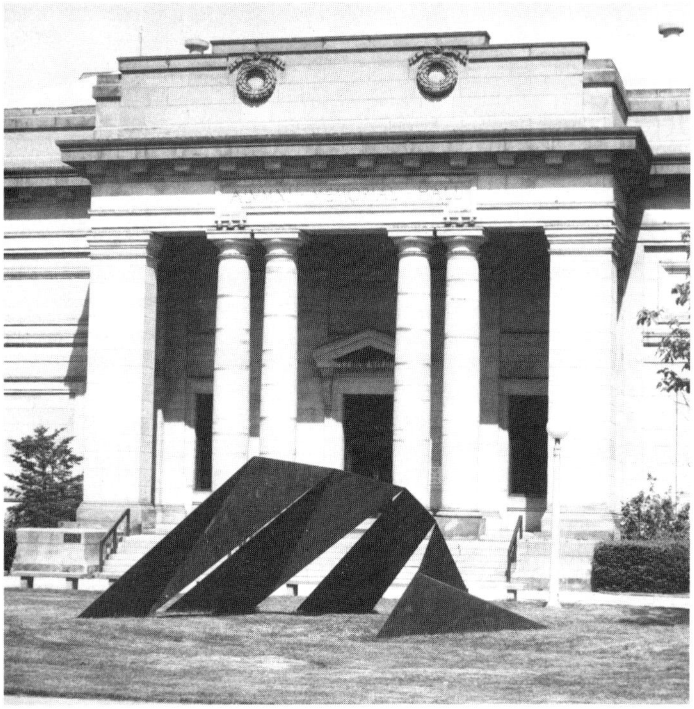

The University of Michigan Museum of Art, Ann Arbor. Courtesy the University of Michigan Museum of Art.

The celebrated English ceramicist Bernard Leach was brought for a seminar, and the department's ceramics program under Abernathy and **William Lewis** developed rapidly. In the 1960s filmmaking courses were added, cooperative programs were developed with the music school, and courses concentrating on the black experience in art began, as did a program to provide students with practical experience in design firms. During this decade, an M.F.A. program was also added.

The University of Michigan finally established a School of Art as a separate college in 1974. The new school moved from the cramped quarters of the architectural department's building to a major new facility designed specifically for the teaching of art. Under the direction of its dean, George Bayliss, dozens of visiting artists were recruited, and their workshops, seminars, lectures, and demonstrations became an integral part of the school's programming. In the 1970s, the School of Art emerged as a center of art education that allowed students increased flexibility in planning their own curriculum. Undergraduates were not required to declare a major nor were they subject to many class requirements after the first year. Students were encouraged to develop their own plans of study and to take advantage of all that the department and the university had to offer.

Michigan State University. Like that of the University of Michigan, the art department of Michigan State University evolved out of the school's engineering department. In the early part of the century, courses were offered in drawing and design as part of a student's basic preparation for an engineering degree. By 1919, however, courses in ceramics and art history had been added to the curriculum, and in 1932 an independent department was created for the art programs.

For its first decade the young department was headed by a painter, Arthur Scheele. In 1945 the well-known art historian Albert Christ-Janer took charge. In his brief two years as chairman, Christ-Janer introduced a successful visiting artist program in which artists of national reputation, diverse backgrounds, styles, and philosophies were brought to East Lansing, sometimes for as little as a day but quite often for as long as a semester. Arnold Blanch, Abraham Rattner, Angelo Ippolito, and Anne Healy were among the many participants in this program.

Under professors Alma Goestch and Katherine Winkler during the 1940s, a strong art education program was developed as well. They kept the art education curriculum within the art department itself, refusing to make it a separate field of study as most other Michigan universities had done. Art education students had to major in a particular medium, such as painting or ceramics, and take the same foundation courses in studio areas as those students not interested in obtaining a teaching certificate. During the 1940s and 1950s these two women provided both the intellectual and social centers for the University's art community, bringing in distinguished guest lecturers and hosting all sorts of gatherings in their house, which had been designed by Frank Lloyd Wright. Students, faculty, and visiting professionals were drawn there for intellectually charged conversation and good company.

Painter Howard Church took over the department during the burgeoning post-World War II period. Church was responsible for hiring many of the faculty members who later played pivotal roles in the department's development. Included in this group were artists such as abstract expressionist **Allen Leepa**, ceramicist **Irwin Whitaker**, and painters **Murray Jones** and **Ralf Henrickson**. Under Church, the department pressed for a strong background for students, stressing basic courses in drawing, anatomy, and art history. Instructors emphasized the mastery of technique rather than the espousal of theory.

The physical plant expanded to include eight "war surplus" buildings along with gallery space in the Student Union Building. In 1958, after years of planning and fund-raising, the department moved into the Kresge Art Center, a building designed to incorporate class, studio, office, and gallery facilities. At the same time, programs leading to both the Bachelor and the Master of Fine Arts degrees were added to the curriculum. Church capped his career by convincing the Midwest College Art Association to hold its 1960 Annual Meeting on the Michigan State University campus, an appropriate honor for the new facilities and expanded programs. That same year Church retired as chairman.

Expansion continued in the 1960s, first under acting head Charles Meyer and then under Erling Brauner. There were nearly a thousand students majoring in art, which necessitated the construction of an additional wing for the Kresge Art Center and a new sculpture building. The department offered programs in painting, drawing, metals and jewelry, graphic design, industrial design, ceramics, sculpture, photography, art education, and art history. Under the direction of Roger Funk during the 1970s, the strength of these areas was kept in balance, with no one major given special emphasis. As a result, Michigan State developed a reputation as an institution dedicated to solid, reliable professional training in the field of art.

Wayne State University. Wayne State University was a relative latecomer as a major center for art education in Michigan. The roots of the existing department are to be found in the programs for art teacher education developed by Jane Betsey Welling at the Detroit Teachers College in the late 1920s. This college merged with City College of Detroit in 1931 to form the institution that would eventually emerge as Wayne State University.

Throughout the 1930s, Welling expanded the curriculum at Wayne State by utilizing the resources available to her in the surrounding art community. Artists such as **Walter Speck** and **Reginald Bennett** were brought in on a part-time basis to teach life drawing and oil painting, respectively. **Samuel Cashwan** taught clay modeling. **Arthur Neville Kirk**, the noted silversmith, gave Saturday classes in crafts and jewelry. The Detroit Institute of Arts textiles curator, Adele Weibel, taught "The History of Art and Museum Study," and puppetry was offered under the guidance of puppeteer **Paul McPharlin**.

By 1936, the programs had grown to the point where it was necessary to create a Department of Art and Art History that was separate from the Department of Art Education. **Wayne Claxton**, a painter from Wisconsin with a background in administration, was appointed to head the newly created department. Claxton continued many of the programs developed by Welling, including the practice of tapping the local art community for part-time teaching talent.

Claxton was a unique and strong personality and the department rapidly became his creation. During the last years of the Depression and throughout the war years, Claxton kept the department going. Even though funds were short, he managed to add faculty, such as art historian Ernst Scheyer and sculptor **G. Alden Smith**. At the same time, Claxton groomed a number of his students for eventual faculty positions once conditions improved, and when World War II ended,

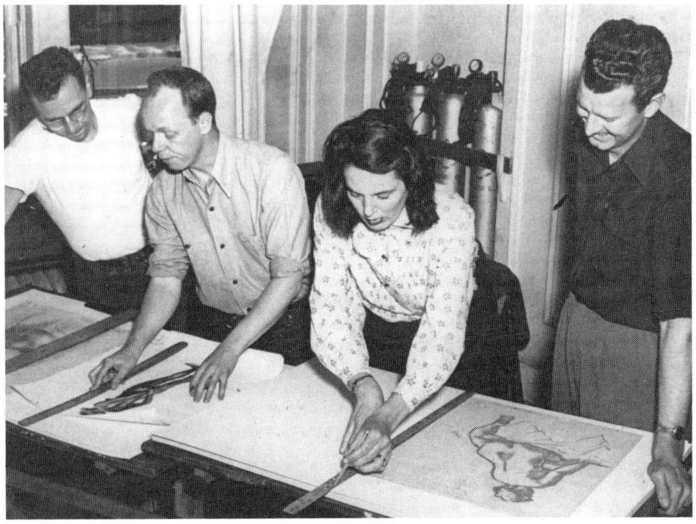

David Mitchell (1918–   ) teaching a class at Wayne State University, ca. 1955. Courtesy Wayne State University, University Archives.

he was able to develop a professional faculty to handle the inevitable expansion.

Claxton was also deeply interested in the ideas of the Bauhaus movement in Germany earlier in the century and particularly in the teachings of Lászlό Moholy-Nagy, who brought the movement to the United States in 1937. Moholy-Nagy promoted his own style of constructivist art, one which not only embodied basic constructivist concepts of an ordered, logical, abstract art assembled from industrial materials but which also emphasized a concern with forms in movement in actual space. Claxton found Moholy-Nagy's interest in movement and the interactions of forms and physical space most important not only for his own work, which in some ways resembled that of Lyonel Feininger, but also from a conceptual point of view for the whole department. The constructivist principles in Moholy-Nagy's *Vision in Motion* (1947) and György Kepes's *Language of Vision* (1944) were made basic to many of the department's classes. Not unexpectedly, the art of both faculty and students often directly responded to the ideas and issues raised by Moholy-Nagy and exalted by Claxton. Under Claxton, the Wayne art department became a department with a most pronounced point of view.

Wayne State's image as a major center for the visual arts was enhanced immeasurably in the early 1950s when the University began construction of one of the first college buildings of the post-World War II era that was intended specifically to be an art center. An effective lobbyist, Claxton worked with others at the University to convince the city and state to provide funds for the structure to be completed by Detroit's 250th birthday. The building was proposed as a community arts center which would serve the city in general as well as the art department directly. In 1956 the Community Arts Building opened on the Wayne State campus, years before similar structures would appear on the campuses of the state's other universities. Claxton retired shortly after the completion of the new structure. He left a faculty of solid professionals and facilities among the best in the state. Thus Wayne State was well prepared for the growth in the arts that would mark the decade of the 1960s.

Faculty member **G. Alden Smith** became chairman of the department in 1960. As chairman, Smith was less concerned than Claxton with imprinting his own particular stylistic and philosophic points of view on the department and sought instead to give his faculty greater freedom and more initiative. Smith decentralized the department's administration. He created a number of semi-autonomous units based around the particular disciplines, and painting, sculpture, printmaking, design, and art history all functioned more or less independently of each other on matters of internal policy.

Smith's laissez-faire approach to the department allowed faculty members the flexibility to develop their areas of interest in ways that made Wayne the most interesting campus in Michigan for art students in the 1960s and 1970s. Students were encouraged to work experimentally and independently.

Smith allowed the faculty to seek out interesting artists from all over the country to serve on the staff, overcoming the parochial tendency of Michigan art schools to look inward for faculty. Important additions were painter **John Egner** from Yale University; printmaker **David Becker**, who had studied at the universities of Wisconsin and Illinois; and painter-printmaker **Aris Koutroulis**, who, besides studying at Cranbrook, had also worked at the John Herron Institute in Indianapolis and the Tamarind Print Workshop before coming to Michigan. More than thirty young artists, often those working in media and styles that were new to Michigan, joined the faculty in the late 1960s alone.

The art department at Wayne State attracted vast numbers of students. Certainly, being urban, relatively inexpensive, and accessible helped enrollment enormously, but more than these attractions, much of Wayne's appeal came from the quality and diversity of its teaching and the experimental, open atmosphere that it seemed to engender.

More than any other Michigan art school, Wayne State became associated with the strong urban art movement that manifested itself in Detroit in the late 1960s and early 1970s. Many of the Wayne State faculty had located their studios in the nearby inner-city neighborhoods, particularly the Cass Corridor. Wayne State students often found studio and living space in the same areas. Furthermore, members of the Wayne State faculty and student body were, in many cases, the key movers behind the projects, exhibitions, galleries, and workshops around which much of the community's activity centered. **John Egner**, for example, was instrumental in the development of the nonprofit Willis Gallery, an alternative space that focused on the works of younger artists experimenting with the use of industrial materials. Faculty member **Aris Koutroulis** and graduate student **James Crawford** created the Michigan Print Workshop, and department chairman G. Alden Smith was a founding member of the Common Ground for the Arts, which, as noted earlier, was one of the first experiments in providing inexpensive cooperative studio space for the city's artists.

Throughout the 1970s, Wayne's art department continued to be a pacesetter in Detroit and Michigan. Its students and faculty consistently drew both local and national critical attention for work that often was the most avant-garde within the state.

Eastern Michigan University. The history of the art department at Eastern Michigan University in Ypsilanti can be traced to courses in drawing first taught in

1893 by an English geographer, Professor John Goodison, when the institution was known as Michigan State Normal College and exclusively devoted to teacher training. Some form of art instruction has remained in the school's curriculum since that time.

For thirty-six years, painter Bertha Goodison, John Goodison's daughter, taught art at the college in Ypsilanti, and from 1918 until her death in 1937, Goodison was in charge of a small faculty. Goodison was herself an "institution" and her principles guided the activities of the department. Her overriding concern was to turn out public school teachers with a thorough training in the fine arts, and under her direction and that of her successor, Orlo Gill, the department became one of the best known and respected centers for art education training in the state. Gill was responsible for developing an annual statewide art education conference held at the college in the late 1930s that later led to the establishment of the Michigan Art Education Association.

Under August Freundlich, the programs of the department were expanded in the 1950s. Freundlich sought to offer a strong major in art and increased the number of credit hours that a student could accumulate in art, even though all programs remained geared to art education. Freundlich's successor, **Kingsley Calkins**, chairman from 1957 to 1979, pushed the department's expansion further by developing major and minor areas of study, expanding credit hours to equal most major art schools, and creating masters programs for both art education and fine arts. Calkins also found more adequate facilities for the department, including a warehouse that became a complete sculpture facility with a bronze foundry.

During the decade of the 1970s Eastern Michigan University's art department emerged as a well-rounded and important center for the arts. Programs were added in ceramics and fiber, as well as a major in multimedia, that stressed video and conceptual art, the first such program in Michigan. Faculty-hiring during the period emphasized the recruitment of artists who were trained at schools with well-known reputations. An extensive lecture series featuring major, often controversial, artists from New York and elsewhere was initiated in the late 1960s and continued throughout the 1970s. The department also developed an active exhibition program that was designed to showcase the talents of artists from both inside and outside of Michigan. **Charles McGee**, one of the state's best-known artists, was hired to direct the university art gallery's programs. By the end of the 1970s, Eastern Michigan University had emerged as one of the state's largest art departments. With thirty-five full-time faculty, and an average enrollment of more than five hundred art majors, the university had joined the ranks of the major art centers in Michigan.

Western Michigan University. A counterpart to Eastern Michigan University was opened as the Western State Normal School in Kalamazoo in 1903. From its beginning, the school had an art department whose aims were directed toward providing public school teachers with a background in art instruction. All of the school's original eighty-eight students attended art classes and, in fact, art instruction was a requirement for every student for nearly two decades.

Amelia Goldsworthy chaired the department from 1905 to 1920. With a staff of only four instructors, Goldsworthy offered one-term courses in methods, drawing, design, applied design, modeling, and art history to teaching candidates in general as well as to prospective art teachers who were following a two-year curriculum.

Lydia Siedschlag served as chairman and director of the Division of Fine Arts from 1924 to 1956. The faculty doubled to consist of eight members, and a three-year program was developed for art education majors. By the end of Siedschlag's tenure, more than one hundred students were listed as majors. During the period, a program of art acquisition for the university was also initiated.

From the mid-1950s to the mid-1960s, the art department experienced rapid growth. The chairman, **Harry Hefner**, oversaw the development of a four-year curriculum, increased the faculty to twelve, and moved the department into a newly constructed art building, Sangren Hall. Steps were also taken to provide full course offerings, with programs added in printmaking, sculpture, ceramics, and textile arts. The enrollment of art education majors increased to over 250.

Charles Meyer, who succeeded Hefner in 1966, carried the expansion of Western's art department into a full-fledged center for art instruction, and degree programs in art were developed, leading to Bachelor and Master of Fine Arts degrees. Printmaking, graphic design, photography, and sculpture developed particular strength. By the time of Meyer's retirement in 1977, Western Michigan University boasted thirty full-time instructors, ranking it with the largest college art departments in Michigan.

In the 1970s, Western hosted a number of workshops, exhibitions, and other events that were aimed at expanding the horizons of its faculty and students and at the same time making the department more visible in the state's art community. The sponsorship of a "National Print and Drawing Annual" exhibition, beginning in 1968, attracted entries and top artists from around the country. Workshops concentrating on aspects of printmaking, such as photogravure, papermaking, and cliché-verre, were held concurrently. Major printmakers came to conduct the workshops, judge the exhibition, and lecture. Similar workshops were developed in the field of sculpture around the processes of forging and smithing, again attracting national attention.

Northern Michigan University. Northern Michigan University has been the center for art instruction in the Upper Peninsula since shortly before the turn of the century. As far back as 1899, the year of the school's founding as the Northern Michigan Normal College, courses were offered in drawing and geography. In 1902 serious training in the arts began at the school, when Grace Spaulding, a graduate of Pratt Institute who had also studied in Florence and Paris, became instructor of art courses at the school. Spaulding brought to the school the sophistication and commitment needed to make the fine arts a vital part of the school's curriculum. For thirty-five years, Spaulding acted virtually as a one-woman department: teaching, exhibiting, and keeping the school and the community of Marquette abreast of artistic developments in New York and Chicago. In 1946 Cleobelle Harrison, a graduate of the Master of Fine Arts program at Wayne State University, became the key mover in the continuing development of the department. Harrison, who directed the department until 1965, was instrumental in improving the art programs in the public schools of the Upper Peninsula by creating art education extension programs.

The department underwent major growth and reorganization following the transformation of the school from a college of education to a full-fledged university in 1963. Ronald Gorski, who became chairman in 1965, oversaw the development of a curriculum that would accommodate the needs of those students who were not necessarily interested in preparation for art education degrees. The reshaping of the curriculum placed great demands on the four-person faculty that comprised the department. Instructors were asked to provide studio experience in three or four areas of study. Space and equipment were improvised, with the faculty often finding resources in discarded materials and unoccupied old buildings.

In the 1960s and 1970s, Gorski and his faculty shaped the department at Northern Michigan University into a major center, offering Bachelor of Science, Bachelor of Arts, and Bachelor and Master of Fine Arts degrees in art education programs, with instruction in such areas as filmmaking, printmaking, and drawing. Study was also offered in cognate courses in psychology and sociology that had bearing on the visual arts. By the end of the 1970s, the art department of Northern Michigan University had grown to include a dozen full-time faculty and more than 260 visual arts majors.

Taken together, Michigan's universities have provided training for literally thousands of Michigan artists. They have also provided much needed employment to the state's fine arts graduates. Thus, their strength has contributed significantly to the overall health of Michigan's artistic community.

Art Galleries

The marketing of art in the first half of the twentieth century was principally conducted through personal contacts, special exhibitions, and nonprofit galleries. Until the art scene began to expand after World War II, there were very few private galleries in Michigan.

From 1906 until 1931 the most important exhibition space showing contemporary art was the salesroom sponsored by the Detroit Society of Arts and Crafts, which was devoted to the exhibition and sale of the works of both American and European craftsmen and included some pieces by Michigan artists. In the 1930s the Detroit Society of Arts and Crafts converted its salesroom into a nonprofit gallery that showed the work of truly avant-garde figures from both sides of the Atlantic. Exhibitions by faculty members of the Society's school were also scheduled on occasion.

The Detroit Artists Market, opened in 1932 as the Young Artists Market, has been one of the most effective nonprofit galleries for Michigan artists. Initiated by Mrs. H. Lee Simpson, a patron of the arts from Grosse Pointe, and Robert Tannahill, art collector and supporter of many Detroit art institutions, the Artists Market was designed to provide artists suffering the effects of the Depression with a subsidized space where their work could be exhibited and sold. The Market soon expanded to accept the work of artists within fifty miles of Detroit and was able to provide some of the area's best-known artists with a much-needed source of income.

As the Detroit Artists Market developed, it created an unusual system for choosing works that would be shown in its galleries, using a process built around three juries. A lay jury drawn from the Artists Market membership would make the first selection of younger artists and their work. A professional jury of recognized artists then looked at the rejected works and made further suggestions as to whether the works should be included or not. A third jury made up of individuals with a long-standing connection to the art community selected the works of more established artists.

For most of the 1930s and in the early 1940s, the Detroit Artists Market served as an important outlet for hundreds of artists. The demands of the war effort, however, halted its activities until 1948. The Market's influence grew considerably in the 1950s and 1960s when it began to offer one-person shows and when its members began to accept abstract art. A number of critically acclaimed exhibitions took place. By the 1970s the Market began to emphasize the jury system less and turned to the concept of selection made by a strong director. Douglas Semivan, art director of the Detroit Artists Market from 1974 to 1979, preferred to present work that was experimental and not necessarily as salable as most of the pieces in exhibitions of the previous decade. The group- and one-person shows of this period were most often given to artists creating new kinds of works in a diverse range of styles, while the gallery space surrounding the main floor exhibition area featured inexpensive works for sale.

The list of artists who exhibited at the Detroit Artists Market from its beginnings in the 1930s through the decade of the 1970s reads like a "Who's Who" in Michigan art. In the early years, work by **Mary Chase Stratton**, **John Carroll**, and **David Fredenthal** appeared, followed by that of **Marshall Fredericks**, **Liselotte Moser**, **Mary Jane Bigler**, **Wallace Mitchell**, **Constance Richardson**, and **Wayne Claxton**. In the 1970s the market remained vital by showing the works of artists such as Patricia Quinlan, **John Piet**, Diane Carr, John Hegarty, and Nancy Pletos.

The nonprofit artists market concept also was adopted by the Flint Institute of Arts, which established the Flint Artists Market in 1947. This organization served as the only effective marketing center for local artists for the next thirteen years, when other galleries began to open in the area.

Commercial Galleries

The profit-making galleries that existed in Michigan before World War II were, with one exception, interior decorating establishments that sold some European and American paintings, for the most part undistinguished ones. The Hanna Gallery of Detroit stands as an exception. Founded in 1864 as the Detroit Art Store, the gallery underwent a number of name changes, but remained, throughout its sixty years of existence, the city's prestige market for fine art. The Hanna Gallery occasionally exhibited the work of Michigan artists, such as marine painter Robert Hopkin in the 1890s and Elsie Carpell and Nell Witters of Saginaw and **Leon Makielski** of Ann Arbor in the 1920s.

The first commercial gallery to become significant in the life of the Detroit art community was the Little Gallery, established in Birmingham in 1949 by Peggy DeSalle. The former wife of painter **Zoltan Sepeshy** and well known in her own right, DeSalle opened her small suburban gallery with the idea of showing the works of contemporary American artists and craftsmen on a continuing basis. Particularly in its first years, the gallery's exhibitions drew heavily from the faculty and students of the Cranbrook Academy of Art, including sculptor **Glen Michaels**, and painters **Wallace Mitchell**, Sepeshy, and **Mary Jane Bigler**.

With the Little Gallery's commitment to rotating exhibitions, Michigan artists for the first time had access to a gallery within the state that made a true financial commitment to their works. Survival for the Little Gallery, as for all the commercial galleries that followed in its footsteps, was in part a matter of actively creating a market for the works handled. Thus, the marketing of Michigan artists' works had entered a new phase.

The Little Gallery's lead was followed shortly by a number of galleries that opened in Michigan in the early 1950s. In 1951 Robert Garelick established a gallery in Detroit that showed artists working in the social-realist vein, and artist-designer Robert Hanamura and architect Wally Kazawa opened the Chiku-Rin Gallery to show the works of artists interested particularly in good interior design, such as **Murray Jones**, **Harry Bertoia**, and Dorothy Sturm as well as the internationally known Jacques Villon and Stanley Hayter. In the same year, the Circle Gallery was founded by artist Morris Barazini and his wife Gail. The Circle Gallery moved in 1954 to Okemos and showed Michigan artists **Charles Pollock**, **David Mitchell**, **Lindsey Decker**, and Donald Thrall.

Beginning in the late 1940s, Jessie Forsythe operated an informal gallery in her Ann Arbor home. In 1954 she established the Forsythe Gallery in downtown Ann Arbor. Her original intent was to provide University of Michigan faculty members with a nearby space for regular shows of their works. In the 1950s, Forsythe handled work by **J. T. Abernathy**, **Frank Cassara**, **William Lewis**, **Thomas McClure**, **Chet La More**, and **Richard Wilt**. By the 1960s, the list had expanded to include many artists from outside Ann Arbor as well: **Charles Culver**, **Zubel Kachadoorian**, **Louise Nobili**, and **Marie Woo**. Through the 1970s, other artists were included, among them **Stefan Davidek** and **Bruce McCombs**.

The most substantial period of growth for galleries in the Detroit area came in the late 1950s and early 1960s, as dozens of galleries opened. In 1958 Donald and Florence Morris, in partnership with Bernard Cohen, opened a Detroit gallery that became the first in Michigan to show the works of major contemporary American and European artists on a regular basis. The Donald Morris Gallery brought in pieces by Willem DeKooning, Arshille Gorky, Milton Avery, and Arthur Dove, as well as works by Fernand Léger, Alberto Giacometti, and Henry Moore. At the same time, the gallery introduced regular exhibitions of African art.

The impact of the Donald Morris Gallery was not immediate, for few of the area's artists took advantage of its offerings. To build interest, Morris initiated a series of lectures and seminars dealing with various aspects of contemporary art, choosing well-known Michigan art world figures such as printmaker **Emil Weddige** and Detroit Institute of Arts curator of modern art, Franklin Page, to participate. A similar series was conducted on the themes and motifs of African art. By the 1970s, the Donald Morris Gallery was one of the most successful galleries in the Midwest and had gained a national reputation. At a new location in Birmingham, the gallery continued to exhibit a variety of works from artists of international reputation as well as certain Michigan artists such as painter **Robert Wilbert** and structurist **David Barr**.

Robert Wilbert was involved in developing a gallery in 1958 when the owner of a frame shop asked him to help organize shows for an adjacent space. Wilbert ran the AAA Gallery in Detroit for the next two years, gathering around him a group of artists from across the state who constituted the Michigan avant-garde of the time: **Gerome Kamrowski**, **Allen Leepa**, **Stefan Davidek**, Carl Van Duser, Harry Brorby, and **Wayne Claxton**. Milton Cohen of the University of Michigan staged multimedia happenings and other experiments with kinetic art. Under Wilbert's direction, the AAA Gallery provided a valuable outlet for the works of a number of serious artists in Michigan.

Robert Hanamura initiated his second gallery venture in 1962 by opening the Hanamura Gallery in downtown Detroit. The new gallery was directed toward avant-garde art and also gave more attention to the crafts, often pairing the works of Michigan craftsmen with compatible painters and sculptors. Respected ceramicists Toshiko Takaezu, Howard Kottler, and **William Lewis** exhibited at the gallery, as did painters **Murray Jones**, **Aris Koutroulis**, and Jens Plum and printmaker William Hamady. The Hanamura Gallery drew the attention of contemporary architects, students, and other gallery owners to its exhibitions and was frequently singled out by critics for the quality and boldness of its shows. The gallery, however, did not attract enough patrons to sustain itself and closed in 1966.

The J. L. Hudson Gallery was opened in the mid-1960s by the department store of that name in its downtown Detroit headquarters. This was a groundbreaking attempt by a major department store to run a professional gallery handling first-rate twentieth-century works. Under the direction of Albert Landry and Joy Emery, the Hudson Gallery held exhibitions of such internationally known artists as Alexander Calder, Jacques Lipchitz, Joseph Cornell, Frank Stella, and Andy Warhol. The works of Michigan artists were also occasionally presented: **Robert Broner**, **Sarkis Sarkisian**, and Gordon Newton, as well as **Paul Collins** of Grand Rapids. The J. L. Hudson Gallery closed in 1974 due mostly to the inability of the gallery to attract enough clientele to visit its downtown Detroit location.

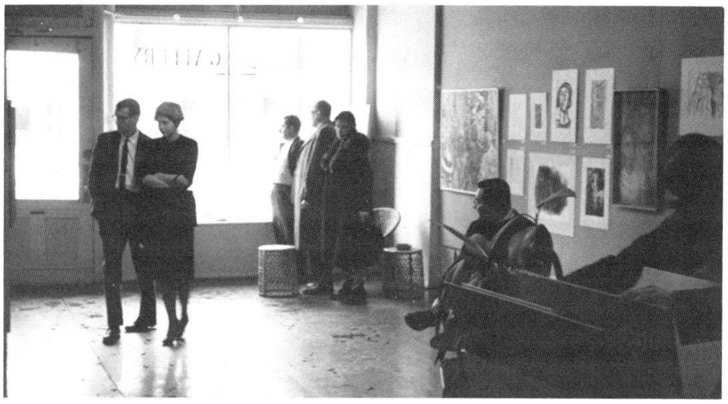

Visitors in the AAA Gallery, Detroit. The Archives of American Art, AAA Gallery Papers. G. J. Karres, Photographer.

The Gertrude Kasle Gallery opened in the Fisher Building in the New Center area of Detroit also in the mid-1960s. A strong supporter of abstract expressionism and other New York movements, Kasle was convinced that there should be at least one gallery where such work could be seen on a regular basis. Until her gallery closed in 1976, Kasle presented many shows of works by emerging artists on the national scene, such as Helen Frankenthaler, Robert Goodnough, Grace Hartigan, Paul Jenkins, Robert Natkin, and Larry Rivers. Kasle also made a commitment to Michigan artists whom she felt were of comparable stature, including **Brenda Goodman**, Ian Hornak, **Aris Koutroulis**, and **Julius Schmidt**. Kasle added a unique element to her gallery by accompanying exhibitions with informal lectures and discussions in which the exhibiting artist would discuss his or her work with anyone who wanted to join in. She also arranged to show films on artists, present poetry readings and other live performances, and coordinate openings with the other galleries in the area so that artists might have a chance to meet with each other in Detroit.

In addition to the galleries just cited, dozens of others opened all over the state and many paid serious attention to the works of Michigan artists. For example, the Arwin Gallery in Detroit devoted its shows to artists working in a representational manner, such as **Sarkis Sarkisian**, **Walter Midener**, and **John Pappas**, and the Arts Extended Gallery provided space for black artists to exhibit works dealing with black experience.

One of the most intriguing experimental galleries in Michigan, Gallery 7, emerged just as the new decade of the 1970s began. In 1969 **Charles McGee**, a black artist with a considerable reputation in the Midwest, organized an exhibition at the Detroit Artists Market of works by accomplished black artists who were still relatively unknown in the wider art community. "Seven Black Artists" included the works of James Strickland, **Lester Johnson**, Robert Murray, James King, Jr., Charles McGee, **Harold Neal**, and **James Lee** and was met with considerable interest. Inspired by the show's success, McGee founded Gallery 7 in the same year and shortly thereafter opened the Charles McGee School of Art with an all-black faculty on Detroit's northwest side.

Gallery 7 immediately became a focal point for black art in Michigan. Artists who were relatively unknown, such as Allie McGhee, MacArthur Binion, **Alfred Hinton**, and **Lester Johnson** all exhibited there and in some cases also taught at the school. More established black artists like Hale Woodruff and Jacob Lawrence also worked with the gallery on exhibitions. In the mid-1970s Gallery 7 moved into the Fisher Building in the New Center area of Detroit and McGee opened his gallery to all artists. McGee recognized that black artists could not remain isolated but had to exhibit within a larger context if they were to continue to develop. Artists who showed at Gallery 7 in the Fisher Building included Maggie Citrin, **Michele Oka Doner**, Robert Stahl, David McDonald, and Robert Murray, as well as MacArthur Binion, Alfred Hinton, and Allie McGhee. McGee closed the gallery in 1978 in order to devote more time to his own work and to direct the university gallery for Eastern Michigan University.

The general prosperity of Michigan in the mid-1970s, together with the national boom in the arts, resulted in the opening of many other galleries throughout the state. Significant galleries of the period included the Yaw Gallery in Birmingham, which devoted itself exclusively to the crafts and handled such accomplished ceramists as **Richard DeVore** and **John Glick**; the Susanne Hilberry Gallery, which included **John Egner** and Ellen Phelan among its artists; and the Feigenson-Rosenstein Gallery which took over many of the Cass Corridor artists who had gotten their start at the Willis Gallery. The Halstead 831 Gallery in Birmingham became one of the nation's most important galleries exhibiting fine photography.

Alternative Spaces

In Detroit, Lansing, Grand Rapids, and elsewhere in the state a number of artist-run organizations developed galleries in the 1970s. These concentrated on providing both space and support for artists and exhibitions that profit-oriented and institutional galleries would be reluctant to consider. Existing on shoestring budgets, and often in makeshift spaces, the alternatives opened up new means of exposure for Michigan artists.

The Willis Gallery was a cooperative initiated in 1971 by artists working in Detroit's Cass Corridor, the impoverished yet vital neighborhood near Wayne State University and the Cultural Center. Established in a converted storefront in the heart of the area, the Willis was a place where artists could display their works free from the pressures of a commercial setting. Quality and experimentation were emphasized, with little con-

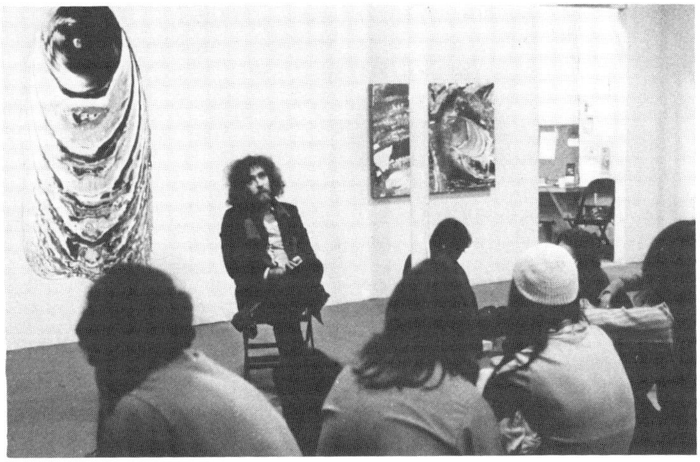

John Perrault at the Willis Gallery, Detroit, November 1971. Carl Schurer, Photographer.

sideration given to the salability of the works exhibited. The founding members acted as a committee to choose other artists to show, and these artists in turn were asked to be involved in deciding on subsequent exhibitions.

During the six years of its existence, the Willis Gallery brought to public attention the works of some of Michigan's most promising younger artists. **John Egner**, Steven Foust, **Michael Luchs**, Ellen Phelan, and **Brenda Goodman** were all given their first important exhibitions at the Willis while they were still relatively unknown. Art critics and museum curators looked to the Willis as the place where "things were happening" in Michigan. The Willis was closely associated with the new school of tough, brutal urban expressionism that came to characterize Detroit art in the 1970s. As the decade progressed, the energy and finances behind the Willis diminished, and, beset with monetary problems, it closed in 1977.

With its closing, artists in southeastern Michigan were again left with too few places to show experimental and noncommercial art. To meet this need, a number of alternative organizations were formed in the late 1970s. The first of these was the Artists Guild of Detroit, which began in 1976 as an artists' cooperative and maintained a rotating schedule of exhibitions in a gallery space located in Detroit's New Center area. Guild members, among them artists Steven Goodfellow, Chris King, Joseph Banush, Edward Fella, and Marilyn Maday, juried all works shown. The selected artists were given a space to show their work and were asked to keep the gallery open for the duration of the exhibition. The Guild provided publicity, mailings, and posters.

The building in which the Guild was located was torn down in 1978. Lacking a specific gallery space, the Guild changed its policy and began to provide artists with funding to stage exhibitions and performances in spaces of their choice. With this approach, the Guild acted much like an artist-run minicouncil for the arts, channeling funds from various government sources directly into the hands of artists whose proposals were judged worthy of support by Guild members and guest jurors.

Through this method, the Guild was responsible for some of the most innovative exhibitions staged in the Detroit area over the following two years. It was also responsible for providing artists with more freedom of action than any support organization had done in the past. Ultimately, all decisions on the funded proposals were left to the artist.

The resulting activities included everything from artist-designed billboards to exhibitions of mail art and artist books. Guild projects utilized spaces which ran the gamut from storefronts with sagging ceilings (an exhibition of the sculpture of Keith Aoki) to the interiors of city buses (seventeen minishows of the works of Detroit photographers). In all, more than two dozen exhibitions, performances, and art events were sponsored by the Guild on a budget that never amounted to more than $5,000 a year. In 1980, the Guild did not receive funding from government grants and shortly thereafter ceased to operate.

Randy Delbeke, Diane Spodarek, and Jean O'Korn founded Alternative Space-Detroit in 1977 to provide Michigan artists with a vehicle for the staging of video, performance, and conceptual art. Alternative Space-Detroit's activities began with a two-day program of performance and video pieces held at Alvin's Finer Delicatessen, a restaurant near Wayne State University frequented by artists, and was organized in conjunction with the Center for Experimental Art and Communication in Toronto.

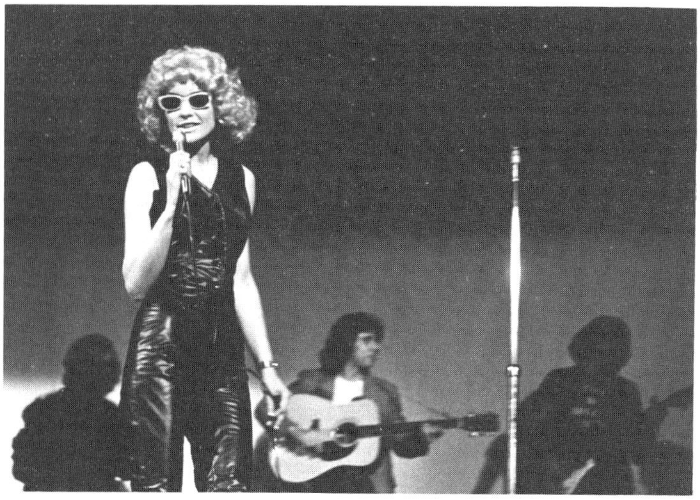

Dangerous Diana [Spodarek] and the Dinettes with Duh Detroit Band in performance at the Detroit Institute of Arts, 1973. The Detroit Institute of Arts, Museum Archives. Robert Vigiletti with Bruce Harkness, Photographers.

Alternative Space-Detroit's most ambitious project took place in 1978, when it co-sponsored the exhibition "New Video and Performance Art in Detroit" as part of the "Works in Progress" series at the Detroit Institute of Arts. The exhibition included eight video works and fourteen performance pieces staged over two evenings and featured artists such as Ray Johnson, Lynn Farnsworth, Jim Hart, and Keith Aoki.

The Contemporary Art Institute of Detroit (CAID) was founded in 1978 by **Charles McGee**, Jean Heilbronn, and Mary Beard. These artists had two goals: to create a continuing program of temporary exhibitions focusing on installation, performance, and nonsalable art in various spaces around Detroit; and to establish a permanent facility, a contemporary art institute, in the city.

CAID's first major undertaking was the staging of "Installations," an exhibition of installation art by more than twenty artists. The site for the exhibition was an aging warehouse near the Detroit waterfront. The artists involved responded to the bleak environment by creating the most extensive exhibition of installation art ever staged in Michigan.

Detroit Focus was the last of the Detroit-based "alternative spaces" to emerge in the 1970s. Focus was the direct result of a general meeting of artists, critics, curators, and administrators that was called to protest the inadequate plans made by the Michigan Council for the Arts to showcase the visual arts at its 1978 Michigan Congress for the Arts. It was decided that an artist-sponsored juried exhibition should be held at the time of the Michigan Congress for the Arts. The momentum surrounding the mounting of this temporary exhibition intensified the local artist community's interest in having some sort of permanent artist-run space and led to the establishment Detroit Focus. Focus renovated space for a gallery in the Greektown area of Detroit and began to sponsor a wide range of exhibitions designed to involve large segments of the art community. Still functioning today, the organization uses outside jurors of some stature, theme shows, and extensive mailings to draw artists. Along with the exhibitions, Focus also sponsors various programs that seek to promote dialogue among artists.

Detroit Focus has been particularly successful in finding funding for its operations from various government sources such as the Detroit Council for the Arts and the Michigan Council for the Arts. These successes, in addition to the wide participation of artists fostered by the organization, made Focus one of the most viable of "alternative space" galleries and assured its survival into the 1980s.

Michigan was by no means New York City, but by the 1970s it had developed a substantial and healthy network of galleries, both commercial and artist-run. Artists in the state could show their work and in many cases it was successfully marketed. Furthermore, Michigan galleries exhibited a sufficient variety of work to allow the region's artists to keep in touch with many contemporary developments. The commercial necessities of the gallery business, as elsewhere, often precluded Michigan galleries from presenting the more unorthodox art forms, but, for the most part, galleries were receptive to the works of the state's artists. Certainly by the 1970s they had become a significant factor in the careers of a great many Michigan artists.

Public Patronage and the Visual Arts in Michigan

Government patronage for the visual arts in Michigan dates back to the Great Depression. Until the terrible days of the 1930s, there was only occasional public support for artists, mostly through commissions for a statue or a mural for a new courthouse, city hall, or the like. Even in the prosperous days of the 1920s, public commissions were infrequent. Most Americans felt that support for the arts should come from the private sector, if they thought about such matters at all.

The Public Works of Art Project

The Depression produced a crisis in the arts of such magnitude that it forced a reexamination of the role of public patronage, for the very survival of the arts was severely threatened. Private individuals and corporations were too preoccupied with basic financial survival to give any attention to the needs of artists. Artists throughout the country found it nearly impossible to continue with their work and still make a living.

Fortunately, several individuals with connections to the Roosevelt administration were concerned that the conditions caused by the Depression could conceivably result in the loss of creative output of a whole generation of Americans. In 1933, George Biddle, an upperclass artist from Philadelphia, and Edward Bruce, an expert on silver for the U.S. Treasury Department and an accomplished painter, responded to the problems of the American visual artist by proposing a program of government patronage designed both to enhance public buildings with works of art and to provide relief for artists. After weeks of political maneuvering, their proposal received the backing of Harold Ickes, administrator of the massive U.S. Public Works Administration. Ickes eventually released funds for public works that could be used for the employment of artists, and the Public Works of Art Project was created.

In 1933 a little more than one million dollars was allocated to the Public Works of Art Project (PWAP) to employ 2,500 artists and 500 laborers on a weekly basis across the nation for four winter months to decorate public buildings and parks. By this one unprecedented act in the history of the visual arts in the United States, the federal government became the most important patron in the nation as an employer of artists on a regular basis. Even more startling, this form of government patronage eliminated the traditional concept of paying an artist for a specific commission. For the first time, artists in America were placed on a payroll, contracted like any other hourly employee, to turn out so much work each day for so much pay. The impact on the art community was immediate, as thousands of artists descended on the various regional headquarters looking for work.

Michigan's experience with the PWAP was fairly typical of that in most other parts of the country. Several hundred artists and others who claimed to be artists showed up for the fewer than fifty positions initially created in Michigan. Michigan was included in a region that encompassed parts of Indiana and Kentucky and all of Ohio, with regional headquarters in Cleveland. William Milliken, director of the Cleveland Museum of Art, was made regional director. Within Michigan, the PWAP was supervised by a board of well-known individuals including Clyde Burroughs and Edgar P. Richardson of the Detroit Institute of Arts, architect Albert Kahn, art critic Florence Davies, and art patron Mrs. H. Lee Simpson. Directives came from Washington by way of Cleveland, and the Michigan board was given a set of guidelines stating what type of projects were permissible, what institutions were qualified to receive work, and even what subject matter was to be emphasized: stress was to be placed on the American scene. Within this framework, however, there was considerable flexibility.

In its brief period of activity, the PWAP managed to employ eighty-four artists to complete sixty-eight projects, most of which were in southeastern Michigan. Outside of Detroit, its suburbs, and Ann Arbor, the PWAP was active only in Grand Rapids, Paw Paw, Flint, Muskegon, Newberry, and Kalamazoo.

Artists in Detroit were commissioned to make stained-glass windows for the Public Library, dioramas for the Children's Museum, a Pewabic tile drinking fountain for Wayne State University, and PWAP artists also created "safety" posters for the Police Department which were widely distributed. By far the most popular projects were those for murals; twenty-nine murals were completed, with twenty-one of these in the Detroit area alone. Thirty-seven artists painted PWAP murals, including ones decorating the Children's Room in the Detroit Public Library, the halls of the Maybury Sanitarium in Northville, and numerous public school auditoriums in Detroit and its suburbs. The McGregor Library in Highland Park commissioned murals depicting characters from Mark Twain, Mother Goose, and Alice in Wonderland.

During the four and one-half months in which the PWAP functioned, the depressed Michigan art scene was transformed into an active and vital one. The PWAP managed to generate commissions for works of art at a rate unheard of even in the boom years of the 1920s.

The Treasury Section of Fine Arts

The U.S. Public Works of Art Project was followed by a number of other programs designed to keep the federal government involved in art patronage. In October 1934 the U.S. Treasury Section of Fine Arts (TSFA) was established to provide artistic embellishment for federal public buildings. This was not a relief measure in the same sense that the PWAP had been, as it did not place artists on a payroll. Instead, artists were commissioned in the traditional way to create a specific work of art for a particular place at a flat fee. Furthermore, the TSFA was much more selective of the artists included and tried to arrange for its commissions to be given to top artists, whether they were actually in need of funds or not. Initially, many of these artists were chosen through a jury system.

The TSFA lasted in one form or another until mid-1943. In the nine years of its existence, it sponsored 1,371 commissions nationwide. Commissions were executed for fifty buildings in Michigan, principally post offices scattered throughout the state. Small towns such as Grayling, Crystal Falls, Iron River, and Munising shared in the program's benefits, as did the cities of Lansing, Grand Rapids, and Detroit. The sculptures and murals sponsored by the TSFA were often the first major works of public art in some of these communities.

Half of the commissions executed in the state were done by Michigan artists. Such Michigan artists as **Zoltan Sepeshy**, **Carlos Lopez**, **David Fredenthal**, James Calder, and **Jaroslav Brozik** were all paid the standard rate of roughly eleven dollars per square foot to paint murals in post office lobbies. Sculptors **Milton Horn** and **Marshall Fredericks** were paid similar amounts for sculptural reliefs. All of the Michigan artists received an average of between six hundred dollars and eight hundred dollars for their work, which was roughly equivalent to what artists from outside the state received.

The works commissioned by the TSFA, as with those done under the PWAP before it, emphasized typical scenes of everyday life in the region. The lumbering town of Manistique received a Fredenthal mural entitled *Logging*; Frankfort, a port on Lake Michigan, was the recipient of *On Board the Car Ferry* by Henry Bernstein. The post office in Michigan's "Cherry Capital," Traverse City, was graced by the *Cherry Picker* by Marion Overby. Urban themes appeared in Michigan's larger cities, with murals entitled *City Workers*, *Chemistry*, and *Change of Shift*. Most notably, William Gropper, one of the important social realists of the 1930s and 1940s, did two commanding murals for the northwestern branch of the post office in Detroit. These twenty- by six-foot murals, entitled *Automobile Industry*, were the largest and most costly ones commissioned by the TSFA in Michigan.

As a result of its late start in Michigan and the relatively few local artists that it employed, the TSFA did not play a key role in the lives of many artists in the state. Other programs were far more crucial to their survival.

The Works Progress Administration's Federal Art Project

Of all of the government programs designed to aid the artist, the Federal Art Project of the Works Progress Administration (WPA/FAP) had the greatest impact on the visual arts in Michigan. Founded in August 1935, the WPA/FAP functioned for the next four years as the United States government's principal effort on behalf of the arts. Unlike the TSFA and the PWAP, the primary concern of the WPA/FAP was for providing work relief. Artists who joined the program were paid a salary to work a specified number of hours per month.

For the first six months of its existence in Michigan, the project was ill-organized and ill-managed, until the young director of the Kalamazoo Institute of Arts, Sylvester Jerry, was hired as director in early 1936. Jerry searched the relief ranks to find as many artists as he could and then went about developing programs and projects that would utilize whatever skills these individuals had. At the same time, using a clause that allowed regional directors to make up twenty percent of their work force from artists not on relief, Jerry was able to improve his staff by hiring sculptor **Samuel Cashwan** and muralist **Gerald Mast** in supervisory positions. Jerry organized eight regional districts within the state, each with an advisory board of local citizens. He also devised the concept of offering institutions a package of several works of art, whereby they could have their facilities enhanced by combinations of murals, sculpture, and easel paintings.

Jerry's shrewdest move of the first few months was the staging of a well-publicized exhibition of WPA/FAP work. Held at the Scarab Club of Detroit in April 1936, the exhibition consisted of the works of some of the better artists on the project. Civic and in-

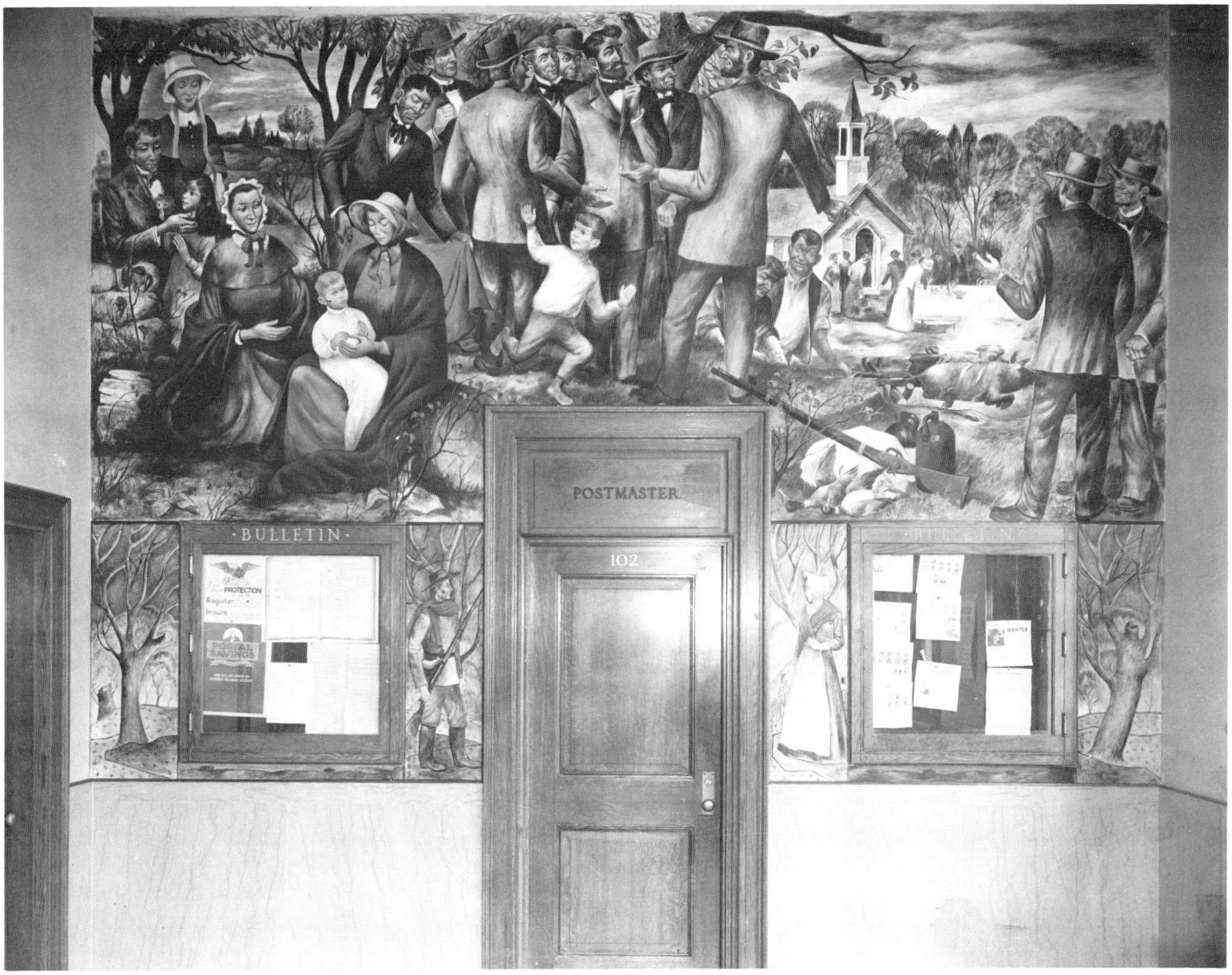

Carlos Lopez (1908–1953). Mural for post office in Birmingham. Commissioned by the Section of Fine Arts in July 1941 and completed a year later. The Archives of American Art.

dustrial leaders from throughout the state came to the exhibition and liked what they saw, and the exhibition drew large crowds of the interested public. By the end of 1936, the fortunes of the WPA/FAP in Michigan were reversed and more than eighty artists were employed. Jerry had dozens of artists at work on projects for the University of Michigan, the Clare (Michigan) High School, and in Detroit at the U.S. Army base at Fort Wayne and the Brodhead Naval Armory.

The WPA/FAP also initiated a number of subprojects that had considerable impact on the public. Artists with lesser skills, for example, were placed on a national program known as the "Index of American Design," which recorded examples of American handicraft antedating 1890 by rendering them in color. The Index was directed by **Paul McPharlin**, a painter and puppeteer, who managed to create a program that captured the interest of both the public and the critics. Quick to recognize the human interest factor in the objects being recorded, McPharlin spent much of his time writing press releases about the uniqueness and diversity of these items. This small subproject thus became the object of much publicity as newspapers across the state printed fascinating stories about the Index's work on everything from hitching posts to ship's figureheads and teacups from the Centennial Exposition.

The WPA/FAP also contributed to the revival of the crafts in Michigan. Late in 1938 an Upper Peninsula Arts and Crafts Project was established at Iron Mountain under the direction of Finnish-American

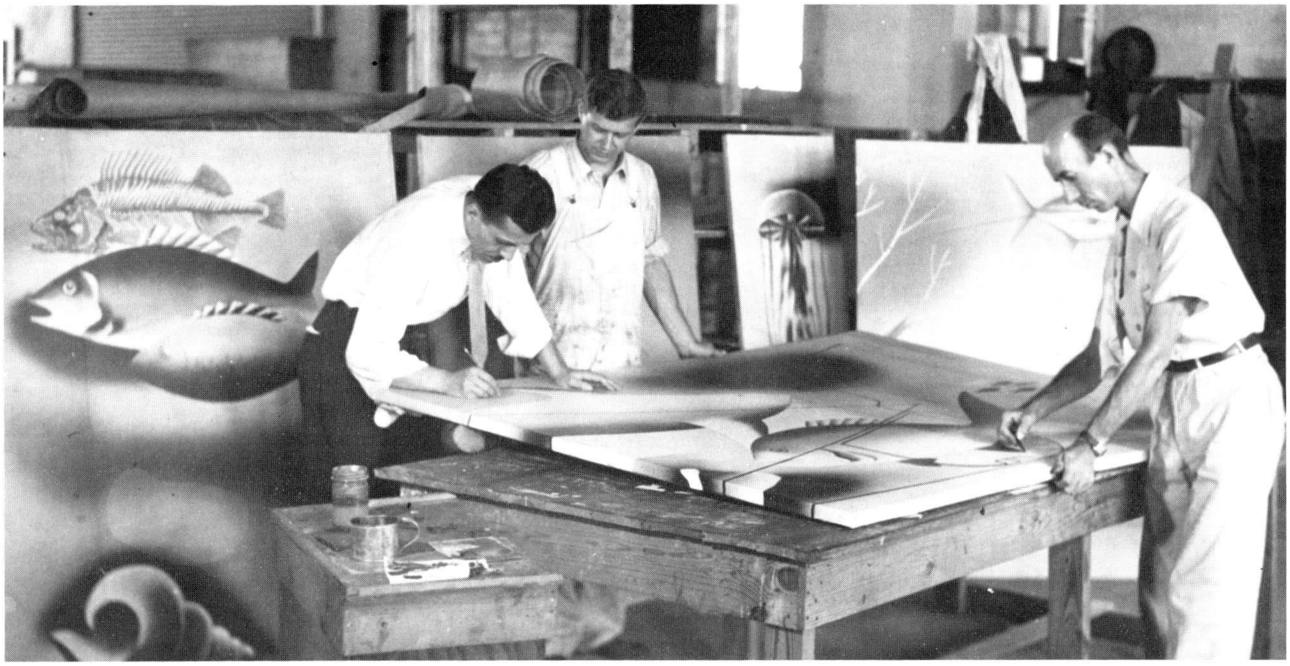

Edgar Yaeger (1904– *) (right) and Gerald Mast (1908–1971) (center) working on a WPA/FAP mural for the Naval Armory in Detroit. The Detroit Institute of Arts, Research Library.*

artist Aarre Lahti. To relieve some of the area's unemployment, Lahti was given the task of encouraging the many area residents of Scandinavian descent to use traditional folk art forms in the creation of craft work. Lahti soon discovered, however, that the supposed skills had all but been forgotten and consequently a retraining program had to be established. By using books on the subject, he managed to set up looms and teach weaving; he helped carpenters and cabinetmakers turn their skills toward more craft-oriented projects. Within a year he had more than seventy artisans involved in the making of everything from curtains to furniture and snowshoes for the use of nonprofit institutions throughout the state. Similar projects were instituted in other parts of Michigan; for example, among the Native American population in the area around Cross Village in the northern Lower Peninsula.

The establishment of the various federal art programs also led to the first experiments in the state with the unionization of artists. In 1936, following the example of New York artists on the WPA/FAP, Michigan artists connected with the project began to organize a union that would serve as a lobbying force as well as an agent for collective bargaining and grievance procedures. By the end of 1938, all of the artists on the Michigan project were members of the American Federation of Government Employees (AFGE), Lodge 322. The AFGE lasted only a year, but was followed by two other unions: the short-lived Professional Division of the Workers' Alliance (November 1937 through June 1938) and the CIO-affiliated United Office and Professional Workers of America, which functioned from mid-1938 until the end of the New Deal.

In Michigan, however, the various artists' unions were not very effective. Although similar unions in New York, Chicago, and other cities were often militant and vocal, staging work-stoppages and sit-ins, no such activities occurred in Michigan. Perhaps the most significant aspect of unionization was the opening of communication between the artists of Michigan and their counterparts in other areas. The national ties that developed would figure significantly in the expanding art world of the post-World War II period.

The decline of the WPA/FAP in Michigan began in 1939 when appropriations were drastically cut at the national level and the administration was moved from Washington to each participating state, leaving it in the hands of a number of state officials who were not particularly interested in the arts. By the early 1940s the project had diminished to the point where most of its emphasis was on handicraft projects, defense poster work, adult education classes, and museum services. The need for the skills of fine artists was gone, and the majority of artists were able to find work in private industry or in teaching. By 1943, the federal projects on the arts disappeared into the war effort.

The federal government, in the nearly ten years it was active as a patron of the visual arts, had a pronounced impact on the Michigan art community, for these projects kept the arts from withering away. Although many of the best-known artists never had to seek its support, for the majority of artists the government projects provided the lifeblood that allowed them to continue to develop by working. Nor should the impact of these projects on the public be discounted, for the work done on them often offered the first experience of contemporary art to many people. For others, the WPA/FAP meant a chance to witness firsthand an artist at work, whether sketching road workers, carving reliefs, painting a mural, or teaching in an adult education class. The federal art projects made art a part of everyday experience for many.

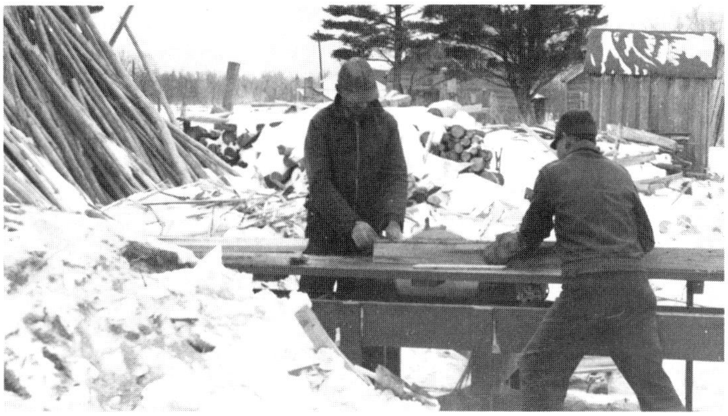

Indians at Cross Village sawing cedar to be used in the construction of furniture designed for the State Conservation Department. Michigan Arts and Crafts Project, February 1941. The Detroit Institute of Arts, Research Library.

The National Endowment for the Arts

After the burst of activity that had characterized the 1930s, it was not until the late 1960s that the federal government again offered support for the arts. Its re-entrance into the field evolved slowly, beginning with the establishment of the National Endowment for the Arts and Humanities in 1965, a composite of the National Endowment for the Arts (NEA) and the National Endowment for the Humanities and their Advisory Councils. The primary purpose of both endowments was to administer grants. In 1969 art administrator Nancy Hanks was named chair of the NEA; her vision and energy provided the impetus for a whole series of programs and actions that allowed the NEA to emerge as a major cultural force. At the same time, Congress dramatically increased the NEA's budget, which suddenly grew to over thirty million dollars. By the late 1970s, the budget approached one hundred million dollars.

Much of the endowment's funding went to established art institutions for the expansion of their services, while another large percentage went directly to the states, in most cases to fund state arts councils (including the Michigan Council for the Arts) which in turn administered local grants to stimulate the arts. The NEA also established programs to place funds directly in the hands of the working artist, such as the artist-in-the-schools program, which brought the creative process into the classroom by funding artists to demonstrate their working processes for primary and secondary school students. This was later expanded to include artist-in-residence programs for both educational institutions and communities, in cooperation with state art councils.

The NEA's most substantial efforts toward aiding the individual artist came with a series of fellowships instituted in 1967 that granted artists and craftsmen funds simply to carry out their work. The NEA grants, ranging up to ten thousand dollars for artists and five thousand dollars for craftsmen, allowed the grantee to decide how best to use the money. A crafts apprenticeship program was also established to allow master craftsmen to hire apprentices. Throughout the 1970s, Michigan artists such as Nancy Pletos, Diane Spodarek, Rosa Patino, and **Robert Piepenberg** took part in all these programs, vying with individuals from other states for the several hundred awards granted each year. Through the NEA, the federal government became by far the most important patron in the nation.

The Michigan Council for the Arts

No organization public or private has been more important to the recent growth of the visual arts in Michigan than the Michigan Council for the Arts. In the 1960s and particularly the 1970s, the Michigan Council served as the state's chief advocate for the arts, providing funds, ideas, and advice to stimulate and support the art community. More than the NEA or any other federal program in support of the arts, the Council became the agency to which most Michigan artists turned for support. In turn, Council's programming reached furthest into the art community.

The concept that individual states should become directly involved with the support of the arts enjoyed a certain vogue around the country in the early 1960s, and state commissions, panels, and councils arose in response. The Michigan Council for the Arts was a product of this concern. The Council began its existence in 1960 as a temporary commission charged with studying the needs of the arts in Michigan. Although powerless and penniless, it nevertheless managed to involve as members many individuals important to the state's artistic life while it studied the arts and lobbied for greater state involvement.

The commission was made a permanent group, the Michigan Council for the Arts, in 1963 but even with this reorganization, it remained a voluntary, financially powerless body until 1966. In that year, the Michigan legislature legally established the council as a permanent state agency for the arts and for the first time provided it with a budget to institute programs. Funding in that first year and the several years that followed was pitifully small. The 1966 budget, for example, consisted of one hundred thousand dollars from the state legislature and fifty thousand dollars from the NEA. In the 1960s the budget never went beyond two hundred thousand dollars. Consequently, the Council was never able to come close to meeting the funding demands placed upon it. As the Council's first director, E. Ray Scott, recalled, "Based on the false assumption that we were going to have the money, we really went out and beat the bushes and encouraged people to apply. We wound up with something like $900,000 in applications and less than $100,000 with which to address these applications."[13]

Despite the woefully inadequate funding of its first years, the Council attempted to provide at least some funding for all of the artistic disciplines. The Council's initial approach to arts programming was by individual discipline. For the visual arts, a coordinator was hired who worked with artists' groups on the creation of projects, making sure they followed up with grant applications, and then "walked" the applicants through the funding process. In 1966, the first visual arts coordinator, sculptor **Jim Pallas**, had about six thousand dollars to work with for all the visual arts in the whole state.

Unlike the federal arts projects of the 1930s and the NEA grants of the 1960s and 1970s, the Michigan Council was not able to provide direct aid to individual artists, and it was decided that the limited funds should be used to create a supportive climate for the arts by centering on projects that could provide exposure for Michigan artists, strengthen artists' organizations and resource institutions in the community, and help artists develop professional skills in handling their business affairs.

The financial strength of the Council grew considerably in the 1970s. Through the support of legislators like Senator Jack Faxon and Governor William H. Milliken, the legislature's allocation for the Michigan Council became second only to New York's in funding for the arts. In 1974 the Council had a budget of over two million dollars, and by 1978 the figure climbed to $4.5 million. This budget allowed the Council to embark on an impressive array of programs that included everything from operational support for major institutions to grants to aid individual artists.

The Council was also instrumental in providing funds for many exhibitions featuring Michigan artists, for example "Contemporary Michigan Craftsmen" held in 1967. A year later, an exhibition of sculpture by such artists as Tom Paul Fitzgerald, **Jim Pallas**, and **John Stephenson** circulated to more than half a dozen cities in the Lower Peninsula. In 1974 the Council lent extensive support to the largest exhibition ever devoted to the work of Michigan artists, "Michigan Focus," by facilitating cooperation among the participating museums, financing the selection process, and underwriting the catalogue.

The Council also helped to finance creative projects directly. In 1972 it began to subsidize the creation of suites of prints by Michigan artists involved with print cooperatives, when a grant was given to the Detroit Workshop of Fine Prints to publish a series of prints made in the medium of cliché-verre. Other funds went to the workshop to produce a suite, "Ten Lithographs by Ten Michigan Artists," followed by a "Bicentennial Suite," both of which were circulated throughout the state for exhibition and sale.

During the 1970s, the Council was active in financing public works of art to put the works of Michigan artists before a wider audience. The Council sponsored "Sculpture in the City," a series of temporary outdoor sculptures in Detroit and other cities; a series of murals painted on the sides of downtown Detroit buildings; and an earthwork by Stan Dolega on Detroit's Belle Isle. The Grand Rapids *Fish Ladder* by **Joseph Edwin Kinnebrew IV**, which functions both as a work of art and as an aid for spawning fish ascending the falls of the Grand River, was also supported by the Council.

One of the Council's most successful and original projects was the Michigan Artrain, a specially equipped train that toured the state. The Artrain was conceived in 1971 as a way to give Michigan's more isolated towns the chance to see works of art. Inside its converted passenger cars were pieces from many different cultures and periods, including a number by contemporary Michigan artists. In a converted baggage car, artists demonstrated their skills by painting, silkscreening, smithing, or throwing pots while visitors gathered around to watch and learn. Artrain was a phenomenal success, for it brought the visual arts to thousands of Michigan residents who had little opportunity to visit museums and galleries or see the creative process in action. The Artrain was expensive, however, for the conversion of the train had cost a hundred thousand dollars and the yearly operating costs were one-and-a-half times that much. Some critics complained that it cost too much for the results it produced; others

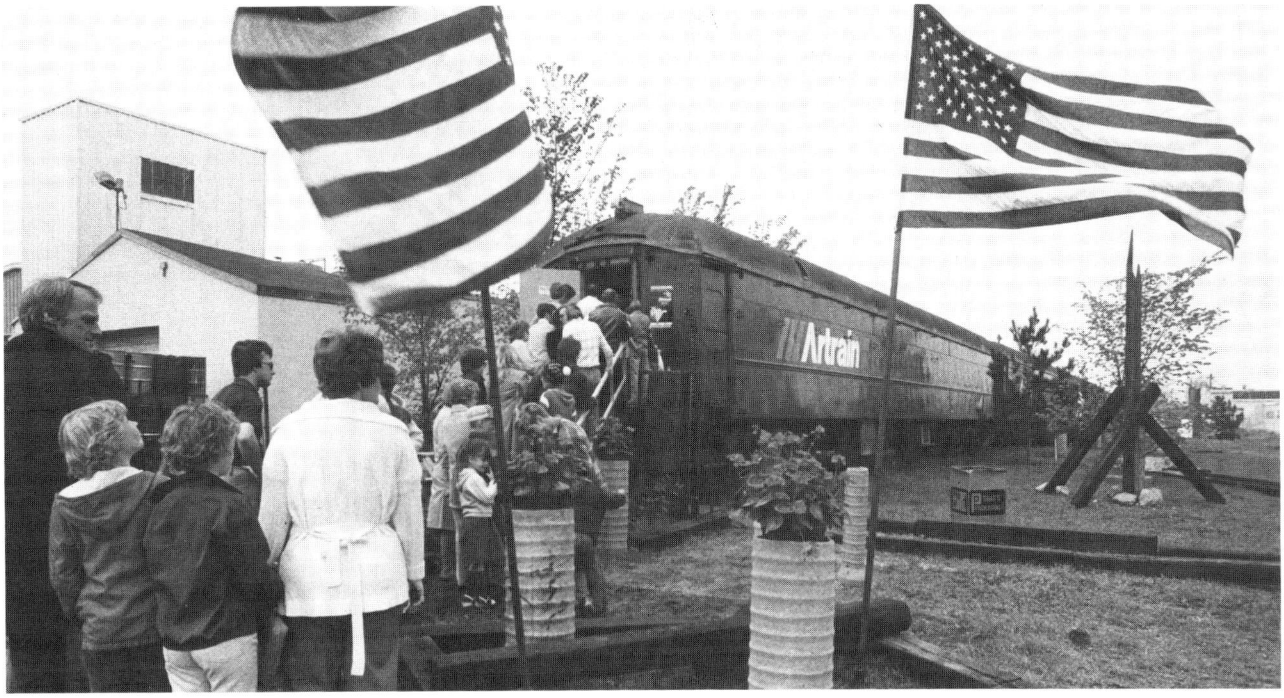

Crowds waiting to visit the Artrain. Courtesy Michigan Artrain.

charged that too few artists benefited. Eventually the Council had to withdraw its direct support, and the Artrain was placed in the hands of a self-sustaining nonprofit organization where it remained through the 1970s.

As its financial strength grew, the Council began to fund more projects that would provide artists with a network of opportunity and support. The Council used its funds to finance artist associations, cooperative galleries, and workshops. Projects that included research on the Michigan art scene and its documentation and publication also received funding from the Council. A computer survey was sponsored in 1976 by the University of Michigan to determine the size, distribution, and type of work done by the state's artists. The survey was subsequently used to help the council plan many things, from mailings to decisions concerning areas for future funding needs. Oral history interviews were conducted with many of the state's most important art figures, and two publications giving information about the state's artists in the nineteenth and twentieth centuries were developed: Arthur Hopkin Gibson's *Artists of Early Michigan* and this book.

Conscious that a healthy art community needs publications to provide arts information and criticism, the Council provided partial funding of periodicals, helping to launch the *Michigan Art Journal* in 1976. The short-lived journal, which ceased publication in 1977, provided articles on the visual arts and a section devoted to the works of selected artists. The *Detroit Artists Monthly* began publication in 1977 and added the dimensions of criticism and interview to its coverage of the Michigan art scene, providing up-to-date commentary on art activity. *Lightworks*, a periodical designed to give literary and visual artists a chance to publish experimental writings and reproductions of visual work, was also first published in 1977 with MCA support.

Two of the Council's most ambitious efforts to develop a supportive atmosphere for the arts evolved in 1976 when plans were made for "Design Michigan" and a major conference involving all the arts. "Design Michigan" was planned as a multifaceted program aimed at making various segments of Michigan society aware of the importance and benefits of good design over a number of years. Generated and organized by the Michigan Council, it included business design conferences, educational packages for schools, touring exhibitions, and television spots highlighting Michigan design accomplishments. But as had happened with the Artrain, "Design Michigan" soon became too large and expensive for the Council to support alone, and in 1978 it was made a state outreach project of the Cranbrook Academy of Art. In this way, the project still received some funds through the Council, but the principal funding came from an amount earmarked by the legislature for the support of certain key cultural institutions in Michigan to provide programs to other institutions and organizations.

The Michigan Congress on the Arts brought together in Detroit representatives from all segments of the state's art world in 1968 in an attempt to build an arts advocacy program that would address numerous issues affecting the arts. Art administrators, MCA members, and artists developed a number of resolutions designed to initiate action on issues as diverse as marketing and the arts, standards for art education, improvement of art criticism, business support of the arts, and the use of electronic media as an art form. In almost all cases, the realization of the goals of these resolutions required long-range planning, and the overall success of the congress has been difficult to ascertain.

The Michigan Council for the Arts also put considerable time and money into special seminars that dealt directly with the professional problems common to working artists, such as marketing, legal protection, contract writing, professional health standards, and health insurance. In 1977 a major symposium was held at the Detroit Institute of Arts on "Issues in the Visual Arts," which brought together experts from both inside and outside the local community to discuss a number of issues facing Michigan artists. Hundreds of artists attended to hear panels and presentations by attorney Tad Crawford, New York critic Robert Pincus-Witten, and curator of the New Museum, Marcia Tucker. Funds were also provided for the development of professional artists associations like the Michigan chapters of Artists Equity and the Women's Caucus for the Arts.

Despite the many and various programs it supported, the Council's efforts did not meet with complete approval from significant segments of the art community. Artists, in particular, criticized the Council for not doing more for them directly. The most common complaint was that the Council's programs put money into the hands of everyone but the artist. In 1978, however, the substantial budget of the council allowed it to respond to some of these demands, and the Support to Individual Artists Program was initiated. An office was established to work directly with artists on the goals of increasing professionalization, exposure, and to stimulate a better market for the working artist. With this new program, the Council became the active agent working to achieve these ends and not merely a funding source for projects initiated by others. The Support to Individual Artists Program was charged with setting up communication networks between artists, building artists' and clients' relationships, establishing social service programs for artists, creating media presentations, and establishing consultancy pools for the benefit of artists. But it was not given the authority to place funds directly in the hands of artists for projects.

The Council in the 1970s was one of the most active and best-financed arts councils in the country. It had also added dramatically to the opportunities available to the state's artists.

Several conclusions can be drawn from this brief overview of the development of the visual arts community in Michigan in the first three-quarters of the twentieth century. First, until after World War II, the art produced in Michigan tended to be provincial. In those years the strongest influence on the course of the state's artistic development most often came from external sources as styles and theories were imported from Europe or the East Coast. The academic painters and sculptors who reigned supreme in the century's first few decades were disciples of European masters. The Arts and Crafts Movement, influential in Michigan for nearly forty years, was a product of England. The "American scene" realism that dominated the Michigan art world in the 1930s was part of a national movement. Abstract expressionism, which in the 1950s influenced practically every Michigan artist then working, was a New York movement that eventually swept much of the country. Even the Cranbrook Academy of Art, which brought fame and glory to Michigan in the 1930s and 1940s for its art and design innovations, was a center of European aesthetics and thought.

Furthermore, many of the social and economic forces that shaped the course of development for Michigan's art community were national in scope. Michigan's artistic destiny in the 1930s was determined by the art programs of the federal government. These programs kept artists employed and even determined the nature of the art they produced. In the 1940s and early 1950s the policies of the federal government, particularly the G.I. Bill, created an economic and artistic boon for the state's universities and helped to generate the explosive growth of the arts in Michigan during the period. Even as late as the 1960s, it was the re-establishment of federal patronage of the arts through programs like that of the National Endowment for the Arts, as well as a growing national interest in supporting the arts, that led to the myriad of art programs which eventually helped to bring so much activity to the Michigan art scene.

But the domination of Michigan's art community for so many years by outside influences did not keep it from making exciting contributions in its own right to the American art world. For example, Michigan had an outstanding record in the Arts and Crafts Movement, establishing such important institutions as the Detroit Society of Arts and Crafts, the Pewabic Pottery, and the Cranbrook Academy of Art. Cranbrook's evolution in the 1930s and 1940s into an American equivalent of the Bauhaus in Germany was truly a major achievement.

Throughout these years many artists created work that could stand on its own merit regardless of how provincial or imitative the general artistic climate. Indeed, during the first half of the century, Michigan produced a number of artists who were recognized and honored on the national scene.

Secondly, those factors that are unique to Michigan and that might have been expected to influence its artistic development did not really have much effect. The superb natural setting that figures so significantly in Michigan's popular image has had little bearing on its artistic life. For decades, artists have visited and worked along the state's shorelines or within its forests but these settings have not inspired an important artistic movement within the state. Michigan never became a center for landscape or seascape painting. It did not produce a major group of ceramicists whose work obviously reflected the influence of natural elements, nor did it witness an identifiable regionalistic movement that drew upon the peculiarities of the land and its people for subject matter.

The influence of the auto industry, so closely identified with Michigan, has also been negligible. There has been no great transfer of ideas and styles between the world of the auto designer and that of the fine artist. Neither has there been much evidence of the automobile as a source of imagery. The presence of the auto industry is seen in the design programs of the state's art schools and art departments, but auto design programs also form part of the curricula of many art schools outside of Michigan. Even the raw art that came out of Detroit in the late 1960s and early 1970s, which occasionally made reference to the automobile, had less to do with the machine itself than with the general urban malaise of the last few decades to which the automobile has been only one contributing factor.

Finally, it is clear that Michigan's greatest period of artistic growth came after the end of World War II. Those years witnessed a phenomenal rise in the number of artists, as increasing numbers of individuals pursued careers in art. The American art world as a whole became enamored with the Bachelor and Master of Fine Arts degrees, and university art departments soon dominated a field where once private art schools had had a commanding presence.

Furthermore, the phenomenal growth of Michigan's schools and departments of art had another consequence. Attracted by substantial salaries and first-rate facilities, Michigan artists were drawn into the educational system to teach others in what was an ever-expanding system. Within a few years, most of Michigan's professional fine artists and craftsmen found themselves tied to the art colleges and universities for their economic well-being.

The postwar period brought other changes as well. From the late 1940s onward, professional organizations proliferated. The new organizations, as a rule, were organized by narrower segments of the art community and for more specific professional goals than their prewar predecessors. Michigan artists made an effort to create an association for practically every conceivable interest group, every medium, every geographical location, and every probable purpose.

The marketing of art also changed. From the nineteenth century through the early 1950s, Michigan artists had sold their art mainly through personal contacts or through institutionally sponsored exhibitions and competitions. In the 1950s and 1960s, however, a great many galleries were established in the state, both commercial and nonprofit, thus providing artists with expanded avenues for the exhibiting and marketing of their work.

None of the changes in the post-World War II period was more important than the end of the provincialism that had characterized most of Michigan's art history in the twentieth century. The greater mobility of artists, coupled with an expanded national art press, made the latest artistic developments and ideas readily available, with the result that regional barriers and differences eventually eroded. Throughout the 1950s and 1960s, Michigan's schools were increasingly staffed by artists who had trained and worked outside the state. Along with these individuals came fresh ideas, styles, and techniques.

At the present time, Michigan possesses a fairly successful and sophisticated visual arts community and can look back on a considerably more than respectable history. In the pages that follow, the careers of many of the individuals who contributed to this history are examined. Taken together, their experiences reveal what it has meant to be an artist in Michigan since 1900.

Notes

1. Edward Rowan, "Directive to PWAP Regional Directors, March 7, 1934," PWAP Central Records, Microfilm roll DC12, Archives of American Art, Smithsonian Institution, Washington, D.C.

2. Edgar P. Richardson, "Introduction," *46th Annual Exhibition for Michigan Artists* (Detroit: Detroit Institute of Arts, 1948), unpaginated.

3. *Annual Exhibition of the Scarab Club at the Detroit Museum of Art* (Detroit, 1915), unpaginated.

4. *Annual Exhibition of the Scarab Club* (Detroit: Detroit Museum of Art, 1917), unpaginated.

5. Ralph Holmes, "Review of the Scarab Annual," *Detroit Times*, January 1, 1928.

6. Quoted in Marion Taylor, "Art Juror Denies Favoritism," *Detroit Free Press*, January 12, 1928.

7. "An Exhibition is Opened," *Detroit Times*, January 4, 1933.

8. Clyde Burroughs, "Michigan Artists Free-for-all Abounds in Fun," *Detroit News*, January 15, 1933.

9. Edgar P. Richardson, "Foreword," *39th Annual Exhibition for Michigan Artists* (Detroit: Detroit Institute of Arts, 1948), p. 2.

10. Joy Hakanson, "Review—Michigan Artist Exhibition," *Detroit News*, January 21, 1973.

11. Quoted in Mary Riordan, *Muskegon Museum of Art, A Preface* (Muskegon, Michigan: Muskegon Museum of Art, 1980).

12. Joy Hakanson Colby, "Paradise: Where the Rent is Free," *Detroit News*, February 26, 1962, p. 8.

13. Ray Scott, interview with the author, Detroit, March 26, 1977. Transcription on file at the Archives of American Art, Smithsonian Institution, Washington, D.C.

BIOGRAPHIES

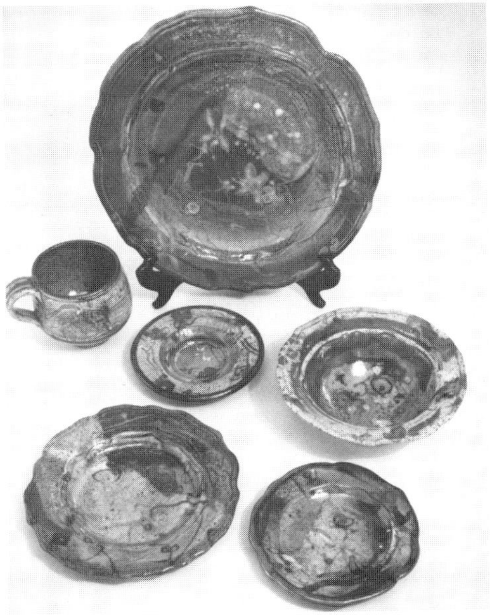

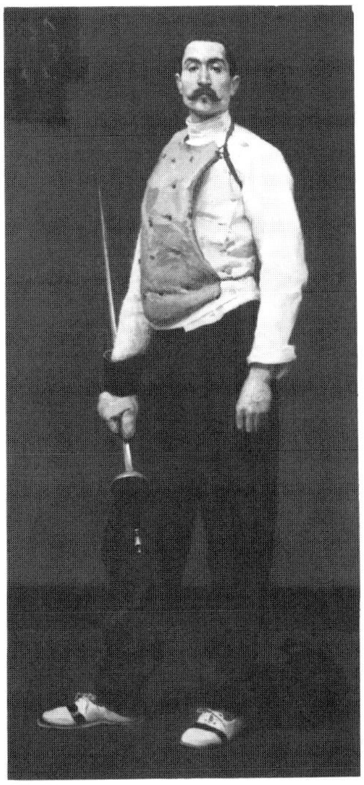

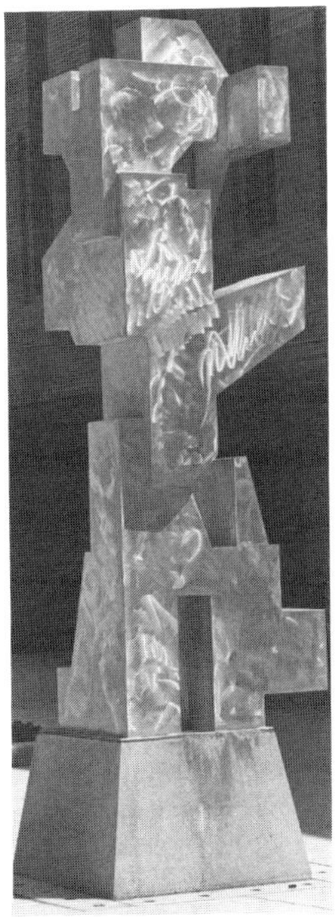

Group Exhibitions: MACE 1964, 1971; *National Religious Art Exhibition*, CAAM 1966; *Objects: USA*, Johnson Wax Collection Touring Show 1969/70*; *Southern Tier Arts and Crafts Exhibition*, Corning Museum of Glass, Corning, N.Y. 1970; *Beaux-Arts Designer/Craftsmen Exhibition*, Columbus Museum of Art, 1972–73, 1975; *The Goldsmith*, NCFA 1974; *Forms in Metal*, Mus Contemp Crafts 1975; *Reprise*, CAAM 1975; *Uncommon Smiths of America*, EMU 1975.

Collections: Johnson Wax Collection of Contemporary Crafts, Racine, Wis.

Sources: *WWAA* 1976; MAR; William Seitz and Rupert Feingold, *Silversmithing*, Radnor, Pa.: Chilton Book Co., 1975.

BARKER, *Charles Arthur*

(b. York, England 1878; d. ?)

Painter/Printmaker. Initially a candidate for the priesthood, Barker chose art instead and studied at the York School of Art and the Royal College of Art in London. The outbreak of World War I interrupted his education and he did not return to art school until 1920, when he resumed studies with Sir Frank Short. At the same time, he began his teaching career and soon became known for etchings (many of which were produced during a 1923 European tour) and for portraits, including several commissioned by members of the royal family. Barker arrived in the United States in 1926 for a sketching tour but shortly thereafter settled in Detroit. He rapidly acquired a reputation as an etcher and for a time taught at the Art School of the Detroit Society of Arts and Crafts. Frank W. Blair of the Union Trust Company commissioned him to produce a series of etchings depicting the construction of the Union Trust Building, and Barker also portrayed Detroit's old buildings in a series published by the Thiebauld Galleries. Known locally for his woodcarving as well, Barker was one of the co-founders of the Crafts Guild in Detroit.

One-person Exhibition: Detroit Civic Theater 1930.

Group Exhibitions: MAE 1928–30, 1932–33 (Dyar Prize 1928, Blair and Smith Prize 1929, Etching Purchase Prize 1932).

Collections: Detroit Historical Museum; Detroit Public Library, Burton Historical Collection; DIA.

Sources: MAR; *DAC News* 17, 1 (January 17, 1932): 10; *DN* 3-12-28; *DFP* 5-4-30.

BARKER, *Laurence*

(b. Houston, Texas 1930)

Papermaker/Printmaker. Barker received a B.A. from Principia College, Illinois (1954), and an M.F.A. from the Cranbrook Academy of Art (1955). He also studied at Atelier 17 in Paris (1956), and at the Long Island workshop of master papermaker Douglass Howell (1962). From 1960 to 1970 he served as head of the printmaking department at the Cranbrook Academy of Art, where he organized the first fine arts papermaking program in the United States (1963). Barker is recognized as the founder of the handmade paper renaissance, and his Cranbrook students included a number of artists who have played major roles in the revival of the medium: Walter Hamady (Shadwell Mill and Perishable Press), **Winifred Lutz** and John Kohler (HMP Papers), and **Aris Koutroulis** and Roland Poska (Fishy Whale Press). In 1970 Barker moved to Barcelona, Spain, where he continues to produce his own paperworks (incorporating unusual mulches such as rag, mohair, and silk with other media). His work is characterized by the use of handformed paper worked with pencil and ink, then embellished with pre-formed and printed papers that are sewn or glued to the work. Barker also produces custom papers and has collaborated with leading artists such as David Hockney, Roy Lichtenstein, Joan Miro, Robert Rauschenberg, and Mark Tobey.

One-person Exhibitions: University of Maine, Orono 1958; AAA Gallery, Detroit, 1961; Olivet College 1967; Galeria Es Portal, Barcelona 1973; Galeria Gari de Sentmenat, Palamas, Gerona, Spain 1973; Galeria Nova Grafica, Barcelona 1973; Gallery 22, Bloomfield Hills 1974; Galeria Skira, Madrid 1975; Upstairs Gallery, Southampton, N.Y. 1977.

Group Exhibitions: *National Exhibition of Prints*, Library of Congress 1957; Weyhe Gallery, New York City, 1956; *Annual*, Philadelphia Print Club 1957–58; MAE 1961, 1963–66 (Arwin Purchase Prize 1964–65); *National Print Exhibition*, Brooklyn Museum 1962; *Michigan Association of Printmakers Biennial* 1963/64, 1967/68; *Contemporary American Printmakers*, Little Gallery, Birmingham 1965; *Michigan Art '67*, BBAA 1967; *Michigan Graphics*, BBAA 1968; *Made in Michigan*, Franklin Siden Gallery, Royal Oak 1970; *National Invitational Print and Drawing Exhibition*, Albion College 1970; *Smithsonian Print Show*, Barcelona 1972; *Fifteen Pop American Artists*, Sala Gaspar, Barcelona 1973; *New Ways With Paper*, NCFA 1977/78*; *Handmade Paperworks of the Seventies*, Alice Simsar Gallery, Ann Arbor 1979 (traveling); *Paper: Metamorphoses*, Florence Duhl Gallery, New York City 1979.

Collections: AIC; Biblioteca Nacional, Madrid; Bibliothèque Nationale, Paris; Brooklyn Museum; Cincinnati Art Museum; Cleveland Art Museum; DIA; Library of Congress; Olivet College.

Sources: Jules Heller, *Papermaking*, New York: Watson-Guptill, 1978; *Am Artist* 41 (August 1977): 39–42; *Print News* 2, 3 (July–August 1980): 2–6; *DN* 4-12-64; *BEcc* 4-16-70; *DFP* 1-27-80.

Sources: *American Art Annual* 1933/34; *WWAA* 1936/37; Bénézit 1976; Burroughs 1936/37; Fielding 1974; Gibson 1975; Mich State Lib 1915; *Detroit Saturday Night* March 7, 1925; *DIA Bulletin* 17, 7 (April 1938): 60; *DMA Bulletin* 1, 15 (October 1907): 6–7; *DMA Bulletin* 13, 1 (October 1918): 2; *International Studio* 47, 184 (June 1912): 280–290; *DFP* 8-4-15, 3-24-18, 4-20-30, 12-4-33, 3-29-36, 8-16-37; *DN* 2-15-20, 2-22-25, 3-18-28, 4-10-38, 10-15-39; *Christian Science Monitor* 4-9-33.

B*ARLOW, Myron*

(b. Ionia, Michigan 1873; d. Etaples, France 1937)

Painter. Barlow received his earliest training from **Joseph Gies** at the Art School of the Detroit Museum of Art. He started his career as a newspaper artist and later studied at the Art Institute of Chicago and in Paris at the École des Beaux-Arts under Jean-Léon Gérôme. He spent most of his career in France but made frequent trips to Detroit, where he maintained a studio in the Fine Arts Building on Grand Circus Park. In 1925 he completed four murals for Temple Beth El (now Wayne State University's Bonstelle Theater) in Detroit. A genre painter, Barlow's favorite subjects were the peasant women who lived in the villages surrounding his studio in northern France. His interior scenes were often compared to those of Vermeer, an artist he much admired. A member of the Scarab Club, the Fine Arts Society of Detroit, and the Société Nationale des Beaux-Arts of France, he was awarded the medal of the Legion of Honor by the French government in 1932.

One-person Exhibitions: Detroit Photographic Company 1918; John Hanna Galleries, Detroit 1920, 1925, 1928; Bonstelle Playhouse, Detroit 1925; Fine Arts Building, Detroit 1936; DIA 1938*.

Group Exhibitions: Académie Colarossi, Paris 1894; *Society of Western Artists*, DMA 1898; *American Painting and Sculpture*, AIC 1901–04, 1906–12, 1917; *Louisiana Purchase Exposition*, St. Louis 1904 (Gold Medal); *Six American Artists Residing in France*, AIC and DIA 1907; *Corcoran Biennial* 1908, 1910; *PAFA Annual* 1908–10; *Carnegie International* 1912–13, 1922; MAE 1912–13, 1916, 1918, 1924–25; *Panama-Pacific Exposition*, San Francisco 1915 (Gold Medal); *American Artists Annual*, DIA 1916, 1918, 1922–25, 1928; *Michigan Art Through 50 Years*, UMMA 1955; *Michigan Art: Yesterday and Today*, FIA 1963.

Collections: City Collection, Etaples, France; Detroit Athletic Club; Detroit Club; Detroit Golf Club; DIA; PAFA; Palais des Beaux-Arts, Douai, France.

B*ARNES, Ernest Harrison*

(b. Portland, New York 1873; d. Detroit, Michigan 1955)

Painter. Barnes received a B.A. and an honorary M.A. (1923) from Hillsdale College and also attended the School of the Art Institute of Chicago and the Art Students League in New York. He later studied under Will Howe Foote and Henry Rankin Poore at the Old Lyme Art School, Connecticut, as well as with Charles H. Davies in Mystic, Connecticut. Barnes joined the faculty at the University of Michigan in 1915 and retired in 1943. He also taught at the Ann Arbor Art Association. He was best known for his impressionistic landscapes.

One-person Exhibitions: Hillsdale College 1908; Arlington Art Galleries, Brooklyn 1912 (two-person)*; Marshall Field & Company, Chicago 1912; Ann Arbor Art Association, Alumni Memorial Hall, U. of M. 1914, 1930 (two-person), 1938; John Hanna Galleries, Detroit 1923, 1929*; Milwaukee Art Institute, 1928; Colony Club, Detroit 1931.

Group Exhibitions: *American Painting and Sculpture*, AIC 1907, 1932; *Annual Exhibition of American Art*, Cincinnati Art Museum 1909–10; *American Watercolor Society Annual*, New York City 1910; *Selected Water Colors by American Artists*, DIA 1911; MAE 1913–24, 1926–28, 1930–38, 1943–46 (Scarab Club 2nd Prize 1916, Preston Prize 1922); *Society of Independent Artists*, Grand Central Palace, New York City 1917–18; *American Artists Annual*, DIA 1920–23, 1926, 1928; *Corcoran Biennial* 1921/22, 1923/24, 1926, 1932; Allied Artists of America, New York City 1935–36; *Michigan Art Through 50 Years*, UMMA 1955.

Collections: DIA; Hillsdale College; Kalamazoo College; MSU; UMMA; WMU.

Sources: *WWAA* 1956; Bénézit 1976; Fielding 1974; Gibson 1975; Kenny 1965; Mallett 1948; *Who's Who in Detroit* 1935/36; *DFP* 2-4-23, 2-3-29; *Hillsdale*

Daily News 6-11-23; *DN* 5-10-25; *Michigan Daily* (U. of M.) 4-23-38.

BARR, David

(b. Detroit, Michigan 1939)

Painter/Sculptor. Barr is one of a small group of artists active in the United States and Canada who call themselves "structurists." He began working with three-dimensional constructed reliefs while an undergraduate at Wayne State University and at about the same time began a correspondence with Charles Biederman, the leading American exponent of structurist theory. After receiving an M.F.A. (1965) from Wayne State University, Barr joined the faculty at Macomb County Community College. He has continued to contribute to the structurist movement by writing a series of articles for *The Structurist*, a periodical published by the University of Saskatchewan. In 1977 Barr received the Michigan Arts Award from the Michigan Foundation for the Arts. In the 1960s and 1970s the emphasis of his work was on traditional structurist wall reliefs in which vividly colored small rectangles of wood are placed in complex patterns on a monochromatic wooden background. Barr has also completed free-standing sculptural forms of painted steel, such as his commissions for Fairlane Town Center in Dearborn and Macomb County Community College.

One-person Exhibitions: Hanamura Gallery, Detroit 1965; Kazimir Gallery, Chicago 1968–69, 1971–72; Evanston Art Center, Ill. 1969; Donald Morris Gallery, Birmingham 1973, 1976, 1979; Richard Gray Gallery, Chicago 1975; Marianne Friedland Gallery, Toronto 1975, 1977; Kent State University 1978.

Group Exhibitions: MAE 1962–66 (Purchase Prize and Kahn Prize 1964); *Flint Invitational*, FIA 1966; *Made in Detroit*, Franklin Siden Gallery, West Bloomfield 1967; *Young Structurists*, Kazimir Gallery, Chicago 1967; *Misalliance*, DAM 1969; *Relief/Construction/Relief*, Museum of Contemporary Art, Chicago 1969*; *Michigan Artists Biennial*, Kresge Art Center Gallery, MSU 1971; *All Michigan II*, FIA 1973/74; *Detroit Art Today: Diverse Directions*, School of Art, U. of M. 1974; *Works In Progress II*, DIA 1976*; *Michigan Sculpture '77*, Macomb County Community College 1977*.

Collections: American Telephone & Telegraph, New York City; Butler Institute; DIA; Fairlane Town Center, Dearborn; Jewish Home for the Aged, Detroit; Macomb County Community College; Westin Hotel, Renaissance Center, Detroit; WSU.

Sources: *WWAA* 1976; MAR; Nawrocki 1980; Barr in *The Structurist* (University of Saskatchewan) 8 (1968): n.p.; Barr in *The Structurist* (University of Saskatchewan) 10 (1970): n.p.; Barr in *Michigan Art Journal* 1, 2 (April 1978): 25; *Art Scene* 1, 2 (November 1967): 22–24; *Art Scene* 1, 3 (December 1967): 17; *Artscanada* 32, 4 (Winter 1975/76): 33–36; *Chicago Midwest Art* 3, 5 (1967): 7; *DFP* 9-25-67, 2-29-76, 4-24-77, 4-23-81.

BARRETT, Bill

(b. Los Angeles, California 1934)

Sculptor. Educated at the University of Michigan (B.S. 1958, M.A. 1969, M.F.A. 1970), Barrett taught at Eastern Michigan University (1960–68). While on the faculty at Eastern, he won numerous prizes in competitions in Michigan. Barrett's early work was characterized by predominantly circular metal forms. His 1971 commission for the University of Michigan Dental School, composed of geometric forms executed in polished aluminum, shows the influence of David Smith. In 1968 Barrett left Michigan for New York City.

One-person Exhibitions: Hanamura Gallery, Detroit 1964; EMU 1965*; KIA 1965; Tadlow Gallery of Fine Arts, Whitehall 1965; Jason Gallery, New York City 1967; *10 Downtown*, New York City 1969; Lantern Gallery, Ann Arbor 1970/71.

Group Exhibitions: MAE 1959–63 (Kahn Prize 1960, Lewis Artist Supply Prize 1962); *West Michigan Annual*, GRAM 1960–62 (Sculpture Award 1960); *Area Show*, KIA 1962 (2nd Prize), 1965 (One-man Show Award); *Michigan Art: Yesterday and Today*, FIA 1963; *Ceramics and Sculpture Show*, Butler Institute 1963, 1966; *Ceramic National*, Everson Museum of Art, Syracuse 1964; *Mid-Michigan Annual*, Midland Art Association 1965 (2nd Prize); *1st Flint Invitational*, FIA 1966; *Michigan Sculpture '68*, Michigan Council for the Arts, First Federal Building, Detroit, 1968; *Contemporary American Sculpture*, Whitney 1970; *Sculpture Guild*, Lever House, New York City 1970–77; *Invitational*, Andre Emmerich Gallery, New York City 1972; *Sculpture in the Fields*, Storm King Art Center, New York 1973/75; *Artrain*, Michigan Artrain Inc. 1977 (traveling); *10 Downtown: Ten Years*, P.S.1, New York City 1977.

Collections: Aldrich Museum of Contemporary Art, Ridgefield, Conn.; Ann Arbor City Hall; Cleveland Museum of Art; EMU Library; Henry Ford Community College; Michigan Education Association, Lansing; Norfolk Museum of Art, Va.; Pennington Park, Patterson, N.J.; Scottsdale Center for the Arts, Ariz.;

Syracuse University; U. of M. Dental School; UMMA; University of the South, Library, Sewanee, Tenn.

Sources: *WWAA* 1978; *Art News* 68, 3 (May 1969): 14; *Art News* 72, 5 (May 1973): 83; *AAN* 10-20-65, 9-20-70, 10-10-71; *The Press* (Ypsilanti) 10-30-65.

BECKER, *David*

(b. Milwaukee, Wisconsin 1937)

Printmaker. Becker studied in Milwaukee at the Layton School of Art and the University of Wisconsin (B.S. 1961). He received an M.F.A. from the University of Illinois at Urbana in 1965 and since then has been a member of the faculty at Wayne State University. Becker has received over twenty-five purchase awards in national and international shows. His meticulously detailed figurative prints are reminiscent of the work of Hieronymus Bosch in their depiction of the strange and fantastic: figures, often nude or encased in mummy-like wrappings, float surrealistically over mysterious landscapes or engage in a variety of morbid activities. Becker is a member of the Society of American Graphic Artists and the Philadelphia Print Club.

One-person Exhibitions: Lawrence Stevens Gallery, Detroit 1968; U. of M., Dearborn 1968.

Group Exhibitions: *Chicago and Vicinity Exhibition*, AIC 1961; *Boston Printmakers Annual* 1965, 1972, 1975–76, 1978–79 (Purchase Awards 1972, 1978, 1979); *Ultimate Concerns*, Ohio State University 1965 (Purchase Award); DAM 1966, 1970; *Midyear Show*, Butler Institute 1967 (Purchase Award), 1968; MAE 1969, 1971; *National Print Show*, Silvermine Guild of Artists, New Canaan, Conn. 1970, 1972, 1974 (Purchase Award), 1976, 1980 (Purchase Award); *Society of American Graphic Artists Annual* 1973 (Purchase Award); *National Exhibition of Prints*, Library of Congress 1973 (Purchase Award), 1975 (Purchase Award); *30 Years of American Printmaking*, Brooklyn Museum 1976* (Purchase Award); *Michigan Association of Printmakers Biennial* 1976 (Purchase Award) 1980 (Purchase Award); *Eight Contemporary American Printmakers*, Albion College 1978; *Biennial International*, Philadelphia Print Club 1979; *Society of American Graphic Artists Annual*, Parsons Exhibition Center, New York City 1979 (Award); *Detroit National Print Symposium*, CAAM 1980.

Collections: AIC; Albion College; Brandeis University, Rose Art Museum; Brooklyn Museum; Butler Institute; DIA; Honolulu Academy of Arts; Hope College; Library of Congress; Madison Art Center, Wis.; New York Public Library; Silvermine Guild of Artists, New Canaan, Conn.; State University of New York, Potsdam and Fredonia; University of Arizona Museum of Art, Tucson; University of Manitoba, Winnipeg.

Sources: WWAA 1980; MAR; *Art News* 74, 7 (September 1975): 48, 49; *Washington Post* 6-7-75.

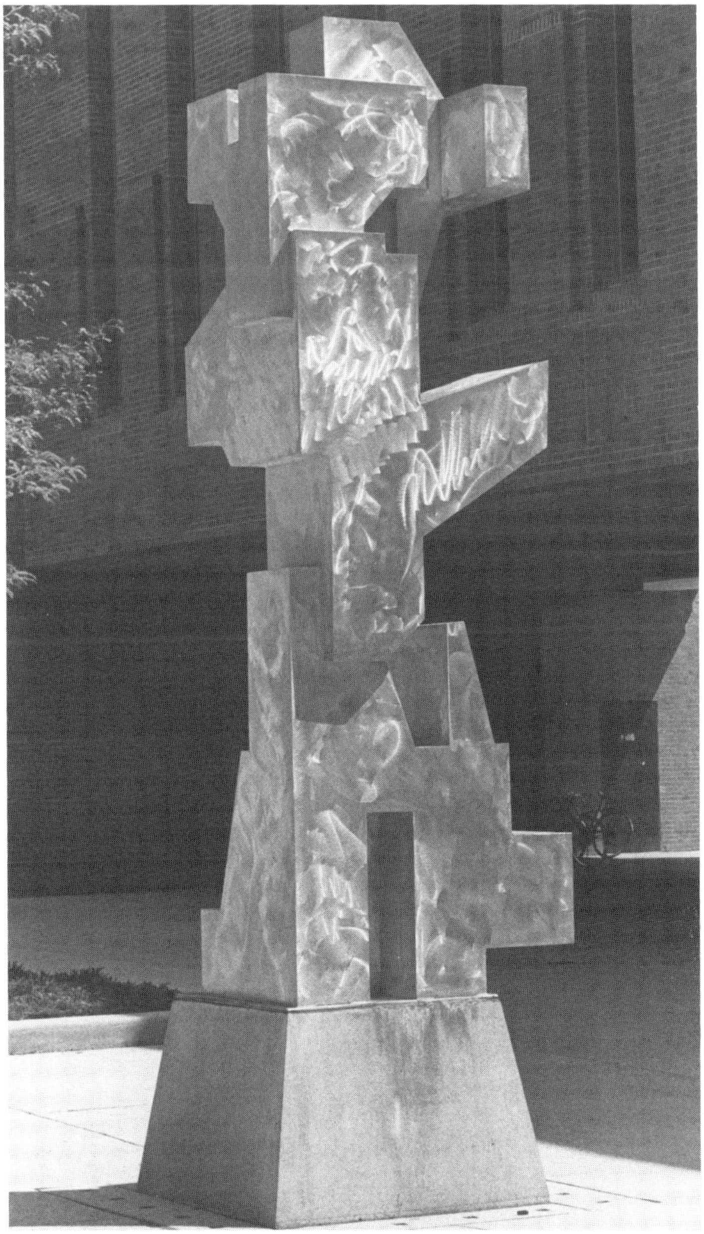

Bill Barrett (1934–). Untitled. *1971. Polished aluminum. h. 15 feet. Collection of the University of Michigan Dental School. Courtesy the University of Michigan, Information Services. Robert Kalmbach, Photographer.*

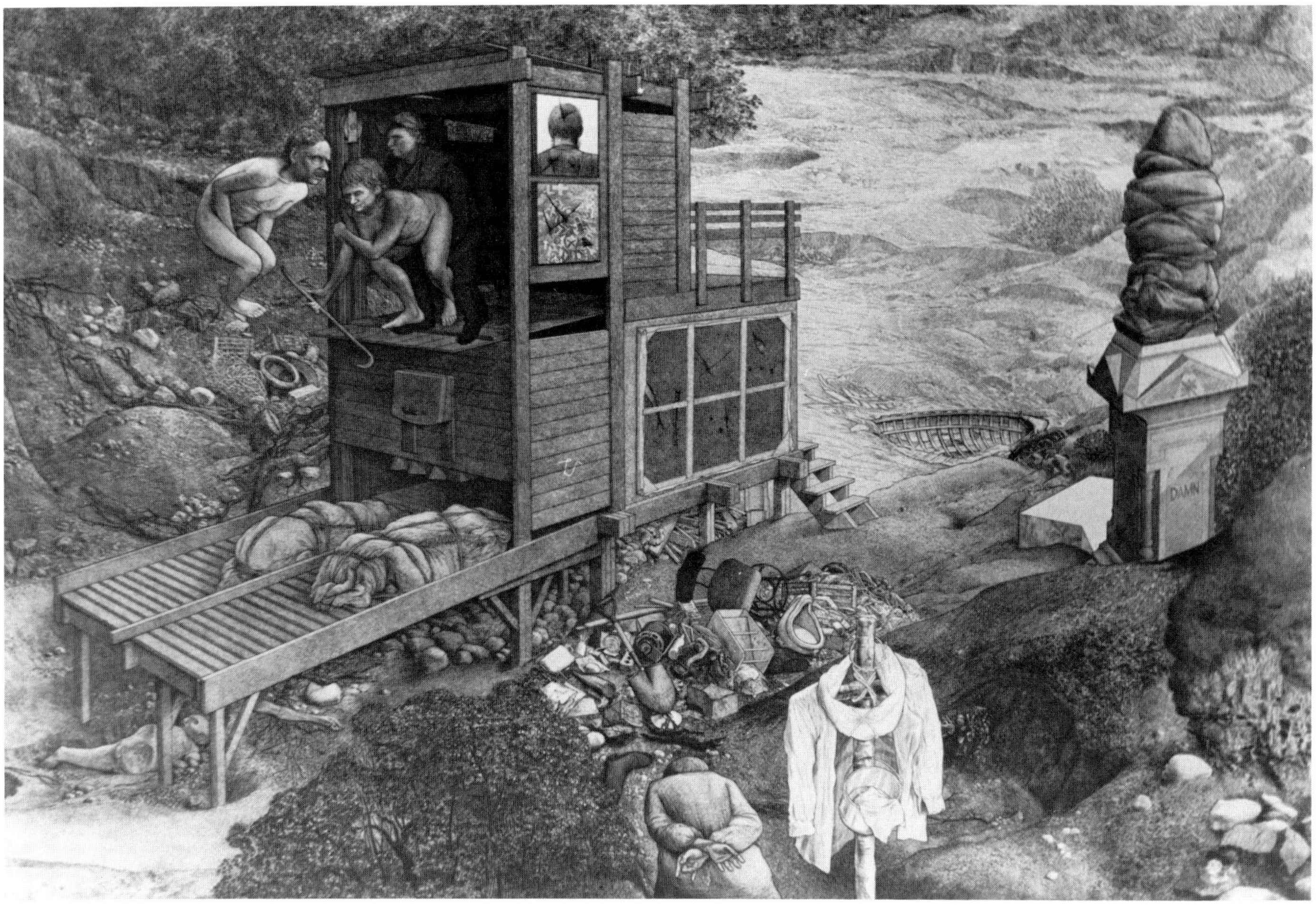

David Becker (1937–). Monuments. 1979. Etching and engraving 21 × 31 inches. Private Collection. Courtesy the artist.

BEERBOHM, *Marvin*

(b. Toronto, Ontario 1908; d. Livonia, Michigan 1981)

Painter. Beerbohm studied with both **John Carroll** and Sam Halpert at the Art School of the Detroit Society of Arts and Crafts (1928–32). During the Depression, under the auspices of the U. S. Treasury Department's Section of Fine Arts, he completed murals for post offices in Belding, Michigan, and Knoxville, Iowa. He also executed murals for Rochester High School and the Detroit Public Library (mural moved to the Smithsonian Institution in 1974) for the Works Progress Administration/Federal Art Project. His commissions in the 1950s included murals for the Harlan Electric Company and Harlan Elementary School in Birmingham as well as a series of stained-glass windows for Sinai Hospital in Detroit. Beerbohm taught at many Detroit institutions, among them the Detroit School of Art (1936–39), Meinzinger's Art School (1848–53), the Jewish Community Center, and the Palette and Brush Club.

One-person Exhibitions: *Commissions for Michigan Artists*, DIA 1952; American Institute of Architects Conference, Mackinac Island 1955; Detroit Historical Museum 1955.

Group Exhibitions: MAE 1931–33, 1935, 1937–40 (Whitcomb Prize 1939); *Corcoran Biennial* 1935, 1937; *American Artists Old and New*, DIA 1937; *PAFA Annual* 1939; *Recent Works by Detroit Artists*, DIA 1944; *West Michigan Annual*, GRAM 1948 (1st Prize); *Gold Medal Mural Exhibition*, Architectural League, New York City 1952; *Michigan Art Through 50 Years*, UMMA 1955; *Drawing U.S.A.*, Minnesota Museum of Art 1963.

Collections: DIA; Harlan Electric Company, Southfield; Harlan Elementary School, Birmingham; Jewish

War Veterans Memorial Home, Detroit; Sinai Hospital, Detroit.

Sources: *WWAA* 1956; AAA 133; MAR; *DN* 7-13-41, 2-15-52, 12-14-52, 8-23-53; *DFP* 11-28-48, 12-14-52.

BEGININ, *Igor*

(b. Rijeka, Yugoslavia 1931)

Painter. Educated at Wayne State University (B.A. 1963, M.A. 1966), Beginin also studied with Kosta Angeli-Radovani in Zagreb, Yugoslavia. He joined the faculty at Eastern Michigan University in 1968, and served as chairman of the Michigan Water Color Society from 1974–77. Beginin is primarily known for his semi-abstract watercolors, several of which have appeared as covers for *Detroit Magazine (Detroit Free Press).*

One-person Exhibitions: Mercy College 1966; Galerie de Boicourt, Birmingham 1967, 1970; Pyramid Gallery, Ann Arbor 1973; Gallery 22, Bloomfield Hills 1974; Creative Arts Gallery, CMU 1976.

Group Exhibitions: *MWCS Annual* 1962–72, 1974–77 (Jaeger Award 1971); *Doctor Collects*, DIA 1965; *Mid-Michigan Annual*, Midland Art Association 1966–67, 1969, 1971, 1975; *Midyear Show*, Butler Institute 1967–69; *National Watercolor Exhibition*, Jackson, Miss. 1968; *Watercolor USA*, Springfield Art Museum, Mo. 1968, 1973.

Collections: Detroit Free Press; Detroit General Hospital; Detroit Trade Center; General Motors Corporation, Detroit; Manufacturers National Bank, Detroit; Blue Cross and Blue Shield of Michigan, Detroit.

Sources: MAR; *BEcc* 12-7-67; *DFP* 10-26-69; *AAN* 2-18-73.

BENNETT, *Reginald*

(b. Devil's Lake, North Dakota 1893; d. Detroit, Michigan 1955)

Painter. Bennett attended the **John P. Wicker** School of Fine Arts in Detroit and later studied with Othon Friesz in Paris. He taught at the Art School of the Detroit Society of Arts and Crafts, the Detroit School of Art, and Wayne State University. During the Depression, Bennett completed a mural for the press room of the old City Hall under the auspices of the Works Progress Administration/Federal Art Project. In 1933 he was one of eight artists selected to execute a mural for the Michigan Building at the Chicago World's Fair, which is now installed in the State Capitol in Lansing. Bennett also painted murals for the residences of prominent Detroiters, including Edsel B. Ford and Ralph H. Booth, and was well known for his caricatures of fellow artists, particularly members of the Scarab Club, of which he was a long-time member.

One-person Exhibitions: Scarab Club, Detroit 1924; Bonstelle Theatre, Detroit 1925; Royal Oak Public Library 1928; Hudson Galleries, Detroit 1931.

Group Exhibitions: MAE 1920–24, 1926–29, 1931–35 (FSPP 1929); *Modern Art Exhibition*, Scarab Club, Detroit 1926; *American Artists Annual*, DIA 1926–29; *Painting and Sculpture from 16 American Cities*, MOMA 1933; New York World's Fair 1939.

Collections: Capitol, State of Michigan, Lansing; DIA; Fordson High School, Dearborn; Northwestern High School, Detroit.

Sources: *WWAA* 1940/41; AAA D318; Burroughs 1936/37; Kenny 1965; *Detroit Saturday Night* November 15, 1942; *DFP* 11-2-24, 5-25-33, 2-12-34; *DN* 11-9-24, 9-27-25, 7-29-28, 8-28-32.

BERG, *Wilfrid*

(b. Muskegon, Michigan 1908)

Painter. Berg received his first art instruction from Wilbur C. Kensler at Muskegon High School, then undertook additional study with Chicago artist, Anthony deYoung. During the Depression, he was commissioned to paint a mural in the Children's Room of the Hackley Public Library in Muskegon under the auspices of the federal government's Public Works of Art Project. Also in conjunction with the government project he constructed historical dioramas for the Muskegon County Museum. After World War II, Berg studied at the Ringling School of Art in Sarasota, Florida, under Hilton Leech, as well as with Jerry Farnsworth. A watercolorist who paints outdoors, Berg is known for his scenes of the Lake Michigan area and his colorful studies of circus life. He divides his time between studios in Muskegon and Florida.

One-person Exhibitions: HAM 1937, 1944, 1949 (two-person); Sarasota Art Association, Fla. 1951; Social Security Office, Muskegon 1974.

Group Exhibitions: *Regional Exhibition*, HAM 1930–present (most years) (Friends of Art Award 1973, 1976).

Collections: Ferris State College; HAM; Muskegon High School; Muskegon Public Library.

Sources: MAR; *Muskegon Chronicle* 2-13-74, 7-10-76.

BERLIN, Rosalind

(b. Saginaw, Michigan 1938)

Textile Artist. Berlin received both a B.A. (1960) and an M.A. (1968) from Michigan State University. She has also studied with such textile artists as Harriet Tidball, **Gerhardt Knodel**, and **Urban Jupena**. A member of the faculty at Delta College since 1968, she has also taught at the Saginaw Art Museum and for the Saginaw Public Schools. In 1975 she opened "The Loominary," a studio/gallery in Saginaw, where she creates wall hangings, upholstery fabric, and loom-shaped garments.

One-person Exhibition: SAM 1969.

Group Exhibitions: *Area Show*, SAM 1961–77 (1st Prize 1963, 1966); *Michigan Artist-Craftsmen Biennial*, GRAM 1965–69, 1973; *Michigan Craftsmen's Council Biennial* 1966–70; *Flint Annual*, FIA 1967 (1st Prize), 1971, 1973; *Mid-Michigan Annual*, Midland Art Association 1967, 1971, 1974; *Craft Invitational*, SAM 1971; *Women '71*, Northern Illinois University 1971; *Filaments '73*, EMU 1973; Upper Peninsula Crafts Conference 1976; *Fiber into Forms*, Calvin College 1977*.

Sources: Harriet Tidball, *Contemporary Costumes: Strictly Handwoven*, New York: Macmillan, 1968; *CH* 33, 2 (April 1973): 51; *Saginaw News* 8-31-75, 10-12-76; *Evening News* (Sault Ste. Marie) 4-19-76.

BERTOIA, Harry

(b. San Lorenzo, Italy 1915; d. Barto, Pennsylvania 1978)

Sculptor. Bertoia came to Michigan in 1930 from his native Italy and attended Cass Technical High School, studying under Mary Davis and Louise Green, then attended the Art School of the Detroit Society of Arts and Crafts, studying under **John Carroll** and **Sarkis Sarkisian**. After only a few months, he entered the Cranbrook Academy of Art and studied painting and drawing with **Zoltan Sepeshy** and **Wallace Mitchell** (1937–39). In 1939 Bertoia was asked by Cranbrook's director, Eliel Saarinen, to reorganize and head the metalworking department. While at Cranbrook, in addition to his work in painting, drawing, and jewelry design, he executed many woodblock prints and a series of innovative monoprints, which were first exhibited in a group show at the Solomon R. Guggenheim Foundation, New York City, in 1943. In the same year, Bertoia moved to California to work with Charles Eames on the latter's new furniture designs. In 1950 he was hired by Knoll Associates, Inc., and developed a series of visually light chairs that were constructed of welded steel rods, which today are considered classics in postwar American design. By 1953 he was devoting all his time to sculpture, developing a unique style which incorporated industrial metalwork techniques such as the flow welding of alloys over metal constructions that leaves a molten metal surface.

His first commission, from architect Eero Saarinen, for a large metallic screen for the General Motors Technical Center in Warren (1953), was followed by numerous commissions for architectural sculpture throughout the world. Bertoia collaborated with such architects as Gordon Bunshaft, William Kessler, I. M. Pei, Kenneth Roche, and Minoru Yamasaki. In addition to large metallic screens and wall reliefs, Bertoia's earlier work included small, textured, bush-like forms and hanging wire spheres. In his later work, he concentrated on kinetic "sound sculptures," consisting of metal rods of varying alloys that produce sound when set in motion. Bertoia won many honors throughout his career, including the Institute Award (1975) from the American Academy of Arts and Letters; the Fine Arts Medal (1955); the Craftsmanship Medal (1956); and the Gold Medal (1973) awarded by the American Institute of Architects.

One-person Exhibitions: Karl Nierendorf Gallery, New York City 1940, 1943, 1947; Knoll Associates, New York City 1951; Fairweather-Hardin Gallery, Chicago 1956, 1961, 1968, 1975; Walker Art Center, Minneapolis 1958; Staempfli Gallery, New York City 1961, 1963, 1968, 1970, 1972, 1976, 1978*; Galleri KB, Oslo 1972, 1976, 1977; Wadsworth Atheneum, Hartford, Conn. 1974; AIC 1975; *Retrospective*, Allentown Art Museum, Pa. 1975*; CAAM, Bloomfield Hills 1980; Benjamin Manzel Gallery, Bala Cynwd, Pa. 1980.

Group Exhibitions: *Corcoran Biennial* 1938; DAM 1939; MAE 1941; *Advance Trends in Contemporary American Art*, DIA 1944; *Graphics*, San Francisco Museum of Modern Art 1945; *Little Show of Works in Progress*, DIA 1946; *American Painting and Sculpture*, AIC 1957, 1961; *Sculpture 1950–1958*, Allen Memorial Art Museum, Oberlin College 1958; U.S. Pavillion, Brussels World's Fair 1958; *Carnegie International* 1958, 1962, 1964; *Contemporary American Sculpture, Painting, Watercolor and Drawing*, Whitney 1958/59; *Recent Sculpture USA*, MOMA 1959, *Contemporary American Sculpture and Drawing*, Whitney 1960, 1962, 1964, 1966; *Contemporary American Painting and Sculpture*, Krannert Art Museum, University of Illinois 1961, 1963; *London Triennial of Sculpture in the Open Air*, Battersea Park

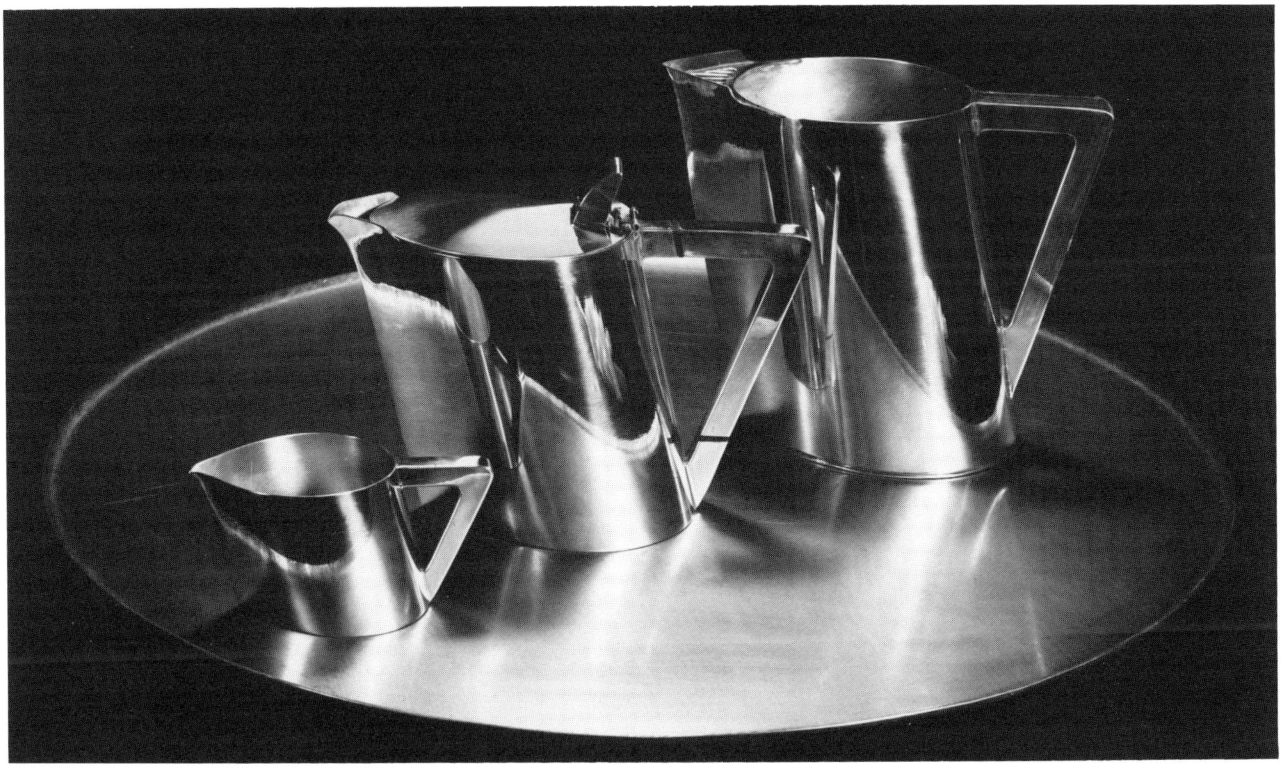

Harry Bertoia (1915–1978). Tray and Pitchers. *Collection of the Cranbrook Academy of Art Museum. Courtesy the Cranbrook Academy of Art Museum.*

1963; *Michigan Art: Yesterday and Today*, FIA 1963; *PAFA Annual* 1964, 1966; *American Sculpture 1900–1965*, FIA 1965; *Modern Consciousness*, NCFA 1975; *Knoll/Herman Miller*, Cranbrook 1975/76; *Arts and Crafts in Detroit 1906–1976*, DIA 1976.

Collections: Albright-Knox Art Gallery, Buffalo; Chase Manhattan Bank of North America; Cranbrook; Denver Art Museum; DIA; Dulles International Airport, Washington, D.C.; FIA; General Motors Tech Center, Warren; Genesee Valley Shopping Center, Flint; KIA; Milwaukee Art Center; MOMA; Northwestern National Life Insurance Building, Minneapolis; Philadelphia Civic Center; San Francisco Museum of Art; Standard Oil Plaza, Chicago; American Consulate, Dusseldorf, Germany; America House, Bremen, Germany; UMMA.

Sources: *WWAA* 1978; AAA Interview; Bénézit 1976; Cummings 1977; *Contemporary Artists*, New York: St. Martin's Press, 1983; *Dictionary of 20th-Century Art*, London and New York: Phaidon, 1973; Jeffrey Eger, *Sonambient: The Sounding Sculpture of Harry Bertoia* (film), Kenesaw Films 1972; Philippe Garner, *20th-Century Furniture*, New York: Van Nostrand Reinhold Co., 1980; Morris E. Guirl, *How Long the Night* (illus. by Bertoia), Grosse Pointe, Mich.: Golden Basket Workshop, 1943; June Kompass Nelson, *Harry Bertoia, Sculptor*, Detroit: WSU Press, 1970; Clifford B. West, *Harry Bertoia's Sculpture* (film) 1965; Bertoia in *Print* 9, 6 (July 1955): 16–17; *Art Dig* 21 (April 15, 1947): 22; *Art News* 44 (October 1, 1945): 28; *Arts and Architecture* 61 (April 1944): 22–24; *Arts and Architecture* 62 (May 1945): 22–23; *Arts and Architecture* 70 (January 1953): 12ff; *Arts and Architecture* 72 (January 1955): 18–19; *Arts Mag* February 1980; *Cranbrook Quarterly* 4, 3 (February 1970): 12; *Interiors* 112 (October 1952): 118ff; *Progressive Architecture* 36 (February 1955): 104ff; *Time* March 31, 1961; *Christian Science Monitor* (Boston) 7-24-43; *NYT* 3-19-61, 11-8-78; *DN* 12-2-62, 6-14-65, 6-26-66.

B*ICK, Georgie Elayne*

(b. Souk-Aras, Tebessa, Algeria)

Textile Artist. Bick learned tapestry weaving in the textile ateliers of the Sisters of Nôtre Dame in her native Algeria. She came to the United States in 1946 and since then has actively worked to promote tapestry as an art form through lectures, workshops, and classes for such organizations as the National Convention of Handweavers, the Michigan League of Handweavers, and numerous guilds throughout the Midwest and Canada. She has acted as a consultant to the Metropolitan Museum of Art in New York and has restored tapestries for various other museum collections. In 1976 she was one of three visual artists to receive the first Michigan Arts Awards, sponsored by the Michigan Foundation for the Arts, in recognition of her contributions to the field. Bick's tapestries are executed in the Gobelin technique in combinations of wool, silk, linen, and gold thread. Her abstract designs are characterized by rich, muted colors, primarily in shades of red, ochre, black, and gray.

One-person Exhibitions: Forsythe Gallery, Ann Arbor 1971, 1973, 1975 (two-person), 1977; Siena Heights College 1975.

Group Exhibitions: *Michigan League of Handweavers Exhibition*, Flint 1968 (1st Prize); MACE 1969; *May Show*, Toledo Museum of Art 1969 (1st Prize); *Ann Arbor Art Association Annual* 1972; *Filaments '73*, EMU 1973; *Annual Exhibition*, Toledo Museum of Art 1975 (Purchase Prize); *Crafts Exhibition*, Bowling Green State University 1975; Société des Beaux-Arts, Paris 1975; *Our Heritage in Weaving*, GRAM 1976; *Women in the Arts Invitational*, NMU 1978.

Collections: Lurcat Museum, Angers, France; Toledo Federation of Art Societies; Toledo Museum of Art; University of Washington, Harriet Tidball Collection.

Sources: MAR; *AAN* 2-20-72, 11-4-73, 10-12-75; *DN* 4-20-76; *BEcc* 4-22-76.

BIGLER, Mary Jane

(b. Columbus City, Indiana 1909)

Painter. Bigler received a B.A. (1941) from Indiana University, then attended Wayne State University (M.A. 1942), where she studied with watercolorist **Helen May**. A member of Wayne State's faculty since 1943, Bigler has been instrumental in promoting watercolor as a significant medium. A founding member of the Michigan Water Color Society she has served on the Society's board of directors for twenty years and as chairwoman for seven. She has also taught watercolor at the Birmingham-Bloomfield Art Association and at the Art School of the Detroit Society of Arts and Crafts. Bigler has spent much time working and studying in Italy, and was instrumental in organizing the Art Studies Abroad program at Wayne State. In 1976 she was one of ten artists honored by the City of Detroit for the nation's Bicentennial, and in 1977 the Michigan State Senate passed a formal resolution recognizing her many contributions to the visual arts. Bigler is well known for her flower paintings and for her use of collage in combination with the watercolor medium.

One-person Exhibitions: DAM 1945 (three-person), 1953; J. Walter Thompson Agency, Detroit 1955; GRAM 1957; Boulevard Photographic, Detroit 1968; Nuovo Carpine Galleria, Rome 1968; Lantern Gallery, Ann Arbor 1970; Little Gallery, Birmingham 1970, 1972, 1977.

Group Exhibitions: National Congress for Women, Washington, D.C. 1938; MAE 1944–45, 1948–61, 1966 (Newberry Prize 1950; MWCS Prize 1960); *MWCS Annual* 1947–present (Merit Award 1947–49, 1953–54, 1956, 1961, 1967, 1971–72); *American Watercolor Society Annual* 1948–55; *International Watercolor Exhibition*, AIC 1949; *Midyear Show*, Butler Institute 1951, 1953, 1957–59, 1962–63, 1966; *American Watercolors, Drawings, and Prints*, MMA 1952; *15 Detroit Artists*, ACA Gallery, New York City 1953; *Michigan Art Through 50 Years*, UMMA 1955; *Midwest Painters Invitational*, GRAM 1960; *Contemporary American Watercolors*, GRAM 1963; *Source Detroit III*, Cranbrook 1972; *Michigan Collects Michigan Art*, Pontiac Creative Arts Center 1976.

Collections: Detroit Board of Education; Detroit General Hospital; DIA; Everson Museum of Art, Syracuse; Ford Motor Company, Dearborn; Manufacturers National Bank, Renaissance Center, Detroit; Michigan Consolidated Gas Company, Detroit; National Bank of Detroit; WSU; Wichita Museum of Fine Arts, Kans.

Sources: *WWAA* 1962; MAR; *Detroit Artists Monthly* 3, 2 (February 1978): 16–18; *DN* 5-28-44, 5-2-48, 12-31-51, 11-10-55, 4-12-59, 9-11-77; *DFP* 7-31-49, 9-6-63, 6-25-72, 9-18-77; *BEcc* 5-19-74, 10-21-76, 9-15-77.

BLACK, James R.

(b. Fenton, Michigan 1935)

Ceramicist. Black attended Flint Junior College (now C. S. Mott Community College) where he studied with **Richard DeVore**, then received both a B.A. (1962) and an M.F.A. (1964) from the University of Michigan. He taught for the University of Michigan's Extension Service in Flint (1962–64) and at the University High School in Ann Arbor (1964–65). He has also been an instructor at the Ann Arbor Potters Guild and at the Left Bank Gallery in Flint. In 1966 he joined the faculty at Schoolcraft College in Livonia. Black is known for large, slab-built vase forms and nonfunctional constructions as well as whimsical "people pots."

One-person Exhibitions: EMU 1964; Left Bank Gallery, Flint 1964; FIA 1965; Hanamura Gallery, Detroit 1965; Lantern Gallery, Ann Arbor 1966; SAM 1967; Alma College 1968; Ferris State College 1969.

Group Exhibitions: *Flint Annual*, FIA 1963–64, 1966–67 (Purchase Prize 1964, 1966), *Area Show*, KIA 1964, 1966; *Decorative Arts and Ceramics Exhibition*, Wichita Art Association, Kans. 1964, 1966 (Purchase Award); *Michigan Artist-Craftsmen*, GRAM 1964, 1966 (Second Prize); *Craftsmen U.S.A. 1966*, Mus Contemp Crafts 1966 (Merit Award); *Ceramic National*, Everson Museum of Art, Syracuse 1966, 1968; *16 Michigan Ceramicists*, Cranbrook 1967; *Ceramics Invitational*, EMU 1968, 1969, *Ceramics Invitational*, School of Art, U. of M. 1970.

Collections: FIA; Midland Center for the Arts; Wichita Art Association, Kans.

Sources: MAR; *CH* 24 (May 1964): 10–11; *FJ* 11-14-65, 12-12-65, 3-27-66; *DN* 10-2-66; *BEcc* 11-3-66, 7-24-69; *DFP* 9-8-67.

B*LOCH, Lucienne*

(b. Geneva, Switzerland 1909)

Painter. Bloch received her earliest art training at the Cleveland School (now Institute) of Art. She also attended the École des Beaux-Arts (1925–29) and studied with Antoine Bourdelle and André Lhote in Paris. For several years, she designed glass sculptures for the Leerdam Glass Works in Holland before her return to the United States in 1932. She first visited Detroit as an assistant to the Mexican painter Diego Rivera while he was working on the *Detroit Industry* murals for the Detroit Institute of Arts. She and her husband, Stephen Pope Dimitroff, also assisted Rivera with the Rockefeller Center murals in New York City. Between 1934 and 1937, under the auspices of the Works Progress Administration/Federal Art Project, she and Dimitroff completed murals for various public buildings, including the House of Detention for Women in New York City. In 1940 they moved to Flint, where Bloch taught ceramics and sculpture at the Flint Institute of Arts and for the Mott Foundation, wrote an art column for the *Flint Weekly Review*, and did illustrations for seven children's books. In 1946 and 1947 Bloch painted murals for the YMCA Gymnasium, the Flint Children's Home, and the children's ward of St. Joseph's Hospital. She and her husband moved to California in 1948, where they have continued to work as muralists and teachers. In 1953 Bloch returned to Michigan to complete a mural for Temple Emanuel in Grand Rapids.

One-person Exhibitions: Delphic Studios, New York City 1933; FIA 1948 (two-person); Ford Gallery, Mill Valley, Calif. 1961.

Group Exhibitions: *New Horizons in American Art*, MOMA 1936; *Exposition des Arts Decoratif*, Paris 1937 (Gold Medal); MAE 1941, 1943, 1945–46; *Flint Annual*, FIA 1941–47 (1st Prize 1945); *Graphic Arts Exhibition*, Wichita Art Association, Kans. 1948; *Seven American Women: The Depression Decade*, Vassar College 1976*.

Collections/Commissions: FIA; Fort Thomas Post Office, Ky.; International Business Machines Corporation, San Jose, Calif.; Marin General Hospital, Calif.; San Francisco National Bank.

Sources: MAR; Bloch, "Murals for Use," in *Art for the Millions*, ed. F. V. O'Connor, Greenwich, Conn.: New York Graphic Society, 1973; *American Magazine of Art* 28 (August 1938): 42; *Time* November 21, 1935; *FJ* 7-28-39, 1-21-41, 11-17-46, 1-18-48, 11-18-53, 7-5-64; *DT* 10-1-44; *GR Herald* 10-27-53, 11-7-53.

B*OHNERT, Thom R.*

(b. St. Louis, Missouri 1948)

Ceramicist. After receiving a B.A. (1969) in ceramics from Southern Illinois University, Bohnert came to Michigan to attend the Cranbrook Academy of Art (M.F.A. 1971), where he studied with **Richard DeVore**. He became an instructor at Mott Community College, Flint, in 1971 and has given lectures, demonstrations, and workshops at the Flint Institute of Arts, the University of Michigan, and the Cranbrook Academy of Art. Bohnert is known for his hand-built ceramic constructions.

One-person Exhibitions: FIA 1976 (two-person); Yaw Gallery, Birmingham 1976.

Group Exhibitions: *Project '70*, DAM; *Cranbrook Alumni Invitational*, DAM 1971; MACE 1971, 1976* (one of six prizewinners); *Ceramics Invitational*, EMU 1971, 1974, 1977; *All Michigan I*, FIA 1971/72; *7th Michiana Regional*, South Bend Art Center, Ind., 1972; *Flint Annual*, FIA 1972–73; *Invitational*, KIA 1973; *Beaux-Arts Designer/Craftsmen*, Columbus Museum of Art 1973, 1975, 1977; *Invitational*, Pewabic Pottery, Detroit 1974; Yaw Gallery, Birmingham 1974; *Clay: Cranbrook Alumni Invitational*, Yaw Gallery 1976; *New Views by Young Ceramists*, Exhibit A, Gallery of American Ceramics, Evanston, Ill. 1976; *Crafts National*, Marietta College, Ohio 1977.

Sources: MAR; *CH* 31, 1 (February 1971): 51; *CH* 32, 2 (April 1972): 48; *CH* 36, 4 (April 1976): 19; *CH* 37, 1 (February 1977): 58; *CH* 37, 4 (June 1977): 43; *CMo* 24, 4 (April 1976): 57; *CMo* 24, 6 (June 1976): 54; *FJ* 12-7-75, 2-29-76; *BEcc* 4-8-76; *DN* 11-7-76.

BOORSMA, Jay

(b. Grand Rapids, Michigan 1893; d. Grand Rapids, Michigan 1955)

Painter. Boorsma studied at the **John P. Wicker** School of Fine Arts in Detroit and the Fontainebleau School of Art in France. He joined the faculty of the Art School of the Detroit Society of Arts and Crafts as an instructor of industrial design in 1929. Appointed director of the school in 1936, he incorporated into its programs his belief that commercial artists and industrial designers should be well-grounded in the fine arts as a supplement to their practical training. During the Depression, Boorsma and **Sarkis Sarkisian** kept the school functioning, literally as a two-man operation, by performing all the necessary functions from teaching to janitorial service. Boorsma was one of the leaders of the Detroit Society of Independents, a group of artists who withdrew from the "Exhibition for Michigan Artists" in 1929 in protest of the jury system, and proceeded to stage their own shows from 1929 to 1933. Boorsma was a modernist whose style was quite controversial in the 1930s. His watercolor landscapes are highly stylized abstractions, characterized by a Japanese-inspired calligraphic line and a palette limited to blues and blacks. When his painting *Waterfalls* won the Founders Society Purchase Prize at the MAE in 1927, it caused a furor. Boorsma retired as director of the Art School of the Detroit Society of Arts and Crafts in 1947 and returned to his native Grand Rapids.

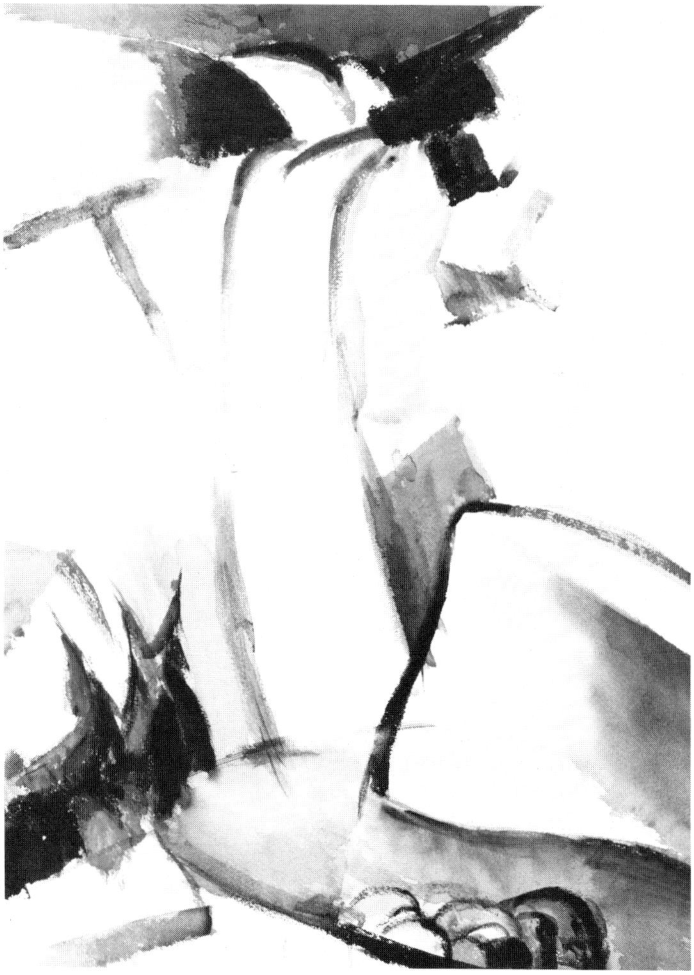

Jay Boorsma (1893–1955). Waterfalls *(Baring Creek Falls, Glacier Park, Montana). 1926. Watercolor. 26½ × 20 inches. Collection of the Detroit Institute of Arts, Gift of the artist.*

One-person Exhibitions: DAM 1936; Modern Art Gallery, DSAC 1938.

Group Exhibitions: *Modern Art Exhibition*, Scarab Club, Detroit 1926; MAE 1925–28, 1931–33, 1935–40, 1944 (FSPP 1927, Scarab Club Gold Medal 1935, Skelton Prize 1937, Haass Prize 1940); *American Artists Annual*, DIA 1928; *National Exhibition of American Art*, Rockefeller Center 1936, 1937; *Great Lakes Exhibition*, Albright Art Gallery, Buffalo 1938; *International Watercolor Exhibition*, DIA 1938; *Contemporary Detroit Painters*, Alger House, DIA 1940; *Michigan Art Through 50 Years*, UMMA 1955; *Arts and Crafts in Detroit 1906–1976*, DIA 1976*.

Collections: DIA.

Sources: AAA D318; *DT* 1-23-27; *DFP* 1-28-27, 2-6-27, 4-2-31, 5-3-36, 4-5-55; *DN* 3-31-29, 10-18-36.

BOSTICK, William

(b. Marengo, Illinois 1913)

Painter/Printmaker/Graphic Designer. Educated at the Carnegie Institute of Technology (B.S. 1934) and Wayne State University (M.A. 1954), Bostick studied with **Zoltan Sepeshy** and **Maija Grotell** at the Cranbrook Academy of Art and with **Carlos Lopez** at the Detroit Art Academy. From 1946 to 1976, he served as administrator and secretary of the Detroit Institute of Arts. Bostick has illustrated several books, including the award-winning *Mysteries of Blair House* (Detroit: Conjure House, 1948), and has designed books and catalogues for the Detroit Institute of Arts, Wayne State

University Press, and the Cranbrook Institute of Science. One of the founders of the Michigan Water Color Society, Bostick is known for his watercolor and lithographic depictions of Detroit's historic buildings. He has taught calligraphy at the Art School of the Detroit Society of Arts and Crafts and at the Grosse Pointe War Memorial. In 1971 he completed thirty-two calligraphic panels for the Resurrection Mausoleum in Justice, Illinois. Bostick is a member and past president of both the Scarab Club and the Midwest Museums Conference. In 1976 he was awarded Wayne State University's Distinguished Alumni Award in recognition of his many contributions to the visual arts in Michigan.

One-person Exhibitions: DAM 1943; Norfolk Museum of Art, Va. 1943; Scarab Club, Detroit 1946; *Commissions for Michigan Artists*, DIA 1960; Grinnell Galleries, Detroit 1963; Arwin Gallery, Detroit 1967, 1975.

Group Exhibitions: MAE 1938–62, 1963 (Purchase Prize); *MWCS Annual* 1948–71 (Jaeger Award 1961); *Michigan Art Through 50 Years*, UMMA 1955; *Scarab Club Gold Medal Exhibition* 1960–64, 1968 (Gold Medal 1962, 1968); *Midyear Show*, Butler Institute 1962; *Prominent Painters and Sculptors in Michigan*, BBAA 1962; *Watercolor Panorama*, FIA 1962; *Arts and Crafts in Detroit 1906–1976*, DIA 1976*.

Collections: CAAM; Detroit Historical Museum; Detroit Public Library; DIA; First Federal Savings & Loan, Detroit; Michigan Consolidated Gas Company, Detroit.

Sources: *WWAA* 1976; AAA, Interview; MAR; *DN* 4-28-41, 3-25-62, 6-2-63; *DFP* 11-21-43, 5-8-60, 5-14-67, 9-2-75, 12-21-75, 1-18-76.

BRAINERD, Owen

(b. Kingston, New York 1924)

Painter/Printmaker. Brainerd received a B.F.A. (1946) and an M.F.A. (1948) from Syracuse University, with additional study at Columbia University under Dong Kingman and at the State University of New York. He taught at Drake University for five years before joining the faculty at Michigan State University in 1957. He has served as an advisor to the Lansing Metropolitan Arts Council and the Michigan Council for the Arts and is past president of the Central Area Chapter of the Artists' Equity Association. Adept in several media, Brainerd has concentrated on serigraphy and painting. In 1959, for the Michigan Board of Education, he completed a freestanding mosaic wall mural, which now hangs in Everett High School in Lansing.

One-person Exhibitions: Des Moines Art Center, Iowa 1955; Dow Art Workshop Gallery, Midland 1959; Northwestern Michigan College, Traverse City 1962; Lantern Gallery, Ann Arbor 1966; Creative Arts Gallery, CMU 1974.

Group Exhibitions: *Art: USA: 58*, Madison Square Garden 1958; *National Print Exhibition*, Library of Congress 1958; *Print Exhibition*, Silvermine Guild of Artists, New Canaan, Conn. 1960; *West Michigan Annual*, GRAM 1960–61, 1965; MAE 1961; Hanamura Gallery, Detroit 1963; *Michigan Art: Yesterday and Today*, FIA 1963; *Michigan Art on Paper*, KIA 1967; *Michigan Art '67*, BBAA 1967.

Collections: Everett High School, Lansing; Iowa Art Education Association; University of Ryukyu, Okinawa.

Sources: *WWAA* 1976; MAR.

BREED, Charles Ayars

(b. Paw Paw, Michigan 1927)

Sculptor. Breed received a B.S. from Western Michigan University and an M.S. from the University of Wisconsin. Originally a metalsmith, Breed was a teacher in the Midland Public Schools when a lecture by a visiting professor from the Massachusetts Institute of Technology on the under-utilization of modern materials by contemporary artists encouraged him to switch to plastics as a medium. In 1961 he received a Dow Foundation grant which enabled him to study plastics technology and electroluminescence. One of the first artists in the country to sculpt with polyester resins, Breed's free-standing sculptures and wall reliefs are characterized by flowing organic forms that are wired with tiny electric lights. Breed served as the Midland Art Council's first artist-in-residence (1961) at the Post Street Workshop, a facility donated by the Dow Foundation to provide studio space and equipment to area artists. He has also served as director of the art program at the National Music Camp at Interlochen (1958–62), and in 1962 joined the faculty at Delta College. Breed also has been active in the development of the Midland Art Council and the Midland Center for the Arts, and is a member of the Michigan Council for the Arts' environmental advisory committee.

One-person Exhibitions: American Craftsmen's Council, Midwest Conference, Kalamazoo 1967; SAM 1968 (three-person); Tadlow Gallery, Whitehall 1970; Midland Center for the Arts 1972.

Group Exhibitions: *Fiber/Clay/Metal*, Minnesota Museum of Art 1955; *Mid-Michigan Annual*, Midland Art

Association 1958, 1963, 1964, 1969, 1971–76 (Grand Prize 1971, 1st Prize 1975); MACE 1962; *Craftsmen U.S.A. 1966*, Mus Contemp Crafts 1966 (Merit Award); *Made of Plastic*, FIA 1968; *Plastic as Plastic*, Mus Contemp Crafts 1968; *Traveling Exhibition*, Smithsonian Institution 1969; *Exhibition 70*, Columbus Gallery of Fine Arts 1970 (Award); *International Small Sculpture Exhibition*, Budapest 1971; *All Michigan I*, FIA 1971/72; *Crafts National*, Marietta College, Ohio 1974.

Collections/Commissions: Dow Chemical Company, Midland; Episcopal Church, Saginaw; Hellenic Orthodox Church of St. George, Bloomfield Hills; Indian River Catholic Church; Midland Center for the Arts; National Education Association, Washington, D.C.; Temple Beth El, Midland.

Sources: *WWAA* 1976; MAR; Irwin Whitaker, *Crafts and Craftsmen*, Dubuque: Wm. C. Brown Company, 1967; Breed in *House Beautiful* February 1962; *DN* 10-25-66; *Midland Daily News* 10-4-71, 9-25-72, 5-17-75; *Bay City Times* 12-19-71.

BRONER, *Robert*

(b. Detroit, Michigan 1922)

Printmaker/Painter. Broner received early training at Cass Technical High School, Wayne State University (M.A. 1946), and the Art School of the Detroit Society of Arts and Crafts. He also studied (1949–52) with Stuart Davis at the New School for Social Research and with Stanley W. Hayter at Atelier 17 in New York. Broner returned to Detroit in 1956 and joined the faculty at the Art School of the DSAC, where he set up one of the first studios for fine art etching in Detroit. He joined the faculty of Wayne State's Monteith College in 1965, and has also taught at the Haystack Mountain School of Crafts in Maine and the University of Haifa in Israel. One of the founders of the Michigan Association of Printmakers, he was instrumental in organizing its biennial statewide exhibition. In addition to his other activities, Broner has written art criticism for the *Detroit Times* and the *Birmingham Eccentric* as well as serving as Michigan correspondent for *Art in America* and *Craft Horizons*. Broner has developed many new techniques in the medium; particularly notable are his imaginative experiments with "found objects." One of the first artists to incorporate printed electronic circuit boards in his prints, he has also used discarded newspaper plates, bits of fabric, wood shingles, kitchen graters, and picture postcards for his intaglio prints. In 1967 one of his etchings, *Paths of Power*, was published in a limited edition by the Detroit Institute of Arts.

One-person Exhibitions: Anna Werbe Gallery, Detroit 1953; Wellons Gallery, New York City 1955; Garelick's Gallery, Detroit 1957, 1960; MSU 1958; Raven Gallery, Detroit 1963; J. L. Hudson Gallery, Detroit 1971*; Rina Gallery, New York 1972; Klein-Vogel Gallery, Detroit 1973; Delsen-Richter Gallery, Tel Aviv 1975; Troy Art Gallery 1976, 1977.

Group Exhibitions: MAE 1941–47, 1953–66; *National Print Exhibition*, Brooklyn Museum 1951, 1953, 1958, 1960, 1964, 1966 (Purchase Prize); *American Watercolors, Drawings, and Prints*, MMA 1952; *Young Printmakers*, MOMA 1953; *New Talent*, Martha Jackson Gallery, New York City 1957; *American Prints Today*, Print Council of America, New York City 1959; *U.S.I.A. Touring Show* 1959, 1964, 1968; *Fourteen Painter-Printmakers*, Weyhe Gallery, New York City 1960*; *Michigan Association of Printmakers Biennial* 1960–76; *Printmaking with Monotype*, Philadelphia Art Alliance 1961; *Made in Detroit*, Franklin Siden Gallery, Detroit 1967; *Two Decades of American Prints*, Brooklyn Museum 1968; *Eight Michigan Artists*, Kresge Art Center Gallery, MSU 1969; *Salon de Mai*, Musée d'Art Moderne, Paris 1969; *Society of American Graphic Artists Annual*, New York 1969 (Purchase Prize); *Pop Graphics*, MOMA 1970; *Monotypes*, Pratt Graphics Center, New York City 1972; *L'Estampe Contemporaine*, Bibliothèque Nationale, Paris 1973.

Collections: AIC; Boston Public Library; Brooklyn Museum; DIA; Israel National Museum, Tel Aviv; Los Angeles County Museum; MMA; MOMA; National Gallery; New York Public Library; Philadelphia Museum of Art.

Sources: *WWAA* 1978; AAA, Interview, 908; Cummings 1977; H. Rasmussen, *Printmaking with Monotype*, Philadelphia: Chilton, 1969; Broner in *CH* 29 (May/June 1969): 52–53; *Art in America* 44 (February 1956): 50–51; *Art News* 54 (May 1955): 53; *Art News* 72 (March 1973): 86; *DN* 2-15-53, 3-5-61, 12-2-62, 2-14-71, 4-25-71; *DFP* 3-3-57, 3-5-61, 11-25-62.

BROSE, *Morris*

(b. Wyshkow, Poland 1914)

Sculptor. Brose arrived in Detroit from his native Poland in 1931. Trained as a watchmaker, he worked at various jobs and eventually established a successful furniture business. During the next fifteen years, he designed furniture, attended drawing classes, and began to make small sculptures in wood and terra cotta. Encouraged by his friend **Sarkis Sarkisian**, he attended night classes at the Art School of the Detroit Society of Arts and Crafts. In 1949 he sold his business and embarked on a new career as a sculptor. Following a short period of study at Wayne State University, he enrolled at the Cranbrook Academy of Art, where he studied with William McVey. In 1954 he made an extended trip to Europe where he met Ossip Zadkine and Jacques Lipchitz. Brose joined the faculty at Cranbrook as an instructor in 1955 and spent the next several summers in Italy researching the Italian bronze foundry tradition. In 1960 he set up a studio in Rome and in the same year was awarded his first one-person show in New York City at the Peridot Gallery.

In 1962 Brose joined the faculty at the Art School of the DSAC and directed the building of the school's foundry on Watson Street. He established the sculpture department at Oakland University in Rochester in 1965, remaining on the faculty there until 1971. He is represented by many commissions in the Detroit area, including a fountain for the J. L. Hudson Company at the Eastland shopping center, *Voyage V* for the Renaissance Center in Detroit, and the monumental *Tzedek* for the Shaarey Zedek Synagogue in Southfield. Brose is best known for his cast and welded bronzes. His work is generally abstract, ranging from pieces based on landscape and figure sources to totally nonobjective groupings of cubic planes and volumes. He also works in wood and with assembled "found" forms.

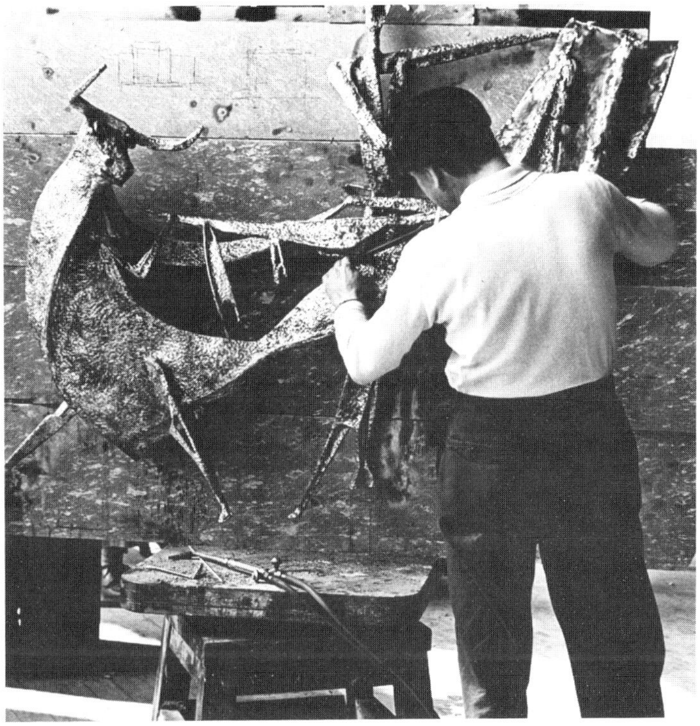

Morris Brose (1914–) working on Matador and Bull. *Courtesy the artist. John C. Andrews, Photographer.*

One-person Exhibitions: Cranbrook 1954; Little Gallery, Birmingham 1955, 1962; DAM 1957; Peridot Gallery, New York City, 1960, 1962, 1965; DIA 1963; Goldwach Gallery, Chicago 1966; Gertrude Kasle Gallery, Detroit 1967*, 1969; J. L. Hudson Company, Detroit 1976; *Retrospective*, Art Gallery of Windsor, Ontario 1977*; Renaissance Gallery, Detroit 1979, 1981.

Group Exhibitions: MAE 1952–60, 1962–63, 1969 (Purchase Prize 1957, Winkelman Prize 1959, FSPP 1962); *PAFA Annual* 1953–54; *American Painting and Sculpture Biennial*, PAFA and DIA 1958, 1959/60; *Contemporary American Sculpture and Drawings*, Whitney 1960, 1963; *American Painting and Sculpture*, AIC 1961; *Prominent Painters and Sculptors in Michigan*, BBAA 1962; *Michigan Art: Yesterday and Today*, FIA 1963; *Recent Sculpture USA*, MOMA 1963, 1965; *Michigan Artists Biennial*, Kresge Art Center Gallery, MSU 1971; *Arts and Crafts in Detroit 1906–1976*, DIA 1976*.

Collections/Commissions: Blue Cross and Blue Shield of Michigan, Detroit; Chase Manhattan Bank, New York City; DIA; Eastland Center, Harper Woods; General Motors Corporation, Detroit; Grace Hospital, Detroit; Grosse Pointe Library; Hirshhorn Museum and Sculpture Garden, Washington, D.C.; Livonia Mall; Westin Hotel, Renaissance Center, Detroit; Shaarey Zedek Synagogue, Southfield; WSU; Zieger Hospital, Detroit.

Sources: *WWAA* 1978; AAA, Interview; MAR; *Art in America* 46, 1 (Spring 1958): 44; *Art News* 61, 1 (March 1962): 44; *Art and Artists* (Detroit) June 1962; *Art Scene* 1, 3 (December 1967): 19–21; *DT* 3-15-59; *DN* 3-22-59, 5-5-63, 1-22-65, 11-5-67, 8-11-68, 6-27-71; *NYT* 2-16-62; *DFP* 4-18-62, 12-25-77.

BROZIK, *Jaroslav*

(b. Pilsen, Czechoslovakia 1904)

Painter/Printmaker. Brozik studied with George Oberteuffer, Allen Philbrick, and Boris Anisfeld at the School of the Art Institute of Chicago (1924–28). He also studied for two summers at the Tiffany Foundation in New York City and spent a year traveling in Europe with his friend, the sculptor Theodore Roszak. He taught for another year at the Municipal Art Gallery in Davenport, Iowa, before arriving in Flint in 1931 as supervisor of the school of the Flint Institute of Arts. During the Depression, under the auspices of the Federal Emergency Relief Administration, Brozik

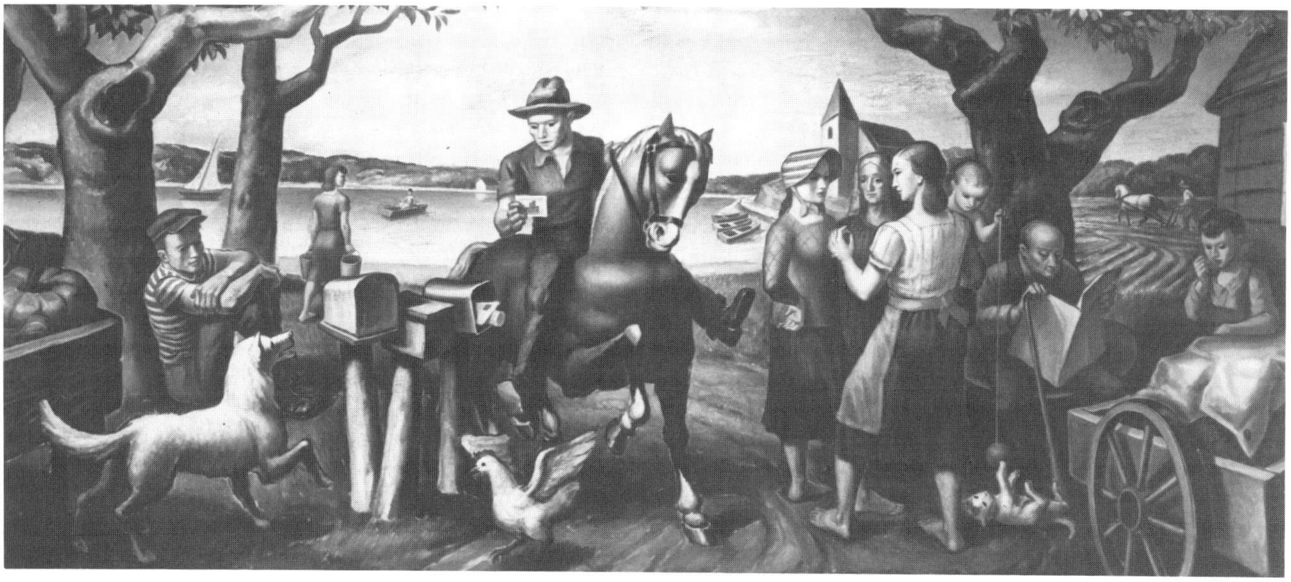

Jaroslav Brozik (1904–). Mural for post office in Howell. Courtesy the artist.

completed murals for Hurley Hospital and the Public Library in Flint. He also received a mural commission for the Howell Post Office from the U.S. Treasury Department's Section of Fine Arts. Part of a small group of American scene painters in Flint, Brozik concentrated on industrial subjects, but he was also known for figure studies and lithographs. He moved to California in 1946.

One-person Exhibitions: Allerton Galleries, Los Angeles 1928; FIA 1932.

Group Exhibitions: *Chicago Artists Exhibition*, AIC 1927–28, 1931–33, 1937 (Jenkins Memorial Prize 1932); *Carnegie International* 1930; *American Painting and Sculpture*, AIC 1930–31, 1938; *International Exposition of Lithography and Wood Engraving*, AIC 1931–32; MAE 1932–40, 1942–43 (Scarab Club Gold Medal 1932, Piper Prize 1939); *Flint Annual*, FIA 1932–44; Michigan State Fair 1934; *National Exhibiton of American Art*, Rockefeller Center 1936–38; New York World's Fair 1939; *1st National Invitational*, GRAM 1940; *Midwest Art Exhibition*, University of Minnesota 1940; *National War Posters Competition*, MOMA 1942; FIA 1943 (six-person).

Collections: FIA; Howell Post Office.

Sources: *WWAA* 1936/37; AAA D133; Cook 1963; Kenny 1965; *Art Dig* 7, 8 (January 15, 1932): 3; *FIA Bulletin* 1941/42; *Time* December 24, 1934; *DN* 1-10-32, 12-31-33, 1-7-34; *DFP* 1-10-32, 12-11-39; *Chicago Evening Post* 1-19-32; *FJ* 2-7-32, 6-7-35, 5-3-36, 3-13-38, 1-6-39, 12-19-39, 11-29-42, 5-24-45.

BULONE, Joseph

(b. Cleveland, Ohio 1922)

Sculptor. Bulone received his education at the Cleveland Institute of Art (1941–43) and at the Cranbrook Academy of Art (1948–52), where he studied with **Carl Milles**. In 1956 he was awarded a Louis Comfort Tiffany grant for sculpture. He began his career as a ceramic sculptor, later worked in bronze (his *Juggler Clown* was commissioned for the Eastland shopping center in Harper Woods in 1957), and most recently in wood. His sculptures are abstract forms derived from the human figure.

One-person Exhibitions: Whitney Gallery, Birmingham 1955; Raven Gallery, Detroit 1961; Little Gallery, Birmingham 1969, 1973, 1977; Olivet College 1971.

Group Exhibitions: MAE 1950–52, 1955, 1959, 1970; *Ceramic National*, Everson Museum of Art, Syracuse 1951; *May Show*, Cleveland Museum of Art 1951, 1953, 1956 (1st Prize, all three years); *Michigan Artist-Craftsmen*, GRAM 1968; *Festival 70*, Grand Rapids 1970 (Sculpture Award); *Silver Medal Exhibition*, Scarab Club, Detroit 1971, 1975 (Best of Show); *All Michigan I*, FIA 1971/72.

Collections/Commissions: Cleveland Museum of Art; Eastland Center, Harper Woods; General Motors Technical Center, Warren; St. Rose of Lima Church, Lima, Tex.

Sources: MAR; Bulone in *CMo* 1, 3 (March 1953): 14–17; *Art in America* 46, 1 (Spring 1958): 44; *DN* 10-9-55; *Wall Street Journal* 8-16-73.

BUTCHER, *Larry D.*

(b. Flint, Michigan 1944)

Painter/Sculptor. After completing a B.S. (1967) and an M.A. (1970) at Central Michigan University, with postgraduate work at the Cranbrook Academy of Art (1971), Butcher joined the faculty of Delta College. He has received considerable recognition for his wood-canvas constructions covered with meticulous drawings.

One-person Exhibitions: J. Walter Thompson Co., Detroit 1970; Xochipilli Gallery, Rochester 1972, 1974; Pyramid Gallery, Ann Arbor 1973; Habatat Gallery, Detroit 1974; University of Hartford, 1975.

Group Exhibitions: *Michigan Artist-Craftsmen*, GRAM 1966 (award); *Flint Annual*, FIA 1966 (purchase prize), 1968, 1970 (award), 1971–72, 1977–79; *The Form of Things Unknown*, DAM 1967; *Mid-Michigan Annual*, Midland Art Association 1967, 1969, 1971/73 (award), 1975, 1977–79; MAE 1970; *Michigan Painters-Printmakers*, GRAM 1973; *Two from Three*, SAM 1974; *Tradition and Invention*, Kresge Art Center Gallery, MSU 1977; *27 Painters*, UMMA 1977.

Collections: CMU; Delta College; Dow Chemical Company, Midland; FIA; First Midland Bank; SAM.

Sources: MAR; *Bay City Times* 8-30-73; *DFP* 10-6-74; *BEcc* 10-10-74; *DN* 10-13-74; *Midland Daily News* 10-10-74, 2-7-79.

CALKINS, *Kingsley*

(b. South Lyon, Michigan 1917)

Painter. Educated at Michigan State Normal College (now Eastern Michigan University) and the University of Michigan (M.A. 1949), Calkins also studied at the Art School of the Detroit Society of Arts and Crafts, the Meinzinger Art School in Detroit, and the Haystack Mountain School of Crafts in Deer Isle, Maine. He joined the faculty at Eastern Michigan University in 1950 and was appointed chairman of the art department in 1960. Under Calkins's direction the department has become one of the major producers of secondary level art educators in Michigan. He has served on the board of the Ann Arbor Art Association and as chairman of the Michigan Water Color Society (1962–65). He completed a mural for the Mayflower Hotel in Plymouth in 1956 and has done several cover paintings for *Ford Times* and *Lincoln Mercury Times*. Known largely for his watercolors for many years, he has more recently concentrated on acrylic polymer. His themes are based on nature and are characterized by an emphasis on natural patterns and textures, such as fish scales, nets, wrinkled walnuts, and cactus.

One-person Exhibitions: Forsythe Gallery, Ann Arbor 1958 (three-person), 1963, 1969, 1971; Anna Werbe Gallery, Detroit 1960; DAM 1962 (two-person), 1968; Gilman Gallery, Chicago 1965; Habatat Galleries, Dearborn 1978.

Group Exhibitions: MAE 1949–52, 1957, 1960–61 (Art Directors Club Prize 1957); *MWCS Annual* 1949–76 (Merit Award 1955); *Watercolor Panorama*, FIA 1952; *Michigan Art Through 50 Years*, UMMA 1955; Michigan State Fair 1955 (1st Prize); *Midyear Show*, Butler Institute 1957, 1959; *Michigan Art: Yesterday and Today*, FIA 1963.

Collections/Commissions: Dayton Museum of Natural History, Ohio; Ford Motor Company, Dearborn; Mayflower Hotel, Plymouth; Michigan Consolidated Gas Company, Detroit; Parke-Davis Company, Detroit; South Bend Art Center, Ind.; Steelcase Corporation, Grand Rapids.

Sources: *WWAA* 1976; MAR; *DT* 5-29-60; *AAN* 4-24-62, 1-12-63, 11-21-67, 5-11-69.

CARROLL, *John*

(b. Wichita, Kansas 1892; d. Albany, New York 1959)

Painter. Carroll attended the Mark Hopkins Art Institute in San Francisco while still a high school student. He entered the University of California in 1913 as an engineering student but dropped out to study painting with Frank Duveneck at the Cincinnati Art Academy. He also studied for a time in Paris and in the early 1920s was a member of the Woodstock Colony in New York. In 1927 he was awarded a Guggenheim Fellowship that enabled him to travel throughout Europe. He had already established a reputation as a "modernistic" painter of sensual women and fashionable por-

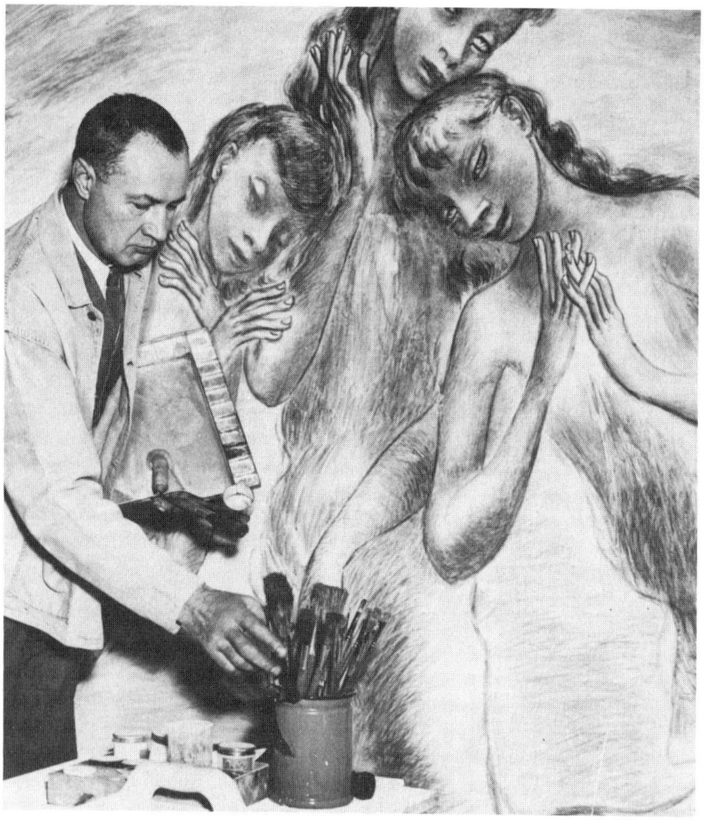

John Carroll (1892–1959) with mural at the Detroit Institute of Arts. Courtesy the Detroit Free Press.

traits when he arrived in Detroit in 1930 to head the painting department of the Art School of the Detroit Society of Arts and Crafts; his acceptance of this position was considered a coup for Detroit. Many prominent Detroiters lined up to have their portraits done by Carroll, among them William R. Valentiner, director of the Detroit Institute of Arts, and local patrons Lillian Henkel Haass and Robert Tannahill.

Awarded a one-person show at the Detroit Institute of Arts in 1930, he was later commissioned by the museum to paint three fresco lunettes in what is now the Robert H. Tannahill American Wing. During his Detroit years Carroll married his second wife, Georgia Finckel, whose physical appearance was to have a dramatic influence in shaping the character of his work. Languid, long-necked female figures with heavy-lidded eyes and elongated hands became a Carroll trademark. In later years, even his portraits became an amalgam of the sitter and Georgia. In 1941 Carroll left the Art School of the DSAC and returned to his farm in upstate New York. He continued to paint, mainly portraits, and for a time taught at the Art Students League in New York City.

One-person Exhibitions: Daniel Gallery, New York City 1924; Rehn Gallery, New York City 1927, 1929, 1931–33, 1936–38, 1940, 1942–46; DIA 1930*; Modern Art Gallery, DSAC 1934, 1937; DAM 1936, 1937; Schaeffer Galleries, San Francisco 1940; Berkshire Museum, Pittsfield, Mass. 1943; *Retrospective*, Albany Institute of History and Art, N.Y. 1963.

Group Exhibitions: *Corcoran Biennial* 1921–26, 1932–51; *American Painting and Sculpture*, AIC 1921–27, 1930, 1940, 1943, 1945 (Silver Medal 1927); *PAFA Annual* 1922, 1924–26, 1930–32, 1934–36, 1938–46, 1948–50, 1952 (Purchase Prize 1922); *Carnegie International* 1922–26, 1928, 1930, 1933–39; *American Artists Annual*, DIA 1922–30, 1937; *Pan-American Exposition*, Los Angeles County Museum 1924 (Gold Medal); *Contemporary American Painting*, Whitney 1932–46; MAE 1934–41 (FSPP 1935, 1941, Scarab Club Gold Medal 1936); *National Exhibition of American Art*, Rockefeller Center 1936–38; New York World's Fair 1939; *Painting in the United States*, Carnegie Institute 1940–49; *Little Show of Works in Progress*, DIA 1946; *Contemporary American Painting*, Krannert Art Museum, University of Illinois 1948, 1950*, 1951; *Michigan Art Through 50 Years*, UMMA 1955; *Arts and Crafts in Detroit 1906–1976*, DIA 1976*.

Collections: Addison Gallery of American Art, Phillips Academy, Andover, Mass.; Brooklyn Museum; Carnegie Institute; DIA; Encyclopaedia Britannica Collection, Chicago; FIA; Indianapolis Museum of Art; International Business Machines Corporation, New York City; Los Angeles County Museum; MMA; PAFA; Toledo Museum of Art; UMMA; Whitney.

Sources: *WWAA* 1956; AAA 76: 649–856; *Current Biography* July 1955; Grace Pagano, ed., *Contemporary American Paintings*, New York: Duell, Sloan, & Pearce, 1945; *Am Artist* 15 (January 1951): 28–34; *American Magazine of Art* 18 (January 1927): 51; *Art News* 28 (May 1930): 22; *Creative Art* 1 (November 1927): 23–27; *Esquire* August 1938; *International Studio* 83 (February 1926): 75–79; *Time* May 4, 1936; *NYT* 11-6-27, 1-7-40, 2-25-43.

CASENELLI, *Victor*

(b. New York, New York 1868; d. Muskegon, Michigan 1961)

Painter. Raised in New York City, Casenelli moved to Cincinnati when he was in his early twenties. Basically self-taught as a painter, Casenelli set up a studio, painted mural decorations for residences and stage backdrops for the Pike Opera House, and gave classes in watercolor. He moved to Muskegon in 1906 and for the remainder of his career divided his time between his home there and studios in Sarasota and St. Augustine, Florida. Casenelli traveled extensively throughout the United States, particularly in the Southwest. His first success was as a painter of Indian scenes, but he later turned primarily to landscape in both oil and watercolor. His sketches of the Lake Michigan shore and woodlands often appeared in local publications and in the Chicago newspapers. In 1929 he was commissioned by the Lumberman's Bank of Muskegon to execute a series of seventeen paintings documenting the history of the city, which now hang in Muskegon Senior High School. His home in North Muskegon was a gathering place for those interested in art, and he was well known throughout the community for his many lectures on artistic techniques and philosophy.

One-person Exhibitions: Lake Harbour Hotel, Muskegon 1911; Marshall Field & Company, Chicago 1911; HAM 1913, 1921, 1924–25, 1936, 1951.

Group Exhibitions: *Cincinnati Art Club Annual*, Cincinnati Art Museum 1894; *Spring Exhibition*, Cincinnati Art Museum 1896; *Regional Exhibition*, Muskegon Art Museum 1927–61; *Michigan Art: Yesterday and Today*, FIA 1963; *Early Michigan Artists*, Kresge Art Center Gallery, MSU 1976*.

Collections: Jackson Public Library; Muskegon Art Museum; Muskegon Senior High School.

Sources: AAA D23; J. Fred Boyd, *My 95 Years in Muskegon*, Ravenna, Mich.: Rogers Publishing, Inc., 1978; *Chicago Examiner* 8-3-11; *Muskegon Chronicle* 8-17-11, 7-24-13, 5-19-28, 12-2-29, 10-1-31, 6-14-33, 12-5-51, 11-17-61, 4-9-72; *GR Herald* 10-18-30.

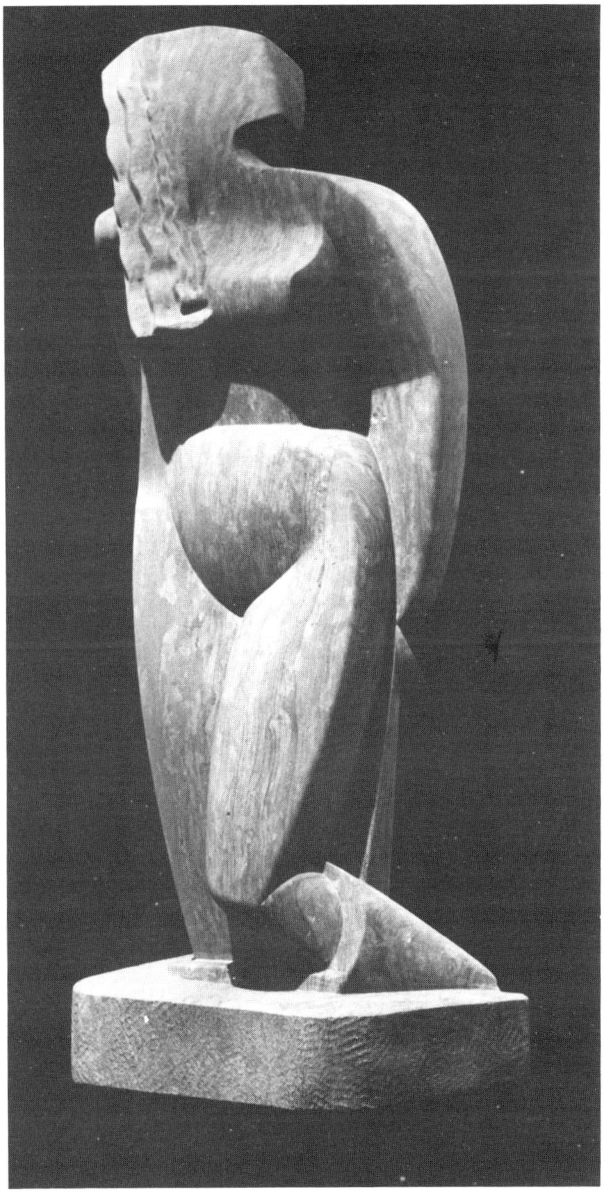

Samuel Cashwan (1900–   ). Nude. *Stone. h. 21 inches. Created under the auspices of the Works Progress Administration/Federal Art Project. The Detroit Institute of Arts, Research Library.*

CASHWAN, *Samuel*

(b. Cherkassi, Russia 1900)

Sculptor. Cashwan arrived in Detroit in 1916 and received his first encouragement in art from Katherine Conover at Central High School. After a period of study with **John P. Wicker**, Cashwan spent a year in New York City at the Architectural League (1919). He also studied under Antoine Bourdelle at the École des Beaux-Arts in Paris (1923, 1926). For a short time, he was an instructor in architectural sculpture at the University of Michigan, then joined the faculty at the Art School of the Detroit Society of Arts and Crafts as head of the sculpture department in 1927. During the Depression, Cashwan, having already established a reputation with his commissions for the Brady Memorial on Belle Isle and the façade of St. Aloysius Catholic Church in Detroit, was appointed supervisor of sculpture for the Works Progress Administration/Federal Art Project in Michigan. His commissions for this project included the Albion Band Shell, several figures for the Music Building at Michigan State College (now Michigan State University), a figure of Tom Thumb for the Children's Room of the Detroit Public Library, a wall relief for the Water Conditioning Plant in Lansing. He established an innovative course in modeling for automotive engineers at the Art School of the DSAC, and for a time taught sculpture at Wayne State University. In 1942 he left the DSAC art school to become a designer for General Motors Corporation. Although he later worked in a more abstract manner in both wood and welded metal, most of the Cashwan's work in Michigan is figurative and carved in stone.

One-person Exhibitions: Bonstelle Playhouse, Detroit 1928; Civic Theater, Detroit 1928; Modern Art Gallery, DSAC 1928, 1936, 1954; DAM 1938 (two-person); Garelick's Gallery, Detroit 1954; EMU 1960; Jewish Community Center, Detroit 1961.

Group Exhibitions: MAE 1920–21, 1924–58, 1961 (Scarab Club Gold Medal 1924; 1937); *American Artists Annual*, DIA 1926; *American Painting and Sculpture*, AIC 1932, 1936, 1938, 1940; *Painting and Sculpture from 16 American Cities*, MOMA 1933; *PAFA Annual* 1934, 1938, 1946; *Painting and Sculpture by Detroit Artists*, DIA 1935; *New Horizons in American Art*, MOMA 1936; *National Exhibition of American Art*, Rockefeller Center 1936, 1938; New York World's Fair 1939; *1st National Invitational*, GRAM 1941; *Americans 1942*, MOMA 1942*; *Origins of Modern Sculpture*, DIA 1946; *Michigan Sculpture Society Exhibition*, DIA 1952; *Michigan Art Through 50 Years*, UMMA 1955; *Arts and Crafts in Detroit 1906–1976*, DIA 1976*.

Collections/Commissions: Brady Memorial, Belle Isle, Detroit; Detroit Public Library; DIA; EMU; First Federal Savings & Loan, Detroit; Highland Park High School; Lincoln Consolidated School, Ypsilanti; Manufacturers National Bank, Detroit; Kresge Art Center Gallery, MSU; National Gallery; General Motors Corporation, Olds Division, Lansing; St. Aloysius Catholic Church, Detroit; Toledo Museum of Art; UMMA; Water Conditioning Plant, Lansing; Westland Shopping Center, Wayne; Wonderland Shopping Center, Livonia; WSU.

Sources: *WWAA* 1953; Hendry 1980A; Nawrocki 1980; *Art News* 40, 20 (February 1942): 22, 29; *Detroit Saturday Night* November 19, 1925; *DIA Bulletin* 7, 4 (January 1926): 42–43; *DFP* 7-19-25, 8-20-25, 11-4-28, 11-18-34, 1-25-42, 8-26-54, 11-22-64; *DN* 8-27-25, 7-3-26, 2-5-28, 7-12-36, 11-17-50; *DT* 1-16-55.

CASSARA, *Frank*

(b. Partinico, Sicily 1913)

Painter/Printmaker. Cassara attended the Detroit School of Art (1933–36), studying under **Walter Speck** and **Reginald Bennett**, and also studied fresco painting with **Jean Paul Slusser**. In 1937 he was awarded a one-year scholarship to the Colorado Springs School of Fine Art. On his return to Detroit, he was appointed supervisor of the easel painting section of the Works Progress Administration/Federal Art Project in Michigan. Cassara completed several murals under the auspices of this project, including those for Thompson School in Highland Park, the Water Conditioning Plant in Lansing, and Fort Wayne in Detroit. He also painted two post office murals, in East Detroit and Sandusky, for the U.S. Treasury Department's Section of Fine Arts. In 1947 Cassara joined the faculty at the University of Michigan, where he completed a master's degree in design in 1954. In 1958 he studied at Stanley W. Hayter's Atelier 17 in Paris. Since the late 1950s, he has concentrated on printmaking. Cassara is known for his abstract color intaglio prints and his development of a unique one-bite white etching ground.

One-person Exhibitions: University of Illinois 1960; FIA 1962; KIA 1962; SAM 1962; Port Huron Museum of Arts and Sciences 1969; Forsythe Gallery, Ann Arbor 1971, 1976.

Group Exhibitions: *International Exhibition of Lithography and Wood Engraving*, AIC 1939, 1940; *National Exhibition of Prints*, Library of Congress 1957, 1960; *Boston Printmakers Annual* 1957 (Gropper Prize), 1958–65; MAE 1960 (Purchase Prize), 1962 (Purchase Prize), 1966; *National Print Exhibition*, Brooklyn Museum 1960; *Michigan Association of Printmakers Biennial 1962, 1968*; *Michigan Painters-Printmakers*, GRAM 1963 (Graphics Award), 1965, 1967 (Purchase Prize); *15 American Printmakers*, Ball State University 1964; *Prints Around the World*, Society of American Graphic Artists, New York City 1965; *Four Printmakers* (in conjunction with *The Graphic Art of Rolf Nesch*), DIA 1969; *Atelier 17: A Retrospective*, Elvehjem Art Center, Madison, Wis. 1977.

Collections: Albion College; Battle Creek Civic Art Center; Bibliothèque Nationale, Paris; DIA; FIA; GRAM; KIA; Library of Congress; Oklahoma Art Center, Oklahoma City; SAM; Stedelijk Museum, Amsterdam; UMMA; University of Maine; United States Information Agency, Washington, D.C.; Wichita Art Association, Kans.

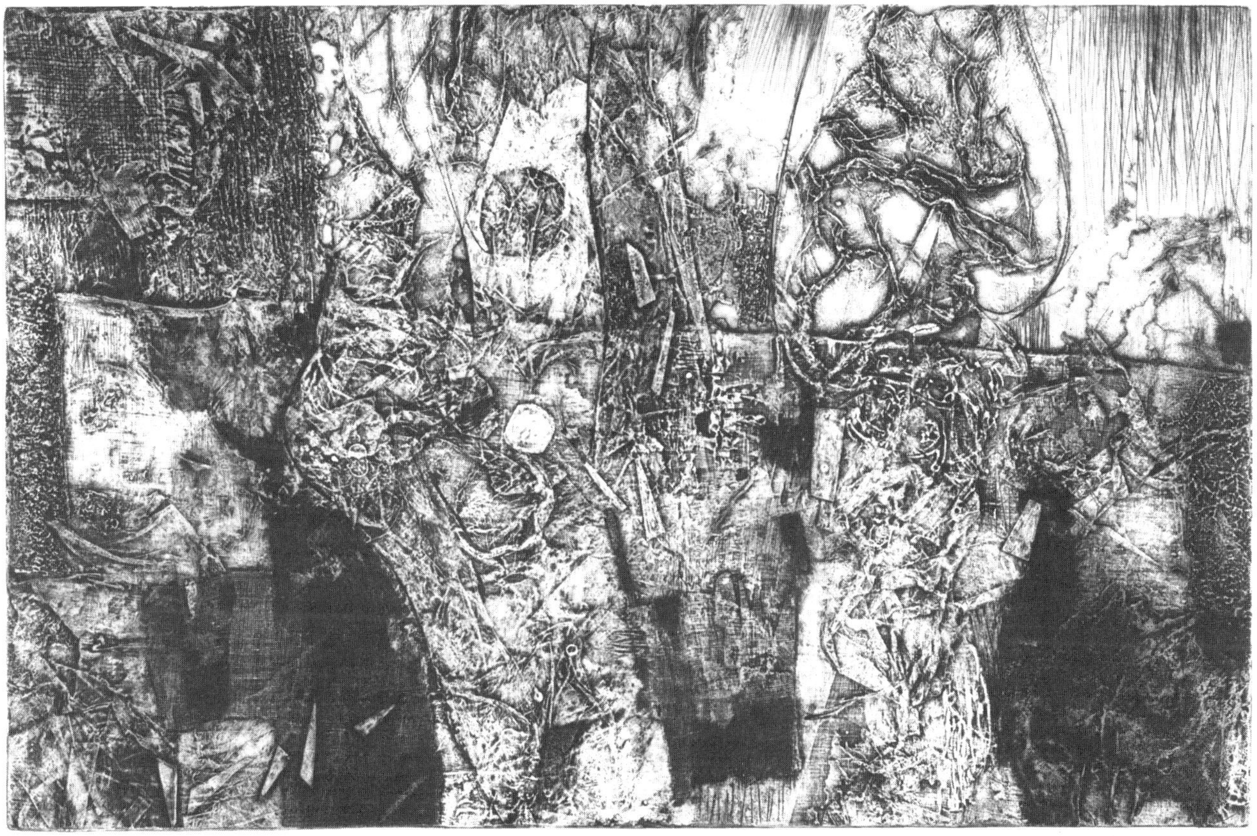

Frank Cassara (1913–). Della Terra. *1962. Intaglio print. 17⅜ × 27⅜ inches. Collection of the Detroit Institute of Arts.*

Sources: *WWAA* 1978; MAR; Cassara in *Artist's Proof* (Summer 1963): n.p.; Ruth Leaf, *Intaglio Printmaking Techniques*, New York: Watson-Guptill, 1976; *AAN* 7-18-71.

CHAFFEE, John

(b. Huntington, West Virginia 1931)

Sculptor. Chaffee received a B.A. (1952) from the University of North Carolina. He also studied at the Art Students League (1956) in New York. He worked as a research engineer in the aircraft and automotive industries for twenty years (1953–73), moving in 1966 to Michigan, where he has served as sculptor-in-residence for the Novi Community Schools (1975–77) and for Schoolcraft College in Livonia (1977–78). He has also participated in the Michigan Council for the Arts' visiting artist program and been active as a member of the visual arts advisory panel. His experience as an engineer has influenced both his technique and imagery. His monumental welded-steel constructions are at once machine-like and yet based on flowing aerodynamic forms. Chaffee has completed commissions for the Novi High School, the City of Algonac (both under the auspices of the Michigan Council for the Arts), and the Luke M. Power Educational Center in Flint.

One-person Exhibitions: Huntington Gallery, W. Va. 1974; Birmingham Gallery 1975; Leland Gallery 1975; Delta College 1976; University of Connecticut 1978.

Group Exhibitions: *Michigan Painters-Printmakers*, GRAM 1970 (2nd Prize); *Invitational*, Ann Arbor Art Association 1971; *Mid-Michigan Annual*, Midland Art

Association 1971; *Mainstreams*, Marietta College, Ohio 1974 (1st Prize), 1975 (Purchase Prize); *Source Detroit*, Cranbrook 1976.

Collections/Commissions: City of Algonac; City of Warren; Industrial Smelting Company, Detroit; Marietta College, Ohio; Mayotte Memorial Chapel, Luke M. Power Educational Center, Flint; Novi High School; Westin Hotel, Renaissance Center, Detroit; Schoolcraft College.

Sources: MAR; *DFP* 10-12-75, 5-9-77.

CLAXTON, *Wayne LeMarr*

(b. Malta, Illinois 1902)

Painter/Illustrator/Designer. Educated at the University of Wisconsin (B.S. 1931, M.S. 1936), Claxton also studied at the Mozarteum in Salzburg, Austria, and in Scandinavia. Prior to his appointment as chairman of the newly established art department at Wayne State University in 1936, he taught at the University of Wisconsin. During his tenure at Wayne State, Claxton was interested in kinesthetics (the study of the effects of body movement on sensory perception) and other theories of visual perception, including those of Gyorgy Kepes and László Moholy-Nagy. He is well known for his drawings of dancers and dancing, and collaborated with his wife, Margaret H'Doubler, to produce the book, *Dance* (New York: Appleton-Crofts, 1940). One of the founders of the Michigan Water Color Society, Claxton also served for ten years as chairman of the professional jury for the Detroit Artists Market and was a frequent contributor to *Ford Times* (the Ford Motor Company's monthly periodical). He retired from the chairmanship at Wayne in 1959 and moved to Arizona.

One-person Exhibitions: Federal Art Center, Laramie, Wyo. 1937; Springfield Museum, Miss. 1944; DAM 1951; Public Museum, Oshkosh, Wis. 1954.

Group Exhibitions: MAE 1936, 1939, 1943–46, 1948, 1950–51, 1957 (Wineman Prize 1951, Newberry and Kahn Prizes 1957); *MWCS Annual* 1947–50, 1954–57 (Merit Award 1947, 1950); *Michigan Art Through 50 Years*, UMMA 1955.

Collections: Beloit Art Gallery, Wis.; DIA; Ford Motor Company, Dearborn; WSU.

Sources: AAA 879; MAR; *DN* 8-25-40, 4-4-50.

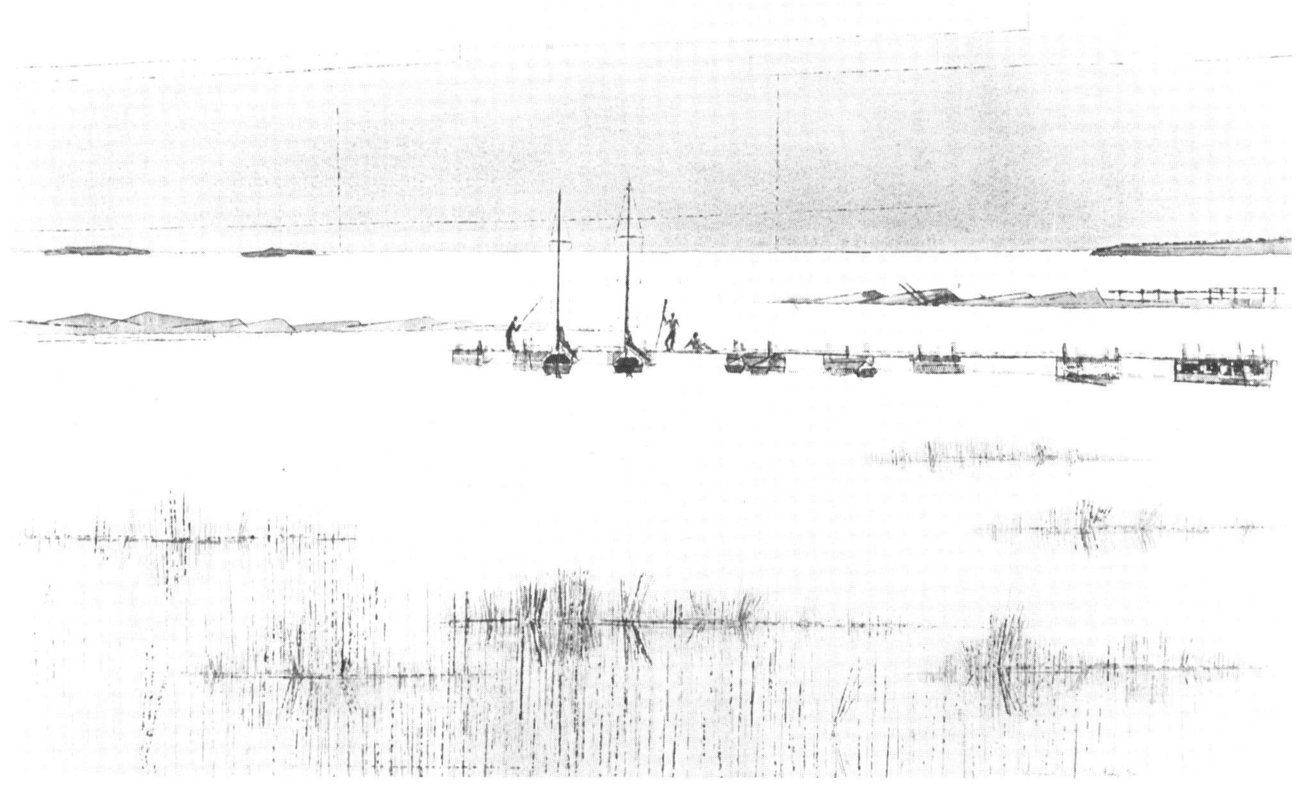

Wayne L. Claxton (1902–). Weborg Point—Door Peninsula. *1950. Watercolor. 14¾ × 24¾ inches. Collection of the Detroit Institute of Arts.*

COHN, Harold

(b. Detroit, Michigan 1908)

Painter. Cohn studied with both Sam Halpert and **John Carroll** at the Art School of the Detroit Society of Arts and Crafts. He taught painting at the Art School of the DSAC from 1935 to 1942, and has also taught at the Jewish Community Center in Detroit and at St. Clair Community College. Cohn is particularly well known for his still lifes and flower studies.

One-person Exhibitions: DAM 1930, 1934, 1937, 1939, 1949 (two-person), 1953 (two-person), 1959; Anna Werbe Gallery, Detroit 1952; WSU 1960; Arwin Gallery, Detroit 1967*.

Group Exhibitions: MAE 1934–35, 1937–47, 1949–56, 1960–61 (Modern Art Prize 1938, 1940, 1943; Scarab Club Prize 1944; McClintock Prize 1946, Myers Prize 1950, Werbe Prize 1953); *American Painting and Sculpture*, AIC 1936, 1938; *Corcoran Biennial* 1937, 1939, 1941, 1947; *National Exhibition of American Art*, Rockefeller Center 1938; New York World's Fair 1939; *Painting in the U.S.*, Carnegie Institute 1941, 1943, 1946–47; *Recent Works by Detroit Artists*, DIA 1944; *Pepsi Cola "Portrait of America" Exhibition*, New York City 1945; *Michigan Art Through 50 Years*, UMMA 1955; *Midyear Show*, Butler Institute 1955, 1956, 1959; *Prominent Painters and Sculptors in Michigan*, BBAA 1962.

Collections: Boston Museum of Fine Arts; Brandeis University; CAAM; DIA.

Sources: *WWAA* 1940/41; AAA 879; MAR; *DN* 10-20-30, 4-7-35, 3-26-39, 4-28-49, 12-4-49, 6-15-52.

COLLINS, Kreigh

(b. Davenport, Iowa 1908; d. Grand Rapids, Michigan 1974)

Illustrator/Painter. Collins studied at art schools in Cincinnati and Cleveland and in Paris (1928, 1931). As a young man he traveled abroad (1928, 1930–31) to North Africa, Spain, and France, sketching experiences which he later used in writing and illustrating travel articles. In 1930 Collins settled in Grand Rapids, subsequently becoming known as an illustrator. During the Depression, he combined his illustrations with his own writings, producing a number of children's books and teaching aids. He also collaborated on an illustrated history of Michigan, *Do You Know* (Detroit: Booth Newspapers, Inc., 1937), which was used extensively in schools and public libraries. An avid sailor, Collins illustrated many articles for major boating magazines. He next turned to adventure comic strips, including "Mitzi McCoy," "Kevin the Bold" (1951–70), and "Up Anchor" (1970–71). A painter of portraits and landscapes, Collins also received numerous mural commissions in Grand Rapids.

One-person Exhibitions: GRAM 1930, 1933.

Group Exhibition: *Paintings by Grand Rapids Artists*, GRAM 1927; *Artists of Grand Rapids*, GRAM and Grand Rapids Historical Museum, 1981*.

Collections: East Church Auditorium, Grand Rapids; East Grand Rapids High School; Grand Rapids Public Library; Grand Valley State College; Newberry High School Auditorium; Ottawa Hills High School; Pioneer High School, Grand Rapids.

Sources: *WWAA* 1973; *Kreigh Collins Papers*, Michigan Room, Grand Rapids Public Library; *GR Press Magazine* 2-20-72; *GR Press* 1-9-74.

COLLINS, Paul

(b. Muskegon, Michigan 1936)

Painter. Primarily self-taught as an artist, Collins studied for a short time at the Kendall School of Design in Grand Rapids. During the 1960s he painted murals in numerous Grand Rapids schools. In 1975 he executed his most ambitious local work, a large-scale mural depicting the life and accomplishments of Gerald R. Ford, at Kent County International Airport. A portraitist who works in "dry oil" (a medium which he developed himself), Collins is best known for his paintings of African men and women, inspired by his travels to Africa (1969–71). Subsequent portrait series have included "Great Black Beautiful Women" and "Sioux Indians." A prominent figure in the Grand Rapids art community, Collins has served on the mayor's committee, "Art for the City Plaza," and on the board of the Emerging Arts Forum (1974–76), an organization that promotes art in the inner city. He also served on the board for the establishment of the C.E.T.A. program in Grand Rapids and is presently on the advisory board of the Kennedy Center for the Performing Arts in Washington, D.C. He has designed theater sets for the Robeson Players, Grand Rapids. His paintings were featured in the film, *Save the Children* (Paramount Pictures, 1973).

One-person Exhibitions: *Great Black Beautiful Women*, Chicago Public Library 1978 and Detroit Historical Museum 1979.

Group Exhibitions: *Area Show*, HAM 1965 (1st Prize); *American Artists*, Butler Institute 1969; *African*

Perspective, American Cultural Center, Dakar, Senegal 1973; *American Heritage*, Corcoran 1973; *Tribal Arts Festival*, New York Public Library at Lincoln Center 1974; *Classic Revival*, Illinois State Museum, Springfield 1975; *Native Americans*, Pueblo Grande Museum, Phoenix, Ariz. 1975.

Collections: Afro-American Museum of Detroit; Creston School, Grand Rapids; Du Sable Museum, Chicago; East Grand Rapids High School; Grand Rapids Public Museum; Grand Rapids Public Schools Instructional Media Center; GRAM; Jefferson Elementary School, Grand Rapids; Kent County International Airport, Grand Rapids; Dr. Martin Luther King Center, Montgomery, Ala.; Palace de la President du Senegal, Dakar; Sigsbee Elementary School, Grand Rapids; South Middle School, Grand Rapids.

Sources: *WWAA* 1978; Cederholm 1973; Paul Collins and Thom La Belle, *Gerald R. Ford: A Man in Perspective*, Grand Rapids: Eerdmans Publishing Co., 1976; Paul Collins and Tom Lee, *Black Portrait of an African Journey*, Grand Rapids: Eerdmans Publishing Co., 1971; Susan E. Meyer, ed., *20 Figurative Painters and How They Work*, New York: Watson-Guptill, 1979; Collins in *Ebony* 28, 8 (June 1973): 46–48ff; *GR Press* 9-9-75, 12-21-75, 2-22-76, 9-17-78.

COPPIN, *John*

(b. Mitchell, Ontario 1904; d. Sarasota, Florida 1986)

Painter/Illustrator. Educated at the Stratford Collegiate Institute in Ontario and at the **John P. Wicker** School of Fine Arts in Detroit, Coppin was well known for his portraits. He painted five Michigan governors, Detroit poet Edgar A. Guest, British actor Alec Guinness, and various other prominent figures. He also completed a mural triptych, *Man and Transportation*, for the Detroit Public Library. Coppin painted many cover illustrations for the Automobile Club of Michigan's *Motor News*, and was the author of *The Haunted House*, a memoir of artist life in the Detroit of the 1920s. He was a member of the Scarab Club.

One-person Exhibitions: Garelick's Gallery, Detroit 1965; Grinnell Galleries, Detroit 1965.

Group Exhibitions: *Scarab Club Annual* 1930–86 (most years) (Gold Medal 1941, 1944, 1946); MAE 1933–38, 1940, 1942–43, 1945–46, 1949–50, 1952 (Popular Prize 1937, 1945, 1949); *Portrait Commissions by Michigan Artists*, DIA 1955.

Collections/Commissions: Blue Cross and Blue Shield of Michigan, Detroit; Detroit Central High School (now Old Main, WSU); Detroit City Hall (now destroyed); Detroit Historical Museum; Detroit Public Library; DIA; Hope College; Michigan Consolidated Gas Company, Detroit; Stratford Festival Theatre, Ontario; Wayne County Courthouse.

Sources: *WWAA* 1962; *DFP* 11-30-45, 2-2-47, 3-30-52, 1-10-54, 1-25-59, 12-29-63, 1-10-65.

CRAWFORD, *James*

(b. Hillsdale, Michigan 1944)

Printmaker/Photographer/Conceptual Artist. Crawford attended Michigan State University (1963–64) and received both a B.F.A. (1967) and an M.F.A. (1969) from Wayne State University, where he worked with **Aris Koutroulis**. A member of Common Ground for the Arts and the Detroit Workshop of Fine Prints, he has also served on the Board of the Michigan Association of Printmakers. In 1976 the Archives of American Art commissioned him to produce a commemorative U.S. Bicentennial edition of three silkscreens, "American Flag Series '76," based on photographs of the world's largest flag, formerly owned by the J. L. Hudson Company. One of Detroit's first conceptual artists, Crawford has created works that range from geometric neon tube sculptures to photographs of piled or stacked objects as well as large outdoor ice installations in public spaces, commissioned by the Detroit Institute of Arts (1970), Detroit Adventure (1973), and the Detroit Department of Parks and Recreation (1975).

One-person exhibitions: WSU 1969; Willis Gallery, Detroit 1972; Detroit Cultural Center (sponsored by Detroit Adventure) 1973; Detroit Public Library 1975; Kern Block, City of Detroit Department of Parks and Recreation 1975; Alma College 1976; Kresge Art Center Gallery, MSU 1976.

Group Exhibitions: DAM 1967–69, 1975; *Michigan Association of Printmakers Biennial*, London Arts Gallery, Detroit 1968; *Plastic in Art*, BBAA 1970; MAE 1972/73; *Michigan Painters-Printmakers*, GRAM 1973; *The Printed Image*, BBAA 1973; *Flint Annual*, FIA 1973–74; *Detroit Artists Invitational*, Detroit Bank & Trust Co. 1974; Willis Gallery, Detroit 1974–75; *Prints From the Collection*, FIA 1975; *A Short Survey of Photography*, Kresge Art Center Gallery, MSU 1975; *Michigan Collects Michigan Art*, Pontiac Creative Arts Center 1976; *Kick Out the Jams*, DIA 1980*.

Collections: AIC; BBAA; Bloomfield Township Public Library; Detroit Bicentennial Commission; Detroit Council for the Arts; DIA; FIA; Ford Motor Company Collection, Dearborn; GRAM; J. L. Hudson Co., Detroit; Michigan Council for the Arts; Midland Center for the Arts; Music Hall, Detroit; Smith Hinchman & Grylls, Detroit; Troy Public Library; UMMA; Your Heritage House, Detroit; WSU.

Sources: MAR; *Kresge Art Center Bulletin* 10, 1 (October 1976): 14; *People's Art 200*, City of Detroit Department of Parks and Recreation, 1977; *DN* 5-21-72, 3-11-73, 1-6-74, 1-19-75, 2-20-75; *DFP* 2-20-75.

CULVER, Charles

(b. Chicago Heights, Illinois 1908; d. Bellaire, Michigan 1967)

Painter. Culver studied with **John P. Wicker** in Detroit (1926–30) and at the Cranbrook Academy of Art (1927–28). During the early years of his career, he worked as a freelance commercial artist for the automotive industry while continuing studies at the Art Institute of Chicago (1934) and at the Art School of the Detroit Society of Arts and Crafts under **John Carroll.** For a short time he taught at the Detroit Art Academy (1937–38). At this time he was also part of a group of young artists, including **Carlos Lopez**, **Ernest Scanes**, and **Frederick Simper**, who became well known for their paintings of the Michigan countryside. By 1946 Culver was spending almost half the year at his studio in northern Michigan; in 1951 he left Detroit and established residence in Bellaire. He returned to Detroit in 1960 when he joined the faculty at the Art School of the DSAC. In addition to his position as head of the watercolor department, Culver was the editor of the school's monthly publication, *Topic and Talk*, and at various times wrote articles for *American Artist*, *Art Digest*, and *Ford Times*, in addition to serving as art critic for the *Detroit Free Press* (1966–67).

Culver was a prolific artist; he had over twenty-five one-person shows in the Detroit area alone. He won fourteen prizes at the "Exhibition for Michigan Artists," including the Scarab Club Gold Medal in 1940 and 1943, and he is represented by fifty-eight works in the Detroit Institute of Arts collection, more than any other Michigan artist. Above all, Culver was a nature painter. In addition to landscapes and village scenes, he also painted a series of semi-abstract works based on rock formations and fossils. But it was for his animal and insect paintings that he was best known. His favorite medium was watercolor and his pallette was predominantly composed of earth tones: gray, sienna, brown and red. Quick, calligraphic brushwork

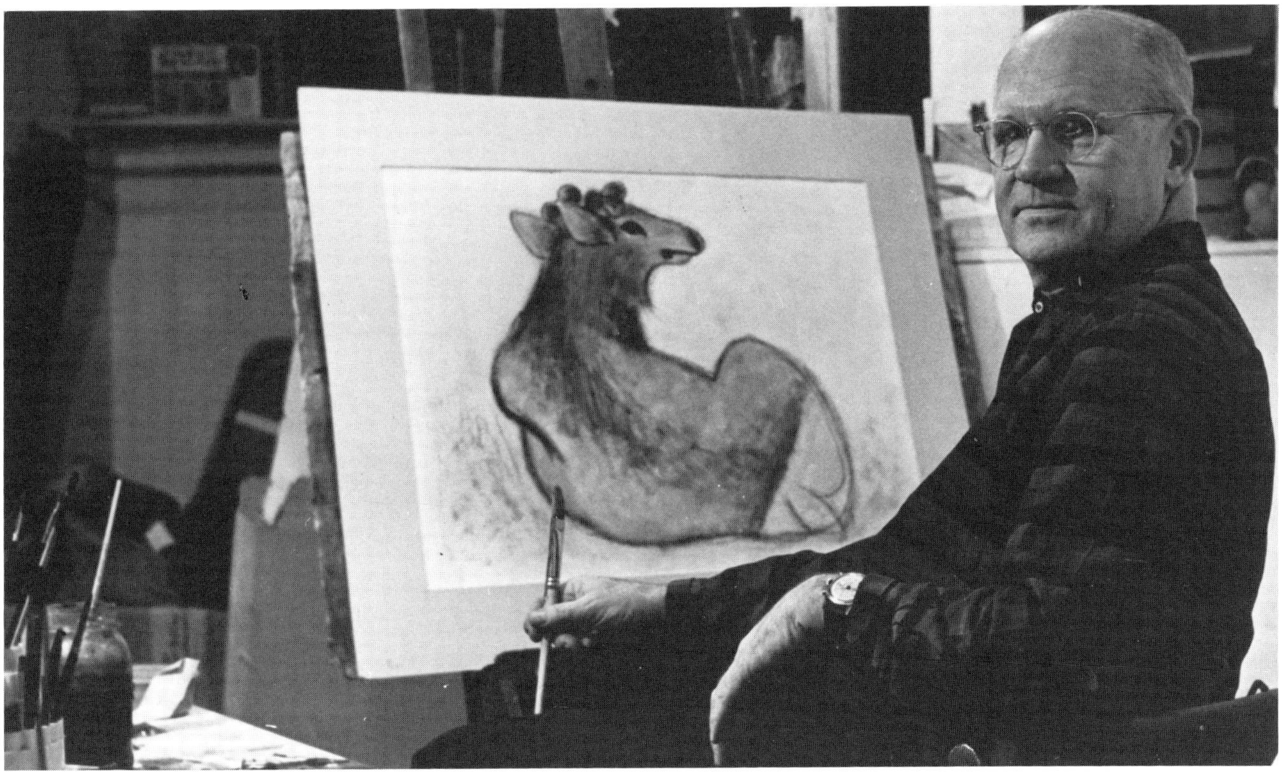

Charles Culver (1908–1967) in his studio. Courtesy the Detroit Free Press.

and simple structural outlines were Culver trademarks.

One-person Exhibitions: Gordon Beer Gallery, Detroit 1936; Detroit Civic Theater 1937; DAM 1938 (two-person), 1939, 1941, 1944, 1946-47, 1949-52, 1959*, 1968; J. L. Hudson Gallery, Detroit 1940, 1945, 1954; 460 Park Avenue Gallery, New York City 1940-41, 1944, 1947; Macbeth Gallery, New York City 1948*, 1950, 1951* Little Gallery, Birmingham 1951, 1958, 1968; Scarab Club, Detroit 1953; KIA 1955; Forsythe Gallery, Ann Arbor 1959; Garelick's Gallery, Detroit 1961*, 1962, 1965*, 1966*, 1967; *Commissions for Michigan Artists*, DIA 1962; FIA 1963; SAM 1964; South Bend Art Center, Ind. 1967 (two-persons).

Group Exhibitions: MAE 1932-44, 1946-57, 1959-61, 1963, 1966 (14 prizes, including Scarab Club Gold Medal 1940, 1943); *National Exhibition of American Art*, Rockefeller Center 1936-37; *American Painting and Sculpture*, AIC 1938; *Great Lakes Exhibition*, Albright Art Gallery, Buffalo 1938; *Contemporary Detroit Painters*, Alger House, DIA 1940; *First National Exhibition*, GRAM 1940; *Corcoran Biennial* 1941; *Recent Works by Detroit Artists*, Metropolitan Art Association of Detroit, DIA 1944; *Annual Exhibition of American Watercolors and Drawings*, AIC 1944, 1946, 1949; *Works in Progress in Michigan II*, DIA, 1949; *Contemporary American Sculpture, Watercolor, and Drawing*, Whitney 1949, 1951; *International Watercolor Exhibition*, Brooklyn Museum 1949, 1951; *MWCS Annual* 1950-67 (Merit Award 1950, 1956, 1958, 1960); *Audubon Artists*, National Academy Gallery, New York City 1950, 1951 (Gold Medal); *Midyear Show*, Butler Institute 1951-52, 1955, 1957, 1961-63, 1966-67 (Purchase Prize 1957, 1967); *Michigan Art Through 50 Years*, UMMA 1955; *Watercolor Panorama*, FIA 1962; *Michigan Art: Yesterday and Today*, FIA 1963; *Arts and Crafts in Detroit 1906-1976*, DIA 1976*; *Michigan Collects Michigan Art*, Pontiac Creative Arts Center 1976.

Collections: Albion College; Butler Institute; CMU; CAAM; DIA; International Business Machines, New York City; Illinois State Museum, Springfield; KIA; Lever House, New York City; Middlebury College; New Britain Museum, Conn.; Northwestern Michigan College; UMMA; U.S. Embassy, Brazil; Whitney; Worcester Art Museum, Mass.

Sources: *WWAA* 1962; AAA D365; MAR; *Am Artist* 24, 6 (June 1960): 34ff; *Art Dig* 18,10 (February 15, 1944): 11; *Art Dig* 23, 1 (October 1, 1948): 15; *Art News* 39, 21 (December 21, 1940): 11ff; *Art News* 43, 1 (February 15-20, 1944): 23; *Art News* 50, 1 (March 1951): 47-58; *Topic and Talk* (Art School of the Detroit Society of Arts and Crafts) November 1967; *DN* 9-27-36, 2-18-40, 11-1-49, 8-30-53, 2-7-65, *NYT* 10-5-41; *DFP* 11-26-28, 2-25-51, 5-11-52, 3-10-63, 9-23-67; *Royal Oak Daily Tribune* 4-2-59; *BEcc* 9-5-68.

DART, Gawaine

(b. Pontiac, Michigan 1929)

Ceramicist/Painter. Dart received a B.S. (1951) from Eastern Michigan University and an M.A. (1952) from Wayne State University, where he studied under **William Pitney**. He has been active in the Michigan Potters' Association as both chairman and board member, and in 1961, with the encouragement of **John Foster**, he was instrumental in organizing the first meeting of the Michigan Craftsmen's Council. He joined the faculty at Henry Ford Community College, Dearborn, in 1957 and became chairman of the art department in 1960. As a painter, Dart concentrates on abstract watercolor landscapes; and as a ceramicist, on reduction-fired stoneware in both functional and sculptural forms.

One-person Exhibitions: Potters Guild, Ann Arbor 1952; Hanamura Gallery, Detroit 1962; Left Bank Gallery, Flint 1965 (two-person); Women's City Club, Detroit 1966; Habatat Galleries, Dearborn 1972, 1974, 1977 (two-person); Creative Arts Gallery, CMU 1973.

Group Exhibitions: *Midwest Designer/Craftsmen*, DIA 1952; MAE 1952, 1953; MACE 1952-54, 1958-64, 1967 (Adler-Schnee Purchase Prize 1967); *MWCS Annual* 1957, 1958; *Octet*, Rackham Gallery, U. of M. 1962; *Craftsmen of the Central States*, Mus Contemp Crafts 1963; *Craftsmen USA*, Milwaukee Art Center 1966; *Michigan Craftsmen's Council Biennial* 1967, 1969, 1971 (Ray Phelps Memorial Prize); *Ceramics Invitational*, EMU 1968, 1969 (Purchase Prize), 1971, 1974.

Collections: Children's Museum, Detroit; Church of the Good Shepherd, Dearborn; EMU; FIA; St. Blaise Parish, Sterling Heights.

Sources: MAR; *CH* 37, 4 (April 1977): 43; *Michigan Challenge* (State Chamber of Commerce) 4, 5 (February 1964): 18.

DAVIDEK, Stefan

(b. Flint, Michigan 1924)

Painter. After early instruction under **Jaroslav Brozik** at the Flint Institute of Arts, Davidek attended the Art Students League in New York City, where he studied with Morris Kantor and Howard Trafton. He returned to Flint in 1947 and was given his first one-person show at the Flint Institute of Arts. Davidek later studied with Fred Mitchell at the Cranbrook Academy of Art (1955). He was one of the first members of the Flint Sculpture Associates/Left Bank Gallery cooperative and has taught at the Flint Institute of Arts, Wayne State University, the Saginaw Art Museum, and at the Haystack Mountain School of Crafts in Maine. Davidek's abstract works are characterized by an emphasis on color and the occasional use of collage elements.

One-person Exhibitions: FIA 1947, 1962; AAA Gallery, Detroit 1958; Left Bank Gallery, Flint 1960; DIA 1962*; Forsythe Gallery, Ann Arbor 1973, 1979.

Group Exhibitions: *Flint Annual*, FIA 1939–76 (1st Prize 1958, 1960, 1961, 1962); *Twenty-Five and Under*, Seligmann Galleries, New York City 1947; MAE 1949-63 (FSPP 1961); *Five Flint Artists*, FIA 1954; *West Michigan Annual*, GRAM 1956, 1957 (Keeler Award), 1960, 1961 (Best of Show), 1967; *Midyear Show*, Butler Institute 1959; *Michigan Art: Yesterday and Today*, FIA 1963; *Contemporary American Watercolors*, GRAM 1963; *2nd Flint Invitational*, FIA 1969*.

Collections: DIA; FIA; HAM; Luke M. Power School, Flint; Mott Children's Clinic, Flint; North Muskegon Community College; St. Luke Catholic Church, Flint.

Sources: *WWAA* 1976; *FJ* 6-15-47, 4-22-50, 11-7-54, 10-1-61, 9-16-62, 3-26-67; *DN* 5-20-61: *AAN* 5-13-73.

DAVIES, John

(b. Kilburnie, Scotland 1901; d. Flint, Michigan 1965)

Painter/Printmaker. Davies received initial training at the Paisley Art Academy in Scotland. He came to the United States in 1923 and studied with Adrian Dornbush at the Flint Institute of Arts, where in 1929 he was the first artist to be given a one-person exhibition. During the Depression, Davies taught painting under the auspices of the Federal Emergency Relief Administration, a forerunner of the Works Progress Administration. One of the founders of the Flint Artists Market, he was also a charter member of the Flint Sculpture Associates/Left Bank Gallery cooperative. From 1949 to 1952, Davies taught at the Flint Institute of Arts, and later taught for both the Mott Foundation and the University of Michigan Extension Service in Flint. Davies worked primarily in watercolor and silkscreen and was well known for landscapes and city scenes. In 1961 he was one of four Flint artists who contributed to a limited edition portfolio of serigraphs issued by the Left Bank Gallery, each depicting a Flint landmark. In 1964 Davies served as president of the Michigan Association of Printmakers.

One-person Exhibitions: FIA 1929, 1936 (two-person), 1950; Left Bank Gallery, Flint 1961, 1964 (two-person), 1970.

Group Exhibitions: *Flint Annual*, FIA 1931–64 (1st Prize in Graphics 1938, 1952, 1956; 1st Prize in Watercolor 1956); MAE 1932–38, 1945, 1954–56, 1960, 1962 (Smith Purchase Prize 1938); *National Exhibition of American Art*, Rockefeller Center 1936; *International Exposition of Etching and Engraving*, AIC 1938; *1st National Exhibition*, GRAM 1940; *Five Flint Artists*, FIA 1954; *Michigan Printmakers Association Biennial* 1962, 1963, 1965; *Mid-Michigan Annual*,

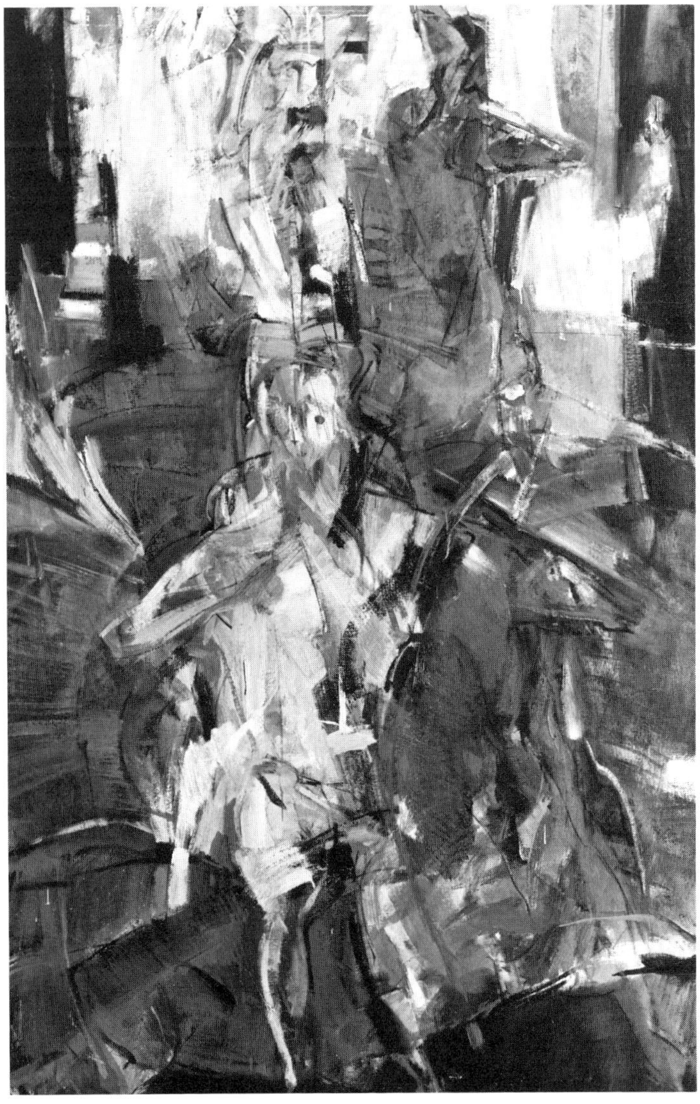

Stefan Davidek (1924–). Rehearsal. *1961. Oil on canvas. 72 × 47¾ inches. Collection of the Detroit Institute of Arts.*

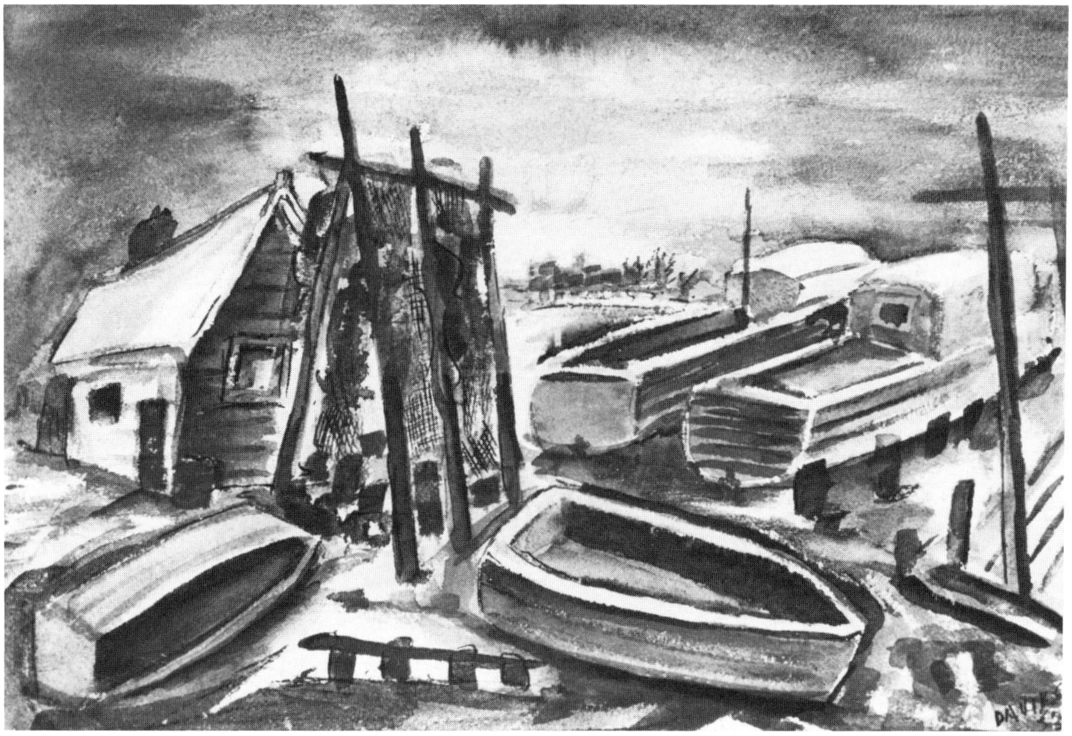

John Davies (1901–1965). Winter Lay-up. *1953. Watercolor. 1st Prize, "Flint Annual," Flint Institute of Arts, 1953. Courtesy the Flint Institute of Arts.*

Midland Art Association 1963 (1st Prize); *Seven Flint Printmakers*, FIA 1963.

Collections: Albion College; DIA; FIA; Flint Public Schools.

Sources: Cook 1963; Kenny 1965; *FJ* 5-10-36, 11-10-36, 3-12-50, 12-27-53, 1-10-56, 3-25-61, 10-20-64, 11-16-65.

DeBLASI, Anthony

(b. Alcamo, Sicily 1933)

Painter. DeBlasi attended the Art Students League in New York City (1957–59), the University of Rhode Island (B.A. 1961), and Indiana University (M.F.A. 1963), where he studied with James McGarrell and Rudy Pozzatti. He joined the faculty at Michigan State University in 1966. DeBlasi's awards include a Louis Comfort Tiffany grant in 1967. His large, color-field paintings are characterized by a solid color ground overlaid with many colors of acrylic paint applied straight from the tube.

One-person Exhibitions: Spectrum Gallery, New York City 1968, 1969, 1971, 1973; DIA 1972*; Albion College 1973 (two-person); Razor Gallery, New York City 1975, 1977.

Group Exhibitions: *Midyear Show*, Butler Institute 1965, 1967; *Michigan Art '67*, BBAA 1967; *National Polymer Exhibition*, EMU 1968; MAE 1969 (Kahn Prize), 1970 (FSPP); DAM 1970, 1971; *All Michigan I*, FIA 1971/72; *Color Directions*, BBAA 1972; *Corcoran Biennial* 1973*; *Full Spectrum*, Michigan Artrain 1978*; *Michigan Artists 80/81: Southwest Region*, GRAM 1980.

Collections: City National Bank, Detroit; DIA; Houston Museum of Fine Arts; Riverside Museum, New York City; Wichita State University.

Sources: *WWAA* 1980; MAR; *Art Forum* 6, 8 (April 1968): 61; *Art Invitational* 14, 1 (January 1970): 87; *Art News* 62, 2 (April 1968): 10; *Art News* 70, 1 (March 1971): 16; *Arts Mag* 42, 6 (April 1968): 65; *Arts Mag* 44, 3 (December–January 1969/70): 57; *Arts Mag* 50, 5 (January 1976): 19.

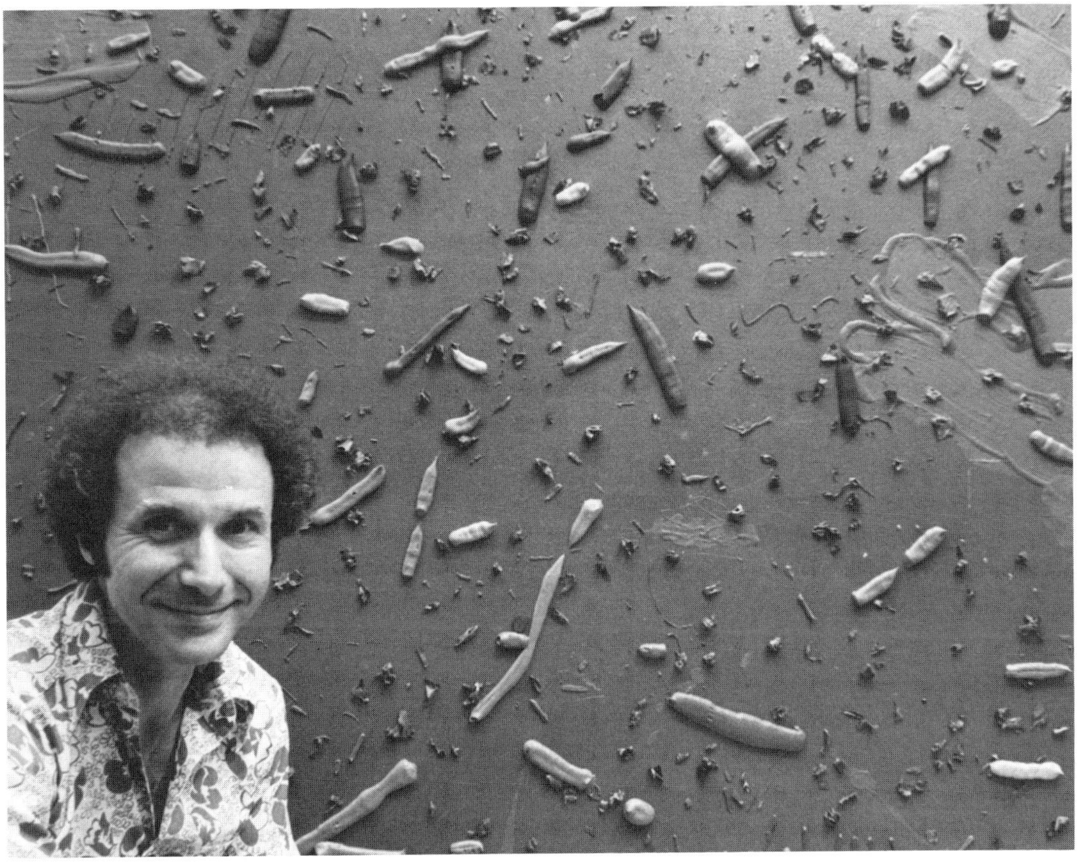

Anthony DeBlasi (1933–) with one of his works. Courtesy the artist.

DECKER, Lindsey

(b. Lincoln, Nebraska 1923)

Sculptor. Decker attended Iowa State Teachers College (1941–42) and the American Academy of Art in Chicago (1942–43) before receiving a B.F.A. (1948) and an M.F.A. (1950) from the State University of Iowa. Following graduation, he joined the faculty at Michigan State University (1950–62). In 1957 he was commissioned by the J. L. Hudson Company to create two sculptural works—a fountain and a wall-screen—for the Eastland Center shopping mall in Harper Woods. The recipient of both a Fulbright Fellowship and a grant from the Italian government, Decker studied for two years in Italy (1957–59). The works Decker created while in Michigan are typically welded metal abstract forms with titles that often refer to the processes of regeneration and reproduction, growth and decay. He left Michigan in 1962.

One-person Exhibitions. KIA 1956; Zabriskie Gallery, New York City 1959*, 1962*; *São Paulo Biennial*, Brazil 1963; Prince Street Gallery, New York City 1969.

Group Exhibition: MAE 1948, 1950, 1952–53, 1955, 1956 (FSPP), 1959, 1961; *Momentum*, AIC 1950–52; Philadelphia Art Alliance 1954; *American Sculpture, Watercolor, and Drawing*, Whitney 1956; *Four American Sculptors*, American Embassy, Rome 1959; *Recent Sculpture USA*, MOMA 1959; *Ten Americans*, Palazzo Venezia, Rome 1959; *Business Buys American Art*, Whitney 1960; *Contemporary Sculpture*, American Federation of the Arts, New York City 1960; *Midwest Sculpture*, Cincinnati Art Museum 1960; *PAFA Annual* 1960; *American Sculpture and Drawing*, Whitney 1960, 1962, 1964; *Michigan Art: Yesterday and Today*, FIA 1963; *Ten American Sculptors*, Walker Art Center, Minneapolis 1963; *American Sculpture 1900–1965*, FIA 1965; *New Talent*, American Federation of the Arts, New York City 1967.

Collections: Albion College; CAAM; DIA; Kresge Art Center Gallery, MSU.

Sources: *WWAA* 1980; Cummings 1977; *Art News* 60 (February 1962): 53; *Arts* 36 (March 1922): 54; *Arts* 24 (May 1960): 60; *Kalamazoo Gazette* 2-4-56, 2-12-56; *DN* 5-17-59; *NYT* 2-4-62.

Hart Benton, took a position as an instructor of graphics and illustration at the Kansas City Art Institute. Benton's influence on DeMartelly can be seen in his works on the subject of rural Midwest life. Like Benton, DeMartelly developed his egg tempera paintings from a three-dimensional plastilene model. During the late 1930s and early 1940s, he began doing etchings for book illustrations, including *Green Mansions* by W. H. Hudson (New York: Peter Pauper Press, 1943). After leaving Missouri, DeMartelly lived briefly (1940–43) in New Hampshire.

He came to Michigan State University in 1943 to teach lithography and drawing and was appointed artist-in-residence in 1946, remaining on the faculty until his death in 1979. He also taught part-time at the Flint Institute of Arts and served as a visiting artist (1954–59) at the Cranbrook Academy of Art. Eventually he moved away from American Scene (regionalist) subject matter, which gave him new freedom to experiment in many media, including pastel, lithography, and oil. In lithography, which remained his prime interest, he developed "indenture," a technique for achieving subtle tonal qualities, and by the mid-1950s was working almost completely in this medium. Throughout his Michigan career, DeMartelly worked in a figurative vein, except for a brief abstract period in the mid-1950s through the 1960s.

One-person Exhibitions: Little Gallery, Birmingham 1958; Midland Art Association, Dow Memorial Library 1964 (two-person); Kresge Art Center Gallery, MSU 1970 (retrospective)*; HAM 1971; GRAM 1974.

Group Exhibitions: *National Exhibition of American Art*, Rockefeller Center 1936; *American Painting and Sculpture*, AIC 1936, 1940–41; *Midwestern Artists*, Kansas City Art Institute, Mo. 1937 (Lighton Prize and 1st Prize, Graphic Arts); *Fifty Prints of the Year*, American Institute of Graphic Arts, New York City 1938*; *Paintings by Artists West of the Mississippi*, Whitney 1938; *American Painting Today*, American Federation of Arts, Washington, D.C. 1939 (traveling); *Contemporary American Sculpture, Drawing and Prints*, Whitney 1939; New York World's Fair, 1939; *Golden Gate Exposition*, San Francisco 1939/40; *International Exhibition of Lithography and Wood Engravings*, AIA 1939–40; *PAFA Annual* 1940–41; *Contemporary American Sculpture, Watercolor, Drawing and Prints*, Whitney 1941; *Artists for Victory*, MMA 1943; *Painting in the U.S.*, Carnegie Institute 1943–46; MAE 1944–45, 1954, 1959 (Jackson Memorial Prize), 1960; *Michigan on Canvas*, J. L. Hudson Gallery, Detroit 1948*; *Midwestern Printmakers*, 1020 Art Center, Chicago 1956 (traveling); *Midwestern University Printmakers*, University of Kansas Museum of Art, Lawrence 1958.

Collections: Bezalet National Museum, Jerusalem; Capitol Savings & Loan, Okemos; Carnegie Institute; CAAM; Encyclopaedia Britannica, Chicago; KIA; MMA; Kresge Art Center, MSU; Tel Aviv Museum; Victoria & Albert Museum; Whitney.

Sources: AAA N86, N100A, John DeMartelly Papers; MAR; Young 1968; Thomas Craven, ed., *A Treasury of American Prints*, New York: Simon and Schuster, 1939; Grace Pagano, ed., *Contemporary American Painting*, New York: Duell, Sloan, & Pearce, 1945; DeMartelly in *Am Artist* 5, 3 (March 1941): 4–9; *Art Dig* 10, 19 (August 1, 1936): 13; *Art Dig* 13, 4 (November 15, 1938): 17; *Art Dig* 13, 17 (June 1, 1939): 25; *Coronet* April 1940; *Life* January 5, 1943; *NYT Book Review* October 6, 1946; *Saturday Review of Literature* February 17, 1940; *The Studio* 129 (June 1945): 198; *NYT* 4-29-41.

DeVORE, Richard

(b. Toledo, Ohio 1933)

Ceramicist. DeVore received a B.E. (1955) from the University of Toledo and an M.F.A. (1957) from the Cranbrook Academy of Art, where he studied under **Maija Grotell**. He established the ceramics program at Flint Junior College, where he taught for nine years before being chosen by Grotell to succeed her as head of the Cranbrook ceramics department in 1966. DeVore received a National Endowment for the Arts grant in 1976, and in 1979 his work was included in the exhibition "A Century of Ceramics in the United States," organized by the Everson Museum of Art in Syracuse, New York. While in Michigan, DeVore established himself as a significant force in contemporary ceramics. Like his mentor, Maija Grotell, his approach stresses aesthetics before practicality. His simple, nonfunctional vessels are characterized by subtly distorted asymmetrical forms with soft matte surfaces. DeVore left Michigan in 1978 to join the faculty of Colorado State University.

One-person Exhibitions: Yaw Gallery, Birmingham, 1971, 1972, 1975, 1978; CAAM 1974; Gallery of American Ceramics, Evanston, Ill. 1974 (two-person), 1975, 1979; Braunstein-Quay Gallery, San Francisco 1976; Drutt Gallery, Philadelphia 1976; Fendrick Gallery, Washington, D.C. 1977; Freudenheim Gallery, Buffalo 1978.

Group Exhibitions: *Ceramic National*, Everson Museum of Art, Syracuse 1954, 1958, 1960, 1962, 1966, 1968; MACE 1956–64, 1966–69, 1971 (Artisans Prize 1964, Michigan Potters' Association Prize 1966, 1971);

Decorative Arts and Ceramics Exhibition, Wichita Art Association, Kans. 1957–60, 1966, 1972; *Midyear Show*, Butler Institute 1957–63, 1965–67; *Young Americans*, Mus Contemp Crafts 1962; *Michigan Art: Yesterday and Today*, FIA 1963; *International Exhibition of Ceramic Art*, Smithsonian Institution 1965; *Craftsmen USA*, Mus Contemp Crafts 1966; *Ceramics Invitational*, EMU 1966, 1968–69, 1971–74; *Objects: USA*, Johnson Wax Collection Touring Show 1969/70*; *International Ceramics '77*, Victoria and Albert Museum 1972; *Beaux-Arts Designer/Craftsmen*, Columbus Museum of Art 1975; *Crafts National*, Marietta College, Ohio 1975; *American Crafts: An Aesthetic View*, Mus Contemp Crafts 1976*; *Concorso Internazionale della Arte Ceramica*, Faenza, Italy 1976; *Michigan Collects Michigan Art*, Pontiac Creative Arts Center 1976; *Michigan Crafts Exhibition*, DIA 1976*; *Contemporary Ceramics: The Artist's Viewpoint*, KIA 1977*; *A Century of Ceramics in the United States*, Everson Museum of Art, Syracuse 1979 (traveling)*.

Collections: Butler Institute; CAAM; Delaware Art Museum; Denver Art Museum; FIA; Joslyn Art Museum, Omaha; Kohler Collection of Contemporary Ceramics, Sheboygan, Wis.; Milwaukee Art Museum; Mus of Contemp Crafts; Philadelphia Museum of Art; St. Louis Art Museum; Utah Museum of Fine Arts.

Sources: MAR; *Art in America* 68, 7 (September 1980): 130–131; *CH* 33, 5 (October 1973): 46: *CH* 34, 2 (April 1974): 54; *CH* 35, 3 (June 1975): 20; *CMo* 23, 1 (January 1975): 35–37; *Philadelphia Arts Exchange* 1, 2 (March/April 1977): 50; *BEcc* 4-27-75; *DFP* 4-27-75, 1-22-78; *DN* 7-11-76, 1-22-78; *Chicago Tribune* 7-19-76.

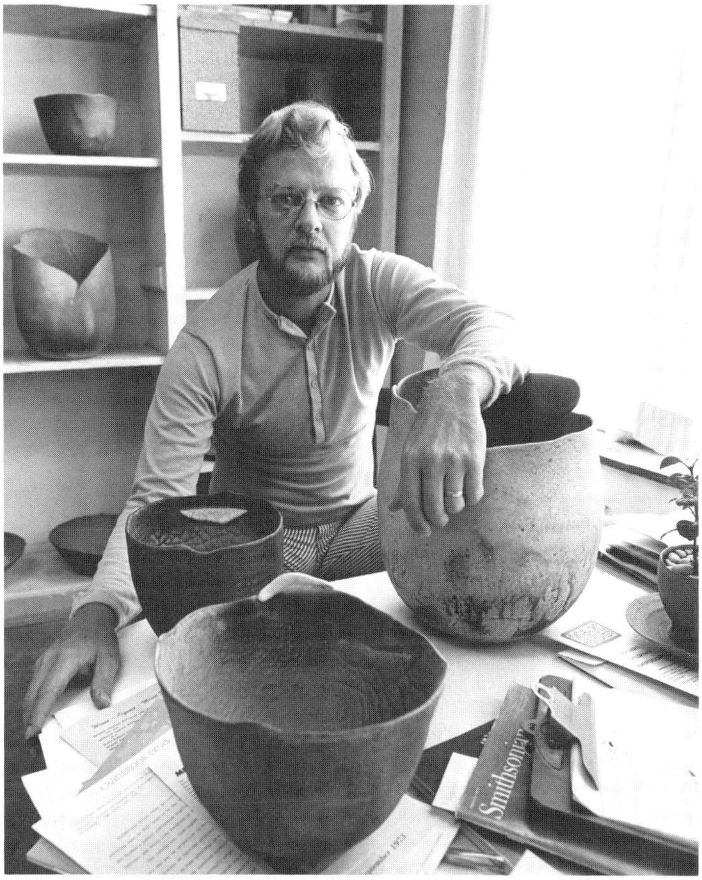

Richard DeVore (1933–) in his office at Cranbrook. Robert Vigiletti, Photographer.

DIEBBOLL, Robert

(b. Grosse Pointe Park, Michigan 1920)

Ceramicist. Diebboll attended Cass Technical High School and Wayne State University and also studied painting with **John Carroll** and **Sarkis Sarkisian** at the Art School of the Detroit Society of Arts and Crafts. He began to study ceramics with **John Foster** in 1948 while teaching at the DSAC and later took instruction with potters Bernard Leach and Shoji Hamada. Employed by the General Motors Styling Division for over twenty-five years, Diebboll also owns and operates the Pines End Pottery in Washington, Michigan. His high-fired stoneware and salt-glazed ceramics are characterized by classic shapes and calligraphically painted surfaces.

One-person Exhibitions: DAM 1949; Women's City Club, Detroit 1949; Pewabic Pottery, Detroit 1974.

Group Exhibitions: MACE 1949–56, 1958, 1960-64, 1966, 1967, 1971 (Webber Prize 1951, Haass Prize 1952, Michigan Potters' Association Prize 1961, 1963, 1964); J. L. Hudson Company, Detroit 1951; *Ceramic National*, Everson Museum of Art, Syracuse 1951–52, 1961, 1965; *Michigan Craftsmen's Council Biennial* 1962; *Sixteen Michigan Ceramicists*, Cranbrook 1967.

Collection: DIA.

Sources: MAR; *Michigan Challenge* (State Chamber of Commerce) 4, 5 (February 1964): 38; *DN* 5-18-41, 1-18-49, 10-30-49; *DFP* 9-18-49.

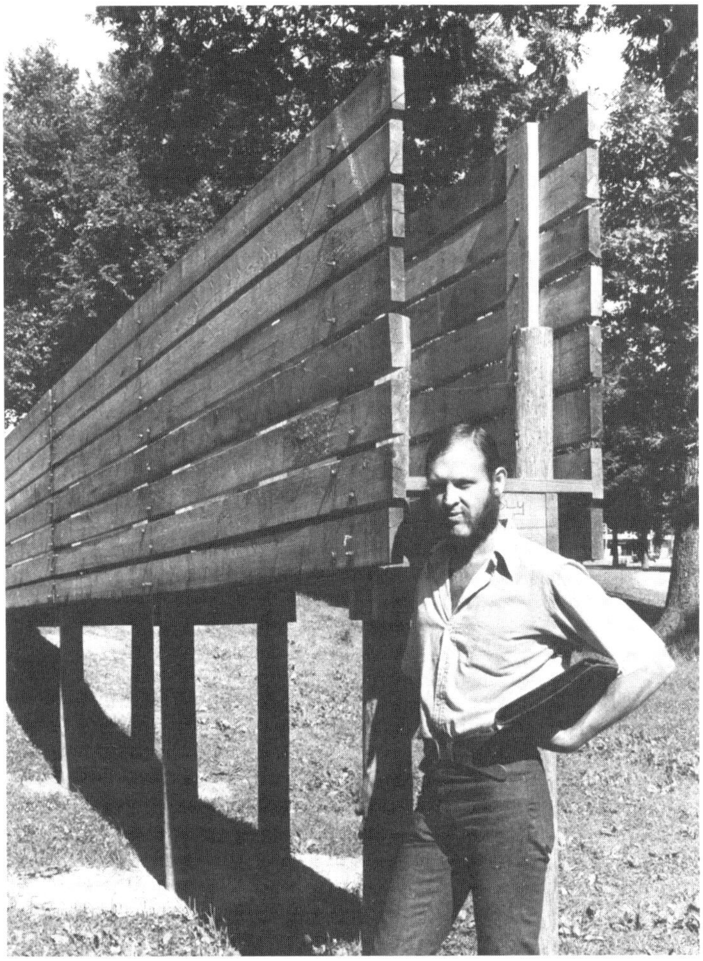

Stan Dolega (1942–) with his sculpture in Clark Park. Courtesy the Detroit News.

DOLEGA, *Stan*

(b. Detroit, Michigan 1942)

Sculptor. Educated at Michigan State University (B.F.A. 1965) and Wayne State University (M.F.A. 1968), Dolega is an environmental sculptor whose works are installed in several public locations in Detroit. These include a metal sculpture on Belle Isle, commissioned by New Detroit, Inc., in 1972, an earthwork play sculpture, also on Belle Isle, and a wooden "bridge" sculpture for Clark Park (1975), both commissioned by the City of Detroit's Department of Parks and Recreation. Dolega has taught at Wayne State University (1960–70) and Wayne County Community College (1974–76) and served as an artist-in-residence at the Oxbow Summer School of Art in Saugatuck (1976). Actively involved in the establishment of the Willis Gallery, Dolega was one of the first artists to set up a studio at Common Ground of the Arts; he has also served as president of the latter group. In 1975 he received a National Endowment for the Arts sculpture fellowship. Dolega moved to Wyoming in 1978.

One-person Exhibitions: Willis Gallery, Detroit 1971 (three-person), 1974, 1976.

Group Exhibitions: *Nine Detroit Artists*, Scarab Club, Detroit 1967; *Common Ground of the Arts*, Scarab Club 1968 (Award); First Federal Building, Detroit 1968; *Michigan Sculpture '68*, MCA 1968; *Common Ground of the Arts*, DAM 1969; MAE 1969–70, 1972; *Festival 70*, Grand Rapids 1970 (1st Prize); *Common Ground of the Arts*, SAM 1973; *Forsythe Saga*, Forsythe Building, Detroit 1973; *Detroit Artists Invitational*, Detroit Bank & Trust Co. 1974*; *Sculpture for a New Era*, Chicago Federal Center 1975; *Sculpture Inside and Out*, School of Art, U. of M. 1975; *Common Grounds of the Arts 10th Anniversary Exhibition*, DAM 1976; *From the Bottom Up: 12 Contemporary Michigan Sculptors*, City of East Lansing 1976; *Works in Progress II*, DIA 1976*; *Michigan Sculpture '77*, Macomb County Community College 1977; *Kick Out the Jams*, DIA 1980*.

Collections: City of Detroit; Federal Building, Wenatchee, Wash.; Oxbow Summer School of Painting, Saugatuck; WSU.

Sources: MAR: Nawrocki 1980; *Detroit Artists Monthly* 3, 5 (May 1978): 4–7; *Michigan Art Journal* 1, 2 (April 1976): 15–17; *DN* 1-20-74, 9-17-74, 10-19-75 (Sunday Magazine), 10-17-76, 6-29-80; *DFP* 5-10-76, 6-11-76 (Sunday Magazine).

DONER, *Michele Oka*

(b. Miami Beach, Florida 1945)

Sculptor. Doner received a B.S.D. (1966) and an M.F.A. (1968) from the University of Michigan, where she studied under **John Stephenson**. She did postgraduate work in lithography with **Aris Koutroulis** at Wayne State University (1972). Doner works primarily in clay, recreating such natural forms as animal skulls, human pelvises, and seed pods that address the themes of birth, death, regeneration, and decay.

One-person Exhibitions: Forsythe Gallery, Ann Arbor 1968 (two-person); Gertrude Kasle Gallery, Detroit 1971 (two-person)*; Gallery 7, Detroit 1976; *Works in Progress IV*, DIA 1978*.

Group Exhibitions: *Wichita National*, Wichita Art Association, Kans. 1966; MACE 1966, 1967 (Malbin

Prize), 1969 (Michigan Potters' Association Prize); *Michigan Craftsmen's Council Biennial* 1967 (Ceramics Prize); *16 Michigan Ceramicists*, Cranbrook 1967; DAM 1968; *Ceramics Invitational*, EMU 1968, 1971, 1977; *Objects: USA*, Johnson Wax Collection Touring Show 1969/70*; MAE 1970; *All Michigan I*, FIA 1971/72; *45 Contemporary Sculptors*, Geijutsu Shincho, Tokyo 1973; *The Plastic Earth: National Ceramics Invitational*, Kohler Arts Center, Sheboygan, Wis. 1973; *Womanart*, SAM 1974*; *Michigan Focus*, DIA 1974/75; *Dolls and Other Effigies*, Kohler Arts Center, Sheboygan, Wis. 1975; *Michigan Crafts Exhibition*, DIA 1976*; *Michigan Collects Michigan Art*, Pontiac Creative Arts Center 1977; *Image & Object in Contemporary Sculpture*, DIA 1979.

Collections: DIA; Johnson Wax Collection of Contemporary Crafts, Racine, Wis.; Kohler Collection of Contemporary Ceramics, Sheyboygan, Wis.; Mus of Contemp Crafts; Steelcase Collection of Contemporary Art, Grand Rapids.

Sources: *WWAA* 1980; MAR; *CH* 27, 2 (March/April 1967): 51–52; *CH* 27, 3 (May/June 1967): 69; *CH* 28, 1 (January/February 1968): 40; *La Revue Moderne*, June 1, 1969, pp. 28–29; *Michigan Art Journal* 1, 1 (January 1976): 22; *Michigan Challenge* (State Chamber of Commerce) 16, 1 (January/February 1976): 9, 21; *Financial Times* (London) 8-30-73; *DN* 1-2-76; *DFP* 6-11-76; *NYT* 1-11-80.

DOUGLAS, *Murray*

(b. Syracuse, New York 1915)

Ceramicist. Douglas received a B.S. (1936) from Wayne State University and an M.A. (1940) and Ph.D. (1956) from Ohio State University. He also studied with **Mary Chase Stratton**; at the Cranbrook Academy of Art; and in Paris. He taught at the Brookside School, Cranbrook, from 1936–50. In 1950 he joined the faculty of Wayne State University and in 1962 became chairman of the art education department. Douglas has been active in the Michigan Potters' Association and has participated in numerous lecture/demonstrations on contemporary design. In 1955 he became the third potter to win the Founders Society Purchase Prize in the "Exhibition for Michigan Artist-Craftsmen." He was awarded the Distinguished Achievement Award at the Wayne State University Centennial Celebration in 1975.

One-person Exhibitions: Eastern Illinois State Teachers College; Ohio State University 1956.

Group Exhibitions: *Ceramic National*, Everson Museum of Art, Syracuse 1939–40, 1946–47, 1949–51, 1954, 1956, 1958; MACE 1948–64 (Heavenrich Prize 1953, FSPP 1955); *National Exhibition of Contemporary Textiles and Ceramics*, Cranbrook 1951; *Craftsmen USA*, Brooklyn Museum 1953; *American Exhibition*, International House, Tokyo 1955; *Michigan Academy of Science, Arts and Letters Annual* 1957*.

Collections: DIA; Eastern Illinois University; Everson Museum of Art, Syracuse; International House, Tokyo.

Sources: MAR; *Who's Who in America* 1972; *Am Artist* 12 (February 1948): 31; *Michigan Challenge* (State Chamber of Commerce) 4, 5 (February 1964): 11; *DFP* 7-18-48; *DN* 7-18-48.

DRAPCE, *Nora*

(b. Daugavpils, Latvia 1886; d. Kalamazoo, Michigan 1968)

Painter. Drapce graduated from the Riga Municipal Art School (later the State Academy of Art) in Latvia, then received a fellowship from the Latvian Culture Fund to study in France and Germany. She emigrated to Kalamazoo in 1950 and joined the staff at the Kalamazoo Institute of Arts as artist-in-residence (1950–62). Her early work was primarily in portraiture. She later turned to landscape in works that explore color and atmospheric effects.

One-person Exhibitions: KIA 1950, 1951 (four-person), 1954 (three-person), 1957, 1962, 1969 (retrospective); Baransky Galleries, New York City 1958*; The Maryland Institute, Baltimore 1964.

Group Exhibitions: MAE 1953, 1956.

Collection: KIA.

Sources: *KIA Bulletin* 5 (September 1962): n.p; *KIA Bulletin* 16 (April 1965): n.p.; *KG* 10-22-50, 10-23-50, 10-29-50, 9-19-62, 6-19-66, 5-7-67, 12-29-68, 1-5-69.

DUNITZ, *Dorothy*

(b. Detroit, Michigan 1919)

Ceramicist. Dunitz was educated at Wayne State University (1936–37) and at the Art School of the Detroit Society of Arts and Crafts. Her slab porcelain vases and wheel-thrown plates are nonfunctional pieces that allude to landscape images. She is a member of the Michigan Potters' Association.

One-person Exhibitions: Claire Pearone, Somerset Mall, Troy 1974 (two-person); Elephant Walk Gallery,

Pittsburgh 1976; *Four Artists*, Gallery 555, Birmingham 1976.

Group Exhibitions: MACE 1964, 1971/72 (Artisans Purchase Prize; Webber Prize); *Michigan Craftsmen's Council Biennial* 1967, 1969; *Salute to the Detroit Artists Market*, J. L. Hudson Gallery, Detroit 1967–72; *Michigan Artist-Craftsmen*, GRAM 1970 (Award), 1972; *Michigan '71*, Midland Art Association 1971; *Michigan Potters' Association Annual* 1971–72; *Crafts National*, Marietta College, Ohio 1976, 1979; *Arts and Crafts in Detroit 1906–1976*, DIA 1976*; *Objects '76*, BBAA 1976; Robert Kidd Associates, Birmingham 1976; *Michigan Ceramics '78*, Pewabic Pottery, Detroit 1978.

Collections: Ford & Earl Design Associates, Warren; Ford Motor Company Headquarters, Dearborn; Lannan Foundation, Palm Beach; Mary McFadden, Inc., New York City; Saks Fifth Avenue Executive Offices, New York City; UMMA.

Sources: MAR; *CH* 31, 2 (April 1972): 52; *CH* 33, 3 (June 1974): 76; *CH* 35, 1 (February 1976): 65; *Vogue Magazine* December 1977, *BEcc* 12-3-71; 3-14-74, 3-28-74, 5-2-76; *DN* 12-5-71, 10-3-76.

EARLE, *Lawrence Carmichael*

(b. New York, New York 1845; d. Grand Rapids, Michigan 1921)

Painter. Earle was raised in Grand Rapids, where his first art lessons were from local artist Marinus Hartung. He studied briefly in New York (1866) before undertaking further studies with Walter Shirlaw in Chicago. At Shirlaw's suggestion, Earle entered the Royal Academy in Munich, where he studied with Ludwig Barth and Franz Wagner. After returning from Europe in 1881, he set up a studio in New Jersey. In 1887 he was made an associate of the National Academy of Design. He returned to Grand Rapids in 1909, after the death of his wife, and soon became active in local art circles. He was a founding member of the Grand Rapids Art Association. Primarily a portraitist (several prominent Grand Rapids citizens sat for him),

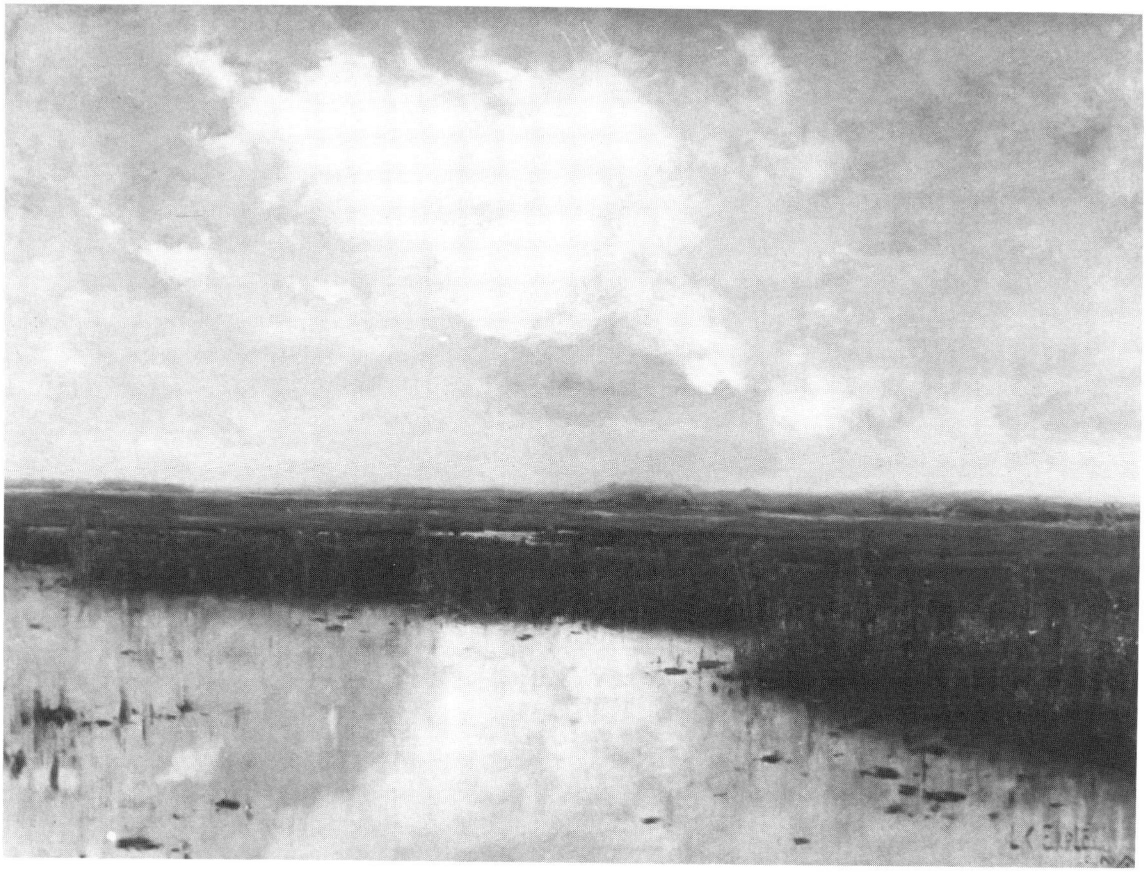

Lawrence Carmichael Earle (1845–1921). Marsh. *Oil on canvas. 35½ × 49 inches. Private Collection.*

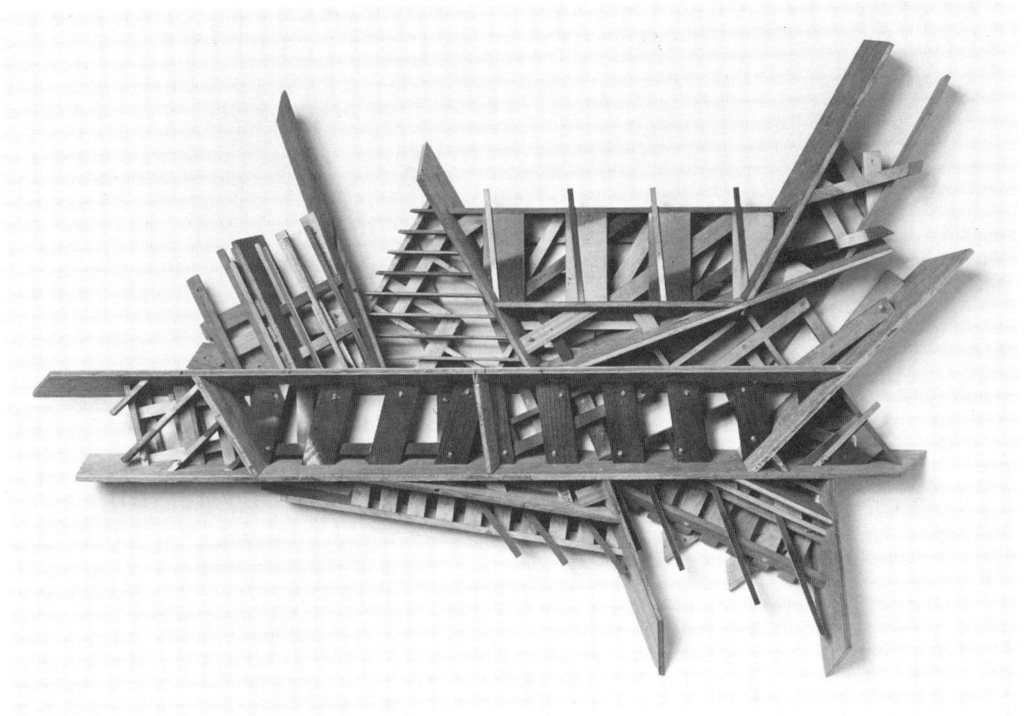

John Egner (1940–). Interceptor. *1977. Spray paint on wood. 27 × 41 × 2½ inches. Collection of Beverly and Norman L. Lippitt, Michigan. The Detroit Institute of Arts, Department of Twentieth-Century Art.*

Earle was also known for his still lifes and genre scenes. Although Earle also worked in watercolor, most of his paintings are in oil, with the painterly brushwork and heavy impasto that is characteristic of the Munich school.

One-person Exhibitions: DMA 1909; Grand Rapids Art Association 1910, 1913, 1929.

Group Exhibitions: *Art Loan Exhibition*, Detroit 1883; *Annual Exhibition*, National Academy of Design, New York City 1888, 1890–92, 1894–99, 1900; *American Painting and Sculpture*, AIC 1901, 1909, 1915; MAE 1913; *Artists of Grand Rapids 1840–1980*, GRAM and Grand Rapids Public Museum 1981*.

Collections: AIC; Butterworth Hospital, Grand Rapids; Chicago National Bank; GRAM.

Sources: *American Art Annual* 1921; Bénézit 1976; Gibson 1975; Fielding 1974; *DMA Bulletin* 3, 3 (July 1909): 36; *GR Herald* 3-2-13; *GR Press* 3-5-13, 11-21-21.

EGNER, John

(b. Philadelphia, Pennsylvania 1940)

Painter/Sculptor. Egner was educated at the Philadelphia College of Art (B.F.A. 1963) and at Yale University (M.F.A. 1966), where he studied with Frank Stella and Jack Tworkov. He joined the faculty at Wayne State University in 1966. An influential member of the original Cass Corridor art community, Egner was one of the founders of the Willis Gallery. He has also been a visiting artist at Albion College and Oakland University. In 1974 he completed a 96′ × 36′ mural, commissioned by Detroit Renaissance, on the exterior of the Park Shelton Hotel in Detroit. One of Egner's consistent concerns as a painter has been with the limitations of the rectilinear picture plane. He has used various methods to modify the flat surface, including cutting the canvas to fit the flow of the paint; building up a domed surface of poured enamel; and, dispensing with the canvas entirely, constructing spray-painted wooden reliefs composed of layers of grids. His most recent works are large-scale, brightly colored abstract paintings in a hard-edge style reminiscent of his mentor, Frank Stella.

One-person Exhibitions: Willis Gallery, Detroit 1971, 1972.

Group Exhibitions: *Forsythe Saga*, Forsythe Building, Detroit 1973; *All Michigan II*, FIA 1973/74; *Detroit Art Today—Diverse Directions*, School of Art, U. of M. 1974; *Detroit Artists Invitational*, Detroit Bank & Trust Co. 1974; *Michigan Focus*, DIA 1974/75; *Antonow, Egner, Faust, Newton*, Willis Gallery, Detroit 1975; *Michigan Artists Biennial*, Kresge Art Center Gallery, MSU 1975; *Michigan Collects Michigan Art*, Pontiac Creative Arts Center 1976; *Michigan Crafts Exhibition*, DIA 1976*; *Works in Progress II*, DIA 1976; *Michigan Sculpture '77*, Macomb County Community College 1977; *Young Americans*, Exxon National Exhibition, Guggenheim Museum 1978*; *At Cranbrook: Downtown Detroit—Twenty-One Artists*, CAAM 1979; *Kick Out the Jams*, DIA 1980*.

Collections: Guggenheim Museum; Park Shelton Hotel, Detroit.

Sources: AAA, Interview; MAR; Nawrocki 1980; *Arts Mag* 52, 6 (February 1978): 140; *Detroit Artists Monthly* 2, 8 (October 1977): 3; *DFP* 11-7-71, 8-4-74, 10-6-74, 7-20-75, 11-6-77, 6-4-68, 5-4-80; *DN* 6-30-74, 11-24-74, 9-2-75, 10-30-77.

ENGSTROM, *Audrey*

(b. Lansing, Michigan 1930)

Metalsmith. Engstrom received a B.A. (1951) from Michigan State University. Trained as a dancer, she became involved first in ceramics and then in metalwork following her marriage to **Robert Engstrom**. From 1961 to 1966 she taught enameling and jewelry-making at the Kalamazoo Institute of Arts. In 1967 she and her husband traveled throughout Scandinavia, conducting research for a proposed book on ancient and modern Scandinavian jewelry. They pursued this project further during a one-year's stay in Oslo in 1969.

One-person Exhibitions (with Robert Engstrom): *Works in Progress*, HAM 1954; GRAM 1959; America House, Birmingham 1968.

Group Exhibitions: MACE 1954–64; *West Michigan Annual*, GRAM 1955–62 (Award for Three-Dimensional Design 1955, 1958); *Contemporary Religious Art*, GRAM 1956; *Fiber/Clay/Metal*, Minnesota Museum of Art 1957, 1959 (Honorable Mention), 1962, 1964 (First Prize in Jewelry); *Decorative Arts and Ceramics Exhibition*, Wichita Art Association, Kans. 1961; *Partners in the Arts*, DAM 1961; *American Jewelry*, Mus Contemp Crafts, 1963; *Michigan Art: Yesterday and Today*, FIA 1963; *Traveling Show of American Crafts*, USIA 1964/66; *Regional Exhibition*, HAM 1965 (Honorable Mention); *Metal Arts Guild Exhibition*, KIA 1977.

Sources: MAR; Polly Rothenburg, *Metal Enameling*, New York: Crown, 1969; Philip Morton, *Contemporary Jewelry*, New York: Holt, Rinehart & Winston, 1970; *CH* 22, 2 (March/April 1962): 25.

ENGSTROM, *Robert H.*

(b. Grand Rapids, Michigan 1922)

Metalsmith. Engstrom received a B.A. (1947) and an M.A. (1952) from Michigan State University, then undertook additional training at the State University of New York at Alfred. He began his career as a potter—he and his wife **Audrey Engstrom** maintained a studio and kiln for four years (1952–56) in Sparta—but soon turned to metalwork. He and Audrey devised a product called *Jet-line Black* for use in the enameling process, and in 1957 he created an enameled copper mural and fireplace screen for the former Win Shuler's Restaurant in Grand Rapids (destroyed in 1977). In 1957 Engstrom joined the faculty at Western Michigan University and in 1961 set up a metalwork studio and began giving classes at the Kalamazoo Institute of Arts. He has also completed a mural, pool, and fountain for the student center at Central Michigan University, a cloisonné cross and candle sticks for the Westwood United Methodist Church in Kalamazoo, and an enameled baptismal font for St. John's Episcopal Church in Sturgis.

One-person Exhibitions (with Audrey Engstrom): *Works in Progress*, HAM 1954; GRAM 1959; America House, Birmingham 1968.

Group Exhibitions: MACE 1954–64, 1967 (Honorable Mention 1963, Weiner Prize 1967); *West Michigan Annual*, GRAM 1954–58, 1961 (First Prize in Ceramics 1954, First Prize for Three-Dimensional Design 1956); *Fiber/Clay/Metal*, Minnesota Museum of Art, 1957, 1959; *Decorative Arts and Ceramics Exhibition*, Wichita Art Association, Kans. 1961; *Partners in the Arts*, DAM 1961; *American Jewelry*, Mus Contemp Crafts 1963; *Michigan Art: Yesterday and Today*, FIA 1963; *Regional Exhibition*, HAM 1965 (Honorable Mention); *Uncommon Smiths of America*, EMU 1975.

Sources: MAR; Polly Rothenburg, *Metal Enameling*, New York: Crown, 1969; Philip Morton, *Contemporary Jewelry*, New York: Holt, Rinehart & Winston, 1970; *CH* 19, 3 (May/June 1959): 28; *CH* 22, 2 (March/April 1962): 31.

ETTL, George

(b. Nittenau, Germany 1940)

Sculptor. Ettl came to the United States from Germany in 1959 and worked as a toolmaker and design apprentice from 1960 to 1966. He attended Wayne State University and by 1969 had received B.A., M.A., and M.F.A. degrees, after spending a year (1968–69) researching Romanesque sculpture in France, Germany, Switzerland, and Italy. From 1966 to 1974 he was on the faculty of Macomb County Community College. He was affiliated with the Willis Gallery group in the Cass Corridor. Ettl's sparse, geometric sculptures combine stone, wood, and other elements with colored plexiglass. He returned to Germany in 1974.

One-person Exhibitions: Birmingham Gallery, 1968; Franklin Siden Gallery (at Common Ground of the Arts), Detroit 1971; PAFA 1971 (two-person); Willis Gallery, Detroit 1972; Sill Gallery, EMU 1973.

Group Exhibitions: MAE 1966, 1971 (Museum Collection Purchase Prize); *Annual Drawing and Sculpture Show*, Ball State University 1967; *Michigan Sculptors*, BBAA 1967 (First Prize); *Midwest Sculpture Show*, Waupin, Wis. 1967 (Honorable Mention); *Michigan Sculpture '68*, MCA 1968 (traveling); *Common Ground*, DAM 1969 (Sculpture Award); *Other Ideas*, DIA 1969*; *Plastic Image*, BBAA 1970; *All Michigan I*, FIA 1971/72 (Purchase Prize); *The Forsythe Saga*, Forsythe Building, Detroit 1973; *Kick Out the Jams*, DIA 1980*.

Collections/Commissions: American Federal Savings, Southfield; American Office Plaza, Courtyard, Southfield; DIA; Holtzman-Silverman Company, Southfield.

Sources: Nawrocki 1980; *DN* 3-21-71, 10-15-72; *DFP* 10-15-72, 8-4-74.

FAIRBANKS, Avard

(b. Provo, Utah 1897)

Sculptor. The son and brother of well-known artists, Fairbanks began modeling at the age of twelve. Encouraged by his family, he joined his father, John B. Fairbanks, in New York City, where he began copying sculpture at the Metropolitan Museum of Art. The youngest scholarship student at the Art Students League, where he studied under James E. Fraser (1910–12), his first public acclaim was received at the age of fourteen when two of his pieces were exhibited at the National Academy of Design. He undertook additional studies in Paris (1913) at the École Nationale des Beaux-Arts under Jean-Antoine Injalbert, and at the Académie Colarossi, the École de la Grande Chaumière, and the École Moderne. He received a B.F.A. (1925) from Yale University; an M.F.A. (1929) from the University of Washington; and an M.A. (1933) and Ph.D. in Anatomy (1936) from the University of Michigan Medical School. He taught at the University of Oregon (1920–27); was the recipient of a Guggenheim fellowship for study in Florence under Dante Sodini (1927–28); and taught at the Seattle Institute of Arts, (1928).

From 1929 to 1947 Fairbanks taught at the University of Michigan, and also lectured statewide through the university's extension service. He also was actively involved with numerous commissions for public sculpture and fountains throughout the United States. Later a dean of the College of Fine Arts at the University of Utah (1947) (becoming professor emeritus in 1965), he subsequently taught at the University of North Dakota for two years before returning to Salt Lake City in 1968 to resume full-time sculpting.

Recognized for his many monuments of Abraham Lincoln and other historic figures, he has also modeled portraits of many prominent persons in universities, industry, medicine, and government, and has designed medals and awards for many societies and businesses, and automobile ornaments for the car industry.

Fairbanks is a fellow of the National Sculpture Society, a member of the Architectural League of New York, the International Institute of Arts and Letters, Circolo Delgi Artisti di Firenzi, and an honorary member of the Society of Oregon Artists. A past chairman of the Michigan Academy of Science, Arts, & Letters, his many awards have included the Herbert Adams Memorial Medal, National Sculpture Society; the Knights of Thermopylae Medal, Sparta, Greece; and the Lincoln Medal of the Sesquicentennial Commission of the Congress of the United States.

One-person Exhibition: Honolulu Academy of Arts 1939.

Group Exhibitions: *Annual*, National Academy of Design, New York City 1911; *Salon des Artistes Français*, Paris 1914; *Panama-Pacific Exposition*, Fine Arts Palace, San Francisco 1915; *National Sculpture Society Exhibition*, Palace of the Legion of Honor, San Francisco, 1929; MAE 1931–35, 1938; Chicago World's Fair 1933; *American Art Today*, Rockefeller Center, New York World's Fair, 1939; *Michigan Art Through 50 Years*, UMMA 1955.

Collections: Bennett Garden, Salt Lake City, Utah; Brookgreen Gardens, S.C.; Brigham Young University; Bush Park, Salem, Ore.; City Hall, Duluth, Minn.; Ewa Plantation School, Honolulu; Ford Theatre Museum, Washington, D.C.; Fort Lewis, Washington; Knights of Thermopylae, Sparta, Greece; Latter-Day Saints Temple, Laia, Hawaii; Latter-Day Saints Temple, Washing-

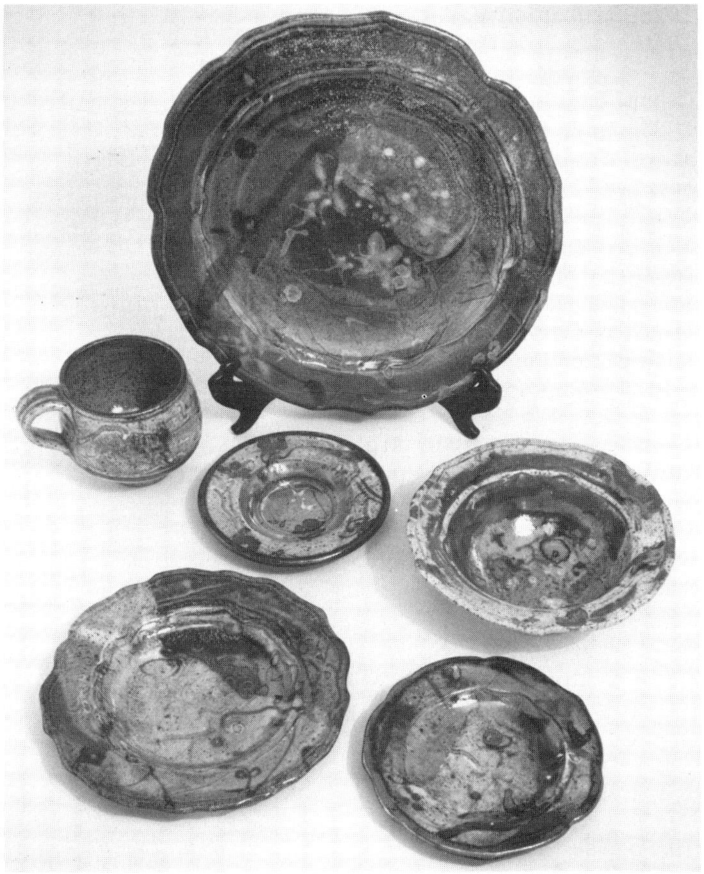

John Glick (1938–). Dinnerware *(for the mansion of the U.S. Vice President). 1979. Reduction-fired stoneware with multiple glazes in various colors. Robert Vigiletti, Photographer.*

Group Exhibitions: *Annual Watercolor Exhibition*, PAFA 1933; MAE 1934, 1941, 1942 (Kahn Prize), 1943 (Newberry Prize), 1944, 1946, 1948, 1949/50, 1952, 1955, 1966 (Tendler Memorial Prize); *International Exhibition of Watercolor*, Brooklyn Museum 1939; *Contemporary American Sculpture, Watercolor, Drawing, and Prints*, Whitney 1941; *International Watercolor Exhibition*, AIC 1941 (traveling); *Tenth Anniversary Exhibition*, Little Gallery, Birmingham 1960; *The American Watercolor*, Sheldon Ross Gallery, Birmingham 1978.

Collections: Avon Township Public Library; DIA; FIA; University of Minnesota; Whitney.

Sources: *WWAA* 1953; MAR; Glassgold and Ed Sully in *Modern Photography* 23, 11 (November 1969): 94–95, 148–153; *New Yorker* September 1938; *DN* 11-24-35, 1-14-40, 10-24-48.

GLICK, John P.

(b. Detroit, Michigan 1938)

Ceramicist. Glick received a B.A. (1960) from Wayne State University, studying under **William Pitney** (whose influence convinced him to focus on functional pottery), and an M.F.A. (1962) from the Cranbrook Academy of Art, studying under **Maija Grotell**. In 1964 he set up a one-person studio and showroom in Farmington, the Plum Tree Pottery. Committed to the educational aspects of his art, Glick provides tours through his pottery and has lectured and given workshops extensively throughout the United States. He has authored numerous articles on ceramics and published technical articles for various craft publications concerning studio management, fuel conservation, and the uses of heat waste. A recipient of numerous awards including two grants from the Tiffany Foundation (1961, 1973), and the National Endowment for the Arts (1974, 1976), Glick is also the recipient of the Michigan Arts Award from the Michigan Foundation for the Arts (1977).

Influenced by Japanese pottery, Glick's handthrown functional stoneware pots are characterized by a uniquely distinctive application of overlapping glazes, oxide brushwork, and patterned sponge-stamping in colors ranging from earth tones and mauves to reds and purples. Since the 1970s, Glick's major interest has been dinnerware, and in 1979 he received a commission from Joan Mondale to do a set for the vice-presidential mansion in Washington D.C. Glick was recently included in the first major survey exhibition of American ceramics, "A Century of Ceramics in the United States 1878–1978," organized in 1979 by the Everson Museum of Art in Syracuse, New York. He is a member of the Michigan Potters' Association.

One-person Exhibitions: Rubiner Gallery, Royal Oak 1967 (two-person), 1970, 1974; Delta College (two-person) 1974; *Exhibit "A"*, Chicago 1974, 1976; *A Ten-Year Retrospective*, Pewabic Pottery, Detroit 1975; Yaw Gallery, Birmingham 1976, 1978, 1980.

Group Exhibitions: MACE 1958, 1960–64, 1966–67, 1971–72 (Rovin Prize 1972); *Fiber/Clay/Metal*, Minnesota Museum of Art 1959, 1962; *Decorative Arts and Ceramics Exhibition*, Wichita Art Association, Kans. 1960; *Five Potters*, Albion College 1968; *Ceramics Invitational*, EMU 1968–69, 1971, 1974; *Objects: USA*, Johnson Wax Collection Touring Show 1969/70*; *Beaux-Arts Designer/Craftsmen*, Columbus Museum of Art 1971, 1973; *Eight Independent Production Potters*, Kansas City Art Institute, Mo. 1976; *Functional Ceramics*, Yaw Gallery, Birmingham 1976; *Michigan Collects Michigan Art*, Pontiac Creative Arts Center 1976; *Soup Tureens: 1976*, Campbell Museum, Camden, N.J. 1976; *12 in Clay*, Cranbrook 1976; *Contemporary Ceramics: The Artist's Viewpoint*, KIA 1977; *A Century of Ceramics in the United States 1878–1978*, Everson Museum of Art, Syracuse 1979* (traveling, also FIA).

Collections: CAAM; Ceramics Monthly Magazine Collection, Columbus; Columbus Museum of Art; Delta College; DIA; EMU; Everson Museum of Art, Syracuse; Johnson Wax Collection of Contemporary Crafts, Racine, Wis.; Kansas City Art Institute, Mo.; U. of M.; Utah Museum of Fine Arts, Salt Lake City; WSU.

Sources: AAA, Interview; MAR; "John Glick, An Artist and His Work" (film), Michigan Council for the Arts 1978; Julie Hall, *Tradition and Change: The New American Craftsman*, New York: Dutton, 1977; Jolyon Hofsted, *Step by Step Ceramics*, New York: Golden Press, 1967; Polly Rothenberg, *The Complete Book of Ceramic Art*, New York: Crown, 1972; Thomas Shafer, *Pottery Decoration*, New York: Watson-Guptill, 1976; Thomas Shafer, *The Professional Potter: How Potters Make a Living at Their Craft*, New York: Watson-Guptill, 1978; Glick in *Studio Potter* 2, 1 (Summer 1973): 4–10; Glick in *Studio Potter* 2, 2 (Winter 1973/74): 46; Glick in *Studio Potter* 4, 1 (Summer 1975): 61–67; Glick in *CMo* 27, 10 (December 1979): 43–62; *CH* 27, 1 (January/February 1968): 46; *CMo* 29, 7 (September 1972): 20–25; *Michigan Challenge* (State Chamber of Commerce) 4, 5 (February 1964): 10–11, 38.

GOOCH, *Donald*

(b. Bloomingdale, Michigan 1907)

Painter/Designer/Illustrator. Gooch received both a B.S. (1935) and an M.S. (1939) from the University of Michigan. He also studied with **Carlos Lopez** at the Detroit Art Academy and at the American School of Painting in Fontainebleau, France (1937). He joined the faculty at the University of Michigan in 1936 and during his tenure there helped develop the program in advertising design and conducted considerable research on the use of pictographic techniques for communicating with nonliterate populations. He is a member and past president of the Ann Arbor Art Association and a charter member of the Michigan Water Color Society. After an early period of "American scene" realism, Gooch's work has been predominantly surrealistic in approach. In 1957 he was one of six local artists, including **Emil Weddige** and **John Coppin**, to be commissioned by the Michigan Consolidated Gas Company to execute a painting depicting some aspect of Michigan's history. In addition to being a painter, Gooch is a book designer and illustrator. He retired from teaching in 1973 and is now professor emeritus at the University of Michigan.

Group Exhibitions: MAE 1934, 1937–39, 1941–43, 1946–48 (FSPP 1947); *Selected Watercolors*, AFA Traveling Show 1941; *Pepsi Cola "Paintings of the Year" Exhibition*, New York City 1946; *MASAL Annual* 1947, 1951 (Award of Merit); *MWCS Annual* 1947–56, 1977 (Merit Award 1947); *Little Show of Works in Progress*, DIA 1948; *PAFA Annual* 1948; *Michigan Art Through 50 Years*, UMMA 1955; *Drawing Invitational*, MSU 1957.

Collections: AFA; DIA; Ford Times Collection, Dearborn; Michigan Consolidated Gas Company, Detroit; Michigan Union, U. of M.

Sources: *WWAA* 1980; MAR; *DN* 1-19-41, 10-17-47; *DFP* 10-21-51; *DT* 10-2-52.

GOODMAN, *Brenda*

(b. Detroit, Michigan 1943)

Painter/Sculptor. Goodman received training at the Art School of the Detroit Society of Arts and Crafts, from **Sarkis Sarkisian**, earning a certificate in 1965 and a B.F.A. in 1972. She taught at various institutions in the Detroit area, including the Art School of Detroit Society of Arts and Crafts (1965–69), Wayne State University (1965–69), the Detroit Institute of Arts (1965–67), the Art Gallery of Windsor (1968–71), and Wayne County Community College (1970–72). In 1976 Goodman moved to New York City where she continues to work in her own very autobiographical and surrealistic style.

One-person Exhibitions: Willis Gallery, Detroit 1973, 1976; Gertrude Kasle Gallery, Detroit 1974; Art Gallery of Windsor, Canada 1976 (two-person); Phyllis Kind Gallery, Chicago 1977 (two-person); Feigenson-Rosenstein Gallery, Detroit 1978, 1980; Pam Adler Gallery, New York 1979.

Group Exhibitions: *J. P. Hunt, Anne Doering, Brenda Goodman*, Willis Gallery, Detroit, 1971; *Michigan Painters-Printmakers*, GRAM 1971; *All Michigan I*, FIA 1971/72*; MAE 1972; *Scarab Club Annual*, Detroit 1972; DAM 1973–75; *Detroit Artists Invitational*, Detroit Bank & Trust Co. 1974*; Forsythe Gallery, Detroit 1974; *Mid-Michigan Annual*, Midland Art Association 1974 (2nd Prize in Drawing); *Michigan Focus*, DIA 1974/75* (Painting Prize); Gertrude Kasle Gallery, Detroit 1975; *Michigan Survey Exhibition*, Cranbrook 1975/76; *Arts and Crafts in Detroit*

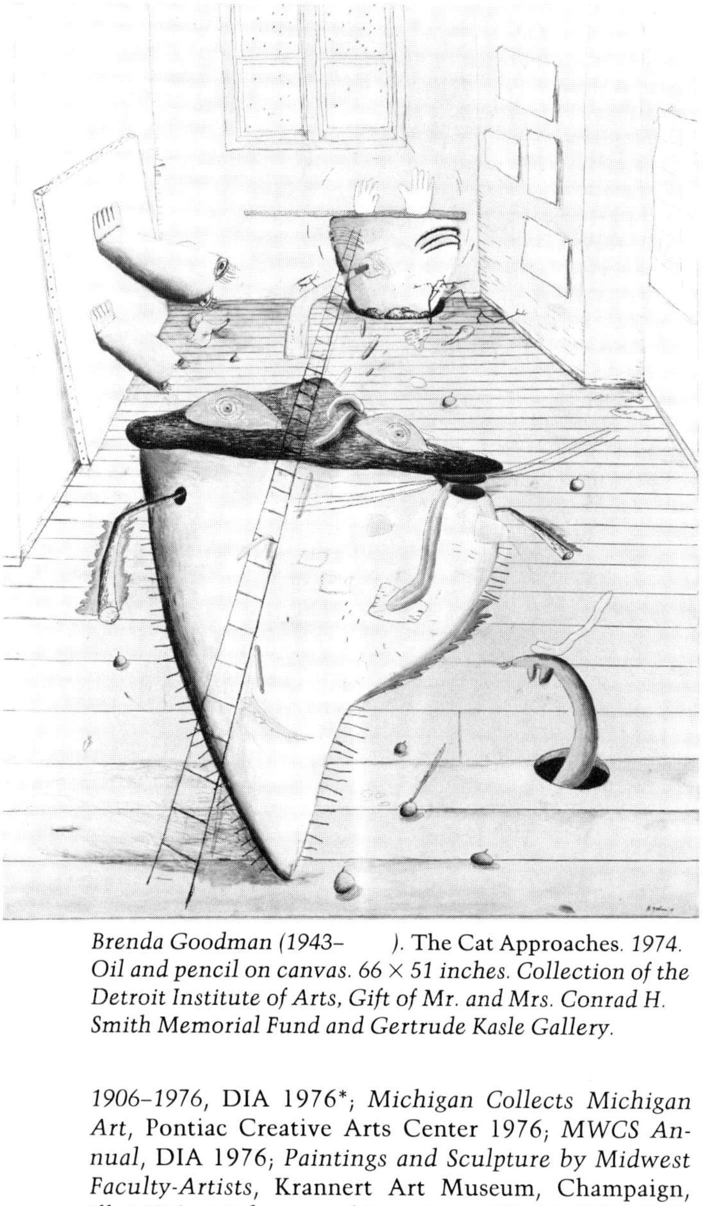

Brenda Goodman (1943–). The Cat Approaches. *1974. Oil and pencil on canvas. 66 × 51 inches. Collection of the Detroit Institute of Arts, Gift of Mr. and Mrs. Conrad H. Smith Memorial Fund and Gertrude Kasle Gallery.*

1906–1976, DIA 1976*; *Michigan Collects Michigan Art*, Pontiac Creative Arts Center 1976; *MWCS Annual*, DIA 1976; *Paintings and Sculpture by Midwest Faculty-Artists*, Krannert Art Museum, Champaign, Ill. 1976; *A Selection of Drawings*, GRAM 1976; Willis Gallery, Detroit 1976; *Memory*, The New Museum (at C Space), New York City 1977; *Double Take*, The New Museum, New York City 1978; *Biennial of Contemporary Art*, Whitney 1979; *Kick Out The Jams*, DIA 1980*.

Collections/Commissions: *Bicentennial Portfolio*, Detroit Workshop of Fine Prints; DIA; Museum of Contemporary Art, Chicago.

Sources: *WWAA* 1976; MAR; *Arts Mag* 53, 1 (June 1979): 16; *Arts Mag* 54, 2 (October 1979): 16; *Detroit Artists Monthly* 1, 2 (December 1976): 2–3; *DIA Bulletin* 54, 2 (1975): 60; *Michigan Art Journal* 1, 1 (January 1976): 16–17; *Moving Out* 5, 1 (1975): 20–25; *New Art Examiner* 7, 7 (April 1980): 1: *DN* 10-21-73, 11-21-76, 9-18-78, 2-26-78.

GRAVES, Oscar

(b. Detroit, Michigan 1921)

Sculptor. Graves attended Wayne State University (1953) and the Cranbrook Academy of Art (1954). From 1952 to 1965 he worked as an apprentice to **Marshall Fredericks**. In Detroit he has been affiliated with the Contemporary Studio and has taught at the Franklin Settlement House, where he executed sculptural memorials to John F. Kennedy and Martin Luther King, Jr. He has also completed bronze figures of Christ and John the Baptist for the Christian Memorial Cemetery in Rochester, and a copper fountain for the Livonia Mall. In addition, Graves is known for his special skills in restoring architectural ornaments, including a ceiling relief for Detroit's Orchestra Hall.

One-person Exhibition: Afro-American Museum, Detroit 1977.

Group Exhibitions: *Afro-American Exhibition*, DIA 1968 (3rd Prize); *Spectrum*, Pontiac Creative Arts Center 1969; *The American Black Artist, Inc.*, Scarab Club 1972; *Art from a Black Perspective*, Detroit Bank & Trust Co. 1977; *Five from Ten*, Pyramid Gallery, Detroit 1979; *Historical Roots: The Black Artist in Michigan*, Detroit Historical Museum 1980.

Collections: Afro-American Museum, Detroit; Christian Memorial Cemetery, Rochester; CMU; Detroit Children's Museum; Franklin Settlement House, Detroit; Harvard Row Mall, Detroit; Livonia Mall; Michigan National Bank, Detroit.

Sources: Cederholm 1973; *DN* 8-18-68, 11-16-77; *DFP* 1-14-80.

GREASON, William

(b. St. Mary's, Ontario 1884; d. Detroit, Michigan 1945)

Painter. Greason studied under Hugh Breckenridge and Thomas Anshutz at the Pennsylvania Academy of the Fine Arts and with Henri Laurens and M. Bashet at the Académie Julian, Paris (1905–07). He came to Detroit in 1910. In 1912 he was given a one-person show at the Detroit Museum of Art. He established the William Greason School of Fine Art in the Fine Arts Building in Detroit and taught summer classes in Douglas, Michigan, where many of his landscapes were inspired by the Lake Michigan shores and the banks of the Kalamazoo River. Although best known for atmospheric landscapes in brilliant colors—deep red, green, and purple—Greason also painted cityscapes and portraits of many Detroiters. He was a member of the Scarab Club in Detroit and the Salamagundi Club, New York City.

One-person Exhibitions: DMA 1912; Bonstelle Theatre, Detroit 1925; Ainslie Gallery, Detroit 1929, Colony Club, Detroit 1932 (two-person).

Group Exhibitions: MAE 1912–14, 1915 (1st Prize), 1917 (Scarab Club Gold Medal), 1918–19, 1921, 1923–27; *PAFA Annual* 1915, 1919, 1921, 1923; *Corcoran Biennial* 1921/22; Hurley Galleries, Detroit, 1928; Palm Beach Art Center 1934 (Honorable Mention); *Paintings and Sculpture by Detroit Artists from the Dr. W. W. Kahn Collection*, DIA 1935; *Artists Professional League Exhibition*, New York World's Fair 1939/40; *Michigan Artists 1901–1951*, DIA 1951.

Collections: DIA; Parliament Building, Regina, Saskatchewan.

Sources: *WWAA* 1940/41; Kenny 1965; *Bonstelle Theatre Program* (Detroit) July 27, 1925; *All the Arts* 3 (June 1920): 47ff; *DIA Bulletin* 4, 2 (November 1922): 15; *Detroit Journal* 4-19-12; *DFP* 4-21-12, 7-8-40, 2-24-41; *Detroit News Tribune* 4-21-12.

GROTELL, Maija

(b. Finland 1899; d. Detroit 1973)

Ceramicist. Grotell graduated from the Central School of Industrial Design in Helsingfors, Finland, then undertook six years (1920–26) of postgraduate study under Albert W. Finch, one of Europe's foremost artist-potters. She emigrated to the United States in 1927 and settled first in New York City, where she taught at the Henry Street Craft School (1928–29), and later at Rutgers University in New Jersey (1936–38). She joined the faculty at the Cranbrook Academy of Art in 1938 as head of the ceramics department, a position she held until her retirement in 1966. Grotell was a major figure in the American crafts renaissance. Like her mentor, Finch, she strove to lift ceramics above the level of mere production of pottery. In her own work she emphasized artistic expression rather than function, and throughout her career was actively engaged in research on glazes. Recognized for their simplicity and monumentality, Grotell's works display a wide range of colors and textures, often incorporating incised abstract motifs based on organic sources. Grotell won many prizes for her work, including the Charles Fergus Binns medal from Alfred University in 1961. Among her original discoveries was the use of chromium and iron in place of uranium to produce an orange coloration. Her students at Cranbrook included Toshiko Takaezu, **John Glick**, and **Richard DeVore**.

One-person Exhibitions: Syracuse University 1967; Cranbrook 1967* (retrospective), 1980 (retrospective); Mus of Contemp Crafts 1968*.

Group Exhibitions: *International Exposition*, Barcelona 1929 (diploma); *American Ceramic Society*, Cleveland 1931; *National Ceramic Exhibition*, Everson Museum of Art, Syracuse 1933, 1934, 1936, 1939, 1946–52, 1956, 1958, 1961 (Honorable Mention 1934, 1941; 2nd Prize 1936; Britannica Prize 1946); *International Exposition*, Paris 1937 (Silver Medal); *Ceramics International*, Everson Museum of Art, Syracuse 1937, 1959, 1961; *Decorative Arts and Ceramics Exhibition*, Wichita Art Association, Kans. 1947, 1951–54 (1st Prize 1947; Purchase Prize 1952); MACE 1949–60 (Haass Prize 1949; Winston Prize 1951; FSPP 1953; Purchase Prize 1955); *Craftsmanship in a Changing World*, Mus of Contemp Crafts 1956; *International Exposition*, Brussels 1958; *La Céramique Contemporaine*, Ostend, Belgium 1959; *Modern American Ceramics*, Royal Copenhagen Porcelain Factory, Denmark 1960; *Clay Form*, UMMA 1961; *Forms from the Earth*, Mus Contemp Crafts 1963; *Michigan Art: Yesterday and Today*, FIA 1963; *Objects: USA*, Johnson Wax Touring Collection 1969/70*; *The Creative Spirit of Cranbrook*, Cranbrook 1972*; *A Century of Ceramics in the United States 1878–1978*, Everson Museum of Art, Syracuse, N.Y. 1979*.

Collections: Alfred University; AIC; Cleveland Museum of Art; CAAM; DIA; Everson Museum of Art, Syracuse; KIA; Mus of Contemp Crafts; Toledo Museum of Art; Walker Art Center, Minneapolis; Wichita Art Association, Kans.

Sources: *WWAA* 1973; AAA 879; MAR; *CH* 28 (September 1968): 42; *CH* 29 (January 1969): 14–23; *CMo* 5, 5 (May 1957): 18–19; *CMo* 22, 1 (January 1974): 58; *CMo* 24, 9 (November 1976): 48–54; *Design* 38 (November 1936): 15; *Design Quarterly* nos. 42–43 (1958): 16, 57; *DFP* 12-23-34; 4-11-77; *DN* 12-23-34, 9-25-38, 2-10-52, 8-28-60, 12-8-73.

GUYSI, Alice Viola

(b. Cincinnati, Ohio 1863; d. Birmingham, Michigan 1940)

Painter. Guysi studied with E. D. Grafton, a watercolorist and portrait artist in Cincinnati, before going to New York City where she studied under William Sartain at the Art Students League. With her younger sister **Jeannette Guysi**, she lived in Paris for four years (ca. 1888–92), studying at the Académie Colarossi and in the studio of the American portraitist Harry Thompson. Guysi exhibited at the Paris Salons of 1891 and 1892. She came to Detroit in the fall of 1896 to organize classes in pastel and miniature painting at the school of the Detroit Museum of Art, and was also instrumental in establishing the museum's Saturday morning art classes. In 1903 she was named Drawing Supervisor for the Detroit Public Schools, and in 1920 was named Supervisor of Applied Art for the secondary schools, retiring in 1934. During her tenure with the public schools, Guysi initiated a unique program of art instruction after school hours for teachers with no specialized art training. She was also known in the area as a lecturer on the history of art and art criticism. Guysi was a member of the Fine Arts Club, Detroit; the Twentieth Century Club, Detroit; Eastern Artists Association; Western Artists Association; and a charter member of the Detroit Society of Women Painters and Sculptors.

One-person Exhibition: DMA 1897.

Group Exhibitions: *Paris Salon* 1891–92; Chicago World's Fair 1893; *Women's Exhibition*, Paris 1894; *Trans-Mississippi Exposition*, Omaha 1897; St. Louis World's Fair 1904; *Michigan Artists*, DMA 1905; *DSWP Annual* 1951.

Collections: Cincinnati Art Museum; Queen City Club, Cincinnati.

Sources: *American Art Annual* 1898, 1917, 1933; AAA, DSWP Scrapbook; *Who's Who in Detroit* 1935–36; Fielding 1974; Gibson 1975; Mallett 1948; Moore 1953; *Detroit Journal* 10-3-96, 1-9-97; *Detroit News Tribune* 10-4-96; *DFP* 10-20-03; *DN* 3-24-40.

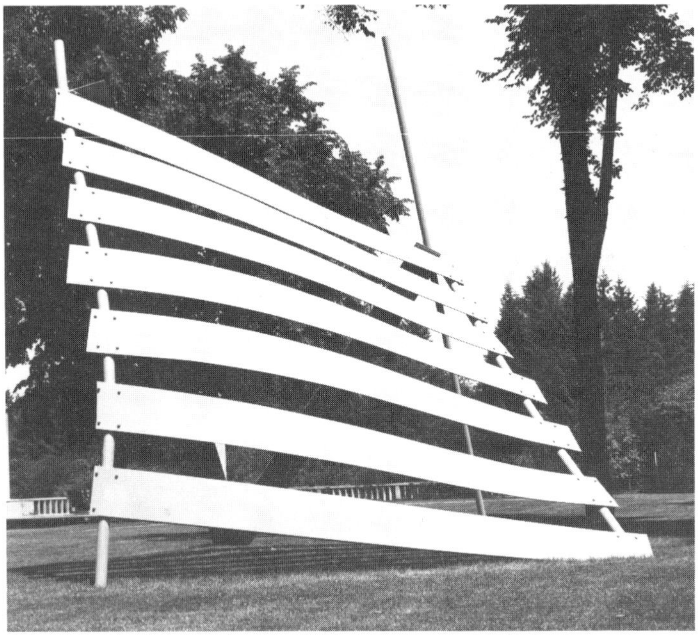

Michael D. Hall (1941–). Ashtabula. *Painted steel. 16 feet 5 inches × 18 feet 6 inches. Private Collection. Courtesy the artist.*

GUYSI, Jeannette

(b. Cincinnati, Ohio 1873; d. Birmingham, Michigan 1966)

Painter/Metalsmith. Guysi, with her older sister **Alice Guysi**, studied with E. D. Grafton in Cincinnati and afterward with William Sartain in New York City. In Paris (ca. 1888–92), she studied at the Académie Colarossi and in the studio of the American portraitist Harry Thompson. At the age of eighteen she was accepted into the 1891 Paris Salon. She then undertook a brief period of study in Boston. Guysi became actively involved in art education in Detroit after her arrival in the city, with Alice, in 1896. She taught at the Art School of the Detroit Museum of Art, serving as principal for a number of years between 1900 and 1910. She was assistant to her sister Alice in the art education department of the Detroit Public Schools (1906–21). Her preferred media were oils and metalwork, and she frequently exhibited locally in both categories. Guysi was a member of the Detroit Society of Women Painters and Sculptors, the Detroit Artists Association, and the Western Art Association.

One-person Exhibitions: DMA 1897, 1903/04.

Group Exhibitions: *Paris Salon* 1891; *Society of Western Artists annual*, AIC 1896; *American Paintings and Sculpture*, AIC 1897, 1903, 1904; *Exhibition of Paintings from the Trans-Mississippi Exposition*, DMA 1898/99; St. Louis World's Fair 1904; *Michigan Artists*, DMA 1905; MAE 1916, 1950; MACE 1949; *DSWP Annual* 1951.

Sources: *American Art Annual* 1898, 1917; AAA, DSWP Scrapbook; *Who's Who in Detroit* 1935/36; Fielding 1974; Gibson 1975; Mallett 1948; Moore 1953; *Detroit Saturday Night* September 9, 1916; *Detroit Journal* 6-2-96, 12-7-96, 1-9-97.

HALL, Michael D.

(b. Upland, California 1941)

Sculptor. Hall attended Western Washington University (1958–60); received a B.A. (1962), studying under Robert Howard, at the University of North Carolina; and later studied ceramics under James McKinnell and sculpture under Hambert Albrizio at the University of Iowa. In 1964 he received a M.F.A. from the University of Washington, Seattle, where he studied under Rudy Autio and Shoji Hamada. Hall taught at the University of Colorado (1965–66) and the University of Kentucky (1966–70), before joining the faculty at the

Cranbrook Academy of Art in 1970. Since the early 1960s Hall has been a major contributor to the revitalization of monumental site sculpture. His linear and planar sculptures, supported in space by tied systems of struts and braces, incorporate architectural images common to the rural Midwestern landscape, such as gates, fences, pipelines, billboards, and other barriers. Hall's many awards include a Guggenheim Fellowship (1973); an Artist's Fellowship from the National Endowment for the Arts (1974); and the Michigan Arts Award given by the Michigan Foundation for the Arts (1978).

Major installations of his work include those at the Hammarskjold Plaza in New York City (1972), Wright State University (1975), and the Detroit Institute of Arts (1977). Hall acted as consultant for "Sculpture Off the Pedestal," an outdoor exhibition devoted to environmental sculpture that was organized by the Grand Rapids Art Museum in 1973. Hall has been instrumental in bringing contemporary outdoor sculpture to Cranbrook; installations have included the work of Robert Stackhouse, William King, Alice Aycock, Tony Rosenthal, and Peter Voulkos. Also a collector of American folk art, Hall is the author of numerous articles and exhibitions catalogues on the subject, including *American Folk Sculpture: The Personal and the Eccentric* (Bloomfield Hills: Cranbrook Academy of Art, 1971).

One-person Exhibitions: Vanderbilt University, 1968; J. B. Speed Art Museum, Louisville, Ky. 1970; Royal Marks Gallery, New York City 1970; Cranbrook 1971; Gertrude Kasle Gallery, Detroit 1971/72; Hammarskjold Plaza, New York City 1972; Everson Museum of Art, Syracuse 1973; Walter Kelly Gallery, Chicago 1975, 1977; DIA 1977*; Feigenson-Rosenstein Gallery, Detroit 1977, 1979.

Group Exhibitions: *Contemporary American Sculpture and Drawing*, Whitney 1968; *Eight American Sculptors*, Equitable Life Plaza, Chicago 1968; *Sculpture of the Month (July)*, New York City Department of Cultural Affairs 1968; *History of American Sculpture*, Sheldon Memorial Art Gallery, University of Nebraska, Lincoln 1970; *Source Detroit*, Cranbrook 1972; *All Michigan II*, FIA 1973/74; *Contemporary American Paintings and Sculpture*, Whitney 1973; MAE 1973 (FSPP); *Michigan Artists Biennial*, Kresge Art Center Gallery, MSU 1973; *Sculpture Off the Pedestal*, GRAM 1973; *Sculpture in the Park*, AIA 1974; *Sculpture for a New Era*, Federal Plaza, Chicago 1975; *From the Bottom Up: 12 Contemporary Michigan Sculptors*, City of East Lansing 1976; *Michigan Collects Michigan Art*, Pontiac Creative Arts Center 1976; *New Works in Clay by Contemporary Painters and Sculptors*, Everson Museum of Art, Syracuse 1976; *Michigan Sculpture '77*, Macomb County Community College 1977; *Scale and Environment: 10 Sculptors*, Walker Art Center, Minneapolis 1977*; *Maquettes and Drawings for Large-Scale Sculpture*, Feigenson-Rosenstein Gallery, Detroit 1979; *Sculpture at Cranbrook 1978–1980*, CAAM 1980*.

Collections: Citizens Fidelity Bank & Trust, Louisville, Ky.; City of Detroit; Cranbrook; DIA; Dickinson College, Carlisle, Pa.; Holtzman-Silverman Company, Detroit; J. B. Speed Art Museum, Louisville, Ky.; Jacksonville Art Museum, Fla.; Princeton University, Art Museum; University of Iowa Museum of Art, Iowa City; University of Washington, Seattle; Wright State University.

Sources: *WWAA* 1978; AAA, Interview; Nawrocki 1980; *Michael Hall—Sculptor* (film), Detroit: Marx-Handley Productions, 1980; *Art in America* 66 (January/February 1978): 120–121; *Art in America* 67 (July/August 1979): 58; *Art News* 69, 3 (May 1970): 66; *Art News* 71, 8 December (1972): 110; *Arts Mag* 49, 10 (June 1975): 34–35; *Michigan Art Journal* 1, 3 (October/November 1976): 11ff; *Monthly Detroit* February 1981.

HANSEN, *Marc*

(b. Salt Lake City, Utah 1925; d. Kalamazoo, Michigan 1977)

Ceramicist. Hansen received a B.A. (1950) from San Jose State College, an M.A. (1952) from Ohio State University, and did postgraduate work at the New York State College of Ceramics at Alfred University. He taught ceramics from 1952 to 1957 at the University of Michigan, from 1957 to 1962 at the Kalamazoo Institute of Arts, and from 1957 to 1977 at Western Michigan University. An early advocate of the necessity for organization among American craftsmen, he was a founding member of the Midwest Designer/Craftsmen Association in 1955 and was also instrumental in organizing the Michigan Potters' Association. In 1975 he was one of twelve ceramicists in the United States who were invited to participate in the International Ceramic Symposium held under the auspices of the International Academy of Ceramics in Gatlinburg, Tennessee. Hansen was known for his crystalline glazes and wrote a definitive early work on this subject for *Ceramics Monthly* (April 1966).

One-person Exhibitions: GRAM 1955; 4 Arts Gallery, Evanston, Ill. 1964 (two-person); AIC 1967 (three-per-

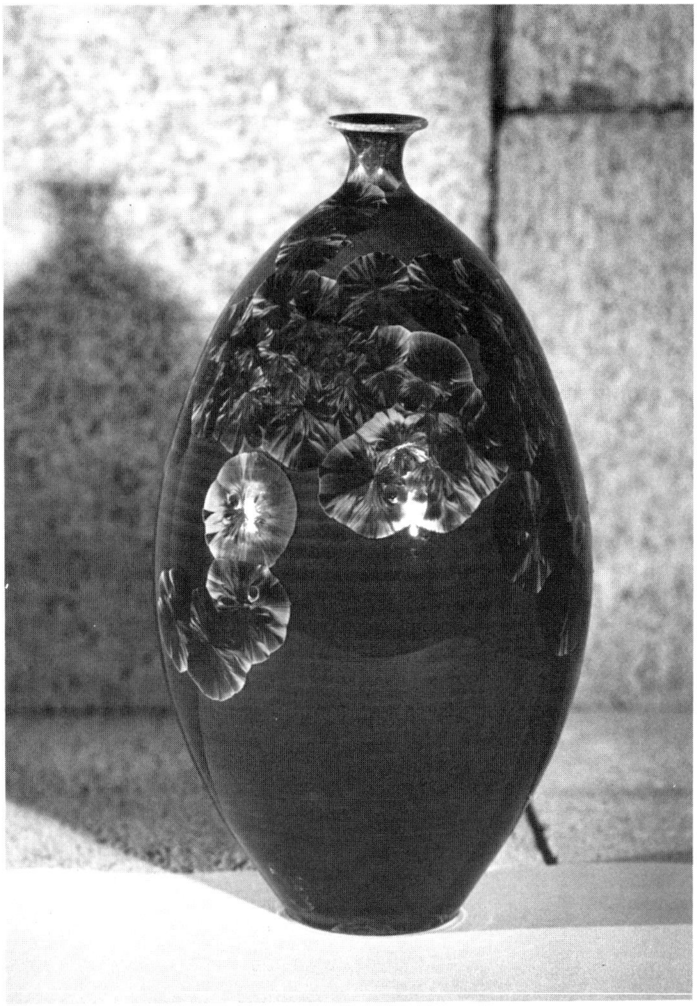

Marc Hansen (1925–1988). Bottle. *Thrown porcelain with transparent brown-blue crystals. h. 3¾ inches. Courtesy Vadra L. Hansen. Douglas Lyttle, Photographer.*

son); KIA 1969; Rubiner Gallery, Royal Oak 1969 (two-person); *Retrospective*, WMU 1977.

Group Exhibitions: *Ceramic National*, Everson Museum of Art, Syracuse 1950, 1956, 1958, 1961, 1965, 1967; *Decorative Arts and Ceramics Exhibition*, Wichita Art Association, Kans. 1954, 1958, 1968, 1970; *Fiber/Clay/Metal*, Minnesota Museum of Art 1955; MACE 1955–58, 1960–63, 1966–68 (Webber Prize 1956); *American Craftsmen*, Smithsonian Institution 1957; *La Céramique Contemporaine*, Ostend, Belgium 1958; *Area Show*, KIA 1959 (1st Prize in Ceramics), 1966; *Michigan Art: Yesterday and Today*, FIA 1963; *Michigan Craftsmen's Council*, BBAA 1967; *Sixteen Michigan Ceramicists*, Cranbrook 1967; *Ceramics Invitational*, EMU 1968–69, 1971, 1974, 1977; *Beaux-Arts Designer/Craftsmen Exhibition*, Columbus Museum of Art 1973.

Collections: Columbus Museum of Art; EMU; FIA; GRAM; HAM; Krannert Art Museum, University of Illinois; UMMA.

Sources: MAR; *Michigan Challenge* (State Chamber of Commerce) 4, 5 (February 1964): 11.

HARDMAN, *Ernest*

(b. Konawa, Oklahoma 1912; d. Detroit, Michigan 1969)

Painter. Hardman was a scholarship student in Cleveland at the John Huntington Polytechnic School of Art and the Cleveland School of Art. When he arrived in Detroit in 1935 he enrolled at the Art School of the Detroit Society of Arts and Crafts, where he studied under **Sarkis Sarkisian** and **Guy Palazzola**. He was also associated with local black arts organizations, including the Pen and Palette Club, where he studied under **Francis DeErdely**; Arts Extended; and the Contemporary Studio Group. Early in his career Hardman concentrated on portraits, later turning to abstract interpretations of children, horses, flowers, and religious themes. Hardman gave classes at his Detroit studio. In 1978 he was posthumously honored as an outstanding member of the black art community of Michigan by the National Conference of Artists.

One-person Exhibitions: National Association for the Advancement of Colored People Headquarters, 1966.

Group Exhibitions: *Pen and Palette Club Annual*, Detroit 1937 (3rd Prize), 1939 (1st Prize), 1940; *Arts Extended Group*, DAM 1952; MAE 1954, 1956–57, 1962; *Columbia Biennial*, Columbia Museum of Art and Science, S.C. 1957; *American Society of African Culture*, Philadelphia Museum of Art 1960 (3rd Prize); *Atlanta University Annual* 1960 (1st Prize); *Downtown Outdoor Arts Festival*, Central Business District Association, Detroit 1960 (2nd Prize); *DAM*, J. L. Hudson Gallery, Detroit 1962; DAM 1962–65; *Midyear Show*, Butler Institute 1963; *National Religious Art Biennial*, Cranbrook 1969; *Historical Roots: The Black Artist in Michigan*, Detroit Historical Museum 1980.

Collections: Atlanta University; Cobo Hall, Detroit; Lagos Museum of Art, Nigeria.

Sources: MAR; *Art and Artist* 1, 2 (March 1960); *Michigan Chronicle* 5-27-44, 2-20-52, 2-29-60, 7-30-66, 8-6-66, 4-26-69; *DFP* 8-28-60, 2-20-64, 9-22-67.

HARRISON, Carole

(b. Chicago, Illinois 1933)

Sculptor. After completing an M.F.A. (1956) at the Cranbrook Academy of Art, Harrison went to England on a Fulbright Fellowship to study at the Central School of Arts and Crafts in London. In 1960 she was awarded a Tiffany Foundation award for excellence in sculpture. In that same year, she joined the faculty at Western Michigan University and established the sculpture department there, remaining as chairperson until 1974, when she left to head the sculpture department at the State University of New York at Fredonia. She has also been an artist-in-residence (1975) for the Ossabaw Island Project, established by **Clifford West**, and at the Oxbow Summer School of Art in 1977. While in Michigan, Harrison concentrated on large-scale, abstract works, cast in bronze and other metals, and primarily based on figurative sources.

One-person Exhibitions: Gallery Four, Detroit 1959; Kasha Heman Gallery, Chicago 1960–61; Gilman Gallery, Chicago 1963–65; Midland Art Center 1963; KIA 1976.

Group Exhibitions: MAE 1955–59, 1963–66; *Exhibition Momentum*, Chicago 1957; *American Painting and Sculpture*, DIA and PAFA 1959; *Young Americans*, DAM 1960; *New Horizons in Sculpture*, McCormick Place, Chicago 1961 (1st Prize); *Area Show*, KIA 1962, 1964–66; *AFA Traveling Show* 1963; *Painting and Sculpture Today (Invitational)*, John Herron Museum, Indianapolis 1967; *75 Women Artists in 75*, Buffalo 1975.

Collections/Commissions: American Federation of Arts, New York City; Battle Creek Civic Art Center; Federal Building, Chicago; HAM; Holland High School; Hope College; KIA; Oak Park Library, Ill.; WMU.

Sources: MAR; Hendry 1980B; *Art in America* 48 (Spring 1960): 143; *Art J* 34, 2 (Winter 1974/75): 155; *Chicago Sun-Times* 11-13-61, 10-28-62, *KG* 3-13-64, 8-21-66, 1-27-70, 9-25-72, 11-8-76.

HEFNER, Harry

(b. Kalamazoo, Michigan 1911)

Painter. Educated at Western Michigan University (B.A. 1936) and Columbia University (M.A. 1939), Hefner also did additional graduate work at Ohio State University. He joined the faculty at Western Michigan University in 1941, served as department head from 1955 to 1965, and retired in 1977. He was awarded the WMU Alumni Association's Teaching Excellence Award in 1977. Hefner has been a visiting professor at Howard University and at the University of Vermont. A member of the Michigan Water Color Society, Hefner works mainly in watercolor in an abstract style.

One-person Exhibitions: Four Arts Gallery, Evanston, Ill. 1964 (two-person); The Gallery, Petoskey 1965; HAM 1966; KIA 1970.

Group Exhibitions: MAE 1962, 1963; *Area Show*, KIA 1962–66, 1970; *American Watercolor Society Annual*, New York City 1963; *West Michigan Annual*, GRAM 1963 (Watercolor Award); *MWCS Annual* 1963 (Merit Award), 1964, 1965, 1971–74; *Michiana Biennial*, South Bend Art Center 1963, 1965 (Watercolor Award, both years); *Mid-Michigan Annual*, Midland Art Association 1964 (1st Prize); *Art on Paper*, KIA 1967.

Collections: Albion College; First National Bank, Kalamazoo; Kalamazoo College; KIA; South Bend Art Center, Ind.; Upjohn Company, Kalamazoo.

Sources: *WWAA* 1976; MAR; *KG* 3-17-63, 5-25-64, 1-7-65, 3-14-65, 4-1-67, 4-13-69; *Muskegon Chronicle* 5-6-66; *AAN* 5-23-71; *Midland Daily News* 2-10-75.

HENRICKSEN, Ralf

(b. Chicago, Illinois 1907; d. East Lansing, Michigan 1975)

Painter. Henricksen graduated from the School of the Art Institute of Chicago in 1931 (B.F.A.) and was awarded the Anna Louise Raymond Traveling Fellowship which enabled him to study at the Académie Colarossi and the Académie de la Grande Chaumière in Paris. From 1953 to 1954 he studied in Mexico and received a M.F.A. (1955) from the Instituto Allende in San Miguel. Employed by the Works Progress Administration/Federal Art Project during the Depression, Henricksen completed murals for several public schools in Chicago and also won U.S. Treasury Section of Fine Arts competitions for post office murals in Monroe, Michigan (mural moved to Monroe Community College in 1971) and Staunton, Illinois (1941). He began teaching at Michigan State University in 1946 and remained there until his retirement in 1973. He also served as director of the University's Summer Art School in Leland, Michigan, for 25 years (1948–73).

One-person Exhibitions: CMU 1965, 1970; Kresge Art Center Gallery, MSU 1973* (retrospective), 1981* (retrospective).

Group Exhibitions: *American Painting and Sculpture*, AIC, 1932, 1935, 1937–38; *International Exhibition of*

Prints, AIC 1934; *Chicago and Vicinity*, AIC 1935 (Prize), 1936–40; *International Watercolor Exhibit*, AIC 1935–36, 1938–42; *New Horizons in American Art*, MOMA 1936; *Annual Watercolor and Print Exhibition*, PAFA 1937; *Pennsylvania Watercolor Society* 1947; *Midyear Show*, Butler Institute 1948; MAE, DIA 1952 (Albert Kahn Watercolor Prize), 1953–55, 1957; *Michiana Biennial, Regional Art Association*, South Bend Art Center 1952, 1957, 1962; *Romance and Realism*, DAM 1957; *Flint Annual*, FIA 1958; *West Michigan Annual*, GRAM 1960–61; *American Painting Today*, GRAM 1961.

Collections: Kresge Art Center Gallery, MSU; Monroe County College; University of Illinois, Urbana.

Sources: *WWAA* 1976; *Kresge Art Center Bulletin* 7, 7 (April 1973); *Michigan State News* 4-4-73.

HERZBERG, *Robert A.*

(b. Fürstenberg-Micklenburg, Germany 1886; d. Detroit, Michigan 1960)

Painter. Herzberg graduated with honors from the School of the Art Institute of Chicago in 1911, after studying with Alphonse Mucha and Will Foote. He also studied with Robert Henri, Thomas Fogarty, and Graham Coots at the Art Students League in New York. In 1913 he came to Detroit. From 1922 to 1934, he was founder and director of the Detroit School of Applied Art, a school organized to instruct pupils in commercial art, design, and illustration to prepare them for professional work. Herzberg is best known for his paintings of famous actors and circus scenes. He followed the Ringling Brothers Circus for two years and did portraits of many celebrities, including Emmet Kelly, Katherine Hepburn, and Orson Welles. He painted many cityscapes of Detroit, including the Old City Hall and scenes along the Detroit river; executed portraits of many public figures, including Attorney General Frank Murphy and Congressman George A. Dondero; and did numerous sketches of Diego Rivera as he painted the Detroit Institute of Arts murals. Originally a strict realist, Herzberg's later style became increasingly abstract.

One-person Exhibitions: Scarab Club, Detroit 1929; Grosse Pointe Yacht Club, Grosse Pointe 1941; J. L. Hudson Gallery, Detroit 1943; Arthur Newton Gallery, New York City 1945, 1947, 1956; DAM 1948–49; Toledo Museum of Art 1958; *Memorial Retrospective*, Anna Werbe Gallery, Detroit 1964.

Group Exhibitions: MACE 1916–18, 1920–22, 1925–27, 1929–30, 1933–38, 1941, 1943, 1945–46, 1952–53, 1955 (Werbe Memorial Prize), 1956–57; *American Artists Annual*, DIA 1919, 1921–23, 1925.

Collections: Atlanta Art Institute; DIA.

Sources: *WWAA* 1956; MAR; Burroughs 1936/37; *Art Dig* 19, 13 (April 1, 1945): 64; *Art News* 44, 5 (April 15–30, 1945): 25; *Public Ledger* (Philadelphia) 1-1-14; *DFP* 2-18-23, 11-4-28, 5-13-30, 6-20-43, 12-5-54; *DN* 2-2-27, 6-22-29, 1-1-33, 10-2-33, 10-5-41, 5-22-43, 6-20-43; *DT* 10-31-39, 11-13-55; *N.Y. Sun* 4-14-45; *N.Y. Herald Tribune* 4-15-45; *BEcc* 11-10-55, 11-17-55, 10-20-60.

HINTON, *Alfred*

(b. Columbus, Georgia 1940)

Painter. Hinton initially studied at Case-Western Reserve University but later received a B.A. (1967) from the University of Iowa, where he studied under Robert Knipschild and Mauricio Lasansky. He moved to Toronto to play professional football for the Toronto Argonauts (1962–67), and later continued his education at the University of Cincinnati, receiving a M.F.A. (1970) in painting and filmmaking. In 1970, he joined the faculty at Western Michigan University. Hinton has been a visiting artist at Saginaw Valley Community College (1973) and the University of Michigan (1975–76). He has served, with **Reginald Gammon**, as coordinator for the Jackson Prison Art Program (1973–74); as Visual Arts Coordinator for the Michigan Academy of Arts and Sciences (1972–74); and since 1970 has also been a member of the Michigan Council for the Arts Advisory Panel. His early work can be characterized as figurative social realism, with particular emphasis on depictions of the black experience in the late 1950s and early 1960s. His more recent paintings consist of either figurative three-dimensional collage or abstract landscapes.

One-person Exhibitions: Kellogg Community College 1971; Gallery Seven, Detroit 1972, 1975; Dome Gallery, Saginaw Valley Community College 1973; Space Gallery, WMU 1974; Gallery II, WMU 1975; Andrews University 1976; CMU 1978.

Group Exhibitions: *Black Artist Exhibition*, Sill Gallery, EMU 1970; *All Michigan I*, FIA 1971/72; Michigan Artrain 1971–72; *National Exhibition of Black Artists*, Smith-Mason Gallery, Washington, D.C. 1971/72; *Black Artists in Michigan Collections*, FIA 1973; *Source Detroit III*, CAAM 1973; *J. L. Hudson Invitational*, J. L. Hudson Gallery, Detroit 1976; London Art Gallery, London, Ontario 1976; *Art From a Black Perspective*, The American Black Artist, Inc., Detroit Bank & Trust Co. 1977; *Black Art: The Known and the New*, Battle Creek Civic Art Center 1977 (traveling); *Historical Roots: The Black Artist in Michigan*, Detroit Historical Museum 1980.

Collection: FIA.

Sources: *Who's Who in Black America* 1976; Elton C. Fox, *Black Artists of the New Generation*, New York: Dodd Mead 1977; *DN* 11-1-70, 5-11-75, 7-1-79; *Battle Creek Enquirer* 2-10-71; *Michigan Daily* (Ann Arbor) 3-19-71; *Saginaw News* 5-11-72; *KG* 10-7-73.

HOFFMASTER, *Maude Miller*

(b. Manistee, Michigan 1883; d. Traverse City, Michigan 1969)

Painter. Largely self-taught, Hoffmaster studied briefly at the School of the Art Institute of Chicago and in Paris with George Ball. For fourteen years, she was on the painting faculty of the National Music Camp at Interlochen, serving as department head from 1942 to 1948, and helped design and organize the Fine Arts Center there. Her painting *The Country Doctor* is reproduced in doctors' offices all over the country.

One-person Exhibitions: Galeries Bernheim-Jeune, Paris 1928; Anderson Gallery, New York City 1929; Crocker Art Gallery, Sacramento 1957.

Group Exhibitions: AIC 1926; *Area Show*, GRAM 1929; MAE 1930, 1933.

Collections/Commissions: Masonic Temple, Traverse City; Munson Hospital, Traverse City; State Hospital, Ypsilanti; Traverse City State Bank.

Sources: *WWAA* 1962; MAR; Gibson 1975; *DN* 2-17-29; *FJ* 10-29-39; *GR Press* 4-21-53; *DFP* 10-6-59; 2-1-67; *Traverse City Record Eagle* 7-2-64, 5-5-66, 10-4-69.

HOLLAND, *Jay*

(b. Detroit, Michigan 1928)

Sculptor. A graduate of Cass Technical High School, Holland received a B.A. (1951) from the Art School of the Detroit Society of Arts and Crafts and an M.A. (1956) from the Cranbrook Academy of Art. He has taught for the Detroit Board of Education (1956–64), the Jewish Community Center (1957–64), and Wayne State University (1968), and has served as chairman of the sculpture department of the Center for Creative Studies since the early 1970s.

One-person Exhibitions: FIA 1963; Hanamura Gallery, Detroit 1963.

Group Exhibitions: MAE 1948–51, 1964, 1966; *Boston Fine Arts Festival* 1959; *Drawing and Sculpture Exhibition*, Ball State Teachers College 1961 (Purchase Award), 1977; *Trends in Michigan Art*, Kresge Art Center Gallery, MSU 1962; *Michigan Art: Yesterday and Today*, FIA 1963; *National Drawing and Sculpture Exhibition*, University of North Dakota 1963 (Merit Award); *Invitational Sculpture Exhibition*, EMU 1971; *Mid-Michigan Annual*, Midland Art Association 1977; *Michigan Artists Biennial*, Kresge Art Center Gallery, MSU 1979.

Commissions: Bell Florist, Birmingham; Dow Chemical Company, Midland; Ira Kaufman Chapel, Southfield.

Sources: MAR; *Lansing State Journal* 3-18-62; *Pontiac Press* 10-11-68; *DFP* 7-14-74, 6-2-79.

HOLM, *Lillian*

(b. New York, New York 1896; d. Bastad, Sweden 1979)

Textile Artist. Holm received her early training from Martha Maas Fjetterstrom in Bästad, Sweden, before coming to the Cranbrook Academy of Art at the invitation of George Booth in 1929. She helped **Loja Saarinen** organize Cranbrook's weaving department, supervising and instructing the many weavers involved in completing Loja Saarinen's designs for the new Kingswood girl's school. Holm returned to Stockholm in 1932 to do graduate work at the Tekniska Skolan and received an M.A. from the Handarbets Vänner. She returned to Cranbrook in 1933 and was appointed head of weaving at the Kingswood School, where she remained for thirty years. In addition to her duties at Cranbrook, she headed the weaving department at the Flint Institute of Arts for twenty-eight years. She was in charge of the weaving department for the Swedish Pavilion at Chicago's Century of Progress Exhibit at the 1933 World's Fair and in 1936 was appointed director of weaving for the Works Progress Administration/Federal Art Project in the Upper Peninsula.

Holm received numerous awards, among them a fellowship to the Goeblins Institute, Paris, in 1933; the Architectural League award at the 1939 World's Fair in New York City; and the Fairchild Publications competition prize in 1940. She is well represented in private collections, including those of Eleanor Roosevelt, who purchased one of her first tapestries done in this country, and Katherine Cornell, for whom Holm executed a portrait of the actress as Cleopatra. In 1964 she was artist-in-residence at the Ossabaw Island Project, established by **Clifford West** in Georgia. Holm retired from Kingswood School in 1965 and at that time was awarded the Cranbrook Founders Medal.

One-person Exhibition: Malmö Museum, Sweden 1947.

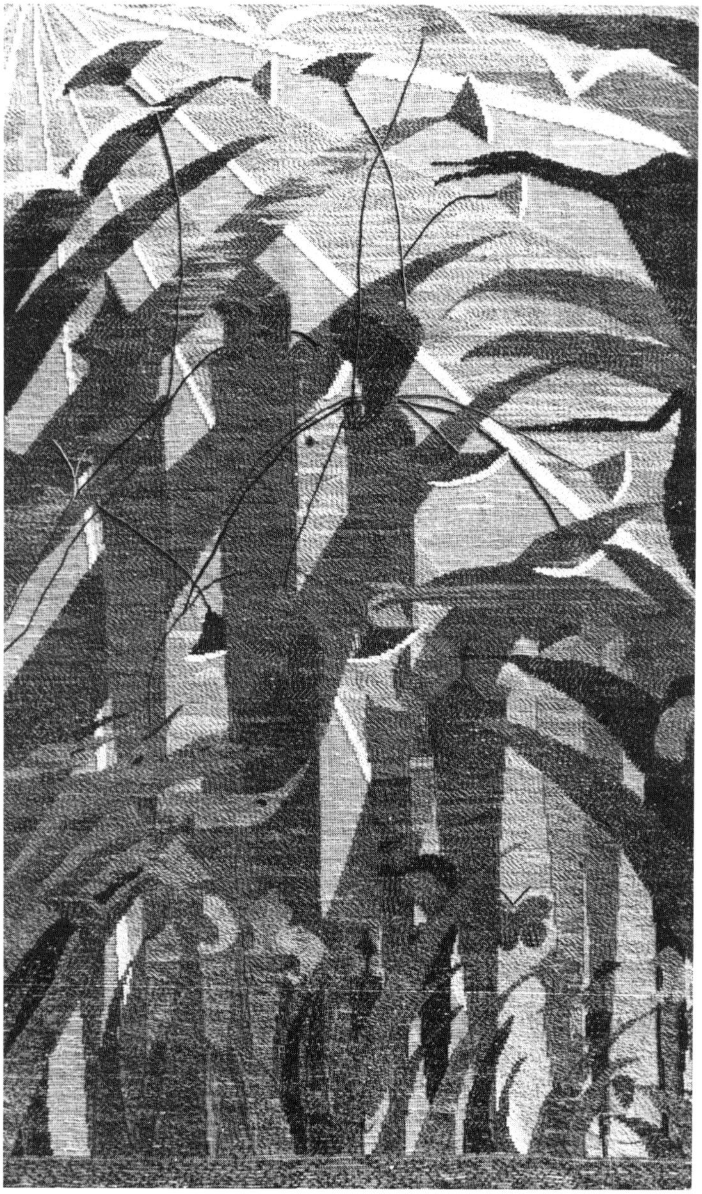

Lillian Holm (1896–1979). The Horizon. *Tapestry. 72 × 90 inches. Collection of the University of Michigan, Gift in memory of Charles Baird. Harvey Croze, Photographer.*

Group Exhibitions: *Craft Show*, DAM 1938; *Flint Annual*, FIA 1940; Philadelphia Art Alliance 1940; *Designer/Craftsmen U.S.A.*, Brooklyn Museum 1940, 1954; MACE 1946–47 (FSPP), 1951–57, 1960–61; *MASAL Annual* 1947–48; American Federation of Arts, New York City 1954/55; *Faculty Show*, FIA 1957; *Michigan Art: Yesterday and Today*, FIA 1963.

Collections: Cranbrook; DIA; FIA; U. of M.

Sources: MAR; *FIA Bulletin* 1942/43; *FJ* 11-15-47, 3-14-65; *Pontiac Daily Press* 5-15-50; *BEcc* 6-6-63.

HONORÉ, Paul

(b. Crawford County, Pennsylvania 1885; d. Philadelphia, Pennsylvania 1956)

Painter/Printmaker. Honoré attended both Cass Technical High School and **John P. Wicker**'s School of Fine Arts in Detroit. He also studied with the English muralist Frank Brangwyn in London. Honoré was one of Detroit's most prolific muralists; between 1925 and 1936 he completed nearly a dozen murals in Michigan, including those for the Players' Club of Detroit, Highland Park High School, the Dearborn Public Library (now the Bryant Branch), and Southeastern High School in Detroit. He was chosen as one of eight local artists to execute a mural for the Michigan Building at the 1933 Chicago World's Fair. In 1923 he received national attention for his development, in conjunction with the Dow Chemical Company, of a mural technique utilizing concrete colored with powdered glass. Honoré used this medium for both the Midland County Courthouse and the Harbor Beach Community Center, maintaining that these outdoor murals would retain the brilliancy of their colors for at least three hundred years.

Honoré was also noted for his work in woodcut illustration. Throughout the 1920s he illustrated a series of children's books, one of which, *Tales from Silver Lands* by Charles J. Finger (Garden City: Doubleday, Page and Co., 1924), won the Newberry Medal in 1926. In 1941 he executed a series of color woodblock prints for a limited edition of Bret Harte's *The Luck of Roaring Camp* (Camden, N.J.: Privately Printed, 1941). Honoré taught landscape painting at the Detroit Conservatory of Music (1915–20) and at the Chestnut Street Settlement in Detroit. In the 1930s he held laboratory classes for aspiring muralists. He was one of the few Michigan artists to refuse mural commissions in conjunction with the Works Progress Administration/Federal Art Project. During the Depression, Honoré made several attempts to devise new ways for communities to support their artists. At one point he suggested a barter system to exchange art works for the necessities of life; he later devised the Paul Honoré Fellowship, in which proceeds from a monthly publication would be used to underwrite the studies of student artists. Honoré was a long-time member of the Scarab Club and had his studio there. He left Detroit in 1940 to found an art colony in Port Deposit, Maryland, with which he was still affiliated at the time of his death.

One-person Exhibitions: DMA 1911; Civic Theater, Detroit 1929.

Group Exhibitions: MAE 1912–29, 1932 (DMA 2nd Prize 1920); *American Artists Annual*, DIA 1917–19, 1921–22, 1925, 1929; *Woodblock Prints in Color by American Artists*, DIA 1919; *Michigan State Fair Ex-*

hibition 1922 (1st prize); *Modern Art Exhibition*, Scarab Club, Detroit 1926; John Hanna Galleries, Detroit 1934.

Collections/Commissions: Baldwin High School, Birmingham; Book Building, Detroit; Dearborn Public Library, Bryant Branch; DIA; General Motors Building, New York City; Harbor Beach Community House; Highland Park High School; Midland County Courthouse; National Research Council Headquarters, Washington, D.C.; People's Church, MSU; Player's Club, Detroit; Scarab Club, Detroit; Southeastern High School, Detroit; UMMA.

Sources: AAA D318; Gibson 1975; Kenny 1965; Mallett 1948: Paul Honoré, *Color, Light and Vision*, Detroit: Privately printed, 1938; *All the Arts* (Detroit) 2 (1919): 103; *DMA Bulletin* 6, 1 (January 1912): 11; *Literary Digest* March 27, 1926; *New York Times Book Review* January 13, 1924, November 3, 1927; *DFP* 4-9-22, 12-16-33, 4-12-56; *DN* 11-9-24, 3-22-25, 11-13-27, 9-22-29, 5-24-36, 5-14-56.

HORN, *Milton*

(b. Kiev, Ukraine, Russia 1906)

Sculptor. Born in a suburb of Kiev, Horn came to the United States with his parents in 1913. He received his first training from Henry Hudson Kitson in Boston and later attended the Beaux-Arts Institute of Design in New York City. From 1927 to 1939, Horn worked in New York City executing sculptural commissions, and for a brief period was employed by the Egyptian department at the Brooklyn Museum. In 1939 he was appointed artist-in-residence at Olivet College, a post he held for ten years (1939–49). While in Michigan, Horn completed a memorial fountain figure honoring Father Shipherd, Olivet's founder; carved reliefs for the Iron River post office; and an interior wooden relief (1944) for the C. D. Wall residence, built by architect Frank Lloyd Wright, in Plymouth. Horn moved to Chicago in 1949.

One-person Exhibitions: *PAFA Annual* 1934; *American Art Today* 1939/40; *Drawings by Contemporary American Sculptors*, Arden Gallery, 1943; *Contemporary American Sculpture, Watercolor and Drawing*, Whitney 1949; *International Exhibition of Sculpture*, Philadelphia Museum of Art 1949; *American Sculpture—1951*, MMA 1951; *New York Artists for Victory Exhibition*, MMA 1951.

Collections: National Academy of Design, New York City; Olivet College; U.S. Post Office, Iron River.

Sources: *WWAA* 1980; AAA 1924; Mallett 1948; Eleanor Bitterman, *Art in Modern Architecture*, New York: Reinhold, 1952; Milton Horn, *Sculpture by Horn*, Olivet, Mich.: Olivet College, 1948; Horn in *Parnassus* 10, 5 (October 1938): 18–20; Horn in *Inland Architect* 8, 10 (June 1965): 9–11; *Art Dig* 26, 9 (February 1, 1952): 12; *Art News* 29 (May 30, 1930): 22; *Art News* 35 (October 31, 1936): 19.

IDEN, *Sheldon*

(b. Detroit, Michigan 1933)

Painter. After initial training at both the School of the Art Institute of Chicago and the Art School of the Detroit Society of Arts and Crafts, Iden received a B.A. (1960) from Wayne State University and an M.F.A. (1962) from the Cranbrook Academy of Art. His teaching positions have included those in the University of Michigan Adult Education Program, the Jewish Community Center in Detroit, and at Wayne State University. In 1969 he joined the faculty at Eastern Michigan University, and in 1971 served as artist-in-residence for the Manistique Public Schools under the auspices of the Michigan Council for the Arts. The recipient of a Fulbright Fellowship in 1962, Iden studied in India, where he visited the Ajanta cave temples, an experience that had a profound influence on his work. The images within the caves, shrouded in darkness yet still visible, inspired Iden to produce his black paintings. These large-scale oils, characterized by black matte backgrounds and shiny, reflective, geometrically shaped "openings," are intended by Iden to duplicate for the viewer his experience of the presence of light within darkness in the Ajanta caves.

One-person Exhibitions: AAA Gallery, Detroit 1962 (two-person); Raven Gallery, Detroit 1962*; Franklin Siden Gallery, Detroit 1971*, 1974; Park West Gallery, Southfield 1975 (two-person); Willis Gallery, Detroit 1976 (two-person); Gallery Renaissance, Detroit 1981 (two-person).

Group Exhibitions: MAE 1959–61, 1966, 1970 (Arwin and Strauss Prizes 1969, Kasle Gallery Prize 1970); *American Painting and Sculpture*, DIA and PAFA 1960; *Annual Drawing and Small Sculpture Exhibition*, Ball State University 1961 (Purchase Award); *Drawing and Sculpture Invitational*, EMU 1964–65; *Made in Detroit*, Franklin Siden Gallery, Detroit 1967; *Other Ideas*, DIA 1969*; *Michigan Artists Biennial*, Kresge Art Center Gallery, MSU 1971; *All Michigan I*, FIA 1971/72 (Honorable Mention); *Michigan Collects Michigan Art*, Pontiac Creative Arts Center 1976; *27 Painters*, UMMA 1976; *10 Years of Drawing*, Pontiac Creative Arts Center 1980.

Collections: Ball State University; City National Bank, Detroit; Cranbrook; DIA; W. B. Doner Agency, De-

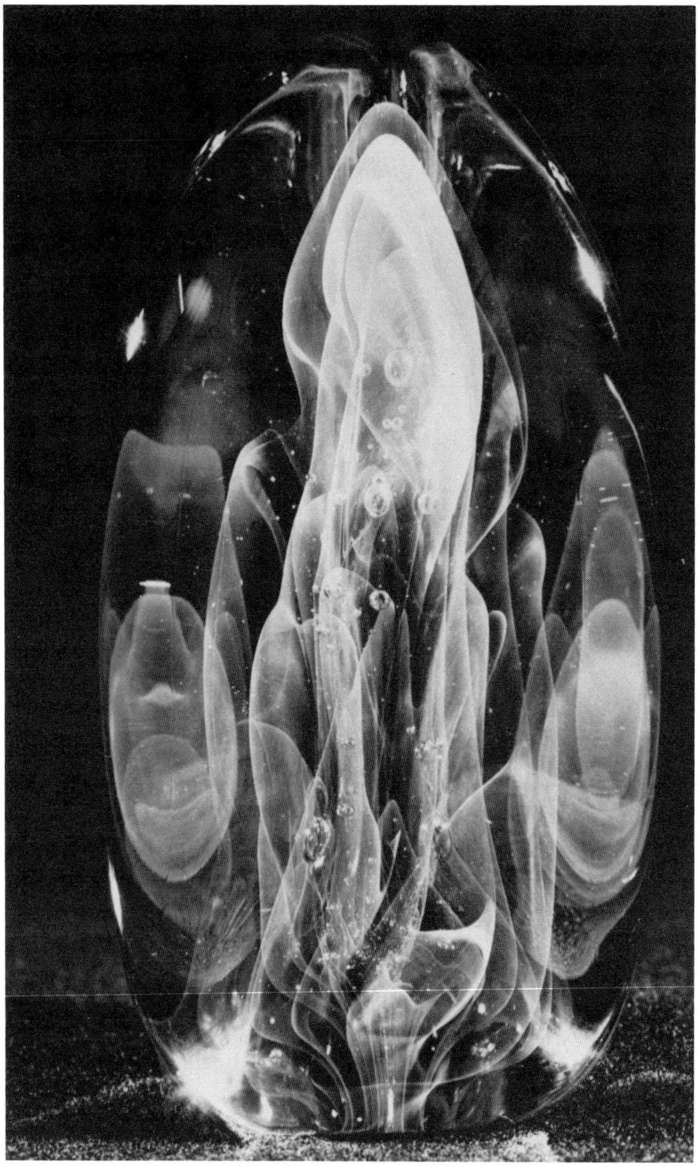

Gilbert C. Johnson (1930–). Paperweight. *Glass. h. 4 inches. Courtesy the artist. John Littleton, Photographer.*

River and Scotten, and was one of ten artists chosen to execute a print for *Time, Place, Image,* a portfolio released by the Michigan Workshop of Fine Prints in 1974. Johnson's early works were primarily watercolor cityscapes but he has since concentrated on abstract acrylic painting, mixed-media assemblage, and sculptural works. A consistent theme of his work has been the celebration of black creativity; he has done several series of paintings dedicated to jazz musicians, including Charlie Mingus, Jimi Hendrix, Miles Davis, Thelonious Monk, and John Coltrane. In his sculptural works, Johnson, a student of African tribal art, uses the traditional African methods of wrapping and binding in conjunction with such materials as wire, steel, rope, and burlap.

One-person Exhibitions: Gallery 7, Detroit 1970, 1975; DAM 1972*; FIA 1973.

Group Exhibitions: Studio 21 Gallery, Detroit 1962; MAE 1964–66, 1970, 1972 (Newberry Purchase Prize and Kahn Prize 1964); *Michigan State Fair Exhibition* 1964–66; *Midyear Show,* Butler Institute 1966; *Watercolor USA,* Springfield Museum of Art, Missouri 1966; Arts Extended Gallery, Detroit 1966, 1968; *Afro-American Exhibition,* DIA 1968; *Seven Black Artists,* DAM 1969*; *Spectrum Invitational,* Pontiac Creative Arts Center 1969; *Black Artists,* EMU 1970; *Contemporary Black Artists in America,* Whitney 1971; *National Exhibition of Black Artists,* Smith-Mason Gallery, Washington, D.C. 1971; *Contemporary American Painting and Sculpture,* Whitney 1972; *Black Artists in Michigan Collections,* FIA 1973; *Michigan Artists Biennial,* MSU 1973; *Michigan Focus,* DIA 1974/75*; *Michigan Collects Michigan Art,* Pontiac Creative Arts Center 1976; *Black Perspectives,* Detroit Bank & Trust Co. 1978; *20th Century Afro-American Art from the DIA Collection,* DIA 1978; *Historical Roots: The Black Artist in Michigan,* Detroit Historical Museum 1980.

Collections/Commissions: Biddle Elementary School, Detroit; City of Hope Medical Center, Los Angeles; DIA; FIA; First Federal Savings & Loan, Detroit; Flint Board of Education; Johnson Publishing Company, Chicago; Michigan Consolidated Gas Company, Detroit; National Bank of Detroit (GM Building); Westin Hotel, Renaissance Center, Detroit.

Sources: *WWAA* 1978; MAR; Cederholm 1973; Nawrocki 1980; *DFP* 8-18-68, 4-6-69, 11-22-70, 12-11-80; *Michigan Chronicle* 12-12-70, 10-30-71, 3-25-72; *DN* 4-9-72, 2-18-73, *FJ* 2-18-73.

JONES, Murray

(b. Durham, North Carolina 1915; d. Galena, Ohio 1964)

Painter. Jones received his formal training at the School of the Art Institute of Chicago (M.F.A. 1939), where he was awarded a foreign travel scholarship which enabled him to work in Tahiti and Latin America. After additional study at Duke University, he joined the faculty at Michigan State University in 1946. In 1959, Jones was awarded a Fulbright Fellowship to Japan; he returned to Michigan State University in 1961, and in 1962 he joined the faculty at Ohio State University. An abstract painter, Jones derived his themes from landscape rather than figurative sources. He experimented with industrial lacquers and incorporated collage elements into much of his work, initially using metal foils and, following his trip to the Orient, various Japanese papers.

One-person Exhibitions: Ferargil Gallery, New York City 1945 (two-person); Circle Gallery, Detroit 1950; Chiku-Rin Gallery, Detroit 1952, 1954; Contemporary Arts Gallery, New York City 1952, 1954, 1957*; DAM 1958; Hanamura Gallery, Detroit 1961, 1964; DIA 1962*; *Retrospective*, Kresge Art Center Gallery, MSU 1965*; Lawrence Stevens Gallery, Detroit 1967.

Group Exhibitions: MAE 1946, 1948 (Purchase Prize), 1949–56, 1957 (Maxon Prize and Gallery 4 Prize), 1959 (FSPP); *West Michigan Annual*, GRAM 1949 (1st Prize), 1956; *Exhibition Momentum*, Chicago 1953; *Michigan Art Through 50 Years*, UMMA 1955; *Contemporary American Painting*, Whitney 1956; *Carnegie International* 1962; *Painters and Sculptors in Michigan*, BBAA 1962.

Collections: Albion College; Columbus Gallery of Fine Arts; DIA; GRAM; Kresge Art Center Gallery, MSU; Oakland Museum of Art, Calif.; UMMA.

Sources: *WWAA* 1962; *Art and Artists* (Detroit) July/August 1964; *Art Dig* 26 (March 15, 1952): 28; *Art J* 24, 3 (Spring 1965): 280; *Art News* 51 (April 1952): 54; *Art News* 53 (April 1954): 54: *Art News* 56 (April 1956): 58; *Art News* 65 (October 1966): 62; *Arts* 31 (April 1957): 69; *DN* 11-19-50, 6-6-54, 3-18-59, 3-29-59, 7-31-60, 2-11-62, 4-12-64, 2-26-67; *DFP* 2-6-58, 2-18-62, 2-19-67; *DT* 3-2-58.

JUNGWIRTH, Leonard D.

(b. Detroit, Michigan 1903; d. Lansing, Michigan 1963)

Sculptor. Jungwirth received his earliest training from his father Joachim Jungwirth, who owned a woodcarving firm in Detroit which specialized in architectural decoration. He also attended **John P. Wicker**'s School of Fine Arts, then received a B.A. (1927) in architectural engineering from the University of Detroit and an M.S. (1940) from Wayne State University. He also studied for a short time at the Royal Academy of Fine Arts in Munich (1929–33). Jungwirth taught sculpture at Wayne State from 1936 to 1940. During the Depression he served as supervisor of the arts and crafts section of the Works Progress Administration/Federal Art Project in Michigan. Under the auspices of this project, he completed a large granite statue, *Father Gabriel Richard*, which still stands at the entrance to Belle Isle in Detroit. Jungwirth joined the faculty at Michigan State University in 1940, where he continued to teach until his death in 1963. His later commissions included a wall relief (the city seal) for the Lansing City Hall, a crucifixion for Christ Church Chapel in Grosse Pointe, and MSU's ceramic *Spartan*. Jungwirth was primarily a carver and often said that he thought in wood. His work is characterized by clearly defined and simplified forms which reflect his carver's approach.

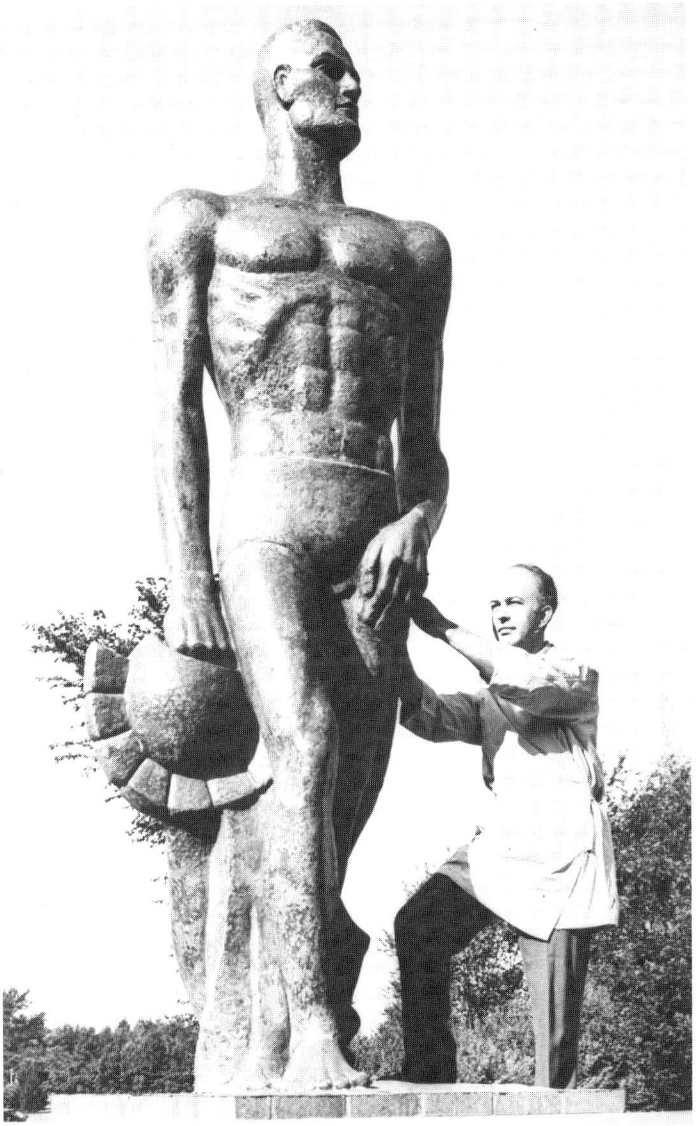

Leonard D. Jungwirth (1903–1963) with Spartan. *Stone. h. 10 feet 6 inches. Campus of Michigan State University, East Lansing. The Detroit Institute of Arts, Research Library.*

One-person Exhibitions: DAM 1938, 1947 (two-person); FIA 1951 (two-person); Anna Werbe Gallery, Detroit 1954; Marygrove College 1957 (two-person); Garelick's Gallery, Detroit 1959; MSU 1963.

Group Exhibitions: *National Exhibition of American Art*, Rockefeller Center 1937; *Michigan Federal Art*

Project Exhibition, DAM 1939; *American Art Today*, New York World's Fair 1939/40; MAE 1939–40, 1943, 1945, 1947–51, 1953, 1955–56 (Kamperman Prize 1937, Skelton and Cantor Prizes 1956); *Origins of Modern Sculpture*, DIA 1946; MACE 1948; *Michigan Artists 1901–1951*, DIA 1951; *Michigan Academy of Science, Arts, and Letters Annual* 1951–55; *Michigan Sculpture Society Exhibition*, DIA 1952; *Michigan Art Through 50 Years*, UMMA 1955; *Michigan Sculpture*, DAM 1958.

Collections/Commissions: Christ Church, Grosse Pointe; City of Detroit; DIA; Grand Haven High School; Lansing City Hall; KIA; MSU; Willow Street School, Lansing.

Sources: *WWAA* 1962; AAA 694–95, 879; Hendry 1980; Nawrocki 1980; *DFP* 4-17-38, 3-5-39, 10-13-40, 11-9-47, 9-14-52; *DN* 11-7-47, 8-22-63.

JUPENA, *Urban*

(b. Jeanette, Pennsylvania 1945)

Textile Artist. Jupena received a B.F.A. (1968) from Philadelphia College of Art and an M.F.A. (1970) from the Cranbrook Academy of Art, where he studied under **Robert Kidd**. From 1970 to 1972 he taught weaving at the Art School of the Detroit Society of Arts and Crafts, and in 1972 became a full-time weaving instructor at Wayne State University. In 1976 Jupena was commissioned to create a wall hanging for the Renaissance Center.

One-person Exhibitions: Art Center, Mt. Clemens 1970; Kingpitcher Gallery, Pittsburgh 1974; Yaw Gallery, Birmingham 1974.

Group Exhibitions: *Contemplation Environments '70*, Mus of Contemp Crafts 1969; MACE 1969, 1971 (Weiner Prize); *Michigan Craftsmen's Council Biennial*, BBAA 1969; *Young Americans*, Mus of Contemp Crafts 1969–71; *Beaux-Arts Designer/Craftsmen*, Columbus Museum of Art 1970; *Boundless Limitations, Designer/Craftsmen VI*, Fort Wayne Art Institute, Ind. 1970 (Prize for Weaving); *Michigan Artists-Craftsmen*, GRAM 1970; *Furs & Feathers*, Mus of Contemp Crafts 1971; *Master Weavers and Protégés*, BBAA 1971; *Space Shelter for Senses—An Experimental Environment*, Mus of Contemp Crafts 1971; *Cranbrook Weavers: Pacesetters and Prototypes*, DIA 1973*, *Con-tex-ture*, Fort Wayne Art Institute, Ind. 1974*; *Arts and Crafts in Detroit 1906–1976*, DIA 1976*.

Sources: MAR.

KACHADOORIAN, *Zubel*

(b. Detroit, Michigan 1924)

Painter. Kachadoorian received his first art training from local portraitist and still-life artist Helen Maynard White. He also studied with **Carlos Lopez** at the Meinzinger Art School in Detroit (1943-44) and privately with **Francis DeErdely**. He attended summer sessions with Francis Chapin at the Oxbow Summer School of Painting and also studied at the Skowhegan School in Maine and the Colorado Fine Arts Center. Kachadoorian lived in France for two years (1950–52), then maintained a studio in New York City. In 1956 he was awarded the Prix de Rome, which enabled him to study at the American Academy in Rome from 1956 to 1960. Upon his return to the United States he accepted a teaching position at the School of the Art Institute of Chicago. He has since taught at the Norton Gallery School in West Palm Beach, Florida; the Birmingham-Bloomfield Art Association; Oxbow Summer School of Painting; Skowhegan School of Painting and Sculpture; and Wayne State University (1967–73). Kachadoorian has also served as artist-in-residence at the Jesse Besser Museum in Alpena, under the auspices of the Michigan Council for the Arts, and in his capacity as art supervisor of the Detroit Repertory Theatre has received two grants from the National Endowment for the Arts. Essentially a figure painter, Kachadoorian works in an abstract expressionist style.

One-person Exhibitions: Scarab Club 1944 (two-person); J. L. Hudson Gallery, Detroit 1945 (two-person), 1947, 1948; Gallery Vivienne, New York City 1947; DAM 1949, 1950, 1953, 1956, 1966; KIA 1946; Galérie Creuze, Paris 1952; Forsythe Gallery, Ann Arbor 1953, 1960, 1961, 1965, 1969; Delacorte Gallery, New York City 1956; Anna Werbe Gallery, Detroit 1959 (two-person); Nordness Gallery, New York City 1960, 1962*, 1964; AIC 1961; Henry Ford Community College, Dearborn 1971; Detroit Repertory Theater 1972.

Group Exhibitions: MAE 1944–64 (Prizes in 1944, 1945, 1955, 1956, 1964); *Five American Painters*, ACA Gallery, Rome 1946; *PAFA Annual* 1948, 1950, 1959; *MWCS Annual* 1949 (Merit Award); *Michigan Art Through 50 Years*, UMMA 1955; *Ten Americans*, Piazza Venezia, Rome 1959; *Contemporary American Paintings and Sculpture*, Krannert Art Museum, University of Illinois 1959; *Midyear Show*, Butler Institute 1960, 1964; *American Painting and Sculpture*, AIC 1961; *Contemporary American Watercolor*, GRAM 1963; *Michigan Art: Yesterday and Today*, FIA 1963; *Corcoran Biennial* 1965; *Made in Detroit*, Franklin Siden Gallery, Birmingham 1967; *Michigan Collects Michigan Art*, Pontiac Creative Arts Center 1976.

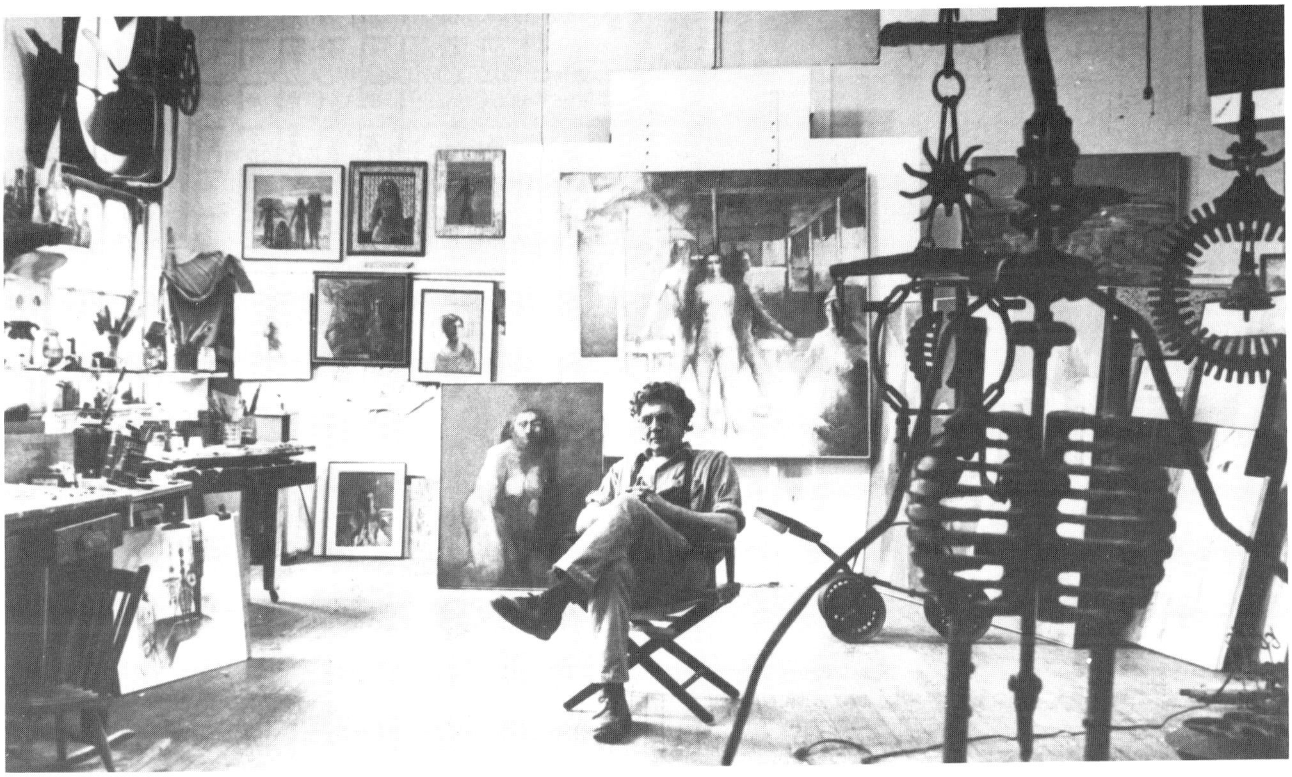

Zubel Kachadoorian (1924–   ) in his studio, 1974. Courtesy the Detroit Free Press.

Collections: AIC; DIA; FIA; NCFA; St. John's Armenian Church, Southfield; Tate Gallery; UMMA; WSU; Worchester Art Museum, Mass.

Sources: *WWAA* 1976; MAR; *Art: USA: Now*, Lee Nordness and Allen S. Weller, eds., New York: Viking, 1962; *Art in America* 2 (Summer 1962): 134; *Arts* 30, 5 (February 1956); 53; *Arts* 30, 7 (April 1956): 8; *Arts* 34, 9 (June 1960): 59; *DN* 1-8-50, 7-8-56, 12-4-68, 1-4-68, 1-14-62, 3-27-66, 2-25-71, 5-19-71; *DFP* 4-23-50, 4-5-56, 4-1-56, 4-10-66, 3-5-67, 9-15-67; *NYT* 4-11-61.

KAMROWSKI, *Gerome*

(b. Warren, Minnesota 1914)

Painter/Sculptor. Kamrowski was educated at the St. Paul School of Art in Minnesota (under Cameron Booth, 1932–35); the Art Students League in New York City (1933–34 and 1938–39); the New Bauhaus in Chicago (1937); and at the Hans Hoffman School of Painting (1938). During the Depression, he worked in Minnesota under the auspices of the Works Progress Administration/Federal Art Project. Toward the end of the 1930s, he returned to New York City, where he was introduced to André Breton and other European Surrealists then living in the city. Kamrowski later became closely associated with Matta. He was one of the first American artists to explore abstract surrealism and the techniques of automatism. In 1946 Kamrowski joined the faculty at the University of Michigan, where he continued to pursue his explorations in abstract surrealism until the late 1950s. In the early 1960s he initiated the Hylozoist Group, which emphasized the use of technological materials and techniques to express surrealistic themes. In 1964 the group held a controversial Hylozoist Arts Festival at the Northland Shopping Center in Southfield at which Ann Arbor's avant-garde ONCE Group also performed. Kamrowski has won many awards, beginning with a Guggenheim Fellowship in 1937. In 1978 he was one of the few Americans to be included in the prestigious "Dada and Surrealism Revisited" exhibition at the Hayward Gallery in London.

One-person Exhibitions: Mortimer Brandt Gallery, New York City 1946; Alexander Iolas Gallery, New York City 1948, 1959; Betty Parsons Gallery, New York City 1948; FIA 1949; *Works in Progress*, DIA 1949; Galérie Creuze, Paris 1950*; Hugo Gallery, New York City 1951; SAM 1954; Battle Creek Civic Art Center 1956; AAA Gallery, Detroit 1958; Gallery Mayer, New York City 1959, 1961; Verve Gallery, De-who is best known for his impressionistic watercolor scenes, has won first prize in watercolor seven times at the Flint Annual. In 1977, one of his watercolors was selected to hang in the Governor's mansion.

One-person Exhibitions: FIA 1947, 1954, 1963, 1969; Scarab Club, Detroit 1960; Albion College 1961; Left Bank Gallery, Flint 1961, 1966, 1971, 1973–74, 1976.

Group Exhibitions: MAE 1934–35, 1937, 1945–46, 1948, 1953, 1955, 1957, 1961; *Flint Annual*, FIA 1936, 1938–41, 1943, 1945, 1949, 1950–55, 1957–60, 1962, 1965, 1967–69, 1972, 1976 (Summerfield Prize 1940; 1st Prize Watercolor 1943, 1956, 1949–51, 1960, 1965); *Five Flint Artists*, FIA 1954; *Area Show*, SAM 1954 (1st Prize), 1962 (1st Prize), 1963 (3rd Prize), 1964 (1st Prize), 1969 (2nd Prize); *Annual Watercolor Exhibition*, Scarab Club, Detroit 1954, 1957, 1961 (1st Prize), 1962, 1964 (2nd Prize); *Mid-Michigan Annual*, Midland Art Association 1960, 1963 (1st Prize); *Michigan Art: Yesterday and Today*, FIA 1963; *Michigan Art on Paper*, KIA 1967; *Scarab Club Annual*, Detroit 1970.

Collections/Commissions: City of Frankenmuth; Ferris State College; FIA; Ford Motor Company, Detroit; McDonald Corporation, Chicago.

Sources: MAR; *FJ* 3-5-61, 4-29-61, 1-21-63, 9-26-76; 1-23-77; *Grand Blanc News* April 1976; 2-17-76.

LARSON, *Julie*

(b. Oneida, New York 1940)

LARSON, *Tyrone*

(b. Detroit, Michigan 1938)

Ceramicists. Julie Larson attended the State University of New York at Buffalo (B.S. 1962) and received an M.A. (1966) from Wayne State University, where she studied with **William Pitney**. Inspired by the example of **John Glick**, she and her husband, Tyrone, who has no formal training in ceramics, set up a production pottery studio in Royal Oak in 1966. Julie taught briefly at the Birmingham-Bloomfield Art Association (1967). The Larson line of production wares includes a variety of handbuilt and wheel-thrown forms such as boxes, covered hexagonal jars, and dinnerware, often luster glazed in gold or platinum. In 1971 the Larsons left Michigan to teach at the Penland School of Crafts in North Carolina.

One-person Exhibitions (joint): Left Bank Gallery, Flint 1968; KIA 1969; Creative Arts Center, CMU 1970; *Art in the Round*, Somerset Mall, Troy 1971.

Group Exhibitions (Julie): MACE 1967 (Honorable Mention), 1969, 1971 (Honorable Mention), 1972; *Traveling Crafts Exhibition*, MCA 1967–71; *Ceramics Invitational*, EMU 1968, 1970; *Designed in Michigan*, BBAA 1968; *Young Americans*, Mus Contemp Crafts 1969; *Exhibition '70*, Columbus Museum of Art 1970 (Beaux-Arts Purchase Prize); *Michigan Design*, FIA 1970; *Contemporary Ceramics: The Artist's Viewpoint*, KIA 1977*.

Group Exhibitions (Tyrone): MACE 1967 (Mt. Clemens Pottery Prize), 1969 (EMU Purchase Prize), 1971–72; *Ceramics Invitational*, EMU 1968, 1970; *Ceramic National*, Everson Museum, Syracuse 1968; *Designed in Michigan*, BBAA 1968; *Exhibition '70*, Columbus Museum of Art 1970; *Craft Multiples*, Smithsonian Institution 1976; *Contemporary Ceramics: The Artist's Viewpoint*, KIA 1977*.

Collections (Julie): CMU; Columbus Museum of Art; North Carolina National Bank, Charlotte; Smithsonian Institution; Utah Museum of Fine Art, Salt Lake City; WSU.

Collections (Tyrone): EMU; Hans Bechtler Collection, Zurich; Henry Ford Community College, Dearborn; Smithsonian Institution; Utah Museum of Fine Art, Salt Lake City.

Sources: MAR; Marjorie Bevlin, *Design Through Discovery*, New York: Holt, Rinehart & Winston, 1977; John Cayne, ed., *The Penland School of Crafts Book of Pottery*, Indianapolis: Bobbs-Merrill, 1975; Polly Rothenburg, *The Complete Book of Ceramic Art*, New York: Crown, 1972; Thomas Shafer, *Pottery Decoration*, New York: Watson-Guptill, 1976; *CH* 31, 1 (February 1971): 47–48; *CH* 31, 4 (August 1971): 47; *CMo* 16, 1 (January 1968): 24; *CMo* 19, 4 (April 1971): 14–16; *Studio Potter* 3, 1 (Summer 1974): 15; *DFP* 8-6-67.

LEACH, *Richard*

(b. Flint, Michigan 1923)

Ceramicist. After initial studies at the Flint Institute of Arts and Michigan State University, Leach earned an M.F.A. (1961) from the State University of New York at Alfred. He joined the faculty at Albion College in 1963. He has taught ceramics at the Kalamazoo Institute of Arts and in 1968 and 1973 directed the Summer School Pottery at the State University of New York at Alfred. Leach has also conducted workshops at the Kalamazoo Institute of Arts (1964, 1973), Southern Illinois University (1974), and John Wesley College, Owosso (1972). Known for his kiln designs, he has constructed kilns in Battle Creek, Albion, Jackson, and Dayton, Ohio. In 1972, Leach and Paul Loukides, a film instructor from Albion, pooled their efforts to create the instructional film, *Throwing on the Wheel: Centering, Opening and Raising* (University of Michigan Audio-Visual Center), which was designed to teach the fundamentals of ceramics to beginning students.

One-person Exhibitions: MSU 1957; HAM 1959; Hanamura Gallery, Detroit 1963 (two-person) 1964, 1967; *Raku*, Fort Wayne Art Institute 1973.

Group Exhibitions: FIA 1950–51; MACE 1956–64 (Webber Prize 1962); *Decorative Arts and Ceramics Exhibition*, Wichita Art Association, Kans. 1957–60; *Michiana Regional Exhibition*, South Bend Art Center, Ind. 1957–60; *Michigan Potters' Association Annual* 1958; *Salon des Refusés*, Scarab Club, Detroit 1960; *Ceramic National*, Everson Museum of Art, Syracuse 1961, 1964 (Purchase Prize); *Fiber/Clay/Metal*, Minnesota Museum of Art 1962; *Midwest Designer/Craftsmen*, KIA 1962; *Ceramic Invitational*, Scripps College, Claremont, Calif. 1963 (Purchase Prize); *Michigan Art: Yesterday and Today*, FIA 1963; New York World's Fair 1964; *Ceramics Invitational*, EMU 1965 (Purchase Prize), 1968, 1977; *Ceramic Arts USA*, Smithsonian Institution 1966; *Sixteen Michigan Ceramicists*, Cranbrook 1967; *Michigan Potters Invitational*, Calvin College 1977.

Collections/Commissions: EMU; Everson Museum of Art, Syracuse; Scripps College, Claremont, Calif.

Sources: MAR; Glenn C. Nelson, *Ceramics*, New York: Holt, Rinehart & Winston 1960; Jack Troy, *Salt Glaze Ceramics*, New York: Watson-Guptill, 1977; Leach in *Studio Potter* 4 (August 1977): 31; *CMo* 20, 7 (September 1972): 49; *Michigan Challenge* (State Chamber of Commerce) 4, 5 (February 1964): 38; *Battle Creek Enquirer* 10-15-68; *GR Press* 9-4-77.

LEE, James

(b. Detroit, Michigan 1927; d. Detroit, Michigan 1975)

Painter/Printmaker. Lee attended Wayne State University and the Art School of the Detroit Society of Arts and Crafts. He taught graphics at the **Charles McGee** School of Arts and was also associated with McGee's Gallery 7. His prints and mixed-media works of oil and cork on canvas are patterned by dots that create an optical effect. A member of the Michigan Association of Printmakers, Lee was its vice president at the time of his death in 1975.

One-person Exhibitions: Highland Park College 1969; Arts Extended Gallery, Detroit 1970; Gallery 7, Detroit 1973.

Group Exhibitions: DAM 1960; *Annual*, Common Ground of the Arts, Detroit 1962; *Michigan Printmakers*, Park Gallery, Detroit 1962; *National Print Exhibition*, Brooklyn Museum 1962; *Michigan Association of Printmakers*, Common Ground of the Arts, Detroit 1966; *Michigan Association of Printmakers Biennial* 1966; *Seven Black Artists*, DAM 1969; *Twenty-Five Black American Printmakers*, Newark, N.J. 1969; *Black Artists Exhibition*, Sill Gallery, EMU 1970; *Contemporary Black Artists in America*, Whitney 1971; *Detroit Art Jazz '71*, DIA 1971; *Artrain*, Michigan Council of the Arts 1971/72; *Art From a Black Perspective*, The American Black Artist, Inc., Detroit Bank & Trust Co. 1977; *Historical Roots: The Black Artist in Michigan*, Detroit Historical Museum 1980.

Sources: Cederholm 1973; *DFP* 4-6-69; *DN* 11-16-69, 3-7-71.

LEEPA, Allen

(b. New York, New York 1919)

Painter. Leepa received his first art training at the Art Students League in New York City, which he attended while still in high school. In 1937 he received a scholarship to the New Bauhaus in Chicago, where he studied with László Moholy-Nagy. He later studied with Hans Hoffman in Provincetown, Massachusetts, Abraham Rattner in New York, and Fernand Léger in Paris, and subsequently received a B.S. (1941) and an M.A. (1942) from Columbia University. He joined the faculty at Michigan State University in 1945, and in

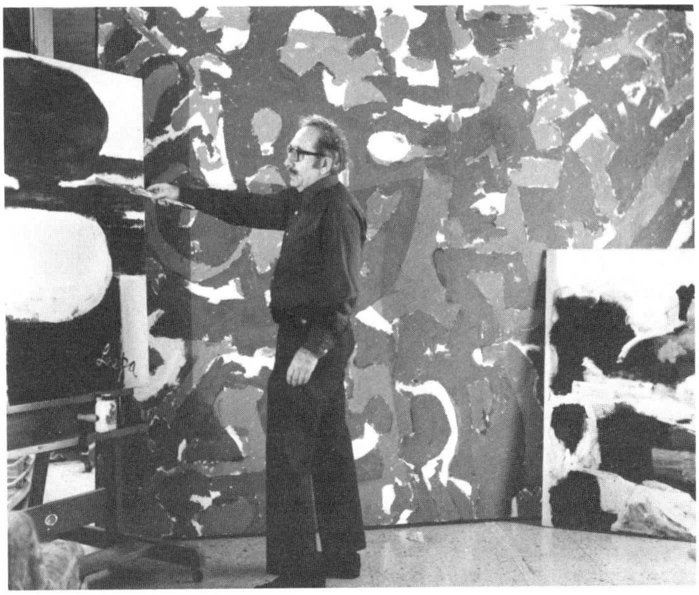

Allen Leepa (1919–) in his studio, 1979. Courtesy the artist.

1950 was a Fulbright Fellow at the Sorbonne. Leepa has written numerous articles on the theory of modern art and two books: *The Challenge of Modern Art* (New York, 1949) and *Abraham Rattner* (New York, 1973). His paintings are large abstract expressionist works characterized by broad brushstrokes.

One-person Exhibitions: Little Gallery, Provincetown, Mass. 1939; Charles Fourth Gallery, New York City 1948 (two-person); Artists Gallery, New York City 1953; AAA Gallery, Detroit 1959; Galérie La Cour d'-Ingres, Paris 1963*; *Retrospective*, DAM 1964, 1975; Forsythe Gallery, Ann Arbor 1976; *Festival of the Arts*, Ferris State College 1978.

Group Exhibitions: *Annual Show*, Brooklyn Museum 1940; *West Michigan Annual*, GRAM 1946, 1948, 1955–56, 1958, 1960 (Keeler Award); MAE 1946, 1954–55, 1959, 1961; Circle Gallery, Detroit 1949; Chiku-Rin Gallery, Detroit 1950; *New Artists*, MOMA 1950; *Salon d'Automne*, Paris 1951; *PAFA Annual* 1951–52; *Michigan Art: Yesterday and Today*, FIA 1963; Musée d'Art Moderne, Paris 1964, 1966; *50 American Printmakers*, AFA 1967; *American Academy of Arts and Letters Annual*, New York City 1968 (Purchase Prize); *27 Painters*, UMMA 1976; *New York W.P.A. Artists Exhibition*, The New School, New York City 1977; *West 80: Art and the Law*, Minnesota Museum of Art, 1980.

Collections: Civic Center, Lansing; GRAM; National Bank of Detroit; Royal Academy, Edinburgh; South Bend Art Center, Ind.

Sources: *WWAA 1980*; AAA, Interview, D313; MAR; *Art Dig* 27, 9 (February 1, 1953): 17; *New Yorker* October 6, 1956; *NYT* 6-10-41, 2-3-53, 9-1-56; *GR Herald* 4-20-58; *DFP* 5-11-58.

LEE-SMITH, *Hughie*

(b. Eustis, Florida 1914)

Painter. Raised in Cleveland, Lee-Smith graduated from the Cleveland School of Art in 1938. During this time he also designed stage sets, acted, and danced for the theatre group of the Karamu Art Association, an organization intended to encourage and develop black talent which he had helped to establish. During the Depression, Lee-Smith was appointed head of the art

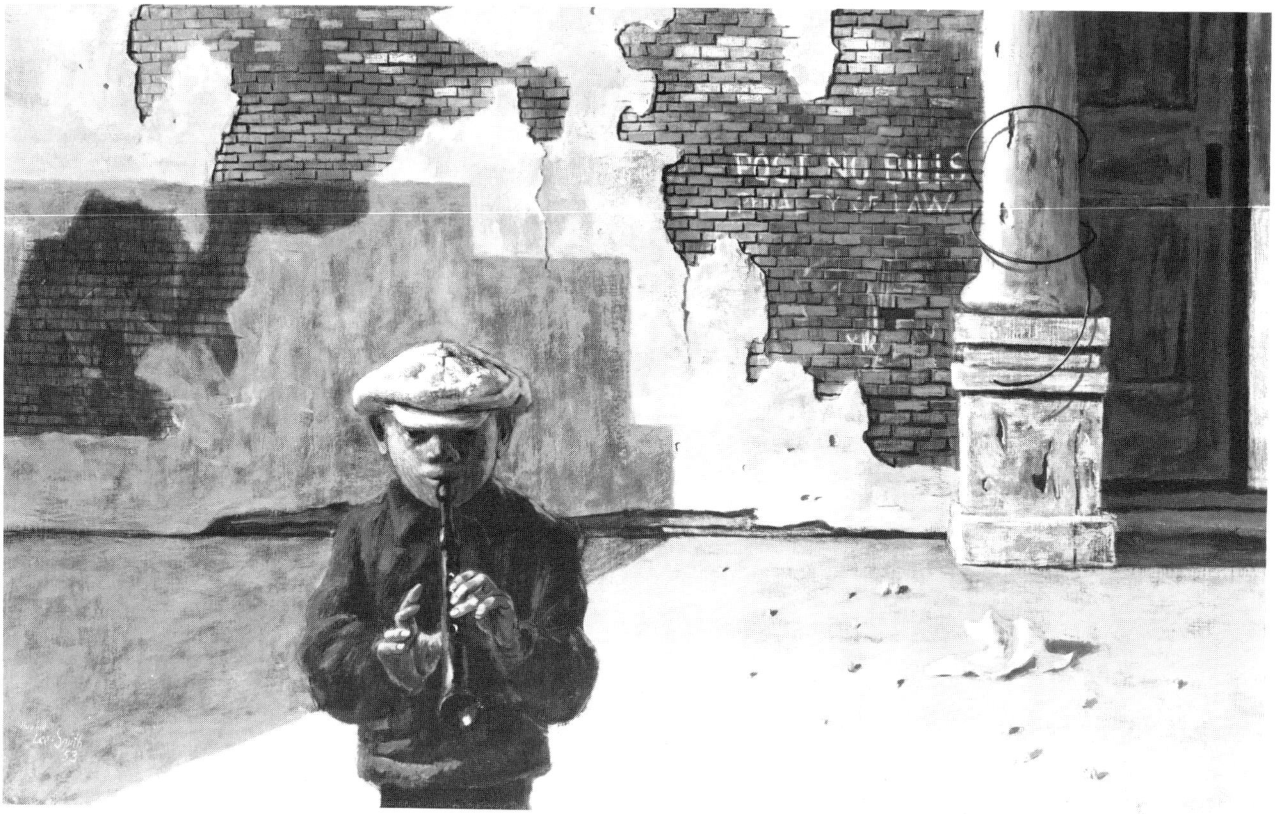

Hughie Lee-Smith (1914–). The Piper. *Oil on composition board. 22 × 35¼ inches. Collection of the Detroit Institute of Arts, Gift of Mr. and Mrs. Stanley J. Winkelman.*

department at Claflin University in Orangeburg, South Carolina, and was also employed by the Ohio Works Progress Administration/Federal Art Project (1938–39). During World War II he served as a Navy artist at the Great Lakes Training Center in Chicago, where he painted a series of murals on black history in the United States. After the war he studied at the Art School of the Detroit Society of Arts and Crafts under **John Carroll** and **Sarkis Sarkisian** and later received a B.S. in art education from Wayne State University. Lee-Smith taught adult education classes in Birmingham and Highland Park as well as at the Grosse Pointe War Memorial (1956–66) and at the Pen and Palette Club (of which he was a member) in Detroit. A promoter of other black artists, he organized an exhibition of Midwestern black artists in 1943.

The first twentieth-century black Michigan artist to achieve national recognition, Lee-Smith's local career culminated in 1953 when he was awarded the Founders Society Purchase Prize at the Michigan Artists Exhibition for his painting, *The Piper*. During his seventeen-year residence in Detroit, Lee-Smith's style developed within the realist tradition. His early paintings of slum children and deteriorating urban landscapes echo the social consciousness of the 1930s, while his later works are more romantic, in the manner of Walter Steumpfig, Edward Hopper, or Eugene Berman. After leaving Detroit in 1958, Lee-Smith taught in Princeton, New Jersey, then served as artist-in-residence at Howard University, Washington, D.C. (1969–71). In 1972 he joined the faculty of the Art Students League in New York City.

One-person Exhibitions: Snowden Gallery, Chicago 1945; South Side Community Art Center, Chicago 1945; Ten-Thirty Gallery, Cleveland 1950 (three-person), 1952, 1955 (three-person), 1956–57, 1960–61, 1966; DAM 1952, 1958, 1961, 1966; Garelick's Gallery, Detroit 1953; Anna L. Werbe Galleries, Detroit 1953–54; Forsythe Gallery, Ann Arbor 1954, 1966; Howard University 1955, 1958; Petite Gallerie, Inc., New York City 1958; Albion College 1959 (two-person); Janet Nessler Gallery, New York City 1960, 1962, 1964; Grosse Pointe War Memorial, 1963; Circle Gallery, Cleveland 1965; Bergman Gallery, University of Chicago 1969; Grand Central Art Galleries, New York City 1969, 1973; Arwin Galleries, Detroit 1971; J. L. Hudson Co., Detroit 1971; San Guiseppi Gallery, Mount St. Joseph College on the Ohio 1974; WMU 1977.

Group Exhibitions: *May Show*, Cleveland Museum of Art 1938–40; *The Negro Artist Comes of Age*, Albany Institute of History and Art, N.Y. 1945; MAE 1950–57; *Negro Artists in Michigan*, Veterans Memorial Building, Detroit 1952; Little Gallery, Birmingham 1955; *MASAL Annual* 1956 (Purchase Prize); Eggleston Gallery, New York City 1957 (Emily Lowe Competition Award); *Annual*, National Academy of Design, New York City 1957–72 (Clarke Prize 1959, Purchase Prize 1963); National Academy Galleries 1958 (Allied Artists Prize); *U.S.I.A. Exhibition* 1958 (traveled to Iron Curtain countries); *PAFA Annual* 1959, 1962; *Midyear Show*, Butler Institute 1960–61; *New Vistas in American Negro Art*, Howard University 1961; *Art of the American Negro*, Harlem Cultural Council, New York City 1966; *Afro-American Artists 1800–1969*, Philadelphia Civic Center 1969; *Black Reflections*, Flint Community Schools 1969 (traveling); *Afro-American Artists: New York and Boston*, Boston Museum of Fine Arts 1970; *Contemporary Black Artists in America*, Whitney 1970*; *Dimensions of Black*, LaJolla Museum of Art, Calif. 1970; The Art Confederation Gallery, Kingston, N.J. 1972; *Black Artists in Michigan Collections*, FIA 1973; *Arts and Crafts in Detroit 1906–1976*, DIA 1976; *Michigan Collects Michigan Art*, Pontiac Creative Arts Center 1976; *Two Centuries of Black American Art*, Los Angeles County Museum of Art 1976* (traveling); *Art From a Black Perspective*, Detroit Bank & Trust Co. 1977; *20th-Century Afro-American Art From the Collection of the Detroit Institute of Arts*, DIA 1978; *Historical Roots: The Black Artist in Michigan*, Detroit Historical Museum 1980.

Collections: Center for Creative Studies, Detroit; Chase Manhattan Bank, New York City; Cleveland Institute of Art; DIA; Flint Board of Education; Golden State Insurance Co., Los Angeles; Howard University; Johnson Publishing Co., Chicago; Kutztown State College, Pa.; Lagos Museum, Nigeria; Museum of Fine Arts, Boston; Museum of the National Center of Afro-American Artists, Washington, D.C.; NCFA; Parrish Museum, Southampton, Long Island; U.S. Navy Art Center, Washington, D.C.; WSU.

Sources: *WWAA 1978*; AAA 694–5, N70-10: 42–174, N69-111: 1–228 (restricted), 829: 1–169; Cederholm 1973; *Artist* 42 (October 1978); 48ff; *DFP* 10-19-52, 1-18-42; *DN* 10-26-52, 12-30-53, 3-21-54, 3-27-55, 12-1-57, 1-12-58, 5-21-58; *NYT* 10-30-58.

LEWIS, *William A.*

(b. Detroit, Michigan 1918)

Painter. Originally trained as a designer, Lewis studied painting with **Carlos Lopez** and **Jean Paul Slusser** while an undergraduate at the University of Michigan. After working as a freelance designer (with Harvey Littleton) and as an illustrator, he joined the University of Michigan faculty in 1949. One of the founders of the Ann Arbor Potters Guild (with **J. T. Abernathy** and Littleton), Lewis is also a member of the Michigan Water Color Society. For ten years he was the University of Michigan's representative to the National Association of Schools of Art. Best known for his large-scale watercolors, Lewis also works in oil, acrylic, and collage. He has had over forty one-person shows and has an equal number of works in corporate and institutional collections throughout the Midwest.

One-person Exhibitions: Forsythe Gallery, Ann Arbor 1953, 1958, 1961, 1963–64, 1966, 1969, 1971, 1976; AAA Gallery, Detroit 1961; GRAM 1961; Battle Creek Civic Art Center 1962; DAM 1962; Albion College 1965; Detroit Historical Museum 1965; Left Bank Gallery, Flint 1966; Arwin Gallery, Detroit 1968, 1977.

Group Exhibitions: *Midyear Show,* Butler Institute 1953, 1958–59, 1961, 1963–65, 1968 (Purchase Prize 1958); MAE 1954 (Contemporary Arts Prize), 1956 (DSWP Prize), 1957, 1961, 1963, 1966; *MWCS Annual* 1955–present (Merit Award 1955, 1957, 1958, Jaeger Award 1972); *Drawings USA,* Minnesota Museum of Art 1956; *MASAL Annual* 1957 (Purchase Award); *West Michigan Annual,* GRAM 1960, 1961 (Keeler Award), 1963, 1966; *Contemporary American Watercolors,* GRAM 1963; *Michigan Painters-Printmakers,* GRAM 1967 (Invited), 1969, 1971.

Collections/Commissions: Albion College; Blue Cross and Blue Shield of Michigan, Detroit; Butler Institute; Church of the Good Shepherd, Ann Arbor; Detroit Bank & Trust Co.; GRAM; Grand Rapids City Hall; KIA; Michigan Consolidated Gas Company, Detroit; Minnesota Museum of Art; Rackham Building and Music School, U. of M.

Sources: *WWAA* 1978; MAR; *DAC News* 52, 2 (February 1967): 59; *AAN* 6-2-57, 3-9-61, 2-4-64, 2-3-66, 9-14-69, 7-4-76; *DN* 8-25-57, 7-21-63, 4-23-64; *GR Press* 1-5-62, 10-1-62; *DFP* 7-15-62.

LOPEZ, *Carlos*

(b. Havana, Cuba 1908, d. Ann Arbor, Michigan 1953)

Painter. Lopez came to the United States in 1919. He attended the School of the Art Institute of Chicago from 1927 to 1930, then spent three years at the Detroit Art Academy (1930–33), where he studied with George Rich and **Leon Makielski.** During the Depression, under the auspices of the U.S. Treasury Department's Section of Fine Arts, Lopez completed murals for post offices in Dwight, Illinois, and Paw Paw, Plymouth, and Birmingham, Michigan. He also painted a mural for the Register of Deeds Building in Washington, D.C. He served as director of the Detroit Art Academy from 1935 to 1937 and subsequently taught at Meinzinger's Art School. In 1942 he was one of eight American artists commissioned by the war department to do a series of paintings of U.S. industry at war. On commission from the U.S. Navy, *Life* magazine, and the Standard Oil Company, he spent the rest of the war years documenting the action in North Africa.

Lopez joined the faculty at the University of Michigan in 1945 and also taught for several summers at the Oxbow Summer School of Art. Lopez's work before the war was very much in the tradition of the "American scene" painters. In the 1940s and 1950s, however, his work became increasingly expressionistic. Most of his work from this period was figurative—performers such as minstrels, clowns, matadors, musicians were a favorite theme—and is characterized by heavy slashing lines, harlequin patterns of color, and introspective, even alienated figures. Lopez also collaborated with his wife, Rhoda Lopez, on ceramic pieces.

One-person Exhibitions: DAM 1936, 1938, 1941, 1945, 1949 (two-person), 1951 (two-person); Hudson Gallery, Detroit 1936; Scarab Club, Detroit 1941; Associated American Artists, New York City 1945; Forsythe Gallery, Ann Arbor 1952; *Memorial Exhibition,* DIA 1953*; *Retrospective,* La Jolla Art Museum Calif., 1963.

Group Exhibitions: MAE 1932–52 (Haass Prize 1936, 1942; Modern Art Prize 1937; Kamperman Prize 1940; Skelton Prize 1941, 1948; Whitcomb Prize 1941, 1942, 1944; Werbe Prize 1943; Maxon Prize 1944, 1952); *National Exhibition of American Art,* Rockefeller Center 1937; *Great Lakes Exhibition,* Albright Art Gallery, Buffalo 1938; *PAFA Annual* 1939, 1942, 1947–49; New York World's Fair 1939; *Corcoran Biennial* 1941, 1947; *Paintings by American Artists,* DIA 1942; *American Watercolors and Drawings,* AIC 1944, 1949; *Pepsi Cola "Portrait of America" Exhibition,* New York City 1944, 1946–48 ($500 award 1947); *Contemporary American Painting,* Whitney 1945; *Painting in the U.S.,* Carnegie Institute 1945; *Contemporary American Painting,* Krannert Art Gallery, University of Illinois, 1948; *Michigan on Canvas,* J. L. Hudson Company, Detroit 1948*; *American Painting Today,* MMA 1950; *Michigan Art: Yesterday and Today,* FIA 1963.

Collections: CAAM; DIA; J. L. Hudson Company Collection, Henry Ford Museum, Dearborn; Naval Hospital, Washington, D.C.; Standard Oil Company, N.J.; UMMA; Whitney.

Sources: *WWAA* 1953: Kenny 1965; *Art Dig* 19, 11 (March 1, 1945): 17; *Art Dig* 22, 2 (October 15, 1947): 8; *Art Dig* 27, 8 (January 15, 1953): 9; *Art News* 44, 3 (March 15, 1945): 27; *Art News* 46, 6 (August 1947):

18–19; *DFP* 2-13-38, 5-4-41, 11-14-43, 11-7-46, 1-11-53; *DN* 8-16-42, 11-30-45, 3-20-49, 1-11-53; *AAN* 1-7-53; *NYT* 1-8-53.

LOREE, *John P.*

(b. New York 1931)

Ceramicist. After receiving an M.F.A. from New York State College of Ceramics at Alfred, Loree taught for two years at New York State College of Education in Buffalo, before coming to Eastern Michigan University in 1962. Known not only as a ceramicist but also as a lecturer/demonstrator, he has given numerous lectures throughout the United States and has served as artist-in-residence at Southern Illinois University in Edwardsville, at Michigan State University, and at the Interlochen Arts Academy. In 1966 he organized and designed the first "Ceramics Invitational" at EMU. In 1969 he taped a half-hour lecture/demonstration, "Two Potters: Hamada of Japan and Loree of the U.S." for commercial television. Loree works predominantly in wheel-thrown porcelain and raku.

One-person Exhibitions: Left Bank Gallery, Flint 1964 (two-person), 1966; DAM 1967 (three-person), 1969, 1971, 1975; Stangers, Birmingham 1968 (two-person); Forsythe Gallery, Ann Arbor 1969 (two-person), 1971; WMU 1975; Hanamura-Hagopian, Detroit 1970 (three-person).

Group Exhibitions: *Decorative Arts and Ceramics Exhibition*, Wichita Art Association, Kans. 1960, 1964, 1966; *Ceramics National*, Everson Museum of Art, Syracuse 1962; Mus Contemp Crafts 1963; MACE 1963, 1972; *Ceramics Invitational*, EMU 1966–71; *Clay/Glass Invitational*, Delta College, Midland 1976, 1977.

Collections: Alden Dow Collection, Midland; Rockefeller Collection, Albany, N.Y.; Royal Ontario Museum, Toronto; Smithsonian Institution.

Sources: MAR; Daniel Rhodes, *Stoneware and Porcelain: The Art of Highfired Pottery*, Philadelphia: Chilton, 1960; *CH* 30, 1 (January/February 1970): 52; *CH* 31, 4 (August 1971): 43; *CH* 37, 2 (April 1977): 54; *CMo* 17, 3 (March 1969): cover; *CMo* 18, 2 (February 1970): 32; *CMo* 20, 4 (April 1972): 18; *DFP* 6-7-70.

LOVING, *Alvin*

(b. Detroit, Michigan 1935)

Painter/Sculptor. Loving received a B.F.A. from the University of Illinois and an M.F.A. from the University of Michigan, then taught at Eastern Michigan University from 1964 to 1968. In 1971 he painted an outdoor mural, an interlocking series of colorful cubes, on the First National Bank Building in Detroit, the first outdoor work commissioned by Detroit Renaissance. Loving left Michigan in 1974.

One-person Exhibitions: Whitney 1969/70*; Gertrude Kasle Gallery, Detroit 1969–71; *Retrospective*, Ohio University, Athens 1974; Notre Dame University 1975: Fischbach Gallery, New York City 1976; Studio Museum of Harlem, New York City 1977.

Group Exhibitions: MAE 1965; *Michigan Art On Paper*, KIA 1967; *Afro-American Exhibit*, DIA 1968 (traveling); *5 + 1*, State University of New York, Stony Brook 1969; *Black Artists Invitational*, EMU 1970; *Contemporary Black Artists in America*, Whitney 1971; *Contemporary American Painting and Sculpture*, Whitney 1972; *Black Artists in Michigan Collections*, FIA 1973; *Blacks: USA: 1973*, New York Cultural Center, New York City 1973; World's Fair, Spokane, Wash. 1974; *American Black Art—The Known and the New*, Battle Creek Civic Art Center 1977 (traveling); *Historical Roots: The Black Artist in Michigan*, Detroit Historical Museum 1980.

Collections: DIA; International Arrivals Building, Kennedy International Airport; Toledo Museum of Art; Trenton Museum; UMMA; Vassar College; Whitney.

Sources: Cederholm 1973; Nawrocki 1980; *Art International* 16, 5 (May 1972): 56–57; *Art International* 17, 6 (Summer 1973): 65–66; *Art News* 70, 2 (April 1971): 83–84; *Art News* 71, 2 (April 1972): 55; *Artforum* 10, 10 (June 1972): 86; *Arts* 44, 3 (December 1969): 56; *Arts* 44, 4 (February 1970): 57; *Arts* 47, 6 (April 1973): 78; *Arts* 47, 7 (May 1973): 61 *Studio International* 179, 921 (April 1970): 187; *DN* 8-18-68, 12-28-69; *DFP* 8-4-74, 10-19-75.

LOWDER, *Dwayne*

(b. Albemarle, North Carolina 1936)

Painter/Sculptor. Lowder received a B.A. (1959) and an M.A. (1963) from the University of North Carolina, Chapel Hill, and came to Michigan in 1963 as the Kalamazoo Institute of Art's first full-time exhibition designer. In 1969 he joined the art faculty at Western Michigan University, and in the same year completed a sculpture for the courtyard of the Kalamazoo Institute of Arts. His works include serigraphs, circular paintings, and sculpture, using aluminum, stained glass, laminated wood or metal, bronze, and acrylic on canvas.

One-person Exhibitions: KIA 1970; WMU 1972; CMU 1973; Albion College 1976.

Group Exhibitions: *International Print Competition*, Seattle Museum of Art 1963 (Purchase Prize); *Michigan Craftsmen and Sculptors*, GRAM 1964; *Area Show*, KIA 1964, 1970 (Award), 1971, 1973 (Award), 1974, 1976; *Michiana Regional*, South Bend Art Center, Ind. 1965; MAE 1965, 1966 (Activities Committee Prize); *Michigan Art on Paper*, KIA 1967; *Eight Michigan Artists*, MSU 1969; *North Carolina Sculpture Invitational*, Duke University Art Museum 1969*; *27 Painters*, UMMA 1976.

Collections: Bundy Art Gallery, Waitsfield, Vt.; KIA; Mint Museum of Art, Charlotte, N.C.; North Carolina Museum of Art, Raleigh.

Sources: Hendry 1980B; *KG* 4-12-73; 11-11-73; 4-25-74, 3-26-76, 2-13-77, 11-9-78; *Daily News* (Midland) 9-4-73.

LUCHS, *Michael*

(b. Portsmouth, Ohio 1938)

Sculptor. Luchs received a B.A. (1961) from Olivet College. He attended the University of Michigan in 1964 and Wayne State University from 1966 to 1968. A member of the co-operative Willis Gallery, he maintained a studio in Detroit's Cass Corridor before moving to Holly, Michigan. In the early 1970s, Luchs began creating both freestanding and wall-mounted constructions using machine parts, wire scrap, wood, and other secondhand materials. His favorite motif is a crouching rabbit. In 1975 he was commissioned by the City of Detroit Parks and Recreation Department to construct a 12-foot steel rabbit in Cass Park (since dismantled).

One-person Exhibitions: Willis Gallery, Detroit 1976; Feigenson-Rosenstein Gallery, Detroit 1977, 1979; Willard Gallery, New York City 1978 (two-person).

Group Exhibitions: MAE, DIA 1970; *Opening Show*, Willis Gallery, Detroit 1971; *12 Statements: Beyond the '60s*, DIA 1972*; *Selections from the Studios at Old Convention Hall*, DAM 1974; *Group Show*, Willis Gallery, Detroit 1974, 1976; *Cass Corridor Artists*, Somerset Mall, Troy 1975; *Detroit Area Artists: Works In Progress II*, DIA 1976*; *Michigan Collects Michigan Art*, Pontiac Creative Arts Center 1976*; *Indoor/Outdoor at P.S. 1*, Institute for Art and Urban Resources, Inc., P.S. 1, Long Island City, N.Y. 1978; *Image and Object in Contemporary Sculpture*, DIA 1979*; *Kick Out The Jams*, DIA 1980*.

Collections: City of Detroit; DIA.

Sources: *Art in America* 67, 4 (July-August 1979): 47–49; *Arts* 53, 5 (January 1979): 25: *New Art Examiner* 7, 1 (section 2) (1979): 3; *DN* 4-8-73, 4-17-77, 2-11-79; *DFP* 7-25-75, 4-10-77, 7-2-78, 7-15-79; *Soho Weekly News* 1-3-80.

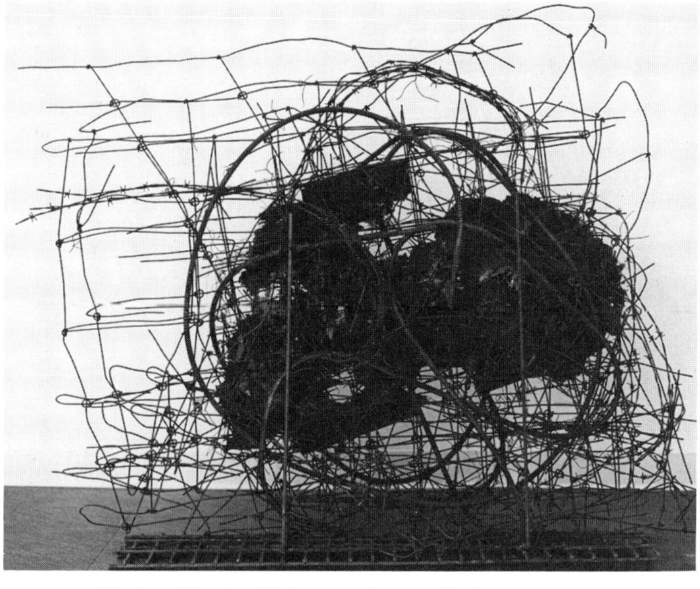

Michael Luchs (1938–). Untitled (#1). 1979. Metal, wood, paint. 45½ × 57 × 12 inches. Private Collection. Courtesy Feigenson-Rosenstein Gallery, Detroit. Brad Iverson, Photographer.

LUTZ, *Winifred*

(b. Brooklyn, New York 1942)

Sculptor. Lutz received a B.F.A. (1965) from the Cleveland Institute of Art and an M.F.A. (1968) from the Cranbrook Academy of Art, where she studied papermaking under **Laurence Barker**. She is known both for hand-processed paperworks (some molded, others freeform) made from such fibers as sisal, jute, milkweed silks and pods, and cotton rags, and for large wooden geometric site-oriented sculpture. Lutz left Michigan in 1974 to join the faculty at Yale University.

One-person Exhibitions: Centro Internazionale de Ceràmica, Rome 1966; Sergel Gallery of Fine Prints, Chicago 1967; Willis Gallery, Detroit 1971 (two-person); GRAM 1973; KIA 1974; Mus Contemp Crafts 1975; Humbolt State University, Aracata, Calif. 1976; Indiana State University 1977; Marilyn Pearl Gallery, New York City 1977–79.

Group Exhibitions: *May Show*, Cleveland Museum of Art 1963–64, 1967; *Annual Ceramics and Sculpture Show*, Butler Institute 1964, 1967, 1973; *Amusement*

Is, Mus of Contemp Crafts 1967; *50 Years—50 Artists*, Cleveland Institute of Art 1967; *Michigan Printmakers Show*, Birmingham 1968; MAE, DIA 1969, 1970/71; *Sculpture Invitational*, Cranbrook 1970; *Michigan Focus*, DIA 1974/75; *Handmade Paper*, MOMA 1976; *Wood*, Nassau County Museum, 1977; *New Ways with Paper*, National Collection of Fine Arts, Washington, D.C. 1978; *Paper as Medium*, Smithsonian Institution Traveling Exhibition Service, Washington, D.C. 1978.

Collections: Albright-Knox Art Gallery, Buffalo; Cleveland Museum of Art; AIC; Crocker Art Museum, Sacramento; Desert Museum, Palm Springs, Calif.; Dewitt Cultural Center, Hope College; GRAM; Oxbow School of Painting, Saugatuck; David Rockefeller, Jr.

Sources: *Artforum* 15, 9 (May 1977): 66–67; *Artforum* 19, 9 (May 1978): 62; *Arts* 51, 9 (May 1977): 26; *Arts* 53, 9 (May 1979): 31; *CH* 37, 3 (June 1977): 62; *CH* 39, 2 (April 1979): 33–35; *NYT* 3-3-78; *Hartford Courant* (Conn.) 10-10-78.

LUX, Gwen

(b. Chicago, Illinois 1910)

Sculptor. Lux began her career in Detroit at age fourteen when she attended classes at the Pewabic Pottery under **Mary Chase Stratton** who encouraged her to pursue further study in Baltimore. She also attended the **John P. Wicker** School of Art in Detroit (1924–25), the Maryland Institute of Arts in Baltimore (1926–27), and the Boston Museum School (1927–28), and studied under Ivan Mestrovic in Yugoslavia (1929). She received her first sculptural commission for Radio City Music Hall, Rockefeller Center, in 1930, exhibited at the Salon d'Automne in Paris the following year, and two years later received a Guggenheim Fellowship (1933) to continue studies in lithography in Paris and also travel to Spain and Morocco. Returning to the United States, she worked for a time as a designer for Steuben Glass in New York City and in 1942 returned to Michigan to head the sculpture department at the Art School of the Detroit Society of Arts and Crafts (1942–46). Lux assisted Mary Chase Stratton in a number of Pewabic Pottery commissions in the Detroit area, including those for the Detroit Institute of Arts and the Bethel Evangelical Church, as well as the Sacred Heart Academy in Grosse Pointe. She is also known for portrait busts, one of which won the Founders Society Purchase Prize at the Michigan Artists Exhibition in 1944. Her later commissions include architecturally scaled sculptures for the Northland Shopping Center in Southfield and the General Motors Technical Center in Warren. She is currently working in Honolulu.

One-person Exhibitions: Delphic Studios, New York City 1933; DAM 1943; Associated American Artists, New York City 1946.

Group Exhibitions: Salon d'Automne, Paris 1931; *Contemporary American Sculpture, Watercolor and Prints*, Whitney 1936; MAE 1942–46; *Recent Work by Detroit Artists*, Metropolitan Art Association, Detroit 1944; *DSWP Annual* 1945 (Prize); *Origins of Modern Sculpture*, DIA 1946; National Academy, New York City 1947 (Honors); *Contemporary American Sculpture, Watercolors and Drawings*, Whitney 1947–48; *National Exhibition of Prints*, Library of Congress 1948; *Little Show of Works in Progress: Recent Works of Founders Society Prize Winners 1935–47*, DIA 1948; *PAFA Annual* 1950–52; *Michigan Artists 1901–1952, In Commemoration of Detroit's 250th Birthday*, DIA 1951; *Michigan Art Through Fifty Years*, UMMA 1955; *Shopping Centers of Tomorrow*, DIA 1955; *Six Former Detroiters*, DAM 1955.

Collections: Aviation Trades High School, New York City; Bethel Evangelical Church, Detroit; Bristol Hospital, Tenn.; CAAM; Dallas Petroleum Club, Tex.; DIA; General Motors Technical Center, Warren; General Wingate School, New York City; KRON-TV Building, San Francisco; Laguna Towers Apartments, San Francisco; Northland Shopping Center, Southfield; Pinnacle Club, New York City; P.S. 19, New York City; Radio City Music Hall; Roosevelt Field Shopping Center, Hempstead, N.Y.; Sacred Heart Academy, Grosse Pointe; *S.S. United States*; State of Hawaii Foundation on Culture and the Arts, State Office Building, Lihue; Steuben Glass, New York City; U.S. Nuclear Ship *Savannah*; Theater, University of Arkansas, Little Rock; Victoria Theater, New York City.

Sources: *WWAA* 1980; Ludwig C. Brumme, *Contemporary American Sculpture*, New York: Crown, 1948; Lillian Pear, *The Pewabic Pottery*, Des Moines, Iowa: Wallace-Homestead Book Co., 1976; *Am Artist* 16, 2 (February 1952): 28–31ff; *Art Dig* 7, 10 (February 15, 1933): 15; *DFP* 2-19-33, 2-4-54, 2-7-54; *DN* 4-28-46, 2-6-47, 12-27-31, 10-23-51, 3-14-54.

MAKIELSKI, Leon

(b. Morris Run, Pennsylvania 1885; d. Ann Arbor, Michigan 1974)

Painter. Makielski was raised in South Bend, Indiana, where he received his first encouragement from local artist L. Clarence Ball. He then attended the School of the Art Institute of Chicago for four years (1903–07), studying under noted portraitist Ralph Clarkson. After winning a foreign study scholarship, he lived in Paris from 1910 to 1913, studying at both the Académie

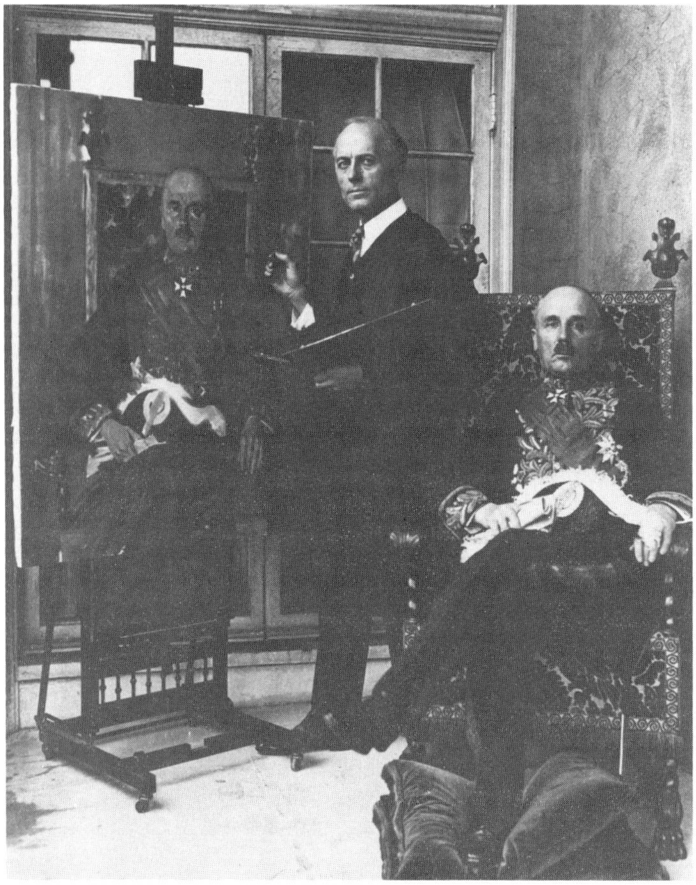

Leon Makielski (1885–1974) painting the portrait of the Polish minister to Washington, 1930. Courtesy the Michigan Artists Registry, The Detroit Institute of Arts, Research Library.

Julian and the Académie de la Grande Chaumière. In 1915 he joined the faculty at the University of Michigan as one of two painters (the other was **Ernest Harrison Barnes**) appointed to the newly established College of Architecture. Makielski remained on the faculty until 1927, when he resigned to devote all his time to portraiture. Among those who sat for Makielski were Robert Frost, at the time a young poet-in-residence at the University; the noted architect Eliel Saarinen; local poet Edgar A. Guest; Detroit Mayor Frank Murphy; the philanthropist S. S. Kresge; President Herbert Hoover; and the Prince of Wales. The University of Michigan owns over fifty of his oil portraits and numerous charcoal drawings of various faculty members.

During the Depression, under the auspices of the Works Progress Administration/Federal Art Project, Makielski and his brother Bronislaw completed several murals, including those for Fordson High School in Dearborn, Royal Oak High School, and Lincoln Consolidated School in Ypsilanti. In addition, he was one of eight Michigan artists chosen to execute a mural for the Michigan Building at the 1933 Chicago World's Fair; all eight of these murals are now in the State Capitol in Lansing.

For over forty years (until 1967), Makielski maintained a studio in Detroit in addition to the one in his Ann Arbor residence. He also taught in Detroit at both the Jewish Community Center and Meinzinger's Art School. A member of the Scarab Club, he often conducted classes in portraiture for his fellow artists.

One-person Exhibitions: The Eagle's Nest, Chicago 1908; South Bend Art Center, Ind. 1914; Alumni Memorial Hall, U. of M. 1915; Ann Arbor Art Association 1920; John Hanna Galleries, Detroit 1926; Bonstelle Playhouse, Detroit 1927; Park Central Hotel, New York City 1930; J. L. Hudson Gallery, Detroit 1931; Scarab Club, Detroit 1938, 1948; Hamtramck Public Library 1957, 1964; Anna L. Werbe Galleries, Detroit 1963; Slusser Gallery, U. of M. 1978.

Group Exhibitions: *Paris Salon* 1911, 1912; *American Painting and Sculpture*, AIC 1912; MAE 1917–35, 1937–38, 1942, 1946, 1950, 1955 (2nd Prize 1917, 1st Prize 1919, 3rd Prize 1921, Hecker Prize 1924, 1925, Popular Prize 1950); *American Artists Annual*, DIA 1919–23, 1925–29; *Michigan State Fair Exhibition* 1922 (2nd Prize), 1924 (1st Prize), 1925; *1st National Exhibition of American Art*, Rockefeller Center 1936; *Polish Paintings*, DIA 1945; *Michigan Art Through 50 Years*, UMMA 1955; *Portraits by Michigan Artists*, DIA 1955.

Collections: City of Ann Arbor; EMU; Federal Building, Detroit; UMMA; Washtenaw County Building; WMU.

Sources: *WWAA* 1956; AAA D318; Fielding 1974; *Detroit Saturday Night* March 27, 1926; *Poland* 9, 11 (November 1928): 699–701, 742–745; *Poland* 11, 12 (December 1930): 728–730; *South Bend News* 3-27-26; DT 1-23-27, 4-24-30, 12-27-31; *AAN* 12-10-30, 11-16-35, 12-30-63, 8-2-70, 11-30-74, 10-1-78; *DN* 12-21-30, 5-1-31, 6-23-63; *DFP* 10-10-37.

MAST, *Gerald*

(b. Topeka, Indiana 1908; d. Ann Arbor, Michigan 1971)

Painter. Mast received his earliest training at the John Herron Art Institute in Indianapolis from William Forsyth. In 1930 he came to Detroit and studied for two years with **John Carroll** at the Art School of the Detroit Society of Arts and Crafts. During the 1930s Mast maintained a studio at the Scarab Club of Detroit and was among the first artists whose work was shown at the Detroit Artists Market. He assisted Carroll with murals for the Detroit Institute of Arts and for two years (1938–39) was supervisor of the mural division

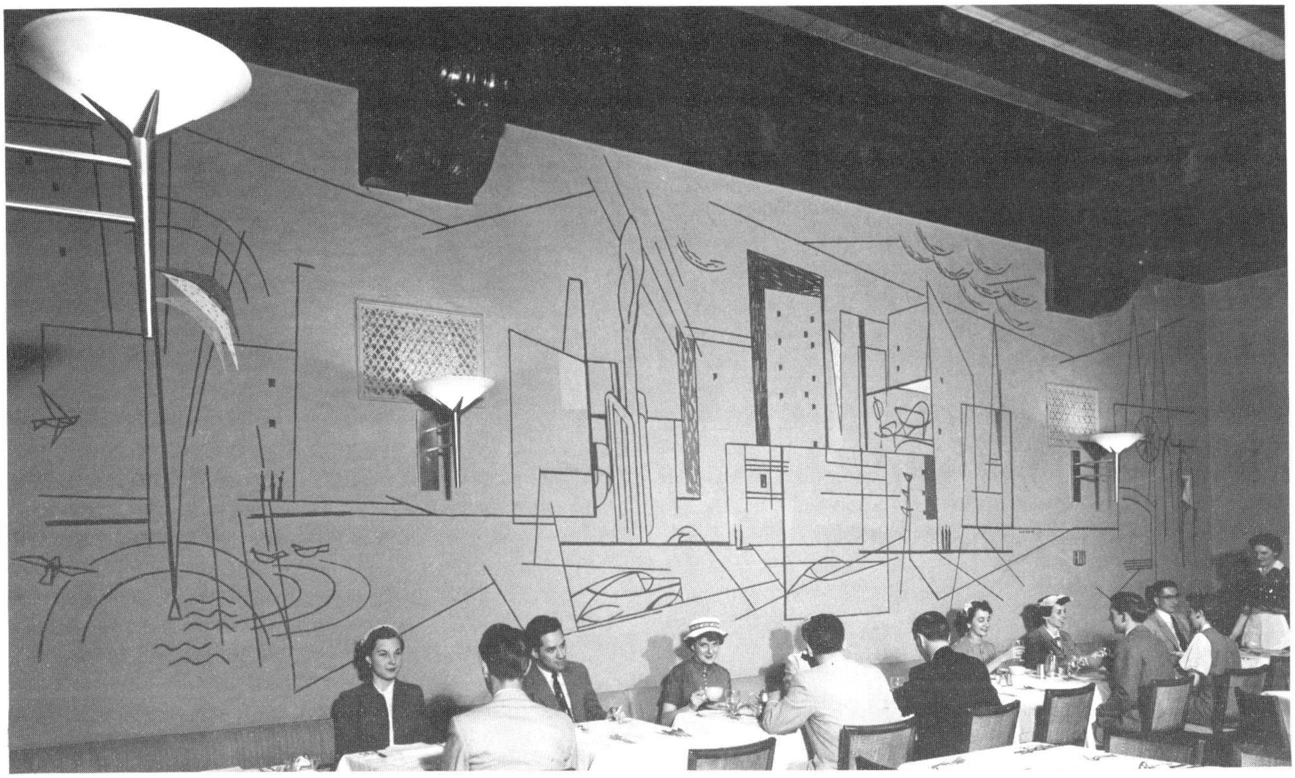

Gerald Mast (1908-1971). Mural for the Morton House, Grand Rapids, 1954. The Archives of American Art, Gerald Mast Papers. Gard, Grand Rapids, photographer.

of the Federal Art Project in Michigan. At that time he completed murals for the Liberty School in Highland Park, the Clare High School, and the Franklin Settlement in Detroit. From 1939 to 1948, Mast headed the mural painting department at the Rhode Island School of Design (receiving a B.F.A. there in 1948). He joined the faculty at the University of Michigan in 1948 and went to Grand Rapids to develop the Art Extension Program, a cooperative effort of the Grand Rapids Art Gallery and the University of Michigan.

Mast later helped establish art education programs in Kalamazoo and Muskegon, and for several years taught summer art courses at the National Music Camp at Interlochen. He remained active as a muralist throughout his years in Grand Rapids; there are numerous examples of his work in the area, including a mosaic panel in the Fountain Street Church. He also designed rugs and tapestries for V'Soske, Inc. of Grand Rapids and did considerable work in portraiture. Mast worked in a variety of styles, ranging from American scene realism to geometric abstraction.

One-person Exhibitions: DAM 1934, 1946; GRAM 1950 (three-person), 1954, 1967; HAM 1964; KIA 1969.

Group Exhibitions: MAE 1931–37, 1938 (Backus Prize), 1939, 1940, 1942 (Newberry Prize), 1943, 1949–52; *Indiana Artists Association* 1932, 1960–65; *1st National Exhibition of American Art*, Rockefeller Center 1936; *Great Lakes Exhibition*, Albright Art Gallery, Buffalo 1938; *Michigan Artists, 1901–1951*, DIA 1951; *West Michigan Annual*, GRAM 1953 (1st Prize), 1955 (Painting Prize), 1956–57, 1963–69; *Michigan Art Through 50 Years*, UMMA 1955; *Midwest Painters Invitational*, GRAM 1960; *Area Show*, KIA 1962, 1964; *Contemporary American Watercolor*, GRAM 1963.

Collections/Commissions: Burton Junior High School, Grand Rapids; Butterworth Hospital, Grand Rapids; DIA; East Grand Rapids High School; Fountain Street Church, Grand Rapids; GRAM; HAM; Herrick Public Library, Holland; KIA; Michigan National Bank, Grand Rapids.

Sources: *WWAA* 1970; AAA 501; Mast in *Design* 41, 7 (March 1940): 6–8; *DFP* 12-4-38; *DN* 3-3-46; *GR Herald* 7-22-51, 4-6-55; *GR Press* 11-5-54, 1-23-56, 8-8-71; *Muskegon Chronicle* 3-22-56.

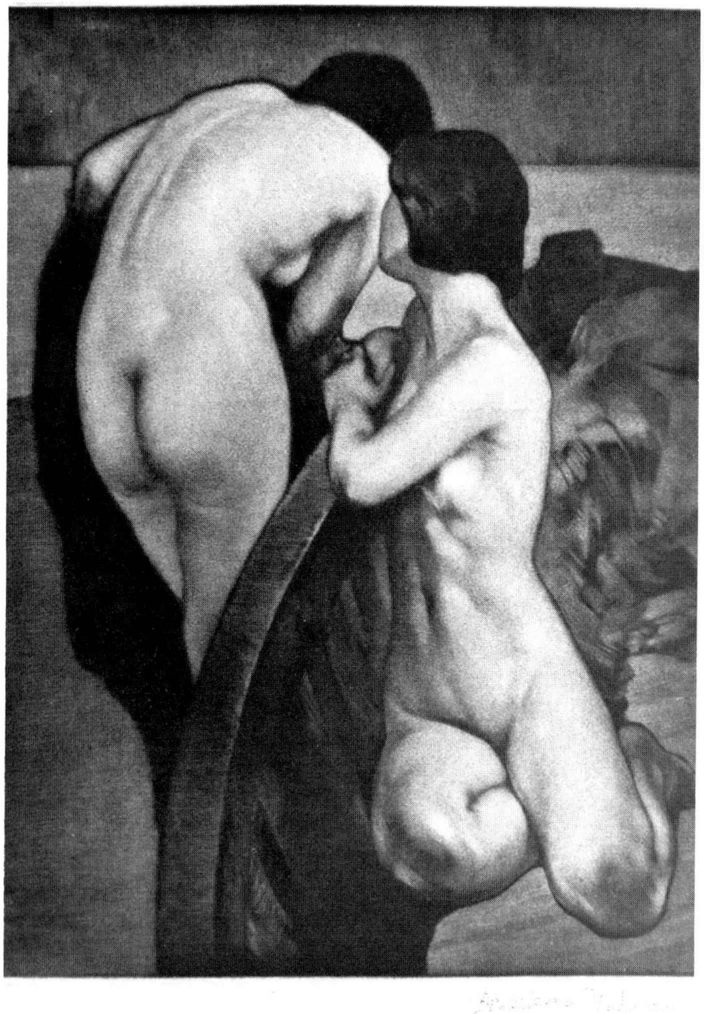

Alessandro Mastro-Valerio (1887–1953). On the Free Shore. *1935. Mezzotint. Courtesy the artist's family.*

MASTRO-VALERIO, Alessandro

(b. San Nicandro Garganico, Italy 1887; d. Ann Arbor, Michigan 1953)

Painter/Printmaker. Mastro-Valerio was educated at the Salvator Rosa Institute in Naples, Italy (1906–12), and came to the United States in 1913. He settled in Chicago and after a brief period as a commercial artist, established a portrait studio near the Loop. Among his patrons were the industralists Harvey S. Firestone and Anheuser Busch. He moved to Ypsilanti in 1919 and received a mural commission the following year from the Ypsilanti National Bank. Mastro-Valerio taught at Ypsilanti Normal College (now Eastern Michigan University) during the summers of 1922 and 1923. He was also on the part-time faculty at the University of Michigan (1924–26) where, after a trip to Italy in 1927, he was appointed to the full-time faculty. In addition to portraits and murals, his oeuvre includes landscapes, seascapes, and figure studies in oil and watercolor. He is best known for his mezzotint prints, particularly his female nudes. His work helped to revive mezzotint as an artistic medium in the United States. A member of the Ann Arbor Art Association, the Chicago Society of Etchers, the Society of Design (Associate 1951), he retired from the University of Michigan in 1952.

One-person Exhibitions: Ann Arbor Art Association 1920 (three-person), 1928 (two-person), 1938; Smithsonian Institution 1936; Forsythe Gallery, Ann Arbor 1967.

Group Exhibitions: *Annual Exhibition by Artists of Chicago and Vicinity*, AIC 1919; MAE 1922, 1924, 1931–35; Chicago World's Fair 1933; *Chicago Galleries Association Exhibition* 1933–34; *International Exhibition of Prints*, AIC 1935–37, 1939; Ann Arbor Art Association 1937, 1939, 1942; *American Art Today*, New York World's Fair 1939; *Fifty American Prints*, Alger House, DIA 1940; *National Exhibition of Prints*, Library of Congress 1945–47, 1952; *Michigan Art Through 50 Years*, UMMA 1955.

Collections: Ann Arbor Art Association; Carnegie Institute; Library of Congress; Los Angeles County Museum of Art; Newark Public Library; New York City Public Library; Smithsonian Institution; Ypsilanti National Bank.

Sources: *WWAA* 1940/41; Mallett 1948; *Am Artist* 6, 7 (September 1942): 4–7; *Am Artist* 6, 8 (October 1942): 21–23; *Art Dig* 9, 5 (December 1, 1934): 20; *Art Dig* 11, 14 (April 15, 1937): 24–25; *Art Dig* 16, 13 (April 1, 1942): 27; *Art Dig* 16, 20 (September 1, 1942): 15.

MAY, Helen

(b. 1890? d. Detroit, Michigan 1957)

Painter. After attending Harvard University and the University of California, May received an M.A. (1939) from Wayne State University. She also studied with André Lhote in Paris; Hans Hoffman and Millard Sheets in California; and **John Carroll** and **Jay Boorsma** at the Art School of the Detroit Society of Arts and Crafts. She taught at the Detroit School of Design (1914–17), Liggett School (1920s), and Wayne State University (1939–47). An influential teacher, her students included **Louise Nobili** and **Mary Jane Bigler**. She was a founder of the Michigan Water Color Society and was active in the Detroit Society of Women Painters and Sculptors, serving as its president during 1935 and 1936.

One-person Exhibitions: DAM 1935 (three-person).

Group Exhibitions: *Detroit School of Design Annual*, DIA 1913, 1915; *Detroit Schools Exhibition*, DIA 1914; MAE 1925, 1927–28, 1930–31, 1932 (Prize), 1933–34, 1943–46, 1948–50; DSWP Argent Gallery, New York City 1932; *DSWP Annual* 1933–34, 1943 (Prize); *First National Exhibition*, GRAM 1940; *Paintings by American Artists*, DIA 1943; *Recent Work by Detroit Artists*, DIA 1944; DAM 1945; *Michigan Painters, Sculptors and Craftsmen*, Alger House, DIA 1946; *MWCS Annual* 1948.

Sources: AAA, DSWP Papers; Moore 1953.

McCHESNEY, *Clifton*

(b. Gary, Indiana 1929)

Painter. After initial training at the Ray-Vogue School of Art and the American Academy of Art in Chicago, McChesney studied with Jack Tworkov at Indiana University (B.A. 1954) and with **Zoltan Sepeshy** at the Cranbrook Academy of Art (M.F.A. 1959). He joined the faculty at Michigan State University in 1960. In 1966 he spent a sabbatical year in Japan, and in 1974 was awarded a Ford Foundation grant which enabled him to return to Japan for another year. Japanese painting and culture subsequently were important influences on his work. An abstract painter, his style is characterized by calligraphic brushwork, translucent oil color, and large scale (some paintings are 20 feet across). Two of his favored formats are based on oriental sources: scroll-like compositions on unstretched canvas, and sequential panels, which he calls *polytychs*, inspired by Japanese folding screens.

One-person Exhibitions: Feingarten Galleries, San Francisco 1961; Little Gallery, Birmingham 1962–65; KIA 1965; Birmingham Gallery 1968–71, 1973–74, 1976; WMU 1970; CMU 1972, Alma College 1973; Albion College 1974; Biwako Museum, Otsu, Japan 1975; Ginza Nova Gallery, Tokyo 1975.

Group Exhibitions: *Art: USA: 59*, The Coliseum, New York City 1959; MAE 1959–61, 1963–64 (Museum Collection Prize 1961, Art Directors Club Prize 1964); *Midyear Show*, Butler Institute 1959, 1961–62; *Michigan Art: Yesterday and Today*, FIA 1963; *Society for Contemporary Arts Exhibition*, AIC 1964; *American Watercolors, Drawings and Prints*, PAFA 1965; *Drawing Invitational*, Albion College 1970; *Source Detroit III*, CAAM 1972; *27 Painters*, UMMA 1976.

Collections: CAAM; DIA; Purdue University; UMMA.

Sources: *WWAA* 1978; MAR; *Voice: Michigan Quarterly Arts Magazine* (Saginaw) 3, 2 (Spring 1963): 10; *DFP* 2-23-64, 2-3-74.

McCLURE, *Thomas*

(b. Pawnee City, Nebraska 1920)

Sculptor. McClure received a B.F.A. (1941) from the University of Nebraska and an M.F.A. (1948) from the Cranbrook Academy of Art; he also studied briefly at Washington State University. After teaching at the School for American Craftsmen at Alfred University in New York (1947) and at the University of Oklahoma (1948), he joined the faculty at the University of Michigan in 1949 as head of the newly established sculpture department. In the early 1950s, McClure was one of the first artists in Michigan to create welded metal sculpture, and since then he has worked almost entirely in metal. He has executed numerous commissions for such architectural firms as Skidmore, Owings & Merrill (the Ford Motor Company Central Staff Office Building in Dearborn), Albert Kahn Associates (the University of Michigan Undergraduate Library), and Rossetti & Associates (the Blue Cross and Blue Shield of Michigan Building in Detroit).

One-person Exhibitions: Little Gallery, Birmingham 1951; University of Oklahoma Museum of Art 1955; Forsythe Gallery, Ann Arbor 1961; Feingarten Gallery, Chicago 1962; UMMA 1962; Wright Gallery, Beloit College, 1963; SAM 1965; Gilman Gallery, Chicago 1968, 1970, 1975.

Group Exhibitions: *Northwest Artists Annual*, Seattle 1942, 1943 (1st Prize), 1944; *Annual Exhibition of Drawings and Prints*, San Francisco 1943; *Ceramics National*, Everson Museum, Syracuse 1947–48, 1950–52; *Ceramic Sculpture Invitational*, Philadelphia Art Alliance 1949; MAE 1949–67 (FSPP 1954); *Michigan Art Through 50 Years*, UMMA 1955; *Eight American Sculptors*, MSU 1957; *Ceramic International*, Everson Museum, Syracuse 1958; *PAFA Annual* 1958, 1960; *American Sculpture Invitational*, Kansas City Art Institute, Kans. 1960; *Contemporary Sculpture 1961*, Cincinnati Art Museum 1961; *Drawings USA*, Minnesota Museum of Art 1961; *Ravinia Festival Sculpture Invitational*, Ravinia Park, Highland Park, Ill. 1961; *Michigan Art: Yesterday and Today*, FIA 1963; *Source Detroit*, Cranbrook 1971; *Circuit: Exhibition of Computer and Electronic Art*, BBAA 1973; *Sculpture Inside and Out*, UMMA 1975.

Collections: Albion College; Beloit College; Congregation Shaarey Zedek, Southfield; DIA; Eastland Shop-

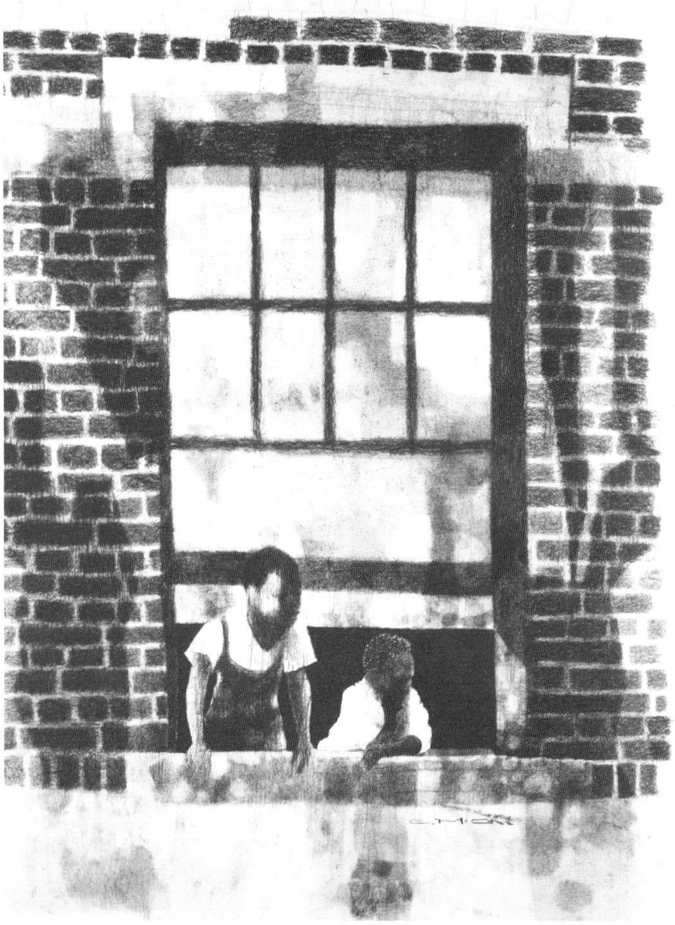

Charles McGee (1924–). Window Watchers. Charcoal. 35½ × 26½ inches. Collection of the Detroit Institute of Arts, Bequest of Robert H. Tannahill.

1917, Walker Prize 1924); *American Artists Annual*, DIA 1916–18, 1920, 1923–24.

Collections/Commissions: Boys' School, Cranbrook; Christ Church, Cranbrook; DIA.

Sources: *WWAA* 1941; AAA, 665, DSWP Scrapbook: Fielding 1974; Gibson 1976; Mallett 1948; Moore 1953; *American Magazine of Art* 16, 10 (October 1925): 542–544; *American Magazine of Art* 20, 6 (June 1929): 311–325; *Pencil Points* 10 (August 1929): 572; *DT* 3-30-24; *DN* 1-11-25, 9-13-25, 4-1-28.

McGEE, Charles

(b. Clemson, South Carolina 1924)

Painter. McGee came to Detroit in 1934 and in 1947 began studies at the Art School of the Detroit Society of Arts and Crafts under **Guy Palazzola**, which he continued part-time for seven years. He was a participant in many of the local art organizations of the 1950s, including the Pen and Palette Club and the Contemporary Studio, which he co-founded with **Henri Umbaji King**, **Leroy Foster**, and **Harold Neal**. In 1967–68 he studied in Spain at both the Escuela Massana and the Barcelona School of Graphics. Returning to Detroit in 1969, he founded the Charles McGee School of Art and, with several other artists, began the cooperative, Gallery 7. The school was nonprofit and had an all-black faculty, all of whom donated their services. The gallery became a showcase not only for local black artists such as **Lester Johnson**, **Alfred Hinton**, **James Lee** and others, but also for nationally known figures such as Romare Bearden and Hale Woodruff. In 1974 McGee closed his school and moved the gallery to the Fisher Building, changing its emphasis first to African sculpture and crafts and later to contemporary art, particularly experimental and conceptional work. The gallery closed in 1978. McGee also developed an art program, funded by the Michigan Council for the Arts, for the inmates at the Wayne County Jail.

A member of the faculty at Eastern Michigan University since 1970, he has also taught at Your Heritage House, the Palette and Brush Club, and Mercy College, all in Detroit, as well as at the Willistead Art Gallery in Windsor. As a member of the visual arts committee of New Detroit, Inc., McGee helped to select the artists commissioned in 1975 to complete ten outdoor murals for the downtown area.

McGee has completed murals for the Pontchartrain Wine Cellars, the Wheeler Art Center, and Northwest Activities Center. He was one of ten local artists commissioned to create a print for the Detroit Bicentennial Suite, and in 1978 was the recipient of the Michigan Foundation for the Arts' Michigan Arts Award in recognition of his many contributions to the visual arts in the state. Although McGee received his first recognition for figurative charcoal studies and screen prints, his work has become increasingly abstract. His recent works range from boldly colored, hard-edge geometrics to all-white splatter paintings incorporating metal plates, plaster, and other materials as part of the surface.

One-person Exhibitions: DAM 1962; Howard University 1962; Grinnell Galleries, Detroit 1964 (two-person); Arts Extended Gallery, Detroit 1965 (two-person); Arwin Gallery, Detroit 1966; Gallery 7, Detroit 1971; Pontiac Creative Arts Center 1977; Midland Center for the Arts 1980.

Group Exhibitions: MAE 1951–52, 1954–59, 1966 (Morgan Prize 1958); *American Painting and Sculpture Biennial*, DIA and PAFA 1959; *New Vistas in American Negro Art*, Howard University, Washington, D.C. 1961; *Midyear Show*, Butler Institute 1961,

1967, *The Negro in American Art*, University of California at Los Angeles 1966; *Afro-American Exhibition*, DIA 1968 (2nd Prize); *Afro-American Artists, 1800–1969*, Philadelphia Civic Center Museum 1969; *Seven Black Artists*, DAM 1969*; *Black Artists Invitational*, EMU 1970; *Contemporary Black Artists in America*, Whitney 1971; *Black Artists in Michigan Collections*, FIA 1973; *Works in Progress II*, DIA 1976*; *Michigan Collects Michigan Art*, Pontiac Creative Arts Center 1976.

Collections: American Embassy, Lima, Peru; Atlanta University; Children's Museum, Detroit; DIA; Engineering Society of Detroit; Howard University, Washington, D.C.; Renaissance Center, Detroit; Smith, Hinchman, & Grylls, Detroit; UMMA; Willistead Art Gallery, Windsor, Ontario.

Sources: AAA, Interview; MAR; Cederholm 1973; Nawrocki 1980; *Art Gallery* 11, 7 (April 1968): 12–25; *DAC News* 52, 2 (February 1967): 59–60; *Detroit Artists Monthly* 3, 2 (February 1978): 13–15; *Negro History Bulletin* 30, 6 (October 1967): 7–9; *DFP* 5-13-62, 5-27-62, 8-18-68, 11-27-77; *DN* 9-5-71, 3-20-77, 4-19-78, 2-4-79, 12-11-80; *Michigan Chronicle* 5-13-72; *AAN* 2-12-78.

McPHARLIN, *Paul*

(b. Detroit, Michigan 1903; d. Birmingham, Michigan 1948)

Puppeteer/Designer. Born in Detroit, McPharlin grew up in New York City and received a B.A. (1924) from Columbia University, an M.A. (1930) from Wayne State University, and a Ph.D. from the University of Michigan. A scholar, critic, and collector in the field of puppetry, McPharlin published and adapted puppet plays, had his own company of puppets, edited the *International Yearbook of Puppetry* (Birmingham: Puppetry Imprints 1938–48, vols. 1–19), and was the author of *The Puppet Theatre in America: A History 1524–1948* (Boston: Plays, Inc., 1969), which remains the most complete study of its kind. McPharlin designed his own puppets, and his collection of examples from around the world formed the nucleus of the Theater Arts Collection at the Detroit Institute of Arts. He taught puppetry and bookmaking at Wayne State University (1938–44) and was Detroit director and later Michigan supervisor of the Works Progress Administration's Arts and Crafts Project (1941–42).

One of the founders and the first president of the Puppeteers of America (1936), McPharlin organized the group's first conference in Detroit in 1937. He also served as director of the Experimental Theatre at the Artisans' Guild and the Marionette Fellowship of Detroit. He left Michigan in 1942 to return to New York City, where he illustrated and designed books for Peter Pauper Press in Mount Vernon and for Hastings House, and contributed numerous articles to *Publishers Weekly*.

He was active in the Typophiles and in the American Institute of Graphic Arts, which included several of his books in its *Fifty Books of the Year* exhibition. After military service (1942–44), he joined an industrial design firm and in 1945 set up his own practice as a free-lance designer.

One-person Exhibitions: Artisans' Guild, Detroit 1935; American Institute of Graphic Arts, Grolier Club, New York City, 1949*; Detroit Public Library 1949.

Group Exhibitions: MAE 1932; *Ballet in Art*, DIA 1952.

Collection: DIA.

Sources: *WWAA* 1040/41; MAR; Burton Historical Collection; Paul McPharlin Collection, Research Library and Theater Arts Department, DIA; McPharlin in *Design and Paper 18*, New York: Marquardt & Co., 1941; McPharlin in *Am Artist* 8, 3 (March 1944): 17–19; *DIA Bulletin* 37, 4 (1957–58): 89; *Publishers' Weekly* October 9, 1948; *DFP* 3-17-35, 3-1-42, 9-29-48; *DN* 8-17-41, 7-26-42.

MELCHERS, *Gari*

(b. Detroit, Michigan 1860; d. Falmouth, Virginia 1932)

Painter. Melchers received his earliest training from his father Julius Melchers, a local woodcarver and architectural sculptor, who was one of the first professional artists to hold art classes in Detroit. At the age of seventeen Melchers entered the Royal Academy at Düsseldorf and after three years there, continued his studies at the École des Beaux-Arts and the Académie Julian under Gustave Boulanger and Jules LeFebvre. In 1884 he established residence in Egmond-ann-Zee, a small Dutch fishing village, where he lived for the next fifteen years, during which he gained an international reputation. He was a frequent prizewinner at all the major international exhibitions (the first American to win a gold medal at Munich). In 1889 he and John Singer Sargent were the only Americans to be awarded the Grand Prize at the Paris Exposition Universelle. His works were acquired by many of the major European and American museums, and he completed mural commissions for the Columbian Exposition of 1893 in Chicago (these murals are now installed in the graduate library of the University of Michigan), and for the Library of Congress (1896).

Throughout his European sojourn, Melchers spent considerable time in the United States. He made

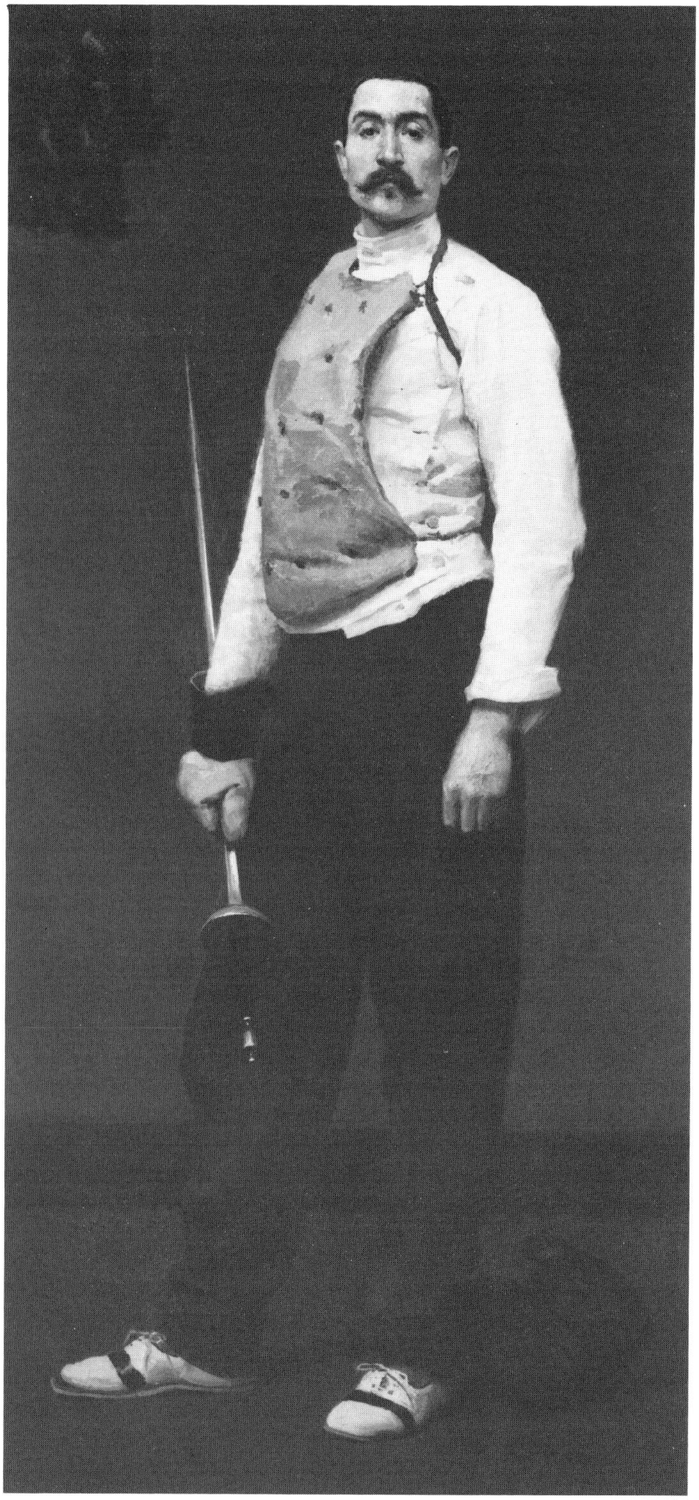

Gari Melchers (1860–1932). The Fencing Master. *ca. 1900. Oil on canvas. 6 feet 9½ inches × 39½ inches. Collection of the Detroit Institute of Arts, Gift of Edward Chandler Walker.*

extended visits to his family in Detroit and for a time had a studio in New York City to facilitate his portrait commissions and mural work. From 1909 to 1914 he served as court painter to the Grand Duke of Saxe-Weimar in Germany, but at the outbreak of World War I returned to the United States. He spent the remainder of his life at his estate near Fredericksburg, Virginia.

Although he never lived in the city after his youth, Melchers has long been considered Detroit's premier artistic "native son." That he was held in great esteem is evidenced by the prominent place accorded him on several important occasions. In 1888 he was awarded the first one-person show at the opening of the Detroit Museum of Art; and again in 1927, when the Detroit Institute of Arts was dedicated, the inaugural exhibition was a Gari Melchers retrospective. In the interim (1922), he had been chosen to execute three large murals for the Great Hall of the new Detroit Public Library. Melchers was well known to the Detroit art community and one of his major commissions, a portrait of President Theodore Roosevelt, was arranged and financed by local patron Charles L. Freer. Melchers achieved his greatest success and is most remembered for his straightforwardly realistic figure studies and genre scenes that were based on the people and traditions of Holland.

Melchers was a member of the National Academy of Design, the Société Nationale des Beaux-Arts, the Munich Secession, the Century Association (president, 1930–32), and the New Society of Artists (president, 1920–28). He was awarded the Medal of the Legion of Honor in 1895 and an honorary LLD by the University of Michigan in 1913.

One-person Exhibitions: DAM 1888; Oehme Galleries, New York City 1906; Montross Gallery, New York City 1911, 1913, 1916; Corcoran 1918, 1928 (two-person), 1933; AIC 1919, 1923; DIA 1927*, 1960*; Milch Galleries, New York City 1928, 1931; Albright Art Gallery, Buffalo 1930; American Academy of Arts and Letters, New York City 1932; Carnegie Institute 1934; Hanna Galleries, Detroit 1935; Memorial Exhibition, Virginia Museum of Fine Arts 1938*; Graham Galleries, New York City 1978*.

Group Exhibitions: *Paris Salon* 1882, 1886, 1888 (3rd Gold Medal), 1900 (1st Gold Medal); *American Painting and Sculpture*, AIC 1891–96, 1901, 1905–07, 1910–13, 1917–18, 1921–25 (First Prize 1891); *Exposition Universelle*, Antwerp 1894 (Medal of Honor); *Carnegie International* 1896–1901, 1907–27; *PAFA Annual* 1896 (Temple Gold Medal), 1898–1926 (most years); *Pan-American Exposition*, Buffalo 1901; *Louisiana Purchase Exposition*, St. Louis 1904; *Corcoran Biennial* 1907–30; MAE 1912, 1915–16, 1920; *Ameri-*

can Artists Annual, DIA 1915–21, 1923–26; *Michigan Art Through 50 Years*, UMMA 1955; *Michigan Art: Yesterday and Today*, FIA 1963.

Collections: AIC; Albright-Knox Art Gallery, Buffalo; Butler Institute; Carnegie Institute; Corcoran; Detroit Athletic Club; Detroit Club; Detroit Historical Museum; DIA; Detroit Public Library; HAM; Library of Congress; MMA; Minneapolis Institute of Arts; Missouri State Capitol; National Gallery, Washington, D.C.; NCFA; Neue Pinakothek, Munich; NPG; PAFA; Parke-Davis Company, Detroit; St. Louis Art Museum; Virginia Museum of Fine Arts.

Sources: AAA, 1180–1182; Bénézit 1976; Burroughs 1936/37; Fielding 1974; Gibson 1975; Kenny 1965, Mich State Lib 1915; Thieme-Becker 1907; Henriette Lewis-Hind, *Gari Melchers*, Painter, New York: William Edwin Rudge, 1928; *American Magazine of Art* 13 (April 1922): 117; *Harper's* 114 (February 1907): 430–439; *International Studio* 31 (March 1907): 11–19; *International Studio* 48 (December 1912): xxvii; *DFP* 10-4-27, 12-1-32; *DN* 11-3-32; *NY Herald Tribune* 11-20-32.

MERIZON, *Armand*

(b. Grand Rapids, Michigan 1920)

Painter. Merizon attended Calvin College and received a scholarship to attend the Vesper George School of Design in Boston. In 1947 he graduated from the Phoenix School of Design in New York City and in 1956 received a fellowship for European study from the Keeler Fund of Grand Rapids. A charter member of the Grand Valley Artists Association, Merizon also taught at the Kendall School of Design in Grand Rapids. In 1966 he was one of the first Michigan artists to have his work chosen to hang in the governor's office. Early in his career Merizon worked as an illustrator for such magazines as *Outdoor Life* and *Field and Stream*. He is best known for Lake Michigan seascapes and for portraits, although he occasionally works in a more abstract vein.

One-person Exhibitions: GRAM 1957, 1966, 1978; Bergsma Gallery, Grand Rapids 1976, 1978.

Group Exhibitions: MAE 1949, 1951; *West Michigan Annual*, GRAM 1956 (Keeler Award), 1957, 1960–61; *Michigan Painters-Printmakers*, GRAM 1966 (Purchase Prize); *Regional Exhibition*, HAM 1977; National Academy of Design, New York City 1978; *Artists of Grand Rapids 1840–1980*, GRAM and Grand Rapids Public Museum 1980*.

Collections: Amway Corporation, Ada; Federal District Court, Grand Rapids; GRAM.

Sources: MAR; *GR Press* 2-1-66, 6-12-77, 5-21-78.

METHEANY, *John M. III*

(b. Mt. Pleasant, Michigan 1935)

Painter. Metheany studied art at Alma College and later received a B.F.A. (1961), an M.A. (1962), and a M.F.A. (1964) from Michigan State University. He joined the faculty of Western Michigan University in 1964. He has also taught at Michigan State University (1962–64), and the National Music Camp at Interlochen (summers of 1963 and 1964). Known for his cubist landscapes inspired by the area around Lake Superior, Metheany has also completed two murals in downtown Kalamazoo.

One-person Exhibitions: The Gallery, Traverse City 1964 (two-person); HAM 1964; WMU 1965, 1973; Four Winds Gallery, Kalamazoo 1967, 1968; Siegel Gallery, Chicago 1967; *Retrospective—The Landscape Years*, KIA 1970; *SAM* 1970; GRAM 1974; Rentschler Gallery, Grand Rapids 1974.

Group Exhibitions: *J. L. Hudson Invitational*, J. L. Hudson Gallery, Detroit 1961–62; *West Michigan Annual*, GRAM 1961–62; MAE, DIA 1962, 1966 (DSWP Prize); *Area Show*, KIA 1964 (Honors), 1967 (Purchase Award), 1969, 1970; *Regional Exhibition*, HAM 1965 (Honorable Mention); *Michigan Painters-Printmakers*, GRAM 1965 (Purchase Award), 1969; *Annual Exhibition*, Allied Artists of America, Inc., New York City 1968; *American Academy of Arts and Letters Biennial*, New York City 1968, 1978 (Hassam Fund Purchase Award); *U. of M. Invitational* 1969–71 (traveling show); *Permanent Collection Exhibition*, University of California, Santa Barbara 1970; *Mainstreams*, Marietta College, Ohio 1970 (1st Prize), 1971.

Collections: GRAM; Kalamazoo College; KIA; MSU; University of California, Santa Barbara; WSU.

Sources: *KG* 1-7-65, 4-18-65, 7-3-66, 4-17-66, 5-17-66, 6-19-66, 11-20-66, 4-1-67, 5-7-70, 8-2-70, 6-10-73; *NYT* 6-9-73.

MICHAELS, *Glen*

(b. Spokane, Washington 1927)

Sculptor. Michaels was educated at the Yale University School of Music, Eastern Washington University (B.A.

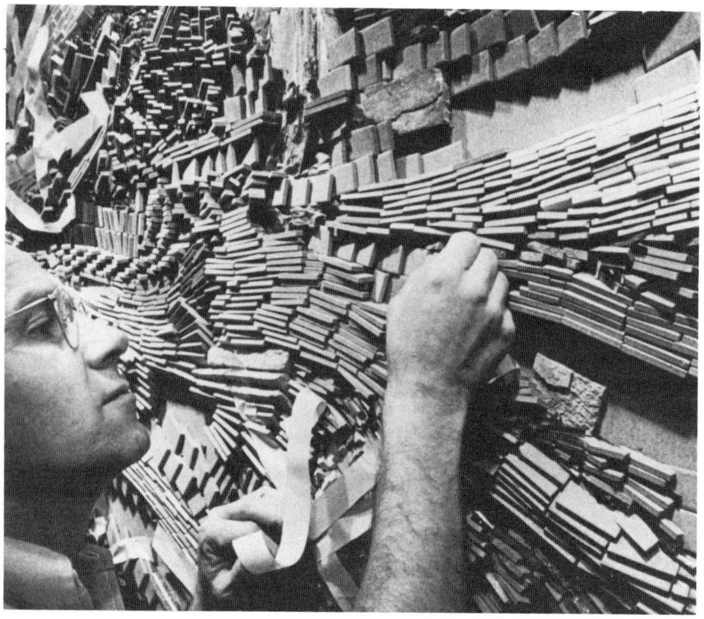

Glen Michaels (1927–   ) working on Assemblage, *a mural for the Manufacturers National Bank, Renaissance Center, Detroit. Courtesy Manufacturers National Bank. Benyas-Kaufman, Photographers.*

1955), and the Cranbrook Academy of Art (M.F.A. 1958), where he studied under **Zoltan Sepeshy**. He taught at Cranbrook from 1958 to 1965, founding in 1959 the Young People's Art Center which was organized as a workshop for community children in all art media. He was an assistant professor in sculpture at Wayne State University (1967–69) and the University of Windsor (1970–71). Originally a painter, his interest in relief sculpture began while he was attempting to bring more texture to his painting by adding foreign materials. Using thousands of tiny pieces of marble, wood, shale, glass, metal, tile, and even plastic, Michaels creates densely organized abstract panels which he calls *assemblages*. Much of his work has an almost woven appearance because of the close juxtaposition of elements. His pieces have been compared to medieval tapestry, and he has taken some of his mural designs to Dutch tapestry weavers for reproduction as textiles. He is represented by many commissions in the Detroit area, including reliefs for the Ford Centennial Library in Dearborn, Manufacturers National Bank (Renaissance Center branch) and Detroit General Hospital.

One-person Exhibitions: Bertha Schafer Gallery, New York City 1960 (two-person), 1962 (three-person); Little Gallery, Birmingham 1960, 1962–63, 1965, 1967, 1969, 1971–72; Robert L. Kidd Associates, Birmingham 1977.

Group Exhibitions: *Collaborator: Artist & Architect*, Mus Contemp Crafts 1962; *Prominent Painters and Sculptors in Michigan*, BBAA 1962; *National Guild Medal Exhibition of Building Arts*, Architectural League of New York 1962–65; *The American Craftsman*, Mus Contemp Crafts 1964; *13th Triennale*, Milan, Italy 1964; *Collector: Object/Environment*, Mus Contemp Crafts 1965; *Michigan Art '67*, BBAA 1967; *International Handcraft Exhibition*, Stuttgart 1967 (Award); *Plastic as Plastic*, Mus Contemp Crafts 1968; *Objects: USA*, Johnson Wax Collection Touring Show 1969/70*; *Sculpture Over Plastic Exhibition*, Smithsonian Institution, 1969/70; *Michigan Collects Michigan Art*, Pontiac Creative Arts Center 1976.

Collection/Commissions: Bulova Watch Company, New York City; Central Pennsylvania National Bank, Philadelphia; Chase Park Plaza Hotel, St. Louis, Mo.; DIA; International Monetary Fund, Washington D.C.; Johnson Wax Collection of Contemporary Crafts, Racine, Wis.; J. Walter Thompson Co., New York City; Manufacturers National Bank Headquarters, Renaissance Center, Detroit; Michigan Bell Telephone Co., Detroit; National Aeronautics & Space Administration, Goddard Space Center, Greenbelt, Maryland; Shaarey Zedek Synagogue, Southfield.

Sources: *WWAA* 1976; AAA 820; MAR; Nawrocki 1980; Edward Mattel, *Meaning in Crafts*, Englewood Cliffs, N.J.: Prentice-Hall, 1959; Louis Redstone, *Art in Architecture*, New York: McGraw-Hill, 1968; *CH* 21, 1 (January/February 1961): 19–22; *CH* 22, 3 (May/June 1962): 29–41; *CH* 24, 3 (May/June 1964): 83: *Design* 7, 9 (September 1963): 30–32; *House Beautiful* September 1969; *Interior Design* February 1967; *New Yorker* July 6, 1968; *NYT* 10-16-60, 1-6-62; *DFP* 6-17-62, 12-5-65; *Chicago Tribune* 9-12-65; *BEcc* 3-5-70, 3-12-70, 11-19-70; *DN* 6-17-72, 10-1-72, 12-4-73, 9-10-78 (Sunday Magazine).

MICHEL, Delbert

(b. Liberty, Indiana 1938)

Painter/Printmaker. Michel received a B.A. (1961) from DePauw University and an M.F.A. (1964) from the University of Iowa, where he studied with Mauricio Lasanski. He joined the faculty of Hope College in 1964 and has also served as a visiting artist (1972–73) at Portsmouth College of Art in England. Michel's abstract works consist of both acrylic paintings on unprimed canvas and silkscreen prints.

One-person Exhibitions: HAM 1967; Kalamazoo College 1971; Forsythe Gallery, Ann Arbor 1974 (two-person), 1975; GRAM 1975.

Group Exhibitions: *Michigan Painters-Printmakers*, GRAM 1965, 1967, 1969 (Award); *Regional Exhibi-*

tion, HAM 1967–69; *Area Show*, KIA 1967, 1975 (Award); *Midyear Show*, Butler Institute 1968 (Purchase Award), 1969; *Michiana Regional*, South Bend Art Center 1968, 1972; *National Drawing and Small Sculpture Exhibition*, Ball State University 1970–71, 1974 (Award).

Collections: Butler Institute; GRAM; HAM; Muskegon Community College; Wooster College, Ohio.

Sources: MAR; *AAN* 11-2-75.

MIDENER, *Walter*

(b. Leignitz, Germany 1912)

Sculptor. Midener attended the Kunst Akademie in Berlin from 1932 to 1936 before emigrating to the United States in 1938. For two years he was an instructor in wood and stone carving at the Henry Street Settlement in New York City and in 1940 won a Tiffany Fellowship for sculpture. Midener also taught at the Cleveland Institute of Art before joining the faculty at the Art School of the Detroit Society of Arts and Crafts as head of the sculpture department in 1946. In addition to teaching, he served as assistant director of the School from 1958 to 1967, was appointed director in 1968, and became president of the board of trustees in 1976. As an administrator, Midener was largely responsible for the accreditation of the School as a degree-granting institution. Maintaining that the study of art could not be separated from higher education, he completed a master's degree at Wayne State University in 1950.

A figurative sculptor, Midener works in a variety of media: cast metal, terra cotta, plaster, stone, and wood. His solid yet sensuous carved wooden figures have received local and national recognition: *Sisters* won the Founders Society Purchase Prize at the Michigan Artists Exhibition in 1952, and his works have been included in four Whitney sculpture annuals.

He has completed numerous commissions, including a series of wooden wall reliefs for the Explorers Room of the Detroit Public Library, a bronze group for the Michigan Cancer Foundation, and a Muntz metal screen for the Pontiac Motor Division of General Motors Corporation. Midener is a member of the Scarab Club, has served as an advisor to the Michigan Council for the Arts, and is presently professor of sculpture and president emeritus of the Center for Creative Studies.

One-person Exhibitions: DAM 1951 (two-person), 1954; Barone Gallery, New York City 1955; *Commissions for Michigan Artists*, DIA 1959; Grosse Pointe War Memorial 1961; *Retrospective*, Pontiac Creative Arts Center 1978*.

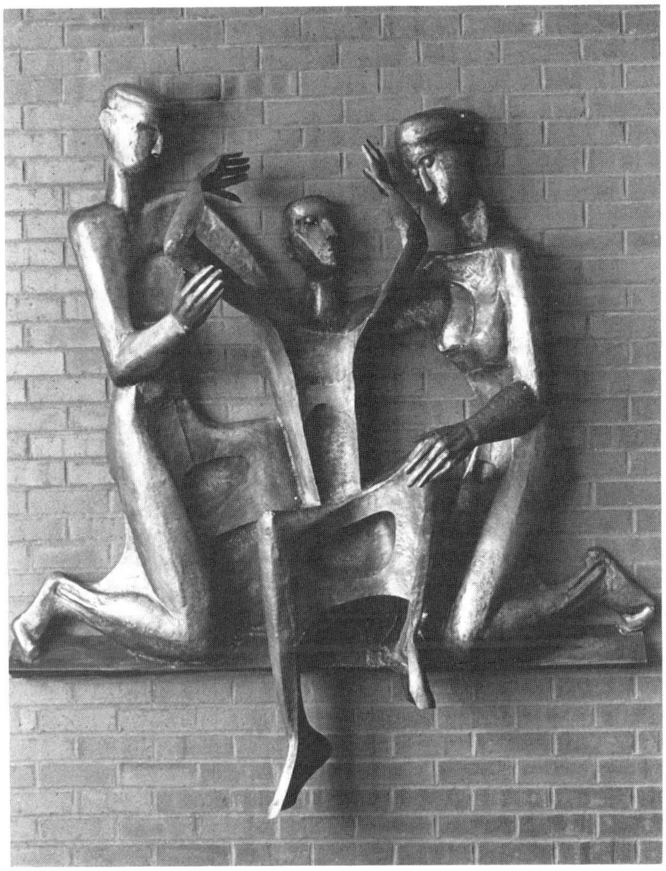

Walter Midener (1912–). Hope. *Collection of the Prentis Comprehensive Cancer Center of Metropolitan Detroit. Photograph courtesy Mary Beard.*

Group Exhibitions: *PAFA Annual* 1941, 1948, 1951, 1953, 1958, 1959/60; MAE 1946–57, 1960–61 (Museum Collection Purchase Prize 1950, FSPP 1952, Winkelman Prize 1955); *Works in Progress in Michigan*, DIA 1949; *Contemporary American Sculpture, Watercolors and Drawings*, Whitney 1950–51, 1953, 1955; *Modellers, Carvers, and Welders*, MOMA 1950; *American Sculpture*, MMA 1951; *Sculpture of the Twentieth Century*, John Herron Art Institute, Indianapolis 1951; *Michigan Art Through 50 Years*, UMMA 1955; *Michigan Art: Yesterday and Today*, FIA 1963; *Governors' National Art Tour* 1966/67; *Arts and Crafts in Detroit 1900–1976*, DIA 1976*; *Michigan Collects Michigan Art*, Pontiac Creative Arts Center 1976*; *Michigan Sculpture '77*, Macomb County Community College 1977.

Collections/Commissions: Berkley Public Library; Bundy Tubing, Detroit; Detroit Public Library; DIA;

FIA; Hebrew Union College, Cincinnati; House of Living Judaism, New York City; Michigan Cancer Foundation, Detroit; Michigan Supreme Court; Pontiac Motor Division, General Motors Corporation, Pontiac; Temple Beth El, Detroit; Temple Beth El, Memorial Park, Livonia; Whitney.

Sources: *WWAA* 1978; AAA, Interview, 103, 880; *Art Dig* 29, 15 (May 1, 1955): 28; *NYT* 4-26-55, 8-6-50; *DFP* 6-5-60; *DN* 1-22-61, 4-25-54, 6-25-62, 7-4-71.

M*IKOLOWSKI, Ann*

(b. Detroit, Michigan 1940)

Painter/Printmaker. Mikolowski attended Cass Technical High School (1956–57), the Center for Creative Studies (1969–71), and Wayne State University (1959–61, 1972–73), where she studied printmaking with **Theo Wujcik** and **Aris Koutroulis**. She has worked as an illustrator for the Chrysler Corporation (1958–61), the Ford Motor Company (1964–66), and the *Detroit Free Presss* (1972–73), and has taught at the Friends School in Detroit and for adult education classes in Port Arthur and Bad Axe (1976–79). Mikolowski's work was included in the *Bicentennial Portfolio* of the Detroit Workshop of Fine Prints. In 1969 Mikolowski and her husband, poet Ken Mikolowski, founded the Alternative Press in Detroit, for the purpose of handprinting original art and poetry by both local and nationally known poets and artists, such as Gordon Newton, **Brenda Goodman**, **Carol Steen**, Bradley Jones, Robert Sestok, Steve Foust, Faye Kicknosway, Allen Ginsberg, Ted Berrigan, and Philip Guston. In 1975 the Press received a National Endowment for the Arts Small Press Grant, and a retrospective exhibition of Alternative Press publications was held at the Detroit Artists Market. In 1974 the Mikolowskis left Detroit and moved the Press to Grindstone City.

Group Exhibitions: *Print Show*, Willis Gallery, Detroit 1972; *The Forsythe Saga*, Forsythe Building, Detroit 1973; *Anything on Paper*, DAM 1974; *Detroit Artists Invitational*, Detroit Bank & Trust Co. 1974; *Figure as Image*, DAM 1974; *The First Five Years: The Alternative Press*, DAM 1974; *Works Under 12*, DAM 1974; *Cheap Stuff*, Willis Gallery, Detroit 1975; *Juried Print and Drawing Exhibition*, Willis Gallery, Detroit 1975; *Self-Portrait*, DAM 1975; *Annual Summer Membership Show*, Willis Gallery, Detroit 1976; *Michigan Collects Michigan Art*, Pontiac Creative Arts Center 1976; *New Work*, Willis Gallery, Detroit 1976; *MWCS* 1977–78; *Mid-Michigan Annual*, Midland Art Association, 1978, 1980 (2nd Prize); *The Alternative Press: The First Ten Years*, Center for Creative Studies, Detroit 1979; DAM 1979.

Sources: MAR; *Lightworks* 10 (Fall 1978): 6–7; *DFP* 2-4-75, 10-4-79; *DN* 6-2-74, 9-30-79.

M*ILES, Cyril Aronson*

(b. Boston, Massachusetts 1918)

Painter/Filmmaker/Conceptual Artist. Miles attended Cass Technical High School and received a B.A. (1942) and an M.A. (1943) from Wayne State University. She also studied with **Sarkis Sarkisian** at the Art School of the Detroit Society of Arts and Crafts. In 1942 Miles joined the faculty at Highland Park Junior College, where she taught until the late 1970s. From 1950 to 1964 she also served as supervisor of art for the Highland Park Public Schools, and has also held teaching positions at the Detroit Institute of Arts and Wayne State University. For several years she operated Cyril's Studio Gallery, a showcase for Michigan artists such as **Mary Jane Bigler**, **Robert Broner**, and **Frank Cassara** as well as for the works of Laszlo Moholy-Nagy and Chicago photographer Arthur Siegal. A charter member and past president (1955) of the Michigan Water Color Society, Miles is also a member of the Michigan Academy of Science, Art, and Letters and the American Craft Council. She has been very active as a lecturer, consultant, and juror and has appeared numerous times on both public and commercial television as an art commentator. Although she began her career as a painter, Miles has increasingly concentrated on collage, and, since 1960, on experimental film. She was one of the first Michigan artists to organize "happenings," at the Bloomfield Art Association in 1965, the Detroit Artists Market in 1967, and the Downey Museum of Art in California in 1968.

One-person Exhibitions: Garden Club Center, Belle Isle, Detroit 1944; DAM 1959, 1967; Women's City Club, Detroit 1962; Studio North Theater, Ferndale 1963; EMU 1964; SAM 1964; Rubiner Art Gallery, Royal Oak 1966; Battle Creek Civic Art Center 1969; Arts Extended Gallery, Detroit 1972; McGregor Public Library, Highland Park 1973.

Group Exhibitions: DAM 1939–72 (most years); MAE 1940–46, 1955, 1957, 1959, 1963, 1965; *International Watercolor Exhibition*, AIC 1941; *MWCS Annual* 1947, 1950–56, 1966–67; Michigan State Fair Exhibition 1951–69; *Drawings USA*, Minnesota Museum of Art 1963; *Michigan Art '67*, BBAA 1967; *The American Flag in the Art of Our Country*, Allentown Art Museum, Pa. 1976; *27 Painters*, UMMA 1976.

Collections: International Business Machines, Southfield; Manufacturers National Bank, Detroit; McGregor Public Library, Highland Park; Metropolitan Federal Savings, Detroit.

Sources: *WWAA* 1976; MAR; Dona Z. Meilach, *Collage and Assemblage: Trends and Technique*, New York: Crown, 1973; *Art and Artists* (Detroit) February/March 1966; *DN* 10-3-44, 3-12-65, 4-16-71; *AAN* 10-1-64; *DFP* 10-31-65, 10-29-67, 5-14-67.

MILLER, *Iris Andrews*

(b. Ada, Ohio 1881; d. Detroit, Michigan 1981)

Painter. Miller studied with William Merritt Chase, Hugh Breckenridge, and Charles Grafly at the Pennsylvania Academy of Fine Arts in Philadelphia (1900–01). Additional classes with Chase were taken by Miller at the New York School of Art (1901–05) and, by invitation, at Chase's summer school in Haarlem, Holland (1903), where she did a series of sketches illustrating Dutch life. These were later published by *Century Magazine* 1906–07) and resulted in other commissions to illustrate stories and articles for various publications. Miller undertook further study at the Art Students League in New York City, under Robert Henri and Everett Shinn (1906–07). She taught Saturday sketch classes at the Detroit Institute of Arts (1924–25), and later in her Detroit studio (1929–50). She was the first woman to be awarded the Detroit Museum of Art Founders Society First Prize (1924), and the second woman to win the Scarab Club Gold Medal (1929), both at the Exhibition for Michigan Artists. Miller was a member of the National Arts Club in New York City, the National Association of Women Painters and Sculptors, and the Detroit Society of Women Painters and Sculptors. Although she painted landscapes and still lifes, Miller is best known for her portraits of prominent Detroiters, painted in the loose brushwork style of her mentor, William Merritt Chase.

One-person Exhibitions: Bonstelle Playhouse, Detroit 1926; Women's City Club, Detroit 1940.

Group Exhibitions: Wolfe Club, New York City 1904 (Portrait Prize); *DSWP Annual* 1910, 1922–24; MAE 1922 (Clark Prize), 1924 (1st Prize), 1925–28, 1929 (Scarab Club Gold Medal), 1931, 1934, 1938, 1940–41, 1955; *Annual*, Scarab Club, Detroit 1922–24; *PAFA Annual* 1924; *Annual Winter Exhibition*, National Academy of Design, New York City 1924, 1929; Old Lyme Art Association, Conn. 1924–25; *Annual Exhibition of Paintings by American Artists*, DIA 1924–29; *Inaugural Exhibition*, Fine Arts Gallery of San Diego 1926; Society of Independent Artists, Detroit 1926; DSWP, Holt Gallery, New York City 1928; *Michigan State Fair*, Detroit 1928 (Prize), 1931 (Prize); DSWP, Port Huron Public Library 1930; DSWP, Argent Gallery, New York City 1932; *California International Exhibition*, The Palace of Fine Arts, San Diego 1935; *Twenty Prominent Detroit Artists*, Y.W.C.A., Detroit 1940; *Michigan Artists 1901–1951: In Commemoration of Detroit's 250th Birthday*, DIA 1951; *Fifty Years of Prize Winning Painting and Sculpture*, Scarab Club, Detroit 1966.

Collections: Children's Home of Detroit, Grosse Pointe; Detroit Golf Club; DIA; Fine Arts Gallery of San Diego; Grace Hospital, Detroit; Kenton Hospital, Ohio; Kenton Public Library, Ohio; Law Club, U. of M.; Liggett School, Grosse Pointe; Michigan Mutual Insurance Building, Detroit; Topeka Church House, Kans.; Wayne County Circuit Court, Detroit; MacKenzie Hall, WSU.

Sources: *WWAA* 1962; AAA, DSWP Scrapbook; Bénézit 1976; Kenny 1965; Mallett 1948; Moore 1953; *Bonstelle Theatre Program* (Detroit) January 4, 1926; *DIA Bulletin* 7, 6 (March 1926): 71; *DN* 11-17-40; *DFP* 5-31-81.

MILLES, *Carl*

(b. Lagga near Uppsala, Sweden 1876; d. Lidingo, Sweden 1955)

Sculptor. As a young man, Milles was apprenticed to a cabinetmaker and attended the Technical School in Stockholm, where he received instruction in woodwork, carving, and ornamental modeling (1895–97). He attended classes at the Académie Colarossi and the École des Beaux-Arts in Paris, and within two years of his arrival exhibited in the 1900 Salon des Artistes Français, which resulted in a visit by the sculptor Auguste Rodin and subsequent assistantship at his Meudon studio. Milles returned to his native Sweden in 1908, and in 1920 was appointed professor of modeling at the Royal Academy of Art in Stockholm. Interested in obtaining commissions in the United States, Milles visited Chicago at the invitation of Holabird & Root, a Chicago architectural firm, and met with George Booth, who urged Milles to come to Cranbrook.

Appointed the first sculptor-in-residence and the director of the Department of Sculpture in 1931, Milles completed his most ambitious commissions during his Cranbrook years. These included the monumental *Fountain of Faith* for the National Memorial Park in Falls Church, Virginia, and statues for the Detroit Civic Center, the Murphy Hall of Justice, radio station WWJ, the Detroit Institute of Arts, the Flint Institute of Arts, and the University of Michigan. Milles was influenced by Swedish folklore and mythology and was known for his handling of water as an integral part of his stylized sculptural groups.

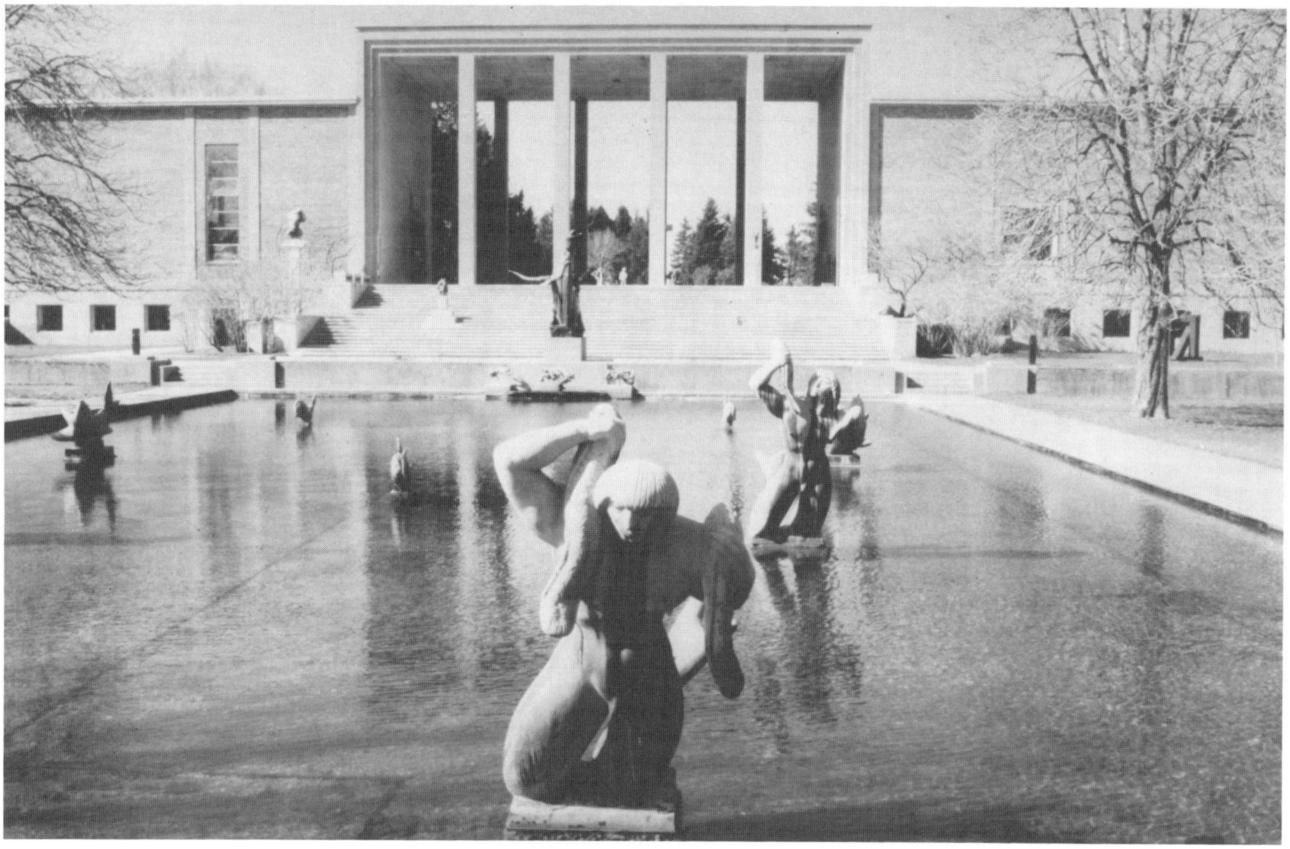

Carl Milles (1876–1955). Fountain in front of Cranbrook Academy of Art Museum. Courtesy the Cranbrook Academy of Art Museum.

In keeping with the Cranbrook "guild" philosophy that emphasized the importance of students serving as apprentices to master artisans, Milles never held formal classes. Instead, he criticized finished designs that were submitted by students and conducted informal discussions at his home. His influence is evident in the work of such students as **Marshall Fredericks** and **Berthold "Tex" Schiwetz**. Because of his precarious health, Milles retired from Cranbrook in 1951.

He later maintained a studio in Rome and also at his home in Lidingo near Stockholm. His numerous awards include the American Academy of Arts and Letters Medal of Merit and gold medals from the Architectural League of New York and the American Architectural Association of New York.

One-person Exhibitions: *Baltic Exposition*, Malmö, Sweden 1914; *Tercentenary Exhibition*, Göteburg, Sweden 1923; Tate Gallery, London 1926/27; Cleveland Museum of Art, 1931; DIA 1931*; St. Louis Art Museum 1931; Brooklyn Museum 1932; Baltimore Museum of Art 1940* (traveling); AIC 1941; Cranbrook 1955; Malmö Museum, Sweden 1955; J. L. Hudson Company, Detroit 1971*.

Group Exhibitions: *Swedish Arts and Crafts Society Exhibition* 1897 (1st Prize); *Paris Salon* 1899, 1900, 1909 (Honorable Mention); École des Beaux-Arts, Paris 1900; Paris World Exposition 1900; *Salon des Arts Decoratifs*, Paris 1925 (Gold Medal); *Exhibition of Modern European Sculpture*, Albright Art Gallery, Buffalo 1927; *A Century of Progress Exhibition*, General Motors Building, Chicago World's Fair 1933; *Painting and Sculpture in the World of Tomorrow*, New York World's Fair 1939; *American Birds and Their Painters and Sculptors*, DIA 1945; *Michigan Painters, Sculptors, and Craftsmen*, Alger House, DIA 1946; *Origins of Modern Sculpture*, DIA 1946; *Michigan Art: Yesterday and Today*, FIA 1963; *American Sculpture 1900–1965*, FIA 1965.

Collections: AIC; Aloe Plaza, St. Louis; CAAM; Cranbrook; Civic Center, Detroit; Des Moines Art Center; DIA; FIA; Michigan Court Building, Chicago; MMA;

Museum of Fine Arts, Houston; Millesgarden, Lidingo, Sweden; Murphy Hall of Justice, Detroit; National Memorial Park Cemetery, Falls Church, Va.; Polytechnical High School, Stockholm; Racine County Court House, Wis.; St. Paul City Hall; Time-Life Building, Rockefeller Center; U. of M., Ann Arbor; Yale University Art Gallery.

Sources: *WWAA* 1953; AAA 812: 1–406; MAR; Bénézit 1976; Nawrocki 1980; Meyric R. Rogers, *Carl Milles*, London: Oxford University Press, 1940; *Milles at Cranbrook*, Bloomfield Hills: Cranbrook Academy of Art, 1960; *American Magazine of Art* 24, 5 (May 1932): 345–354; *American Magazine of Art* 27, 8 (August 1934): 439–441; *Apollo* 20, 115 (July 1934): 31–34; *Architectural Forum* 84, 6 (June 1946): 92–96; *Art Dig* 5, 10 (February 15, 1931): 26; *Art Work* 6, 24 (Winter 1930): 248–255; *Life* March 30, 1953, June 27, 1955; *Parnassus* 6, 1 (January 1934): 7–9; *Time* July 18, 1949; *DN* 2-3-31, 2-8-31, 9-16-34, 6-20-35, 3-27-49; *DFP* 10-25-52, 9-20-55; *NYT* 9-20-55.

MITCHELL, David

(b. Detroit, Michigan 1918)

Painter. Mitchell received training at the University of Iowa under Grant Wood (B.F.A. 1941, M.A. 1942) as well as at the Cranbrook Academy of Art (M.F.A. 1947). In addition, he studied under Hans Hofmann in Provincetown, Massachusetts, and in 1953 received a Fulbright fellowship for study in Rome. Mitchell joined the faculty at Wayne State University in 1947 as a painting and drawing instructor. For three years (1950–53) he served as director of the Crystal Lake Summer Art School in northern Michigan. An abstract painter, Mitchell bases much of his work on landscape or still life subjects. His Italian scenes are characteristic of his style, emphasizing color, bold brushwork, and simple forms. Mitchell presently teaches design at Wayne State University.

One-person Exhibitions: Circle Gallery, Detroit 1951; DAM 1954, 1956 (two-person), 1960 (two-person); WSU 1967.

Group Exhibitions: MWCS 1947 (Merit Award), 1948, 1958, 1967, 1970; MAE 1949 (Newberry Purchase Prize), 1950–53, 1954 (Skelton Prize and Cranbrook Purchase Prize), 1955 (Morgan Prize), 1956–59, 1961; *Midyear Show*, Butler Institute 1950; *Michigan Art Through 50 Years*, UMMA 1955; *Fulbright Painters*, Duveen-Graham Galleries, New York City 1956; *Michiana Regional*, South Bend Art Center, Ind. 1956 (Purchase Prize); *American Painting and Sculpture Biennial*, DIA and PAFA 1959; *Octet*, Rackham Galleries, U. of M. 1960; *Prominent Painters and Sculptors in Michigan*, BBAA 1962; *Michigan Art '67*, BBAA 1967.

Collections: CAAM; DIA; South Bend Art Center, Ind.; University of Iowa.

Sources: MAR; AAA 879; *DFP* 8-21-49, 10-14-56; *DN* 3-16-52, 10-17-54, 10-7-56, 9-28-58, 5-8-60; *NYT* 9-30-56.

MITCHELL, Wallace

(b. Detroit, Michigan; d. Bloomfield Hills, Michigan 1977)

Painter/Sculptor. Wallace received a B.A. (1934) from Northwestern University, attended the Cranbrook Academy of Art for two years, and was awarded an M.F.A. (1936) by Columbia University. He joined the faculty at Cranbrook in 1936 as a painting instructor, then served as director of the Cranbrook Museum from 1956 to 1971, when he was appointed president of the Academy, a position he retained until his death. An abstract painter, Wallace was principally a colorist. Throughout his career he experimented with the organization of geometric forms in space and their effect on color relationships. His earlier paintings are characterized by the use of repeated shapes, such as accordian panels, toothed rectangles, and diamond chains against

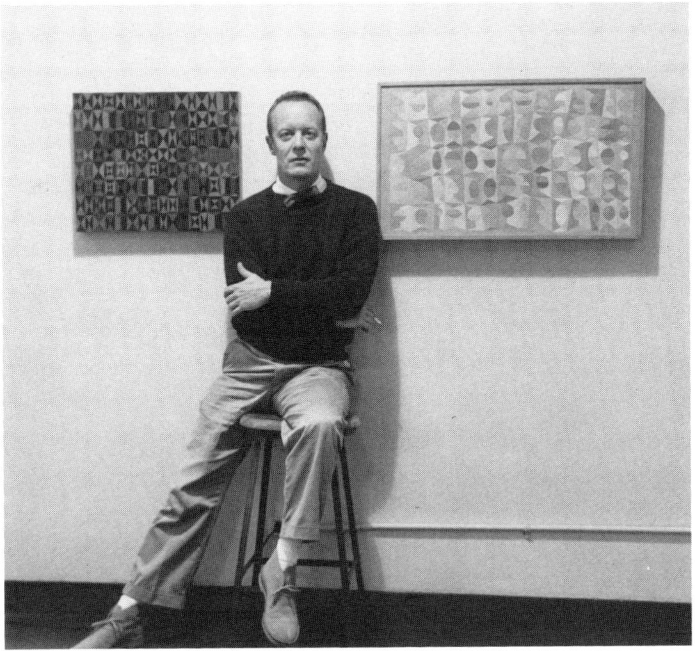

Wallace Mitchell (1911–1977) with paintings at the Cranbrook Academy of Art Museum. Courtesy the Cranbrook Academy of Art Museum.

a neutral background. By the early 1960s he had turned to three-dimensional painted constructions, usually based on a grid format combining circles and squares. Wallace completed several mural commissions, including one for the General Motors Technical Center in Warren (1956) and another for the University of Kentucky Medical Center (1961).

One-person Exhibitions: DAM 1938, 1939, 1955 (two-person), 1963; Bertha Schaeffer Gallery, New York City 1950, 1957–58; Cranbrook 1953*; University of Minnesota 1954*; *Retrospective*, Cranbrook and FIA 1970*; Little Gallery, Birmingham 1974 (two-person); *Memorial Exhibition*, Cranbrook 1977*.

Group Exhibitions: MAE 1936–38, 1940–42, 1944–52, 1955 (Tannahill Prize 1945, 1946, Skelton Prize 1946); *Great Lakes Exhibition*, Albright Art Gallery, Buffalo 1938; *Contemporary Detroit Painters*, Alger House, DIA 1940; *International Watercolor Exhibition*, AIC 1942; *Realities Nouvelles*, Palais des Beaux-Arts, Paris 1948; *Works in Progress in Michigan*, DIA 1948; *The Classic Tradition in Contemporary Art*, Walker Art Center, Minneapolis 1953; *Michigan Art Through 50 Years*, UMMA 1955; *Michigan Art: Yesterday and Today*, FIA 1963; *Flint Invitational*, FIA 1966, 1969; Everson Museum, Syracuse 1973; *Michigan Collects Michigan Art*, Pontiac Creative Arts Center 1976*.

Collections/Commissions: CAAM; Denison, Porter & Bartush, Bloomfield Hills; DIA; General Motors Technical Center, Warren; Guggenheim Museum; University of Kentucky.

Sources: *WWAA* 1976; Cummings 1977; *Art News* 48, 9 (January 1950): 47; *Art News* 56, 6 (October 1957): 59; *Arts* 32, 1 (October 1957): 56; *CH* 37, 2 (April 1977): 10; *DFP* 8-11-50, 10-14-56; *DN* 3-29-53, 12-6-70, 2-6-77; *BEcc* 12-17-70, 3-3-77.

MOSER, Liselotte

(b. Lucerne, Switzerland 1906)

Painter/Textile Artist. Moser studied in Vienna and with Victor Surbek in Bern, Switzerland, before arriving in Detroit in 1927. She received additional training under **John P. Wicker** and at the Art School of the Detroit Society of Arts and Crafts (1927–28). Moser works in many media: oil, watercolor, linoleum block print, calligraphy, and embroidery. She is known for her portraits, landscapes, and botanical studies, the latter characterized by close-up views of small segments of nature. Her embroidered "paintings" usually have mythological or religious themes. One of these, *The*

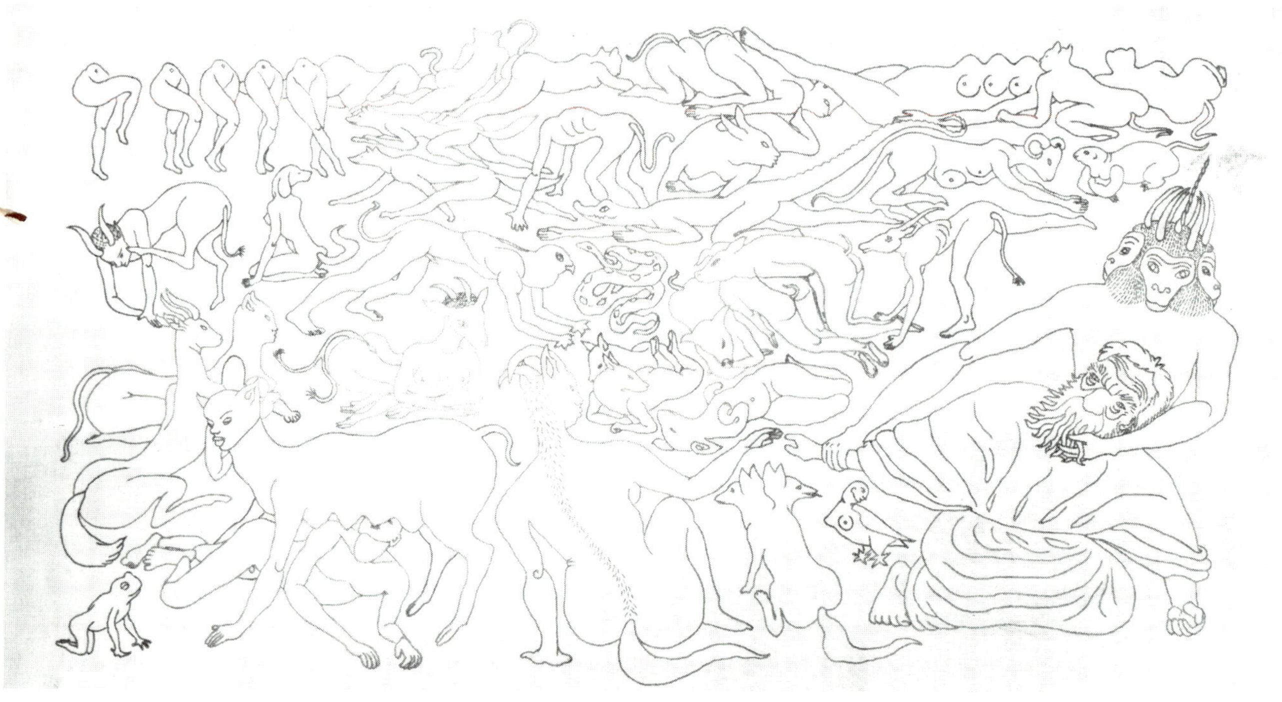

Liselotte Moser (1906–). The Temptation of Saint Anthony. *1949. Embroidery on bleached linen. 23¼ × 42½ inches. Collection of the Detroit Institute of Arts.*

Temptation of St. Anthony, won the Founders Society Purchase Prize at the Michigan Artist-Craftsmen Exhibition in 1949. Since 1964, she has resided in Switzerland.

One-person Exhibitions: DAM 1950, 1954, 1964*.

Group Exhibitions: MAE 1928–31, 1933–57, 1960 (Mrs. Ralph H. Booth Purchase Prize 1937, Mrs. George Kamperman Purchase Prize 1938, Sarah M. Sheridan Prize 1948, David B. Werbe Memorial Prize 1951, Hal H. Smith Memorial Prize 1952, Anthony and Minerva Maiullo Prize 1954 and 1956, Palette and Brush Club Prize 1957); Society of Independents, Detroit 1930; *Great Lakes Exhibition*, Albright Art Gallery, Buffalo 1938; *Adam and Eve Exhibition*, DIA 1942; *Recent Works by Detroit Artists*, DIA 1944; *Michigan Painters, Sculptors, and Craftsmen*, Alger House, DIA 1946; MACE 1947–49 (FSPP 1949), 1951–57, 1962; *Designer/Craftsmen U.S.A.*, Brooklyn Museum 1953; *Michigan Art Through 50 Years*, UMMA 1955; *Arts and Crafts in Detroit 1900–1976*, DIA 1976*.

Collections: DIA.

Sources: MAR; *DFP* 8-14-49, 5-19-53, 9-23-62; *DN* 3-19-50, 1-3-54, 1-10-60, 2-5-64.

MOULTON, *Helmi K.*

(b. Trenary, Michigan 1917)

Textile Artist. Moulton studied with **Katherine Ux** at Central Michigan University where she received a B.S. (1960). After further training at Wayne State University (M.Ed. 1963), she attended a summer session (1967) in Banff, Alberta, with Malin Selander of Sweden. Moulton joined the faculty at Western Michigan University in 1960, where she has been instrumental in introducing weaving to the fine arts program. She has also taught at the University of Michigan Extension in Kalamazoo and at the Kalamazoo Institute of Arts. She has given numerous lectures to professional organizations, including the Annual State Conference of Michigan Art Teachers; the Fine Arts Festival in St. Cloud, Minnesota; the Muskegon Weavers Guild; and the Kalamazoo Weavers Guild. She received the Outstanding Educators of America Award in 1975.

One-person Exhibitions: *Finnish Collection and Weavings by Helmi*, Kalamazoo College 1971; Tadlow Gallery, Holland 1971, 1972 (two-person); Calvin College Fine Arts Center, Grand Rapids 1972; *Weavings and Ceramics*, J. Walter Thompson Co., Detroit 1972 (two-person); America House, Birmingham 1973 (two-person); Creative Art Gallery, CMU 1974 (two-person).

Group Exhibitions: MACE 1964; *Michigan Artists-Craftsmen*, GRAM, 1964, 1966; *Hand of the Craftsmen*, Midland Art Association 1965; *Area Show*, KIA 1966 (Best of Show in Weaving); *Michigan Education Association Purchase Prize Exhibition*, East Lansing 1966; *Collectors Room*, America House, New York City 1967; *U.S. Artists Selected by the American Crafts Council*, Toronto 1967; *Crafts Show*, SAM 1971; *Michigan Traveling Exhibition*, Michigan Craftsmen's Council 1971; *Stitches and Techniques*, Studio 23, Bay City 1972; *Ann Arbor Street Fair*, Ann Arbor 1973*; *Filaments '73*, EMU 1973; *N.O.W. Fine Arts Exhibition*, Episcopal Cathedral, Kalamazoo 1973.

Collections: Calvin College; GRAM; Harriet Tidball Collection, University of Washington, Seattle; WMU.

Sources: MAR; *Who's Who in the Midwest* 1970; American Crafts Council Registry, New York City; Susanna Cuyler, *Rugmaking Technique*, New York: Harper & Row, 1973; *American Home Magazine* October 1967; *KG* 5-13-73.

NAWARA, *Jim*

(b. Chicago, Illinois 1945)

Painter/Printmaker. Educated at the School of the Art Institute of Chicago (B.F.A. 1967) and at the University of Illinois, Nawara joined the faculty at Wayne State University in 1969. Although he works in acrylic and watercolor, Nawara is primarily interested in drawing, printmaking, and photography. In 1974 he undertook a number of projects in a billboard-sized format. Six of these works were shown in Kalamazoo in conjunction with a national print exhibition. In 1975 Nawara's work was included in a suite of works by Michigan artists commissioned by the Michigan Workshop of Fine Prints. Since about 1970, he has concentrated on imaginary aerial views, characterized by a trompe-l'oeil precision and clarity, that draw on his interest in flying, archaeology, cartology, and geology.

One-person Exhibitions: University of Windsor, Ontario 1974; Willis Gallery, Detroit 1974 (two-person), 1976 (three-person); South Dakota Art Center, Brookings 1976 (Purchase Award).

Group Exhibitions: *National Drawing Exhibition*, San Francisco Museum of Art 1970; *National Exhibition of Prints*, Library of Congress 1971; *All Michigan I and II*, FIA 1971/72, 1973/74; *Midyear Show*, Butler Institute 1972–73, 1975 (Purchase Prize 1973); *British Print Biennial*, Bradford, England 1972–76; *Biennial of Graphic Art*, Ljubljana, Yugoslavia 1973; *Drawings USA*, Minnesota Museum of Art 1973, 1975; *Smithsonian Institution Traveling Exhibition* 1973, 1977;

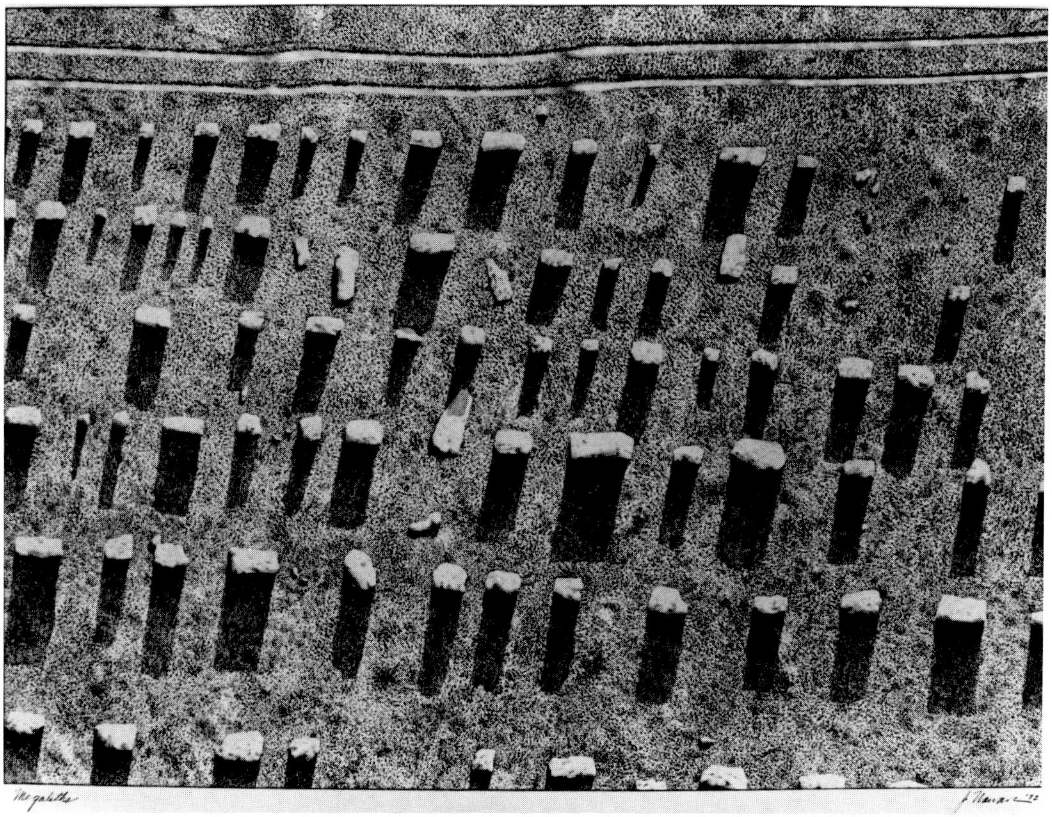

James Nawara (1945–). Megaliths. 1972. Pencil, Private Collection. Courtesy the artist.

Los Angeles Printmaking Society National Exhibition 1974 (Cash Award), 1975; *Michigan Focus*, DIA 1974/75*; *Eleven Michigan Artists*, MSU 1975; *30 Years of American Printmaking*, Brooklyn Museum 1976*; *International Print Biennial*, Krakow, Poland, 1976, 1980; *Michigan Association of Printmakers Biennial*, DIA 1977/78 (Purchase Award); *Detroit-area Printmakers*, Calvin College, Center Art Gallery, 1978; *Return of Realism, Part II*, Meadowbrook Art Gallery, Oakland University, Rochester 1978; *Photography in Printmaking*, Victoria and Albert Museum 1979; *Urban Landscape*, DAM 1979; *Cliché-Verre, Hand-Drawn, Light-Printed*, DIA 1980*; *Road Show*, First Federal Savings of Detroit (sponsor), Detroit 1980*.

Collections: Bradford City Art Gallery, England; Butler Institute; Dulin Gallery, Knoxville; Jagiellonian University, Krakow, Poland; South Dakota State University, Brookings; Springfield Art Association, Ill.; Western Ontario University, London; WMU; WSU.

Sources: MAR; *Arts Mag* 51, 6 (February 1977): 19; *New Art Examiner* 7, 9 (June 1980): 22; *DFP* 3-5-72, 3-13-79; *DN* 5-26-74, 2-15-76, 12-13-78, 3-11-79, 8-5-79.

NEAL, *Harold*

(b. Memphis, Tennessee 1924)

Painter. Neal graduated from the Art School of the Detroit Society of Arts and Crafts in 1953. In 1958 he cofounded, with **Henry Umbaji King**, the Contemporary Studio, the first black owned and operated gallery in the Midwest. He taught at the Oak Park Art Club (1962–68); the Charles McGee School of Fine Arts; for the University of Detroit's "Unicomm" program; and at the Willestead Galleries, Windsor, Ontario; Wayne County Community College; and Washtenaw County Community College. An active figure in the art community, Neal is on the board of the Detroit Council for the Arts. He is known primarily for his genre scenes depicting the black experience.

One-person Exhibitions: Contemporary Studio, Detroit 1960 (two-person).

Group Exhibitions: Atlanta University 1962 (Prize); *30th Anniversary Exhibition*, DAM 1962; *Midyear Show*, Butler Institute 1964; *7 Black Artists*, DAM 1969; *Ten of Detroit's Best Artists*, Bellajar Art Gallery, Detroit 1974; *Michigan Collects Michigan Art*, Pontiac Creative Arts Center 1976; *5 From 10*, Pyramid Gallery of Art, Detroit 1979; *Historical Roots: The Black Artist in Michigan*, Detroit Historical Museum 1980.

Collections: Atlanta University Collection of American Negro Art; Butler Institute.

Sources: *Promenade* (Detroit Council for the Arts Newsletter) 3, 11 (November 1979): 3; *DFP* 4-6-69, 12-11-80; *Michigan Daily* (Ann Arbor) 3-19-71; *DN* 7-22-79.

NEWMAN, *Kirk*

(b. Dallas, Texas 1926)

Sculptor/Printmaker. Newman was educated at the University of Tulsa (B.A. 1949) and the University of Iowa (M.A. 1951). From 1949 to 1956 he served on the faculty of the University of Michigan as an instructor for the art extension program in Kalamazoo. He taught at Kalamazoo College (1957–58) and is presently assistant director of the Kalamazoo Institute of Arts and head of the Institute's school. Newman is known for his life-size realistic figure groups, which are often based on satiric themes. He has completed three outdoor installations in Kalamazoo: a fountain for the Burdick Street Mall, and figure groups for the Kalamazoo Institute of Arts and Bronson Park. The latter group was commissioned as a Bicentennial project by the Kalamazoo Foundation.

One-person Exhibitions: KIA 1964, 1966, 1971; University of New York, Albany 1969; La Boetie, New York City 1970; Pyramid Gallery, Ann Arbor 1971; HAM 1972; GRAM 1974; Fort Wayne Museum of Art, Ind. 1975.

Group Exhibitions: MAE 1950, 1954; *West Michigan Annual*, GRAM 1956, 1957; *Sculpture Midwest*, Rackham Gallery, U. of M. 1958; *Michigan Art: Yesterday and Today*, FIA 1963; New York World's Fair 1964.

Collections/Commissions: Borgess Hospital, Kalamazoo; Bronson Park, Kalamazoo; City of Kalamazoo; HAM; Kalamazoo College; KIA; People's Church, Kalamazoo; Syracuse University; Temple B'Nai Israel, Portage; WMU.

Sources: MAR; Hendry 1980B; *KG* 11-1-64, 11-13-68, 11-24-68, 9-6-71, 6-9-74; *GR Press* 4-23-72.

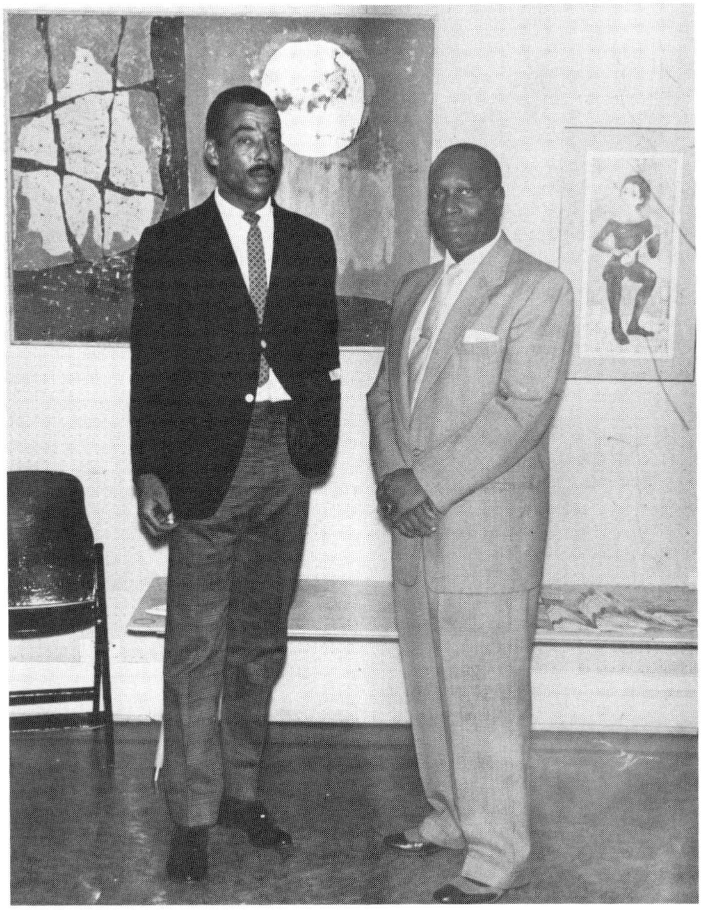

Harold Neal (1924–   ) and Ernest Hardman (1912–1969) (right) during their joint show, Contemporary Studio, Detroit, 1960. The Archives of American Art.

NOBILI, *Louise Jansson*

(b. Detroit, Michigan 1917)

Painter. Nobili received a B.F.A. (1939) and an M.F.A. (1941) from Wayne State University, studying under **Wayne Claxton** and **Helen May**. She also studied with László Moholy-Nagy at the Chicago School of Design and attended the School of the Art Institute of Chicago. Nobili has taught stage design at Wayne State University (1939–43), and interior design at Northwestern University (1943–44). Since 1944 she has taught painting at Wayne State University. A charter member of the Michigan Water Color Society, she is known for her technical innovations with watercolor, particularly that of producing texture by bonding new media into her work. Since the 1950s, her extensive travels have influenced her imagery. In the 1960s she began using new media, such as sand, aluminum, and gold leaf, along with other elements of collage. Her more recent works are three-dimensional watercolors

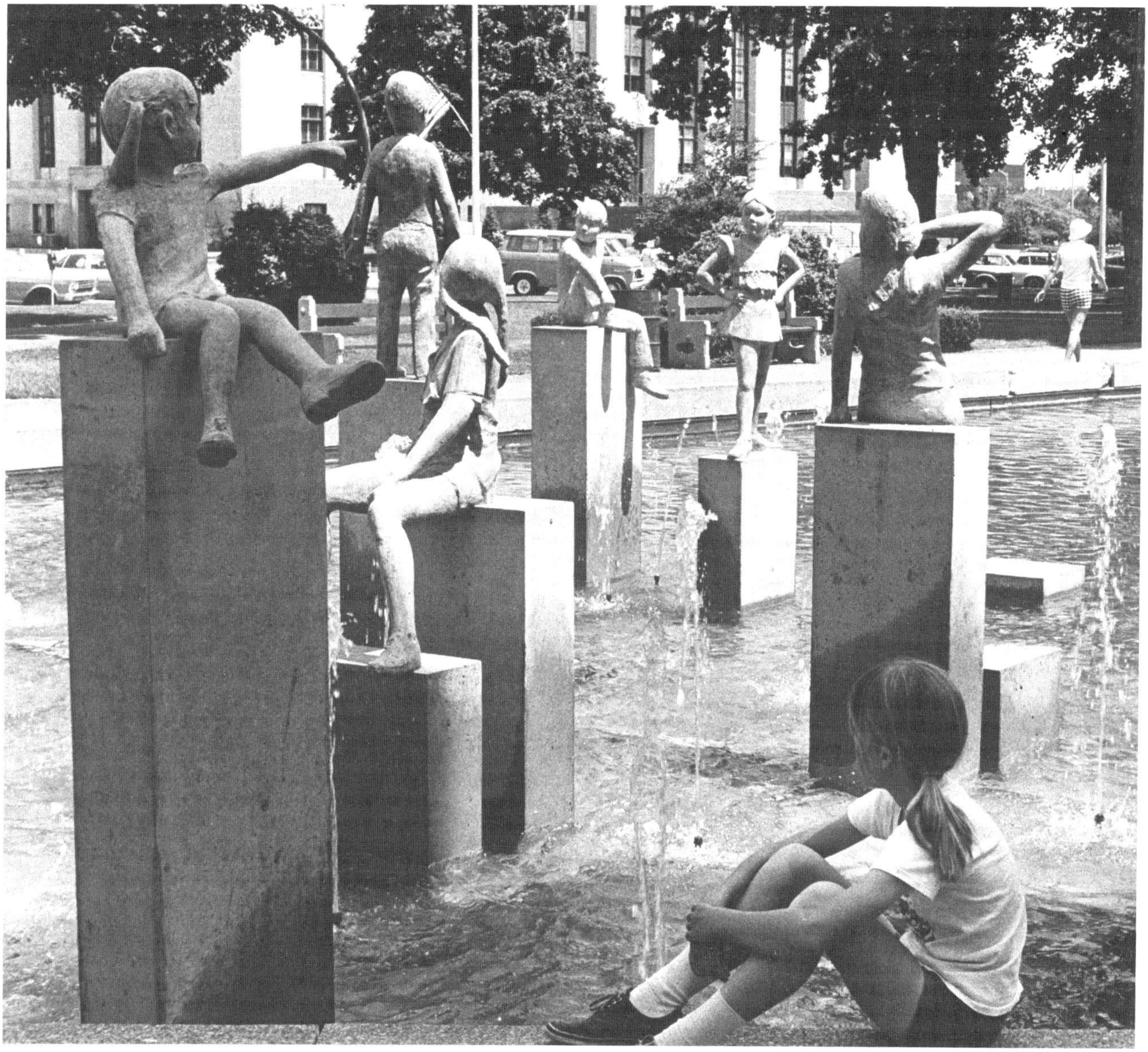

Kirk Newman (1926–). Bicentennial Sculpture. Bronson Park, Kalamazoo. Courtesy the artist.

that stand up like relief sculptures. She also works in acrylic and oil.

One-person Exhibitions: DAM 1945-46, 1947 (two-person), 1948, 1949 (two-person), 1954, 1957, 1961; Forsythe Gallery, Ann Arbor 1957, 1961, 1964, 1967, 1969; Denison University Art Gallery, Granville, Ohio 1955 (two-person); Anna Werbe Gallery, Detroit 1967-68; Galleria il Canale, Venice 1968; J. Walter Thompson Company, Detroit 1962.

Group Exhibitions: MAE 1945 (Newberry Prize), 1946-48, 1950, 1952-53, 1954 (WSU Art Educators Alumni Purchase Prize), 1955, 1956 (FSPP), 1957 (J. Walter Thompson Co., Prize), 1959-60; *American Watercolor and Drawing*, AIC 1948; *MWCS Annual* 1948-51, 1953 (Merit Award), 1954-57, 1958 (MWCS Award), 1959, 1960 (Honorable Mention), 1961, 1962 (MWCS Award), 1963, 1965-68, 1972-74, 1976 (MWCS Award), 1977; *Annual Watercolor Exhibition*, Scarab Club, Detroit 1951, 1953 (2nd Prize), 1954 (3rd Prize), 1957 (Honorable Mention), 1958, 1959 (1st Prize), 1961-63, 1970-71; *International Watercolor Exhibition*, Brooklyn Museum 1953; *Michigan Art Through 50 Years*, UMMA 1955; *Michigan Artists 1901-1951*, DIA 1951; *American Painting and Sculp-*

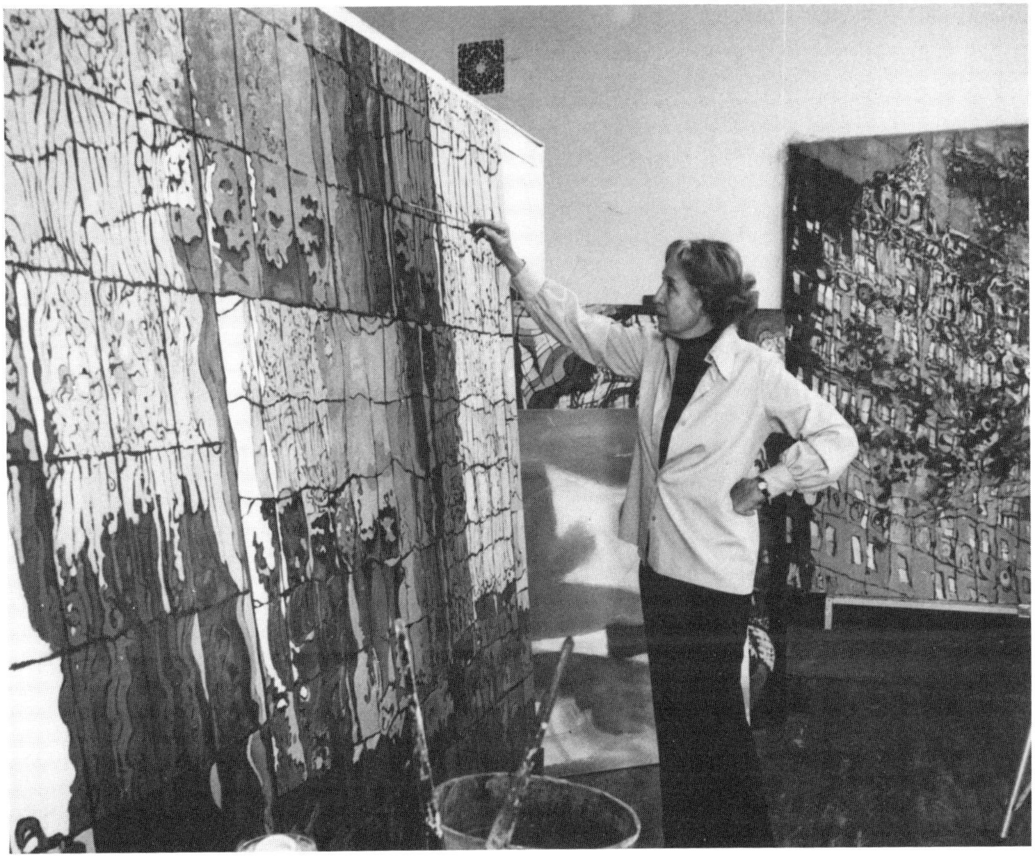

Louise Nobili (1917–) in her studio, 1976. The Archives of American Art, Louise Nobili Papers.

ture Biennial, PAFA and DIA 1958; *Midyear Show*, Butler Institute 1958, 1960–62, 1966–67, 1975–76; *Watercolor Panorama, An International Survey*, FIA 1962; *Prominent Painters and Sculptors in Michigan*, BBAA 1962; *West Michigan Annual*, GRAM 1963; *Contemporary American Watercolors*, GRAM 1963; *Michigan Art: Yesterday and Today*, FIA 1963; *Michigan Collects Michigan Art*, Pontiac Creative Arts Center 1976; *Mainstreams 77*, Marietta College, Ohio 1977.

Collections: American Airlines, Dallas; Blue Cross and Blue Shield of Michigan, Detroit; Butler Institute; Detroit Bank & Trust Co.; Detroit General Hospital; DIA; the Etruscan Foundation, Sienna, Italy; First Federal Savings & Loan Association, Detroit; Ford Motor Company, Dearborn and Detroit; Ford Times Collection of American Art, Dearborn; Steelcase Collection of Contemporary Art, Grand Rapids; UMMA; WSU Alumni Association; WSU Medical Building.

Sources: MAR; AAA 695, Interview; *Detroit Artists Monthly* 2, 3 (March 1977): 8–9; *DFP* 10-28-45; *DN* 1-13-46; 1-17-46, 10-20-57, 5-15-66, 12-5-67, 12-2-76, 12-5-76, 12-20-76; *AAN* 3-29-70; *Pittsburgh Post Gazette* 8-15-75.

NYGARD, *Alfred F.*

(b. Copenhagen, Denmark 1870; d. Grand Rapids, Michigan 1941)

Sculptor. At an early age Nygard was apprenticed to a sculptor and carver in his native Copenhagen. After a brief period of military service, he emigrated to America at the age of twenty-three. Attracted to Grand Rapids because of its furniture industry, he worked there briefly before settling in Detroit around 1892. By 1894, he was a partner in the firm of Nygard, Marty, & Mildner, which specialized in architectural decoration. Nygard also taught Saturday modeling classes at the Art School of the Detroit Museum of Art (1896–97) under the auspices of the Detroit Architectural Sketch Club and was one of the original faculty members at the Detroit School of Design (ca. 1911). Well known for his intricate ornamental carving in both stone and wood, Nygard did decorative work for many of the city's finest buildings, including the Detroit Opera House (since demolished), and collaborated with architects such as Alfius Chittenden; Donaldson & Meir; Albert Kahn; George Mason; McKim, Mead, & White; and Leonard Willike. He also carved furniture, some of which was shown at the World's Columbian Exposition in Chicago in 1893. He was an honorary member of the Scarab Club and the designer of the Scarab Club gold medal. His later years were spent in Grand Rapids.

Group Exhibitions: World's Columbian Exposition, Chicago 1893; *Architectural Exhibition, Detroit Architectural Club and the Society of Arts and Crafts,* DMA 1900, 1909; *MAE* 1915–16, 1918–19.

Sources: Gibson 1975; *DN* 11-26-23, 1-24-24, 12-6-25; *GR Herald* 12-8-29.

OREAR, *Gordon*

(b. Minneapolis, Minnesota 1923)

Ceramicist. Trained as a chemist, Orear first studied ceramics with Grover Cole at the University of Michigan. He also attended the Art School of the Detroit Society of Arts and Crafts for two years (1950–52), studying under **John Foster**. From 1957 to 1964, he directed the pottery studio at Greenfield Village, Dearborn, in addition to teaching ceramics at the Detroit Institute of Arts and the University Center for Adult Education in Detroit. In 1969 Orear joined the faculty of the Art School of the Society of Arts and Crafts, where he became chairman of the ceramics department in 1973. He was a founding member of the Michigan Potters' Association, and belongs to the Michigan Craftsmen's Council and the American Craftsmen's Council. Orear's commissions include three ceramic pieces for the Johnson Foundation in Racine, Wisconsin (1960), and an indoor ceramic garden for the First National Bank of Chicago (1972). He has also worked closely with several Detroit design firms, including W. B. Ford Associates and Ross Roy, Inc.

Since the late 1960s Orear's work has become increasingly nonfunctional. Concentrating on one form, a wheel-thrown stoneware cylinder, he produces sculptural constructions in a severely geometric format that often incorporates added metallic elements. An intriguing characteristic of these unglazed forms is their retention of an opening, a remnant of their functional beginnings as containers.

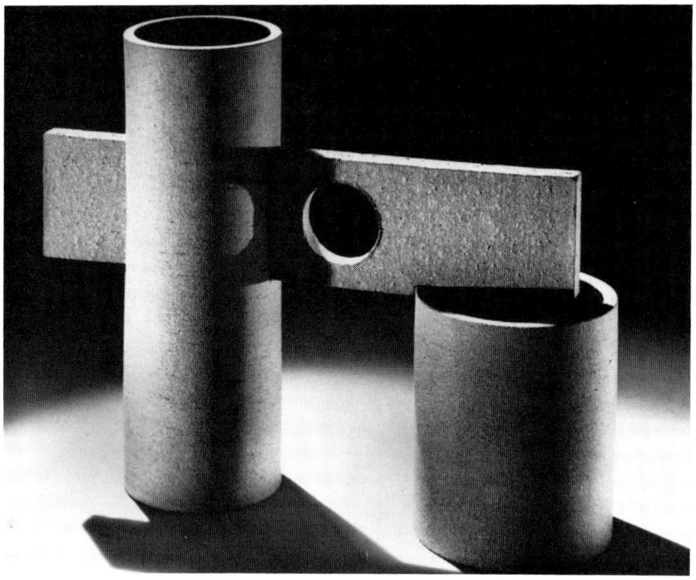

Gordon Orear (1923–). Untitled. *Nemo Warr, Photographer.*

One-person Exhibitions: Gallery 4, Detroit, 1958 (two-person); Hanamura Gallery, Detroit 1964; America House, Birmingham 1968; Battle Creek Civic Art Center 1969 (two-person); Somerset Mall, Troy 1974 (two-person); Galleria del "BATIK," Rome 1977.

Group Exhibitions: MACE 1951–72 (Webber Prize 1956); *Decorative Arts and Ceramics Exhibition,* Wichita Art Association, Kans. 1954–56; *Ceramic National,* Everson Museum of Art, Syracuse 1954–56, 1964; *New Directions,* DAM 1966; *16 Michigan Ceramicists,* Cranbrook 1967; *Michigan Council for the Arts Traveling Show* 1967/68, 1969/71; *EMU Ceramics Invitational* 1968–69, 1971, 1974, 1977, 1979; *Detroit Invitational,* Pewabic Pottery, Detroit 1971; *Objects and Images,* Parrish Art Museum, Southampton, N.Y. 1971; *Contemporary Crafts of the Americas,* Colorado State University Traveling Show 1975/77*.

Collections/Commissions: Detroit Bank & Trust Co.; First National Bank, Chicago; Johnson Foundation, Racine, Wis.; Kelsey Hayes Company, Detroit; Michigan Consolidated Gas Company, Detroit; Sears, Roebuck & Company, Chicago.

Sources: MAR; Leon Nigrosh, *Clayworks,* Worcester, Mass.: Davis Publications, 1975; *CH* 22, 5 (September/October 1962): 40–41; *CH* 24, 3 (June 1964): 39; *CH* 32, 2 (April 1972): 52; *CMo* 29, 4 (April 1972): 18; *Interiors* June 1973; *Michigan Challenge* (State Chamber of Commerce) 4, 5 (February 1964): 38; *Studio Potter* 2, 2 (Winter 1973/74): 23–29.

ORTMAN, George Earl

(b. Oakland, California 1926)

Painter. Ortman studied at Arizona State Teachers College, Tempe; the California College of Arts and Crafts, Berkeley (1947–48); Atelier 17, New York City, with Stanley William Hayter (1949); Académie André Lhote, Paris (1950); and the Hans Hoffman School of Fine Arts, New York City (1950–51). In 1965 he was awarded a Guggenheim Fellowship, and in 1966 a Ford Foundation Grant to the Tamarind lithography workshop. He has taught at the School of the Visual Arts, New York City (1957–66), serving as co-chairman of the fine arts department (1963–65); at New York University School of Education, New York City (1963–65); at Princeton University (1966–69); and at the Honolulu Academy of Fine Art (1969–70), before his appointment as head of the painting department at the Cranbrook Academy of Art. Involved with the co-op galleries in New York in the 1950s, Ortman held his first one-person exhibition in 1953. His work is characterized by three-dimensional painted and collaged constructions that employ a variety of geometric symbols, such as crosses, arrows, squares, and circles.

One-person Exhibitions: Tanager Gallery, New York City 1953; Stable Gallery, New York City 1957, 1960; Howard Wise Gallery, New York City 1962–64, 1967, 1969; David Mirvish Gallery, Toronto 1964; Walker Art Center, Minneapolis 1965*; Harcus Krakow Gallery, Boston 1966; Portland Museum of Art, Maine 1966; The Art Museum, Princeton University 1967*; Middlebury College, Vt. 1969*; Indianapolis Museum of Art 1971*; J. L. Hudson Gallery, Detroit 1971; WMU 1972; FIA 1976; Lee Hoffman Gallery, Detroit 1976; Gertrude Kasle Gallery, Detroit 1976.

Group Exhibitions: *Salon de Mai*, Paris 1950; *4 Painters*, Tanager Gallery, New York City 1952; *New Forms, New Media*, Martha Jackson Gallery, New York City 1959; *American Painting and Sculpture*, AIC 1961–62; *Carnegie International* 1962, 1964, 1967, 1970; *60 Years of American Painting*, Whitney 1963; *Towards a New Abstraction*, The Jewish Museum, New York City 1963; *Contemporary American Painting*, Whitney 1963, 1965, 1967, 1973; *American Painting*, Stedelijk Museum, Amsterdam 1964; *History of Geometric Painting in America*, Whitney 1964; *Contemporary American Painting and Sculpture*, Krannert Art Museum, University of Illinois, Urbana 1965, 1969*; *300 Years of American Painting*, Whitney 1966; *Tamarind Print Exhibition*, MOMA 1967; *Michigan Collects Michigan Art*, Pontiac Creative Arts Center 1976; *27 Painters*, UMMA 1976; *Tenth Street Days, The Co-ops of the 50's*, Soho (various galleries), New York City 1977.

Collections: Albright-Knox Art Gallery, Buffalo; Chase Manhattan Bank, Zurich; Detroit Bank & Trust Co.; Honolulu Academy of Art; Indianapolis Museum of Art; Los Angeles County Museum of Art; MOMA; The Newark Museum; Oakland Museum of Art, Calif.; Smith, Hinchman & Grylls, Detroit; Walker Art Center, Minneapolis.

Sources: *WWAA* 1978; AAA, Interview: Cummings 1977; Fielding 1974; *Dictionary of 20th-Century Art*, London and New York: Phaidon, 1973; *Art in America* 51 (April 1963): 80–83; *Art in America* 51 (December 1963): 30; *Art International* 6 (April 1962): 42–44; *Art News* 64 (November 1965): 32–35; *Art Voices* 6 (Summer 1965): 67–68.

OUGHTON, Lawrence David

(b. Rochester, New York 1945)

Ceramicist. After receiving a B.F.A. (1968) from the Kansas City Art Institute, Oughton attended the Cranbrook Academy (M.F.A. 1971). He has taught ceramics at the National Music Camp in Interlochen and at Adrian College. In 1973 he joined the faculty at Delta College. Oughton was instrumental in organizing the annual "Delta Clay/Glass Invitational," first held in 1974. He has conducted demonstrations throughout the state on body and face casting in porcelain, a technique he has perfected.

One-person Exhibitions: SAM 1971; Birmingham Art Gallery 1971, 1972 (two-person); Habatat Gallery, Dearborn 1974; Xochipilli Gallery, Rochester 1974 (two-person); Artforms Gallery, Detroit 1976; Jesse Besser Museum, Alpena 1976; Sycamore Gallery, Mason 1976 (two-person).

Group Exhibitions: *Young Americans*, Mus of Contemp Crafts 1969; MACE 1969, 1971; *Exhibition '70*, Columbus Gallery of Fine Arts 1970; *Magnificent Objects*, Yaw Gallery, Birmingham 1970; DAM 1970, 1973–74; *Forms: Fiber/Clay/Metal*, Fine Arts Gallery, State University of New York, Oneonta 1971; *Furs and Feathers*, Mus of Contemp Crafts 1971; *Mid-Michigan Annual*, Midland Art Association 1971, 1974, 1976; *Beaux-Art Designer/Craftsmen*, Columbus Museum of Art 1972–73; *Prospectus: Toledo Annual Exhibition*, Toledo Museum of Art 1973; *Invitational*, SAM 1973–75; *Area Show*, SAM 1973, 1976–77; *Invitational*, Pewabic Pottery, Detroit 1974; *Ceramics Invitational*, EMU 1974–77; *Masks, Hysterical and Historical*, SAM 1975; *Invitational*, Ella Sharp Museum, Jackson 1976.

Sources: MAR; Leon Nigrosh, *Clayworks*, Worcester, Mass.: Davis Publications, 1975; *CH* 36, 4 (April

1976): 63; *CH* 37, 4 (April 1977): 43; *CMo* 23 (December 1975): 59–61; *BEcc* 10-3-74, 12-9-76; *DN* 10-13-74; *Saginaw News* 1-13-75, 3-26-75; *Midland Daily News* 2-10-75, 10-13-75, 10-26-75; *DFP* 11-27-75, 6-26-77.

OVERVOORDE, *Chris Stoffel*

(b. Rotterdam, The Netherlands 1934)

Painter/Printmaker. Overvoorde attended the Kendall School of Design, Grand Rapids (1961) and Grand Rapids Junior College (1961–63) before receiving a B.S.D. (1964) and an M.F.A. (1966) from the University of Michigan. In 1966 he joined the art department at Calvin College and was appointed chairman in 1979. Overvoorde served as chairman of the visual arts exhibition for Festival '73 in Grand Rapids and has also participated in various Michigan Council for the Arts committees, including the Visual Arts Advisory Panel, which he chaired from 1975 to 1978. In 1976 he was commissioned by the Dutch Immigration Society to do four paintings on the theme of the cultural contributions of Dutch Americans as a Bicentennial project. Overvoorde is best known for his woodcuts on religious themes and his atmospheric watercolors, which show the influence of his study of Dutch landscapes.

One-person Exhibitions: Grand Valley Art Association, Grand Rapids 1962; Lantern Gallery, Ann Arbor 1967; University of Windsor Gallery 1967; HAM 1969; Grand Haven Art Center 1972; Forsythe Gallery, Ann Arbor 1973, 1979; Hefner's Gallery, Grand Rapids 1974, 1978; Alma College Gallery 1975; Battle Creek Art Center 1975; CMU 1975; GRAM 1975.

Group Exhibitions: *Regional Exhibition*, HAM 1962 (1st Prize), 1967, 1968 (Walker Shaw Award), 1969, 1970, 1973, 1976–77; *West Michigan Annual*, GRAM 1963; *MWCS Annual* 1963, 1965–66; MAE 1965; *Michigan Painters-Printmakers*, GRAM 1965, 1967; *Michiana Biennial*, South Bend Art Center, Ind. 1966 (Graphics Award); *National Religious Art Exhibition*, Cranbrook 1966/67; *Michigan 100*, Battle Creek Civic Art Center 1975 (Graphics Award).

Collections: Alma College; Calvin College; GRAM; Grand Rapids City Hall; HAM; University of Windsor.

Sources: MAR; *AAN* 4-5-66, 1-10-67; *GR Press* 1-11-76, 11-19-78.

PALAZZOLA, *Guy*

(b. Kalamazoo, Michigan 1919, d. Ann Arbor, Michigan, 1978)

Painter. Palazzola received a diploma (1940) in painting from the Art School of the Detroit Society of Arts and Crafts, where he studied under **Sarkis Sarkisian** and **John Carroll**. He joined the DSAC staff in 1942, serving as assistant director from 1950 to 1957. In 1958 he was appointed to the faculty at the University of Michigan. Palazzola also taught at the Crystal Lake Summer Art School and was well known throughout Michigan for his lectures and demonstrations to amateur groups. He gained an even wider audience through his hosting of several University of Michigan educational television series, including *Meet the Masters*, *The Painter's Art*, and *Painting with Palazzola*. Totaling over 100 programs, these series have been seen on public TV stations throughout the United States. A painter of great technical competence, Palazzola worked in a variety of styles. In 1975 Palazzola received the University of Michigan's Distinguished Faculty Award.

One-person Exhibitions: Collector's Gallery, Chicago 1961; DIA 1961 (two-person); DAM 1967.

Group Exhibitions: MAE 1938–40, 1942–44, 1948–61, 1965, 1970 (Friends of Modern Art Prize 1939, Sheridan Prize 1940, 1956, Purchase Prize 1949, Skelton Prize 1950, FSPP 1951, 1960); *American Painting and Sculpture*, AIC 1951; *Michigan Art Through 50 Years*, UMMA 1955; *Midyear Show*, Butler Institute 1955, 1957–58 (Purchase Awards), 1960–63 (Invited 1961); *Young American Painters*, AFA Traveling Show 1957/58; DAM 1958–71; *West Michigan Annual*, GRAM 1959–62 (1st Prize 1959); *Midwest Painters Invitational*, GRAM 1960; *Michigan Art: Yesterday and Today*, FIA 1963; *Michigan Art '67*, BBAA 1967; *All Michigan I*, FIA 1971/72; *Art and Crafts in Detroit, 1900–1976*, DIA 1976*; *Michigan Collects Michigan Art*, Pontiac Creative Arts Center 1976.

Collections: Butler Institute; Corcoran; DIA; GRAM; UMMA.

Sources: AAA, Interview; MAR; *Prize-Winning American Paintings*, N.Y. 1959, 1960, 1961; *Art in America* 45, 1 (January 1957): 30–31; *DFP* 8-3-52, 4-14-52, 3-12-67; *DN* 3-20-55, 3-12-67, 4-30-67; *AAN* 1-28-76, 11-28-76.

PALLAS, Jim

(b. Detroit, Michigan 1941)

Sculptor. Educated at Wayne State University (B.F.A. 1963, M.F.A. 1965), Pallas joined the faculty at Macomb County Community College in 1965. He has also served as visual arts coordinator for the Michigan Council for the Arts (1967). Although he began his career in the more traditional medium of welded metal sculpture, Pallas began creating kinetic sculptures in the late 1960s. His sculptures are "performing" pieces that depend on a combination of computer logic and environmental stimuli to produce patterns of light, sound, and movement. A conceptual artist, Pallas's concern with verbal and visual symbolism is also reflected in his investigation of moving systems of information, such as his *Phoney Vents* in which participants receive unannounced phone calls containing a pre-recorded "message."

One-person Exhibitions: Allan Stone Gallery, New York City, 1978; *Works in Progress IV*, DIA 1978*.

Group Exhibitions: MAE 1964, 1965 (Redstone Prize), 1972; *Misalliance*, DAM 1969; *Michigan Collects Michigan Art*, Pontiac Creative Arts Center 1976; *Michigan Sculpture '77*, Macomb County Community College 1977.

Collections: City of Detroit, Washington Boulevard Plaza; DIA.

Sources: MAR; *Detroit Artists Monthly* 3, 2 (February 1978): 10–11; *Michigan Art Journal* 1, 1 (January 1976): 13–15; *DN* 6-8-75, 11-5-76, 2-19-78, 11-20-80; *DFP* 2-26-78; 6-9-78, 1-31-80; *Washington Post* 11-19-80.

PARDUCCI, Corrado

(b. Pisa, Italy 1900)

Sculptor. Parducci arrived in New York City from his native Italy in 1904. He studied modeling under Albin Polosek at the Richmond Hill Settlement House in Greenwich Village and then served an apprenticeship with the architectural firm of Zari & Ricci. He arrived in Detroit in 1924 and collaborated with Smith, Hinchman & Grylls on sculptural design for the downtown branch of Detroit Public Library. Parducci was particularly active during the building boom in Detroit in the 1920s, and his work can be seen on such Detroit landmarks as the Guardian Building, the Buhl Building, the Penobscot Building, the Fisher Building, and the Federal Courthouse. Other major commissions included exterior reliefs for the Kalamazoo County Courthouse and the Civic Auditorium in Grand Rapids. Parducci also worked on the residences of such prominent Detroiters as Senator James Couzens, Alvin MacCauley, Louis Mendelsohn, the Fisher brothers, and Mr. and Mrs. Alfred Wilson's home at Meadowbrook. After World War II, he was primarily occupied with church and mausoleum work. He was elected as honorary member of the Detroit Chapter of the American Institute of Architects in 1958.

Collections: Blessed Sacrament Cathedral, Detroit; Book Tower, Detroit; Buhl Building, Detroit; Detroit College of Law; Detroit Free Press Building; Downtown Branch, Detroit Public Library; Duns Scotus College, Detroit; Federal Building, Detroit; Fisher Building, Detroit; Grand Rapids Civic Auditorium; Guardian Building, Detroit; Kirk in the Hills, Bloomfield Hills; Kresge Headquarters (now Detroit Institute of Technology), Detroit; Masonic Temple, Detroit; Meadowbrook Hall, Rochester; Penobscot Building, Detroit; Rackham Building, U. of M.; Rackham Fountain, Detroit Zoo, Royal Oak; St. Aloyius Church, Detroit; St. John's Seminary, Detroit; St. Peter's Cathedral, Marquette; Shrine of the Little Flower, Royal Oak; Trinity Lutheran Church, Detroit.

Sources: Hendry 1980; Hendry 1980A; Hendry 1980B; *Michigan Society of Architects Monthly Bulletin* 50, 10 (October 1975): 3–6; *DFP* 5-10-31, 3-13-76 (Magazine), 11-12-79; *DN* 3-22-73.

PAPPAS, John L.

(b. Florina, Greece 1899; d. Detroit, Michigan 1976)

Painter. A Greek immigrant, Pappas came to the United States via Saginaw in 1914 and later settled in Detroit (1916). He studied at the **John P. Wicker** School of Fine Arts, Detroit, and later taught at the Wicker School (1930), at the Art School of the Detroit Society of Arts and Crafts, and at the Lakeside Palette Club in Saint Clair Shores. Pappas owned two downtown restaurants, including "Jolly Jim," a downtown artists' "hang-out" that was open twenty-four hours a day and where he did most of his painting in the basement. Essentially a landscape painter, Pappas was known for his oils and watercolors that were inspired by his visits to ancient Greek villages and ruins such as the Parthenon. He was a member of the Scarab Club.

One-person Exhibitions: Bonstelle Playhouse, Detroit 1928 (two-person); Detroit Galleries 1931; J. L. Hudson Gallery, Detroit 1934; Gronyn & Lowndes Galleries, Rockefeller Center 1934; DAM 1937, 1939–41, 1947.

Group Exhibitions: MAE 1928, 1929 (Walker Prize), 1930, 1932–34, 1935 (Haass Prize), 1936–38, 1939 (Scarab Club Gold Medal), 1940 (Honorable Mention),

1941–48, 1950–52, 1955–57, 1960–71; *Carnegie International* 1930; *American Painting and Sculpture*, AIC 1931; *Scarab Club*, Detroit 1938–39; DAM 1938–39, 1942, 1944, 1949, 1951, 1957; *American Art Today*, New York World's Fair 1939; *Golden Gate International Exposition*, San Francisco Museum of Art 1939; *Great Lakes Exhibition*, DIA 1939; Rackham Gallery, U. of M. 1939; *American Artists Annual*, DIA 1940; *Contemporary Detroit Painters*, Alger House, DIA 1940; *Grosse Pointe Artists Association*, Alger House, DIA 1942; *Metropolitan Art Association of Detroit*, DIA 1944; *Michigan Art Through 50 Years*, UMMA 1955.

Collections: DIA.

Sources: *Art and Artists* 4,2 (July/August 1964): 12–13; *DN* 9-4-32, 1-24-37, 10-17-37, 1-29-39, 5-5-40, 2-16-41, 11-23-41; *DFP* 9-7-33.

PAPPAS, John Nick

(b. Detroit, Michigan 1934)

Sculptor. Educated at Wayne State University (B.F.A. 1958, M.F.A. 1959), Pappas taught briefly at Wayne State and worked as a clay modeler for an automotive company before joining the faculty at Eastern Michigan University in 1961. Winner of a Prix de Rome fellowship in 1966, he spent a year working in Rome where he became acquainted with the Italian sculptor Giacomo Manzu. Returning to the United States in 1967, he helped design the new sculpture building at Eastern Michigan University and developed an innovative course that combined sculpture and drawing. A figurative sculptor who works in the traditional medium of cast bronze, Pappas has constructed his own foundry in Ypsilanti. In 1972 he won a statewide competition for a sculpture for the Detroit headquarters of Blue Cross and Blue Shield of Michigan. His monumental group of fourteen figures is one of the largest bronze statuary pieces cast in the United States in the past twenty years.

One-person Exhibitions: Forsythe Gallery, Ann Arbor 1963 (two-person); Hanamura Gallery, Detroit 1965; Arwin Gallery, Detroit 1967, 1971–72, 1973 (two-person), 1977–78; Wilna Gallery, Chicago 1971–72.

Group Exhibitions: *Michigan Art: Yesterday and Today*, FIA 1963; *Drawings U.S.A.*, Minneapolis Museum of Art 1963, 1965 (Purchase Prize); MAE 1963 (Medow Memorial Prize), 1970; *West Michigan Annual*, GRAM 1964; *American Academy Annual*, Rome 1967; *Formes Humaines*, Rodin Museum, Paris 1968; *Mainstreams*, Marietta College, Ohio 1969.

Collections/Commissions: Beyer Hospital, Ypsilanti; Blue Cross and Blue Shield of Michigan, Detroit; City of Hillsdale; EMU; Michigan Education Association, Lansing; Minnesota Museum of Art; WSU.

Sources: MAR; *Detroit Artists Monthly* 3, 2 (February 1978): 2; *Ypsilanti Press* 5-22-69, 4-3-70, 8-15-76; *DN* 8-15-76 (Sunday Magazine), 12-18-77; *DFP* 11-22-77; *AAN* 11-12-77.

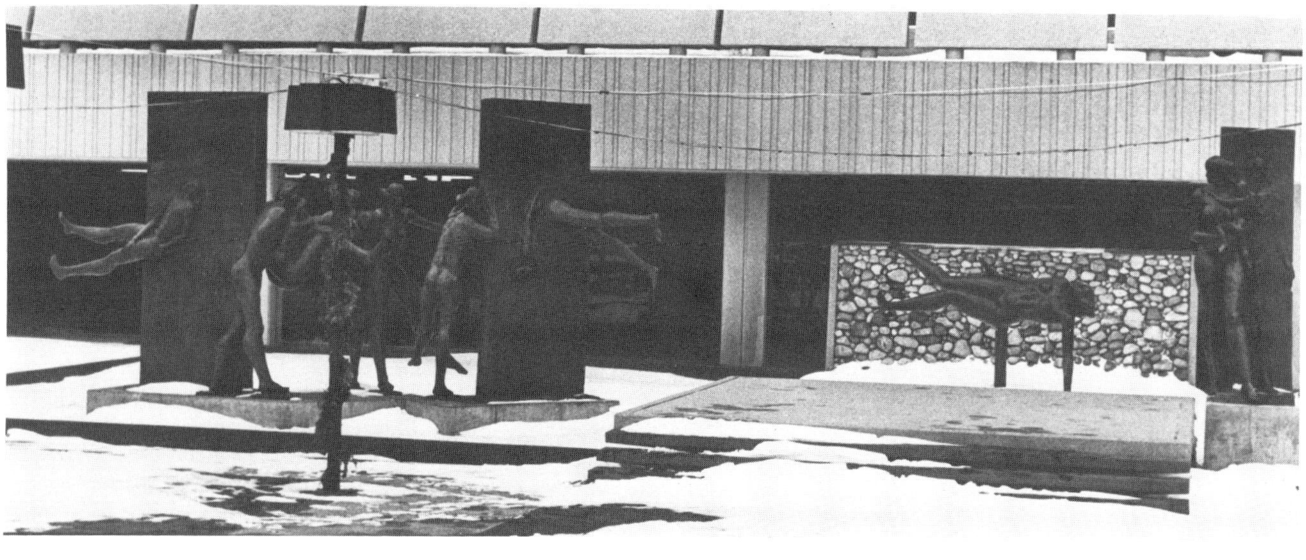

John Nick Pappas (1934–). Commission for Blue Cross and Blue Shield of Michigan, Headquarters, Detroit. Courtesy the Detroit Free Press.

PAPSDORF, Frederick

(b. Dover, Ohio 1887; d. Detroit, Michigan 1978)

Painter. Papsdorf achieved fame in the 1940s as Detroit's "Milkman Painter." Employed as a shipping clerk for the Borden Milk Company, he began to paint when he was nearly fifty. Primarily self-taught, he briefly attended evening classes at the Detroit Institute of Arts. His instructor, **Sarkis Sarkisian**, recognized his unique style and advised him against further formal study. His flower paintings, rural landscapes, and domestic scenes were purchased by such Detroit area collectors as Robert Tannahill, William R. Valentiner, John S. Newberry, and George Kamperman. In 1943 he was included in the Museum of Modern Art's *Realist and Magic Realists* exhibition.

One-person Exhibitions: DAM 1938–39, 1950, 1952, 1966, 1973, 1976; DSAC 1941; Perls Gallery, New York City 1943*, 1945*, 1948; KIA 1944 (three-person).

Group Exhibitions: *Contemporary Detroit Painters*, DIA 1940; *Contemporary American Painting*, Whitney 1940; *New Year's Show*, Butler Institute 1942, 1946, 1949; *Painting in the United States*, Carnegie Institute 1944–48; *PAFA Annual* 1944–47, 1950; MAE 1948–63; *Michigan Art Through 50 Years*, UMMA 1955.

Collections: Butler Institute; DIA; MOMA; St. Louis Art Museum; Whitney.

Sources: AAA 981; *Art Dig* 18, 1 (October 1, 1943): 8; *Art Dig* 19, 20 (September 15, 1945): 17; *Art Dig* 22, 15 (May 1, 1948): 15; *Art News* 44, 11 (September 1-30, 1945): 21; *DAC News* 42, 7 (July 1957): 26–27; *New Yorker* September 29, 1945; *Newsweek* October 1, 1945; *Time* October 11, 1943; *DN* 1-15-39, 1-21-40, 1-15-61, 2-2-66; *DFP* 10-3-43, 6-27-48.

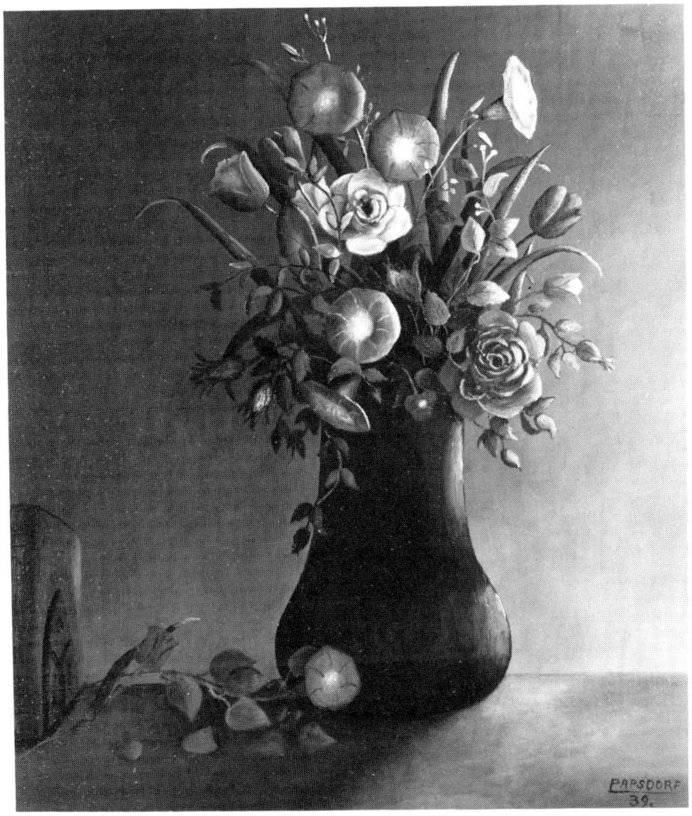

Frederick Papsdorf (1887–1978). Flowers. *1919. Oil on canvas. 20⅛ × 18 inches. Collection of the Detroit Institute of Arts, Gift of Robert H. Tannahill.*

PARISH, Tom

(b. Hibbing, Minnesota 1933)

Painter/Printmaker. Parish studied at the College of William and Mary, Williamsburg, Virginia, and at the Pennsylvania Academy of the Fine Arts. He received a B.F.A. (1957) from the University of Pennsylvania, an M.A. (1961) from the University of North Dakota, and two Cresson Traveling Scholarships, which allowed him to study in Europe (1955, 1966). Parish taught at Joliet Junior College (1961–64) in Illinois and at St. Louis County College (1964–67) in Missouri, before accepting a teaching position at Wayne State University in 1967. Parish was one of the original members of the Willis Gallery co-op and has served on the Arts Advisory Board of New Detroit, Inc.

One-person Exhibitions: Gilman Galleries, Chicago 1966, 1971; University of Windsor, Ontario 1972; Martha Jackson Gallery, New York City 1974; DAM 1978; WSU 1976, 1978; Willis Gallery, Detroit 1980 (two-person).

Group Exhibitions: Barone Gallery, New York City 1955; Philadelphia Print Club 1955–57; Philadelphia Art Alliance 1957; PAFA 1958; Northwest Printmakers, Seattle 1959; *Boston Printmakers Exhibition*, Museum of Fine Arts, Boston 1963; *Midyear Show*, Butler Institute 1964, 1965 (Purchase Award); *Fifty Years of American Realistic Painting Since the Armory Show*, FIA 1966; *American Painters*, Allentown Museum, Pa. 1968; *Contemporary American Painting and Sculpture*, Krannert Art Museum, University of Illinois 1969*; *Landscape Now*, DAM 1972; *New Images*, Martha Jackson Gallery, New York City 1973; *The Forsythe Saga I & II*, Forsythe Building, Detroit 1973, 1976; *Detroit Artists Invitational*, Detroit Bank & Trust Co. 1974; *Print Show*, Brooklyn Museum 1974; *Salute to '76*, Martha Jackson Gallery, New York City 1976; *Tradition and Invention*, Kresge Art Center Gallery, MSU 1976; *27 Painters*, UMMA 1976; Sheldon Ross Gallery, Birmingham 1977; *Selected from Detroit*, Pontiac Creative Arts Center 1978.

Collections: Butler Institute; Kemper Insurance Company, Chicago; Kresge Foundation, Lansing; Lewis College, Lockport, Ill.; University of North Dakota, Grand Forks.

Sources: MAR; *Arts and Artists* 8 (November 1973): 52; *Arts* 48 (May 1974): 68–70; *Detroit Artists Monthly* 3, 6 (June 1978): 5–6; *Chicago Daily News* 12-10-66; *DN* 4-11-76, 12-4-78.

PAULUS, *Francis Petrus*

(b. Detroit, Michigan 1862; d. Detroit, Michigan 1933)

Painter/Printmaker. Paulus received initial training at the Pennsylvania Academy of Fine Arts and later studied at the Royal Academy of Fine Arts in Munich under Robert Loefftz. He returned to Detroit in 1889 and helped organize the first classes at the Art School of the Detroit Museum of Art. After a short stay, he returned to Europe, where he attended the École des Beaux-Arts in Paris, studying under Léon Bonnat. In 1895, he returned to Detroit and with **Joseph Gies** founded the Detroit Art Academy, where he remained as co-director until 1903. For a time he also directed an art school in Ann Arbor (1896–98). Paulus left Detroit in 1903 and traveled extensively throughout Europe before settling in Bruges, Belgium, where he remained until the outbreak of World War I. He was one of the founders of the Detroit chapter of the Society of Western Artists and was an early member of the Scarab Club. He was also a member of the National Arts Club, the Munich Etching Society, the Chicago Society of Etchers, and the Internationale Société de la Gravure en Noir. Paulus worked in both oil and pastel, and although he painted many portraits, he was best known for his scenes of Bruges: quaint canals, bridges, and street scenes. He was also an etcher of note.

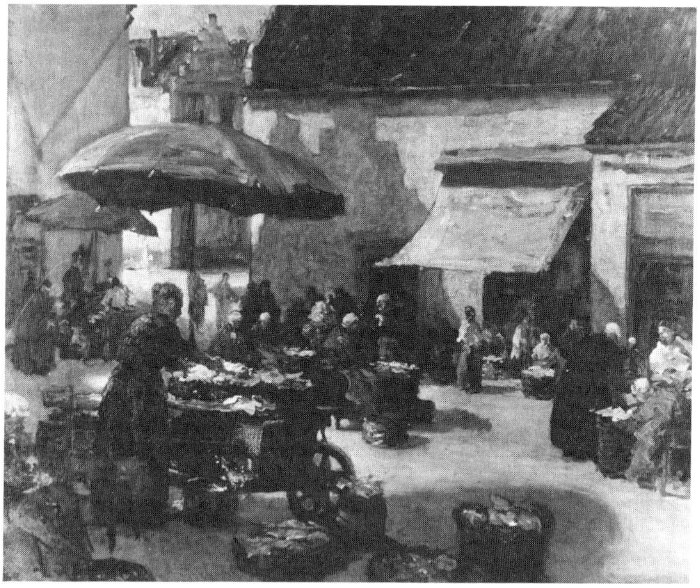

Francis Petrus Paulus (1862–1933). Fish Market at Bruges. *ca. 1918. Oil on canvas. 34 × 40 inches. Collection of the Detroit Institute of Arts.*

One-person Exhibitions: DMA 1902, 1910, 1915; GRAM 1911; DIA 1919, 1928*; John Hanna Galleries, Detroit 1924; Bonstelle Theatre, Detroit 1925.

Group Exhibitions: *2nd Exhibition*, DMA 1889; *American Painting and Sculpture*, AIC 1895, 1897, 1905; *Society of Western Artists* 1897–98, 1902; *Watercolors, Pastels, and Miniatures*, AIC 1899; *Summer Exhibition*, DMA 1903; *Paris Salon* 1904–12; *Paintings by Michigan Artists*, DMA 1905; *PAFA Annual* 1910–11; MAE 1911–12, 1914–19, 1924–26, 1930 (1st Prize 1914, 3rd Prize 1917, FSPP 1926); *Chicago Society of Etchers Annual*, AIC 1913; *American Artists Annual*, DIA 1917–20, 1923–26; *Michigan Art Through 50 Years*, UMMA 1955.

Collections: DIA; Hudson Public Library; Indianapolis Museum of Art, Ind.; Library of Congress; Marygrove College, Detroit; McGregor Public Library, Highland Park; Musée d'Art Moderne, Brussels; New York Public Library; Oakland Art Museum, California.

Sources: AAA N102; *American Art Annual* 1933; Bénézit 1976; Burroughs 1936/37; Fielding 1974; Gibson 1975; Kenny 1965; Mallett 1948; Mich State Lib 1915; *All the Arts* (Detroit) 3, 3 (March 1920): 19–23; *American Magazine of Art* 17 (June 1926): 293; *Brush and Pencil* (Chicago) 3, 3 (December 1898): 160; *International Studio* 55 (April 1912): 141; *DFP* 2-1-20, 2-3-33; *NYT* 2-3-33.

PEDERSON, *Roy*

(b. Madison, Wisconsin 1931)

Ceramicist. After studying ceramics with Carleton Ball and Harvey Littleton at the University of Wisconsin, Pederson received a B.S. (1956) and an M.S. (1957). He also studied with **John Stephenson** at the University of Michigan, concentrating mainly on stoneware. Pederson's studio is located in a carriage house in Plymouth, and his gas kiln is constructed inside the water tower of the former Daisy Air Rifle Company. He has taught for the Northville Public Schools since 1957, while also teaching at Eastern Michigan University and for the Ann Arbor Potters Guild. In 1972 he was a participant in the Michigan Artrain, giving pottery demonstrations.

One-person Exhibitions: EMU 1962; South Bend Art Center, Ind. 1966; Battle Creek Civic Art Center 1967 (two-person).

Group Exhibitions: *Midwest Designer/Craftsman Show*, AIC (later Smithsonian traveling exhibition) 1957; MACE 1958 (Webber Prize), 1960–62, 1966, 1968; *Michiana Regional*, South Bend Art Association, Ind. 1958–60, 1962; Hanamura Gallery 1961; *Michigan Art: Yesterday and Today*, FIA 1963; *Michigan Crafts Council Exhibition*, Birmingham 1965; Rook's Gallery, Pontiac 1965; *Michigan Council for the Arts Traveling Exhibition* 1967; *Ceramic Invitational*, EMU 1969; Hartland Art Show 1976.

Sources: MAR; Thomas Sellers, *Throwing on the Potter's Wheel*, Columbus, Ohio: Professional Publications, 1960; *CH* 27, 1 (February 1957): 40; *CMo* 7, 2 (February 1959): 35; *CMo* 7, 4 (April 1959): 35; *CMo* 11, 4 (April 1963): 26–27; *CMo* 18, 2 (February 1970): 32.

PERRAULT, *Ida Marie*

(b. Detroit, Michigan 1874; d. Detroit, Michigan 1930)

Painter. Born in Detroit, Perrault studied first under John Ward Dunsmore at the Detroit School of Art, then at Art School of the Detroit Museum of Art, and, finally, for seven years in Paris, The Hague, and Brussels. Upon her return from Europe in 1911, she was given a one-person show of her paintings and sketches at the Detroit Institute of Arts and became known for her sensitive portraits of mothers and children. After a second trip abroad, she returned to Detroit in 1918 due to World War I, and later became noted for her dolls and marionettes in native and historical costumes as well as for her illustrations for children's books. Perrault also worked as an interior designer, executing commissions for decorative panels and fire screens.

One-person Exhibition: DIA 1911*.

Group Exhibitions: Detroit Art Association 1893; MAE 1919, 1922 (Detroit River Club Prize for Best Work by a Woman Artist), 1924 (Founders Society 2nd Prize), 1925, 1930; *DSWP Annual* 1930.

Collections: Aesthetic Club, London; Detroit Public Library; Société des Americaines, Paris; Ten Club, Paris; Toledo Public Library.

Sources: Gibson 1975; *Detroit Journal* 9-28-1894, 12-15-1894, 1-23-20; *News Tribune* 1-19-1896; *DFP* 12-6-08, 10-8-11, 10-15-11, 3-16-19; *DN* 1-4-23, 1-24-24, 11-2-25.

PIEPENBURG, *Robert*

(b. Detroit, Michigan 1941)

Ceramicist. After graduating with an M.A. (1965) from Eastern Michigan University, Piepenburg began his extensive teaching career at Highland Park High School as a woodworking instructor. From 1967 to 1969 he taught drawing at Highland Park Community College and has been teaching ceramics at Oakland Community College in Farmington since 1969. In 1973 he received an M.F.A. from Eastern Michigan University and since then has given numerous workshops and lectures throughout the country and locally at the Michigan Potters' Association, Michigan State University, the Flint Institute of Arts, and the University of Michigan. He is the recipient of a National Endowment for the Arts Fellowship for 1980/81 and is the author of *Designs in Wood* (New York: Bruce Publishing, 1969) and *Raku Pottery* (New York: Macmillan Publishing 1972).

One-person Exhibitions: Habatat Galleries, Dearborn 1972; Yaw Gallery, Birmingham 1972 (three-person), 1973; Artforms Gallery, Detroit 1973 (two-person); EMU 1973; Alma College 1974; Bates College, Lewiston, Maine 1974; Greenwich House Pottery, New York City 1974; University of Windsor, Ontario 1974; The Gallery, Ann Arbor 1975; J. Walter Thompson Co., Detroit 1975; Midland Center for the Arts 1979; Robert Kidd Gallery, Birmingham 1980; Mill Gallery, Milford 1981.

Group Exhibitions: *Michigan Artist-Craftsmen Exhibition*, GRAM 1972 (1st Place Award); *Detroit Invitational*, Pewabic Pottery, Detroit 1972; *Ceramic Invitational*, EMU 1972, 1974, 1977, 1980; MACE 1972; *Michigan Potters' Association Annual* 1972 (1st Place), 1977–78, 1981; *Beaux-Arts Designer/Craftsmen*, Columbus Museum of Art 1972–73; *Invitational*, DAM 1972; *All Michigan II*, FIA 1973/74; *Mid-Michigan Annual*, Midland Art Association 1974, 1977; *Ceramics West Invitational*, Utah State University, Logan 1975–77; *Clay-Glass Invitational*, Delta College 1975; 1977–78; *Michigan Crafts Exhibition*, DIA 1976 (Award); *Film/Video Competition*, University of Nevada, Las Vegas 1977; *Michigan Sculpture '77*, Macomb County Community College 1977; *Video/Audio Installations*, Willis Gallery, Detroit 1977; *Vision '77*, Banff Centre, Alberta 1977; *National Raku Exhibition*, Peter's Valley Craftsmen, Layton, N.J. 1977–78; *Michigan Artists Biennial*, Kresge Art Center Gallery, MSU 1981*.

Collections: Cadillac City-County Building; DIA.

Sources: MAR; Polly Rothenberg, *The Complete Book of Ceramic Art*, New York: Crown, 1972; *CH* 33, 2 (February 1973): 69–70; *CH* 34, 3 (June 1974): 70; *CH* 34, 6 (December 1974): 62; *CMo* 21, 9 (November 1973): 32–33; *CMo* 23, 1 (January 1975): 27; *CMo* 23, 4 (April 1975): 32; *Studio Potter* 2, 2 (Winter 1973/74): 28–29.

PIET, John

(b. Detroit, Michigan 1946)

Sculptor. Piet studied at the Art School of the Detroit Society of Arts and Crafts (B.F.A. 1973) and Wayne State University (M.F.A. 1975). He has worked as a clay modeler for General Motors Corporation and taught sculpture and ceramics at Wayne County Community College (1971–76). Recipient of two Ford Foundation Grants (1967, 1972) and a National Endowment for the Arts Fellowship (1973), Piet co-organized the "Forsythe Saga" exhibition in 1973, the "Detroit Artists Invitational" in 1974, and the "Michigan Sculpture '77" exhibition at Macomb County Community College. Piet creates large, graceful painted steel structures, groupings of several small pieces in varying configurations, and large free-standing cylindrical pieces. He is presently an instructor at Macomb County Community College.

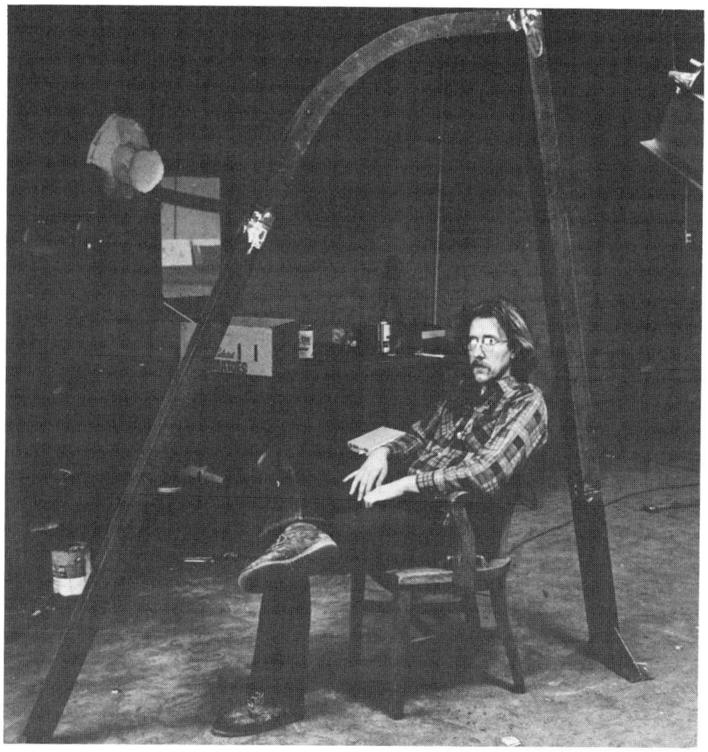

John Piet (1946–   ) in his studio, Detroit, October 1972. Carl Schurer, Photographer.

One-person Exhibitions: Willis Gallery, Detroit 1974, 1976.

Group Exhibitions: *All Michigan I and II*, FIA 1971/72, 1973/74; *Sculpture Walk*, Central Business District Association, Detroit 1972; *Forsythe Saga*, Forsythe Building, Detroit 1973; DAM 1974; *Detroit Artists Invitational*, Detroit Bank & Trust Co. 1974*; *Michigan Focus*, DIA 1974/75 ($1,000 Sculpture Award)*; *Cass Corridor Artists*, Somerset Mall, Troy 1975; *Sculpture Inside and Out*, School of Art, U of M. 1975; *Arts and Crafts in Detroit 1906–1976*, DIA 1976*; *15 Contemporary Sculptors*, MSU 1976; *7 for 76*, Eastern Illinois University 1976; *Michigan Sculpture '77*, Macomb County Community College 1977; *At Cranbrook: Downtown Detroit*, CAAM 1979; *Kick Out The Jams*, DIA 1980*.

Collections: Fort Street Plaza, Detroit Bank & Trust Co.; Grand Circus Park, Detroit Parks and Recreation Department; K-Mart Corporate Headquarters, Troy; Pingree Park, Detroit, Inc.; The Roostertail, Detroit.

Sources: MAR; Nawrocki 1980; *People's Art 200*, City of Detroit Department of Recreation Pamphlet 1977; *Monthly Detroit* October 1980; *DFP* 6-22-75, 9-7-75, 3-7-76, 7-3-80; *DN* 3-31-74, 6-12-75, 10-19-75, 2-29-76, 3-7-76, 3-21-76.

PITNEY, William

(b. Eastport, New York 1914)

Ceramicist. Pitney graduated from the Pratt Institute, New York City, in 1942. He also attended the State University of New York at Alfred, earning an M.F.A. (1950) in ceramics. In 1950 he joined the faculty at Wayne State University, where he subsequently headed the ceramics division until his retirement in 1972. His students included **Julie Larson**, **John Glick**, and Carolyn Judson. Pitney was instrumental in the establishment of both the Michigan Potters' Association and the Michigan Craftsmen's Council. He is currently owner and operator of The Pot Shop in Sharon, Connecticut.

One-person Exhibitions: DAM 1952; Women's City Club, Detroit 1955; Habatat Galleries, Dearborn 1976; Hillsdale College 1978 (two-person).

Group Exhibitions: *Ceramics National*, Everson Museum of Art, Syracuse 1950–61; MACE 1951–52,

1954, 1956–58, 1960, 1962–64; *Designer/Craftsmen U.S.A.*, Brooklyn Museum 1953*; *Regional Designer/Craftsmen, USA*, DIA 1953; *Ceramic International*, Everson Museum of Art, Syracuse 1958; *La Ceràmique Contemporaine*, Ostend, Belgium 1959; *Modern American Ceramics*, Royal Copenhagen Porcelain Factory, Denmark 1960; *Bowls-Plates-Platters*, Habatat Galleries, Dearborn 1976.

Sources: MAR; Pitney in *Michigan Challenge* (State Chamber of Commerce) 4, 5 (February 1964): 10–11, 38; *CH* 24, 3 (May/June 1964): 57; *DN* 3-25-51.

PLUM, *Jens*

(b. Rochester, New York 1926)

Painter. Plum received a B.F.A. (1954) from Wayne State University and an M.F.A. (1956) from the Cranbrook Academy of Art, where he studied under **Zoltan Sepeshy**. He joined the faculty at Michigan State University in 1965. Plum is best known for his oil still lifes and charcoal figure studies.

One-person Exhibitions: Hanamura Gallery, Detroit 1965; KIA 1965; CMU 1974; Battle Creek Civic Art Center 1978.

Group Exhibitions: *PAFA Annual*, 1959, 1961; MAE 1959, 1961, 1972; *Area Show*, KIA 1963–66; *Midyear Show*, Butler Institute 1965; *Michigan Painters-Printmakers*, GRAM 1961, 1967, 1971 (Purchase Prize); *Michigan Art '67*, BBAA 1967; *All Michigan I*, FIA 1971/72; *Michigan Focus*, DIA 1974/75; *27 Painters*, UMMA 1976.

Collections: City National Bank, Detroit; GRAM; Kresge Corporation, Troy; Manufacturers National Bank, Detroit.

Sources: MAR; *DN* 3-7-65.

PLUM, *Nancy Manes*

(b. Providence, Rhode Island 1932)

Ceramicist. Plum received a B.A. (1954) from Antioch College and an M.F.A. (1956) from the Cranbrook Academy of Art, where she studied with **Maija Grotell**. She received an M.A. (1957) from Mills College in Oakland, California, and also studied with Marguerite Wildenhain at the Pond Ford Pottery in California. From 1957 to 1959, she taught ceramics and weaving at New Mexico Highlands University in Las Vegas. Plum presently teaches at the Lansing Potters Guild and maintains a studio in Okemos. Her stoneware is characterized by simple, functional shapes and warm, earthy glazes.

One-person Exhibitions: *America House*, Birmingham 1970; Battle Creek Civic Art Center 1977; Hanamura Gallery, Detroit 1979 (two-person).

Group Exhibitions: MACE 1955–57 (Fleischman Prize), 1958, 1960 (Haass Prize), 1961–62, 1963 (Webber Prize), 1972; *Young Americans*, Mus Contemp Crafts 1956, 1958, 1962; *Ceramic National*, Everson Museum of Art, Syracuse 1956, 1961; *Fiber/Clay/Metal*, Minnesota Museum of Art 1957 (Purchase Prize); *West Michigan Annual*, GRAM 1961; *Michiana Regional*, South Bend Art Center, Ind. 1962, 1970; *Michigan Art: Yesterday and Today*, FIA 1963; *Midwest Designer/Craftsmen*, Columbus Museum of Fine Arts 1970, 1973; *Ceramics Invitational*, EMU 1971, 1974; *Objects 76*, BBAA 1976; *Michigan Ceramics 1979*, Pewabic Pottery, Detroit 1979.

Collections: DIA; Minnesota Museum of Art; Witte Memorial Museum, San Antonio.

Sources: MAR; *DIA Bulletin* 36, 3 (1956–57): 75–76; *Michigan Challenge* (State Chamber of Commerce) 4, 5 (February 1964): 38; *DN* 8-25-63; *BEcc* 8-13-70.

POLLOCK, *Charles*

(b. Denver, Colorado 1902)

Painter/Printmaker. Pollock began his career in the early 1920s as a newspaper artist for the *Los Angeles Times*. He then studied at the Otis Art Institute in Los Angeles (1923–24) and at the Art Students League in New York City with Thomas Hart Benton (1927–28). During the Depression, he taught school in New York City, traveled in the Southwest and California with his brother Jackson, and worked for the special skills division of the Federal Resettlement Administration. He came to Detroit in 1937 as a political cartoonist and layout editor for the United Autoworkers union paper. He subsequently became acquainted with Sylvester Jerry, head of the Works Progress Administration/Federal Art Project in Michigan, who appointed him technical supervisor of mural painting and graphics for the project. Pollock completed murals for the Water Conditioning Plant in Lansing and for the auditorium at Michigan State College (now Michigan State University). He joined the faculty at Michigan State in 1942 and remained on the staff until 1968, teaching etching, lettering, and book design. He is the author of a text, *Lettering and Handwriting in the College Curriculum*, published in 1949. In 1966 Pollock was awarded both a Guggenheim Fellowship and a National Endowment for the Arts grant. Although he began his career as a painter of the American scene, Pollock since the 1960s has concentrated on abstract collage and color-field painting. He presently resides in Paris.

One-person Exhibitions: KIA 1964; *Retrospective*, Kresge Art Center Gallery, MSU 1964; Henri Gallery, Alexandria, Va. 1966; Gertrude Kasle Gallery, Detroit 1966-68.

Group Exhibitions: *American Painting and Sculpture*, AIC 1931; *PAFA Annual* 1934, 1941; *Corcoran Biennial* 1935, 1967*; MAE 1937-39, 1941, 1945, 1949; *International Exposition of Lithography and Wood Engraving*, AIC 1938; New York World's Fair 1939; *200 American Watercolors*, NCFA 1941; *International Exposition of Watercolor*, AIC 1942; *Contemporary American Painting*, Whitney 1963; *Michigan Art '67*, BBAA 1967.

Collections/Commissions: DIA; Kresge Art Center Gallery, MSU; UMMA; Water Filtration Plant, Lansing; Whitney.

Sources: *WWAA* 1962; AAA 1097; *DN* 1-16-66, 6-18-67.

PONSEN, *Tunis*

(b. Wageningen, The Netherlands 1891; d. Chicago, Illinois 1968)

Painter. Ponsen arrived in Michigan from his native Holland in 1913, after studying under Louis Raemaekers and August Falise. He received further training from a local Muskegon artist, Wilbur C. Kensler, then attended the School of the Art Institute of Chicago, studying under Karl Buehr and George Oberteuffer. After his graduation in 1925, Ponsen divided his time between Chicago and Muskegon, with periods of study in Paris and in Provincetown, Massachusetts, with Charles Hawthorne. He completed many commissions for Muskegon area collectors, including landscapes based on local scenes and a number of portraits. In 1929 one of his paintings was chosen by popular vote to become the first oil painting acquired for the collection of the Flint Institute of Arts. After 1931 Ponsen resided in Chicago. At the time of his death, he was on the faculty at the Chicago Academy of Fine Arts.

One-person Exhibitions: HAM 1921 (three-person), 1922, 1923, 1925, 1927, 1931, 1967; Chicago Galleries Association 1950 (two-person).

Group Exhibitions: MAE 1927-28, 1930-34, 1936-37; *American Painting and Sculpture*, AIC 1927, 1929 (Cahn Prize), 1930; *Regional Exhibition*, HAM 1927-31; *PAFA Annual* 1931; *Century of Progress Exhibition*, Chicago 1933.

Collections: City of Chicago; FIA; HAM; Northwestern University.

Sources: *WWAA* 1962; Bénézit 1976; *Art Dig* 24, 8 (January 15, 1950): 11; *Muskegon Chronicle* 6-6-31, 11-2-67.

RADELL, *Renée*

(b. Birmingham, Alabama 1929)

Painter. Educated in Detroit at Cass Technical High School, the Art School of the Detroit Society of Arts and Crafts (Diploma 1953) and Wayne State University, Radell taught at Oakland University in Rochester before joining the faculty at Mercy College of Detroit in 1962. Two important aspects of Radell's work are images of women and themes of social and political satire.

One-person Exhibitions: DAM 1952; Garelick's Gallery, Detroit 1959*, 1961*; Tasca Gallery, New York City 1965-66; Shuster Gallery, New York City 1967, 1969, 1971; J. Walter Thompson Company, Detroit 1968; University of Windsor, Ontario 1968; Hillsdale College 1976.

Group Exhibitions: *MWCS Annual* 1951-53, 1957-58 (1st Prize 1951, 1952); MAE 1953, 1957 (Taylor Prize), 1960; *Midyear Show*, Butler Institute 1957, 1960-61, 1963, 1967, 1969; *Michigan Painters-Printmakers*, GRAM 1969; *Womanart*, SAM 1974 (Invited); *Mainstreams*, Marietta College, Ohio 1968 (1st Prize), 1974-75.

Collections: Brother Rice High School, Birmingham; DIA; Douglas MacArthur School, Southfield; Mercy College, Detroit.

Sources MAR; *Art News* 66, 7 (November 1967): 62; *Arts Mag* 42, 2 (November 1967): 55; *Arts Mag* 43, 5 (March 1969): 63; *Arts Mag* 54, 3 (January 1971): 68; *University of Windsor Review* 12, 1 (Fall/Winter 1976): 66-76; *DN* 8-5-50, 1-11-59, 1-9-66, 2-24-74 (Sunday Magazine); *Rochester News* 12-8-61; *DFP* 10-20-68, 2-22-69; *GR Press* 7-12-70; *Hillsdale Daily News* 2-2-76.

RAMSAY, *Theodore K.*

(b. Cedar Rapids, Iowa 1936)

Sculptor/Painter. Ramsay received a B.F.A. (1958) and M.F.A. (1961) from the University of Iowa, where he

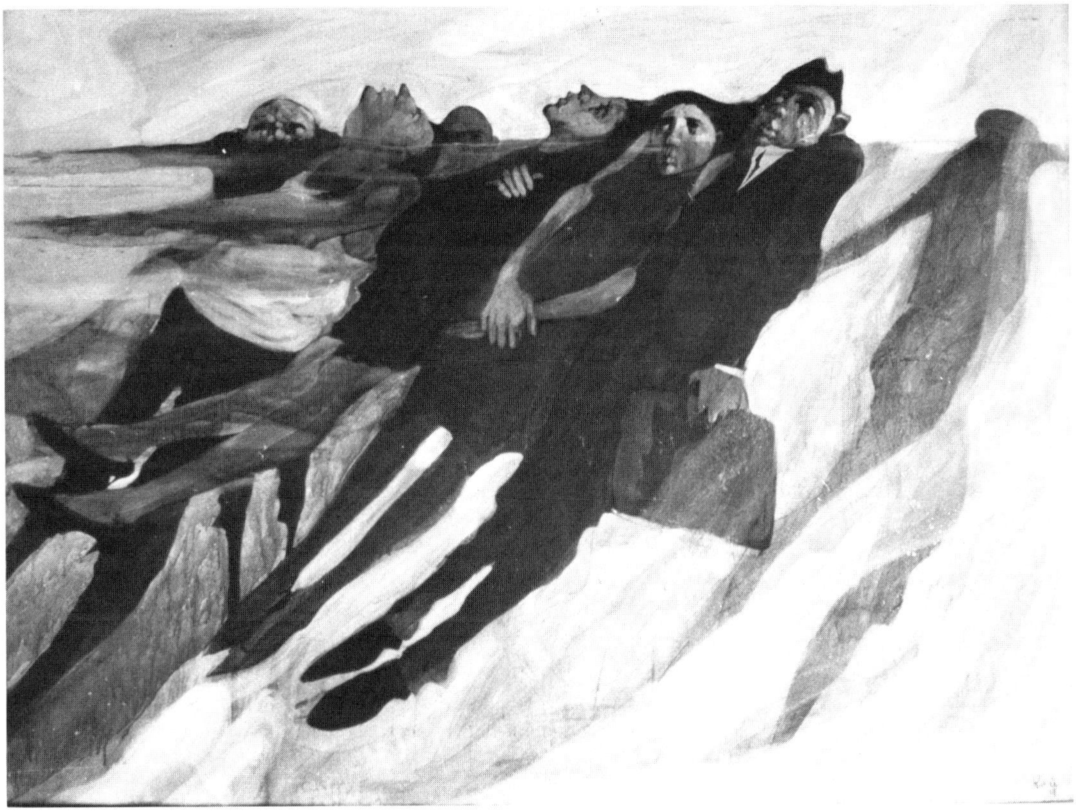

Renée Radell (1929–). The Tide. *1967. Courtesy the artist. Marc Radell, Photographer.*

studied under James Lechay and Mauricio Lasansky. He taught at the University of Iowa (1962–65) before joining the faculty at the University of Michigan. In 1976 he received a certificate in papermaking from the International Institute of Experimental Papermaking in Santa Cruz, California, and during 1977–78 was guest artist at the Twinrocker Incorporated Papermill in Brookston, Indiana. Between 1967 and 1975 Ramsay concentrated on polyester and epoxy bas-relief sculptures. In 1976 he switched media and began experimenting with bas-relief sculptures in handmade rag-paper. He has given numerous workshops, demonstrations, and lectures on papermaking and in 1976, under the auspices of the Michigan Council for the Arts and the Mott Foundation, held a series of workshops in Flint on mold-making.

One-person Exhibitions: Four Winds Gallery, Kalamazoo 1966; Albion College 1968; FIA 1968 (two-person); GRAM 1969; J. Walter Thompson Company, Detroit 1969; Alma College 1971; University of Wisconsin, Oshkosh 1971, 1979; Gertrude Kasle Gallery, Detroit 1972*, 1974; SAM 1973; Birmingham Gallery 1974; Henry Ford Community College 1977.

Group Exhibitions: *Area Show*, KIA 1966 (1st Prize); MAE 1966; *Midyear Show*, Butler Institute 1966; *Mid-Michigan Annual*, Midland Art Association 1966 (1st Prize), 1967 (2nd Prize), 1978; *Art on Paper*, KIA 1967; *Flint Annual*, FIA 1968 (1st Award, Drawing); *Made of Plastic*, FIA 1968; *Michigan Graphics*, BBAA 1968; *Plastic Image*, BBAA 1970; *Projects 70*, DAM 1970; *All Michigan I and II*, FIA 1971/72, 1973/74; *Sculpture Inside and Out*, School of Art, U. of M. 1975; Gilman Gallery, Chicago 1977; Kathryn Markyl Gallery, New York City 1977; *Silver Medal Exhibition*, Scarab Club, Detroit 1977–78; *Innovations in Paper*, BBAA 1978; *Somerset Invitational*, Troy 1979–80.

Collections: Albion College; Blue Cross and Blue Shield of Michigan, Detroit; City of Flint; Des Moines Art Center; EMU; Flint Community Schools; K-Mart Corporation, World Headquarters, Troy; Michigan Education Association, Lansing; Sioux City Art Center, Iowa.

Sources: MAR; Ramsay in *Michigan Art Journal* 1, 1 (January 1976): 24–25; *Michigan Alumnus* 80 (May 1974): 27–28; *AAN* 4-27-75; 3-6-77; *BEcc* 1-3-80.

RAYNOR, Louis

(b. New York 1917)

Ceramicist. After receiving a B.A. and an M.A. from the State University of New York at Alfred, Raynor joined the faculty of Michigan State University in 1946, where he served as head of the ceramics department.

One-person Exhibitions: *Works in Progress in Michigan*, DIA 1948; Kresge Art Center, MSU 1967; Creative Arts Gallery, CMU 1971 (two-person); Sycamore Gallery, Mason 1976; Freeman Gallery, East Lansing 1978 (two-person).

Group Exhibitions: *Ceramics National*, Everson Museum of Art, Syracuse 1947, 1949 (Honorable Mention), 1952, 1954, 1956, 1958, 1961, 1965; MACE 1947–50, 1952–54, 1955, 1956 (FSPP), 1960, 1961 (Fleischman Prize), 1963, 1964; *Annual Exhibition of Ceramic Art Invitational*, NCFA, Washington, D.C. 1953, 1955, 1957; *Decorative Arts and Ceramics Exhibition*, bition, Wichita Art Association, Kans. 1954; *Craftsmanship in a Changing World*, Mus of Contemp Crafts 1956; *International Ceramics Exhibition*, Smithsonian Institution 1958 (Best of Show), 1961; *Fiber/Clay/Metal*, St. Paul Art Center, Minn. 1959, 1961–62; *Michigan Art: Yesterday and Today*, FIA 1963; *National Ceramics Invitational*, Smithsonian Institution 1965 (Best of Show), 1967 (1st prize for stoneware); Hanamura Gallery, Detroit 1967, 1969–71; *Ceramics Invitational*, EMU 1971, 1974, 1977.

Collections: Brooklyn Museum; DIA; MMA; PAFA; Smithsonian Institution; U. of. M.

Sources: *CMo* 23, 6 (June 1975): 79; *Michigan Challenge* (State Chamber of Commerce) 4, 5 (February 1964): 11; *DN* 10-24-48; *Escanaba Daily* 4-24-64.

RHODES, Curtis

(b. Butler, Missouri 1939)

Printmaker/Sculptor. Rhodes was educated at Kansas University (B.F.A. 1962) and Ohio University (M.F.A. 1966). He joined the faculty at Western Michigan University in 1966. The recipient of a National Endowment for the Arts fellowship (1974/75) and two Ford Foundation Grants, Rhodes has been instrumental in developing the printmaking program at Western Michigan University. He has also been an artist-in-residence at the Oxbow Summer School of Art and has served as an advisor on the Visual Arts Panel of the Michigan Council for the Arts. Rhodes was one of ten artists chosen to execute a print for the Bicentennial portfolio of prints sponsored by the Michigan Council for the Arts.

One-person Exhibitions: Left Bank Gallery, Flint 1968; KIA 1969; Willis Gallery, Detroit 1974.

Group Exhibitions: *Midyear Show*, Butler Institute 1960; *Flint Invitational*, FIA 1966 (Purchase Prize), 1969; *Michigan Art on Paper*, KIA 1967; *Michigan Artists Biennial*, Kresge Art Center Gallery, MSU 1969; *All Michigan I*, FIA 1971/72; *Michigan Painters-Printmakers*, GRAM 1973; *Mid-Michigan Annual*, Midland Art Association 1977; *Handmade Paper*, Smithsonian Institution Traveling Exhibition 1978/80.

Collections: FIA.

Sources: MAR.

RICHARDSON, Constance

(b. Indianapolis, Indiana 1905)

Painter. Richardson attended the Pennsylvania Academy of the Fine Arts (1925–28). In 1930 she moved to Detroit where her husband, Edgar P. Richardson, had taken a position as assistant director of the Detroit Institute of Arts. A landscape painter, Richardson finds her subjects in the covered bridges and small towns of New England, and the farmland of the Midwest, as well as the mountains and deserts of the West, which she depicts in a traditional technique that is notable for its painstaking overglazing.

One-person Exhibitions: Schaeffer Gallery, New York City, 1938; DAM 1938, 1941, 1950; MacBeth Gallery, New York City 1944*, 1946, 1950; M. H. deYoung Memorial Museum, San Francisco 1947; Wildenstein Gallery, New York City 1955; Kennedy Galleries, New York City 1960*, 1963, 1966, 1970*.

Group Exhibitions: *Painting and Sculpture from 16 American Cities*, MOMA 1933; MAE 1934–54, 1956–61 (Skelton Prize 1938, Sheridan Prize 1939, Tannahill Prize 1941, Museum Collection Prize 1952); *American Painting and Sculpture*, AIC 1936–37, 1940–42, 1945; *National Exhibition of American Art*, Rockefeller Center 1938; *Contemporary Detroit Painters*, DIA 1940; *Romantic Painting in America*, MOMA 1944; *Contemporary American Painting*, Whitney 1944–46; *American Painting Today*, MMA 1950; *Michigan Art Through 50 Years*, UMMA 1958; *American Landscape: A Changing Frontier*, NCFA 1966*; *Currents of Expansion: Painting in the Midwest 1820–1940*, St. Louis Art Museum 1977*.

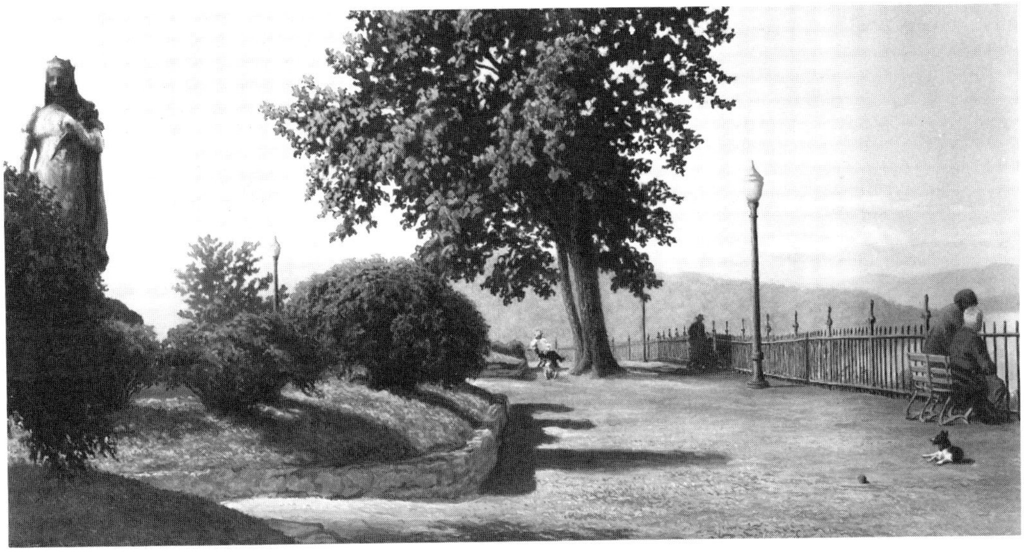

Constance Richardson (1905–). Parade Hill South. *1951. Oil on masonite. 16 × 30 inches. Collection of the Detroit Institute of Arts.*

Collections: Columbus Museum of Art; DIA; GRAM; Indianapolis Museum of Art; PAFA; SAM; UMMA; Whitney.

Sources: *WWAA* 1978; AAA 267; *Am Artist* 25, 1 (January 1961): 20–25; *Art Dig* 20 (May 1, 1946): 17; *Art Dig* 24, 9 (February 1, 1950): 19; *Art News* 45 (May 1946): 35; *Art News* 48 (February 1950): 51; *NYT* 4-3-38, 2-27-44, 4-28-46, 1-20-60; *DN* 5-15-38, 4-27-47, 11-5-50, 9-20-55; *DFP* 9-28-55.

ROBBERT, Paul A.

(b. Holland, Michigan 1928)

Painter/Printmaker. Robbert received both a B.A. (1954) and an M.F.A. (1955) from Michigan State University. In 1959 he joined the faculty at Western Michigan University, where he has been instrumental in broadening printmaking activities. He has been a frequent lecturer and workshop participant at the Kalamazoo Institute of Arts, where he also designed the printmaking facilities. He works in a variety of media, including watercolor, acrylic, gouache, and woodcut.

One-person Exhibitions: KIA 1964 (two-person); Midland Art Council 1966; KIA 1974.

Group Exhibitions: MAE 1960, 1962, 1963 (Smith Memorial Prize), 1966, 1970/71 (Phyllis King Weiner Prize); *Area Show*, KIA 1964 (award); *Michiana Regional*, South Bend Art Center 1964 (award), 1965 (award); *All Michigan I*, FIA 1971/72; *All Landscape*, DAM 1972.

Collections: Albion College; DIA; Kalamazoo College, KIA; South Bend Art Center.

Sources: MAR; *KG* 1-14-62, 12-13-64, 1-7-65, 3-14-65, 5-30-65, 11-6-66, 11-20-66, 5-7-67.

ROLAND, Arthur

(b. Detroit, Michigan 1935)

Painter. Roland attended the Meinzinger School of Art in Detroit and Wayne State University (1959–61); he also studied with Jon Lockard (1961–63) and **Leroy Foster** (1962–66). In Detroit, he has taught at Your Heritage House (1973–75), the Detroit Institute of Arts (1976–77), and Wayne County Community College (1976–77). Roland served as program chairman for "Art From a Black Perspective," a 1977 exhibition sponsored by The American Black Artist, Inc., Detroit, of which he is currently the associate director. He received first prize at "PUSH Expo '72" in Chicago, and his work was also shown in the film *Save the Children* (Paramount, 1972). Roland has served on the Detroit Bicentennial Committee (1975), and the Detroit Council for the Arts steering committee (1975).

One-person Exhibitions: Hamtramck Public Library 1968; Manufacturers National Bank, Detroit 1969–70; AAA Gallery, Detroit 1970; Detroit Bank & Trust Co. 1971; First Independence Bank, Detroit 1974.

Group Exhibitions: *UAW Art Festival*, Detroit 1966 (2nd Prize), 1967 (2nd and 3rd Prizes), 1968 (1st Prize); *Afro-American Exhibition*, DIA 1968 (traveling); *Russell Woods Annual*, Detroit 1968; *National Exhibition of Black Artists*, Smith-Mason Gallery, Washington, D.C. 1971; New Jersey State Museum, Trenton 1971; *The American Black Artist, Inc.*, Scarab Club, Detroit 1972; *Art From a Black Perspective*, The American Black Artist, Inc., Detroit Bank & Trust Co. 1977; *5 From 10*, Pyramid Gallery of Art, Detroit 1979; *Historical Roots: The Black Artist in Michigan*, Detroit Historical Museum 1980.

Collections: Ann Arbor City Hall; Catholic Archdiocese of Detroit; Chaney Elementary School, Detroit; EMU; Howard University, Washington, D.C.; Johnson Publishing Co., Chicago; Whitney Young Middle School, Detroit.

Sources: MAR; Cederholm 1973; *Cass Technician* (Detroit) September 18, 1972; *Ebony* December 1975; *Michigan Chronicle* 4-3-71, 2-19-72; *DN* 2-9-72, 8-9-74, 8-26-74; *DFP* 11-10-72, 9-2-74.

ROLSHOVEN, *Julius*

(b. Detroit, Michigan 1858; d. New York, New York 1930)

Painter. Rolshoven attended both the Cooper Union School of Art and the Plessman Academy in New York City before embarking on a course of European training that included study under Hugo Crola in Düsseldorf (1877–78), Ludwig Loefftz in Munich, and Adolphe Bouguereau and Tony Robert-Fleury in Paris (1885–90). While in Munich, he met the American painter Frank Duveneck, became a member of Duveneck's circle, and studied with him in Florence (1883–84). Rolshoven gave private lessons in Paris and London before settling in Florence in 1907, where he purchased and restored a fourteenth-century castle which remained his studio-residence until his death in 1930. Although a resident of Italy, Rolshoven made many trips to the United States. During World War I, he lived and worked in Santa Fe, New Mexico, became a member of the Taos Society of Artists, and acquired a considerable reputation for his Indian paintings. He was often in Detroit, and in addition to frequent exhibitions of his work at the Detroit Museum of Art (now the DIA) and local galleries, Rolshoven received numerous portrait commissions from Detroiters, including local art patron and industrialist Dexter M. Ferry.

His canvases reflect the brilliant technique favored by the Munich school. He was particularly well known for his skill in painting beautiful textures and rich fabrics. His favored subjects were sensuous nudes, figures from myth and legend, and picturesque European scenes. Rolshoven won many honors throughout a long career, including the coveted Hors de Concours (exempting his works from the jury process) at the Paris Salon. He was an associate of the National Academy of Design and a member of the Société Nationale des Beaux-Arts in Paris, the Munich Secession, and the Scarab Club of Detroit.

One-person Exhibitions: Cincinnati Art Museum 1905, 1919; Artists Guild of Chicago 1912; DMA 1912, 1916*; Scarab Club, Detroit 1916; John Hanna Galleries, Detroit 1921; Carper Galleries, Detroit 1923; Wright Galleries, Detroit 1923; Reinhardt Gallery, New York City 1924; Central Gallery, New York City 1927–29; DIA 1931; Grand Central Galleries, New York City 1954; *Memorial Exhibition*, Museum of New Mexico Art Gallery, Santa Fe 1959*.

Group Exhibitions: *Art Loan*, Detroit 1883; *1st Annual Exhibition*, Merrill Hall, Detroit 1887; *Opening Exhibition*, DMA 1888; *Paris Salon* 1889 (Silver Medal), 1890 1899, 1902; *American Painting and Sculpture*, AIC 1903, 1905, 1910, 1912–13, 1921–23; *Louisiana Purchase Exposition*, St. Louis 1904 (Silver Medal); *Michigan Artists*, DMA 1905; *Corcoran Biennial* 1907–09, 1921–26; *Exhibition of Oriental and American Art*, Ann Arbor Art Association 1910; *Pan-American Exposition*, Buffalo 1910 (Bronze Medal); *Carnegie International* 1911–12; MAE 1912–15, 1921, 1927; *American Artists Annual*, DIA 1916, 1918–22, 1924–26, 1928–29; *Taos Society of Artists Exhibition*, DIA 1919; *PAFA Annual* 1928; *Michigan Art Through 50 Years*, UMMA 1955.

Collections: Brooklyn Museum; Christ Church, Detroit; Cincinnati Art Museum; Detroit Athletic Club; DIA; Minneapolis Institute of Art; Museum of New Mexico Art Gallery, Santa Fe.

Sources: *American Art Annual* 1931; *Dictionary of American Biography* 16: 123; Burroughs 1936/37; Fielding 1974; Gibson 1975; Kenny 1965; Mich State Lib 1915; Van Deren Coke, *Taos and Santa Fe: The Artists' Environment*, Albuquerque, N. Mex.: University of New Mexico Press, 1963; *Art Dig* 5 (December 1930): 15; *Art News* 29 (December 1930): 14; *Art News* (April 1931): 10; *DMA Bulletin* 1, 15 (October 1907): 4; *Detroit Saturday Night* December 13, 1930; *DFP* 1-4-12, 12-8-30; *DN* 13-9-16, 12-9-30, 12-30-30; *NYT* 12-30-28, 12-8-30.

ROSENTHAL, *Stanley*

(b. Chicago, Illinois 1942)

Printmaker. Rosenthal received a B.F.A. (1964) from the Carnegie Institute of Technology and an M.F.A. from Wayne State University (1967). He has taught at the University of Detroit, Macomb County Community College, and Mercy College. Rosenthal has managed the Oxbow Summer School of Art in Saugatuck (1968–73) and now teaches printmaking at Wayne State University. A member of Common Ground of the Arts, Rosenthal has also served as director of intaglio printing at the Detroit Workshop of Fine Prints (1974–76) and since 1975 has been on the board of directors of the Michigan Association of Printmakers. In addition, he has contributed to the Oxbow Print Portfolio (Chicago, 1967) and was also one of ten local artists chosen for the United States Bicentennial Portfolio published by the Detroit Bicentennial Committee in 1975. Rosenthal's photo intaglio prints employ the human figure as an allegorical reference to nature.

One-person Exhibitions: DAM 1962 (three-person); Aquinas College, Grand Rapids 1975; Klein-Vogel Gallery, Royal Oak 1975.

Group Exhibitions: *National Print and Drawing Show*, Northern Illinois University, DeKalb 1969, 1971 (Purchase Prize); *May Show*, Cleveland Museum of Art 1969–73 (Awards 1971–73); *Ten American Printmakers*, Southern Methodist University 1970; Society of American Graphic Artists, New York City 1971; *Eight Invited Artists*, U. of M. 1972; *Michigan Printmakers*, Habatat Gallery, Dearborn 1972; *Midwest Printmakers*, University of Wisconsin, Oshkosh 1972; *Art on Paper*, DAM 1973; *History of the Aquatint*, DIA 1973; *National Print and Drawing Exhibition*, Oklahoma City Art Center 1974, 1975 (Award), 1976; *Color Print USA*, Texas Tech University, Lubbock 1975 (Purchase Prize); *The Art of Poetry*, NCFA, Smithsonian Institution 1976; *Michigan Printmakers*, Somerset Mall, Troy 1976; *Michigan Association of Printmakers*, DIA 1977 (Drawing and Print Club Purchase Award); *Bradley University National Print and Drawing Show*, Peoria, Ill. 1978 (Purchase Prize); *Detroit Area Printmakers*, Calvin College 1978.

Collections: DIA; Henry Ford Community College, Dearborn; S.S. Kresge World Headquarters, Troy; National Bank of Detroit; Texas Tech University, Lubbock; University of California.

Sources: MAR; *DN* 10-5-75.

RUSH, *Jon*

(b. Atlanta, Georgia 1935)

Sculptor. Rush attended the School of the Art Institute of Chicago (1953–55) and later received a B.F.A. (1959) from the Cranbrook Academy of Art, where he studied under **Berthold "Tex" Schiwetz**. He taught at the Columbus Gallery of Fine Arts (1959–62), before joining the faculty at the University of Michigan in 1962. In 1970 Rush was awarded a Tiffany Foundation Grant. His work is characterized by large-scale geometric forms constructed from stainless or Cor-Ten steel.

One-person Exhibition: Columbus Gallery of Fine Arts 1962.

Group Exhibitions: MAE 1959, 1964, 1966 (Detroit Foundry Prize), 1971; *Michigan Art: Yesterday and Today*, FIA 1963; Donald Morris Gallery, Birmingham 1963; *Octet Show*, Rackham Galleries, U. of M. 1963; *Sculpture and Sculptors' Drawings*, EMU 1964; American Academy, Rome 1965; *Michigan Sculpture*, BBAA 1967; *Cranbrook Alumni*, DAM 1971; *Michigan Sculptors*, EMU 1971; *All Michigan I*, FIA 1971/72; *All Michigan II*, FIA 1973/74; SAM 1974; *Sculpture Inside and Out*, U. of M. School of Art, 1975; *Fifteen Michigan Sculptors*, City of East Lansing 1976.

Collections: Columbus Gallery of Fine Arts; Concordia College, Fort Wayne; Somerset Mall, Troy; U. of M. School of Art.

Sources: *WWAA* 1978; MAR.

SAARINEN, *Loja*

(b. Helsingfors, Finland 1879; d. Bloomfield Hills, Michigan 1968)

Textile Artist/Sculptor. Saarinen graduated from the Konstföreningen in Helsinki, Finland (1899), and then studied sculpture in Paris at the Académie Colarossi. She returned to Helsinki in 1903 and was employed commercially in sculpture, interior decoration, and photography. She came to America with her husband Eliel Saarinen in 1923; they lived briefly in Evanston, Illinois and in Ann Arbor, before Eliel was hired by George Booth as resident architect for the Cranbrook Educational Community in 1924. In 1928, Loja Saarinen founded at Cranbrook what would later become one of the most productive weaving departments in the United States. Heavily influenced by the Swedish craft tradition, Saarinen was one of the first artist-craftsmen to bring Scandinavian design to America and to create and coordinate a building's interior fabrics in association with the architect in order to achieve an integrated design. Her most extensive effort was for Kingswood School, Cranbrook, for which her studio designed and wove tapestries, rugs, curtains, and upholstery. Saarinen brought to America two artists she had known in Sweden: **Lillian Holm** and **Marianne Strengell**. In addition to designs for Cranbrook, her studio received commissions for residential work throughout the Detroit area and also produced original designs by Charles Eames and Frank Lloyd Wright. Saarinen retired from the weaving department in 1942.

Her work is characterized by simplified geometric designs in subtle light and dark contrasts, with a frequent use of complementary colors.

One-person Exhibitions: Architectural League of New York, New York City 1931; DIA 1932; Norfolk Museum of Art and Science, Va. 1937; Cincinnati Museum of Art 1938; Toledo Museum of Art, 1938; Berea College, Ky. 1943; Jacques Seligmann Gallery, New York City 1957 (two-person); Cranbrook 1980*.

Group Exhibitions: *The Architect and Industrial Art*, MMA 1929, 1934; *Decorative Arts From Cranbrook*, DIA 1931; *Exposition Internationale des Arts et des Techniques*, Paris 1937 (Silver Medal in sculpture); *Exhibition of Contemporary Decorative Arts*, Toledo Museum of Art 1938; New York World's Fair 1939; *Contemporary American Industrial Art*, MMA 1940; *Exhibition of Modern Textiles*, UMMA 1940; *Outstanding Michigan Craftsmen in Weaving, Ceramics and Metal, Honoring Loja Saarinen*, BBAA 1963; *Creative Spirit of Cranbrook*, Cranbrook 1972/73*; *Cranbrook Weavers, Pacesetters and Prototypes*, DIA 1973.

Collections: CAAM; Chrysler Corporation, Detroit; Cranbrook; Richard Hudnut Salon, New York City; Tabernacle Church of Christ (now First Christian Church), Columbus, Ind.; Yardley Shop, New York City.

Sources: *WWAA* 1940/41; MAR; Albert Christ-Janer, *Eliel Saarinen*, Chicago: University of Chicago Press, 1948; *Detroit Saturday Night* December 26, 1931; *BEcc* 4-04-63; *DN* 8-30-42, 6-23-57, 4-01-63, 1-31-65.

SAILORS, *Robert D.*

(b. Grand Rapids, Michigan 1913)

Textile Artist. A graduate of Olivet College, Sailors also studied at the School of the Art Institute of Chicago. He taught weaving at the Grand Rapids Art Museum (University of Michigan Extension Program) before enrolling as a student at the Cranbrook Academy of Art. In 1949 he opened a weaving studio, Contemporary Textiles, near Grand Rapids. Sailors has designed fabrics for the Celanese Corporation of America, La France Industries, and several Frank Lloyd Wright homes. He uses both hand and power looms and is known for his handwoven draperies, upholstery fabric, rugs, and Roman shades, which incorporate such materials as foil, plastic, leather, and wood slats.

One-person Exhibitions: GRAM 1956.

Group Exhibitions: *International Textile Exhibition*, Greensboro, N.C. (1st Prize) 1944; MACE 1944, 1954; Royal Museum of Art, Toronto 1945; *Decorative Arts and Ceramics Exhibition*, Wichita Art Association, Kans. 1946; *Cranbrook Faculty*, GRAM 1947; *Contemporary Textiles and Ceramics*, Cranbrook Museum of Art 1949; *International Contemporary Weavers*, GRAM 1965.

Collections/Commissions: Big Boy Restaurants; Celanese Corporation of American; La France Industries; Miami Beach Hotel, Fla.

Sources: *WWAA* 1947; *BEcc* 4-06-44; *GR Press* 2-13-47, 11-5-48, 11-14-48, 11-3-56, 3-19-58, 6-17-65, 5-3-70; *DFP* 11-28-48.

SARKISIAN, *Sarkis*

(b. Smyrna, Turkey 1909; d. Detroit, Michigan 1977)

Painter. Sarkisian emigrated to Detroit with his family at the age of thirteen and received his first training from **John P. Wicker**, whose approach to teaching was later to be reflected in Sarkisian's own philosophy of art education. Awarded a scholarship by Dr. and Mrs. George Kamperman, he later attended the Art School of the Detroit Society of Arts and Crafts, where he studied with **John Carroll** for two years (1931-32). In 1932 he became the first of the DSAC graduates to be appointed to the faculty. By 1941, he was head of the painting department, and his teaching was the determining factor in the development of generations of young artists, among them, **Robert Broner, Leroy Foster, Brenda Goodman, Richard Jerzy, Guy Palazzola,** and **Carol Wald**. From 1947 until his retirement in 1967, in addition to his teaching duties, he served as director of the School, guiding its postwar expansion and influencing the direction of its development. Among his contributions were his policy of making the School available to minority students and his hiring of working artists as faculty members, a practice that reflected his belief that university training was not necessarily essential for an artist-teacher.

As an artist, Sarkisian was known for his still lifes, figure studies, and portraits. He worked in many styles throughout a long career during which he won both local and national recognition. He was the only artist to win the Founders Society Purchase Prize three times, for works as diverse as the cubist-inspired *Still Life with Grapes and Figs*; the early *Student*, with its suggestions of Carroll's influence; and his realistic portrait, *Anna Werbe*.

One-person Exhibitions: Gordon Galleries, Detroit 1931; Hotel Fort Shelby, Detroit 1932; DAM 1935-37, 1939, 1947, 1951 (two-person), 1955 (two-person), Women's City Club 1958; *Sarkis, Yesterday and To-*

day, DAM 1965*; Arwin Gallery, Detroit 1973; *Memorial Exhibition*, DIA 1977*; DAM 1978.

Group Exhibitions: MAE 1928-61, 1963 (FSPP 1938, 1949, 1967; Skelton Prize 1942); *American Painting and Sculpture*, AIC 1931-32, 1935-36, 1938, 1941, 1943; *Painting and Sculpture from 16 American Cities*, MOMA 1933; *Contemporary American Art*, Whitney 1934; *PAFA Annual* 1934, 1936-37, 1949, 1951, 1958, 1960; *Corcoran Biennial* 1935, 1949-53, 1955; *National Exhibition*, Rockefeller Center 1936, 1938-39, *Great Lakes Exhibitions*, Albright Art Gallery, Buffalo 1938; *Golden Gate International Exposition*, San Francisco 1939 (Honorable Mention); New York World's Fair 1939; *American Artists Annual*, DIA 1940, 1942; *Works in Progress*, DIA 1948; *Mid-year Show*, Butler Institute 1951-53, 1955 (2nd Prize); *Michigan Art Through 50 Years*, UMMA 1955; *Michigan Art: Yesterday and Today*, FIA 1963; *Arts and Crafts in Detroit, 1906-1976*, DIA 1976*; *Michigan Collects Michigan Art*, Pontiac Creative Arts Center, 1976*.

Collections/Commissions: Butler Institute; Church of the Incarnation, Detroit; DIA; Flint Armory; Ford Motor Company, Dearborn; St. Mary's Episcopal Church, Detroit; UMMA.

Sources: *WWAA* 1976; AAA 591-593, Interview; *DIA Bulletin* 37, 1 (1957-58): 16; *Impresario* November 11, 1973; *DN* 5-31-31, 6-5-32, 10-3-58, 6-14-59, 11-21-65, 8-27-67, 3-26-72; *DFP* 11-4-34, 7-24-49, 2-23-60, 12-26-65, 1-25-77.

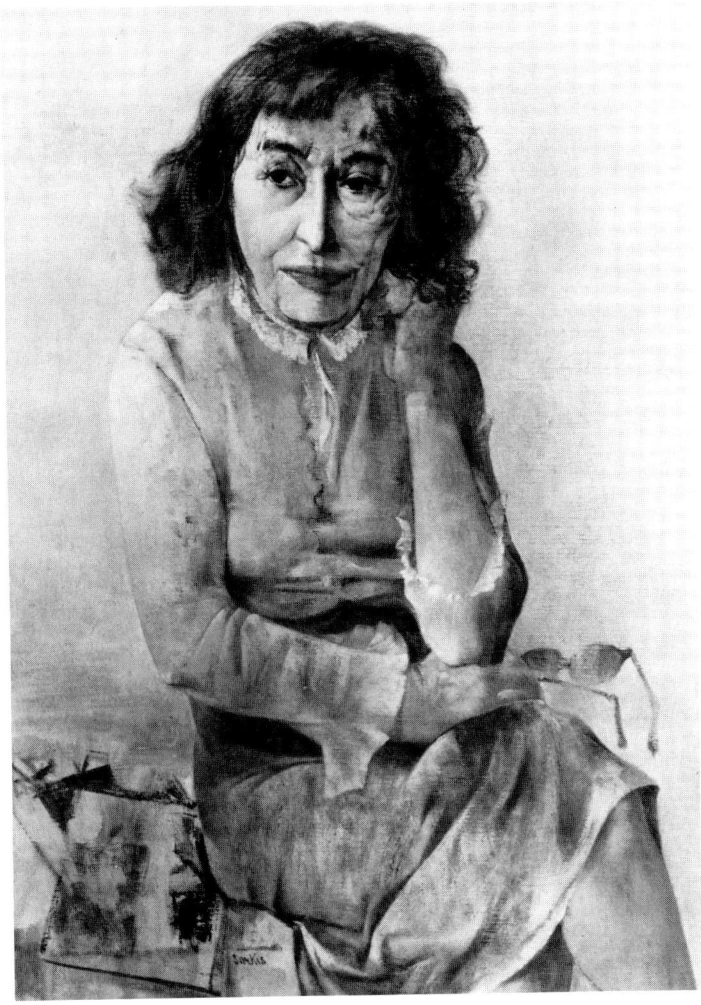

Sarkis Sarkisian (1909–1977). Anna Werbe. *Oil on canvas. 37 × 26 inches. Collection of the Detroit Institute of Arts. Winner of the Founders Society and the Leon and Josephine Winkelman Foundation Purchase Prizes at the "Exhibition for Michigan Artists," 1957.*

SCANES, *Ernest William*

(b. Lorain, Ohio 1909)

Painter. Educated in Detroit at Cass Technical High School, studying under Mary Davis and Louise Green, Scanes also attended the **John P. Wicker** School of Fine Arts, Detroit (1929-31); the Art School of the Detroit Society of Arts and Crafts (1929-31); and the Cranbrook Academy of Art, under **Zoltan Sepeshy** (1931-41). From 1932 to 1952 he worked as a staff artist for the General Motors Corporation and from 1952 to 1972 was the art director of its public relations department. Scanes is well known for his watercolors of Michigan scenes. He also designed a mural for the General Motors Building at the 1939 New York World's Fair. A charter member of the Michigan Water Color Society, he is also a member of the Scarab Club and the Michigan Academy of Science, Arts, and Letters.

One-person Exhibitions: DAM 1940, 1950 (two-person).

Group Exhibitions: MAE 1933, 1935-46, 1948-49/50, 1952-56, 1963; *Great Lakes Exhibition*, Albright Art Gallery, Buffalo 1938; DAM 1938, 1940, 1950; *Annual Watercolor Exhibition*, AIC 1938-39, 1941; *American Painting and Sculpture*, AIC 1938-40; New York World's Fair 1939; *First National Invitational*, GRAM 1940; *MWCS Annual* 1947-51, 1954, 1956, 1959 (Honorable Mention), 1961-63, 1974 (Honorable Mention), 1968; *Watercolor Exhibition*, Scarab Club, Detroit 1949-50, 1953, 1955, 1961-62 (Awards 1953, 1963); *Michigan Art Through 50 Years*, UMMA 1955; *Graphic Art by Michigan Artists*, DIA 1962.

Collections: DIA; Milwaukee Art Institute.

Sources: *WWAA* 1947; AAA D133; MAR; *DN* 10-27-40, 5-8-49; *DFP* 1-15-50.

SCHIWETZ, Berthold ("Tex")

(b. Cuero, Texas 1909; d. Dexter, Michigan 1971)

Sculptor. Schiwetz attended business school at Texas A&M University, College Station, and studied sculpture at the Museum of Fine Arts in Houston under William McVey who urged him to enroll at the Cranbrook Academy of Art in 1939 to study under **Carl Milles**. He worked with Milles until the beginning of World War II, then served as his assistant again after the war. Between 1949 and 1955 Schiwetz regularly went with Milles to his studios at Millesgarden near Stockholm and to the American Academy in Rome. After Milles's death in 1955, Schiwetz stayed at the academy to supervise the completion of his mentor's final fountain commissions for the Volker Memorial in Kansas City and the Metropolitan Museum of Art in New York. Returning again to Cranbrook, Schiwetz served as head of the sculpture department (1956–62).

In 1962 he was commissioned to do a fountain sculpture for Oakland University in Rochester. He then spent several years working in his studio at the Bruno Bearzi Foundry in Florence. He returned to the United States in 1966, settling at Ossabaw Island off the coast of Savannah, Georgia, where he served on the board of the Ossabaw Island Project and sketched wildlife, shore birds, and shells in preparation for later pieces of sculpture. He returned to Michigan in 1967 to set up a studio in Bloomfield Hills and two years later moved to an old church in Dexter.

Schiwetz worked primarily in bronze and was known for fountains and garden sculpture that were distinguished by playful animal forms and mythological or biblical themes. During his last years in Michigan he also modeled small objects in wax and bronze, such as trees, birds, people, and other products of his whimsical imagination.

One-person Exhibitions: Worcester Art Museum, Mass. 1957/58* (traveled to Sculpture Center, New York City 1958*); Birmingham Gallery 1971* (retrospective).

Group Exhibitions: MAE 1956; *Contemporary American Art*, FIA 1958; PAFA 1960; *National Religious Art Exhibition*, Birmingham 1960 (1st Prize), and Cranbrook 1962; *Prominent Painters and Sculptors in Michigan*, BBAA 1962; *Michigan Art: Yesterday and Today*, FIA 1963; *Michigan Collects Michigan Art*, Pontiac Creative Arts Center 1976.

Collections: Brookside School, Cranbrook; CAAM; Cleveland Museum of Art; Cranbrook Academy of Art; FIA; General Mills Offices, St. Paul; Good Samaritan Hospital, Portland, Ore.; Millesgarden, Lidingo, Sweden; Oakland University, Rochester; Ossabaw Island Project Foundation, Savannah, Ga.; Philadelphia Public Parks; Worcester Art Museum, Mass.

Sources: AAA 812-14; Clifford B. West, *Tex Schiwetz* (film); *Arts* 31, 1 (October 1956): 12; *Arts* 32, 6 (March 1958): 61–62; *DFP* 5-5-57, 12-29-57, 11-21-71; *DN* 12-9-57; *NYT* 2-16-58; *Christian Science Monitor* 6-9-60.

SCHMIDT, Julius

(b. Stamford, Connecticut 1923)

Sculptor. Schmidt attended Oklahoma A&M College, then received a B.F.A. (1953) and an M.F.A. (1955) from the Cranbrook Academy of Art. He also studied under Ossip Zadkine in Paris and at the Accademia di Belle Arti in Florence. From 1952 to 1959 he served as chairman of the sculpture department of the Kansas City Art Institute. He subsequently held teaching positions at the Rhode Island School of Design and the University of California. In 1962 he returned to Cranbrook to head the sculpture department. Schmidt received a Guggenheim Fellowship in 1964, enabling him to travel in France, Italy, and Greece. While at Cranbrook, Schmidt designed and equipped one of the most extensive art school foundries in the United States, with facilities for casting metal in over twenty methods, including lost wax, ceramic shell, styrofoam vaporization, and core-sand. The core-sand process, in which the sculptor carves directly on the sand block to form a mold, was developed by Schmidt from an industrial process. His textured, totem-like cast-iron columns have won him national and international recognition. Schmidt's later work at Cranbrook was characterized by interlocking ovoid forms and dissected cylinders reminiscent of finely tooled machine parts. Schmidt left Michigan in 1970 to head the sculpture department at the University of Iowa.

One-person Exhibitions: Silvermine Guild of Artists, Conn. 1953; Kansas City Art Institute, Mo. 1957; Nelson Gallery of Art, Atkins Museum of Fine Art, Kansas City, Mo. 1958; Santa Barbara Museum of Art, Calif. 1961; Otto Gerson Gallery, New York City 1961, 1963; Franklin Siden Gallery, Detroit 1964; Kansas City Art Institute, Mo. 1966; Talladega College, Ala. 1966; Gertrude Kasle Gallery, Detroit 1967, 1972.

Group Exhibitions: MAE 1952, 1954; *Mid-American Annual*, Nelson Gallery of Art, Atkins Museum of Fine Arts, Kansas City, Mo. 1957 (1st Prize Purchase Award); *New Talent USA*, AFA Gallery, New York City 1958; *Contemporary American Painting and Sculpture*, Krannert Art Museum, University of Illinois 1958, 1961, 1964–65, 1967, 1971; *Sixteen Americans*, MOMA 1959*; *American Painting and Sculpture*, AIC 1960; *Annual Exhibition of Sculpture and Drawings*, Whitney 1960, 1962–63, 1966; *Carnegie International* 1961–62; *Contemporary Trends in Painting and Sculpture*, Kresge Art Center Gallery, MSU 1962; *Michigan Art: Yesterday and Today*, FIA 1963; *Sculpture in the Open Air*, Battersea Park, London 1963; *10 American Sculptors*, Walker Art Center, Minneapolis 1963; *American Sculptors 1900–1965*, FIA 1965; *Flint Invitational*, FIA 1967, 1969.

Collections: AIC; Albright-Knox Art Gallery, Buffalo; CAAM; Chase Manhattan Bank; DIA; FIA; Kalamazoo Art Center; Krannert Art Museum, University of Illinois, Urbana; MOMA; Nelson-Atkins Museum of Art, Kansas City, Mo.; Princeton University, The Art Museum; Santa Barbara Museum of Art, Calif.; UMMA; University of Nebraska Museum of Art, Lincoln; Walker Art Center, Minneapolis; Washington University, St. Louis; Whitney.

Sources: *WWAA* 1980; MAR; Cummings 1977; *NYT* 9-30-62 (Magazine); *DN* 4-29-62, 4-14-64, 1-30-66 (Magazine), 5-7-72, 9-25-69; *BEcc* 9-24-64, 6-24-65, 5-25-67, 10-16-69; *DFP* 9-27-64, 5-14-72.

SCHNEE, *Ruth Adler*

(b. Frankfurt am Main, Germany 1923)

Textile Artist. Schnee came to Detroit with her family in 1939 and graduated from Cass Technical High School in 1942. She then received a fellowship to study at the Harvard School of Architecture and Design under Walter Gropius and later received a B.F.A. from the Rhode Island School of Design and an M.F.A. from the Cranbrook Academy of Art. In 1947 she opened a studio devoted to the design and printing of contemporary textiles. From 1949 to 1977 Schnee and her husband, Edward, owned and managed Adler Schnee/Fine Design, a retail outlet in Detroit. Schnee has received many awards, including the American Institute of Decorator's Award (1947–48), the House and Garden Award (1948), the Chicago Tribune Award (1948), and the Museum of Modern Art and the Architectural Institute of Decorators "Good Design" Award in 1958. She has also received many major public and private design commissions and has worked closely with Detroit architects Louis Redstone and Minoru Yamasaki.

Group Exhibitions: MACE 1947, 1949–51, 1954–55, 1956 (Mr. and Mrs. Henry Hopkins, Jr., Prize), 1958; *Works in Progress in Michigan: Painting by Gerome Kamrowski and Charles Culver, Sculpture by Walter Midener, Textiles by Ruth Adler, Ceramics by Lydia Winston*, DIA 1949; *Designer-Craftsmen U.S.A.*, DIA

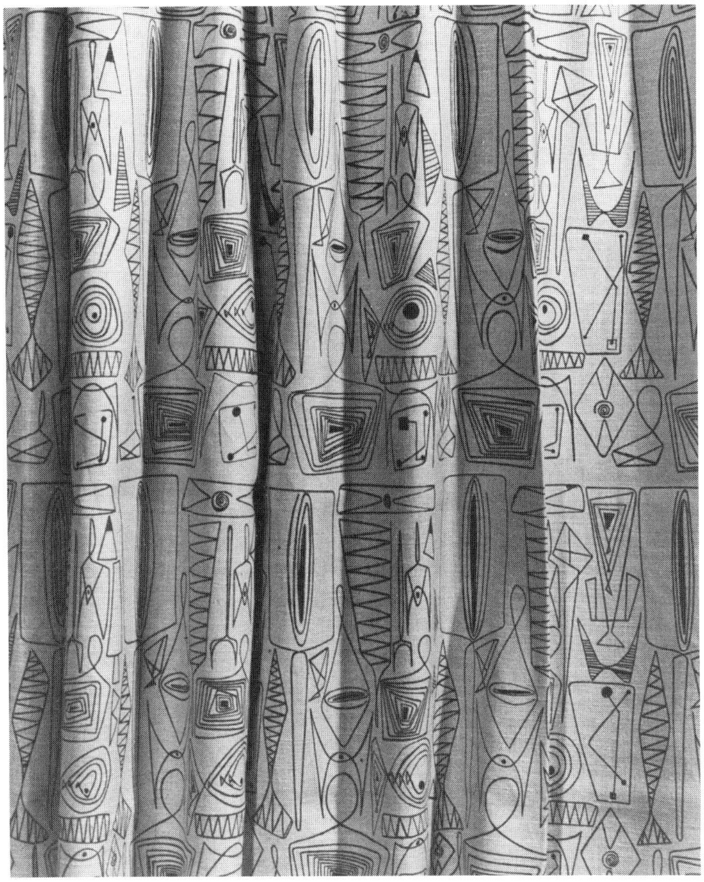

Ruth Adler Schnee (1923–). Wireworks. ca. 1953. Drapery fabric. Courtesy the artist.

1953; *American Institute of Architects: Honor Awards and Michigan Craftsmen Exhibition*, DIA 1955.

Collections: Children's Museum, Detroit; Detroit Public Schools: Krolik, Bell, Peck, and Glazier elementary schools; DIA; International Institute, Detroit; Museum of American Crafts, New York City; Victoria and Albert Museum; Walker Art Center, Minneapolis.

Sources: *Design* 51, 5 (February 1950): 20–21, 23; *DN* 9-18-49; *Christian Science Monitor* 11-1-50; *DFP* 6-19-55, 10-1-50.

SEPESHY, *Zoltan*

(b. Kassa, Hungary 1898; d. Birmingham, Michigan 1974)

Painter. Sepeshy attended the Royal Academy of Art in Budapest, studying under Julius Aghazy and Kernstock Karoly, where he received a master's degree in art and art education. He also studied in Vienna and Paris before emigrating to the United States in 1921. From 1922 to 1925 Sepeshy worked for Detroit architect Albert Kahn as an architectural draftsman. In 1926 he was appointed painting instructor at the newly founded Art School of the Detroit Society of Arts and Crafts. In 1930 at the invitation of **Eliel Saarinen**, whom he had met while working for Kahn, Sepeshy joined the staff at the Cranbrook Academy of Art. He served as head of the painting department and as resident artist and, at Saarinen's death in 1947, became the second director of the Academy. He was appointed president in 1959 and retired in 1966. Throughout his thirty-five year tenure at Cranbrook, Sepeshy played an important role in its growth and development. His flexibility of approach to art instruction was largely responsible for Cranbrook's national accreditation as a degree-granting institution in 1960.

From 1930 to 1960, Sepeshy achieved both national and local recognition. In 1947 he became the first Michigan artist to win the top prize in the Carnegie Institute's annual exhibition in Pittsburgh. A master of tempera painting, Sepeshy developed a special technique, which he outlined in his definitive work, *Tempera Painting* (New York: American Studio Books, 1946). Although adept at figure studies and portraits, Sepeshy was best known for his Michigan scenes: city streets, small towns, the Lake Michigan beaches, harbor scenes, and industrial sites. In addition, he was a muralist whose commissions included Fordson High School, Dearborn (1928); the Lincoln Park Post Office (now destroyed), done under the auspices of the U.S. Treasury Section of Fine Arts; the Michigan Building at the Chicago World's Fair (1933); the Rackham Building, Detroit (1941); and the Federal Bank & Loan Company, Kalamazoo (1950).

Seldom totally abstract, many of his works nevertheless display a cubist-inspired simplification of forms into geometric patterns and flattened space. Others, particularly his figure studies, combine realism with an expressionist feeling for line and color.

One-person Exhibitions: Bonstelle Theatre, Detroit 1925; John Hanna Galleries, Detroit 1926; Newhouse Galleries, New York City 1932; Cranbrook 1932, 1950, 1966, 1974; Marie Sterner Galleries, New York City 1936; Midtown Galleries, New York City 1938, 1941, 1946, 1950, 1953-54, 1956, 1961; DAM 1940; Kansas City Art Institute, Mo. 1947; Philadelphia Art Alliance 1950; M. H. deYoung Memorial Museum, San Francisco 1952; *Zoltan Sepeshy: Forty Years of His Work*, Syracuse University and Cranbrook 1966*; Little Gallery, Birmingham 1969, 1974 (two-person).

Group Exhibitions: MAE 1921-56 (2nd Prize 1925, Kahn Prize 1935, 1940, Skelton Prize 1939, 1943, Haass Prize 1945, Scarab Club Prize 1946, Maiullo Prize 1952, Maxon Prize 1942, 1953, Associated Gallery Prize 1955); *American Artists Annual*, DIA 1922, 1924-29, 1940, 1942; *PAFA Annual* 1927-28, 1930, 1932, 1936, 1941-54; *American Painting and Sculpture*, AIC 1932, 1936, 1938, 1940-45; *Painting and Sculpture from 16 American Cities*, MOMA 1933; *National Exhibition*, Rockefeller Center 1936-38; New York World's Fair 1939; *Golden Gate Exposition*, San Francisco 1939/40 (2nd Prize); *Corcoran Biennial* 1939-51, 1955; *Painting in the U.S.*, Carnegie Institute 1940, 1943-49 (1st Prize 1947); *Contemporary American Painting*, Whitney 1940, 1945-48, 1952; *Contemporary American Painting*, MMA 1943; *Pepsi Cola "Portrait of America" Exhibition*, New York City 1944-48 (Award 1946); *Michigan on Canvas*, J. L. Hudson Company, Detroit 1948*; *Midyear Show*, Butler Institute 1953, 1957, 1961 (invited), 1963; *Michigan Art Through 50 Years*, UMMA 1955; *Michigan Art: Yesterday and Todayy*, FIA 1963; *The Creative Spirit of Cranbrook*, CAAM 1972*, *Arts and Crafts in Detroit 1900-1976*, DIA 1976*; *Michigan Collects Michigan Art*, Pontiac Creative Arts Center 1976*; *Currents of Expansion: Painting in the Midwest, 1820-1940*, St. Louis Art Museum 1977*; *American Painting*, Muskegon Museum of Art, 1980.

Collections: AIC; Butler Institute; Cass Technical High School, Detroit; Cranbrook; Dallas Museum of Fine Art; DIA; Encyclopaedia Britannica, Chicago; FIA; GRAM; HAM; International Business Machines, New York City; KIA; MMA; NAD; National Academy of Budapest; PAFA; St. Louis Art Museum; Tel Aviv Museum, Israel; Toledo Museum of Art; UMMA; Walker Art Center, Minneapolis; Wichita Art Museum, Kans.

Sources: *WWAA* 1976; AAA, Interview: Grace Pagano, ed., *Contemporary American Painting*, New York: Duell, Sloan, & Pearce, 1945; *Am Artist* 8, 7 (September 1944): 5, 8-9; *Art Dig* 6, 15 (May 1, 1932): 20; *Art Dig* 10, 10 (February 15, 1936): 15; *Art Dig* 13, 5 (December 1, 1938): 7; *Art Dig* 16, 9 (February 1, 1942): 17; *Art Dig* 24, 10 (February 15, 1950): 13; *Life* May 27, 1940; *Time* October 20, 1947; *DN* 11-22-25, 2-25-32, 1-2-36, 5-7-50, 4-6-52, 8-29-65, 6-8-72, 6-9-74; *DFP* 5-8-32, 12-8-57, 7-19-74; *Christian Science Monitor* 1-25-36, 7-6-40; *NYT* 2-11-36, 11-7-38, 3-25-61, 7-20-74.

SIMPER, *Frederick*

(b. Mishawaka, Indiana 1914)

Painter. Self-taught as an artist, Simper was an instructor in the Department of Watercolor and Commercial Art at the Art School of the Detroit Society of Arts and Crafts (1948-51) and the Birmingham Bloomfield Art Association (1968-70). He also has been art director at D'Arcy-MacManus & Masius Advertising, Detroit (1949-80).

One-person Exhibitions: DAM 1949 (two-person), 1951 (two-person); Arwin Galleries, Detroit 1968, 1978.

Group Exhibitions: MAE 1939/40–56, 1959–61, 1966 (Prizes in 1942, 1949, 1953, 1955, 1959–61); DAM 1943; *Michigan Painters, Sculptors and Craftsmen*, Alger House, DIA 1946; *MWCS Annual* 1947–50, 1951 (Merit Award), 1956, 1960, 1964–65, 1967–68, 1970–71, 1972 (MWCS Award), 1973, 1975; *Work in Progress in Michigan*, DIA 1949; *Annual Watercolor Exhibition*, Scarab Club, Detroit 1950, 1951 (3rd Prize), 1959, 1968 (2nd Prize), 1970; *Michigan Artists*, BBAA 1962; *Watercolor USA*, Springfield Art Museum, Mo. 1964.

Collections: DIA; South Bend Art Center, Ind.; U.S. Embassy Collection.

Sources: *WWAA* 1978; MAR.

SLUSSER, Jean Paul

(b. Wauseon, Ohio 1886; d. Ann Arbor, Michigan 1981)

Painter/Art Historian. After receiving a B.A. from the University of Michigan in 1909, Slusser studied for a year at the University of Munich, returning to the University of Michigan to complete an M.A. in 1911. He subsequently attended the Boston Museum of Fine Arts School (1913–15), studying under Philip Hale, and the summer sessions (1914–17) of the Art Students League at Woodstock, New York, where he studied with Henry Lee McFee. While in Boston he served as the art critic for the *Boston Herald*. After World War I, he lived in New York City where he worked as a free-lance writer and as assistant to Henry McBride, art critic for the *New York Herald*. In 1925 he joined the faculty at the University of Michigan, replacing **Leon Makielski** as painting and drawing instructor, a position he held until his retirement in 1956.

During the Depression he executed a mural for the Blissfield Post Office under the auspices of the U.S. Treasury Department's Section of Fine Arts. Appointed the first director of the University's Museum of Art in 1946, Slusser developed an ambitious exhibitions and collections program. He was an active member of the Ann Arbor Art Association, serving as its president from 1940 to 1944. In addition, Slusser was one of the founders of the Michigan Museums Council, and served as art critic for the *Ann Arbor News*.

He worked in many media, including oil, woodblock, and etching, but is best known for his watercolor landscapes and still lifes. Trained as an impressionist, his later work became increasingly abstract.

One-person Exhibitions: Dudensing Galleries, New York City 1926; Ann Arbor Art Association 1926, 1935, 1978; Gordon Galleries, Detroit 1927–28, 1930, 1942; DAM 1935; 1941 (two-person), 1942; J. L. Hudson Galleries, Detroit 1936; MacBeth Gallery, New York City 1942.

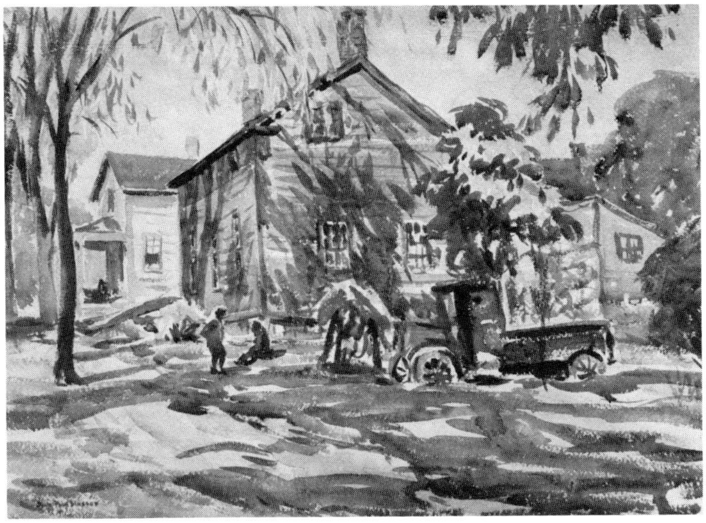

Jean Paul Slusser (1886–1981). The Green Cottage. *1932. Watercolor on white paper. 15¼ × 22-3/16 inches. Collection of the University of Michigan Museum of Art, Gift of the Ann Arbor Art Association, 1972.*

Group Exhibitions: MAE 1926–28, 1930–35, 1937–52, 1960–61 (Walker Prize 1928, FSPP 1931, Whitcomb Prize 1945); Ann Arbor Art Association 1926–81 (most years); *American Painting and Sculpture*, AIC 1932; *Contemporary American Sculpture, Watercolor and Drawings*, Whitney 1934, 1939; *Corcoran Biennial* 1935; *Great Lakes Exhibition*, Albright Art Gallery, Buffalo, 1938; New York World's Fair 1939; *Michigan Painters, Sculptors, and Craftsmen*, DIA 1946; *MWCS Annual* 1947–present (Merit Award 1947, 1st Prize 1951); *Michigan Art Through 50 Years*, UMMA 1955.

Collections: Blissfield Post Office; DIA; UMMA.

Sources: *WWAA* 1966; AAA 498; Fielding 1974; Kenny 1965; *Art News* 41, 14 (December 1942): 27; *DN* 5-1-27, 4-20-30, 3-8-36, 9-24-39, 3-15-42; *AAN* 9-23-63, 9-17-78.

SMITH, G. Alden

(b. Glencoe, Illinois 1912)

Sculptor. Educated at the School of the Art Institute of Chicago (B.F.A. 1938, M.F.A. 1945), where he studied under architectural sculptor Emil Zettler and received a scholarship to travel in the Orient and the Middle East, Smith joined the faculty at Wayne State University in 1940. Largely responsible for the development of the sculpture department, Smith also instituted the

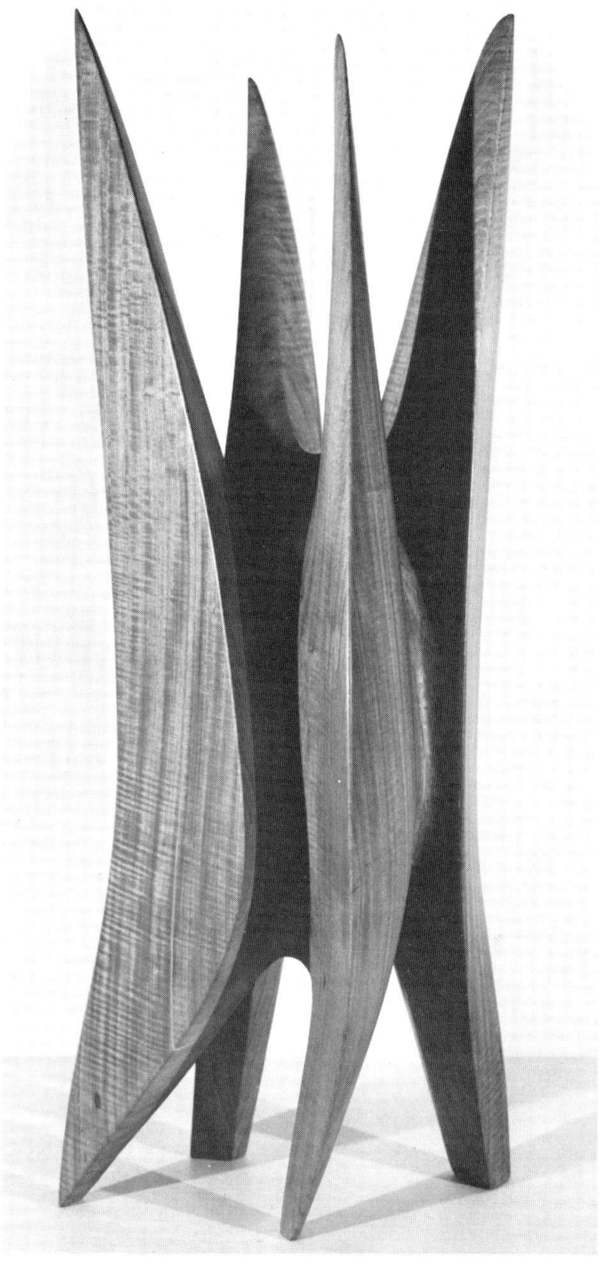

G. Alden Smith (1912–   ). Quartet. *1955. Walnut. h. 34¾ inches. Collection of the Detroit Institute of Arts.*

first photography classes at Wayne. In 1960 he was appointed chairman of the art department, a position he held until 1977 when he returned to full-time teaching. He was one of the original members of Common Ground for the Arts, a studio cooperative in Detroit's Cass Corridor. He works in a variety of media, including steel, bronze, and plexiglass, but has a particular affinity for wood, particularly exotic tropical varieties such as rosewood, granadilla, and lignum vitae. His carved wooden pieces are abstract, usually large, and often embellished with metal.

One-person Exhibitions: Women's City Club, Detroit 1956; DIA 1969*; *Retrospective*, WSU 1975.

Group Exhibitions: MAE 1942, 1944–45, 1947, 1950, 1952, 1954–62, 1965–66 (Skelton Prize 1955; FSPP 1966); *Recent Works by Detroit Artists*, DIA 1944; *Origins of Modern Sculpture*, DIA 1946; *Michigan Sculpture Society Exhibition*, DIA 1952; *Michigan Academy of Science, Arts and Letters Annual* 1957 (Sculpture Award); *Opening Exhibition*, Common Ground, Detroit 1962; *Prominent Painters and Sculptors in Michigan*, BBAA 1962; *Michigan Art: Yesterday and Today*, FIA 1963; *Michigan Sculpture*, MCA Touring Show 1968; *Michigan Collects Michigan Art*, Pontiac Creative Arts Center 1976; *Michigan Sculpture '77*, Macomb County Community College 1977.

Collections/Commissions: DIA; Hudson's Oakland Mall, Troy; Purdy Library Court and State Hall, WSU; Sentinel Building, Detroit.

Sources: AAA, Interview; Nawrocki 1980; Smith in *Michigan Art Journal* 1, 1 (January 1976): 20–21; *DFP* 3-4-56, 8-7-49, 4-20-75; *DN* 5-6-60, 4-20-75.

SMITH, Henrietta ("Letta") Crapo

(b. Flint, Michigan 1862; d. Boston, Mass. 1921)

Painter. A descendent of a prominent Michigan family (her grandfather was Governor Henry H. Crapo), Smith's earliest art training was in china painting. She undertook formal studies with William Merritt Chase in New York and in the late 1890s went to Paris to study at the Académie Julian. While there, she became the first Michigan woman to show in the Paris Salon. After several years abroad, including a period of study with George Hitchcock in Holland, she returned to Detroit in 1903. She was a member of the Detroit Watercolor Society and the Detroit Society of Women Painters, serving as president of the latter group from 1908 to 1915. Smith also studied privately in Detroit with **Julius Rolshoven** and spent one winter in Tokyo, studying with a Japanese printmaker. She was best known for her portraits, often done in pastels, and her genre scenes, usually interiors in the "Dutch manner" then popular.

One-person Exhibition: DMA 1907*.

Group Exhibitions: *Michigan Artists*, DMA 1890; *Paris Salon* 1901–02; *American Painting and Sculpture*, AIC 1902–03, 1908; *Summer Exhibition*, DMA 1903; *Watercolors, Pastels, and Miniatures Exhibi-*

tion, AIC 1903–05; *Louisiana Purchase Exposition*, St. Louis 1904 (Bronze Medal); *Paintings by Michigan Artists*, DMA 1905; *DSWP Annual*, DMA 1905–11; *PAFA Annual* 1909.

Collections: DIA; Hurley Hospital, Flint.

Sources: *American Art Annual* 1921; Bénézit 1976; Gibson 1975; Kenny 1965; Mich State Lib 1915; Moore 1953; *DMA Bulletin* 1 (July 1907): 14; *FJ* 6-3-62.

SMITH, Judson D.

(b. Grand Haven, Michigan 1880; d. Woodstock, New York 1962)

Painter. The son of a decorator and sign painter, Smith spent his childhood in Grand Rapids. He studied under **Joseph Gies** and **John P. Wicker** at the Detroit Art Academy and received the Anna Scripps Whitcomb Scholarship in 1898 to the Art Students League in New York City, where he studied with John Twatchman, Kenyon Cox, and muralist John La Farge. Smith returned to Michigan in 1903 and during the early years of his career was employed as an interior designer and mural painter with the J. Vinton Company and Albert Kahn, and also worked from his own studio in Bloomfield Hills. He did the decorations in the George Booth house in Bloomfield Hills and, with his brother Perry, carried out the artistic work for the "Cranbrook Masque," a production written especially for the dedication of the Greek theater on the George Booth Estate (ca. 1916). He also did murals for Detroit's old Pontchartrain Hotel, and a series of six murals for the Detroit Free Press Building, *The Spirit of Progress* (1917).

Leaving the state in 1921, he traveled to Europe and then settled that same year in Woodstock, New York. He taught at the Woodstock School of Art (1922–24), and in 1930 founded the Woodstock School of Painting and Sculpture in barns adjacent to his home. He continued to receive numerous mural commissions throughout the late 1930s and 1940s. During the Depression, he served as regional supervisor for the State of New York's Works Progress Administration/Federal Art Project. Smith's style ranged from cubism in the 1920s to more realistic portraits and landscapes in the 1930s.

By 1946 his work had changed radically to an abstract style that was related to the work of Mark Tobey and Bradley Walker Tomlin, who was Smith's close friend and neighbor. He stopped painting in 1952 and spent the last decade of his life experimenting with metalwork.

Smith served as visiting professor at many institutions across the country, including the Kalamazoo Institute of Arts, and also juried numerous national shows, including the prestigious Carnegie International. Smith was a member of the American Society of Painters, Sculptors, and Engravers; the director of the Salons of America; and for many years served as director and treasurer of the Woodstock Art Association.

One-person Exhibitions: Durand Ruel Gallery, New York City 1947; Woodstock Art Association, N.Y. 1949; Hacker Gallery, New York City 1950; Philadelphia Art Alliance 1950; Stevens College, Columbia, Mo. 1951 (two-person); Woodstock Art Gallery, N.Y. 1952* (retrospective).

Group Exhibitions: MAE 1926 (Scarab Club Gold Medal); *Golden Gate Exposition*, San Francisco Museum of Art 1939/40; *Carnegie International* 1931 (1st Honorable Mention), 1933–34, 1936–40, 1943, 1945–47; *American Painting and Sculpture*, AIC 1932 (Logan Prize); *Contemporary American Painting*, Whitney 1932/33, 1934, 1936, 1938, 1944, 1947–50, 1953; *Municipal Art Exhibition*, Rockefeller Center 1934; *Abstract Painting in America*, Whitney 1935; *National Society of Mural Painters*, Whitney 1940; *Virginia Biennial*, Virginia Museum of Fine Arts 1942; *Contemporary American Paintings*, Worcester Art Museum 1945 (1st Honorable Mention); *Painting in the United States*, Carnegie 1945; *Woodstock: An American Art Colony, 1902–1977*, Vassar College Art Gallery 1977*.

Collections: DIA; Virginia Museum of Fine Arts, Richmond; Whitney; Woodstock Artists Association, N.Y.

Sources: WWAA 1962; AAA, Judson Smith Papers; MAR; Bénézit 1976; Gibson 1975; Kenny 1965; Smith in *The Art of the Artist*, New York: Crown Publishers, 1951; *American Magazine of Art* 23, 6 (December 1931): 473; *Art Dig* 13, 4 (November 15, 1938): 5–6; *Art Dig* 23, 18 (July 1, 1949): 14; *Art Dig* 25, 6 (December 15, 1950): 24; *Art News* 46, 3 (May 1947): 45.

SPECK, Walter

(b. Detroit, Michigan 1896; d. Claremont, California 1979)

Painter/Sculptor. Speck attended the **John P. Wicker** School of Fine Arts in Detroit, the Académie Colarossi and the Académie Moderne (studying under Othon Friesz) in Paris, and the Art Students League in New York City. He worked as a surveyor and draftsman for the City of New York for three years and in 1925 took part in the Tacno-Arica boundary survey in South America. As a result of his trip to South America, Speck became interested in ceramics and on his return to Detroit in 1927 set up a kiln in his garage. He continued to paint and held teaching positions at the Art

School of the Detroit Society of Arts and Crafts and at Wayne State University. In 1933 he organized the Detroit School of Art, which he directed until 1938 when the Depression forced its closing. Under the auspices of the Works Progress Administration/Federal Art Project, Speck completed murals in Michigan for the Roosevelt High School in Wyandotte, the Officer's Mess at Fort Wayne, the Ferris School in Highland Park, and the State Reformatory at Ionia. He also completed a mosaic panel for Hurley Hospital in Flint and was one of eight artists chosen to execute, for the Michigan Building at the 1933 Chicago World's Fair, a mural which is now in the Michigan State Capitol in Lansing. At the same time he continued his work in ceramics, helping to organize the ceramics section of the Federal Art Project in Michigan, and becoming well known for his small, brightly colored, ceramic animals. In Detroit, Speck taught at Meinzinger's Art School and Marygrove College. He also taught at the National Music Camp at Interlochen before moving to California in 1960.

One-person Exhibition: DAM 1949.

Group Exhibitions: MAE 1922, 1925, 1928–42, 1954 (Walker Memorial Prize 1930, Scarab Club Gold Medal 1933, Burroughs Prize 1954); *Modern Art Exhibition*, Scarab Club, Detroit 1926; *International Exposition of Lithography*, AIC 1930; Society of Independents, Detroit 1930, 1933; *American Art Today*, New York World's Fair 1939; *Origins of Modern Sculpture*, DIA 1946; MACE 1946–50, 1952; *Michigan Sculpture Society*, DIA 1952; *Michigan Art: Yesterday and Today*, FIA 1963.

Collections: Children's Museum of Detroit; DIA; UMMA.

Sources: MAR; AAA D133; Gibson 1975; *DFP* 9-9-56.

STANLEY, *Jane C.*

(b. Detroit, Michigan 1863; d. Ann Arbor, Michigan 1940)

Painter. Basically self-taught as an artist, Stanley began painting watercolors during a 1925–26 trip to Europe. She was a charter member of the Detroit Society of Women Painters and Sculptors and was also active in the Ann Arbor Art Association, the Art Club of Detroit, and the American Federation of the Arts.

One-person Exhibitions: Bonstelle Playhouse, Detroit 1926–27; John Hanna Galleries, Detroit 1928, 1938; Ann Arbor Art Association 1931, 1938; Argent Gallery, New York City 1942* (two-person).

Group Exhibitions: *DSWP Annual*, Detroit 1905, 1921, 1923, 1930, 1933–34, 1951; *Annual Exhibition of the Society of Western Artists*, DIA 1910; MAE 1925–26, 1928–33, 1935; *Annual Watercolor Exhibition*, PAFA 1925, 1928–29, 1931; DSWP, Argent Gallery, New York City 1932; Ann Arbor Art Association 1937.

Collections: UMMA.

Sources: AAA, DSWP Scrapbook; Bénézit 1976; Fielding 1974; Gibson 1975; Kenny 1965; Mallett 1948; Moore 1953; *Art Dig* 15, 5 (December 1, 1940): 21; *Art News* 26, 16 (January 21, 1928): 16; *Art News* 38, 5 (November 4, 1939): 12–16; *Bonstelle Theatre Program* (Detroit) December 13, 1926, October 31, 1927; *DN* 10-4-25, 2-13-27, 1-1-28, 1-25-31, 10-23-38; *DFP* 11-6-27, 11-2-40.

STARK, *Shirley*

(b. New York, New York 1927)

Sculptor/Printmaker. A Detroit resident between 1951 and 1970, Stark studied at the University of Detroit; with **G. Alden Smith** at Wayne State University; at the Museum of New Mexico, Santa Fe; and at the Art Students League, New York City. She taught for the Detroit Public Schools Cultural Environment Programs at the Children's Museum (1967), and at the Arts Extended Gallery, Detroit (1962–69). Stark has given lectures on Afro-American painters and sculptors throughout the country. In 1975 she was appointed Visiting Andrew Mellon Professor in Sculpture at Carnegie Mellon University, Pittsburgh. Stark's abstract stone sculptures explore themes of nature and ritual.

One-person Exhibitions: Arts Extended Gallery, Detroit 1967; Stables Gallery, Taos, N.Mex. 1972; Johnson Gallery, University of New Mexico, Albuquerque 1974; Eastern New Mexico University, Portals 1975; Art Gallery of Windsor, Ontario 1977* (two-person).

Group Exhibitions: *Ohio Ceramic and Sculpture Show*, Butler Institute 1962, 1968; Russell Woods Annual, Detroit 1963–64; Arts Extended Gallery, Detroit 1964–71; AAA Gallery, Detroit 1966; *Arts Extended Group*, Hamtramck Public Library 1966; Bloomfield Art Association, Birmingham 1967; Dayton Art Institute 1967; *Michigan Painters-Printmakers*, GRAM 1967; *Southern Sculptures: '67*, Southern Association of Sculptors 1967 (traveling); *Afro-American Exhibition*, DIA 1968; *Drawing and Small Sculpture Show*, Ball State University Art Gallery 1968; *Broadside Press Portfolio*, Detroit Public Library 1969; Gallery 7, Detroit 1969; *Annual*, Carnegie Institute Museum of Art 1975; *Historical Roots: The Black Artist in Michigan*, Detroit Historical Museum 1980; *Forever Free: Art by African-American Women 1862–1980*, Illinois State University, Normal 1981 (traveling).

Collections: Children's Museum, Detroit; Jerome Foundation, St. Paul; Midland Federal Savings Bank, Denver; Museum of New Mexico, Santa Fe; Roswell Museum, N.Mex.; Wulitzer Foundation, Taos, N.Mex.

Sources: *WWAA* 1978; *Who's Who Among Black Americans 1977–78*; Leaonead Pack Bailey, *Broadside Authors and Artists*, Detroit: Broadside Press, 1974; Elton C. Fax, *Black Artists of a New Generation*, New York: Dodd, Mead & Co., 1977; *Art and Artists* (Detroit) April/May 1966; *Michigan Challenge* (State Chamber of Commerce) 9, 9 (June 1969): 54–55; *Peterborough Transcript* (N.H.) 4-1-76.

STEEN, *Carol*

(b. Detroit, Michigan 1943)

Metalsmith/Sculptor. Steen received a B.A. (1965) from Michigan State University and then studied at the Oxbow Summer School of Painting. She received an M.F.A. (1971) from the Cranbrook Academy of Art. She taught at Southfield Senior High School from 1965 to 1969, the Art School of the Detroit Society of Arts and Crafts from 1971 to 1974, and at the University of Michigan in 1975 on a Ford Foundation Grant. Her work is sculptural, ranging from highly polished free-standing pieces to serial wall reliefs of steel or other metal.

One-person Exhibitions: *Metal*, DIA 1973*; Little Gallery, Birmingham 1975; Gallery 7, Detroit 1976; 55 Mercer, New York City 1978.

Group Exhibitions: DAM 1967–69; *Michigan Artist-Craftsmen Exhibition*, GRAM 1968, 1970; *Michigan Craftsmen's Council Biennial* 1969, 1971; *Mid-Michigan Annual*, Midland Art Association 1969, 1971; *Women '71*, DeKalb, Ill. 1971; MACE 1971 (FSPP), 1976*; *Detroit Artists Invitational*, Detroit Bank & Trust Co. 1974*; *Forms in Metal*, Mus Contemp Crafts, 1975*; *Arts and Crafts in Detroit*, 1906–1976, DIA 1976*; *Five Sculptors*, Willis Gallery, Detroit 1976; *Whitney Counterweight*, Whitney 1977.

Collections: DIA; Mus of Contemp Crafts.

Sources: MAR; *DN* 9-23-73, 9-19-76 (Sunday Magazine), 9-18-77; *DFP* 12-7-75, 9-19-76.

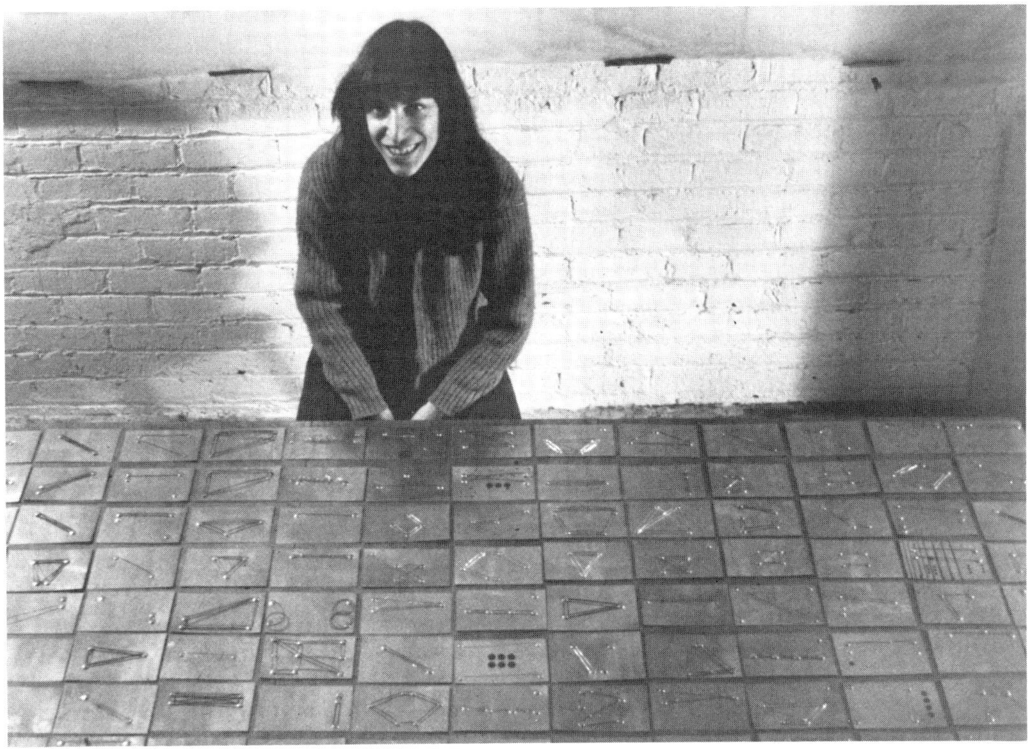

Carol Steen (1943–) with one of her works. Robert Vigiletti, Photographer.

tended the School of the Art Institute of Chicago for three years and also studied in New York City with William Merritt Chase and Leonard Ochtman. For a time he conducted drawing classes in New York City before returning to Detroit in 1902. Swift then divided his time between his studio on Adams Avenue and his summer home in Chippewa Cove near Harbor Springs. Although he also painted city scenes, it was for his misty, impressionistic landscapes, inspired by the northern Michigan woods and lake country, that Swift became known. He was one of the first Detroit artists to experiment with photography as an art form. With the publication of *Fagots of Cedar* (Chicago, Tomorrow Press, 1907), he began a career as a poet that eventually overshadowed his activities as a painter. Often called the "poet laureate" of Michigan, he published several more volumes, including *The Blue Crane and Shore Songs* (New York, J.T. White & Co., 1918) and *Green Bench Writs and Opinions* (Harbor Springs, Privately Printed, 1929).

During the Depression, Swift gained considerable notoriety for his caustic, almost daily letters to the editors of various Detroit newspapers. In these, he railed against government "handouts" (he refused to take part in the Federal Art Project), castigated the authorities for their neglect of the veterans of the Spanish-American War, and advocated that all writers, artists, and architects should be exempt from taxes.

One-person Exhibitions: Healy Shop Galleries, Detroit 1920; Drury Lane Theater, Detroit 1935; Harbor Springs Public Library 1937.

Group Exhibitions: *Pastels, Watercolors, and Miniatures Exhibition*, AIC 1906; MAE 1911–15, 1917–26, 1928–37, 1940 (Society of Art, Poetry, and Music Prize 1936); *Paintings by Detroit Artists*, Detroit Photographic Company 1918; *American Artists Annual*, DIA 1919–24, 1926, 1928; *Michigan State Fair Exhibition* 1925 (1st Prize); National Arts Club, New York City 1927, 1929, 1935, 1937, 1938; *West Michigan Annual*, GRAM 1929; Society of Independent Artists, Detroit 1930–34.

Collections: Detroit Public Library, Duffield Branch; DIA; Harbor Springs Public Library; Lochmoor Golf Club, Grosse Pointe; Michigan State Library; Petoskey High School.

Sources: WWAA 1936/37; AAA 919–920; Gibson 1975; Kenny 1965; Mallett 1948; Swift in *Michigan History Magazine* 14 (Spring 1930): 233–241; *All the Arts* (Detroit) 3, 4 (April 1920): 20–22, 57; *DFP* 2-21-15, 4-1-23, 5-8-33, 10-6-45; *DN* 2-10-35, 10-5-45; *GR Herald* 1-19-36.

TEED, *Douglas Arthur*

(b. Utica, New York 1864; d. Detroit, Michigan 1929)

Painter. At the age of fourteen, Teed opened a studio in his native Utica, New York, executing landscapes which later paid for extensive travel and study in Europe and North Africa. Returning to the United States (ca. 1912), he exhibited and sold work done abroad, which later enabled him to study additional years in Egypt, Algiers, and Morocco. After a brief stay in New York, Teed settled in Detroit (ca. 1917 or 1918) and opened a studio in the Fine Arts Building. He painted portraits of the state and public officials of New York and was also a landscapist, but he was best known to Detroiters for his boldly colored open air market and bazaar scenes and people, subjects that were influenced by his extensive travels in North Africa. In 1927 he executed a series of some forty to fifty panel paintings for the Oriental Theatre (since demolished) in Detroit.

One-person Exhibitions: John Hanna Gallery, Detroit 1920; Bonstelle Theatre, Detroit 1925; Crafts Guild, Detroit 1929 (memorial exhibition).

Group Exhibitions: *Annual Exhibition of Paintings by American Artists*, DIA 1918, 1921–28; MAE 1919–22, 1924–27, 1929; *Inaugural Exhibition*, Fine Arts Gallery of San Diego 1926; Hurley Galleries, Detroit 1928; *Paintings and Sculpture by Detroit Artists from the Dr. W. W. Kahn Collection*, DIA 1935.

Collections: Arnot Art Museum, Elmira, N.Y.; The Detroit Club.

Sources: Kenny 1965; *Bonstelle Theatre Program* (Detroit) February 2, 1925; *The Club Woman* (Detroit) 19 (September 1926): 24–26; *Detroit Saturday Night* November 2, 1929; *DN* 7-22-20, 2-22-25, 8-21-27, 5-25-29; *DFP* 5-24-29.

THOMAS, *Richard*

(b. Marion Center, Pennsylvania 1917)

Metalsmith. Thomas received a B.S. (1940) in art education from State Teachers College in Indiana, Pennsylvania; and an M.F.A. (1948), under **Zoltan Sepeshy**, from the Cranbrook Academy of Art. He has served as supervisor of art education for the public schools of Conneaut, Ohio (1941) and head of the metalsmithing department at the Cranbrook Academy of Art, where in 1948 he established the first college degree program in metalsmithing. A noted lecturer in his field, Thomas is the author of two texts, *Metalsmithing for the Artist*, Philadelphia: (Chilton, 1960) and *Course of Study-*

Metalsmithing (A.C.C. Press 1963). He is also the recipient of a 1979 National Endowment for the Arts grant. Primarily interested in liturgical art, Thomas has received many commissions from churches throughout the Detroit area.

Group Exhibitions: MACE 1952; *The Architect and the Craftsman Work Together*, DIA 1955; *Michigan Craftsmen*, DIA 1955; *The American Craftsman*, Mus Contemp Crafts 1964; *Copper II*, University of Arizona 1979.

Collections: Ascension Lutheran Church, Birmingham; Augustinian Chapel, Oxford; Christ Church, Cranbrook; Cleveland Public Auditorium; College Lutheran Church, East Lansing; Congregation Beth Shalom, Oak Park; Convent Chapel, Greensburg, Pa.; Diocese of Northern Michigan, Menominee; First Congregational Church, Port Huron; First Methodist Church, Birmingham; Henry Ford Hospital, Protestant Chapel, Detroit; Kingswood School, Cranbrook; Our Shepherd Church, Birmingham; Saint Michael's Episcopal Church, Toledo; United Methodist Church, Birmingham; Valparaiso University.

Sources: AAA 926; Julie Hall, *Tradition & Change: The New American Craftsman*, New York: Dutton, 1977.

UX, *Katherine*

(b. McBain, Michigan, ca. 1910?)

Textile Artist. Ux received a B.A. from Western Michigan University, an M.A. (1938) from Columbia University, and did postgraduate work at the School of the Art Institute of Chicago; the Art School, Stockholm, Sweden; Cranbrook Academy of Art; and Haystack Mountain School of Crafts, Deer Isle, Maine. She was on the faculty of Central Michigan University from 1944 until her retirement in 1978, and has been involved with many other aspects of art education. In 1966 she was given the Michigan Art Education Association award for outstanding work in art education. In 1975 she received the distinguished alumni award from Western Michigan University. Ux has done extensive research in the weaving techniques and crafts of both the ancient and contemporary Indians of the Americas, and is nationally known for her fabric designs and knotting techniques.

One-person Exhibitions: EMU 1965; Studio 23, Bay City 1966; Left Bank Gallery, Flint 1966; Purdue University 1966; Fine Arts Gallery, Birmingham 1970 (three-person); Creative Arts Gallery, CMU 1971; SAM 1973; KIA 1975.

Group Exhibitions: MACE 1954, 1958, 1960–64; *Fiber/Clay/Metal*, St. Paul Art Center, Minn. 1955; *Western Michigan Artists*, GRAM 1961, 1970; *Michigan Art Yesterday and Today*, FIA 1963; Mus of Contemp Crafts 1963; *Michigan Craftsmen's Council Biennial* 1967, 1979 (1st Prize); *Cranbrook Academy of Art Invitational* 1969; *Fiber Art by American Artists*, Ball State University 1971; *Cranbrook Weavers: Pacesetters and Prototypes*, DIA 1973; *Filaments '73*, EMU 1973.

Collections: Cooper-Hewitt Museum, New York City; Joslyn Art Museum, Omaha; KIA; Minnesota Museum of Art, St. Paul; Smithsonian Institution.

Sources: MAR; *Who's Who in American Women* 1970; *CH* 24 (May/June 1964): 23–24; *BEcc* 1-29-70.

VIGILETTI, *Sylvia*

(b. Chatham, Ontario 1933)

Glass Artist. Originally a fiber artist, Vigiletti switched to glass in 1968. She studied at the Center for Creative Studies and at the Toledo Museum of Art glass workshop under such artists as **Gilbert Johnson**, Richard Ritter, Mark Peiser, and Biz Littell. She was a teaching assistant at summer workshops in Naples, New York

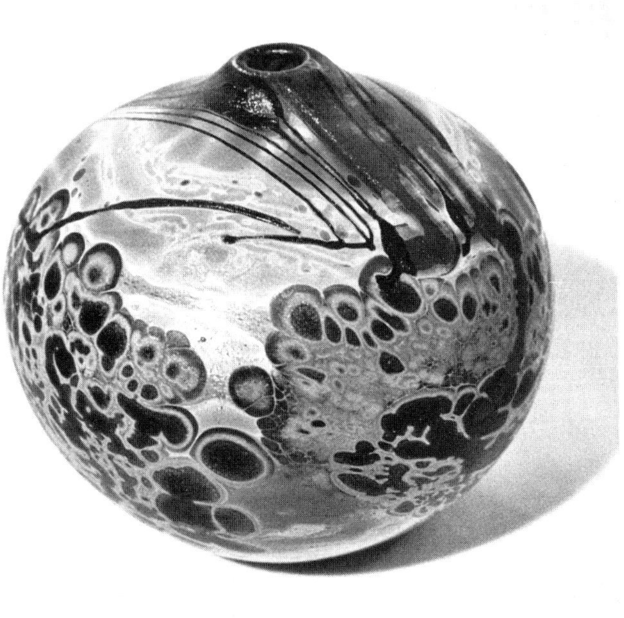

Sylvia Vigiletti (1933–   ). Bottle. *1978. Glass. h. 5 inches. Collection of the Detroit Institute of Arts.*

(1947–77), and has been active in the Michigan Glass Guild and the Michigan Craftsmen's Council. Since 1973 she has served on the crafts advisory board for the Michigan Council for the Arts. In 1977 she was commissioned by the Birmingham-Bloomfield Art Association to create a limited edition of hand-blown glass. Vigiletti concentrates primarily on functional pieces executed in the off-hand glassblowing technique.

One-person Exhibitions: J. Walter Thompson Gallery, Detroit 1974; Creative Arts Gallery, CMU 1975 (two-person); *Artisans Unlimited*, Courtyard Gallery, Birmingham 1976 (three-person).

Group Exhibitions: MACE 1971; *Michigan '71*, Midland Art Association 1971; *Southern Tier Art Show*, Corning Museum of Glass, N.Y. 1972; *Beaux-Arts Designer/Craftsmen*, Columbus Museum of Art 1972–73, 1975; *Regional Glass Invitational*, EMU 1973 (Purchase Prize); *U. S. Glass Invitational*, Habatat Galleries, Dearborn 1973–75, 1977; *Scarab Club Glass Exhibition*, Detroit 1974 (Honorable Mention), 1975, 1977 (Purchase Prize); *Miniature Exhibit*, Texas Tech Museum, Lubbock 1975 (Purchase Prize); *Glass Art Society Exhibit*, Corning Museum of Glass, N.Y. 1976; *Objects '76*, BBAA 1976; *Clay/Glass Invitational*, Delta College 1977, 1978 (Purchase Prize); *Contemporary Glass 1976 International*, Corning Museum of Glass, N.Y. 1977; *Michigan Artists Biennial*, MSU 1977*; *National Paperweight Exhibition*, Habatat Galleries, Dearborn 1977; *Prints and Glass*, Troy Art Gallery 1978.

Collections: Delta College; EMU; Museum of Arts and History, Port Huron; Texas Tech Museum, Lubbock.

Sources: MAR; *Glass Art Registry*, Portland, Oreg.; *BEcc* 5-17-76, 10-7-76, 2-10-77; *DFP* 3-27-77; *Southfield Eccentric* 11-10-77; *Royal Oak Tribune* 1-5-78.

V*IGLAND, Alan*

(b. Elberta, Michigan 1941)

Ceramicist. Vigland received a M.F.A. (1968) from Michigan State University, where he studied with **Louis Raynor**. Upon graduation, he began the Vigland Pottery in Benzonia, where he is a full-time studio potter, specializing in functional pottery, with an emphasis on experimental glazing. From 1968 to 1977 he was a part-time ceramics instructor at Northwestern Michigan College and in 1972–73 taught at Interlochen Arts Academy. Vigland has been involved in many workshops, including those for the Midland Arts Council and the Ontario Crafts Council in Windsor, both in 1977.

One-person Exhibitions: Creative Arts Gallery, CMU 1970, 1975; Left Bank Gallery, Flint 1971; Delta College 1973; Habatat Gallery, Dearborn 1975; Indiana University/Purdue University, Fort Wayne 1978.

Group Exhibitions: MACE 1966, 1976; *Michigan Art on Paper*, KIA 1967; *Traverse City Arts Council Exhibition* 1971–76 (Honorable Mention 1971; Best of Show 1974); *Beaux-Arts Designer/Craftsmen*, Columbus Museum of Art 1975; *Ceramics Invitational*, EMU 1975, 1977; *Clay–Glass Invitational*, Delta College 1976–78; *Lidded Container Show*, Habatat Gallery, Dearborn 1978.

Collections/Commissions: Albion College; CMU; First Congregational Church, Benzonia; MSU; St. Francis Catholic Church, Traverse City.

Sources: MAR; *Studio Potter* 2, 2 (Winter 1973/74): 28–29.

V*IZZINI, Michael*

(b. Detroit, Michigan 1914)

Metalsmith. Vizzini studied at Cass Technical High School in Detroit and Wayne State University. He later taught evening classes at Cass Tech before joining the faculty of the Art School of the Detroit Society of Arts and Crafts in 1956. One of the founding members of the Michigan Silversmiths Guild, Vizzini has served as the group's treasurer and president. In 1962 he was the first artist to occupy a studio at Detroit's Common Ground for the Arts under an arrangement by which he taught two hours each week in exchange for rent.

One-person Exhibitions: DAM 1960 (two-person); SAM 1964 (three-person).

Group Exhibitions: DAM 1948; MACE 1948–49, 1951–52, 1954, 1956, 1960–61, 1962 (Ford Purchase Prize); *Works in Progress*, DIA 1950/51; *Designer/Craftsmen USA*, Brooklyn Museum 1953; *Craftsmanship in a Changing World*, Mus Contemp Crafts 1956; *Fiber/Clay/Metal*, Minnesota Museum of Art 1959; *Sculpture Invitational*, EMU 1963; *Area Show*, SAM 1964; *CCS at DAM*, DAM 1977.

Collections/Commissions: Center for Creative Studies, Detroit; Christ Church Episcopal, Grosse Pointe; Pontiac Motor Division (Administration Building), Detroit.

Sources: *CH* 24, 3 (May/June 1964): 88; *DN* 11-14-48, 1-16-77; *DT* 3-20-49, 5-29-60; *DFP* 7-20-52, 2-10-57, 12-25-60, 12-1-71.

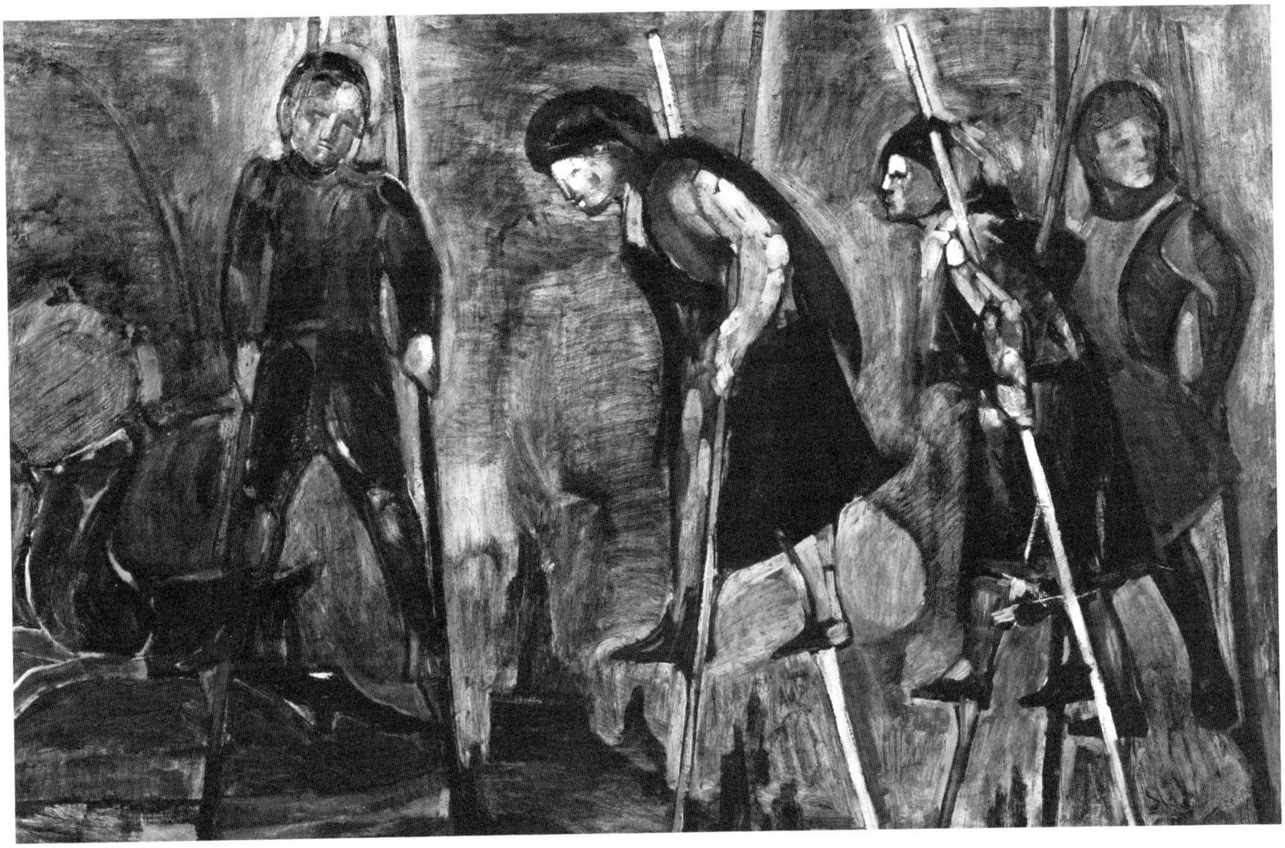

Carol Wald (1935-). Children on Stilts. 1960. Oil on masonite. 30½ × 48 inches. Collection of the Detroit Institute of Arts.

WALD, Carol

(b. Detroit, Michigan 1935)

Painter/Illustrator. Educated at Cass Technical High School in Detroit and at the Art School of the Detroit Society of Arts and Crafts (1954–58), under **Sarkis Sarkisian**, Wald later studied at the Cranbrook Academy of Art and the Skowhegan School of Painting in Maine. She has taught at the Art School of the Detroit Society of Arts and Crafts; at the Flint Institute of Arts; and in East Jordan, Michigan, under the auspices of the Michigan Council for the Arts' artists-in-the-schools program. The recipient of several fellowships, including a residency at the McDowell Colony, New Hampshire, in both 1968 and 1971, Wald also won a national competition to execute a U.S. Bicentennial painting, *The New Spirit of 76*, as a companion piece to George Willard's original in the Cleveland City Hall. She began her career as a painter and, in the 1960s won many local prizes for her expressionistic studies of women and children.

Since the early 1970s she has worked primarily in collage and photography. A collector of printed memorabilia from the Victorian era, Wald combines these existing images in three-dimensional multiple-image collages that are surrealistic in their juxtaposition of disparate elements and distortions of scale. Her works have appeared in the *New York Times, Saturday Review, Ms Magazine, Time, Life, New York Magazine,* and *Womensports*. She is also the author of a book, *Myth America: Picturing Women 1865–1945* (New York: Pantheon Books, 1975), an exploration of the use of stereotypical images of women in print media. In 1978 she was commissioned by First Federal Savings & Loan of Detroit to execute two large works, *Detroit's Past* and *Detroit's Future*. Since 1971, Wald has resided in New York City.

One-person Exhibitions: Raven Gallery, Detroit 1961; Garelick's Gallery, Detroit 1963, 1964, 1968–69; FIA 1964; Scarab Club, Detroit 1966; Rubiner Gallery, Royal Oak 1967, 1973; DAM 1971; *Images Gallery*, New York City 1974; Terry Dintenfass Gallery, New York City 1974; O. K. Harris Gallery, New York City 1975; Pontiac Art Center 1978.

Group Exhibitions: MAE 1955–61, 1966, 1971 (Taylor Purchase Prize and American Association of University Women Prize in 1960); Detroit Art Festival 1960

(1st Prize); *West Michigan Annual*, GRAM 1962; Michigan State Fair 1963–64, 1966, 1970 (1st Prize); *Midyear Show*, Butler Institute 1965, 1966; *Drawings U.S.A.*, Minnesota Museum of Art 1968; *Watercolor U.S.A.*, Springfield Art Museum, Mo. 1969; *New Directions*, DAM 1970; *All Michigan I*, FIA 1971/72; *National Exhibition*, Society of Illustrators, New York City 1974, 1975 (Gold Medal), 1976; *The American Flag in the Art of Our Country*, Allentown Art Museum, Pa. 1976; *Arts and Crafts in Detroit 1900–1976*, DIA 1976*; *Michigan Collects Michigan Art*, Pontiac Creative Arts Center 1976.

Collections: City of Cleveland; City of Detroit; DIA; EMU; Minnesota Museum of Art, St. Paul; National Gallery.

Sources: AAA 64; MAR; *Am Artist* 41 (July 1977): 78–81; *People Magazine* May 17, 1976; *DT* 6-12-60; *DFP* 6-16-63, 11-18-78; *DN* 4-3-64, 9-5-65, 9-18-66, 11-24-68, 4-9-71, 6-29-75, 7-30-76; *FJ* 7-4-70.

WALKER, *James A.*

(b. Connersville, Indiana 1921)

Painter/Printmaker. Walker received a B.S. (1946) from Western Michigan University, an M.A. (1949) from Teachers College, Columbia University, and an M.F.A. (1961) from Michigan State University. He taught at Flint Northern Community High School (1956–66) and at the National Music Camp at Interlochen (Summer 1963), before leaving Michigan in 1966 to join the faculty at Kent State University. Originally a watercolorist, Walker has concentrated on serigraphy since the early 1960s.

One-person Exhibitions: Norfolk Museum of Art, Va. 1953; Gallery Arkep, New York City 1962; Left Bank Gallery, Flint 1962 (two-person); SAM 1963 (three-person); CMU 1964; FIA 1964; Tadlow Gallery of Fine Art, Whitehall 1964; Kellogg Community College 1965; Women's City Club of Detroit 1965; Henry Ford Community College 1967.

Group Exhibitions: *Flint Annual*, FIA 1957–62, 1964, 1966 (Graphics Prize in 1961, 1962, 1964); *Michigan Association of Printmakers Biennial* 1962, 1966; *West Michigan Annual*, GRAM 1962; *Area Show*, SAM 1962 (1st Prize), 1965 (Purchase Prize); *MAE* 1963; *National Print Competition*, University of North Dakota 1963 (award); *Seven Flint Printmakers*, FIA 1963; *Area Show*, KIA 1963–64; *National Print Exhibition*, Brooklyn Museum 1964; *Michigan Painters-Printmakers*, GRAM 1965–67; *Bicentennial Exhibition*, Battle Creek Civic Art Center 1976.

Collections: Albion College; FIA; GRAM; Henry Ford Community College; KIA; Michigan Academy of Science, Arts, and Letters, Ann Arbor; Norfolk Museum of Art, Virginia; Upjohn Company, Kalamazoo; WMU.

Sources: *WWAA* 1978; MAR; *FJ* 1-14-62, 7-15-62, 9-27-64.

WALTENSPERGER, *Charles*

(b. Detroit, Michigan 1871; d. Detroit, Michigan 1931)

Painter. Educated in Detroit at the Julius Melchers School and at the Art School of the Detroit Museum of Art under **Joseph Gies**, Waltensperger received the first two-year James E. Scripps Scholarship from the Museum school in 1890, which enabled him to study in France at the Académie Julian. After returning to Detroit from Europe, he worked as a commercial artist for the *Detroit Free Press* and as a designer for the Calvert Lithographing Company. For a time he also illustrated books by C. B. Lewis, a well-known humorist, but later abandoned commercial art to work seriously in oils. His repeated visits to Laaren, Holland, are reflected in the Dutch interior scenes for which he was well known. Waltensperger also painted coastal scenes and crayon and pastel figure studies. He was a member of the Scarab Club.

One-person Exhibitions: Crowley-Milner Co., Detroit 1929.

Group-Exhibitions: *MAE* 1911–22, 1924–27, 1929 (Hopkin Memorial Prize 1916); *Exhibition of American Artists*, DIA 1916–22, 1924–29; *Painting and Sculpture by Detroit Artists from the Dr. W. W. Kahn Collection*, DIA 1935; *Michigan Artists 1901–1951: In Commemoration of Detroit's 250th Birthday*, DIA 1951.

Collections: DIA.

Sources: AAA; Gibson 1975; Mallett 1948; *Detroit Journal* 8-3-1893, 9-29-93, 12-15-93, 12-29-94; *DFP* 6-14-25, 12-13-31; *DN* 12-1-29.

WARNER, *Douglas W.*

(b. Tulsa, Oklahoma 1930)

Printmaker/Sculptor/Painter. Warner received a B.F.A. (1953) from Oklahoma State University and an M.S. (1957) from the University of Wisconsin. He did additional graduate work at the University of Tulsa, the University of Michigan, and Michigan State University. Warner has taught at Oklahoma State University, the Philbrook Art Center in Tulsa, and the Flint Institute of Arts. In 1957 he joined the faculty of Flint Community Junior College. Warner began his career as a sculptor but more recently has concentrated on drawing, creating abstract, symmetrical, grid constructions in pencil, often in combination with charcoal.

One-person Exhibitions: Artist's Workshop, Tulsa, Okla. 1957; EMU 1959 (two-person); Yaw Gallery, Birmingham 1970 (two-person); FIA 1973 (two-person); KIA 1973 (four-person); U. of M. 1973 (two-person); Xochipilli Gallery, Rochester 1974 (two-person), 1977.

Group Exhibitions: *MWCS Exhibition* 1958, 1959 (1st Prize), 1960; *Flint Annual*, FIA 1958–61, 1962 (1st prize in sculpture; 1st Prize in Drawing), 1963, 1964 (1st Prize in Sculpture), 1965–68, 1971–72, 1975, 1977 (1st Prize in Painting); *Annual Drawing Exhibition*,PAFA 1959; *West Michigan Annual*, GRAM 1959; *MAE* 1959–61, 1965; *Faculty Exhibition*, FIA 1959–60, 1962, 1964, 1966–69, 1971, 1974; *Invitational Drawing Exhibition*, KIA 1960; Hanamura Gallery, Detroit 1962; *Drawing U.S.A.*, Minnesota Museum of Art 1963; *Mid-Michigan Annual*, Midland Art Association 1963 (1st Prize in Drawing), 1964, 1972–73, 1975 (Purchase Prize); *Michigan Painters and Printmakers*, GRAM 1963, 1971; *American Sculpture 1900–1965*, FIA 1965; *Michiana Regional*, South Bend Art Center, Ind. 1972; *27 Painters, UMMA* 1976; *National Exhibition of Prints and Drawings*, Oklahoma Art Center 1977 (1st Prize in Drawing); *Artrain*, MCA 1978 (Purchase Prize).

Collections: British Museum; Chrysler Corporation, Detroit; FIA; HAM; KIA; Michign Artrain; Minneapolis Institute of Art; MSU; Smithsonian Institution.

Sources: MAR; *FJ* 4-03-66; 4-08-73, 5-29-77, 11-27-77; *AAN* 6-17-73; *Rochester Eccentric* 4-08-74; *BEcc* 5-13-77.

WATSON, Ronald

(b. Grand Island, Nebraska 1941)

Sculptor/Painter. Watson attended the University of Nebraska (B.F.A. 1964, M.F.A. 1967). He taught at Northern Michigan University before joining the faculty at Aquinas College in Grand Rapids in 1968, where he has been chairman of the art department since 1971. Watson has served on advisory panels for both the National Endowment for the Arts and the Michigan Council for the Arts. In 1973 he was a consultant and site foreman for the "Sculpture Off the Pedestal" exhibition at the Grand Rapids Art Museum, and in 1974 was project director for the National Endowment's grant for the installation of *Earthwork* by Robert Morris in Belknap Park, Grand Rapids. A 1975 recipient of a National Endowment for the Arts fellowship, Watson is the founder and director of the Urban

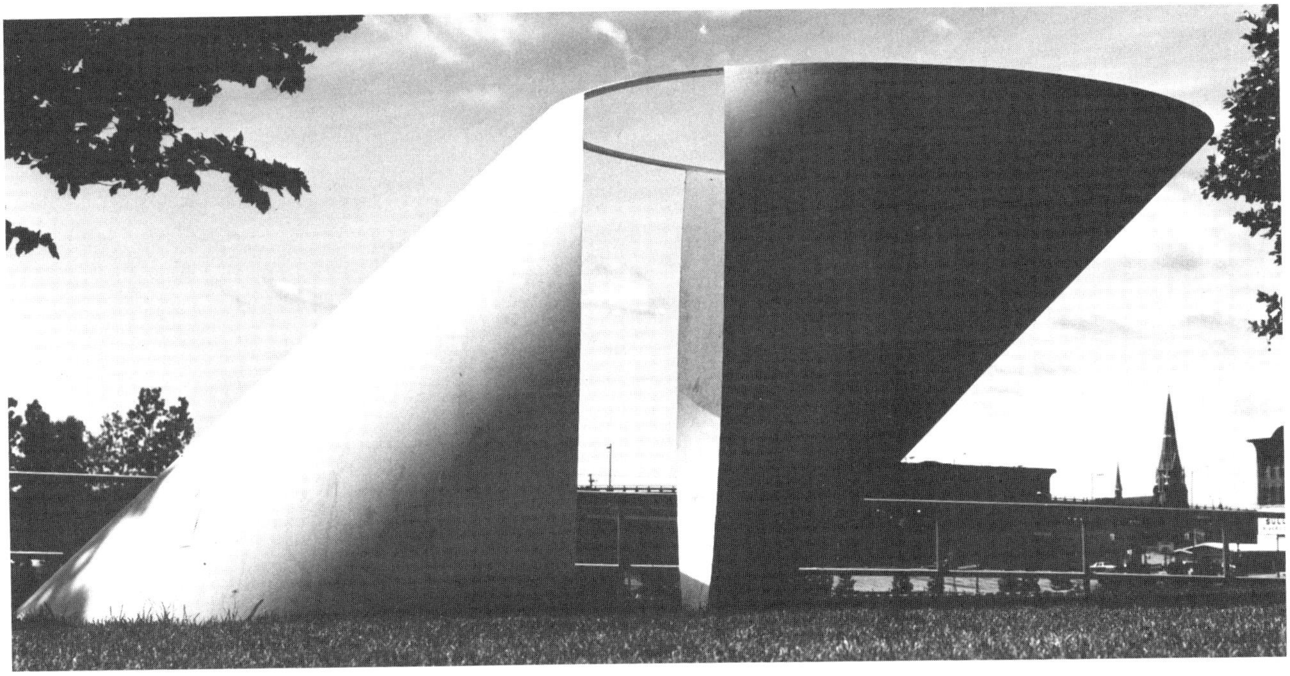

Ronald Watson (1941–). Solar Painting: The Terminator. *1975. Painted steel. 6 × 6 × 14 feet. Justice Park, Grand Rapids. Balthazar Korab, Photographer.*

Institute for Contemporary Art in Grand Rapids. In both sculpture and painting, he is concerned with light and color. Watson's polyester resin and fiberglass paintings are translucent panels supported by grids that change with the quality of light which filters through them. His sculpture, *Solar Painting,* recently installed in Justice Park, Grand Rapids, is a painted steel cylinder that is bisected by a slit-like opening through which are visible changing patterns of reflected light.

One-person Exhibitions: Grand Valley State College, 1970; GRAM 1973; Adrian College 1977; Ohio State University 1978.

Group Exhibitions: *Sculpture for a New Era,* Federal Plaza, Chicago 1975; *An Evening Without Feathers,* Urban Institute for Contemporary Art, Grand Rapids 1978*; *Full Spectrum,* Michigan Artrain 1978–79*; *Art in Public Places,* Ferris State College 1979*.

Collections: City of Grand Rapids; Coopers & Lybrand, Inc., Grand Rapids; Ferris State College, GRAM; Standard Oil, Inc., Chicago.

Sources: MAR; Hendry 1980A; Watson and Joseph Kinnebrew in *Michigan Art Journal* 1, 3 (September/October/November 1976): 12–13, 27; *New River* (Grand Rapids) January 1977: pp. 10–12; *GR Press* 1-22-78.

WEBER, *Albert J.*

(b. Chicago, Illinois 1919)

Painter/Printmaker. Weber attended Northwestern University and the Oxbow Summer School of Painting in Saugatuck (1946–48), then received a B.F.A. (1950) from the School of the Art Institute of Chicago and an M.F.A. (1952) from Mexico City College. He was awarded a Fulbright fellowship in 1952 for travel in Latin America and subsequently spent several years in Spain before joining the faculty at the University of Michigan in 1955. He has also held teaching positions at the Centro de Estudios Universitarios in Mexico City, the Oxbow Summer School of Painting, and the University of Michigan Extension Service in both Dearborn and Battle Creek. He is a member of the Ann Arbor Art Association and has served on its board of directors. Weber's work combines traditional subject matter, such as landscapes, nudes, and interiors, with an abstract expressionist style that is characterized by strong brushwork and vivid color.

One-person Exhibitions: Cromer and Quint Gallery, Chicago 1953; Forsythe Gallery, Ann Arbor 1959, 1962; Angeleski Gallery, New York City 1961; Sill Gallery, EMU 1966.

Group Exhibitions: *Current American Prints,* Carnegie Institute 1949 (Purchase Award); *National Exhibition of Prints,* Library of Congress 1949; *National Print Exhibition,* Brooklyn Museum 1949–50, 1958; *PAFA Annual* 1950, 1959/60; *Arte Abstracto,* Museo de Arte Contemporaneo, Madrid 1954; *Midyear Show,* Butler Institute 1957, 1959 (Purchase Award), 1961 (Purchase Award); MAE 1959–60, 1966, 1970; *Art: USA: 58,* Madison Square Garden 1958; *Ann Arbor Group,* Riverside Museum, New York City 1959; *American Painting Today,* GRAM 1961; *All Michigan I,* FIA 1971/72.

Collections: Butler Institute; Carnegie Institute; Olivet College; Panellit Corporation, Skokie, Ill.

Sources: *WWAA* 1976; MAR; *Arts Mag* 35, 8–9 (May/June 1961): 98; *Chicago Sun Times* 9-4-55; *Michigan Daily* (U. of M.) 5-9-56; *AAN* 4-30-59, 2-7-62, 12-7-75.

WEDDIGE, *Emil*

(b. Sandwich, Ontario 1907)

Painter/Printmaker. Weddige first became interested in printmaking while studying at Michigan State Normal College (now Eastern Michigan University) with Orlo Gill. After receiving a B.A. (1934), Weddige studied at the Art Students League in New York City with Morris Kantor and Emil Ganso before returning to Ann Arbor. He received an M.S. in design from the University of Michigan in 1937 and then joined the faculty, remaining there until his retirement in 1974. Although he began as a painter, he concentrated primarily on printmaking since the early 1950s. He helped develop the printmaking program at the University of Michigan and in 1952 founded the Michigan Printmakers Society. From 1955 to 1959 he maintained a studio in Paris where he met Fernand Léger and worked with Edmond Desjobert. In 1962 Weddige received a Ford Foundation grant to work at the Tamarind Lithography Workshop in Los Angeles.

A pioneer in the renaissance of color lithography, Weddige is the author of a widely used text, *Lithography* (Scranton, Pa.: International Textbook Co., 1966). He has completed commissions for the Dow Chemical Corporation (on the history of paper) and the University of Michigan (a history of the University, in honor of its sesquicentennial). Weddige was also a founder and the first president of the Michigan Water Color Society and was instrumental in the development of Michigan's Artrain.

One-person Exhibitions: Contemporaries Gallery, New York City 1953*; DAM 1953 (two-person); Rackham Memorial Building, Detroit 1954; *Commissions for Michigan Artists*, DIA 1957; GRAM 1958, 1968; Park Gallery, Detroit 1959 (two-person), 1961; KIA 1959, 1973; Forsythe Gallery, Ann Arbor 1959, 1964; Herbinet Gallery, Paris 1960; Arwin Gallery, Detroit 1967; Birmingham Gallery, Birmingham 1969, 1973, 1975.

Group Exhibitions: Chicago World's Fair 1933; MAE 1935–56 (FSPP 1942, McClintock Prize 1945, Newberry Prize 1948, Hal H. Smith Prize 1949); New York World's Fair 1939; *National Exhibition of Prints*, Library of Congress 1945, 1950–51, 1955, 1959; *Works in Progress*, DIA 1946; *MWCS Annual* 1947–49, 1956 (Merit Award 1948); *National Print Exhibition*, Brooklyn Museum 1948, 1950–51, 1956; *Society of American Graphic Artists Annual*, New York City 1950, 1953, 1956; *American Color Print Society Annual*, New York City 1950, 1954, 1957 (Klein Award), 1958, 1965, 1968, 1971; *Michigan Art Through 50 Years*, UMMA 1955; *Michigan Association of Printmakers Biennial* 1960–68; *Michigan Art '67*, BBAA 1967.

Collections: Bibliothèque Nationale, Paris; MMA; National Gallery; Library of Congress; Brooklyn Museum; Philadelphia Museum of Art; DIA; GRAM; FIA; KIA; UMMA; Jesse Besser Museum, Alpena; Parke Davis & Company, Ann Arbor; Michigan Consolidated Gas Company, Detroit.

Sources: *WWAA* 1976; AAA 950, 987–990, Interview; *Art Dig* 27, 8 (January 15, 1953): 19; *Art News* 48, 2 (April 1949): 60; *Art News* 51, 10 (January 1953): 15; *Art News* 53, 1 (March 1954): 59; *DAC News* 52 (February 1967): 56–62; *Look Magazine* December 1953; *AAN* 12-17-42, 3-5-53, 10-30-63, 2-27-67, 1-17-72; *DN* 5-26-52, 3-15-53, 3-5-61.

WEIDENAAR, Reynold H.

(b. Grand Rapids, Michigan 1915)

Printmaker/Painter. After receiving early training at the Kendall School of Design (1935–36) in Grand Rapids, Weidenaar attended the Kansas City Art Institute (1938–40). While there he began a correspondence with Bertha E. Jacques, founder of the Chicago Society of Etchers, who encouraged him and helped him to acquire an etching press. In 1944 he traveled in Mexico on a Guggenheim Fellowship, in 1948 was awarded a Tiffany Scholarship, and in 1949 was elected an associate of the National Academy of Design.

Weidenaar is best known for his work in color mezzotint. One of his works in this medium, *Bridge Builders*, was commissioned as a presentation print for the Society of American Graphic Artists in 1965. He is also the illustrator of numerous books, including his own *Our Changing Landscape* (Hyannis, Mass: Wakebrook House, 1970), Willis F. Dunbar's *Michigan* (Grand Rapids: Eerdmans, 1965), and Anne Zeller's *A Sketchbook of Michigan* (Grand Rapids: Baker Book House, 1980).

In 1965 Weidenaar completed a fresco mural for the La Grave Avenue Christian Reformed Church in Grand Rapids. He has taught life drawing at the Kendall School of Design since 1956, and maintains a studio in Grand Rapids. Weidenaar is a member of Allied Artists of America; the American Artists Professional League; the Michigan Academy of Science, Arts, and Letters; the Silvermine Guild of Artists; and the Society of Western Artists.

One-person Exhibitions: Smithsonian Institution 1942*; HAM 1943, 1965; GRAM 1946*, 1966; Norfolk Museum, Va. 1947; Print Club, New York City 1949; *Three Regionalist Printmakers*, Pratt Graphics Center, New York City 1975.

Group Exhibitions: *National Academy of Design Annual*, New York City 1940, 1949–53, 1954 (John Taylor Arms Award); MAE 1941, 1942 (Print Purchase Prize), 1943–45, 1946 (Giern Prize), 1947–48, 1949 (Giern Prize), 1951–52, 1953 (Smith Prize), 1954, 1956 (Smith Prize); *National Exhibition of Prints*, Library of Congress 1943–46, 1951, 1956–57; *Society of American Etchers* 1945 (Noyes Memorial Prize); *National Print Exhibition*, Brooklyn Museum 1951, 1958; *West Michigan Annual*, GRAM 1956, 1960–61, 1967; *Midyear Show*, Butler Institute 1957, 1958–59, 1961 (invited), 1963 (invited); *Society of Western Artists*, San Francisco 1959 (1st Prize), 1962; *100 Fine Prints*, Kennedy Galleries, New York City 1974.

Collections: Boston Museum of Fine Arts; Brooks Memorial Art Gallery, Memphis, Tenn.; Carnegie Institute; DIA; GRAM; HAM; Honolulu Academy of Fine Arts; MMA; National Gallery of South Wales; Philadelphia Museum of Art; Smithsonian Institution; Society of American Graphic Artists, New York City; Wadsworth Atheneum, Hartford, Conn.

Sources: *WWAA* 1980; AAA 879; Weidenaar in *Am Artist* 12, 7 (September 1948): 52; Weidenaar in *Am Artist* 20, 10 (December 1956): 24; *Art Dig* 22, 15 (May 1, 1948): 37; *Art Dig* 23, 16 (May 15, 1949): 19; *Print Review* No. 4 (1975); *Washington Star* 3-22-42, 11-17-47; *Christian Science Monitor* 5-4-42, 5-23-42; *Kansas City Star* 10-27-44; *DFP* 5-1-49; *GR Press* 5-22-63, 6-16-74.

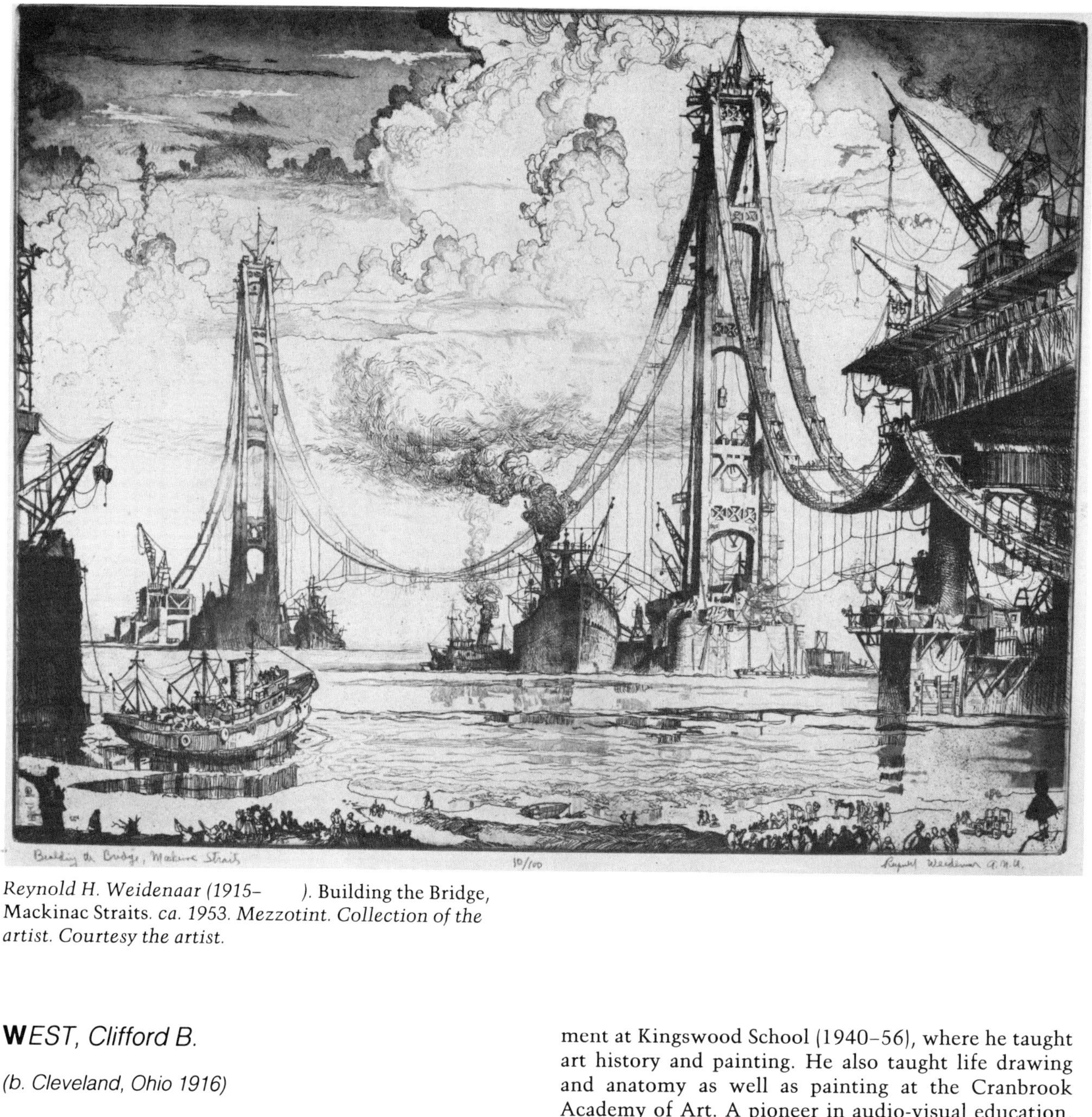

Reynold H. Weidenaar (1915–). Building the Bridge, Mackinac Straits. *ca. 1953. Mezzotint. Collection of the artist. Courtesy the artist.*

WEST, *Clifford B.*

(b. Cleveland, Ohio 1916)

Painter/Filmmaker. West attended the Cleveland School of Art (1933–37), graduating with a certificate in portrait painting. He enrolled the following fall at the Cranbrook Academy of Art and studied under **Zoltan Sepeshy**, **Carl Milles**, Eliel Saarinen, and **Maija Grotell**. In 1939 he was awarded the Prix de Rome by the American Academy in Rome. He also studied with Boardman Robinson and Arnold Blanch at the Colorado Springs Fine Arts Center and received a B.A. (1940) from Adams State Teachers College, Alamosa, Colorado. Returning to Cranbrook, West received an M.F.A. (1948), then served as head of the art department at Kingswood School (1940–56), where he taught art history and painting. He also taught life drawing and anatomy as well as painting at the Cranbrook Academy of Art. A pioneer in audio-visual education, he began making films on Renaissance art while at Kingswood because of the shortage of art history teaching aids; since then he has made numerous films on such artists as Edvard Munch and Rolf Nesch as well as his Cranbrook colleagues: Milles, **Harry Bertoia**, and **Berthold "Tex" Schiwetz**.

A mural painter during the 1930s, West executed commissions for the Stockholm Restaurant, Detroit (1936); Fox and Hounds Inn, Birmingham (1939, later removed); Engineering Society, Rackham Building, Detroit (1940, destroyed in fire); Penobscot Building, Detroit (1948); and the Veterans Memorial Building, Detroit (1949). With David Fredenthal in 1938, he executed three murals for the New York World's Fair.

In 1969 West was awarded the Fine Arts Medal from the Michigan Academy of Science, Arts, and Letters. He was instrumental in the founding of Ossabaw Island Project Foundation in Georgia in 1961 and served as its president (1961–75). Presently living in Italy, he continues to exhibit extensively and is still active in film production.

One-person Exhibitions: Butler Institute 1938; Massillon Museum, Ohio 1938; Cranbrook Academy 1942; Bonestell Gallery, New York City 1946; DIA 1948; FIA 1948; Little Gallery, Birmingham 1961; United States Information Service, Florence, Italy 1962; American Consulate, Florence, Italy 1965; Moss Museum of Art, Norway 1974; American Embassy, Oslo 1975; Birmingham Gallery 1976.

Group Exhibitions: *May Show*, Cleveland Museum of Art 1934–37; National Academy of Design, New York City 1937, 1938; AIC 1937, 1939, 1943–45; Denver Art Museum 1937, 1939, 1943; MAE 1938, 1940–42, 1944–50, 1953; *Midyear Show*, Butler Institute 1940, 1945–46, 1948; *Artists for Victory*, MMA 1942; Woodstock Art Association, New York 1944–46; Corcoran 1947, *Contemporary American Painting and Sculpture*, AIC 1948; *Michigan Academy of Science, Arts, and Letters Annual* 1948; PAFA Annual 1948; *Flint Annual*, FIA 1949 (1st Prize); Massillon Museum, Ohio 1953–54; *MACE* 1956; Cranbrook 1979.

Collections: Basilica of San Lorenzo, Florence; British Arts Council, London; Brooklyn Museum; Casa Contenta Hotel, Guatemala; City National Bank, Penobscot Building, Detroit; Colorado State Historical Society, Denver; Cranbrook; Foreign Department, Government of Norway, Oslo; Iowa State Teachers College, Ames; Massillon Museum of Art, Ohio; MMA; Munch Museet, Oslo; National Gallery, Oslo; New York Public Library; Veterans Memorial Building, Detroit.

Sources: *WWAA* 1980; AAA, Interview; MAR; *Michigan Art Journal* 2, 1 (Winter 1977): 15–18; *BEcc* 10-3-63, 4-10-69, 10-14-72, 10-27-73, 10-28-76.

WHITAKER, *Irwin*

(b. Wirt, Oklahoma 1919)

Enamelist/Ceramicist. Whitaker received a B.A. (1947) from San Jose State College in California and an M.F.A. (1949) from Claremont College in California. He taught ceramics for one year at Southern Oregon College and joined the faculty of Michigan State University in 1950. He works primarily in enamel and has written a number of books, including *Crafts and Craftsmen* (Dubuque, Iowa: William C. Browne, 1967) and *A Potter's Mexico* (Santa Fe: University of New Mexico Press, 1978), co-authored with Emily Whitaker.

One-person Exhibitions: Kresge Art Center Gallery, MSU 1969, 1973, 1976; WMU 1970; Birmingham Gallery 1975.

Group Exhibitions: *Works in Progress*, DIA 1951; *MACE* 1951–62, 1963 (Activities Committee Prize), 1964; *Ceramics National*, Everson Museum of Art, Syracuse 1951 (Honorable Mention), 1952, 1954, 1960; *Decorative Arts and Ceramics Exhibition*, Wichita Art Association, Kans. 1953; *Midwest Designer/Craftsmen* Joslyn Art Museum, Omaha 1954; *West Michigan Annual*, GRAM 1953, 1970; *Area Show*, KIA 1956, 1970; *American Craftsmen*, Smithsonian Institution 1959; DAM 1961; Cranbrook 1961; *Michigan Art: Yesterday and Today*, FIA 1963; *Ceramic Invitational*, Scripps College, Claremont, Calif. 1970.

Collections: DIA.

Sources: MAR; Whitaker in *CH* 17, 5 (October 1957): 32; *Kresge Art Center* (MSU) *Bulletin* 3, 2 (November 1969): n.p.

WICKER, *John P.*

(b. Saginaw, Michigan 1860; d. Detroit, Michigan 1931)

Painter. Wicker studied at the Académie Julian in Paris under William Bougereau, Tony Robert-Fleury, and Fernand Corman. Returning to Michigan after seven years abroad, he conducted classes for a time in Saginaw before arriving in Detroit in 1902. Shortly thereafter he joined the faculty of the Detroit Art Academy, then directed by its founder, **Joseph Gies**. Upon Gies's retirement in 1910, Wicker became director of the school, which was re-named the Wicker School of Fine Arts. For the next twenty years, Wicker was acknowledged as Detroit's foremost art teacher. His school was the first in Detroit to encourage the study of "modernist" art, including the work of Van Gogh, Matisse, Gauguin, and the Fauves. **Sarkis Sarkisian, Jay Boorsma, Paul Honoré, John L. Pappas, Edgar Yaeger,** and many other Michigan artists studied with Wicker. For six consecutive years Wicker students won the coveted Anna Scripps Whitcomb Scholarship for study abroad. Although he considered himself a "failed artist," ruined by his academic training, Wicker's work was widely known and respected.

Group Exhibitions: *Paris Salon* 1903–04; *Louisiana Purchase Exposition*, St. Louis 1904; *MAE* 1911–13,

1922, 1924–31 (Scarab Club Gold Medal 1925); *Amerjuican Artists Annual*, DIA 1924–29; *Michigan Art Through 50 Years*, U. of M. 1955.

Collection: DIA.

Sources: Burroughs 1936/37; Gibson 1975; Kenny 1965; *DN* 3-15-16, 2-11-25, 6-16-29, 2-15-31, 7-11-31; *DFP* 2-13-31.

WILBERT, *Robert*

(b. Chicago, Illinois 1929)

Painter. Wilbert received his formal training at the University of Illinois (B.F.A. 1951; M.F.A. 1954) under Warren Doolittle and Abraham Rattner. After graduation he came to Michigan to teach at the Flint Institute of Arts and at Flint Junior College. He joined the faculty at Wayne State University in 1956. For two years (1958–60) he was the director of the AAA Gallery in Detroit. During his tenure at the gallery, such Michigan artists as **Gerome Kamrowski**, **Stefan Davidek**, **Allen Leepa**, and Leonard Zamiska were given their first one-person showings in Detroit. The gallery also showcased one of the first sound and light performances by Ann Arbor artist Milton Cohen. In the early 1960s, after an early period of abstract expressionist work, Wilbert turned to a more realistic approach, retaining, however, the strong brushwork, formal concerns, and vibrant color of his earlier style. He is adept in both oil and watercolor and is best known for his still-lifes, although, figure studies, portraits, and landscape are also important aspects of his work.

One-person Exhibitions: SAM 1958; AAA Gallery, Detroit 1959; University of Illinois 1960; Park Gallery, Detroit 1962*; Donald Morris Gallery, Birmingham 1964, 1967, 1972–73, 1977; *Two Views of Reality*, J. B. Speed Museum, Louisville, Ky. 1975 (two-person).

Group Exhibitions: *American Watercolor, Drawings and Prints*, MMA 1952; *Midwest Designer/Craftsmen*, AIC 1952, 1954; MAE 1955, 1959–61, 1966 (MWCS Prize), 1969 (Werbe Prize), 1970 (Prize for oil painting); *West Michigan Annual*, GRAM 1956 (Award), 1958, 1960; *Michiana Regional*, South Bend Art Center, Ind. 1957–58, 1960 (Award), 1962 (Award); *MWCS Annual* 1957–60, 1962 (Jaeger Award 1957, 1959; Merit Award 1958); *Midyear Show*, Butler Institute 1960, 1962–63; *Watercolor, Drawings, and Prints*, PAFA 1961, 1963; *Michigan Art: Yesterday and Today*, FIA 1963; *Eight Michigan Artists*, MSU 1971; *Detroit Art/Diverse Directions*, UMMA 1974; *27 Painters*, UMMA 1976; *Works in Progress*, II, DIA 1976*.

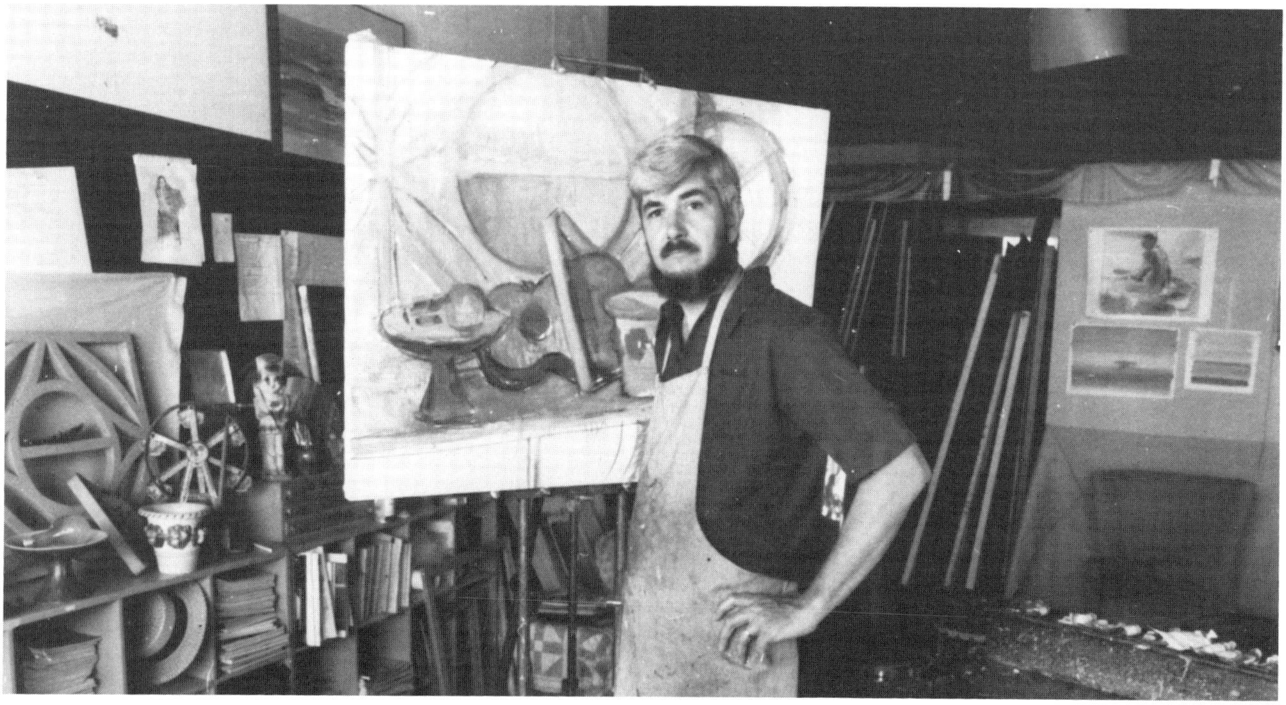

Robert Wilbert (1929–   ) in his studio, 1976. The Archives of American Art, Robert Wilbert Papers.

Collections: Kresge Art Center Gallery, MSU; SAM; South Bend Art Center, Ind.; Upjohn Company, Kalamazoo; WMU; WSU.

Sources: *WWAA* 1976; AAA, Interview; *New Art Examiner* 7, 7 (April 1980) 1 (section 2); *DN* 11-23-58, 4-19-59, 11-11-62, 12-13-64, 5-21-67, 4-16-72; *DFP* 4-16-72, 6-5-77.

WILLIAMS, *Mildred E.*

(b. Detroit, Michigan 1892; d. Detroit, Michigan 1967)

Painter/Printmaker. A native Detroiter, Williams studied at the **John P. Wicker** School of Fine Arts, Detroit; the Pennsylvania Academy of the Fine Arts, Philadelphia, under Hugh Breckinridge; the Art Students League, New York City, under Robert Henri, George Luks, Mahonri Young, and etcher Joseph Pennell (1919–22); and privately with John Sloan in New York City. Williams also traveled abroad for additional study 1923–24, 1929), working mainly in and around Paris and Brittany. In 1924 she was included in the Salon des Indépendants exhibition in Paris.

Returning to Detroit in 1923, Williams established a studio on Woodward Avenue and also maintained a studio in New York City for more than fifteen years. She was employed by the federal government's Works Progress Administration Graphic Arts Section in New York City and the Public Works of Art Project in Detroit in 1933 and 1934. During this time, she executed six murals depicting familiar classical children's stories for the McGregor Memorial Library in Highland Park.

A member of the Michigan Academy of Science, Arts, and Letters, and the Birmingham Society of Women Painters and Sculptors, Williams was also an active member of the Detroit Society of Women Painters and Sculptors, becoming a life member in 1942. She taught privately in Birmingham for many years and was an instructor of portrait painting at the Bloomfield Art Association. Williams was known for her portraits and decorative flower studies.

One-person Exhibitions: Bonstelle Theatre, Detroit 1925; John Hanna Galleries, Detroit 1925; Orkil Farms, West Simsbury, Conn. 1939.

Group Exhibitions: *Merrill Hall Exhibition*, DMA 1886; MAE 1915, 1918, 1921–22, 1924–25, 1927–29, 1934–43, 1946, 1956–57 (Prizes in 1925, 1936, 1939–40); *Annual Exhibition of Paintings by American Artists*, DIA 1923–24, 1927–29; Salon des Indépendants, Paris 1924; *PAFA Annual* 1926, 1928 (Award); *DSWP*, Holt Gallery, New York City 1928; *50 Prints of the Year*, American Institute of Graphic Arts and DIA 1930 (traveling); *DSWP Annual* 1933–34, 1936; *American Artists Annual*, AIC 1936; *Corcoran Biennial* 1937; *American Federation of the Arts Exhibition*, Carnegie Institute 1941 (traveling); *Adam and Eve Exhibition*, DIA 1942; *Paintings by American Artists*, DIA 1943; *Recent Work by Detroit Artists sponsored by the Metropolitan Art Association*, DIA 1944; *Michigan Painters, Sculptors, and Craftsmen*, Alger House, DIA 1946; *Michigan Academy of Science, Arts, and Letters Annual* 1948–49, 1951–54, 1957; New York Public Library 1957.

Collections: Detroit Historical Museum; DIA; Library of Congress; McGregor Public Library, Highland Park; New York Public Library; PAFA; Staten Island Museum.

Sources: *WWAA* 1962; Fielding 1974; Kenny 1965; Mallett 1948; Moore 1953; *The Afterglow* (Detroit) 1, 2 (April 1925): 20–21; *Bonstelle Theatre Program* (Detroit) May 25, 1925; *Detroit Saturday Night* 4-11-25; *DFP* 2-10-24, 4-12-25, 6-21-25, 9-2-67.

WILT, *Richard*

(b. Tyrone, Pennsylvania 1915)

Painter. Educated at the Carnegie Institute of Technology in Pittsburgh (B.A. 1938) and the New School for Social Research in New York City, Wilt joined the faculty at the University of Michigan in 1947. His other teaching positions included those at the Oxbow Summer School of Art, the Carnegie Institute, and Wayne State University. In 1953 he received an M.A. from the University of Pittsburgh. Characteristic of his work is the use of a variety of methods to achieve surface texture, including blotting and bleeding of color, beaded and veined pigment, and scored lines. He is well known both for his figurative works, which usually feature inert, vacant-eyed, almost surrealistic children, and for his intricately detailed depictions of tropical foliage, inspired by a 1960 sabbatical in the Caribbean.

One-person Exhibitions: ACA Gallery, New York City 1948; Albion College 1949; GRAM 1950; Little Gallery, Birmingham 1950; DAM 1952, 1962, 1967 (two-person); Institute of Contemporary Art, Boston 1952; Forsythe Gallery, Ann Arbor 1953, 1958 and then biennally to 1974; Garelick's Gallery, Detroit 1959*; DIA 1961*; Amel Gallery, New York City 1962, 1963; KIA 1965; Kresge Art Center Gallery, MSU 1969.

Group Exhibitions: MAE 1947–63 (Maxon Prize 1949, 1959, Museum Collection Prize 1951, Kahn Prize 1953, 1961, FSPP 1960, Newberry Prize 1961); *Mid-year Show*, Butler Institute 1948–49, 1951, 1953–55,

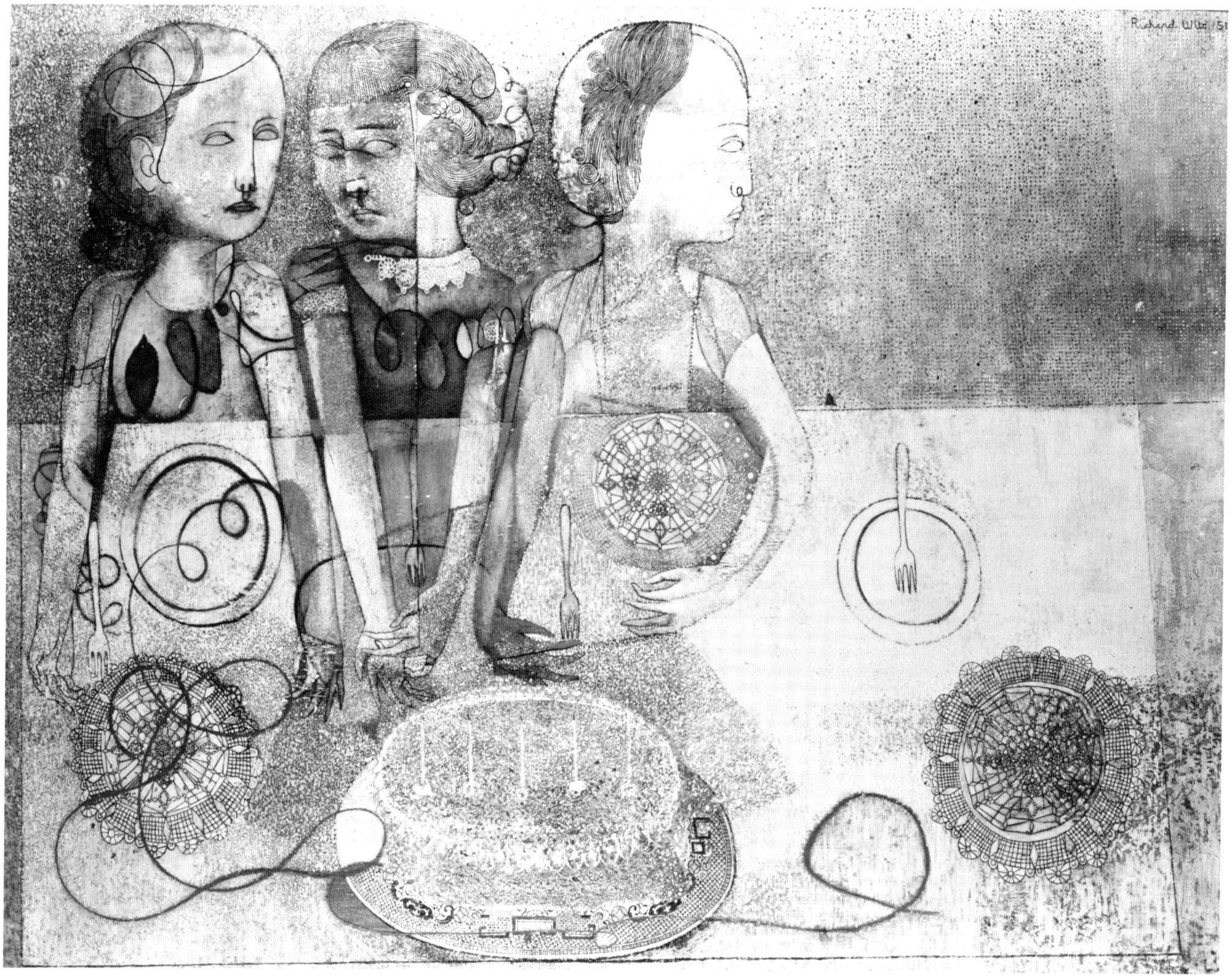

Richard Wilt (1915–). Birthday Cake. *1951. Oil on masonite. 29¾ × 39¾ inches. Collection of the Detroit Institute of Arts.*

1957–59, 1961–62, 1967 (Invited 1959, 1961); *American Watercolors and Drawings*, AIC 1949; *Five Americans*, AFA Traveling Show 1951/52; *MWCS Annual* 1954, 1957–59, 1964, 1967, 1972, 1975, 1977 (Merit Award 1964, 1972); *Michigan Art Through 50 Years*, UMMA 1955; *American Painting and Sculpture*, AIC 1957; *Midwest Painters Invitational*, GRAM 1960; *Drawing U.S.A.*, Minnesota Museum of Art 1962; *Contemporary American Painting and Sculpture*, Krannert Art Museum, University of Illinois 1963; *Contemporary American Watercolors*, GRAM 1963; *Michigan Art: Yesterday and Today*, FIA 1963.

Collections: Butler Institute; Carnegie Institute; DIA; Illinois State Museum; KIA; Krannert Art Museum, University of Illinois; Kresge Art Center Gallery, MSU; UMMA.

Sources: *WWAA* 1962; MAR; *Art News* 61, 3 (May 1962): 60; *Art News* 62, 7 (November 1963): 51; *DN* 11-15-59; 4-15-62, 5-7-67; *DFP* 4-11-62; *NYT* 5-5-62; *AAN* 12-7-75.

WONNACOTT, *Gladys*

(b. Chicago, Illinois 1920)

Textile Artist. Wonnacott received a B.S. in Design (1962) from the University of Michigan, after also studying at the Art Institute of Chicago. Prior to World War II she was an occupational therapist and in 1947 opened her own studio in Chicago. In 1951 she moved to Baldwin, Michigan. Intermittent with her work as a therapist, Wonnacott has taught at Eastern

Michigan University and Lake Superior State College. From 1947 to 1955 she inaugurated, edited, and published the still existing *Warp and Weft*, a periodical for handweavers. She specializes in handwoven, hard surface fabrics.

One-person Exhibitions: Little Gallery Studio, Chicago 1947; Chicago Public Library 1949; Rochester Art Center, Minn. 1951; Memphis Academy of Art, Tenn. 1952; GRAM 1954; HAM 1956; U. of M. 1959; EMU 1962; Traverse City Public Library 1963; Lake Superior State College 1975.

Group Exhibitions: *American Institute of Decorators National Traveling Exhibition* 1947; *International Textile Exhibition*, University of North Carolina, Greensboro 1948 (3rd Prize), 1949 (1st Prize); *Chicago Weavers Guild*, AIC 1949; *International Trade Fair*, Chicago 1950; *American Craftsmen's Invitational*, University of Illinois 1952; *Northwestern Michigan Arts and Crafts Exhibition*, Traverse City 1953 (three 1st Prizes); *34 American Artists*, University of Minnesota 1955; *Michigan Artist-Craftsmen*, GRAM 1962; *Fiber/Clay/Metal*, Minnesota Museum of Art 1962–63; *First Invitational Craft Exhibition*, NMU, Marquette 1977.

Collections: NMU; U. of M.

Sources: MAR.

WOO, Marie

(b. Seattle, Washington 1928)

Ceramicist. After attending the California College of Arts and Crafts, Woo received a B.A. from the University of Washington. She studied ceramics with **Maija Grotell** at the Cranbrook Academy of Art and received an M.F.A. (1956), then taught for three years at the University of Michigan. She received a Horace Rackham Research Grant (1959) to travel to Japan, where she spent three years working, teaching, and doing research, primarily on glazing. Upon her return to the United States, she taught at the University of Washington for one year, then returned to the Far East to teach at Chulalongkorn University in Bangkok for three years. She established a studio in Birmingham in the late 1960s and has taught at various places in Michigan, including the Birmingham-Bloomfield Art Association; Pewabic Pottery, Detroit; Center for Creative Studies; and Michigan State University. Woo works in both stoneware and porcelain, with an emphasis on thrown work.

One-person Exhibitions: Gallery Four, Detroit 1969 (two-person); Creative Arts Gallery, CMU 1974; Troy Art Gallery 1976 (two-person); Pewabic Pottery, Detroit, 1978 (two-person).

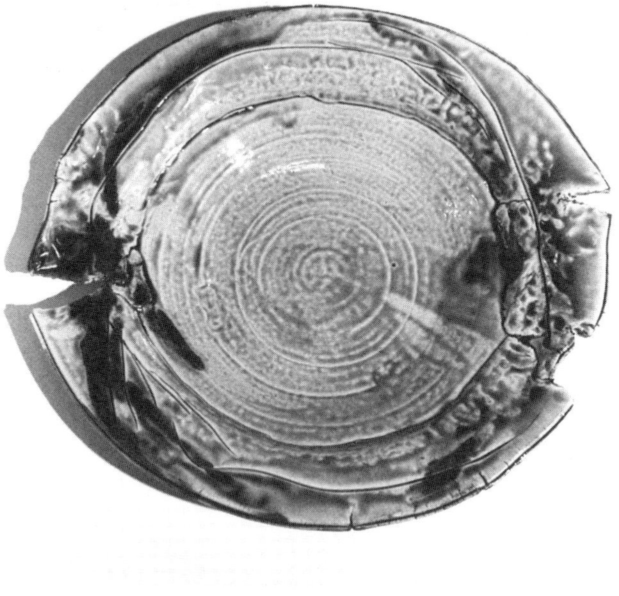

Marie Woo (1928–). Plate. ca. 1975. Robert Vigiletti, Photographer.

Group Exhibitions: *Decorative Arts and Ceramics Exhibition*, Wichita Art Association, Kans. 1955–58; MACE 1955–59, 1960 (Webber Prize), 1962 (Winston Prize), 1975–76; *Ceramic National*, Everson Museum of Art, Syracuse 1956 (Purchase Prize), 1961; *Young Americans*, Mus of Contemp Crafts 1956–58; *Ceramics International*, Everson Museum of Art, Syracuse 1958; *La Ceràmique Contemporaine*, Ostend, Belgium 1959; *Midwest Designer/Craftsmen* 1959 (Best in Ceramics); *Modern American Ceramics*, Royal Copenhagen Porcelain Factory, Denmark 1960; Mitsukoshi Gallery, Tokyo 1962; *Third International Exhibition*, Prague 1962; *Tenth International*, Smithsonian Institution 1965 (Freeman Award); *A Decade of Ceramic Art 1962–1972*, San Francisco Museum of Modern Art 1972; Rubiner Gallery, Royal Oak 1974–75; *Invitational*, Somerset Mall, Troy 1974–77; *Michigan Collects Michigan Art*, Pontiac Creative Arts Center 1976; Pewabic Pottery, Detroit 1977.

Collections: Everson Museum of Art, Syracuse; DIA; Smithsonian Institution.

Sources: *Michigan Challenge* (State Chamber of Commerce) 4, 5 (February 1964): 11; *Studio Potter* 2, 2 (Winter 1973/74): 28–29; *DN* 4-26-59; *Oakland Press* 2-3-76; *BEcc* 3-25-76.

WOOD, Marcia

(b. Paw Paw, Michigan 1933)

Sculptor/Painter. Wood received a B.A. (1955) from Kalamazoo College and an M.F.A. (1956) from the Cranbrook Academy of Art. She has also undertaken graduate study at the Courtauld Institute of Art in London, and at Harvard University. A member of the faculty at Kalamazoo College since 1965, she previously served as an art consultant to the Kalamazoo Public Schools as well as teaching at the National Music Camp at Interlochen and Philadelphia College of Art. Wood creates sculpture in many media, including bronze, terra cotta, stainless steel, and cast aluminum. In 1980, she won a statewide sculpture competition, sponsored by the National Endowment for the Arts, which led to the installation of one of her works on the Washington Boulevard mall in downtown Detroit.

One-person Exhibition: KIA 1975.

Group Exhibitions: *Michigan Artist-Craftsmen*, GRAM 1966 (Honorable Mention); *Battle Creek 100*, Battle Creek Civic Art Center 1967; *Michigan Art on Paper*, KIA 1967 (Sequoia Press Award); *Mid-Michigan Annual*, Midland Art Council, 1974–75.

Collections/Commissions: Battle Creek Civic Art Center; City of Detroit; Hope College.

Sources: MAR: *KG* 10-10-65; 10-7-66, 2-24-67, 6-25-67, 4-29-69, 11-24-74, 10-12-75.

WUJCIK, Theo

(b. Detroit, Michigan 1936)

Printmaker. Educated at the Art School of the Detroit Society of Arts and Crafts, Wujcik also studied at the Creative Graphics Workshop in New York City and with Garo Antreasian at the University of New Mexico (1967). In 1964 he received a Tiffany Foundation Award and in 1968 a Ford Foundation Grant to the Tamarind Lithography Workshop in Los Angeles. While at Tamarind he worked with such artists as Karl Kasten, Billy Al Bengston, and Michael Meyer as well as with Jasper Johns at Gemini G.E.L., also in Los Angeles. Wujcik taught graphics at the DSAC art school from 1965 to 1970, and in 1969 co-founded the Detroit Lithography Workshop with **Aris Koutroulis**. In 1970 he joined the staff of the University of South Florida. Wujcik has revived many "antiquated" techniques in printmaking, such as stipple etching and silverpoint. In 1977 he was awarded a National Endowment for the Arts Fellowship for printmaking.

One-person Exhibitions: Stables Theatre, Detroit 1963; University of South Florida, Tampa 1973; Brook Alexander, Inc., New York City 1976; Donald Morris Gallery, Birmingham 1978.

Group Exhibitions: *Forty Michigan Artists*, Raven Gallery, Detroit 1960; MAE 1963 (Scarab Club Award), 1965; *Michigan Association of Printmakers Biennial* 1963; *Boston Printmakers Annual* 1964–65, 1967; *National Print Exhibition*, Brooklyn Museum 1964, 1970, 1976; *Michigan Painters-Printmakers*, GRAM 1967; *Intaglio Prints by Michigan Artists*, DIA 1969; *Prints by Seven*, Whitney 1970; *Contemporary Prints*, DIA 1974; *American Master Drawings and Watercolors*, Yale University 1976*; *Drawings of the 70's*, AIC 1977.

Collections: AIC; Boston Museum of Fine Arts; Brooklyn Museum; DIA; Jesse Besser Museum, Alpena; Library of Congress; Los Angeles County Museum; MOMA; UMMA; U. of M.; Whitney.

Sources: MAR; *Art and Artists* (Detroit) June/July 1962; *Arts Mag* 51 (December 1976): 31; *Print Collector's Newsletter* 4, 2 (May/June 1973): 38; *Print Collector's Newsletter* 7, 5 (November/December 1976): 150; *Print Collector's Newsletter* 8, 2 (May/June 1977): 44; *DT* 6-5-60.

YAEGER, Edgar

(b. Detroit, Michigan 1904)

Painter. Yaeger attended both **Robert Herzberg**'s Detroit School of Fine and Applied Art and the **John P. Wicker** School of Fine Arts. He won the Founders Society Purchase Prize in 1932 and in that same year became the seventh Wicker student to win the Anna Scripps Whitcomb Traveling Scholarship awarded by the *Detroit News*. He subsequently studied in Paris with André Lhote, Marcel Gromaire, and Othon Friesz (at the Académie Ranson). Returning to Detroit in 1935, Yaeger joined the Works Progress Administration/Federal Art Project and completed murals for the Brodhead Naval Armory and the Public Lighting Commission Building in Detroit. He eventually executed murals for the Grosse Pointe City Hall, Grosse Pointe South High School, the Children's Hospital of Detroit (later demolished), the Ford School in Highland Park, and the Men's Union Dormitory at the University of Michigan. Yaeger was one of the founders of the Grosse Pointe Artists Association and taught for many

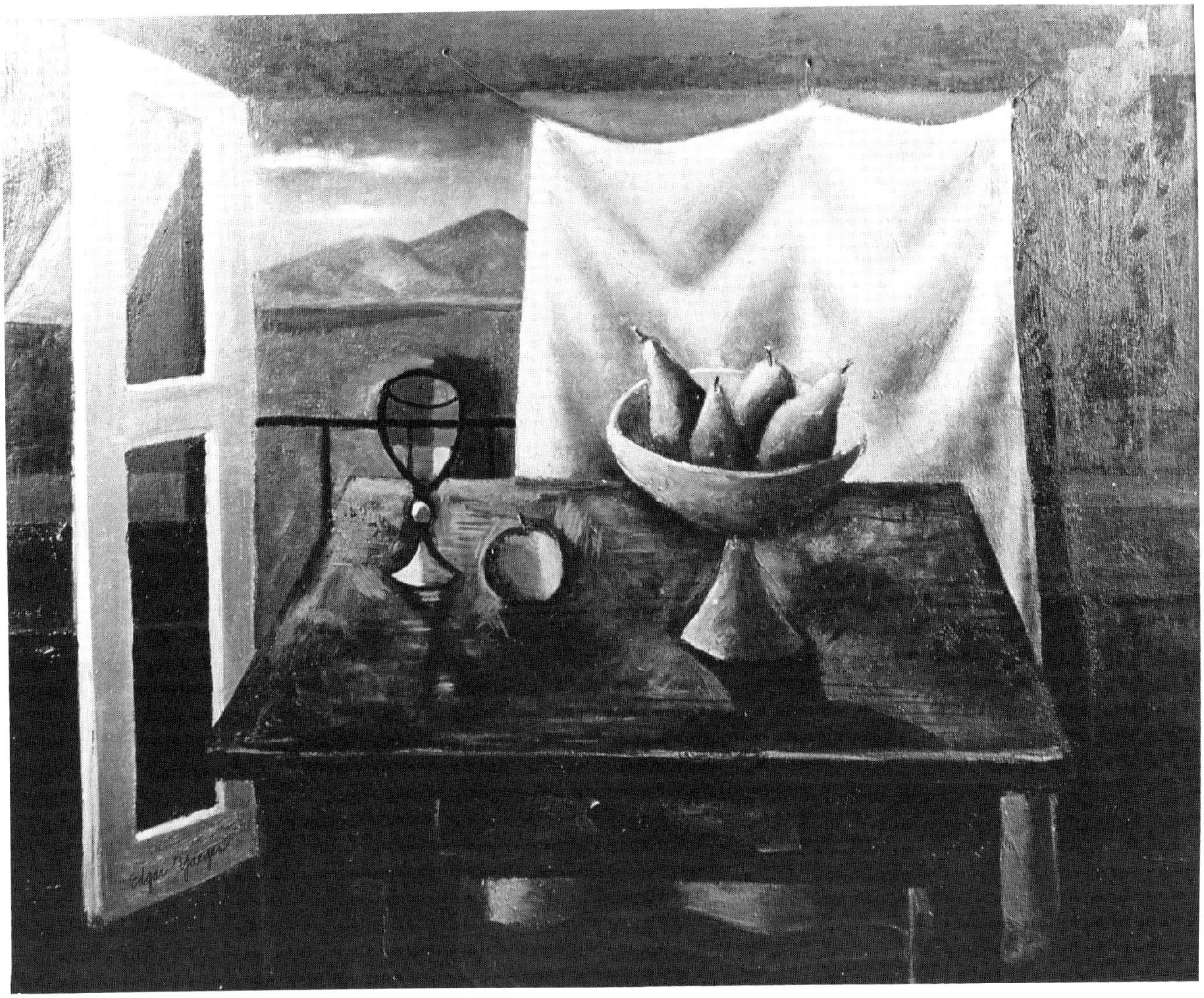

Edgar Yaeger (1904–). Still Life. *Commissioned by the Works Progress Administration/Federal Art Project. The Detroit Institute of Arts, Research Library*

years at the Grosse Pointe War Memorial. He also was active as a stage designer for the Wayne State University Theater Guild and the Detroit Symphony.

One of the earliest abstract artists in Michigan, Yaeger was influenced by both Picasso and the Italian forerunner of surrealism, Giorgio de Chirico. His paintings are notable for their pure, flat color, stylized human figures, and decorative sense of pattern. Although he painted typically cubist still lifes, Yaeger was also well known for his fantasy landscapes, characterized by solitary figures, empty spaces, and a dreamlike quality.

One-person Exhibitions: Ann Arbor Art Association 1936; DAM 1938, 1939 (two-person), 1940, 1943, 1948, 1949 (two-person), 1951; Women's City Club, Detroit 1958; Grosse Pointe Galleries 1959; Four Winds Gallery, Kalamazoo 1968.

Group Exhibitions: *Modern Art Exhibition*, Scarab Club 1926; MAE 1926–44, 1946, 1948–51, 1953–54, 1956–59 (Zeigen and Boulevardier Prize 1930, Kamperman Prize 1935, HAASS Prize 1939, Burroughs Prize 1950); *Carnegie International* 1930; *Corcoran Biennial* 1930; *PAFA Annual* 1931, 1934; *American Painting and Sculpture*, AIC 1931–32, 1938; *Painting and Sculpture from 16 American Cities*, MOMA 1933; *New Horizons in American Art*, MOMA 1936, *National Exhibition*, Rockefeller Center 1936–38; *Great Lakes Exhibition*, Albright Art Gallery, Buffalo 1938; *Golden Gate Exposition*, San Francisco 1939/40; *Recent Works by Detroit Artists*, DIA 1944; *MWCS An-*

nual 1947–51 (Merit Award 1949, 1951); *Michigan Art Through 50 Years*, UMMA 1955.

Collection: DIA.

Sources: *WWAA* 1953; AAA; Kenny 1965; *Art and Artists* (Detroit) October/November 1962; *DN* 5-25-32, 1-4-31, 11-5-33, 3-3-40, 2-27-49, 3-13-51, 3-17-57, 12-3-78; *DFP* 1-8-38, 2-26-39, 5-17-42; *Grosse Pointe News* 6-6-57; *DT* 8-23-59; *KG* 7-14-68.

ZIRBES, Georgette

(b. Chicago, Illinois 1940)

Ceramicist. Zirbes received a B.A. (1962) from DePauw University. During a summer session in 1963, she studied with master potter Shoji Hamada at San Jose State College, and later graduated with an M.A. (1964) from Ohio State University. She received a Fulbright Grant for study in Japan at the Kyoto City College of Fine Art in 1964 and stayed through 1967 for further study and construction of her own studio and kiln. Zirbes has taught briefly in New York City, at Washtenaw Community College in Michigan, and at the Ann Arbor Potters Guild, as well as at Eastern Michigan University. She has been on the faculty of the University of Michigan since 1970, and has given numerous demonstrations, lectures and workshops including one at the Detroit Institute of Arts in 1970. She received a National Endowment for the Arts Craftsmen's Fellowship for 1975/76.

One-person Exhibitions: Fulbright Commission, Tokyo 1966 (two-person); Greenwich House Pottery, New York City 1967 (two-person); KIA 1969 (two-person); Creative Arts Gallery, CMU 1970; State University of New York, Fredonia 1975.

Group Exhibitions: *Ceramic National*, Everson Museum of Art, Syracuse 1965; *Beaux-Arts Designer/Craftsmen*, Columbus Museum of Art 1969 (Purchase Prize), 1970, 1972–74, 1977; *Ceramics Invitational*, EMU 1969 (Purchase Prize), 1971, 1974 (Purchase Prize), 1977; *Michigan Craftsmen's Council Traveling Show* 1969; MACE 1971 (Michigan Potters' Association Prize); *Michigan '71*, Midland Center for the Arts, 1971; *Pots That Potters Admire*, Pewabic Pottery, Detroit 1971; *Women '71*, Northern Illinois University 1971; *Michigan Potters' Association Annual*, Pewabic Pottery, Detroit 1972; *Crafts National*, Marietta College, Ohio 1974; *Michigan Artists Biennial: Tradition and Invention*, Kresge Art Center Gallery, MSU 1977.

Collections: Columbus Museum of Art, EMU; State University of New York, Fredonia.

Sources: MAR; *DFP* 4-21-70.

ABBREVIATIONS

AAA	Archives of American Art, Smithsonian Institution, Washington, D.C.
AAN	*Ann Arbor News*
AFA	American Federation of Arts, New York
AIC	Art Institute of Chicago
AID	American Institute of Design, New York
Am Artist	*American Artist*
Art Dig	*Art Digest*
Art J	*Art Journal*
Arts Mag	*Arts Magazine*
BBAA	Birmingham-Bloomfield Art Association (formerly Bloomfield Art Association)
BEcc	*Birmingham Eccentric*
Bénézit 1976	Bénézit, E., ed., *Dictionaire des Peintres, Sculpteurs, Dessinateurs et Graveurs*. 1911. Reprint. Paris; Librairie Grund, 1976.
Burroughs 1936/37	Clyde Burroughs. "Painting and Sculpture in Michigan." *Michigan Historical Magazine* 20 (1936): 395–409 and 21 (1937): 39–54, 142–157.
Butler Institute	Butler Institute of American Art, Youngstown, Ohio
CAAM	Cranbrook Academy of Art Museum, Bloomfield Hills
Carnegie Institute	Museum of Art, Carnegie Institute, Pittsburgh
Cederholm 1973	Cederholm, Theresa Dickason, comp. and ed. *Afro-American Artists: A Bio-bibliographical Directory*. Boston: Trustees of the Boston Public Library, 1973.
CH	*Craft Horizons*
CMo	*Ceramics Monthly*
CMU	Central Michigan University, Mt. Pleasant
Cook 1963	Cook, Joyce Slocum. "The Flint Institute of Arts, 1928–1963." Mimeographed and bound. Flint Institute of Arts, 1963.
Corcoran	Corcoran Gallery of Art, Washington, D.C.
Cranbrook	Cranbrook Academy of Art, Bloomfield Hills
Cummings 1977	Cummings, Paul. *A Dictionary of Contemporary American Artists*. 3rd ed. New York: St. Martins Press, 1977.
DAC News	*Detroit Athletic Club News*
DAM	Detroit Artists Market
DFP	*Detroit Free Press*
DIA	Detroit Institute of Arts
DMA	Detroit Museum of Art (former name of the Detroit Institute of Arts)
DN	*Detroit News*
DSAC	Detroit Society of Arts and Crafts (the Art School of the DSAC is now the Center for Creative Studies)
DSWP	Detroit Society of Women Painters (and Sculptors)
DT	*Detroit Times*
DTr	*Detroit Tribune*
EMU	Eastern Michigan University, Ypsilanti
FIA	Flint Institute of Arts
Fielding 1974	Fielding, Mantle. *Dictionary of American Painters, Sculptors, and Engravers*. Greens Farms, Conn., 1974.
FJ	*Flint Journal*
FSPP	Founders Society Purchase Prize
Gibson 1975	Gibson, Arthur Hopkin. *Artists of Early Michigan*. Detroit: Wayne State University Press, 1975.
GRAM	Grand Rapids Art Museum
GR Herald	*Grand Rapids Herald*
GR Press	*Grand Rapids Press*
HAM	Hackley Art Museum (now the Muskegon Museum of Art)

Hendry 1980	Hendry, Fay L. *Outdoor Sculpture in Lansing*. Okemos: Iota Press, 1980.
Hendry 1980A	Hendry, Fay L. *Outdoor Sculpture in Grand Rapids*. Okemos: Iota Press, 1980.
Hendry 1980B	Hendry, Fay L. *Outdoor Sculpture in Kalamazoo*. Okemos: Iota Press, 1980.
Hirshhorn	Hirshhorn Museum and Sculpture Garden, Smithsonian Institution, Washington, D.C.
Hodgman 1966	Hodgman, Katherine and Robinson, Cornelia. "An Art Center Grows in the Midwest." Printed in looseleaf binder. Kalamazoo Institute of Arts, 1966.
Kenny 1965	Sister Kenny. "A History of Painting in Michigan 1850 to World War II." M.A. thesis. Wayne State University, 1965.
KG	*Kalamazoo Gazette*
KIA	Kalamazoo Institute of Arts
MACE	Exhibition for Michigan Artist-Craftsmen (at DIA)
MAE	Exhibition for Michigan Artists (at DIA)
Mag of Art	*Magazine of Art*
Mallett 1948	Mallett, Daniel Trowbridge. *Mallett's Index of Artists*. 1935. Reprint. New York: Peter Smith, 1948.
MAR	Michigan Artists Registry
MASAL	Michigan Academy of Science, Arts, and Letters
MCA	Michigan Council for the Arts
Mich State Lib 1915	Michigan State Library. *Biographical Sketches of American Artists*. 3rd. ed. rev. 1915. Reprint. Lansing, 1924.
MMA	Metropolitan Museum of Art, New York
MOMA	Museum of Modern Art, New York
Moore 1953	Moore, Julia Gatlin. *A History of the Detroit Society of Women Painters and Sculptors, 1903–1953*. River Rouge: Victory Printing Co., 1953.
MSU	Michigan State University
Mus Contemp Crafts	Museum of Contemporary Crafts (now the American Craft Museum, New York)
MWCS	Michigan Water Color Society
National Gallery	National Gallery of Art, Smithsonian Institution, Washington, D.C.
Nawrocki 1980	Nawrocki, Dennis. *Art in Detroit Public Places*. Detroit: Wayne State University Press, 1980.
NCFA	National Collection of Fine Arts, Washington, D.C.
NMU	Northern Michigan University, Marquette
NPG	National Portrait Gallery, Smithsonian Institution, Washington, D.C.
NYT	*New York Times*
PAFA	Pennsylvania Academy of the Fine Arts, Philadelphia
SAM	Saginaw Art Museum
Thieme/Becker 1907	Thieme, Ulrich, and Becker, Felix. *Allegemeines Lexicon der Bildenden Künstler*. 1907. Reprint. Leipzig: E. A. Seeman Verlag, 1967–.
UMMA	University of Michigan Museum of Art, Ann Arbor
U. of M.	University of Michigan, Ann Arbor
USIA	United States Information Agency, Washington, D.C.
Whitney	Whitney Museum of American Art, New York
WMU	Western Michigan University, Kalamazoo
WPA/FAP	Works Progress Administration/Federal Art Project
WSU	Wayne State University, Detroit
WWAA	*Who's Who in American Art*. New York: R. R. Bowker, 1936–80.
Young 1968	Young, William, ed. *Dictionary of American Artists, Sculptors, and Engravers*. Cambridge, Mass.: Wm. Young and Co., 1968.

SOURCES CONSULTED

Archives and Libraries

Much of the information available on Michigan artists consists of newspaper clippings, small pamphlets, exhibition announcements, and other ephemera that is scattered among a variety of repositories, including libraries, institutional archives, museum files, and manuscript collections. Not every such source investigated can be enumerated here, but the holdings listed were used extensively.

Midwest Area Center of the Archives of American Art

The Midwest office of the Archives has recorded on microfilm the personal papers of a number of Michigan artists (journals, sketchbooks, scrapbooks, correspondence, exhibition catalogues, photographs, etc.) as well as the records of such Michigan institutions as the Scarab Club, the Hanna Galleries, and the Detroit Society of Arts and Crafts.

Partially as an adjunct to the creation of this book, the Archives conducted over 75 taped interviews with Michigan artists, critics, educators, gallery owners, and museum staffers. Most of these have been transcribed and are also available to scholars.

The Detroit Institute of Arts, Research Library

The Research Library maintains a large collection of printed materials from various arts institutions in Michigan and around the country (American Art Institutions Collection). Post-1945 material, which usually consists of pamphlets, catalogues, programs, annual reports, and so forth, predominates in this collection.

The Library also maintains a file on all artists who entered either the "Exhibition for Michigan Artists" or the "Exhibition for Michigan Artist-Craftsmen" throughout the entire course of their respective histories. This card file contains some biographical information as well as listing the works entered in the exhibitions and indicating any prizes won.

Also of interest to the researcher is the Library's clipping file, part of which has been recorded on microfiche. In this file can be found magazine and newspaper articles, dealers' announcements, small catalogues and pamphlets, obituary notices, and other information on both artists and institutions.

Finally, the Library houses the Michigan Artists Registry (MAR). Originally intended as a data bank on contemporary Michigan artists, this registry was established in 1975 by Sylvia Wilkinson under the auspices of the Michigan Council for the Arts. When the research for this book was completed, the files that resulted were incorporated into the Registry, creating perhaps the most comprehensive body of materials available on Michigan artists. The MAR files contain items such as curricula vitae, press clippings, magazine articles, exhibition pamphlets, and photographs, all of which were gathered primarily from the artists themselves or their descendants, although in many cases copies of documents from other repositories have been added.

The Detroit Public Library, Fine Arts Department, Biographical Files

Arranged alphabetically by artist's surname, these files contain a wide variety of newspaper clippings, announcements, and other information on Michigan artists.

Books and Articles

American Art Annual. 1898–1935.

Ann Arbor Potters Guild. *Ann Arbor Potters Guild 10th Anniversary*. Ann Arbor, 1959.

Barrie, Dennis. "The History of the Development of the Visual Arts Community in Michigan, 1900–1980." Ph.D. diss. Detroit: Wayne State University, 1983.

Bénézit, Emanuel, ed. *Dictionaire des peintres, sculpteurs, dessinateurs et graveurs*. 1911. Reprint. Paris: Librarie Grund, 1976.

Burroughs, Clyde. "Painting and Sculpture in Michigan." *Michigan Historical Magazine* 20 (1936): 395–409 and 21 (1937): 39–54, 142–157.

Clayton, Wallace E. *The Growth of a Great Museum: An Informal History of the Detroit Institute of Arts.* Detroit Institute of Arts, 1965.

Colby, Joy Hakanson. *Art and a City: A History of the Detroit Society of Arts and Crafts.* Detroit: Wayne State University Press, 1956.

Cook, Joyce Slocum. "The Flint Institute of Arts, 1928–1963." Bound Typescript. Flint Institute of Arts, 1963.

Cranbrook Academy of Art, Museum of Art. *The Creative Spirit of Cranbrook: The Early Years.* Exh. cat. 1973.

Detroit Artists Monthly. Vols. 1-3 (1976–78).

Detroit Institute of Arts. *Arts and Crafts in Detroit 1906–1976: The Movement, The Society, The School.* Exh. cat. 1976.

Detroit Institute of Arts. *From the Inside: The Archives of the Detroit Institute of Arts 1883–1945.* 1980.

Detroit Institute of Arts. *Kick Out the Jams: Detroit's Cass Corridor 1963–1977.* Exh. cat. 1980.

Detroit Institute of Arts. *Bulletin of the Detroit Institute of Arts* (formerly *Bulletin of the Detroit Museum of Art*). Vols. 1–68 (Annual Reports for 1904–1980).

Dunbar, Willis Frederick. *Michigan: A History of the Wolverine State.* Grand Rapids, Michigan: William B. Erdmans Co., 1965.

Fielding, Mantle. *Dictionary of American Painters, Sculptors, and Engravers.* Rev. ed. Stratford, Connecticut: Art Reference Publishers, 1974.

Gibson, Arthur Hopkin. *Artists of Early Michigan: A Biographical Dictionary of Artists Native to or Active in Michigan, 1701–1900.* Detroit: Wayne State University Press, 1975.

Harrington, Freda. *Up From the Basement: A History of the Art Education Department at Wayne State University, 1927–1977.* Detroit: Wayne State University Press, 1977.

Hodgman, Kathryn, and Cornelia Robinson. "An Art Center Grows in the Midwest." Typescript. Kalamazoo Institute of Arts, 1966.

Huckle, Doris, comp. *Artists North: First Regional Collector's Guide.* East Jordan, Michigan: The Necessary Press, 1978.

Isbell, Egbert R. *A History of Eastern Michigan University, 1849–1965.* Ypsilanti, Michigan: Eastern Michigan University Press, 1965.

Kenny, Sister M. Kilian. "A History of Painting in Michigan from 1850 to World War II." M.A. thesis. Wayne State University, 1965.

Kresge Art Center. *Early Michigan Paintings.* Exh. cat. East Lansing: Michigan State University, 1976.

Lorch, Emil, and Jean Paul Slusser. *The Ann Arbor Art Association, 1909–1959: A Survey of Fifty Years.* Ann Arbor Art Association, 1959.

Mallett, Daniel Trowbridge. *Mallett's Index of Artists.* 1935. Reprint. New York: Peter Smith, 1948 (includes 1940 supplement to original edition).

Michigan Art Journal. Vol. 1, issues 1–4 (1976).

Michigan State Library. *Biographical Sketches of American Artists.* Lansing: Michigan State Library, 1915.

Moore, Julia Gatlin. *A History of the Detroit Society of Women Painters and Sculptors, 1903–1953.* River Rouge: Victory Printing Co., 1953.

Nawrocki, Dennis Alan, with Thomas J. Holleman. *Art in Detroit Public Places.* Detroit: Wayne State University Press, 1980.

O'Connor, Francis V., ed. *Art for the Millions: Essays from the 1930s by Artists and Administrators of the WPA Federal Art Program.* Boston: New York Graphic Society, 1973.

Parks, Alma Forest. "A City Survey, The Arts in Detroit." *Negro Digest,* November 1962.

Pear, Lillian Myers. *The Pewabic Pottery: A History of its Products and its People.* Des Moines: Wallace-Homestead Book Company, 1976.

Riordan, Mary. *The Muskegon Museum of Art: A Preface.* Muskegon Museum of Art, 1980.

Sweeney, J. Gray. *Artists of Grand Rapids, 1840–1980.* Exh. cat. Grand Rapids Art Museum and Grand Rapids Public Museum, 1981.

Vexler, Robert I. *Detroit: A Chronological and Documentary History.* Dobbs Ferry, New York: Oceana Publications, 1977.

Who's Who in American Art. New York: R. R. Bowker, 1936–80.

Yasko, Karal, comp. "List of Murals Painted in Michigan Under the Auspices of the Treasury Department." U.S. General Services Administration, Washington, D.C., 1977.

Young, William, ed. *Dictionary of American Artists, Sculptors, and Engravers.* Cambridge, Massachusetts: Wm. Young and Company, 1968.

Your Heritage House. *In Retrospect: The Pen and Palette Club.* Detroit: Your Heritage House, 1982.

Classification of Artists by Medium

Areas of focus include:

Ceramics	Metalsmithing
Conceptual Art	Painting
Design	Papermaking
Enamel	Printmaking
Film	Puppetry
Glass	Sculpture
Illustration	Textiles

Note: Many artists listed in this volume are known for work in more than one medium. Additional areas of concentration are cited in parentheses following the respective artist's name.

Ceramics

Abernathy, J. T.
Anthony, James H.
Black, James R.
Bohnert, Thom R.
Dart, Gawaine (painting)
DeVore, Richard
Diebboll, Robert
Douglas, Murray
Dunitz, Dorothy
Foster, John A.
Foster, Kenneth
Glick, John P.
Grotell, Maija
Hansen, Marc
Kline, Svea (sculpture)
Larson, Julie
Larson, Tyrone
Leach, Richard
Loree, John P.
Orear, Gordon
Oughton, Lawrence David
Pederson, Roy
Piepenburg, Robert (sculpture)
Pitney, William
Plum, Nancy Manes
Raynor, Louis
Speck, Walter (painting)
Stephenson, John (sculpture)
Stephenson, Suzanne
Stratton, Mary Chase Perry
Vigland, Alan
Whitaker, Irwin (enamel)
Woo, Marie
Zirbes, Georgette

Conceptual Art

Crawford, James (printmaking)
Miles, Cyril Aronson (painting, film)

Design

Claxton, Wayne LeMarr (painting, illustration)
Gooch, Donald (painting)
Kinnebrew, Joseph Edwin IV (sculpture)
Knodel, Gerhardt (textiles)
McPharlin, Paul (puppetry)
Warner, David (sculpture, painting)

Enamel

Whitaker, Irwin (ceramics)

Film

Miles, Cyril Aronson (painting, conceptual art)
West, Clifford B. (painting)

Glass

Johnson, Gilbert C.
Vigiletti, Sylvia

Illustration

Bacon, Irving R. (painting)
Claxton, Wayne LeMarr (painting, design)
Collins, Kreigh (painting)
Coppin, John (painting)
Fredenthal, David (painting)
Wald, Carol (painting)

Metalsmithing

Bambas, Thomas R.
Engstrom, Audrey
Engstrom, Robert
Fike, Philip (printmaking)
Kenney-Eagen, Fred
Kenney-Eagen, Marion
Kirk, Arthur Neville
Krentzin, Earl
Steen, Carol (sculpture)
Thomas, Richard
Vizzini, Michael

Painting

Alten, Mathias J.
Anthony, James H. (printmaking)
Bacon, Irving R. (illustration)
Barker, Charles Arthur (printmaking)
Barlow, Myron
Barnes, Ernest Harrison
Barr, David (sculpture)
Beerbohm, Marvin
Beginin, Igor
Bennett, Reginald
Berg, Wilfrid
Bigler, Mary Jane
Bloch, Lucienne
Boorsma, Jay
Bostick, William (printmaking)
Brainerd, Owen (printmaking)
Broner, Robert (printmaking)
Brozik, Jaroslav (printmaking)
Butcher, Larry D. (sculpture)
Calkins, Kingsley
Carroll, John
Casenelli, Victor
Cassara, Frank (printmaking)
Claxton, Wayne LeMarr (illustration, design)
Cohn, Harold
Collins, Kreigh (illustration)
Collins, Paul
Coppin, John (illustration)
Culver, Charles
Dart, Gawaine (ceramics)
Davidek, Stefan
Davies, John (printmaking)
DeBlasi, Anthony
DeErdely, Francis
DeMartelly, John S. (printmaking)
Drapce, Nora
Earle, Lawrence Carmichael
Egner, John (sculpture)
Fisher, George Harold
Fleming, Ray Frost
Flyn, Alexander
Foster, Leroy
Fredenthal, David (illustration)
Fursman, Frededrick
Gamble, Roy C.
Gammon, Reginald
Garretson, Della
Garretson, Lillie
Gies, Joseph
Glassgold, Harry (printmaking)
Gooch, Donald
Goodman, Brenda (sculpture)
Greason, William
Guysi, Alice Viola
Guysi, Jeannette
Hardman, Ernest
Hefner, Harry
Henricksen, Ralf
Herzberg, Robert A.
Hinton, Alfred
Hoffmaster, Maude Miller
Honoré, Paul (printmaking)
Iden Sheldon
Ives, Percy
Johnson, Lester (sculpture)
Jones, Murray
Kachadoorian, Zubel
Kamrowski, Gerome (sculpture)
King, Henri Umbaji
Koutroulis, Aris (printmaking)
Kozlow, Richard
Kryzanowski, Roman
La More, Chet (printmaking, sculpture)
LaRiviere, Rodolphe
Lee, James
Leepa, Allen
Lee-Smith, Hugie
Lewis, William A.
Lopez, Carlos
Loving, Alvin (sculpture)
Lowder, Dwayne (sculpture)
Makielski, Leon
Mast, Gerald
Mastro-Valerio, Alessandro (printmaking)
May, Helen
McChesney, Clifton
McCormick, John William
McEwen, Katherine
McGee, Charles
Melchers, Gari
Merizon, Armand
Metheany, John M. III
Michel, Delbert (printmaking)
Mikolowski, Ann (printmaking)
Miles, Cyril Aronson (film, conceptual art)
Miller, Iris Andrews
Mitchell, David
Mitchell, Wallace (sculpture)
Moser, Liselotte (textiles)
Nawara, Jim (printmaking)
Neal, Harold
Nobili, Louise Jansson

Ortman, George Earl
Overvoorde, Chris Stoffel (printmaking)
Palazzola, Guy
Pappas, John L.
Papsdorf, Frederick
Parish, Tom (printmaking)
Paulus, Francis Petrus (printmaking)
Perrault, Ida Marie
Plum, Jens
Pollock, Charles (printmaking)
Ponsen, Tunis
Radell, Renée
Ramsay, Theodore K. (sculpture)
Richardson, Constance
Robbert, Paul A. (printmaking)
Roland, Arthur
Rolshoven, Julius
Sarkisian, Sarkis
Scanes, Ernest William
Sepeshy, Zoltan
Simper, Frederick
Slusser, Jean Paul (art history)
Smith, Henrietta ["Letta"] Crapo
Smith, Judson D.
Speck, Walter (sculpture)
Stanley, Jane C.
Strickland, James Dudley
Swift, Ivan
Teed, Douglas Arthur
Wald, Carol (illustration)
Walker, James A. (printmaking)
Waltensperger, Charles
Warner, Douglas W. (printmaking, sculpture)
Watson, Ronald (sculpture)
Weber, Albert J. (printmaking)
Weddige, Emil (printmaking)
Weidenaar, Reynold (printmaking)
West, Clifford B. (film)
Wicker, John P.
Wilbert, Robert
Williams, Mildred E. (printmaking)
Wilt, Richard
Wood, Marcia (sculpture)
Yaeger, Edgar

Papermaking

Barker, Laurence (printmaking)
Lutz, Winifred (sculpture)

Printmaking

Anthony, James H. (painting)
Barker, Charles Arthur (painting)
Barker, Laurence (papermaking)
Becker, David
Bostick, William (painting)
Brainerd, Owen (painting)
Broner, Robert (painting)
Brozik, Jaroslav (painting)
Cassara, Frank (painting)
Crawford, James (conceptual art)
Davies, John (painting)
DeMartelly, John S. (painting)
Fike, Philip (metalsmithing)
Glassgold, Harry (painting)
Honoré, Paul (painting)
Keller, Germaine (sculpture)
Kirby, Kent Bruce
Koster, Marjory
Koutroulis, Aris (painting)
La More, Chet (painting, sculpture)
Lang, Henrietta Dean
Lee, James
Mastro-Valerio, Alessandro (painting)
McCombs, Bruce
McConnell, James
McCormick, John William (painting)
Michel, Delbert (painting)
Mikolowski, Ann (painting)
Nawara, Jim (painting)
Newman, Kirk (sculpture)
Overvoorde, Chris Stoffel (painting)
Parish, Tom (painting)
Paulus, Francis Petrus (painting)
Pollock, Charles (painting)
Rhodes, Curtis (sculpture)
Robbert, Paul A. (painting)
Rosenthal, Stanley
Stark, Shirley (sculpture)
Stewart, Paul
Walker, James A. (painting)
Warner, Douglas W. (sculpture, painting)
Weber, Albert J.
Weddige, Emil (painting)
Weidenaar, Reynold (painting)
Williams, Mildred E. (painting)
Wujcik, Theo

Puppetry

McPharlin, Paul (design)

Sculpture

Barr, David (painting)
Barrett, Bill
Bertoia, Harry
Breed, Charles Ayars
Brose, Morris
Bulone, Joe
Butcher, Larry D. (painting)
Cashwan, Samuel
Chaffee, John

Decker, Lindsey
DeGiusti, Sergio
DeLuca, Joseph
Dolega, Stan
Doner, Michele Oka
Egner, John (painting)
Ettl, George
Fairbanks, Avard
Fredericks, Marshall
Goodman, Brenda
Graves, Oscar
Hall, Michael
Harrison, Carole
Holland, Jay
Horn, Milton
Johnson, Lester (painting)
Jungwirth, Leonard (painting)
Kamrowski, Gerome
Keller, Geramine (printmaking)
Kinnebrew, Joseph Edwin IV (design)
Kline, Svea (ceramics)
LaGrone, Oliver
La More, Chet (painting, printmaking)
Loving, Alvin (painting)
Lowder, Dwayne (painting)
Luchs, Michael
Lutz, Winifred (papermaking)
Lux, Gwen
McClure, Thomas F.
Michaels, Glen
Midener, Walter
Milles, Carl
Mitchell, Wallace (painting)
Newman, Kirk (printmaking)
Nygard, Alfred F.
Pallas, Jim
Pappas, John Nick
Parducci, Corrado
Piepenburg, Robert (ceramics)
Piet, John
Ramsey, Theodore K. (painting)
Rhodes, Curtis (painting)
Rush, Jon
Saarinen, Loja (textiles)
Schiwetz, Berthold ["Tex"]
Schmidt, Julius
Smith, G. Alden
Speck, Walter (painting)
Stark, Shirley (printmaking)
Steen, Carol (metalsmithing)
Stephenson, John (ceramics)
Warner, Douglas W. (painting, printmaking)
Watson, Ronald (painting)
Wood, Marcia (painting)

Textiles

Auvil, Eleen
Berlin, Rosalind
Bick, Georgie Elayne
Holm, Lillian
Ingvarson, Ruth
Jupena, Urban
Kidd,Robert
Knodel, Gerhardt (design)
Moser, Liselotte (painting)
Moulton, Helmi K.
Saarinen, Loja (sculpture)
Sailors, Robert D.
Schnee, Ruth Adler
Strengell, Marianne
Ux, Katherine
Wonnacott, Gladys